Repeating and
Multi-Fire Weapons

ALSO BY GERALD PRENDERGHAST

*Richard III and the Princes in the Tower:
The Possible Fates of Edward V
and Richard of York* (McFarland, 2017)

*Britain and the Wars in Vietnam:
The Supply of Troops, Arms and Intelligence,
1945–1975* (McFarland, 2015)

Repeating and Multi-Fire Weapons

A History from the Zhuge Crossbow Through the AK–47

GERALD PRENDERGHAST

McFarland & Company, Inc., Publishers
Jefferson, North Carolina

LIBRARY OF CONGRESS CATALOGUING-IN-PUBLICATION DATA

Names: Prenderghast, Gerald, 1954– author.
Title: Repeating and multi-fire weapons : a history from the Zhuge crossbow through the AK-47 / Gerald Prenderghast.
Other titles: History from the Zhuge crossbow through the AK-47
Description: Jefferson, North Carolina : McFarland & Company, Inc., Publishers, 2018 | Includes bibliographical references and index.
Identifiers: LCCN 2018006135 | ISBN 9781476666662 (softcover : acid free paper) ∞
Subjects: LCSH: Firearms—History. | Machine guns—History. | Military weapons—History.
Classification: LCC U884 .P74 2018 | DDC 623.4/424—dc23
LC record available at https://lccn.loc.gov/2018006135

BRITISH LIBRARY CATALOGUING DATA ARE AVAILABLE

ISBN (print) 978-1-4766-6666-2
ISBN (ebook) 978-1-4766-3110-3

© 2018 Gerald Prenderghast. All rights reserved

No part of this book may be reproduced or transmitted in any form or by any means, electronic or mechanical, including photocopying or recording, or by any information storage and retrieval system, without permission in writing from the publisher.

Front cover photograph © 2018 iStock

Printed in the United States of America

*McFarland & Company, Inc., Publishers
Box 611, Jefferson, North Carolina 28640
www.mcfarlandpub.com*

Acknowledgments

With grateful thanks to the following: Bonhams for their kind permission to use images from their archive. James D. Julia Auctioneers, Fairfield, Maine (http://www.jamesdjulia.com), and most especially their graphic designer, Ms. Lisa Oakes, for her invaluable help and unfailing kindness. Max Popenker, operator of the World Guns website.

Table of Contents

Acknowledgments   v
Preface   1
Introduction   3
Glossary   5

Section I: Early Repeating Weapons

One. Repeating Weapons from the Ancient World   11

Section II: Without Black Powder

Two. Perkin's Steam Gun and Other Oddities   20

Section III: The Black Powder Era

Three. Early Military Rockets   32
Four. Early Black Powder Weapons   40
Five. Early Repeating Pistols and Colt's Percussion Revolvers   52
Six. The Rimfire Revolver and Rollin White's Patent   69
Seven. Pinfire and Centerfire Revolvers   85
Eight. Repeating Rifles and Shotguns   97
Nine. Early Machine Guns and Repeating Cannon   115
Ten. The Gatling Gun: Gatling's 150-Year-Old Masterpiece   128

Section IV: The Smokeless Powder Era

Eleven. Maxim's Automatic Machine Gun: "The Devil's Paintbrush"   138
Twelve. Smokeless Powder and Repeating Rifles   150
Thirteen. Self-Loading or Semiautomatic Pistols   178

Section V: The Machine-gun Era

Fourteen. The Development of Repeating and Multi-fire Weapons in the Early 20th Century   211

Fifteen. Light Machine Guns in World War I	224
Sixteen. Medium and Heavy Machine Guns in World War I	252
Seventeen. Submachine Guns, Semiautomatic Rifles and Postwar Changes	288
Eighteen. Light Machine Gun Development After World War I	317
Nineteen. Heavy Machine Gun and Automatic Cannon Development After World War I	360
Twenty. Assault Rifles and the Rise of the "Woolworth's" Gun	397
Twenty-one. Perspectives	413
Chapter Notes	417
Bibliography	423
Index	425

Preface

Weapons capable of firing more than once without reloading have always been something of an obsession for the military mind, but it was innovations introduced in the nineteenth and the early part of the twentieth century that really made this sort of device a reality.

Consequently, this book covers what might arguably be called the most significant period during which repeating and multi-fire weapons were designed and invented; the years from the first appearance of the repeating crossbow in A.D. 200 to the development of the Bren and MG 34 light machine guns before the beginning of World War II. With the exception of the Kalashnikov AK-47 and a few later assault rifles, weapons manufactured during and after World War II are not included here. The beginning of World War II and the appearance of the enormous variety of weapons which that conflict engendered, although intrinsically interesting, really marked something of a quiescence in the development of multi-fire and repeating weapons. Technologically, most of the problems involved in design and even manufacture had been solved, and semiautomatic and automatic weapons would continue to be produced on the same tested principles, with relatively little technological variation, in the period during and after World War II. Perhaps more importantly, such weapons are more than adequately covered by a number of modern writers well versed in their myriad complications. For the sake of completeness, however, a selection of books about modern weapons is included in the bibliography.

The book is arranged chronologically and consequently describes a number of what might be considered the most significant weapons from a particular period in some detail, while including a more general, less complete description of the more unfamiliar weapons from the same era. Brief technical details concerning the operation of these weapons are included, but those readers specifically concerned with such matters would be advised to consult the relevant technical manuals. Unfortunately, it soon became pretty clear that the author's decision about the significance (or otherwise) of selected guns, particularly in the later sections referring to smokeless weapons, might not be received with universal agreement, and for that, my apologies.

Although this publication is not intended as an antiques guide, many of the weapons from this period are regarded as highly collectible. Consequently, an assessment of their auction values was felt to be appropriate and consequently is included, with pricing based on results from auctions between 2006 and 2016.

Any attempt at pricing should be regarded as a guide only. Consultation with a reputable auction house is the only reliable way to make a definitive assessment of a weapon's value.

Where possible, values are listed as "NRA Good" or "NRA Fine," a system for determining the relative condition of a weapon, which is based on the National Rifle Association classification.

The text is based upon information contained in standard texts and obtained from original documents from the National Archives of Great Britain, the National Archives of America, and the U.S. Patent Office.

Introduction

A repeating weapon may be conveniently thought of as any device capable of successively firing a number of projectiles without reloading. This group differs from traditional multi-fire weapons, a category including arms such as the Nock volley gun or a conventional muzzleloading cannon charged with canister, which discharge a number of projectiles simultaneously, after which reloading is required.

Although they were not numerous or widely used in military operations, repeating weapons were produced before the appearance of reliable black powder muskets and revolving weapons. Arguably the most famous of these early repeaters was the repeating crossbow, developed by the Chinese in the 2nd century, but it was the invention of black powder and, more importantly, a reliable means of ignition in the form of the percussion cap, that really ushered in the period of rapid development of this type of firearm.

It is perhaps not surprising that multi-fire weapons, as opposed to true repeaters, were the first group to be fully exploited for military purposes, although it would be more correct to say that what was developed was rather multi-shot ammunition, both grapeshot and canister being used in the conventional muzzleloading cannon of the period. The first readily available repeating firearm, both because of its relative cheapness and the numbers produced, was Colt's revolver, although in the high-pressure environment of America's nineteenth-century manufacturing industry, Sam Colt was not without his imitators and competitors. Despite the marked success of Colt's early Walker revolver, which was rapidly followed by his Pocket and Navy models, revolving cylinder rifles do not seem to have shared in this financial bonanza. Colt certainly produced one, the Colt Model 1855 revolving rifle, offered as a carbine, rifle and musket, but only around 15,000 were produced. Their tendency to fire several chambers simultaneously, sometimes removing the user's fingers in the process, soon became well known and consequently did nothing to enhance their popularity. Repeating rifles only began to take a real grip upon the popular mind with the appearance the Volcanic range of magazine pistols and rifles, which were rapidly followed by the Henry rifle, produced by the same New Haven Arms Company, and finally the various models of Winchester, manufactured in a huge assortment of models and calibers.

Alongside the development of repeating pistols and rifles, larger weapons of strategic value were also being produced by inventors such as Agar, Nordenfeldt and Gatling. Gatling's invention was a particularly successful multi-fire weapon, although it was not a true, fully automatic machine gun, its rate of fire being determined by the rotation of a firing handle that operated the mechanism. The fully automatic machine gun had to wait until 1883, when Hiram Maxim developed a weapon with a mechanism operated by the recoil generated by a previously expended cartridge. The weapon would fire continually for as long as the ammunition lasted and the operator kept the firing button depressed. Perhaps needless to say, such an innovation changed forever the way in which wars were fought, and it was weapons developed from Maxim's original design, as well as military incompetence, which were largely responsible for the horrific casualties sustained during massed infantry attacks in World War I.

Weapons development slowed down in the aftermath of World War I, although the lessons of that bloody conflict were sufficiently well learned to cause several European armies to begin to seriously examine the role of the light machine gun as a means of supporting advancing infantry. The British Army's contribution to these developments was the excellent and well respected Bren gun, while Germany also began producing their MG34 and the later, much improved MG42 for use during World War II. The period of weapons development covered here is brought to a close with the Kalashnikov AK-47, included because its unique manufacturing characteristics and longevity set it apart from its more complex contemporaries, another "Woolworths" gun in the cheap and cheerful tradition of the ubiquitous and frequently derided STEN.

Glossary

ACP or Automatic Colt Pistol cartridge This designation refers to a cartridge designed for use in several Colt semiautomatic pistols. There is a large range of ACP cartridges:
- .25 ACP. Designated in Europe as: 6.35 × 16mmSR.
- .32 ACP. Designated in Europe as: 7.65 × 17mm Browning SR or 7.65 Browning.
- .380 ACP. Designated in Europe as: 9mm Browning or 9 × 17mm.
- .38 ACP (now obsolete).
- .45 ACP, used in the M1911 and M1911A.

Automatic fire
- **Fully automatic operation:** This term refers to a weapon in which it is only necessary to hold down the trigger or firing button for the weapon to continue operation until the cartridge delivery system, be it magazine or belt, is empty. A number of weapons offer a choice between semiautomatic and fully automatic operation. Examples of fully automatic weapons include the Maxim machine gun, the Vickers machine gun and the Hotchkiss M1909.
- **Semiautomatic or self-loading:** This refers to a weapon, pistol, revolver, rifle or carbine in which the only requirement to fire a single round is to pull the trigger, all other operations being carried out by the weapon's mechanism. Unlike fully automatic operation, the trigger must be operated to fire each succeeding shot. Examples include the Colt M1911 and M1911A pistols, the Webley-Fosbery automatic revolver, and the Mauser C96 pistol.

Automatic weapons: U.S. legal position As with all automatic weapons offered for sale in America, any gun registered with the federal government (BATFE) before May 1986 may be held and fired legally on a firearms permit as a transferable NFA or Class III firearm. The information offered here is for guidance only and the relevant federal authorities should always be consulted when considering the purchase of such a weapon.

Fully automatic firearms may not be owned legally in Britain.

Bolt mechanisms—Bolt action
- **Conventional bolt action:** This term describes a mechanism in which the bolt of a weapon is operated manually, the breech being opened and closed by means of a handle welded to the bolt, most commonly placed on the right-hand side of the weapon. In operation, the handle is raised to the vertical, unlocking the bolt, and is then pulled sharply back, opening the breech and ejecting the used (spent) cartridge case. This action also cocks the firing pin, although this may occur as the bolt is closed, depending upon the design of the rifle. Finally, a new cartridge (round) is placed into the breech, the bolt is pushed forward, and the handle returned to its original horizontal position.
- **Straight-pull bolt-action:** In a straight-pull action, the bolt lever can be cycled without rotating it, hence producing a reduced range of motion by the shooter, with the goal of increasing the rifle's rate of fire. It has never been a popular mechanism, because the locking mechanism of such an arm is usually expensive to manufacture. This usually prices such a weapon out of normal military contracts, as in the case of the Ross rifle.

Bolt mechanisms—Semiautomatic and fully automatic
- **Open bolt:** This type of mechanism is found in a fully automatic firearm when operation requires the bolt to be pulled back and locked before firing, thus leaving the chamber open. The cartridge is subsequently stripped from the magazine by the action of the bolt when the trigger is pulled. Weapons with this type of operation include the Sten gun and MP 40.
- **Closed bolt:** This type of mechanism is found in a fully automatic firearm when operation requires the bolt to be pulled back and then pushed forward before firing, chambering the cartridge and cocking the striker mechanism, thus leaving the chamber closed. Weapons with this type of operation include the Browning M1919 and M2 as well as the Bren and MP 34.

"Open-bolt" designs tend to be cheaper to manufacture than the more complex "closed-bolt" types and are not so prone to the dangerous phenomenon known as "cooking off." This occurs when the firing chamber becomes so hot that the chambered cartridge fires spontaneously without the trigger being squeezed, which makes the "open-bolt" design more suitable for weapons designed for constant, fully automatic operation.

Bullet   Initially, muzzleloading firearms used a round lead ball, cast by the user from a mold supplied with the weapon. As firearms became more sophisticated and accurate, bullets also changed, becoming more aerodynamic and specialized for particular roles.
- **Spitzer bullet:** This is a bullet in which the front is drawn out to a fine point, for better aerodynamic performance. The term originated in Germany in the late 19th century as *Spitzgeschoss* (trans: *pointed projectile*), before being anglicized to "Spitzer."

Cartridge (*aka* metal cartridge, metal case or round)   A brass cylinder, with a flat base, which holds the powder and ball used in a firearm. The base of the cartridge holds a highly volatile substance used to ignite the charge and fire the weapon, serving the same function as the percussion cap. In common shooting parlance, a single cartridge is also referred to as a "round." There are three common types:
- **Rimfire:** These cartridges have the priming compound enclosed in the base of the cartridge, which is of thin brass. The hammer strikes the rim of the cartridge and thus fires the round. Due to the necessity for a thin base, rimfire cartridges were not suitable for heavy powder loads.
- **Pinfire:** A rarer cartridge type than the other two, mostly confined to European arms. The cartridge case is fitted with a pin, which goes through the wall of the case, and ignites the primer. Cylinders fitted to these arms have a characteristic slot machined in the top edge of each cylinder to receive the pin of the cartridge. Revolvers using this type are also, of necessity, always of open-frame design.
- **Centerfire:** Weapons using this type of cartridge are by far the most commonly encountered design. It is the cartridge of choice for most modern weapons larger than .22 in caliber, although many early weapons were chambered for larger rimfire rounds (.38, .32, .41). Centerfire cartridges consist of a hollow cylinder, closed at one end by a substantial brass base plate, termed the "head," which has a hole for the priming cap or primer to fit into the center of the base of the cartridge case. This primer consists of a metal cup containing the priming material and, depending upon its design, an "anvil." Upon firing, the weapon's firing pin strikes the base of the primer, crushing the priming material between the cup and the anvil and firing the cartridge. This anvil may be either contained in the primer (Boxer primer) or manufactured as part of the case (Berdan primer). Rimmed cartridges are differentiated from the more modern rimless ammunition, by having an "R" included in their size: e.g., the .303 British is designated as 7.7 × 56mmR, showing it to be a rimmed cartridge. The base of the cartridge or "head" usually has caliber and manufacturer's information stamped upon it and this is referred to as the cartridge **"head" stamp.**

In addition to the three main types, a number of other designs of cartridge were manufactured for short periods during the nineteenth century. These included Allen & Wheelock's lipfire cartridge, Moore's teatfire cartridge, Plant's cupfire cartridge, and Silas Crispin's ludicrously dangerous belted cartridge.

Charge   The charge refers to the amount of propellant contained in a weapon or cartridge, while the load refers to powder, wad and ball.

Coaxial   A weapon fitted to a tank or aircraft which can only fire in one direction and has no mechanism to allow either elevation or traverse.

Cyclic rate or rate of fire   These terms are synonymous and refer to the rate at which the mechanism of a fully automatic machine gun could fire, usually measured as rounds per minute or rpm.

Frames (revolvers and revolving rifles)   That part of the revolver which holds the lock and trigger mechanism and to which the breech lug and barrel are attached.

Open frame refers to a revolver with only a single strap, either above or below the cylinder, joining the frame and the barrel.

Solid frame describes a revolver in which a strap is present above and below the cylinder. This may be a real solid frame, in one piece, as is found in Adam's revolvers. Alternatively it may be a two-piece frame, superficially resembling a true solid frame, in which the top strap and lower section of the breech lug are located in recesses in the lock-frame. This type is found in Ball's revolver and some cheaper Adam's copies.

Finish
- **Bluing:** This is a process in which steel is partially protected against rust, and is named after the blue-black appearance of the resulting black iron oxide finish.
- **Parkerizing:** This is a method of protecting a steel surface from corrosion and increasing its resistance to wear through the application of a chemical phosphate conversion coating. It is considerably more effective than the older bluing process and gives the weapon a matte gray appearance.

Frizzen   The part of a flintlock mechanism which is struck by the flint to cause the spark that ignites the powder in the pan and fires the weapon.

Head stamp   The base of the cartridge or "head" usually has caliber and manufacturer information stamped upon it, and this is referred to as the cartridge head stamp.

Indexing (of a revolver cylinder)   This refers to the action of aligning the cylinder exactly with the barrel of a revolver, so as to allow the ball to enter the bore of the weapon cleanly and without impinging on the side walls of the barrel. In modern revolvers from the time of Colt's percussion weapons, this is carried out automatically by the internal mechanism, but in earlier flintlock arms, like Nock's seven-barreled pocket pistols, Collier's revolver and Puckle's "machine gun," this operation was carried out manually by the user.

Land service   Literally any sort of service on land, including conventional infantry and Special Forces, along with vehicles or other types of land transport, including armored vehicles. **Air service** similarly refers to any deployment involving aircraft or airborne forces, while **Naval service** refers to waterborne operations, including deployment in naval vessels or with waterborne forces such as the Royal Marine Commandos.

Load   The load in a muzzleloading weapon refers to the entire contents of the barrel or breech, i.e., the powder, the patch (if present), and the ball.

Lock mechanisms   This book uses the following classification with reference to lock mechanisms and is the typical system for most British and some American publications.

Single-action: This refers to a weapon in which the hammer has to be cocked manually, before it is fired by pulling the trigger. Examples of this type of weapon are Colt, Remington and Manhattan revolvers. It is by far the commonest type of action found in flintlock, percussion and early metal cartridge weapons.

Self-cocking: In weapons fitted with this mechanism, the gun is fired by pulling the trigger, which causes the hammer to move backwards until automatically released, thus firing the charge in the chamber. The hammer cannot be cocked manually. Early Adams and Webley-Bentley revolvers are the most commonly encountered arm with this type of mechanism. Such weapons may be readily be identified by the absence of a hammer spur. In some American publications, this system may be found referred to as "double-action only."

Double-action: This mechanism, as its name suggests, is a combination of the two previous types. The hammer of a double-action weapon may be cocked and then fired, or alternatively, it may be fired by simply pulling the trigger. This mechanism combines the advantages of both types, in that rapid fire is possible by simply pulling the trigger, while if greater accuracy is required, the weapon may be used in single-action mode. Beaumont-Adams and 4th Model Tranter revolvers have this type of mechanism.

Hesitating: This type is a modification of the self-cocking mechanism, in that one pull of the trigger cocks the weapon, while the second pull fires it. It is much less common than the other types, and examples include a few early Adams, Tranter and Starr revolvers. Both Tranter and Starr revolvers, in fact, are equipped with two triggers, one to cock the weapon and the second to fire it.

Receiver The casing that houses the operating mechanism of a firearm. In a semiautomatic or fully automatic weapon, the receiver usually holds the bolt and its operating system, collectively termed the bolt carrier group, and the trigger mechanism, together with both the ejection port and magazine housing. In a revolver, this component may be referred to as the "body" or "frame" of the weapon.

RFC Royal Flying Corps. This was the corps in the British army responsible for aircraft operation until a separate service, the Royal Air Force, was formed in 1918.

RNAS Royal Naval Air Service, a section of Britain's Royal Navy responsible for operating aircraft and light cars equipped with Vickers machine guns. Amalgamated with the Royal Flying Corps in 1918 to form the Royal Air Force.

Royal Small Arms Factory, Enfield More usually abbreviated to RSAF, Enfield, this was the factory that produced British military rifles, muskets and swords from 1816 until its closure in 1988.

Royal Ordnance Factory (ROF) These were factories run by the British government for the manufacture of arms and munitions. Sites included Fazakerley in Liverpool, Maltby in South Yorkshire, and the city of Leeds.

Sights This term describes any device used to assist in aligning or aiming a weapon by eye. Most frequently, they take the form of fixed iron sights or optical devices.

- **Fixed iron sights:** Fixed iron sights are typically composed of two components: a rear sight mounted perpendicular to the line of sight and a front sight that may be a post, bead or ring. **Open sights** have a shaped notch in the rear sight, which may have a variety of conformations; square, rectangular, circular or triangular are the most common.
- **Aperture sights** have a circular hole, often with a cross-wire, to replace the notch in the open pattern sight.
- **Optical sights:** This category includes any sight that uses an optical device to align a weapon, such as telescopic sights, reflector sights, or red-dot laser imaging sights.

Glossary

Stocks
- **Full-stock:** The stock (combined butt and fore grip) in a rifle or musket of this type extends the full length of the barrel, terminating at or near to the muzzle. Examples include the Pennsylvania rifle, Brown Bess musket, Lee Enfield rifles, and Colt's Model 1855 rifle.
- **Half-stock:** The stock in a rifle or musket of this type ends somewhere short of the muzzle. Examples include Henry and Winchester rifles and carbines, Spencer rifles and carbines, and Browning's Harmonica rifle.

Striker This is a mean of firing a cartridge employing a heavy firing pin directly connected to the spring providing the energy to impact the primer. It differs from a firing pin, which is a lighter component that serves to transfer energy from a spring-loaded hammer to the primer. Striker mechanisms are generally simpler than those fitted to hammer-fired weapons, because they combine the functions of hammer and firing pin in one component.

Waffenamt This organization was the German Army Weapons Agency. It was the center for research and development for weapons, ammunition and army equipment to the German Reichswehr, and later to the Wehrmacht.

War Department The War Department was the British government department responsible for the supply of equipment to the armed forces of the United Kingdom and the pursuance of military activity. In 1857 it became part of the War Office. Within the War Office the name "War Department" remained in use to describe the military transport services of the War Department Fleet and the War Department Railways.

War Office (UK) The War Office was a department of the British government responsible for the administration of the British Army between about 1684 and 1964, when its functions were transferred to the Ministry of Defence. It operated alongside the Admiralty, which was responsible for the Royal Navy, and the Air Ministry, which controlled the RAF. All objects that are the property of the War Office are stamped with that department's "Broad Arrow."

Section I: Early Repeating Weapons

CHAPTER ONE

Repeating Weapons from the Ancient World

Much has been written about the technological advances in warfare during the nineteenth century. A number of writers have dated the real beginning of modern, "sophisticated" warfare from the time of the American Civil War, which saw innovations such as the Gatling gun, muzzleloading rifle, and trench warfare. Of particular note, in the context of this period, was the introduction of the repeating firearm, most especially Colt's ubiquitous revolver and the Henry and Spencer lever-action magazine rifles. However, these were not the first repeating weapons to be used in organized warfare, and in order to find the first incidence of a repeater's use in battle, it is necessary to return to China during the 4th century B.C.

The Chinese Repeating Crossbow

Also known as the "Zhuge" crossbow after its inventor, the earliest archaeological evidence of a repeating weapon, in this case a crossbow, was found in Tomb 47 at Qinjiazui, Hubei Province, and has been dated to the 4th century B.C., during the Spring and Autumn period. However, most authorities attribute Zhuge Liang (A.D. 181–234), a famous military adviser of the Three Kingdoms period, with the invention of this simple and uniquely deadly weapon. He improved the design and developed a type that shot two or three bolts at once and could be used on massed formations. There are several designs, usually differentiated by their size, deployment and the number of bolts they could fire without reloading.

DESIGN

Whatever its size, a Zhuge crossbow consists of a conventional recurve crossbow with a magazine mounted on the stock to which the bow is fixed, the bowstring being arranged to move through a slot running the length of the base of the magazine. The magazine is hinged to the stock by the firing lever and secured by metal pins.

OPERATION

Once the operator has filled the magazine with the requisite number of bolts of an appropriate size, the firing lever is pushed forward, which in turn moves the magazine forward and secures the string in the trigger mechanism. Pulling back on the firing lever moves the string back, flexing the bow. As the lever reaches the end of its travel, a bolt drops into the firing slot on the shaft, whereupon the string is released and the bolt fired. To continue firing, the lever is simply moved forward and jerked back repeatedly until the magazine is empty, which a trained operator using one of the smaller hand-held types could achieve in approximately 15 seconds, usually firing the weapon from the hip. In addition to the small crossbows used by individual soldiers, larger weapons were also developed. The most common was an antipersonnel weapon, with two magazines, capable of discharging two bolts in a single operation and operated by two men. Larger weapons were also developed to act as siege weapons or for the defense of castles, employing heavier bolts and

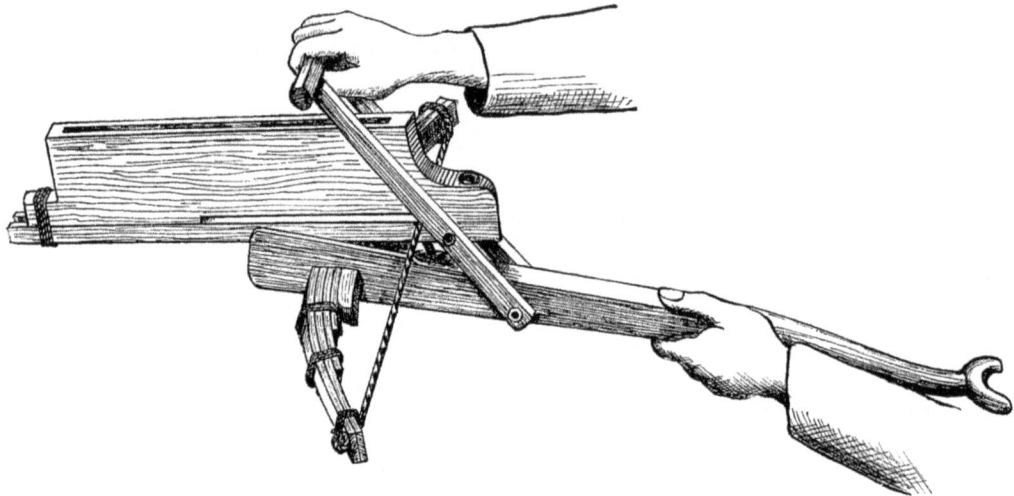

First stage in the operation of a repeating crossbow, in which the firing handle is moved forward, which simultaneously pushes the magazine forward and secures the string over the sear on the firing handle.

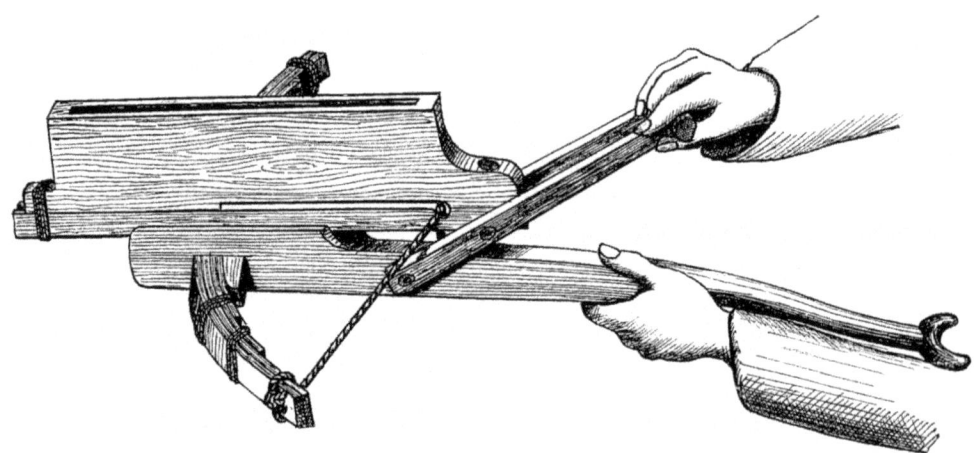

Second stage in the operation of a repeating crossbow, in which the firing handle is moved back, the string released and the bolt fired.

usually mounted on a castle wall or positioned to defend gates or doorways. There are also modern records which show repeating crossbows mounted on naval vessels.

The only major problem users experienced with this weapon was excessive wear on the bowstring. To counteract this deleterious effect, the strings were substantially constructed, being made of twisted animal sinew, reinforced with duck or goose quills.

Variations

- One-man antipersonnel weapon, fired from the hip.
- Two-man antipersonnel weapon, with two magazines, capable of discharging two bolts in a single operation.
- A siege weapon, employing heavier bolts and usually mounted on a castle wall or positioned to defend gates or doorways.

Military Service

Organized use of the crossbow by Chinese military forces began in the 4th century B.C., although repeating crossbows only began to become widespread in China during the 11th century, some 1,500 years later.[1] They became the principal weapon of the infantry during the Song (959–1126), Ming (1368–1644) and Qing (1644–1912) dynasties, and large bodies of infantry men seem to have been equipped with this weapon. Some accounts describe 100 men discharging 2,000 bolts in 15 seconds, while achieving hits at a range of up to 200 meters.

The Polybolos or Repeating Ballista

Development

The Original Ballista

The ballista was a weapon originally developed by the ancient Greeks from their crossbow siege weapons. Like the original crossbow, it consisted of a substantial stock upon which the bolt was laid prior to firing and a windlass to draw the string back to the trigger release or "nut." However, in place of the bowstave or "prod" of the conventional crossbow, a ballista had a heavily built frame on either side of the stock, containing twisted skeins of horsehair or some other strong material, into which had been inserted a substantial piece of timber to act as a lever. The ends of the two pieces of timber or levers protruded from the left- and right-hand boxes, and the bowstring was secured between them so as to produce a torsional force in the skeins in the box when it was drawn back to the nut.

Firing a ballista is a relatively simple process and similar to the technique used for a conventional crossbow. The bowstring is wound back using the windlass until it engages the "nut," whereupon a bolt is placed in position in the firing slot of the stock, with its nock resting in the string. All operators then stand clear, the trigger is depressed, and the string flies forward, driving the bolt out of the weapon and towards the target. Ballistae came in various sizes, from the portable Greek cheiroballista and Roman scorpio to the cart-mounted Roman carroballista. The Roman legions were very well supplied with this type of artillery, and each legion would have had approximately sixty of each type, i.e., one scorpio and one carroballista serving with each *century* of 100 men.[2]

The Polybolos

The Polybolos (Greek: "multi thrower") was a repeating ballista or torsion crossbow which is thought to have been invented by Dionysius of Alexandria, a Greek engineer working at the Rhodes arsenal in the 3rd century. Philo of Byzantium, a Greek engineer and mathematician who also lived in the 3rd century B.C., described a weapon similar to the polybolos, a catapult that could fire repeatedly without a need to reload. He left a detailed description of the mechanism, which was reputed to place successive bolts into the firing slot of the weapon without any manual intervention.

Modern replica of a relatively small ballista, probably used to throw missiles of between two and three pounds (courtesy Oren Rozen: CCA-SA-3.0).

OPERATION

The polybolos is thought to have differed from an ordinary ballista in that it had a wooden magazine, capable of holding several dozen bolts, over the cradle that holds the bolt prior to firing (the mensa). To operate the weapon, the windlass fitted to the end of the weapon was rotated counterclockwise with the trigger claw raised, which drove the mensa forward towards the bowstring, where a metal lug pushed the trigger under the trigger claw, and so secured the string. With the string locked into the trigger mechanism, the windlass was then rotated clockwise, drawing the mensa back. As the mensa was being drawn back, a round wooden pole in the bottom of the magazine rotated, dropping a single bolt into the firing tray. As the mensa continued its backward motion, it encountered another raised lug, which depressed the trigger mechanism and fired the bolt. Upon firing, the direction of the windlass was immediately reversed, driving the mensa forward, to secure the string and repeat the firing operation. Firing rates were thought to be in excess of ten bolts per minute, approximately five times the rate of fire of a conventional ballista, which could usually only manage around two shots every minute.

MILITARY SERVICE

Conventional ballistae saw considerable service, especially with Phillip of Macedonia and his son Alexander the Great, as well as later with the Roman legions. Unfortunately, no records exist of the polybolos being used in any battle.[3]

The Korean Hwacha or "Fire Cart"
DEVELOPMENT

The hwacha (aka: hwach'a) or fire cart was a device capable of simultaneously launching large numbers of *singijeons* or fire arrows. It was developed by Korean scientists for use from fortified positions against large bodies of troops, a role it fulfilled perfectly during the Japanese invasion of 1593 to 1598. It consisted of a two-wheeled cart carrying a board drilled with rows of holes and into which a fire arrow or singijeon was inserted. The capacity of individual hwacha was variable, but some weapons of this type were constructed so as to be capable of firing approximately 200 singijeons in a single salvo.

The development of the singijeon itself was more significant than the design for the hwacha, which was in principle only a simply constructed platform capable of securely holding multiple rockets. Gunpowder and the technology for manufacturing rockets and cannon reached Korea in the late fourteenth century (around 1380), and the rockets and *singijeon* that were subsequently developed saw use in campaigns to extend Korea's northern borders in 1388, and as coastal defense weapons against the Japanese when they tried to invade Korea in the 1590s.

These fire arrows were manufactured in three sizes: a large 52cm rocket, a 13cm medium rocket, and a small fire arrow. The largest singijeon was usually launched from some type of hand-held gun by ignition of a fuse in the paper tube that comprised the body of the rocket. This fuse would continue to burn after the weapon had been launched, until it reached the primitive warhead, which then exploded. Time and distance of the flight of

The front section of a hwacha, showing the singijeons in position with their attached black powder charges (courtesy Kai Hendry: CC-BY-2.0).

an individual rocket was determined by the amount of gunpowder contained in the paper body tube, and was adjusted before launch to ensure that the missile covered the required distance to the target before detonation, maximum range being between one and two kilometers. Medium singijeons were of a similar construction and function to the larger weapon, although range seems to have been limited to 150 meters. Despite its smaller capacity, the warhead on a medium rocket was still powerful enough to make a crater 30 cm deep in a mound of sand. The smallest singijeon was simply an arrow with a gunpowder pouch attached near the iron head of the shaft. Usually launched in multiples of 100 by a hwacha, the attached gunpowder container acted as the propellant and had an incendiary rather than an explosive function.

Operation

A hwacha was a simple two-wheeled handcart fitted with a substantial wooden launch pad approximately 50 cms in diameter and drilled with between 100 and 200 round holes. In order to fire the weapon, fused gunpowder igniters were first placed into the separate launching holes. Singijeons with their attached gunpowder containers were then also positioned in these launching holes, care being taken to ensure the arrow's gunpowder charge was adjacent to the igniter. The individual fuses from the igniters were then spliced together and the weapon was ready to fire. The launcher was set at right angles to the horizontal bed of the cart, and elevation could be altered by repositioning the handles that were used to push the cart. Traversing was effected in a similar way, by lifting the handles and simply pointing the cart in the direction of the enemy. Once aligned satisfactorily, the main fuse was lit, and after a short period the arrows were launched almost simultaneously, with an effective range of approximately 100 meters.[4]

Military Service

At the siege of Haengju, a Korean army of approximately 2,500 soldiers was besieged by an opposing Japanese force of over 10,000 troops. The Korean general, Kwon Yul, decided to make his stand on a low hill called the Haengju. On the summit he constructed a fortified earthwork, which was reinforced with a wooden palisade. Arms and food supplies were quickly moved into the fort and the walls were further reinforced by 40 hwachas. The Japanese attacked on the morning of 12 February 1593 but were repulsed after nine successive attacks and 1,000 casualties. Their losses were mainly inflicted upon densely packed bodies of Japanese troops by the hwachas, guns and mortars of the Koreans. The attackers retreated, but despite a significant defeat for the forces of the Shogun, the Japanese did not leave Korea until 1598.[5]

Table One: Comparison of the repeating crossbow, polybolos and hwacha

Weapon	Repeating crossbow	Polybolos	Hwacha
Makers	Seems to have been made by specialized craftsmen as the construction, particularly the trigger mechanism, is quite complex.	Various Greek armies; Romans may have adopted the weapon but archaeological evidence is lacking	Korean government

One. Repeating Weapons from the Ancient World

Weapon	Repeating crossbow	Polybolos	Hwacha
Period of production	Possibly 4th century B.C. until 1900 (2,300 years)	First appeared in the 3rd century B.C.	1380–1650
Production	No reliable records but certainly several million	No archaeological evidence, which suggests few weapons built	Between 1,000 and 10,000
Military service	Chinese Imperial Army, particularly during the period of the Three Kingdoms	None recorded	Border conflicts 1380; coastal defense 1300–1500 Japanese invasion of Korea 1592–1598
Crew	1 man for the small antipersonnel design; 2 men for the larger antipersonnel weapon, with a double magazine; 2 men (gunner and loader) for the larger siege weapons	Probably two: a gunner and loader	Variable; enough to load 100–200 arrows quickly, so probably 5 or 6 men
Weight	1-man weapon: 2–3 lb (1–1.5 kgs) 2-man weapon: 4–5 lbs (2–2.5 kgs) Siege weapon: over 100 lbs (50 kgs)	Approximately 15 kgs	Approximately 30 kgs, not including the cart
Length	1 man: 2 ft (70 cms) 2 man: 3 ft (1 meter) Siege weapon: 6–8 ft (2–3 meters)	Variable but approximately 1 meter; these were anti-personnel rather than siege weapons	Individual arrows: approximately 1 meter; Cart dimensions: variable
Mechanism	Conventional recurve or crossbow with magazine and repeating mechanism	Self-loading ballista, powered by torsion "springs"	Fire arrows using a gunpowder propellant, with a simple tube launcher
Sights	None fitted; smaller, one-man weapon usually fired from hip	None fitted; weapon seems to have been used at close range by instinctive alignment	None fitted. Alignment was achieved by moving the cart on which the device was mounted towards the enemy and then estimating elevation.
Maximum range	80–120 meters	Approximately 100 meters	100 meters
Rate of fire	Rate of fire was approximately 10 bolts in 15 seconds for the smaller one-man type, slightly longer for the bigger siege weapons. Reloading of the small, one-man weapons probably took less than a minute with practice, although the larger weapons would have taken considerably longer.	Ten bolts per minute. Reloading: probably around five minutes, the time necessary to fill the magazine with bolts	100–200 arrows simultaneously. Reloading: probably 30 minutes, depending upon expertise of the loading crew

Organ Guns

Although known in most English gunnery texts as "organ guns" because of their resemblance to the pipes of a church organ, such multi-barreled weapons were also known as ribauldequins, rabaulds, ribaults, ribaudkins, "chars de cannon" and "orgues des bombardes." They were essentially an early attempt to produce a muzzleloading volley gun, consisting typically of a collection of barrels of the same caliber secured to a frame, which was mounted on a two-wheeled cart and firing a small shot of 1 lb or less. In action, they were loaded individually before each barrel was fired as nearly simultaneously as possible, and the wheels of the carts were often fitted with blades or pikes for further protection from enemy infantrymen. The distance between the touchholes of the individual barrels was a major disadvantage in these weapons and often resulted in the delivery of a spasmodic volley, with the barrels usually going off in not very rapid succession. Leonardo da Vinci addressed this problem with a design of his own in which the barrels were arranged in a fan with the breeches of the individual barrels grouped closely together, although the weapon does not appear to have ever been used on a battlefield. Despite Leonardo's modification and their considerable use by many European armies, no professional gunner seems to have been sufficiently interested to attempt any improvement in the weapon's design, and organ guns showed little development in their three hundred years of service on the battlefield.

Military Service

The first record of a ribauldequin or organ gun being used on a European battlefield dates from 1339, when guns of this type were employed by the army of Edward

Polish artillery piece incorporating twenty barrels, fired simultaneously. The barrels are angled to ensure that the shot spreads when fired to cause maximum damage (courtesy Maciej Szczepańczyk: CC 3.0).

Early 16th-century volley gun, constructed for use by the armies of the Ottoman Empire.

III in France during the Hundred Years' War, although the Chinese had been using such weapons for a considerable period before their introduction to Europe. These early English guns had twelve barrels, thus firing volleys of twelve balls, although the number of barrels could vary considerably; later weapons used by the Milanese army and other participants in the Italian Wars (1494–1559) had only nine barrels. Ribauldequins were also used by the army of Ghent (1382), which had 200 guns of this type, and the Burgundians, who are recorded as having an establishment of approximately 2,000 organ guns of various designs and types in 1411. Organ guns were also deployed later by both sides during the Wars of the Roses (1455–1487). In the Second Battle of St. Albans (17 February 1461), it was Burgundian mercenaries under the command of the Yorkist Earl of Warwick who utilized the weapon against the Lancastrian Army, although this did not prevent the Yorkists' subsequent defeat. Despite their slow rate of fire, multi-barreled artillery pieces continued to be used in battles during the 16th and 17th century, and the army of Charles I is known to have deployed a double-barreled cannon in the English Civil War (1642–1651). It does not seem to have been a very effective weapon, since it could only fire a 2 oz ball or a small quantity of grapeshot.

These multi-firing organ guns were not an outstanding success, being extremely heavy and difficult to move from point to point on the battlefield. More importantly, while the multiple barrels gave a reasonable volume of fire, this advantage was rendered insignificant because of the long periods during which the gun was idle and the gunners were defenseless while they reloaded the weapon. The main advantage of such a weapon lay in positioning it at a critical point on the battlefield, where its single volley could have the most deleterious effect upon the enemy. Such a placement obviously had to be carefully considered, given the unwieldy nature of these early multi-firing guns.[6]

Table Two: Specification of the Ribauldequin or "Organ Gun"

Manufacturers	Gun founders in England and upon the Continent, probably by special order of the king or Board of Ordnance
Period of production	1339 until 1670
Production	Difficult to assess, but probably several thousand. Burgundian army in 1411: 2,000 guns Army of Ghent: 200 guns
Military service	Hundred Years' War (1337–1453) Wars of the Roses (1455–1487) Italian Wars (1494–1559) English Civil War (1642–1651)
Crew	Probably several men: a gunner, to aim and fire the weapon; five or six loaders to charge the multiple barrels.
Weight	Approximately 1,000 lbs
Length/barrel length	Total length probably around ten ft/barrels between four and six ft
Mechanism	Muzzleloading multiple barrels, ignited via a touchhole using a slow match.
Sights	None. Weapon was simply pointed in the general direction of the enemy and fired.
Maximum range	Approximately 1,000 meters
Rate of fire	Very slow, given the time necessary to load ten or twelve barrels individually. Probably around ten to fifteen minutes for an experienced crew.

Section II: Without Black Powder

CHAPTER TWO

Perkins's Steam Gun and Other Oddities

Steam Guns

In general terms, steam guns differ very little from more conventional black powder weapons. Replacing steam with evolved gas from the explosion of black powder requires changes associated with the delivery of the propellant, but such weapons, with perhaps the exception of the unfortunate Winan's Steam Gun, are instantly recognizable as projectile weapons, although not all were capable of repeating or multi-fire operation.

Archimedes and Leonardo

The first device to make practical use of steam for firing a cannonball was described in the late fifteenth century by Leonardo da Vinci (1452–1519), although he generously attributed the original concept to Archimedes (circa 287 B.C.–212 B.C.), who had previously described the procedure for making such a weapon in the 3rd century B.C. Leonardo referred to his weapon as an "architonnerre" and the record of its construction was hidden amongst his papers until it was rediscovered by Étienne-Jean Delécluze of the French Institute, who published Leonardo's description of the gun in the magazine *L'Artiste* in 1841. While not strictly a repeating weapon, the device is included here because the basic principle upon which it worked did not rely upon pressure generated by a separate steam engine, marking a significant departure from the later steam guns, which relied on the technical advances inherent in steam technology. Consequently, the architonnerre serves to demonstrate the innovations in weapon manufacture which were achieved even before the outpouring of technology that typified the nineteenth century.

The Architonnerre

This device was simply a steam-powered cannon, which operated by generating steam almost instantaneously from boiling water in the cannon's "breech," instead of using the gas generated by the explosion of a charge of black powder.

Operation

Archimedes's steam cannon consisted of a muzzleloading cannon of almost conventional design fitted with a strong metal tube connecting the breech to a copper boiler, which was fitted with a screw-in stopper, designed to act as a safety valve. The tube from the breech terminated below the water level inside the boiler, describing an inverted U above the level of the water, in the manner of a siphon. Charcoal was used to heat the breech of the cannon and the boiler, until the metal of the cannon's breech became red hot and the water in the copper container boiled vigorously. Steam was allowed to escape from the boiler via the screw-in safety valve, thus preventing a dangerous excess of pressure.

With all these preliminaries carried out, the cannon was now ready to fire. The firing sequence was begun by closing the safety valve, causing an immediate increase in pressure in the boiler, which forced the boiling water contained there along the siphon tube into the cannon's breech, the bend in the tube preventing the boiling liquid from returning to the boiler. In the breech, the boiling water met the red-hot metal walls of that component and was instantly converted into steam, and the sudden increase in pressure resulting from this conversion forced the cannonball out of the muzzle of the gun.

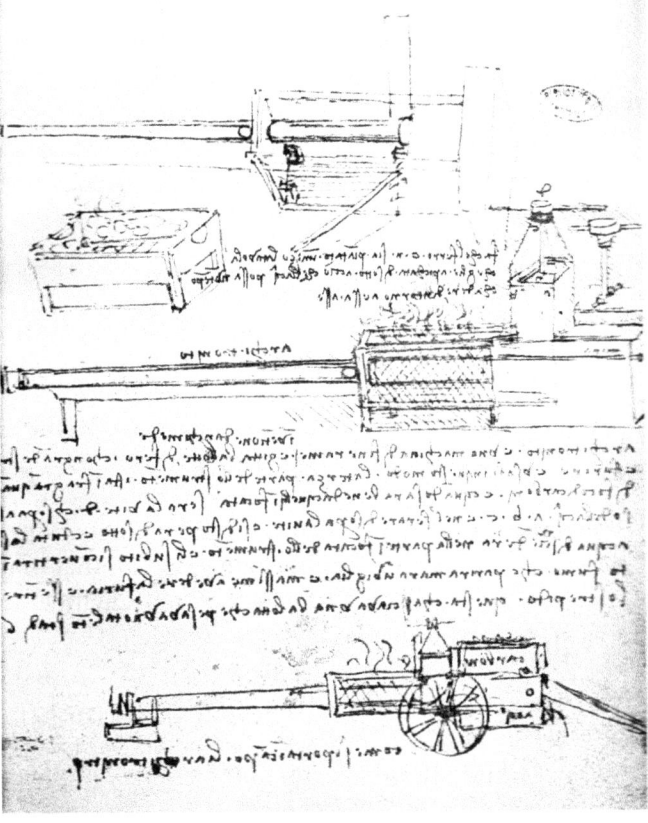

Original drawing of Leonardo da Vinci's Architonnerre steam-powered cannon, claimed to be capable of firing a projectile weighing 30 kgs.

Leonardo's original notes give this description:

> The *Architonnerre* is a machine of fine copper, which throws balls with a loud report and great force. It is used in the following manner:—One third of this instrument contains a large quantity of charcoal fire. When the water is well heated, a screw at the top of the vessel which contains the water must be made quite tight. On closing the screw above, all the water will escape below, will descend into the heated portion of the instrument, and be immediately converted into a vapor so abundant and powerful, that it is wonderful to see its fury and hear the noise it produces. This machine will carry a ball of a talent in weight (approximately 32 kilos or 68 lbs).

Perkins's Steam Gun

During the early half of the nineteenth century the search for repeating or quick-firing firearms was fast becoming something of an obsession with the military establishment, and many and diverse were the multi-shot weapons offered to the British Army during that period. Between Waterloo and the start of the American Civil War, a number of innovative designs were produced, such as Gatling's multi-fire weapon and Agar's "Coffee Mill" gun. More obscure weapons were also introduced, including designs like the Treeby "Chain" gun and a frankly bizarre "Revolving Cannon" that saw limited service with the Confederate forces during the Civil War. Few of these weapons, however, could match an earlier, radically innovative design demonstrated to the Duke of Wellington on 6 December 1825 by an American, Jacob Perkins.

JACOB PERKINS (1766–1849)

Perkins was born in Massachusetts in 1766, and after a career spent in a variety of engineering and metalworking concerns, he came to England in 1818, accompanied by a group of skilled workers who had worked in his American engraving and manufacturing business. Soon after his arrival in England, he became interested in steam as a power source, eventually developing a single-cylinder engine with a working pressure of 800 psi, which was an exceptional piece of engineering for that time. Using an engine with similar characteristics, on 15 May 1824, he took out English Patent 4592/1824 for the weapon which came to be known as Perkins's Steam Gun.

THE LONDON TRIAL AND MILITARY REACTION

Perkins offered his gun to the military in 1825 and somehow managed to attract the attention of the Duke of Wellington, then Master-General of the Ordnance, who authorized a trial of the gun at Perkins's factory near the present-day Regent's Park Canal. These tests were subsequently reported in the *Times* on 6 December 1825, their reporter apparently finding the gun's performance quite impressive.

First, Perkins fired his device over a range of about 35m against an iron target, using lead musket balls, which were completely shattered by their impact on the target. His next test involved firing at a target consisting of eleven 1-inch-thick deal (pine) boards arranged in a line, which the musket balls passed through completely. To give some idea of the effect this would have had against human tissue, a firearm that could propel a ball through a plank of deal only a ¼ inch thick had been shown to be sufficiently powerful to fatally wound an enemy soldier. As a final test, the gun was fired against a ¼-inch iron plate, which had been specially produced at the Woolwich Arsenal, and the first shot from Perkins's weapon also passed completely through this target. The gun was then fitted with a circular magazine before being used to perforate a 3m plank over its entire length, showing its effective lateral movement and multiple firing performance. This test was then duplicated on a plank that had been fixed vertically, with similar results. Perkins was not unaware of the financial constraints the military labored under in peacetime, either, and he was quick to explain his gun's advantages in that connection: "One pound of coal burned for raising steam will throw as many balls as four pounds of gun powder." He also claimed to be able to construct a gun "big enough to fire a one-ton ball from Dover to Calais."

Despite an enthusiastic reception from the old Duke and his companion, the Duke of Sussex, who left the trial crying, "Damn'd wonderful—damn'd wonderful," the military establishment proved unreceptive, citing a number of disadvantages. Amongst their objections were the length of time it would take to get steam up in the event of an attack (approximately 2 hours). Also, with the boiler alone weighing 5 tons, the weight of the complete gun was so much that it would have been extremely difficult to move across even the most forgiving terrain. Moreover, the experts felt that the generator and other components would be unreliable in the field as a consequence of developing major leaks under the high pressure of steam. These objections overrode the gun's more obvious advantages, and the government refused to consider the weapon. Unfortunately for Perkins, his later attempts to interest the French military were to confirm these shortcomings in the most unequivocal manner.

Perkins refused to be discouraged by the British rejection, however, and when the French government became interested in the weapon, he built another gun to their order, this time designed to fire four-pound balls at a rate of between 200 and 300 per minute. With construction complete, he arranged another trial at Greenwich, in the presence of the future Bourbon Prime Minister, Jules de Polignac, and a group of French military engineers. Unfortunately, after the Greenwich trial and further tests at Vincennes, near Paris, the French concluded: "The steam gun, after what is considered a fair trial, does not possess the power of throwing a ball more than half the distance that a common cannon of the same caliber did."

The difficulty appears to have arisen because, unlike gunpowder, which produces its propulsive pressure by a rapid initial expansion of gas, pressure in the steam gun was applied to the ball constantly until it left the muzzle. With the small, relatively tight-fitting ball such as that used in a conventional musket, the 900 psi of the steam gun was sufficient to produce performance comparable or even exceeding that of a conventional arm. Unfortunately, the larger, less carefully made ammunition used in the French tests seems to have allowed large quantities of steam to escape past the ball, and so reduced the pressure to a point that rendered the weapon largely ineffective.

Perkins's gun ended its days as an exhibit in the Adelaide Gallery of Practical Science, a museum and exhibition center designed to demonstrate new inventions of all kinds, although most of the exhibits originated from Perkins's fertile brain. A central feature of the exhibition was, of course, the steam gun, which was fired several times each day, discharging a load of seventy balls in four seconds, against a target approximately seventy feet from the gun. Scientific exhibitions at the Adelaide Gallery came to an end around 1840, and the steam gun was moved again, finally becoming an exhibit in the Tower Armouries. Perkins handed control of his manufacturing business to his son in 1835, when he was 69, and lived in semiretirement with his son and daughter-in-law until he died on 30 July 1849.

Operation

The construction of the gun was quite unique, although the principle upon which it worked was relatively simple. It was similar to that used in a modern air rifle, although in Perkins's invention steam replaced the compressed air of the modern gun. A steam engine, originally designed by Perkins himself and capable of producing a working pressure of 900 psi, was connected via a throttle valve to the rear of a massively constructed steam-tight firing chamber. The barrel of the gun, which was of "musket" bore (.75 caliber) and about 6 ft (approximately 2 meters) long, was welded to the front of this firing chamber, with a direct, open connection between the two components. The firing chamber bore a hopper into which the ammunition was placed, and a handle appears to have been used by the operator to open the bottom of the hopper periodically and thus fire the weapon. Aiming was by the adjustment of a swivel joint fitted between the firing chamber and the throttle valve, which allowed the barrel to be orientated in almost any direction. From an examination of the drawings and original text of the trials, firing was probably carried out in the following manner:

Once the steam engine had achieved an adequate pressure, the lead or iron musket balls used as ammunition were placed in the hoppers. The gun was then presumably aimed using the swivel joint, and once it was satisfactorily positioned, the throttle valve was opened to the desired extent and the gun was ready to fire. Firing was achieved by simply turning the handle attached to the ammunition hopper, which allowed a ball to fall into the firing chamber, steam pressure then expelling it down the barrel. Although this sounds simple, there must have been some very careful design and precise machining involved in the manufacture of the firing chamber, in order to prevent the pressure from simply blowing the musket balls out of the hopper during the loading cycle, instead of firing them down the barrel. Presumably the passage of steam was prevented as the hopper moved over the breech to deposit the individual musket balls, the pressure being reapplied when the breech was effectively closed as the handle continued the loading cycle.[1]

Antiques and Memorabilia

After Perkins's death, his unique gun was transferred to the Tower Armouries, and the firing mechanism is currently on display in the White Tower (circa 2016).

Winan's Centrifugal Steam Gun

Perkins was not the only inventor to see the advantages of steam, although the weapon named after Maryland industrialist Ross Winan but developed by the two Ohio inventors William Joslin and Charles Dickinson, did not work on the same principle as Perkin's weapon. Rather than steam pressure, the Joslin-Dickinson gun relied upon a steam engine to rotate the breech assembly, thus generating sufficient force to expel the two-ounce steel balls that were used as ammunition. In operation, this breech and barrel assembly was accelerated to a speed of approximately 200 rpm, whereupon the ammunition was dropped into a hopper mounted on top of the barrel. Subsequent expulsion of the ammunition was controlled by a spring-loaded catch that opened as the barrel reached its firing position.

After completing their initial design, Joslin and Dickinson had a major disagreement some time in 1859 and subsequently parted company. Dickinson patented the gun under his own name and managed to secure enough financial backing to build a gun to a modified design during 1860. Although his backers were a group of Boston financiers and Dickinson had constructed a prototype of the gun while living there, for some reason he moved the finished weapon to Baltimore, Maryland, where he appears to have demonstrated it to the City Council in February 1861, presumably in the hope of attracting more financial backing.

Unfortunately for Dickinson, the Civil War broke out two month later, on 12 April

1861, and a week after that, in the wake of the Baltimore Riot, the gun was seized by the city police. This is the point at which Ross Winan enters the story. The gun was taken to his works by the police, although it was soon moved from there and placed in a public display with other weapons seized by the city authorities. Winan, however, had previously obtained a contract from the Baltimore Board of Police to produce a variety of munitions for that force; and this, together with his involvement in Secessionist politics and the presence of the gun in his workshop, was sufficient to give impetus to the story that he had in his possession a powerful steam-powered weapon which was to be used against Union troop trains passing through the town on their way to Washington. His alleged involvement even led to Winan's being detained by federal forces, although he was released after only two days. The steam gun was even eventually returned to his machine shop for repair at the *city's* expense.

Dickinson clearly had an eye for the main chance, however, because when the repaired gun was returned to him, he promptly made plans to move it to Harpers Ferry, where it was claimed he intended to sell it to the Confederacy. Unfortunately, he and his gun were captured before he could contact his prospective buyers and the gun was returned to the federal camp at Relay, Baltimore, by the Union troops who had captured it.

Although it apparently worked well enough to impress the Baltimore City Council in February 1861, the gun itself never seems to have seen action, and after being used as an exhibition piece for some years after the war, it was sold for scrap late in the 19th century. The design was resurrected in 2014 for the U.S television series *Mythbusters*. Using the original specifications, the team certainly managed to produce a steam machine gun which would fire around 400 rounds per minute, with an impressive range of approx-

Artist's impression of Winan's steam cannon, showing the shield installed to protect the gunners and the steam boiler.

imately 700 meters. Unfortunately, its function as a weapon was less than impressive, because when fired against a pig's carcass, the steel ball being used as ammunition failed to even penetrate the outer skin. It seems doubtful if the 19th century weapon was much more effective.

Antiques and Memorabilia

Originally exhibited in Lowell, Massachusetts, before being sold for scrap at the end of the nineteenth century. The weapon constructed by the *Mythbusters* team is now on display in Elkridge, Maryland.[2]

Table Three: Perkins's and Winan's Steam guns

Weapon	Perkins's Steam Gun	Winan's Centrifugal Steam Gun
Manufacturers	Perkins Manufacturing Co., Hyde Park	Joslin and Dickinson were originally inventors, but U.S. patent was in Dickinson's name
Period of production	Production between 1825 and 1826	One prototype, made by Dickinson in 1860
Production	Two prototype guns: First demonstrated to the Duke of Wellington and his staff; second demonstrated to Jules de Polignac and his engineers	Single prototype
Military service	None	None
Crew	Possibly two: gunner and loader	Two: gunner and loader
Weight	In excess of five tons, with the steam generator	Several tons
Length	Total length; between 3 and 4 meters Barrel length: Approximately one meter	2–3 meters
Mechanism	Semiautomatic operation using high-pressure steam	Self-loading, steam-driven centrifugal cannon
Ammunition	.75 caliber musket ball or 4 lb cannonball, delivered from a hopper communicating with the breech of the gun	.75 caliber musket balls
Sights	None	None
Maximum range	Approximately 1500 meters	Not recorded for the original
Rate of fire	Claimed to be approximately 1000 rpm (rounds per minute)	Not recorded for the original

The Holman Projector

Although the nineteenth-century steam guns had proved ineffective, the Royal Navy used a weapon working on a similar principle as a cheap, simple and quite surprisingly effective AA (antiaircraft) gun during the early years of World War II. Called the Holman Projector, it was originally designed for use as an antiaircraft weapon and was fitted to trawlers and a number of the Navy's smaller craft from early in 1940 until the end of 1941.

Designed and manufactured by Holmans, a machine and hydraulic tool manufacturer based at Camborne, in Cornwall, the Projector was produced in three models, MK I, Mk II and Mk III. It had significant advantages over more sophisticated AA guns, since it could be produced using only cast iron and mild steel, both of which were fairly easy to obtain at this period of the war. Also, it required no expensive machining in its construction, which meant Projectors could be produced quickly and in large numbers. All three types used either compressed air or high-pressure steam to fire an explosive projectile at an enemy aircraft. They were intended primarily as defensive weapons for British merchant ships, which had been suffering heavy losses from Luftwaffe aircraft flying anti-shipping sorties, until enough stocks of more conventional antiaircraft weapons became available. The low altitude at which such strikes often took place, especially during skip-bombing by the Focke-Wulf Fw 200 Condors or torpedo attacks by Heinkel He 111s, led the Admiralty to consider that even a weapon with the limited range of the Holman could usefully screen a vessel, by unnerving the pilot of the attacking aircraft and distracting the bomb aimer. Unfortunately, the Holman's short range made it less useful against bombing attacks from high altitude, but forcing the Luftwaffe to bomb from a greater height would significantly reduce the effectiveness of their attacks, and the weapon was far cheaper and easier to build and install in large numbers than conventional antiaircraft weapons.[3]

Holman Projector in action, showing the inclinometer sight and the ammunition tins grouped on the weapon's base.

Operation

The problem with Perkins's self-loading gun, which had appeared when he tried to scale up the design to fire 4-pounder cannonballs, was that the steam pressure from his engine could only be provided in a constant stream, rather than a single, concentrated burst, which was how the propellant gas was evolved in a conventional black powder weapon. Consequently, any equalities in the bore of his weapon allowed steam to escape.

While this was not problematic in the original, musket-bore weapon, it became increasingly significant as the caliber of the weapon increased. This effect did not occur with the first, single-shot Holmans, which were designed to use a jet of compressed air or steam impinging immediately upon the projectile in the barrel at the pressure required, and did not require a constant pressure to be maintained throughout their operation.

Mk I Holman Projector

The ammunition used in this device was constructed in the form of an open-topped metal container, holding a Mills bomb fitted with a 3.5-second fuse, the Projector itself consisting of a 1.5-meter unrifled steel barrel into which this specially manufactured ammunition was dropped by the loader, after pulling the pin of the Mills bomb, with the grenade's safety lever retained by the side wall of the container. Upon reaching the bottom of the barrel, the base of the tin can instantly triggered the weapon's pneumatic system and the projectile was then fired from the barrel, the container and grenade separating and the Mills bomb subsequently exploding at the top of its trajectory. The high-pressure tanks supplying the weapon contained enough air to fire fifty grenades and their accompanying tin cans to a height of around 180 m.

The Mk I Projector was successfully trialed in February 1940, and an order was subsequently placed by the Royal Navy for 1000 of the Mk I models. Its success in

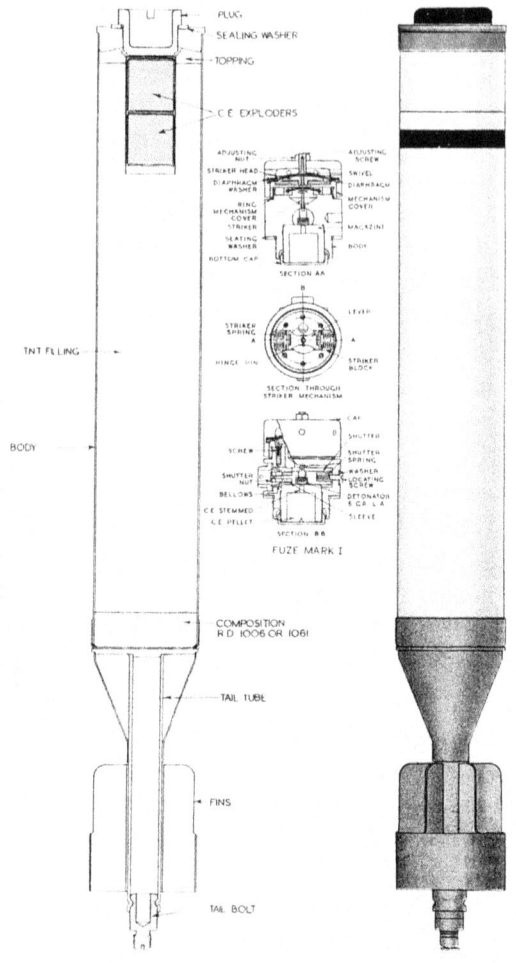

H.E. (high explosive) shell specifically designed for the Holman Projector, showing the external appearance, the explosive TNT filler and the fuse mechanism.

action justified all of the confidence the manufacturers reposed in the weapon, the first confirmed success coming only three weeks after the initial batch had been installed, when a Heinkel aircraft was reported damaged by Projector fire. Although an experienced crew was able to achieve a firing rate of about thirty rounds per minute, complete destruction of an enemy aircraft was uncommon. However, the grenades fired by the projector had one significant advantage over conventional AA weapons, because they produced a large cloud of dense, black smoke, absent for some unexplained reason from ground-based explosions involving this type of Mills bomb. Consequently, firing a large number of projectiles in quick succession at the leading aircraft of a flight gave following pilots the impression that

Left: No. 5 Mk1 Mills bomb, with part of case removed to show the base plug, detonator, cavity that contained the explosive in a live weapon, and the safety lever, with the projecting "ear" of the case to allow correct orientation in darkness. The spring-loaded striker is located above the detonator (courtesy Jean Louis Duboise). *Right*: No. 36 M Mk1 Mills bomb showing the brass plug sealing the hole through which the granular explosive was poured into the case of the bomb (courtesy Jean Louis Duboise).

the target vessel was armed with something far more dangerous than a smooth-bore grenade thrower. Often, this had the result of causing them to break off their original attack on the merchant ship doing the firing, although they might then attempt another run from a greater height. Sometimes attacking pilots were persuaded to break off their attack altogether, especially as merchant vessels always traveled in convoy with other ships fitted with some sort of AA defense, who would have all been using the attacking aircraft for target practice.

Mk II

The second version of this weapon, the Mk II Projector, was developed after a request from the Royal Navy for a weapon that used steam instead of compressed air, so as to equip older, steam-driven ships, particularly those in Britain's enormous trawler fleet, which were operating as mine sweepers and fishing vessels. Unfortunately, the original, automatic design was of no use when used with steam power, the harsh weather conditions the trawlers experienced and the steam itself serving to corrode and finally jam the valves of the adapted automatic mechanism, so a manual trigger had to be incorporated into the design.

In order to demonstrate the new weapon's versatility, a trial was arranged at Aldershot, with Winston Churchill himself in attendance. Unfortunately, the organizers brought no grenades, assuming that ammunition would be available from the Army, who were overseeing the trials at one of their major bases. No ammunition was forthcoming, however, so there was every prospect that the trial would be abandoned, until one bright young man thought of the bottles of beer that had been brought to drink with lunch. The smoothbore Projector was able to fire these rather unusual projectiles successfully, and all struck the target squarely with a very impressive splash. The Prime Minister commented on the weapon afterwards: "A very good idea, this weapon of yours. It will save our cordite."

Despite the apparent success of the Aldershot trial, the Mk II Projector was found to be extremely inaccurate when fired at moving targets more than a few hundred meters away from the operating vessel. Fewer than twelve aircraft were confirmed as shot down by the weapon in its first year of service, although a large number of reports were received in which Luftwaffe aircraft were described as turning away from an attack after salvos from a ship's Holman Projector were launched, so it clearly had a significant deterrent value. Within the Admiralty, the Projector was certainly perceived as a useful interim weapon in the early years of the war, when other, more effective antiaircraft weapons, such as the Oerlikon 20mm cannon, were in short supply. Consequently, the Mk II was eventually fitted to a wide variety of ships, including armed trawlers, mine sweepers, motor gunboats, and even some older destroyers.

Mk III

In 1941, production of a new Mk III Holman Projector began, featuring a semiautomatic mechanism capable of firing specially designed, multiple projectiles in a single salvo to a height of around 300 meters. An order was placed by the Admiralty for one thousand weapons, for fitting to coastal gunboats and other light craft, where the light recoil of the weapon would be a distinct advantage, outweighing the Projector's shortcomings. Plans were also drawn up for a Mk IV version of the semiautomatic weapon, with a shorter barrel and swivel base, to facilitate operation aboard these smaller craft, but by the time design work was complete, more advanced weapons had made the Projector obsolete.

Ammunition

All three types of Projector were designed to use a No. 36M Mk1 Mills bomb as ammunition, as well as their own specialized H.E and illuminating projectiles. Patented by William Mills, an employee at the Mills Munition Factory in Birmingham, the initial design was accepted into the British Army as the "Mills Bomb, No. 5 Mk1" early in 1915. Subsequent improvements, in particular the application of a coating of shellac to prevent dampness from reaching the internal mechanism of the fuse, resulted in the acceptance in 1918 of the No. 36M Mk1 Mills bomb, which was the British army's issue hand grenade from that time until it was replaced in 1972 by the L2 series of grenades. Originally, the No. 36M Mk1 had been fitted with a seven-second fuse, but the fighting in France during 1940 showed that this was too long a delay, and the standard fuse was modified after Dunkirk to give a delay of only four seconds.

Viewed externally, a Mills bomb consists of an oval case with deep serrations covering the side walls, which were originally intended to give a secure grip when throwing, and a security pin and lever projecting from the striker assembly, which was screwed into the top of the casing. To load the weapon, explosive filler was poured through a small circular hole in the top of the case, which was then closed with a plug. A detonator was then fitted into a larger hole in the bottom of the grenade, which was closed with a larger base plug. Finally, the striker mechanism, with its security pin and lever attachment, was screwed into the fuse well in the top of the complete grenade; this lever was protected by metal "ears" flanking the top of the case, which were fitted as an aid to correctly orientating the bomb in darkness. Unfortunately the oval shape of the Mills 36M did not lend itself to the conformation of the Holman's barrel, so bombs used in the Projector were placed in round tins that fitted the barrel more snugly. This modification allowed the compressed air pulse to fire the projectile effectively and the fuse delay was also decreased to 3½ seconds, presumably thus ensuring that the bombs exploded at the very top of their flight.[4]

Table Four: Specification of Holman Projector Mks I, II, III

Manufacturers	Holmans of Camborne, Cornwall
Period of production	1940 to the end of 1914
Production	Mk I—approximately 1,000 Mk II—probably at least 1,000 Mk III—approximately 1,000
Military service	Fitted to trawlers, mine sweepers and small inshore craft between 1940 and 1941.
Crew	Two: Loader and aimer
Weight	Several tons, but the weapon was permanently mounted aboard a ship, near either a source of compressed air or steam, so was not portable.
Length/barrel length	Approximately two meters/approximately 1.5 meters
Mechanism	Mk I: Compressed air mortar Mk II: Steam-powered mortar Mk III: Steam-powered, semiautomatic mortar Mk IV: Steam-powered, semiautomatic mortar
Ammunition	No. 36M Mk1 Mills bomb, fitted with 3.5-second fuse and enclosed in a metal case. Specialized H.E shell Specialized, parachute-mounted illuminating shell Projectile loaded at the muzzle, as in a conventional mortar
Sights	Circular wire frame and inclinometer, fixed to the muzzle and projecting on the left side
Maximum range	Mk I: 150–160 meters Mk II: 120–150 meters Mk III: 300 meters
Rate of fire	Thirty rounds per minute, with an experienced crew

Museums and Artifacts

Holman projectors are included in exhibits at these museums:

The King Edward Mine museum (kingedwardmine.co.uk), located near Troon, in Cornwall.

The Canadian War Museum (www.warmuseum.ca), 1, Vimy Place, Ottawa, Ontario, K1A0M8.

Section III: *The Black Powder Era*

CHAPTER THREE

Early Military Rockets

Although rockets are not invariably thought of as a multi-fire weapon, they are usually fired simultaneously from either banks or on multiple single launchers, and because their effects were similar to other early weapons of this type, they are included here. The Chinese were the first country to introduce rockets for military purposes, the weapon being adopted in turn by the Mongols under Genghis Khan around 1250, when his armies overran and conquered northern China. He found Chinese rocket experts amongst the subject peoples in that region, and these men were subsequently "persuaded" to work for him. Progress in this sort of technology was relatively slow, but by the middle of the sixteenth century the rocket was well known in Europe, described first in the works of Conrad Hess, although the British had to wait until 1767 and the First Anglo-Mysore War for their first experience of the weapon's effectiveness.[1]

Indian and Napoleonic Rockets

TIPU SULTAN AND THE ANGLO-MYSORE WARS

Hyder Ali was responsible for the wholesale introduction of rockets into Mysorean military organization when he came to power in 1761. There were approximately 1,200 specialist rocket troops in the Army of Mysore when an attack by his troops on an outpost manned by the British East India Company precipitated the First Anglo-Mysore War (1767–1769). Rockets did not figure prominently in that conflict, but in the Second Anglo-Mysore War (1779–1784), troops of the British East India Company were defeated in 1780 at the Battle of Pollilur, because a rocket is thought to have destroyed most of the British ammunition train. Hyder Ali died in 1782, and when his eldest son, Tipu Sultan, succeeded to his father's throne, he increased the numbers of rocket specialists in his army as well as improving their strategic use. The Third Anglo-Mysore War began in 1789, over the disputed ownership of two forts in Cochin, but luck as well as the British were against Tipu Sultan. He was forced to sign a humiliating treaty and turn over two of his sons as hostages in 1792, in order to end the war and prevent further British depredations. Two years later, in 1794, still discontented by British rule, he began to conspire with the French, now represented by their Republican officials, to throw the British out of Mysore first, and eventually the whole of India. Unfortunately for both Tipu Sultan and Bonaparte, Nelson destroyed the French Navy at the Battle of the Nile in 1798, and the British, having learned of the Sultan's diplomatic efforts, were then able to send three columns of British and Indian infantry to lay siege to his capital of Srirangapatna, where he was killed on 4 May 1799.[2]

Mysorean Rocket Technology

Mysorean rockets were certainly much better than the similar, contemporary European weapons. Hyder Ali's rocket scientists had developed a projectile that used an iron cylinder to hold the firing charge, instead of the paper component installed in European rockets, allowing a much greater quantity of propellant to be used and greatly increasing the weapon's range. Although these rockets were claimed to be able to travel over 1,500 meters, accuracy was still a problem. However, the Sultan's scientists seem to have quickly discovered that the problem of the inaccuracy of single rockets could easily be rendered insignificant by firing them in large numbers simultaneously as rocket batteries. Hyder Ali also increased his rocket's effectiveness by mounting them on small, highly mobile carts and training a special corps of rocket men to operate the weapons. Tipu Sultan was an even greater advocate of rockets than his father, and after he assumed command of the army in 1782, his Mysorean rocket corps began an expansion, which eventually saw it number over 5,000 trained men. By this period, his Rocket Corps were highly experienced in the idiosyncrasies of their weapons and were able to aim them effectively by setting the launcher at an angle calculated from the diameter of the rocket cylinder and the distance from the launcher to the target. To make them even more gruesomely effective and add to their psychological impact, blades were mounted on the sticks, making their flight extremely erratic as their speed dropped, and causing the blades to rotate, resulting in terrible injuries to anyone caught in their path. Some of the rockets also had pierced cylinders, turning them into effective incendiaries.

Table Five: Specification of Mysorean rockets

Manufacturers	Mysorean rocket scientists attached to the court of the Sultan
Period of production	1761 until 1799
Production	No records, but certainly many thousands

Military service	Army of Mysore in:
	    First Anglo-Mysore War (1767–1769)
	    Second Anglo-Mysore War (1779–1784)
	    Third Anglo-Mysore War (1789–1792)

Crew	No record, but probably two: loader and aimer, with ancillaries to move the carts
Weight	Individual rockets weighed only a few ounces, but they were fired from a cart weighing several hundred kilos
Ammunition	Individual rockets weighing only a few ounces, loaded individually by hand
Sights	Aimed by pointing the cart in approximately the right direction
Maximum range	1,500 meters
Rate of fire	Fired in batteries, so rate of fire would be determined by the time taken to reload the battery

Congreve's Rocket

Tipu Sultan's death had a number of repercussions for British India, but there were also unexpected benefits in the field of armament technology. After the fall of Srirangapatna, 600 launchers, 700 serviceable rockets and 9,000 empty rocket cases were found there. British experience of the effectiveness of the Sultan's rockets led to the transfer of much of that Mysorean rocket equipment to the Woolwich Arsenal, where it came eventually to the attention of the son of the Comptroller, one William Congreve. Congreve began his own experiments in rocket technology in 1804, buying and modifying European rockets with his own funds, before examining the Mysorean weapons. Eventually he produced his first successful rocket design, a missile with a 6-lb iron warhead and an effective range of 1,500 yards, produced to his design at the Royal Arsenal, Woolwich.

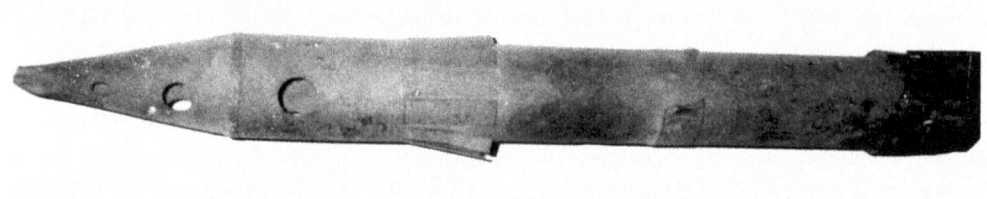

Original casing from a Congreve rocket.

Reproduction of a painting showing the effect of Mysorean rocket artillery on British troops.

Congreve had begun by building rockets with cardboard ignition chambers, much like a modern firework, but by 1806, he had perfected a design using sheet iron for the case. He also discovered how the composition of the gunpowder used as propellant needed to be adjusted to suit the size of the rocket, an innovation he was quick to introduce when making his subsequent weapons. By 1806 he was able to produce a 32-lb rocket capable of traveling over 3,000 meters. Records for 1813 show Congreve rockets as a regular feature of the two troops of the Rocket Battery, RHA, and available in three distinct classes, categorized by weight, like artillery cannon:

- **Heavy rockets:** These were explosive rockets, the largest weighing three hundred pounds, with a warhead between five and six feet in length and a stick of approximately 25 ft, larger warheads requiring a longer stick. Rockets of this size were little used, because of their expense and the difficulties inherent in transporting them.
- **Medium rockets:** These had warheads between two and four feet in length, of between 24 to 42 lbs in weight and constructed as shot, case shot, or explosive ordnance (shell). Stick length varied from 15 to 20 ft, depending upon the size of the warhead; larger warheads, not unexpectedly, required a longer stabilizing stick. Usually a naval weapon, it was rockets of this type which were used against Baltimore in 1814.
- **Light rockets:** These weapon had warheads between 16 to 25 inches long which weighed between 6 and 18 lbs and like the medium rockets, were constructed as shot, case shot, or explosive ordnance. The length of the stabilizing stick varied from 8 to 14 ft, as before depending upon the weight of the warhead in use.

Light rockets appear to have been the most common weapon of this type in use with the British Army during the Napoleonic Wars, although the Royal Navy found the medium type significantly more useful, commissioning two purpose-built ships to utilize the weapon, HMS *Erebus* and HMS *Galgo*. *Galgo* had originally been a merchantman before being converted first to a warship, then to a rocket ship, by having 21 angled tubes or "rocket scuttles," each firing a 32-lb rocket, installed in place of her broadside. These scuttles were fitted with iron shutters to prevent the rockets' exhaust from entering the vessel and setting it on fire. *Erebus* was similarly equipped, although to an improved design, and she also had the more interesting career, being the ship that participated in the attack on Baltimore in 1814 and inspired Francis Scott Key to compose what became America's national anthem, "The Star-Spangled Banner."

In December 1815, Congreve demonstrated a new design, in which the stabilizing stick was screwed into the center of the base of the rocket case. This design was accepted by the Army in 1817 and used in service until 1867, when it was replaced by Hale's rocket. Although the range of Congreve's rockets was similar to that which was possible with a 6-pounder smoothbore cannon, the rate of fire was significantly higher. More importantly, the overall saving in weight meant that fewer horses were needed to transport the equipment, approximately 105 horses for a full rocket troop, while an artillery troop with the same potential firepower needed more than double that number, at around 220. This was important, especially during the Peninsular Campaign, where horses were hard to come by and even harder to feed well enough to keep in reasonable condition.

Rockets, however, were not without disadvantages, particularly when considering their medium- to long-range accuracy and reliability. An example of the problem was described by Captain Mercer, commanding G Troop, RHA, during the retreat from Quatre Bras, in June 1815:

> The rocketeers had placed a little iron triangle in the road with a rocket lying on it. The order to fire is given—port-fire applied—the fidgety missile begins to sputter out sparks and wriggle its tail for a second or so, and then darts forth straight up the chaussée. A gun stands right in its way, between the wheels of which the shell in the head of the rocket bursts, the gunners fall right and left.... Our

rocketeers kept shooting off rockets, none of which ever followed the course of the first; most of them, on arriving about the middle of the ascent, took a vertical direction, whilst some actually turned back upon ourselves—and one of these, following me like a squib until its shell exploded, actually put me in more danger than all the fire of the enemy throughout the day."

Naval Service

The Royal Navy adopted Congreve's rocket into service in 1805, and its first operational use was in an attack on Bolougne in the autumn of that year. The attack was not very successful, but the Navy persisted with the new invention and achieved a number of significant successes with the rockets during the Napoleonic Wars. Most notable of these were the attack on Bolougne in 1806, the burning of Copenhagen in 1807, Cochrane's attack on the French fleet in the Aix/Basque roads in 1809, and the attack on Flushing by the rocket ship HMS *Galgo* in 1809. In 1812, the United States declared war on Britain, and Congreve's rockets figured quite prominently during the War of 1812. They were deployed with the Royal Marines at Fort Oswego, at Lundy's Lane, and during the Chesapeake Campaign, while the Royal Navy used them during their unsuccessful attack on Baltimore.

Army Service

Rockets were not accepted into service with the British Army until 1813, when the newly formed Rocket Brigade joined Crown Prince Bernadotte's Army of the North, where they fought successfully in the battles of Gohdre and Leipzig. In January 1814, the unit was renamed the 2nd Rocket Troop, RHA, and were sent to Holland to serve under Sir Thomas Graham, but returned in time to fight at Waterloo under the command of Captain Whinyates. Previously, in September 1813, Wellington had also reluctantly accepted the services of another rocket unit, initially called the "Rocket Company" but later renamed the 1st Rocket Troop, RHA, which fought at the Crossing of the Ardour and the Battle of Toulouse, before being sent to America to participate in the expedition against New Orleans.

Congreve rockets remained in service until the Crimean War, where they were used at the Battle of Inkerman, being superseded in 1867 by the Hale rocket.[3]

Antiques and Collectible Memorabilia

The nature of Congreve's rockets mean that they usually deteriorated very quickly. Consequently, few examples have survived to the present, and these are mostly museum specimens. The best collection is housed in the Royal Artillery's FIREPOWER Museum, which is located within the old Woolwich Arsenal site. Occasionally, objects associated with the two Rocket Troops, RHA, may also be found at auction, such as shoulder flashes or items of a similar nature.

Hale's Rocket

Congreve was not the only inventor interested in military rockets during the nineteenth century. In 1844, William Hale patented a new type of rocket, based on Congreve's final design, but incorporating angled exhaust holes instead of a stabilizing stick. Exhaust gases expelled through these holes caused the rocket to spin, in a manner analagous to a rifle bullet, giving far greater stability in flight than the Congreve.

WILLIAM HALE

Born in Colchester in 1797, Hale is thought to have been without a formal education, being taught initially by his grandfather, before finishing his training in science and engineering largely through his own efforts. His first British patent was granted in 1827 for what was effectively an early form of jet propulsion, utilizing an Archimedean screw to supply propulsive power by driving a stream of water through the stern of a vessel.

In 1839, he moved to Woolwich, where he began a series of trials intended to improve the performance of the Congreve rocket, principally by replacing the stick with a system which created spin-stabilization, in a manner analogous to a bullet from a rifled firearm. His first rocket patent was granted in January 1844, and in 1846 he sold the manufacturing rights for his rocket to the U.S. government for $20,000. The U.S. Army subsequently used them in the Mexican War (1846–1848). Some of Hale's rockets saw service in the Crimea (1854–1856), but it was not until 1867 that the weapon was accepted into service with British forces, replacing the earlier Congreve and Boxer rockets. Hale rockets were used in action by the British Army in Abyssinia and a number of colonial wars. Their last use on active service was in Sierra Leone in 1899, although the weapon was not finally declared obsolete until after World War I, in 1919. As well as seeing service with the British Army, Hale rockets also played a relatively minor role in the U.S. Civil War, only one federal rocket unit having been recruited as a rocket battalion in the 24th New York Battery. Unfortunately, no record for Confederate units equipped with Hale's rockets appears to be still in existence, although it is known that they were in use by Southern troops, and a number of unexploded rockets have been excavated in recognizable condition from Civil War battlefields.[4]

HALE'S ROCKET DESIGN

The rocket itself was an elongated cylinder, made initially of rolled sheet iron, although later a mild steel case was introduced. The nose or warhead was rounded to improve the

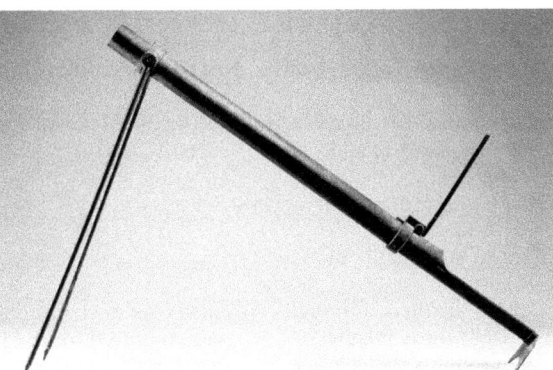

Hale rocket launcher from left side, showing the supporting bipod and sighting apparatus (courtesy James D. Julia Auctioneers, Fairfield, Maine. www.jamesdjulia.com).

Hale rocket in non-excavated condition (the only known example). This is a later pattern, with the rotation vents at the base of the head, rather than in the base, and so may have either a Federal or Confederate States provenance (courtesy James D. Julia Auctioneers, Fairfield, Maine. www.jamesdjulia.com).

missile's aerodynamics and filled with the type of ordnance required: shot, case shot, or an explosive shell. A wooden plug was then inserted, followed by the black-powder propellant; the plug was intended to separate propellant and charge and thus prevent premature ignition of the warhead. The rear end was threaded to screw into the body of the rocket, securing charge, plug and propellant firmly into position. On its outer, lower surface, the plug was fitted with three angled "fins," which directed the propellant exhaust gases so as to cause the rocket to spin in flight and thus assume a more stable trajectory. In a later development, Hale moved the steering vents forward so that they exited from the base of the head, which resulted in greater stability in flight.

Hale rockets ranged in size from 3 lbs up to 100 lbs, although the 9- and 24-pound rockets were the size most commonly used by the British. Launchers were similar to the device used for the Congreve, being in the form of a fairly simple trough for land-based rockets and a tube screwed to a convenient vertical surface when used on shipboard. Hale rockets had an effective range of approximately 2,000 yards.[5]

Table Six: Congreve's and Hale's rockets

Weapon	Congreve rocket	Hale rocket
Manufacturers	Royal Arsenal, Woolwich	Various U.S. government arsenals: 1846 until 1865; Royal Arsenal, Woolwich: 1865 until 1899
Period of production	1806 until 1867	1846 until 1899, with British and U.S. forces, including the CSA (Confederate States Army)
Production	Not recorded, but probably several million	Not recorded, but probably several million
Military service	Napoleonic Wars: battles of Gohdre, Leipzig and Waterloo. War of 1812: attack on Baltimore. Crimea War: battle of Inkerman.	U.S. Army: Mexican war, Civil War (both sides)
Crew	Usually six men, although most of these men were required for the placing of the rocket tubes, rather than actually firing the weapon.	Usually six men, although most of these men were required for the placing of the rocket tubes, rather than actually firing the weapon.

Weapon	Congreve rocket	Hale rocket
Weight	Several kilograms, for a single launcher	Several kilograms, for the single launcher
Length/Barrel length	Launcher, approximately 2 meters	Launcher, approximately 1.5 meters
Ammunition	Heavy rocket: 300 lbs, 10 meters in length Medium rocket: 24–42 lbs, 7 to 8 meters in length Light rockets: 6–18 lbs, 3.5–5 meters in length Loaded by hand into the individual launchers and fired by lighting a linked fuse, usually to produce a salvo	Rockets were produced in sizes from 3 lbs up to 100 lbs; 9- and 24-lb rockets were mostly used by the Royal Artillery. Loaded by hand into the individual launchers and fired either individually or by a multiple fuse
Sights	Pointed in the general direction of the enemy and fired	Pointed at enemy and fired
Maximum range	Approximately 3,000 meters for the larger types	2,000 meters
Rate of fire	Determined by the skill and experience of the crew but perhaps one salvo per minute.	Determined by the skill and experience of the crew but perhaps one salvo per minute, similar to the Congreve.

Antiques and Memorabilia

Although it might seem hard to believe, Hale rockets and even complete launchers not infrequently find their way into auction sales in the U.S., although they are very rarely seen in Britain. Hale rockets and their associated equipment found in the U.S. almost invariably have a Civil War provenance, and this factor, together with their rare appearance, means that prices at auction tend to be alarmingly high.

Values

Launchers : NRA Good: $10,000–$12,000; NRA Fine: $28,000–$31,000.
Rockets: Excavated grade: $2,000–$2,500; Mint or Museum grade: $7,500–$10,000.

CHAPTER FOUR

Early Black Powder Weapons

Early Types of Ignition and Repeating Weapons

The main barrier to the development of repeating weapons during the first half of the nineteenth century was the lack of a reliable, self-contained ignition system. Even the development of the fulminate percussion cap, which had its first trial by the Board of Ordnance at the Royal Arsenal, Woolwich in 1820, did not improve matters very much in the field of heavy artillery, although it did usher in the era of repeating hand weapons. Prior to the development of the fulminate cap, however, the ignition systems fitted to the general run of firearms were of three distinct types, either matchlock, wheel lock or flintlock. There were also a number of developmental stages within these major divisions, and flintlock weapons, in particular, were a final design produced from experiences with forerunners like the snaphaunce.[1]

THE MATCHLOCK

Matchlock weapons, as their name suggests, were fired by means of a slowmatch, held in some sort of simple lever arrangement, called the serpentine, which was mounted in front of the flash pan. A weapon of this type was loaded by ramming a charge of powder and a ball down the barrel; the priming pan, sited at the breech, was then loaded with a finer grade of powder. The matchlock was fired by the simple expedient of pulling a lever, which emerged from the bottom of the weapon and was connected to the serpentine. Operation of this lever drove the serpentine into the pan, igniting the fine priming powder, which flashed through the hole between the pan and the barrel, termed the touchhole, igniting the charge and firing the weapon. A further development of this system was the snapping matchlock, in which the serpentine was spring-loaded and operated by a button, trigger, or in some cases a short string entering the mechanism. Reliability and accuracy were not outstanding features of these devices, and the musketeer was usually required to spend most of his time twirling the match between his fingers to keep it alight. Nor were they especially cheap, since it was estimated that a soldier on sentry duty for a year would use up over a mile of slowmatch. They were not produced regularly as repeating weapons, although their conformation would not prohibit the production of a multi-fire pistol or musket, similar to Nock's volley gun. At least one arm is recorded with a cylinder having five chambers.[2]

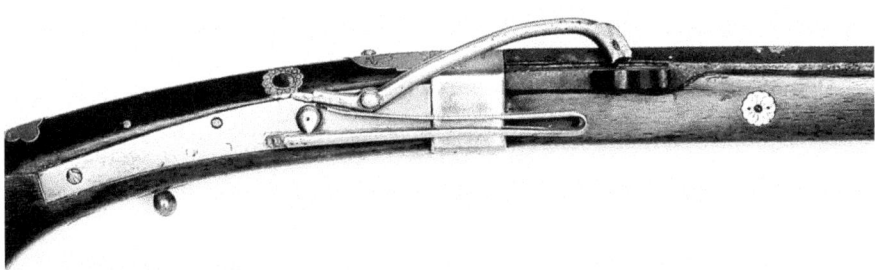

Matchlock musket, showing the serpentine without its characteristic fuse, the activating spring and the trigger (by kind permission of Bonhams).

THE WHEELOCK

Wheelock weapons were the next stage in firearms development and were seen by most users as a decided improvement over the unreliable match lock system. Wheelocks are believed to have originally been devised by Leonardo da Vinci, early in the sixteenth century, although German guns made around that date are also recorded.

Similar in operation to the flint and wheel system in an old-fashioned cigarette lighter, this type of ignition system consists of a roughened iron wheel that bears against a piece of pyrites. When ready to fire, the mechanism of the wheel was wound up by means of a key or wrench and the flash pan pulled back. Pulling the trigger drew a stop pin out of the wheel, allowing it to turn at considerable speed, which produced sparks from the pyrites and ignited the priming, sending a flash through the adjacent touchhole. Wheelocks were expensive to make, and so they did not replace the matchlock as the military weapon of choice, although they are commonly found as well-made and beautifully decorated sporting guns. Multi-fire weapons such as a volley gun or "duck's foot" pistol can be constructed using this system, but production of such an arm capable of firing successive shots was fraught with considerable difficulties, as well as being expensive, so few weapons of this type were made.[3]

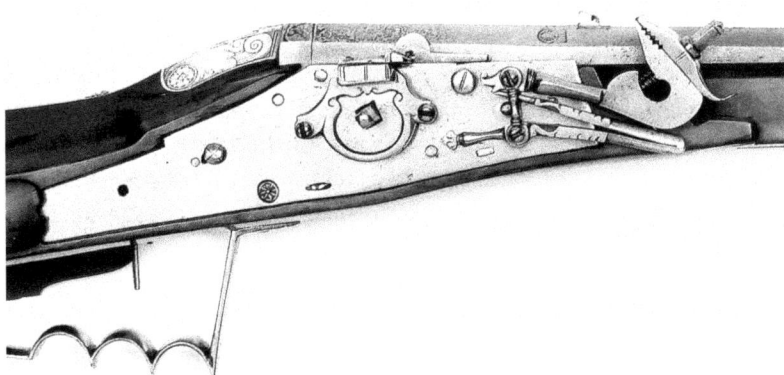

A wheellock musket, showing the hammer and the square lug that was used to wind the mechanism. The trigger guard also incorporates a hand grip to aid the shooter's control of the weapon (by kind permission of Bonhams).

The Flintlock or Snaplock

Flintlock mechanisms produced the next major advance in ignition systems, the earliest probably being of Spanish origin, produced sometime before 1550.[4] This type of lock works by driving a flint against a steel or frizzen, the resulting sparks igniting a powder charge to fire the weapon. *Snaplock* is a general, collective term that may be accurately applied to all weapons with locks operating on this principle.

The snaphaunce was an early form of this type. At first, the steel and pan cover were separate, and the cover was opened by hand before firing. In later weapons, steel and pan were combined as in the flintlock, although because such weapons had no half-cock, they were often constructed so as to allow the steel to be swiveled sideways, giving a safe carry with the cock down.

Experts are still speculating upon the flintlock's origin, but the earliest true flintlock, possessing a combined steel and pan cover, along with a vertically operating sear mechanism giving full- and half-cock, was designed by a Frenchman, Martin le Bourgeouys, some time between 1615 and 1627.[5] Flintlock weapons heralded the introduction of the "half-cock" as a safety device, where the hammer may be set at an intermediate position between "full-cock" and rest. The mechanism was arranged so that pulling the trigger would not fire the weapon when the hammer was set at half-cock, although in poorly made guns, a sharp blow could induce the hammer to fall, sometimes with fatal results. Loading was simply a matter of setting the weapon at half-cock, pouring a measured powder charge down the barrel, and then afterwards ramming home a lead ball. The ball for a rifled weapon was generally encased in a patch of cloth or cartridge paper, to ensure a snug fit against the grooves in the barrel. After loading, a small quantity of fine priming powder was placed in the pan, the frizzen closed and, once the weapon was set at full-cock, it was ready to fire. Pulling the trigger caused the hammer to fall, whereupon the flint struck the frizzen, simultaneously producing a shower of sparks and driving the frizzen and its attached pan upwards so that the sparks could fall on to the powder and ignite it. The powder flash then ignited the charge, via the touchhole, and the weapon fired … unless it was raining, or the powder was damp, or one of a dozen other little problems prevented it. Shooting a flintlock weapon is certainly a trial of both character and patience, and fighting a duel with one must have been a severe test of nerve! This type of arm may be found as smoothbore or rifled pistols and longarms, as well as shotguns and multi-barreled repeaters. All types may be single- or double-barreled, with double-barreled weapons significantly rarer, and as either muzzle- or breech-loaders, a good example of the latter being the turn-barrel or turn-off barrel pistol. In this design, the barrel is unscrewed at the breech and the load and ball inserted from here, although such a system seems to possess little advantage over the conventional muzzleloading arm.

Flintlocks do not lend themselves very readily to the incorporation of a true repeating mechanism, since the lock assembly is too cumbersome to result in an easily used, reliable design. One inventor, Elisha Collier, did produce a reliable, hand-turned flintlock revolver, but it was expensive as well as complex to produce, and does not seem to have been sufficiently popular to be an economic proposition for the inventor.

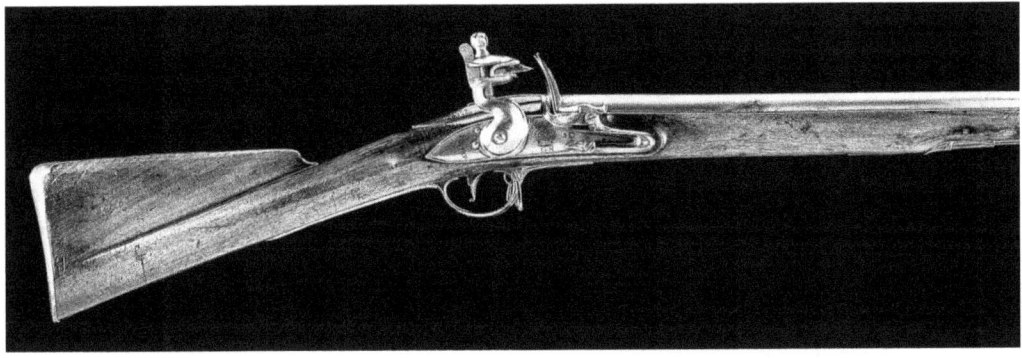

Brown Bess musket of the type issued to the British army between 1717 and 1850 (by kind permission of Bonhams).

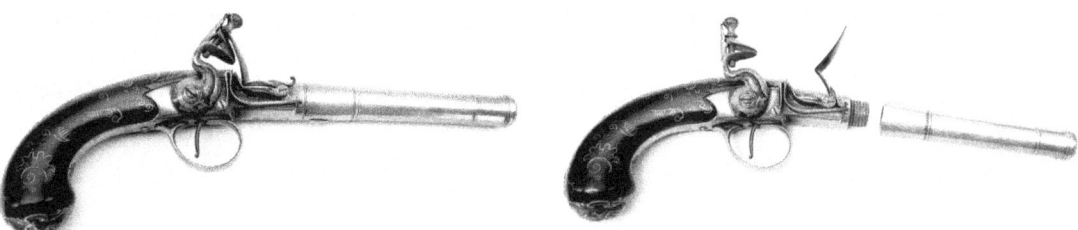

Left: Flintlock, breech-loading turn-barrel pistol. *Right:* Turn-barrel pistol with barrel removed for loading.

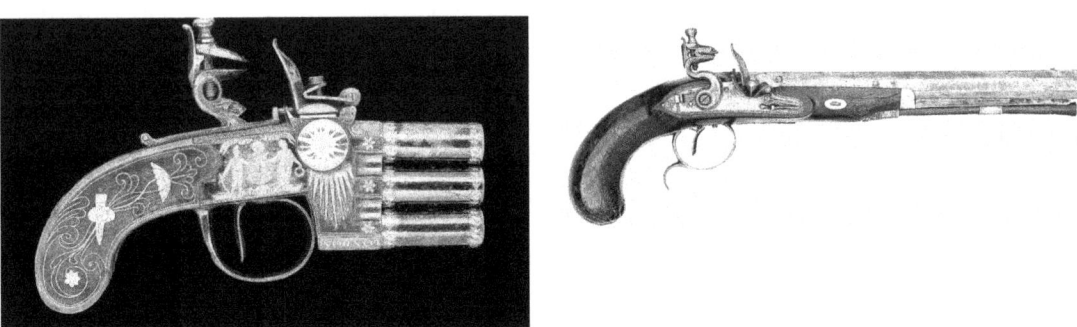

Left: **Three-barreled flintlock pistol.** *Right:* **Flintlock dueling pistol by Manton showing the spurred trigger guard and sparse sights characteristic of these weapons (both photographs by kind permission of Bonhams).**

THE CAPLOCK OR PERCUSSION SYSTEM

The first weapons of this type began to appear around 1820 and they soon became popular, being simpler to load and construct than comparable flintlock arms, as well as being more reliable to shoot. These inherent advantages also ensured that many good quality flintlock arms were subsequently converted to percussion ignition.

Percussion weapons look superficially similar to flintlocks, except the large, cumbersome frizzen pan is replaced by a small cone or "nipple" that communicates with the barrel via a narrow hole, termed the flashhole, bored through its center. Muzzleloading guns were charged in the conventional manner, the powder charge and a ball being forced down the barrel with the hammer at half cock. A copper percussion cap, containing fulminate of mercury, was then placed on the cone and the hammer brought to full cock. Squeezing the trigger caused the hammer to fall on the cap, which ignited the explosive fulminate material, sending a flame through the flashhole and into the barrel, igniting the charge and firing the weapon. Both muzzle- and breech-loading percussion arms were constructed at various periods; the Sharp's carbine was a particularly common American example of a breech-loading percussion rifle. Its compact construction meant that the percussion system was inherently more flexible than any of its predecessors. This allowed the construction of weapons capable of multiple firings, most important of these being the many designs of percussion revolving pistol and rifle.[6]

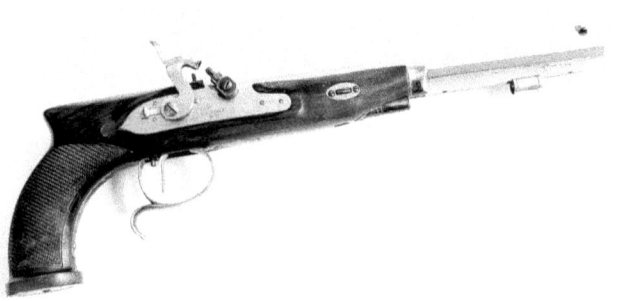

Replica percussion pistol, produced to the design used by H.W. Mortimer.

Tape primers

The standard percussion system, which used a single copper cap placed on the nipple of a weapon each time it was charged, had quickly proved vastly superior to the earlier flintlock. On the battlefield, however, it still had distinct disadvantages. It was relatively slow, and in cold weather, the tiny percussion cap was awkward for a soldier with stiff fingers to seat. Firearms inventors were not slow to appreciate these problems, and a number of solutions were devised based on primers enclosed in a single strip or tape.

French patent documents describing what was probably the first tape primer were taken out by Monsieur Leboeuf de Valdehon as early as 1821 (the first patent for a percussion cap in Europe was only granted in 1818). Unfortunately, no example of his weapon is known to exist. It may be that the system proved too difficult to manufacture and so never left the drawing board. In 1834, however, M.C.L. Stanislaus, Baron Heurteloup, designed his own tape priming system, although this did have a similar action to the earlier weapon. In particular, the hammer of both weapons cut and fired the primer in a single operation, and because of the problem of "chain firing" inherent in these locks, this system was adopted by most of the later inventors who developed tape primers.[7]

De Valdehon had apparently used individual straws to hold the priming material for his lock, and this may have been one reason for its lack of success. Heurteloup, however, decided upon something more substantial and enclosed the priming material for his gun in a soft metal tube. The Baron's first musket had a conventional side-hammer lock, with the priming loaded in the butt, but he soon replaced this with an improved model, which featured an under-hammer lock, the primer now being inserted under the barrel. His guns proved so successful that Britain's Ordnance Department conducted two trials of them, in 1837 and 1842. Although the British never adopted the Baron's rifle, they were used by some specialist corps in the French, Belgian and Russian armies.

A number of other inventors also produced guns using locks with priming material incorporated in a continuous coiled strip, but unfortunately, they all suffered from the same fatal design flaw. The priming material used in all these weapons was potassium chlorate (the same material that was used in slow match), and if the ignited portion of tape was not completely isolated by the initial hammer strike, the flames would "jump" past the hammer and burn through the entire roll of priming, rendering the weapon useless, if not positively dangerous, for the shooter. However, in 1845 a Baltimore dentist and inventor brought a final sophisticated flourish to the tape primer and produced a device that was to see service in both the Crimea and the U.S. Civil War.[8]

Maynard's tape priming lock

Edward Maynard, inventor of the tape primer that bears his name, was born in Madison, New York, in 1813. He was initially intent upon a military career, but ill health forced him to leave West Point after only a few months. He then made a successful career change, qualifying as a dentist four years later, in 1835. He was very successful, establishing a practice in Baltimore and Washington and numbering congressmen and presidents amongst his patients. Maynard also registered a number of patents for dental equipment, although he was most famous for his firearms inventions. His first and best known patent was for a tape priming system, which has come to be known to collectors as the "Maynard lock," for which he was issued a U.S. patent in 1845.

Maynard's innovation was to use two strips of paper with pellets of fulminate glued between them, instead of the clumsy metal tapes used by Continental inventors. This

Lock of a Massachusetts Arms Company pistol, designed for a tape primer and showing the "MAYNARD'S PATENT" stamp on the cover of the tape holder (courtesy James D. Julia Auctioneers, Fairfield, Maine. www.jamesdjulia.com).

entirely solved the problem of tapes burning through as well as allowing the lock to be much smaller, although it did give rise to a number of other disadvantages. The lock that used this primer consisted of a conventional, single-action hammer and trigger mechanism, mounted on a thick metal lock plate, with the percussion cone mounted in the breech of the barrel adjacent to the hammer. Superficially, it resembled a conventional percussion lock, and could even function as one if tape primers were unavailable, as a Maynard lock worked perfectly well if it was primed with a conventional percussion cap. However, it differed from the more usual percussion conformation in having a compartment machined in the lock plate between the hammer and trigger assembly, which was covered with a flat, hinged plate, often bearing the relevant patent information. This chamber was divided into two sections: the small, upper section containing either a prong or a star-shaped wheel that served to move the tape through a gap in the top of the lock and onto the percussion cone each time the hammer was cocked; and the larger, lower section holding the tape roll.[9]

Operation

In use, the tape roll is inserted in the lower compartment, the free end then being led through the upper compartment and out of a slot in the top of the lock until a pellet rests on the cone, with the hammer resting over it at half-cock. This is the critical part of the operation because if the primer is not properly positioned for this first shot, the mechanism will not deliver any subsequent pellets correctly. The weapon is then loaded and the hammer brought to full cock, which moves a pellet into position on the cone. Squeezing the trigger causes the hammer head to fall on the pellet, its sharpened edges cutting the pellet from the roll and simultaneously firing the fulminate, ensuring that only a single priming charge will be ignited and almost eliminating the possibility of the fulminate roll suffering a chain fire.

In dry conditions and using a weapon free of dirt and moisture, Maynard's system functioned well. So well, in fact, that in 1845 the U.S. government contracted for 300 muskets

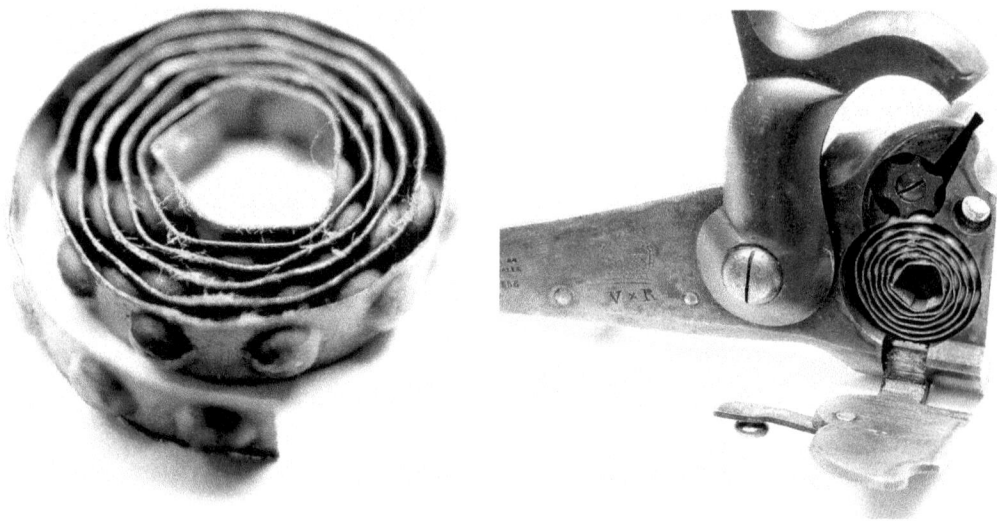

Left: A Maynard priming tape. *Right:* The lock of a Green's carbine showing how the tape priming roll was positioned for shooting.

to be fitted with the system so that trials could be conducted. These trials proved successful, and the federal government decided to adopt the system, buying Maynard's patent for payment of a royalty of $1.00 per rifle and later fitting it to their new 1855 rifle.[10]

Military use of Maynard's primer

Unfortunately, the system proved unreliable under wartime conditions. The British Army tried it in the Crimea, using the Greene carbine to which Maynard's lock was fitted, but the primers frequently misfired, the system did not feed reliably, and most importantly, the tapes themselves proved very susceptible to damp. After encountering similar problems, although not before producing nearly 60,000 of the 1855 Springfield rifle-muskets, the American Ordnance Department tried to remedy the situation by making the primers out of foil, instead of paper. This brought about a slight improvement, but the Maynard priming system was really too unreliable for military use, and soldiers seem to have frequently preferred to prime their Model 1855 rifles in the conventional manner, with a single percussion cap. Many Model 1855 Springfields saw service during the American Civil War, and Confederate soldiers who were issued these weapons must have found this feature particularly useful.

Weapons fitted with the Maynard primer included:

- Model 1855 U.S. percussion rifle-musket
- Model 1855 U.S. percussion rifle
- Sharps Model 1851 breech-loading carbine
- Sharp's Model 1855 U.S. Carbine and Sharp's Model 1855 British Carbine
- The Greene carbine, British and U.S. types
- Massachusetts Arms Company revolvers

The Massachusetts Arms Company produced a number of revolver models fitted with Maynard primers, after the disastrous result of the patent infringement case brought against them by Sam Colt. It was claimed that these weapons were manufactured with Maynard primers as a selling point in order to offset the disadvantage of their hand-revolved cylinders, a necessity after Col. Sam's litigious activities.[11]

Nineteenth-Century Warfare and Weapons Development

Firearms began to have a role in conventional warfare from the late medieval period. Richard III was apparently supplied with cannon and experienced artillerymen at the Battle of Bosworth Field, although hand-held weapons supplied to individual troops were a much later innovation. Matchlock muskets were the first issued military long-arm, coming into general use with Continental armies from about 1600 until 1690, when they were fairly quickly superseded by the flintlock musket. Battles continued to be fought with flintlocks from the end of the seventeenth century until about 1838, when a percussion musket was accepted into service with the Guards regiments of the British army as the P 1838 (Pattern 1838), the new Brunswick percussion rifle having been introduced to the Rifle Brigade a year earlier, in 1837. The first U.S. purpose-built percussion musket was the Springfield

Model 1842, the French having begun production of both a percussion musket and rifle slightly earlier, in 1839, although many of their original Model 1777 Charleville muskets were also converted to percussion. Repeating weapons were not generally issued to troops in any army until the acceptance of the M1886 bolt-action Lebel rifle by the French Army in 1887, although both Henry and Spencer repeating rifles and carbines did see limited use in the U.S. Civil War, particularly with cavalry units. It is of interest to note that in both the U.S. and British Army, the usual reason given for senior officers' reluctance to introduce this plainly superior type of weapon was that it would encourage troops to waste ammunition, presumably making the peacetime armies of these two countries more costly to run and leading to protests from the civilians who were obliged to find the money for military expenses!

Napoleonic Warfare

The period of European conflict usually termed the Napoleonic Wars began in 1793 with the First Coalition and lasted until 25 March 1802, when Britain signed the Treaty of Amiens. War broke out again in May 1803 and lasted until 1815, when an army composed of Allied troops defeated Bonaparte for the last time, sending him into exile on St. Helena.

The period from 1793 until 1815 places the battles fought during this period firmly in the flintlock era. Consequently, it is no surprise to find that the usual infantry weapon of the period was a muzzleloading, smoothbore musket and bayonet, with artillery consisting mainly of smoothbore cannon of various sizes, although rocketry was also included amongst the resources of the Royal Artillery. Primitive multi-fire weapons were in general use, although it would be more accurate to say that it was multi-shot ammunition rather than purpose-built, multi-shot artillery that was employed on Napoleonic battlefields.

Canister and Grapeshot

Multi-shot ammunition came in two forms for the Napoleonic artillerymen: grapeshot and canister. Grapeshot was usually supplied as a mass of small cannonballs or even slugs packed into a canvas bag. It came in various sizes, depending upon the cannon to be served; some bags for 24-pounder naval guns used individual grapeshot of four- or even six-lb cannonballs. Firing was simply a matter of charging the gun with the required amount of black powder, ramming home the bag of grapeshot, pointing the weapon at the enemy, and firing. Canister differed from grapeshot in being a more effective antipersonnel weapon, the projectile consisting of a tin or iron container filled with musket balls and closed with wood or metal plugs, with a canvas bag of black powder attached to one end. To load, the case was simply rammed down the barrel of the cannon, the bag was pierced with a metal quill, and the weapon fired in the conventional manner. Both grapeshot and canister were reserved for use at close ranges of less than 100 meters. Case shot was a later, slightly more sophisticated modification of the original canister, consisting of a shell filled with musket balls set off after firing by a timed fuse.

Although smoothbore cannons have significant limitations in both range and accuracy, one advantage they had over more finely machined, modern artillery pieces is the ease with which ammunition could be produced to serve them. This is particularly true of any gun which it became necessary to convert to fire multi-shot ammunition, since, if they were lacking a supply of factory-made grape or canister, gunners could improvise by loading nails, scrap iron, glass or stones into their guns. This makeshift load seems to have proved just as effective at dispersing enemy formations as the rounds issued by the War Department.[12]

Canister shot of the type used in the U.S. Civil War (courtesy the Minnesota Historical Society: License: CC A-S-A 3.0).

VOLLEY GUNS

Volley guns were arms produced with multiple barrels, usually seven, fitted with a single lock intended to discharge all barrels simultaneously. Most common of these seven-barreled guns were those produced by Henry Nock for sale to the Royal Navy, although the gun was actually invented by James Wilson, who presented it to the Board of Ordnance of testing on 29 July 1779. The Board felt it to be a practical weapon but probably of more use to the Navy than Britain's land forces, and so referred Wilson to the Lords Commissioners of the Admiralty, who gave the job of making two prototypes to Henry Nock. The guns consisted of a single, conventional flintlock hammer and trigger mechanism, the frizzen pan connecting via the touchhole to a bell-shaped firing chamber screwed to the central barrel, which was surrounded by the other six. In operation, when the charge in the firing chamber was ignited, this fired the central barrel, which in turn fired the six surrounding barrels simultaneously, each peripheral barrel being connected to the central barrel by its own hole. Nock constructed this arrangement by brazing the barrel group together

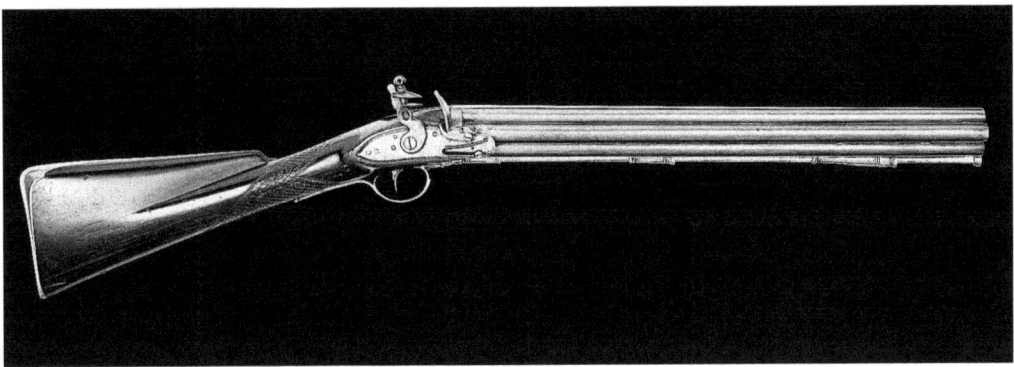

A Nock volley gun (by kind permission of Bonhams).

around the central barrel and then drilling each barrel separately, so that a hole was produced in the external surface of the peripheral barrels as well as between each barrel and the central barrel. The external hole proved useful, because the screw plug which closed it when firing could be easily removed to allow the gun to be cleaned of the powder residue that accumulated when using the weapon for a prolonged period. Nock's gun had been originally intended to be used in the "fighting tops" of British warships, but unfortunately, muzzleloading weapons in this position had an alarming tendency to set fire to the surrounding rigging, which made the volley gun unpopular with naval officers and resulted in its never seeing significant active service.[13]

The Crimean War (October 1853–February 1856)

After Waterloo, there was little pressure in the British army during peacetime to introduce new weapons, especially as such innovations resulted in increased expenditure for the taxpayer. Percussion muskets were introduced in 1838, but most of these were modified from the original Brown Bess, and the British army did not have a percussion service rifle until 1851. This was the P1851 Minié rifle, and although it did a certain amount of destruction at Inkerman during the Crimean War, its flawed construction meant it was subsequently withdrawn. It was replaced by the muzzleloading Enfield Pattern 1853 percussion rifle-musket, which began to be issued to Crimean troops in February 1855.[14]

The Crimean War was a nineteenth-century conflict in which Imperialist Russia fought against an Allied army composed of forces from France, Britain, the Ottoman Empire and Sardinia. British and French activity centered on Sevastopol in the Crimean Peninsula in a siege that lasted from September 1854 until August 1855. The Russians offered peace terms in March 1856, after a number of other countries had joined the Allied armies. The war was characterized by extremes of incompetence on both sides, culminating in the Battle of Balaklava and the Charge of the Light Brigade. It was yet another war where casualties from disease far exceeded those killed in action, or as the Royal Navy were wont to cryptically put it, "The Doctor's bill exceeded the Butcher's bill." In this case, of just over 21,000 British soldiers who died in the Crimea, 4,800 were killed in action or died of wounds, while over 16,000 men died of disease. However, there had been changes since the days of Waterloo. The Crimean War was the first major international conflict that was reported by a specialized corps of war correspondents, most notably William Russell of the *London Times*. This complete coverage was only possible because a telegraph line was installed between Balaklava and the British HQ in March 1855, which allowed the journalists to relay their stories back to their home office with a minimum of delay. It was also the first war to be extensively photographed, most notably by Roger Fenton. At about the same period the British army also managed to get a rudimentary railway working, although it does not seem to have made a significant contribution to the supply problem.

Technology was certainly being adapted the needs of the military during this period, although the geographical constraints imposed by the conformation of the Crimea Peninsula did not allow as much use of new technology as would be possible in later wars.

In particular, with the exception of revolvers bought as personal arms by forward-looking officers, repeating firearms played no part in any of the battles of this conflict. This contrasted sharply with the situation that arose in the War between the States, which began only five years after the end of the Crimean debacle.[15]

The American Civil War (April 1861–May 1865)

This was the first war in which technology had a really major role to play, with strategic use being made of railways, trench systems, infantry rifles (many of them imported P53 Enfield rifles), ironclad warships, even submarines and reconnaissance balloons. A number of strategic multi-fire weapons were deployed by both sides. This war also saw the first use of a Gatling gun at the siege of Petersburg, Virginia, albeit only the earliest, relatively inefficient percussion version. Despite this influx of new technology, much that was old remained. Cannon were still muzzleloading, and the most ubiquitous multi-fire weapon on the Civil War battlefield was still a smoothbore cannon loaded with grapeshot or canister, much like their forerunners at Marengo and in the Peninsular War. Modern repeating weapons were, however, issued as personal arms, all cavalry and artillerymen on both sides having some make of revolver, while weapons such as the Henry and Spencer rifles also found their way to a number of small, specialist corps and were often privately purchased by those who could afford such a weapon. The improved technology was reflected in the casualty lists: a total of 200,000 killed in action nearly 400,000 dead from disease, 60,000 dead in prison camps and nearly 500,000 wounded in action. The total of more than a million killed or wounded, in a conflict that only deployed a total of 3 million on both sides, means a casualty rate of just over 38 percent. This compares quite favorably, however, with World War I, which saw total military casualties (dead, wounded and missing) of over 39½ million for a total deployment by both sides of about 68 million men, casualties of approximately 58 percent.[16]

Table Seven: Comparison of military casualties: Crimea, U.S. Civil War, World War I and World War II

War	Total deployment by both sides	Killed or missing	Wounded	Total casualties (killed and wounded)	% casualties: total deployment
Crimea War	1.7 million men	700,000	200,000	900,000	53%
U.S. Civil War	3 million men	660,000	500,000	1.16 million	38%
World War I	68 million men	17.6 million	21.2 million	39.8 million	58%
World War II	98.7 million men	19.8 million	22.6 million	42.4 million	43%

All figures are, of necessity, the most generally accepted approximations.

CHAPTER FIVE

Early Repeating Pistols and Colt's Percussion Revolvers

Repeating and Multi-Barrel Pistols

The length of time required to charge and prime a muzzleloading pistol meant that many inventors tried to produce an arm that was capable of firing successive shots without reloading. The usual solution to this problem, and incidentally one still in use today, was to produce a weapon with two or more barrels, exemplified by modern smoothbore shotguns and the smaller four-barreled "Derringer"-pattern pistols.

Double-barreled and occasionally triple-barreled flintlock and percussion pistols were produced by a number of makers, both with fixed barrels and as "turn-over" pistols, one particularly unusual type being known as the "duck's foot" pistol. This was a weapon with four barrels radiating from the single lock in a manner reminiscent of a duck's foot, hence its popular name amongst collectors. The barrels were fired simultaneously from the single lock when the trigger was pulled, giving the weapon a similar effect to the larger volley guns. It was exceedingly uncomfortable to shoot, according to contemporary accounts. It also suffered from the major disadvantage of being fearsomely inaccurate, so that anyone standing in front of the muzzles was in danger, whether friend or foe.[1]

Although multi-barreled weapons were the most common solution to the problem of multi-firing before the invention of the percussion cap, a number of other mechanisms were also used. As well as the various designs of revolving pistol, with a number of barrels

"Duck's-foot" pistol from above, showing the four barrels and the flintlock mechanism (courtesy James D. Julia Auctioneers, Fairfield, Maine. www.jamesdjulia.com).

Five. Early Repeating Pistols and Colt's Percussion Revolvers 53

Left: Percussion "turn-over" pistol, constructed with two barrels. After firing the first barrel, the user twisted the barrels through 180 degrees to bring the percussion cone of the second barrel under the hammer. *Right:* Flintlock tap-action pistol made by Twigg of London (both photographs by kind permission of Bonhams).

usually turned by hand in an early form of the pepperbox revolver, two other types predominated: "Roman candle" guns, which incorporated a system using successively loaded charges of powder and a pierced ball; and the magazine gun, whose powder and shot were stored in sealed containers or magazines within the gun. The shooter was required to operate some form of cycling mechanism to deliver the rounds to the breech for firing, in much the same way as a modern centerfire arm such as a Winchester rifle.[2]

SUPERIMPOSED CHARGE OR "ROMAN CANDLE" GUNS

Pistols, muskets and rifles that fired one bullet and then a second and often subsequent loads using only the first ignition have been known since the beginning of the fifteenth century. They are referred to by collectors as "Roman candle" guns, because one shot follows another in a manner reminiscent of the firework of that name. Pistols of this design are found with matchlock, wheelock and flintlock ignition systems. In their simplest form they utilized bullets in which a hole had been drilled through the center of the ball, this hole then being filled with some sort of combustible material to act as a fuse. Balls and charges were loaded successively, care being necessary to ensure each ball was a tight fit and that the fused holes in the bullets were correctly aligned, parallel to the axis of the barrel. Pulling the trigger operated the lock mechanism and thus ignited the first powder charge, which in turn fired the ball from the muzzle and ignited the combustible material in the ball beneath. When the fuse burnt through, it ignited the powder charge below it, the whole process repeating itself until every ball had been fired. Some muskets were produced with this mechanism which their makers insisted were capable of reliably firing between seven and ten balls in rapid succession, although the time required to reload after firing in order to ensure successful ignition of each charge must have been considerable.[3]

HAND-TURNED REVOLVING PISTOLS

The manufacture of firearms with a number of barrels that were turned by hand appears to have begun in Britain around 1770. Manufacture of a true revolver—with a cylinder indexed by an internal mechanism—only began in Britain some fifty years later, with a flintlock weapon produced by an American, Elisha Collier. Mechanical repeating arms had been seen previously as too unreliable to be seriously considered as a weapon because their mechanisms were unsuitable for hard, extended use, but Collier's more robust design changed this attitude and the gun became very popular with many who tried it. Unfortunately, the mechanism that automatically turned the cylinder when the hammer was cocked gave so much trouble that Collier dispensed with it in later guns and reverted to turning the cylinder by hand.

Nock's flintlock pistol

Henry Nock was particularly well known as a maker of "multi-barrel" firearms, producing the large-caliber, seven-shot "volley gun," which was adopted by the Royal Navy as well as a sturdy, small caliber flintlock pepperbox with seven barrels. Small pistols of this type were also produced by a number of other makers, and the design may not have originated with Nock.

Whoever their maker, these little pistols are technologically interesting. They were usually small-caliber, most often 120 bore, single-action, hand-rotated pocket pistols, their seven barrels being screwed into a single, substantial breech-piece, each barrel having its own separate pan formed as part of that breech-piece. Projecting from the rear of the breech-piece was a spindle, which inserted into the lock of the pistol and was fitted with a two-pronged "thumb" screw in the frame, bearing on this spindle and securing each barrel in turn before firing. A metal collar was fixed to the lock frame, covering the main priming pan and intended to prevent the priming powder from spilling out of the individual pans in the breech block. The hinged steel and pan cover were also mounted on the top of this collar.

Nock seven-barrel revolving pistol, showing the flintlock mechanism and the key on the left side of the breech that was loosened to allow the barrels to be rotated (by kind permission of Bonhams).

Loading the pistol was relatively time-consuming. Each barrel was first unscrewed from the breech, using a suitable key inserted in the muzzle, and powder and shot placed in the breech cup, whereupon the barrel was replaced. Following that operation, priming was poured through an opening in the metal collar, filling the large main pan, and the barrels rotated to allow a priming charge to fall into each of the smaller pans in the breech block. The central hammer was then cocked, the pan cover closed, and the first barrel fired in the normal way.

After firing, the thumbscrew was loosened slightly and the barrel assembly turned by hand against the pressure of a flat spring. This spring bore in turn on a ratchet cut in the head of the spindle and thus placed the pan of the next barrel correctly over the hammer. The pressure of this ratchet spring could be changed by a second thumbscrew, and it was important that both ratchet and locking screws were properly adjusted if the mechanism was to function correctly. Finally, in order to fire the weapon again, the pan cover had to be returned to its horizontal position. The central barrel had no separate pan, but was fired from the pan of one of the barrels fixed around it, resulting in the simultaneous discharge of those two barrels.[4]

The First English Revolver: Collier's Flintlock Design

The first revolver to be manufactured in England appeared in 1818, when a flintlock weapon of this type was produced by an American, Elisha Collier. It was quickly shown to have a more robust mechanism than previous weapons of this type and proved to be at least as reliable as a conventional flintlock, even in the mud and rain of the hunting fields. Collier's original revolver design was something of an innovation. To operate the weapon, the cylinder's chambers were first loaded with powder and ball in the usual way and the priming magazine in the frizzen (or steel) filled with powder. The cylinder, the mouth of which was countersunk to allow it to be seated into a corresponding cone on the barrel, was then drawn back against the pressure of the chamber spring, which served to seat the cylinder and barrel firmly together when firing. With the cylinder drawn back, it was rotated counterclockwise against the pressure of a second, helical spring. When this second spring had sufficient tension, the cylinder was allowed to move forward and re-engage the barrel cone.

In order to operate the weapon, the hammer of the single-action mechanism was cocked and the trigger pulled, discharging the first chamber under the hammer. Re-cocking the hammer for a second shot caused a small hook, linked to the hammer, to catch in a circular notched skirt, which was attached to the rear of the cylinder. This hook then drew the cylinder back, against the pressure of the cylinder spring, thus allowing the second, helical spring to rotate the cylinder to the next chamber. As the chamber came opposite the barrel, the hook encountered one of the notches in the cylinder skirt, which caused it to disengage, and thus allowed the cylinder spring to push the chamber mouth onto the barrel cone. The frizzen or steel was then snapped down by the user, causing a linkage to rotate the plug in the bottom of the priming magazine and deposit a quantity of priming powder into the flash pan; sufficient powder was carried in the magazine to charge the pan each time the frizzen was closed. Unfortunately, Collier soon found this method of cylinder rotation too problematic to be reliable. As a result, most of his pistols and long-arms have hand-rotated cylinders, the cylinder being simply pulled back, turned, and then allowed to snap into place. Even without the mechanically rotated cylinder, the guns were reliable and popular, although the design was never accepted by the military, despite Collier's efforts to elicit Royal favor. Sam Colt is thought to have bought a Collier revolver during his stay in London, and it was claimed that he used some of the features in his early Patterson revolvers. Apart from the use of a revolving cylinder to deliver successive loads to the

Collier flintlock revolver, showing the cylinder and giving an indication of the high quality of manufacture of these guns (courtesy James D. Julia Auctioneers, Fairfield, Maine. www.jamesdjulia.com).

barrel, however, the mechanism of Colt's revolvers does not share any significant features with Collier's weapon. At least, that was the decision of the U.S. courts, when Colt sued the Massachusetts Arms Co. for patent infringement and won.[5]

Table Eight: Specification of the Collier flintlock revolver

Manufacturers	Elisha Collier, weapons being made by hand in one of his London workshops
Period of production	Between 1818 and 1827, when Collier retired
Production	Reliable figures not available, but probably significantly fewer than 1,000 weapons
Military service	None, although Collier did attempt to interest the military in his pistol
Weight	Approximately 2½ to 3 lbs when loaded
Length/Barrel length	Approximately 15 inches/approximately 7½ inches
Mechanism	Single-action, muzzleloading with manually turned cylinder
	Cavity in frizzen pan, supplying priming powder
Ammunition	Loose powder and shot, ignited by a flintlock mechanism
Sights	Post front sight
	Conventional slotted rear sight
Maximum accurate range	15 ft (5 m)
Rate of fire	Powder delivery from the frizzen pan would probably have slowed operations, but a full cylinder might have been discharged in approximately 30 seconds by an experienced user

The Percussion System

Most of the work (and hence the expense) in both Nock and Collier's weapons involved modifications to the flintlock ignition, to ensure that such weapons could be re-primed and fired repeatedly. So it is hardly surprising that cheap and effective multi-shot firearms were not produced in significant numbers until the invention of the percussion cap. Since a weapon with several barrels revolving around a central spindle is much easier and, more importantly, cheaper to produce than a conventional revolver, the first weapons of this type manufactured commercially in Britain were pepperbox pistols, also known as "self-revolving" or "repeating" pistols. Many gunmakers in both London and Birmingham made these handy little weapons, in varying degrees of quality. They consist of either 3, 5 or 6 barrels, brazed onto a central spindle and fitted with a percussion cone at the breech. Both bar-hammer and under-hammer types were produced, and they usually have a self-cocking mechanism, although single- and double-action types are known.[6]

Six-barreled pepperbox made by John Cooper of London. This weapon has a ring trigger with the hammer mechanism mounted within the breech.

MAGAZINE PERCUSSION PISTOLS

Although the pepperbox revolver is probably the most common early revolving pistol encountered, it was by no means the only design that was offered for sale. Thomas Cochran patented another multi-shot system in 1835, which he called a turret revolver, although the guns were in fact made by C.B. Allen of Springfield, Massachusetts. Instead of using a round cylinder, revolving vertically within the frame of the gun, Cochran's system used a magazine or charge carrier made in the form of a flat disc, mounted horizontally. Its edge was drilled to form a number of chambers for the charge, complete with a percussion cone that was screwed into the chamber between the arms of the ratchet that locked the disc in place, before it was fired by the underhammer lock. The system was used in both revolvers and rifles, but it does not seem to have been very popular, perhaps because the shooter stood as good a chance of being shot when he pulled the trigger as the target he was aiming at![7]

COCHRAN MODEL 1837 PERCUSSION REVOLVER

These revolvers were produced as a modification of Cochran's longarm design, with horizontal rotary cylinder, but made by C.B. Allen of Springfield Mass, who may have instructed Poole to take out the English patent. Cochran's rifle was also made and retailed by J. Wilkinson of Pall Mall.

Production numbers

Not recorded, but from their frequency at auction, probably several hundred. These were single-action, .36 caliber under-hammer percussion revolvers with a hand-

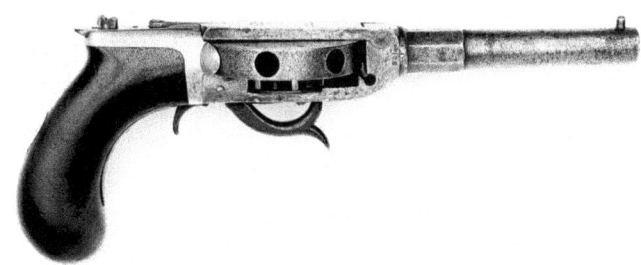

Cochran turret revolver from the right side showing the openings in the circular magazine intended to receive the loads of powder and ball (courtesy James D. Julia Auctioneers, Fairfield, Maine. www.jamesdjulia.com).

turned horizontal cylinder that had seven chambers. Further details of these interesting, American-made weapons are recorded in Flayderman.[8]

Values

NRA Good: $5000–$6,500; NRA Fine: $15,000–$18,000

Harmonica pistols

Several designs of both percussion and pinfire harmonica pistols are recorded and known to have been offered for sale, their name derived from the shape and function of the magazine. Most notable amongst the makers of this type of pistol was the French gunsmith M.J. Jarre, although despite the excellent quality of his guns, they seem to have been neither popular nor particularly successful. Conformation of these guns is similar, whoever made them; each is a pistol of conventional shape with a rectangular breech opening. This opening was designed to accept the magazine, which consisted of a steel bar drilled with a number of percussion chambers. Each chamber was fitted individually with a cone (or nipple) designed to accept a conventional percussion cap, with the cones usually sited in a cavity in the upper surface of the magazine. Each chamber was loaded in the usual manner with powder and ball and the chambers were then capped. After loading, the slide is inserted in the breech of the gun, the first chamber is correctly positioned over the breech-end of the barrel, and the slide is locked in position. When the hammer is cocked, the weapon is now ready to fire. After firing, the mechanism securing the slide magazine is released, the slide is repositioned so that the second chamber is in line with the barrel, and having once again been locked into position, the hammer only needs to be cocked to make the gun ready to fire the second load. Pinfire weapons were similar, except the chambers were loaded with the appropriate caliber of pinfire cartridge, which were ignited by the hammer operating in a similar manner to the earlier percussion weapons.[9]

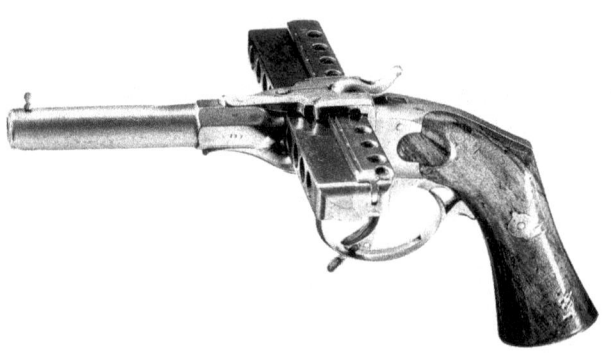

Jarre harmonica pistol, with the magazine inserted, ready for firing (courtesy Rock Island Auction Company).

Values

NRA Good: $5000–$6,500; NRA Fine: $10,000–$12,000

Pistols using either the Kalthoff or Lorenzoni mechanisms[10] do not seem to have been produced in significant numbers, if at all, probably because these devices, with their large breech mechanisms, would have been cumbersome when fitted to a weapon of pistol length and caliber.

Transition Percussion Revolvers

The early pepperbox revolvers were the basis for a later design, the "transition" pattern revolver, a cheaper, inferior development in revolver technology that paralleled that of Colt's and Adam's weapons. Early examples of this type were open framed, with a self-cocking bar hammer, the primitive mechanism for which was contained in a lock frame, to which the arbor was attached. A five- or six-chambered cylinder with vertical percussion cones revolved upon this arbor, the barrel locating over the end and secured by a wedge, screws or a "wing" nut to the single lower frame bar. A final modification to the lock mechanism, in the form of a "pin stop" fitted to the trigger, crudely indexed the cylinder in line with the barrel, although users may well have found it safer to confirm the indexing of the cylinder by hand. Given the conformation of many transition revolvers, it is tempting to assume that at least some could have been produced by converting pepperbox revolvers. However, this does not appear to be the case, since there is only one recorded example of such a conversion. The cost and practical problems involved also seem to suggest that converting even a well-made pepperbox would not have been an economic proposition.

These transition revolvers were generally neither robust nor well designed. They were inaccurate, and were prone to multiple discharges because of the absence of partitions between the percussion cones. Some of the cheaper examples also seem to have allowed excessive quantities of gas to escape from the union between the cylinder and the barrel. Their chief attraction was probably their cheapness and simplicity when compared to the weapons of their larger competitors. However, if the number of examples still in collections is any reflection of their popularity, they

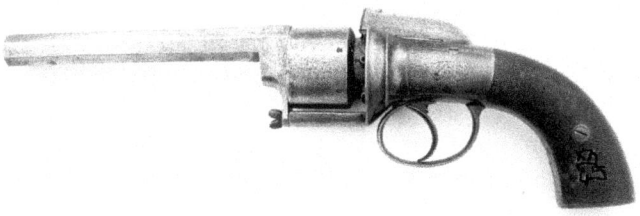

Early transition revolver, of inferior construction, showing the bar hammer and wing nut securing the barrel and breech to the frame.

must have sold reasonably well. Such weapons certainly served to fill a gap in the market until Adam's and, particularly, the mass-produced revolvers made at Colt's London factory, became so cheap that they drove many conventional gunmakers out of business.[11]

Conventional Percussion Revolvers

Revolver manufacture marked one of the first attempts at mechanized firearms production in Britain and the U.S. Although barrels, lock plates and stocks for military arms had previously been produced to a sealed pattern, the weapons still had to be assembled or "set up," and the variation between the components produced meant this could only be done by a gunsmith in his workshop. Most of the pepperbox and transition revolvers had also been hand-made, but Sam Colt changed all that. His factories in Hartford and London turned out revolvers whose parts were interchangeable, at least within a specific model, and this pointed the way for gun makers like Robert Adams and William Tranter. These innovations did not affect the whole of the British trade, however, and in Birmingham, for example, revolvers sold by Joseph Bentley and the Webley brothers were hand-made by pieceworkers until well into the late 1850s. Revolvers, unlike their forerunners the single-shot flintlock and percussion pistols, could now be produced quickly and at reasonable cost by these industrial methods, although the initial outlay for the manufacturer was high. A Manton percussion pistol, for example, retailed at around £55 in 1830, while Colt was selling his Colt Dragoon revolver in London twenty years later for £6, which included a bullet mold and wrench for the percussion cones. This went up to £7.50 for a cased weapon, complete with accessories. Despite this cut-price policy, he still made sufficient profit to leave an estate worth $15 million when he died in 1862.[12]

Sam Colt and His Early Revolvers

Samuel Colt was born on 19 July 1814 at Hartford, Connecticut, the third son of a merchant, Christopher Colt. Sent to sea in 1830 when he was sixteen, Colt came home a year later, bringing with him a wooden model embodying the basic design for a revolving pistol. It is traditionally claimed that he got the idea from examining the mechanism of the ship's wheel, although it seems more likely that the basis was actually the pawl and lever system of the capstan.

However the idea came about, by 1836, Colt had launched the Patent Arms Manufacturing Company of Paterson, New Jersey, making a range of .28, .31 and .36 caliber pocket, belt and holster pistols, all chambered for 5 shots. The venture proved short-lived, but a number of Colt's largest No. 5 pistols found their way to Texas, where the Rangers used them very effectively against the Comanches. It was here that Colt's revolver came to the notice of Ranger Captain Sam Walker.

Captain Walker suggested some modifications to the original design, which Colt incorporated into a new six-shot, .44 caliber pistol. Walker then went to Washington to try to convince the government to buy Colt's pistol. He must have been persuasive because eventually the Army bought 1,000 of the new pistols for use during the Mexican War of 1846. By the time the war ended in 1848, Colt was finally on his way.

He established his famous factory in Hartford, Connecticut, in 1847, and despite initial financial problems, it was from here he manufactured, in turn, the Walker and Dragoon model pistols before designing, in 1848, one of his most successful weapons, the .31 caliber Pocket Model. Over 300,000 of these revolvers in various models and barrel lengths were sold before production ceased in 1878, five years after the introduction of the Model P centerfire cartridge revolver. His next revolver, the Colt Navy (or Ranger size, as it was originally called) of 1851, did nearly as well, selling over 250,000 before manufacturing ended in 1873. Between 1853 and 1859, Colt also had a factory assembling and manufacturing revolvers in London.[13]

PATERSON COLTS

These are the revolvers produced during Colt's ill-fated venture at Paterson, New Jersey. All were single-action and were made in three frame sizes: pocket, belt and holster.

The smallest revolver produced during this period was known as the No. 1 pistol. Of .28 caliber, it had grips that were flat at the bottom, unlike the bevels on the later models. Models No. 2 and No. 3 were of .31 caliber and also differed from No. 1 in both size and the shape of the grips. A No. 4 pistol never appears to have been planned, and the final arm in the series is the No. 5, .36-caliber and largest and most popular of all the Paterson Colts.

Characteristically, the trigger on all these pistols sits within the frame, and there is no trigger guard. Cylinders may have round or "square back" rear shoulders, and serial numbers cannot generally be seen without disassembly, although some specimens have numbers on the bottom of the butt.

Internally, Patersons were complex, perhaps over-complex, with a number of small springs and other parts that did not react well to black-powder fouling, a factor certainly contributing to their lack of success. Everywhere, that is, except Texas.

Pocket Model Paterson revolver (No. 1)

Manufactured between 1837 and 1838, this model has the distinction of being the smallest percussion revolver Colt ever made.

Serial numbers: 1–500.

Barrels are .28 caliber, in lengths from 1¾ to 4¾ inches and octagonal in shape, without a loading lever. There is also a rare "Ehlers" model, also known as the Fourth Model Ehlers, which does have a factory-fitted loading lever.

Barrel addresses appear on the top barrel flat and have the following format:

Patent Arms M'g Co Paterson, N.J.—Colt's Pt

The Ehler's Model has the M'g missing, with a space where the marks are removed from the manufacturing die, giving it the following appearance:

Patent Arms Co Paterson, N.J.—Colt's Pt

Cylinders have five chambers, with a "Centaur" scene, the single word COLT and the original four horse-head Colt trademark all roll-engraved. Butt plates are of varnished walnut with a blue finish on all metal parts, including the hammer.

Belt Model Paterson revolver (No. 2)

Manufactured between 1837 and 1840, Models 2 and 3 differ only in the grip shape and small points of detail, the most significant being the addition of a factory-fitted loading lever to some late Model 3s.

Serial numbers: 1–850, shared with the No. 3 Model.

Barrels are .31 caliber, octagonal with lengths varying from 2½ to 5½ inches, and without a loading lever. Barrel address, as usual, on top flat in the following format:

Patent Arms M'g Co Paterson, N.J.—Colt's Pt

The No. 2 revolver also has an "Ehlers" variant, sometimes known as the Fifth Model Ehlers, which has an attached loading lever, a capping channel on the recoil shield, and a cylinder with rounded rear shoulders. The barrel address is identical to the smaller Fourth Model Ehlers. Cylinders have five chambers, and are roll-engraved in the same way as the Pocket Model No. 1. Butt plates are polished walnut and all metal parts, including the hammer, are blued. No. 2 revolvers are twice as heavy as a Pocket of corresponding barrel length, and this offers a quick means of differentiating between the two types.

Belt Model Paterson revolver (No. 3)

This weapon is really a variation of the No. 2, which Colt manufactured with differently shaped grips. The two models share the same serial number series, although the No. 3 Model is never found with the shorter, 2½-inch barrel, and some have factory-fitted loading levers. All other features are identical.

Holster Model Paterson revolver (No. 5)

Serial numbers: 1–1000, in a series separate from the other models.

Also known as the "Texas Paterson," this revolver, manufactured between 1838 and 1840, is the most popular Paterson amongst Colt collectors because of its historical associations with the early Texas Rangers.

No. 5 revolvers are .36 caliber, with an octagonal barrel that may be 4, 7½, 9 or 12 inches in length, 7½- and 9-inch Models being designated "Standard." The barrel address is on top barrel's flat, and is identical to that found on the Model No. 1. Cylinders are 5-shot, with roll engraving of a stagecoach scene, incorporating the word "COLT." Rear shoulders may be round or square, and some specimens have a capping cutout in the recoil shield. Butt plates are polished walnut grips. Metal parts are blued, except the hammer and frame, which are case-hardened. Weapons with "U.S. War Department" or other "martial" markings are worth considerably more than standard specimens. Forgers know this, too, so any Paterson offered for sale, however it is marked, warrants a very careful inspection, especially since even a good specimen can fetch over $100,000 (U.S.). As might be expected, given their provenance, Patersons in general tend to be more popular with the American market than amongst UK buyers.

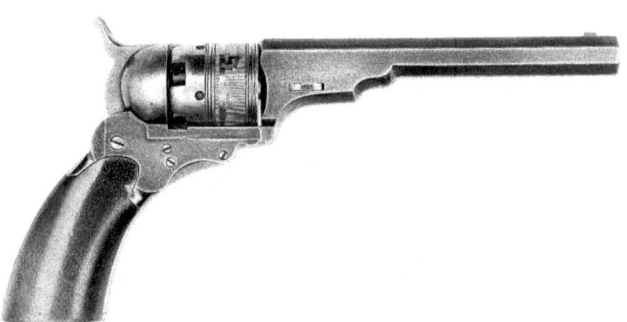

Belt Model Paterson (No. 3) revolver, from the right, showing the trigger folded back into the frame and securing wedge (courtesy James D. Julia Auctioneers, Fairfield, Maine. www.jamesdjulia.com).

Values

Colt No. 1 revolver: NRA Good: $15,000–$20,000; NRA Fine: $40,000–$45,000
Colt No. 2 revolver: NRA Good: $15,000–$20,000; NRA Fine: $40,000–$45,000
Colt No. 3 revolver: NRA Good: $20,000–$25,000; NRA Fine: $48,000–$60,000
Colt No. 5 revolver: NRA Good: $40,000–$50,000; NRA Fine: $100,000–$150,000

WALKER COLTS

Only 1,100 of these enormous handguns were ever produced, manufacturing beginning at Hartford in 1847. With a barrel of 9½ inches, a weight of 4lbs 9oz, and a cylinder holding sixty grains, nearly twice that of later revolvers, it was the most powerful percussion handgun ever produced commercially. This large powder charge proved to be its undoing, however, because with a full load, cylinders and barrels both had a tendency to rupture. It was quickly replaced by the Colt 1st Model Dragoon, which used a slightly smaller charge, 50 grains, and so was not prone to the Walker's defects. Manufacturers of modern-day replica Colt percussion revolvers generally recommend a charge of between 15 and 20 grains, using which such weapons still shoot with consistent accuracy.

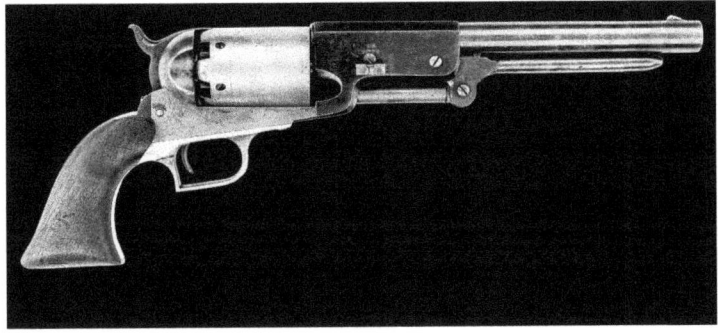

A Walker Colt, showing the loading lever, which, having no securing catch, frequently moved down when the weapon was fired, jamming the cylinder. Many users secured the lever by tying it to the barrel (courtesy James D. Julia Auctioneers, Fairfield, Maine. www.jamesdjulia.com).

Values

Their rarity and the mystique surrounding them mean that any Walker Colt that comes up for sale fetches an incredible price at auction, the record currently being U.S. $920,000, in October 2008. Fortunately, Uberti make an accurate replica, although possession in the UK requires a FAC. However, this does make them a perfect area for the fakers, so careful inspection of any Walker offered for sale is a clear necessity. To put this even further into perspective, Flayderman states that only about 100 to 110 of these revolvers are still in existence.

COLT DRAGOON

Colt Dragoons were made in four models: the extremely rare Whitneyville, followed by 1st, 2nd and 3rd Models. Total production for all three models was 18,700.

Weighing only 4lb 2oz, with a 7½-inch barrel and shorter cylinder, they were significantly lighter than the Walker, although even with this weight reduction, a Dragoon is still awkward to handle and fire. Nor did they have the same aggravating tendency to cylinder and barrel disintegration. As a final innovation, Dragoons were fitted with a catch at the end of the barrel, which retained the loading lever. This prevents the lever from falling down during shooting and thus driving the rammer into the cylinder, preventing the cylinder from turning and thereby jamming the action. Old-timers who used the Walker often tied the loading lever to the barrel with string or rawhide to prevent this sort of accident.

Externally, the three models may be differentiated by the trigger guard, the shape of the bolt stops in the cylinder, and the presence or absence of pins on the cylinder between the percussion nipples, although there are a number of less significant differences. Described by Colt as "Holster" or "Cavalry" pistols, all are of .44 caliber, chambered for six shots.

Colt 2nd Model Dragoon revolver, showing the characteristic round barrel (courtesy James D. Julia Auctioneers, Fairfield, Maine. www.jamesdjulia.com).

Variations are also recorded in the type of mainspring used, the older "V" spring being replaced in later 3rd Models by flat springs, which were easier to both make and replace.

Values

Original cost of these arms in Britain in 1854 was £6.00 ($24 U.S.), complete with bullet mold and wrench, or £7.00 ($28 U.S.) in a wooden case complete with caps, flask, bullet mold and wrench. Colt Dragoons rarely appear at auction in the UK, but one cased example of a Hartford-English 3rd Model at a London auction house had a reserve price of £30,000–£35,000, in 2006.

All models: NRA Good: $5,000–$7,000; NRA Fine: $20,000–$30,000

Colt's later percussion revolvers

Colt went on to produce a number of other percussion revolvers, all single-action weapons in a variety of calibers, with open frames except the Model 1855 or Root revolver. These included, in roughly chronological order:

- The Model 1849 Pocket revolver: .32 caliber, cylinders with five or six chambers.
- The Model 1851 Navy revolver: .36 caliber, cylinders with six chambers.
- The Root or Model 1855 Sidehammer Pocket revolver: .36 caliber, cylinders with six chambers. Colt's only solid-frame percussion revolver.
- The Model 1860 Army revolver: .44 caliber, cylinders with six chambers.
- The Model 1861 Navy revolver: .36 caliber, cylinders with six chambers.

Colt Pocket Model revolver. At .31 in caliber, this proved a popular alternative to the Dragoon, with nearly 500,000 manufactured before production ceased (courtesy James D. Julia Auctioneers, Fairfield, Maine. www.jamesdjulia.com).

All these revolvers were routinely converted to use rimfire or centerfire cartridges, either as factory-made conversions or conversions by private gunsmiths.[14]

American Percussion Revolver Manufacturers

In America, the major manufacturers of percussion revolvers included[15]:

- **Allan & Wheelock:** Produced weapons in .31 and .34 caliber, five-chambered Pocket Model, and .36 caliber, six-chambered Navy Model.
- **Manhattan:** Produced weapons in .31 caliber, five- or six-chambered Pocket Model, and .36 caliber, five- or six-chambered Navy model.
- **Remington:** Produced weapons in .31, .36 and .44 caliber revolvers, with five- or six-chambered cylinders.
- **Rogers & Spencer:** Produced weapons in .44 caliber, 6-chambered Army revolver.
- **Springfield Arms Co.:** Produced weapons in .31, .36 and .40 caliber, 6-chambered Belt, Navy and Dragoon Model revolvers.
- **Starr Arms Co.:** Produced weapons as double-action revolvers, .36 caliber Navy, .44 caliber Army, and a single-action .44 caliber Army Model, all with six-chambered cylinders.
- **Whitney Arms Co.:** Produced weapons in .31 and .36 caliber revolvers, with six-chambered cylinders.

English Percussion Revolver Manufacturers

Major English makers included[16]:

- **Adams:** Produced weapons in 38, 54, 80, 90 120 bore, self-cocking and later double-action weapons with five-chambered cylinders.
- **Bentley**: Single- and double-action revolvers produced in a variety of calibers by Bentley and many smaller Birmingham gunmakers under license.
- **Le Mat:** Originally designed by a New Orleans physician, Dr. J.A. Le Mat, these guns were mainly manufactured in Belgium, but were also made under license by the Birmingham firm of Tipping & Co. They were of an unconventional design, having a cylinder with nine chambers firing through an upper, .42 caliber rifled barrel, with a second, .63 caliber smoothbore barrel designed for a shotgun charge, below this conventional barrel. The design was reliable when the guns were properly constructed, but unfortunately, many of the examples that found their way into the hands of Confederate forces were not well finished or properly assembled. As a result, the gun gained a reputation for unreliability that was not wholly deserved.[17]
- **Tranter:** Produced weapons in 38, 54, 80, 90 120 bore with five-chambered cylinders and Tranter's unique "hesitating" mechanism.
- **Webley:** "Long spur" revolvers manufactured as 38, 54, 80, 90 120 bore weapons with five- or six-chambered cylinders.

In addition, there were numerous small gunmakers producing revolvers by traditional methods, using hand tools and often working from a room in their homes.

Proof figures from the London House confirm the revolver's increasing popularity after 1851. Beginning in that year, 954 revolvers were submitted for proof, this figure

An Adams 5-shot self-cocking percussion revolver (courtesy James D. Julia Auctioneers, Fairfield, Maine. www.jamesdjulia.com).

A Webley "Long-Spur" single-action percussion revolver (courtesy James D. Julia Auctioneers, Fairfield, Maine. www.jamesdjulia.com).

Later Le Mat revolver, this example showing signs of considerable wear, so probably a Confederate-issued weapon (courtesy James D. Julia Auctioneers, Fairfield, Maine. www.jamesdjulia.com).

increasing over sixfold in 1852, to 6,121 weapons. There was a further increase in 1853 to 13,916, clearly showing the sudden rise in their popularity. These figures include Colt and Adams revolvers as well as pepperbox and transition weapons, so determining what proportion of the year's output was represented by each design is difficult.[18]

Continental Percussion Revolver Manufacturers

Percussion revolvers were also produced in Europe, and major Continental makers included[19]:

- Ancion & Cie: Produced Adams and Beaumont-Adams revolvers under license from Deane, Adams & Deane and L.A.C.
- **Auguste Francotte:** A famous maker of high quality revolvers, Fancotte produced Adams, Beaumont-Adams and the LeMat "grapeshot" revolvers under license from their respective patentees.
- **Giraud & Cie:** Responsible for the Continental production of Le Mat's revolver, which was noted for their shoddy workmanship and unreliable shooting characteristics.

Table Nine: General specification of pepper box, transition and percussion revolvers

Weapon	Pepperbox revolver	Transition revolver	Percussion revolver
Makers	USA: Most gunmakers, particularly Allen & Thurber. UK: Numerous, including most of the better quality London and Birmingham gunmakers. Continental: Most gunmakers, but weapons from this source tended to be more ornate than comparable UK or American guns.	USA: Leavitt & Wesson produced to compete with Colt. Massachusetts Arms Company (MA Co). UK: Various but usually the smaller London and Birmingham gunmakers.	U.S.: Colt, Remington, Allan & Wheelock. UK: Adams, Tranter, Webley. Continental: Le Mat, numerous makers in Liege.
Period of production	1835–1860	Approximately from 1850 until 1870	1837–1873
Production	Reliable figures not available, but probably between 50,000 to 100,000 weapons.	Reliable figures not available, but probably fewer than 50,000 pistols.	Colt: over 1 million of all models. Remington: more than 250,000 of all models. UK manufacturers: probably fewer than 100,000.
Military service	No official military contracts, but many of these pistols were probably bought as private purchases by serving officers.	Some MA Co revolvers were purchased by the federal government during the Civil War and many were probably purchased as private weapons by military personnel.	Crimea War (British Army) U.S. Civil War (Federal forces and CSA) U.S. Indian Wars before 1873.
Weight	Between 6oz and 1½ lbs	Similar to a conventional percussion revolver, between 2½ and 3 lbs, although MA Co did make a Pocket Model which may have been lighter.	Between 1½ and 4½ lbs
Length/Barrel length	Extremely variable: 6 inches–15 inches in length/ 3 inches–7 inch barrels	Total length between 9 and 15 inches/ 4½ and 8 inch barrels	Total length between 9 and 15 inches/ 4½ and 8 inch barrels
Frame type	Only a lock frame, with barrels brazed to a central rod	Open frame	Open or solid frame
Mechanism	Single action or self-cocking. Muzzleloading with cylinder indexed either manually or by some internal mechanism	Single or double action. Muzzleloading, cylinder indexed by internal mechanism	Single, self-cocking or double action. Cylinder turned and indexed by an internal mechanism.
Ammunition	Loose powder and ball individually loaded into each barrel, before being capped	Loose powder and ball loaded into individual chambers of the cylinder.	Muzzleloading with loose powder and ball or factory-made foil cartridges.
Sights	Not usually fitted	Leaf or pillar front sight, fixed rear sight, when fitted	Leaf front sight, fixed rear sight in the top of the hammer or frame

Weapon	Pepperbox revolver	Transition revolver	Percussion revolver
Maximum range	Approximately six feet (2 meters)	10 ft (3 meters)	60 ft (20 meters)
Rate of fire	5 to 10 seconds, since these were usually double-action guns. Reloading: Between 5 and 10 minutes.	Similar to a conventional single-action revolver, approximately 5 to 10 seconds. Reloading: Between 5 and 10 minutes, depending upon expertise.	A loaded Colt revolver may be discharged in between 5 and 10 seconds, depending upon the dexterity of the user. Reloading can take up to ten minutes, depending upon expertise.

CHAPTER SIX

The Rimfire Revolver and Rollin White's Patent

Development of the Self-Contained Metal Cartridge

Percussion weapons, especially revolvers, had quickly become popular in the more sparsely populated areas of America and saw much use by both civilians and the military, especially during the American Civil War. However, they still had a number of significant disadvantages. The process of loading remained relatively slow, since the loading materials themselves, consisting of powder flask, bullets, caps and wads, were cumbersome. Although significantly better than the flintlock, they were not completely impervious to the effects of weather. Dissatisfaction with the percussion system led to the search for a self-contained load and eventually resulted in Smith & Wesson's rimfire cartridge, patented in 1860.

Invented by Louis Flobert in 1845, the first rimfire cartridge was simply a tiny bullet pushed into the mouth of a percussion cap, the fulminate in the cap acting as both primer and propellant. The round itself was used solely for target shooting in the specially designed galleries of German beer halls. The idea was seized upon by the American, Walter Hunt, who devised a rifle to use this type of cartridge, which was subsequently manufactured by the firm of Robbins & Lawrence. Robbins & Lawrence produced only a small number of rifles, but one of their employees, B. Tyler Henry, recognized the potential of the idea and went to Horace Smith. Together with his partner Daniel Wesson, Smith founded the Volcanic Firearms Company. Smith & Wesson sold Volcanic to Oliver Winchester in 1855, founding their own company in 1856 to manufacture the first rimfire revolvers, while Winchester used a larger rimfire cartridge in the original Henry rifle and the later repeating rifles that still bear his name.

In a rimfire cartridge, as the name implies, the fulminate priming material is formed into a ring around the lower rim of the case. This means that the metal of the base must be thin enough to allow the hammer of the weapon to act through it on the priming material. That, in turn, makes it difficult to manufacture a rimfire case with even a moderately heavy charge. Rimfire ammunition is now usually available only in .22 caliber because of this restriction, although early weapons, such as the Spencer and Henry rifles as well as some converted Colt and Remington revolvers, were chambered for rimfire ammunition with calibers up to .56 inches (approx. 14 mm).

Continental gunmakers favored another, earlier type, the pinfire cartridge, which consisted of a metal case with fulminate priming fired by a pin projecting above the surface of the cartridge. This pin fit into a groove in the top of the cylinder, and the cartridge fired when the hammer struck the pin. Lefaucheux revolvers, amongst others, are chambered for this round. Such weapons are characterized by an open-frame design, a hammer similar in shape to that found on many percussion revolvers, and a cylinder slotted on the top face of each chamber to accept the pin of the cartridge.

The final development in the field was the centerfire cartridge, in which the priming material is contained in a metal cup or primer that fits into the center of the base of the cartridge case. Upon firing, the weapon's firing pin strikes the base of the primer, crushing and igniting the priming material between the cup and an "anvil," contained either in the primer (Boxer primer) or produced as part of the case (Berdan primer). Most ammunition in use today is of this type.[1]

The Rimfire Revolver and the Demise of Percussion Ignition

Smith & Wesson were the first major firearms manufacturer to produce a practical cartridge revolver using a rimfire cartridge, although their design did not meet with universal approval. Many found the cartridge lacked stopping power, and moreover, their products, particularly the cartridges, were difficult to obtain. Smith & Wesson, however, had one very significant advantage over their competitors.

In 1855, an inventor called Rollin White had taken out an American patent that contained a claim for "extending the chambers through the rear of the cylinder for the purpose of loading them at the breech from behind." Smith and Wesson approached White and offered him generous terms for the exclusive use of his patent, which made them the only company able to manufacture any weapon in which a metal cartridge was loaded into the rear of a cylinder until White's patent expired in 1869. More importantly, under this agreement, he was also obliged to take legal action against any company infringing his patent. White was forced to take up the legal cudgels against patent offenders with depressing frequency, and although suit was successfully brought against the Bacon Manufacturing Co., the Manhattan Firearms Manufacturing Co., and a number of others, the cost of litigation forced White into bankruptcy.

Smith & Wesson's appetite for litigation and their universal success against patent transgressors deterred the big companies, like Colt, from using White's idea, and they were forced to look for another way of chambering a revolver to accept a metal cartridge.[2]

The First Smith & Wesson Revolvers

Smith & Wesson produced their first rimfire revolver in 1857, under the protection of Rollin White's original patent. It continued to be manufactured by the company until 1860, when production ceased in favor of the Second Issue revolver, and was typical of the company's early rimfire weapons. Later weapons included the .32 caliber Model No. 2 Army revolver, before the company switched to the production of revolvers chambered for centerfire cartridges.

Smith & Wesson No. 1 revolver, 1st Issue

Total production: 11,671 revolvers.

Single-action, solid-frame revolver, with a plain cylinder chambered for seven .22 caliber rimfire cartridges. Barrel is octagonal, with company name and address inscribed. This revolver features a unique, "tip-up" frame opening mechanism with the barrel hinged to the forward end of the top strap, which allows the cylinder to be completely removed for loading. The frame is of silver-plated brass with a removable side-plate, cylinder and barrel are in blued steel, and rosewood butt-plates are most usual. A blade front sight and rudimentary rear sights are fitted. Six types are recognized by collectors within this First Issue, and there were Second (1860–1868) and Third (1868–1881) issues, also with a number of type modifications.[3]

 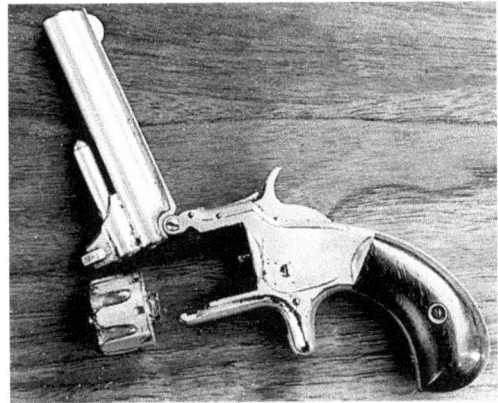

Left: Smith & Wesson No. 1 revolver, .22 caliber, from the right (courtesy James D. Julia Auctioneers, Fairfield, Maine. www.jamesdjulia.com). *Right*: Smith & Wesson No. 1 revolver opened for loading.

Values

Price is dependent upon type. The "First Type" revolvers are usually the most sought-after and expensive.

NRA Good: $600–$5,000; NRA Fine: $2,000–$13,000

Table Ten: Specification of Smith & Wesson No. 1: First Issue revolver

Period of production	Between 1857 and 1860
Production	11,671 pistols
Military service	Commonly seen as private purchases during the U.S. Civil War
Weight	Approximately 16 oz
Length/Barrel length	Approximately 7 inches/barrel 3¼ inches
Frame type	Solid frame, with "tip-up" mechanism for loading
Mechanism	Single action
Ammunition	Chambered for seven .22 caliber short rimfire cartridges
Sights	Blade front sight
Maximum accurate range	20 ft (60 m)
Rate of fire	A loaded Smith & Wesson No. 1 revolver may be discharged in between 5 and 10 seconds, depending upon the user's ability. Reloading would take approximately 1–3 minutes, again depending upon the user's familiarity with the weapon.

Other Manufacturers of Rimfire Revolvers

After the expiration of Roland White's patent, other manufacturers began to produce rimfire weapons. These included:

AMERICAN MANUFACTURERS[4]

- Allen & Wheelock: Rimfire and lipfire revolvers in calibers between .22 and .44, cylinders with six or seven chambers.
- Colt: Rimfire revolvers in .38 and .44 caliber, cylinders with six chambers.
- Remington: Rimfire revolvers in .38 and .41 caliber, cylinders with six chambers.

BRITISH MANUFACTURERS[5]

- Tranter: Rimfire revolvers in calibers between .230 and .44, cylinders with five, six or seven chambers.
- Webley: probably only acting as a retailer of Continental arms.

CONTINENTAL MANUFACTURERS

Numerous small gun makers, particularly in Liege, probably including Francotte and Ancion et Cie.

Rollin White and the Smith & Wesson Patent

Rollin White began work as a gunsmith in his elder brother's shop in Williamstown, Virginia, in 1837. Having finished his apprenticeship, in 1849 he went to work for Colt, turning revolver barrels on a lathe, and it was during this period that he used the company workshop and two rejected cylinders to produce his own "bored-through" cylinder. White's patent application, dated 3 April 1855, shows a revolver with a single percussion cone mounted on top of the frame and a flat magazine, containing the paper or linen cartridges, fixed to the left of the hammer, with an opening adjacent to the cylinder. The revolver was apparently single action and is shown in the patent drawings with a ring trigger, similar in conformation to an under-hammer pepperbox.

Cocking the hammer served to drive forward a piston that pushed a fresh cartridge from the spring-loaded magazine into the topmost chamber. When the hammer fell, the piston retracted sufficiently to allow a fresh cartridge to be pushed into position from the magazine, ready to be moved into the adjacent cylinder by the piston when the hammer was cocked again. Despite its undoubted mechanical ingenuity, unfortunately White's 1855 revolver required the single percussion cone to be capped before each shot, slowing down the rate of fire considerably, although there is a suggestion that he may have intended to incorporate a Maynard primer into the design to solve this problem. It also seems very doubtful if the complex mechanism, which includes three tiny cog wheels to actuate the hammer mechanism, would have been proof against the fouling that commonly bedevils users of black powder weapons, even to the present day.

White never manufactured his 1855 Model revolver but he did form a company in 1861, in Lowell, Massachusetts, to produce a copy of the Smith & Wesson .22 caliber revolver. Called the Rollin White Arms Company, it produced approximately 5,000 of these small caliber revolvers before White's association with the company ended, all of which were marketed through Smith & Wesson's retail outlets. Subsequently, the company became the Lowell Arms Company.[6]

White's Competitors

Perhaps more accurately referred to as Smith & Wesson's competitors, these companies fell into two broad groups. The first were those who copied the Smith & Wesson breech-loading design, while the second group comprised a few manufacturers who tried to circumvent the patent by using systems incorporating metal cartridges, but which could not be designated "breech-loading" for the purposes of an action for patent infringement.

Many of what may be termed the "breech-loading" group suffered badly when White was forced into legal action by the conditions under which he had sold his patent to Smith & Wesson. Several of these manufacturers, including the Bacon Manufacturing Company, Manhattan Fire Arms Manufacturing Company, and E.A. Prescott of Massachusetts, settled matters by selling their revolvers to Smith & Wesson. Such arms often bear a stamp in the form:

PAT. APRIL 3, 1855
or
made for Smith & Wesson

Some revolvers may be found that bear both stamps, although not all weapons that were the subject of this litigation bear the relevant markings. Few, if any, Manhattan .22 caliber revolvers, for example, are so marked.

The second and, perhaps not unexpectedly, smaller group included revolvers patented and produced by Colt (the Thuer revolvers), the Brooklyn Arms Company (aka Slocum revolver), Moore's Patent National Firearms Company, the Plant Manufacturing Company, and Lucius Pond. While they had no trouble with White and his lawyers, many of these arms did not work as well as the Smith & Wesson rimfire revolvers, and some, such as Silas Crispin's revolver with its belted-rim cartridge, were so unsafe they saw few, if any, sales.[7]

Revolvers Not Covered by White's Patent

Metal cartridge conversions of Colt percussion revolvers

The men running the Colonel's firm since his death in 1862 were not about to give up their overwhelming share of the revolver market to Smith & Wesson's new product without a fight. Prior to the expiration of White's patent, the Colt company patented a system, in 1868, for converting Colt percussion revolvers to use a specially developed centerfire cartridge, loaded from the front.

This system was invented by a Colt employee, Alexander Thuer, and is consequently referred to as a "Thuer conversion" by collectors. The conversion process involved machining off the rear of the percussion cylinder and fitting a breech ring containing a firing pin and ejector button. Special tapered cartridges, also designed by Thuer, were loaded into the front of the cylinder, to be fired when the revolver hammer struck the firing pin of the conversion ring, which, in turn, struck the primer of the cartridge. After firing, the cases were ejected by bringing the ejector button round under the hammer, which was then "snapped" to push the spent case forward out of the cylinder.

Thuer's system was ingenious, but too complicated and unreliable for commercial success. It was soon superseded, although the revolvers themselves are now seen as very desirable by collectors.

With the expiration of White's patent in 1869, Colt abandoned the complexities of Thuer's system and began to market a new conversion based originally on Colt's 1860 Army revolver. This conversion, which had been developed by another employee, C.B. Richards, looked superficially like a Thuer conversion in that it also had a breech plate in front of the cylinder. But cartridges were loaded from the rear of the cylinder through an aperture in the breech plate, after opening the loading gate fitted onto the right flash shield. As in the Thuer revolver, a cartridge was fired when the hammer struck the integral firing pin of the breech plate, which was then driven forward to strike the primer. As a further refinement, a rod ejector was fitted in place of the original loading lever, although for reasons best known to the factory and designer, the enclosing sleeve of the ejector stopped some distance short of the cylinder. The original barrel and breech were also retained and a rear sight fitted to the breech plate.

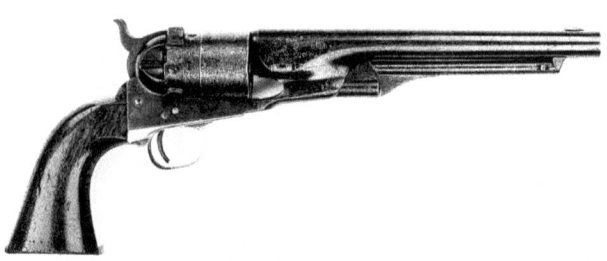

Colt Model 1860 Army revolver converted to accept Thuer cartridges. This weapon shows the characteristic retention of the under-barrel loading lever, which was used to seat the cartridges (courtesy James D. Julia Auctioneers, Fairfield, Maine. www.jamesdjulia.com).

Richards-Mason conversion, this weapon with a shorter, round, engraved barrel and ivory butt plates. The loading gate is similar in shape to that found on the later Model "P" (courtesy James D. Julia Auctioneers, Fairfield, Maine. www.jamesdjulia.com).

From around 1873, an improved Richards-Mason conversion was adopted, despite Colt's having by then put their new Model P into full production. This system retained the breech plate, but dispensed with the integral firing pin. Instead, the breech plate was machined out at the top, to allow the hammer nose to strike the cartridge directly. In addition, the ejector sleeve reached to the front of the cylinder. Depending upon the model, converted weapons of this type may have a barrel and breech of a new design, especially made for these revolvers, or retain the original components. All these conversions have barrels retained by a wedge through the breech and are exactly similar in this respect to Colt's percussion revolvers.

Unfortunately, Colt still had large numbers of components for their percussion weapons, which would have to be scrapped if they produced an entirely new metal cartridge revolver. Consequently, between 1868 and 1873, when Colt's famous Model P, more commonly known as the "Peacemaker," completed development, as well as performing conversions, Colt also sold factory-new revolvers converted for rimfire and centerfire cartridges. This explains why revolvers of all models may be found as cartridge conversions, and also why many bear serial numbers within the original percussion series.

Colt revolvers with Thuer conversion

Manufactured between 1869 and 1872, with a total production of approximately 5,000.

Converted revolvers are similar in all respects to the standard percussion Models, including barrel, frame and serial number markings, except for the presence of the breech plate and ejection mechanism. The breech plate is marked at the breech end of the cylinder:

PAT.SEP.
15.1868

Colt revolvers recorded with the Thuer conversion include:

- Model 1849 Pocket
- Model 1851 Navy
- Model 1860 Army
- Model 1861 Navy
- Model 1862 Police
- Model 1862 Pocket Navy

Thuer conversions are also known for the Model 1855 Dragoon, the Model 1855 Root revolver, and the Model 1855 Sidehammer rifle, although these last three are rare.

Values

All Models: NRA Good: $4,500; NRA Fine/Excellent: $15,000

Dragoon and Root revolvers and sidehammer rifles will have higher values because of their rarity.[8]

Thuer cartridges showing the rimless base (courtesy James D. Julia Auctioneers, Fairfield, Maine. www.jamesdjulia.com).

Colt revolvers with the Richards conversion

Converted revolvers are similar in all respects to the standard percussion Models, including barrel address, frame, trigger guard and serial number markings and are chambered for the .44 caliber Colt centerfire cartridge. Richard conversions are mainly characterized by; a breech plate with an integral rear sight and an ejector rod cylinder which terminates a significant distance from the front edge of the main cylinder, although there are other, minor differences. The original barrel and breech is retained in this conversion and loading levers are not fitted or removed from original percussion weapons and the hole in the breech lug plugged. A transition Model between the Richards and Richards-Mason conversions is known, characterized by Richards pattern barrel and case ejector and a Richards-Mason pattern breech plate and hammer.[9]

Values

NRA Good: $1,500; NRA Fine/Excellent: $4,000
Examples marked U.S. and with a government inspector's mark:
NRA Good: $3,000–$4,000; NRA Fine/Excellent: $12,000

Colt revolvers with the Richards-Mason conversion

This conversion is characterized by: a breech plate without a rear sight, this plate being cut away at the top to allow the hammer to strike the cartridge; an ejector tube that reaches the front edge of the cylinder; and, on some models, a specially manufactured round barrel and breech. Loading levers were not fitted or were removed from original percussion weapons returned to the factory, and the hole in the breech was plugged.[10]

Colt revolvers recorded with the Richards-Mason conversion include:

- Model 1849 Pocket
- Model 1851 Navy
- Model 1860 Army
- Model 1861 Navy
- Model 1862 Police
- Model 1862 Pocket Navy

Values

NRA Good: $3,000–$4,000; NRA Fine/Excellent: $12,000 (Flayderman 2008)

OTHER MANUFACTURERS OF METAL CARTRIDGE REVOLVERS
NOT COVERED BY WHITE'S PATENT

The Brooklyn Firearms Company revolvers

Brooklyn Arms "Slocum" front-loading Pocket Model revolver

Manufactured by the Brooklyn Firearms Company of Brooklyn, New York, from 1863 to 1864, under an American patent registered to Frank Slocum, then resident in Brooklyn.

Production: Estimated to be over 10,000 weapons. Details of frame numbering not available.

Single-action, solid-frame revolver, with spur trigger, in .32 caliber rimfire. Only one type produced with a 3-inch round barrel and plain cylinder with five chambers. The cylinder design is unique in that the chambers are made in two parts, an inner, sliding tube contained within a fixed, hemispherical outer chamber.

The chamber to be loaded is turned until it is in the correct position, adjacent to the rod fitted on the right hand side of the revolver, below the barrel and forward of the cylinder. The inner cylinder tube is moved forward over this rod, allowing access to the outer cylinder, into which a conventional .32 caliber rimfire cartridge is placed. The inner tube is then returned to its original position, securing the cartridge against the rear of the cylinder, which is pierced with a notch to allow the hammer nose access to its base. After firing, the procedure is reversed, the spent case being simply tipped from the outer chamber after the inner tube has been moved forward.

Frames are in brass, usually engraved and frequently silver-plated, with blued steel barrel and cylinder, both of which are also usually engraved. Butt plates are most frequently walnut, although ivory and other materials were also used, and they have a characteristic, although unconventional, shape.

Barrels are stamped:

B. A. CO. PATENTED APRIL 14, 1863

Although these revolvers were complex and probably expensive to make, the numbers produced and sold seem to indicate that they were both popular and reliable, although unfortunately, no record of their use in either a military or civilian capacity has so far been recorded.

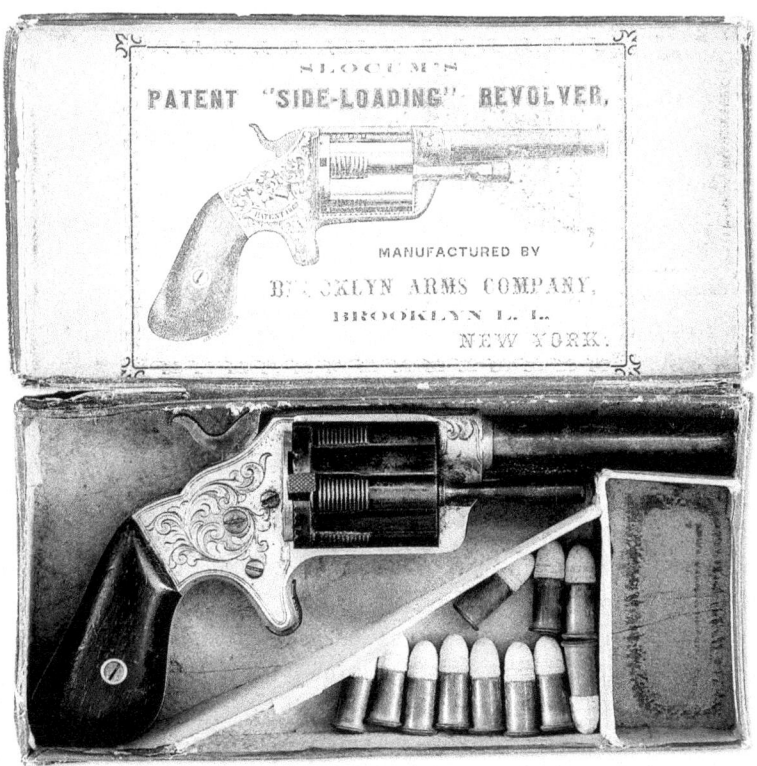

Brooklyn Arms Slocum revolver in its characteristic box, with some rather corroded cartridges (courtesy James D. Julia Auctioneers, Fairfield, Maine. www.jamesdjulia.com).

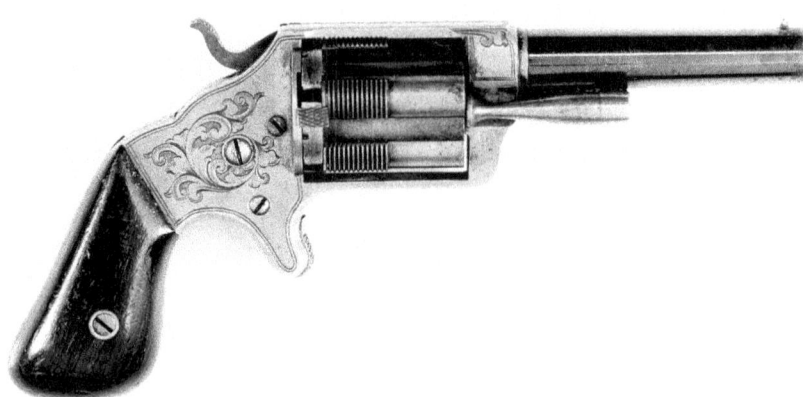

Brooklyn Arms revolver from right (courtesy James D. Julia Auctioneers, Fairfield, Maine. www.jamesdjulia.com).

Values

NRA Good: $750; NRA Fine: $1,100

Incidentally, the Brooklyn Firearms Company also produced conventional .32 caliber and .22 caliber breech-loading revolvers.[11]

Moore's Patent Firearms Company revolvers

Moore's .32 caliber front-loading "teat-fire" revolvers

Manufactured by Moore's Patent Firearms Company from 1864 to 1866, then by its successor the National Firearms Company, Brooklyn, New York, from 1866 to 1870. Although Moore produced these revolvers, the patent for the cartridge was owned by David Williamson, another resident of Brooklyn during this period.

Production: Approximately 30,000 revolvers in the various models, by both companies.

Single-action, open-frame, spur-trigger revolver in .32 caliber with 3¼-inch round barrel. Frame is engraved brass. The cylinder, which is often engraved as well, has six chambers loaded from the front via a small, triangular gate, hinged at the bottom and screwed to the breech lug in front of the barrel. Each chamber is pierced at the rear to accept a protrusion or "teat" extending from the base of the cartridge, which gives the round its name and characteristic appearance. When Williamson designed the first of these cartridges, they were produced with a flat teat. This caused several problems, including some difficulty in seating the round properly in the chamber, so the inventor later changed the design to incorporate a round teat, for which he took out a new patent in 1869. However, these "round-teat" cartridges did not fit properly in the guns designed for the earlier round, needing a slight modification to the chamber to allow them to be loaded and fired in weapons with frame numbers of around 8000 and lower, although the point in production where the new chambering was introduced still awaits clarification.[12] Later weapons, possibly those designed for the "round-teat" cartridge, were fitted with a hooked cartridge extractor. Butt plates are in either walnut or gutta-percha (an early plastic made from rubber).

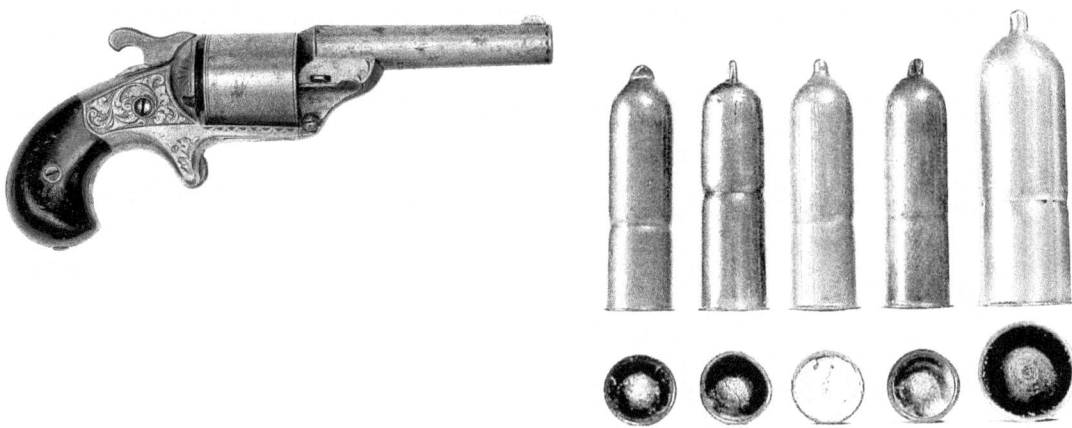

Left: Moore's .32 caliber teat-fire revolver (by kind permission of Bonhams). *Right:* Selection of Teat-fire cartridges. From left to right: 1: Williamson's first cartridge design, with the flat teat. 2: Cartridge turned sideways to show the flattened conformation of the teat. 3: Later cartridge with round teat made under Williamson's second cartridge patent of 1869. 4: Misfired cartridge. 5: Rare .45 caliber teat-fire cartridge, apparently produced only with the round teat (courtesy www.old ammo.com).

Distinguishing marks (barrel and cylinder)

Revolvers without hooked extractor: Barrel addresses take the following form, depending upon the date of manufacture:

Before 1866:

MOORE'S PATENT. FIREARMS CO. BROOKLYN, N.Y.

After 1866:

NATIONAL ARMS CO, BROOKLYN N.Y.

Another stamp is found around the rear circumference of the cylinder and takes the following form:

D. WILLIAMSON'S PATENT JAN. 5, 1864

In earlier revolvers, specifically those with the "MOORE'S PATENT" barrel address, cylinder patent marks may take this form:

D. WILLIAMSON'S PATENT JANUARY 5, 1864

Revolvers with hooked extractor (all after 1866): Barrel addresses take the following form:

NATIONAL ARMS CO, BROOKLYN N.Y.

Another stamp is found around the rear circumference of the cylinder and takes the following form:

D. WILLIAMSON'S PATENT JUNE 5—MAY 17, 1864

The smaller .32 caliber weapon was apparently popular with both sides in the Civil War and was carried as a privately purchased side arm, despite the obvious problems with ammunition supply. Weapons with an authentic Civil War history may therefore be encountered, although the usual precautions should be taken before final purchase.

Values

NRA Good: $800; NRA Fine: $1,100

National Arms Co. Large Frame Teat-fire revolver

Production: Very limited, and given the barrel address, probably produced after 1866, although a more precise date is currently unavailable.

Single-action, solid-frame revolver, chambered for .45 caliber "teat-fire" cartridge and with a 7½-inch barrel. Cylinder is plain, unfluted and bears no patent stamps. Chambered for six cartridges, which are loaded in a similar manner to the smaller .32 caliber weapon, although only the later "round-teat" cartridges were produced for this revolver. Frames are silver-plated brass and usually bear no markings. "Bird's-head" butt, with walnut butt plates.

Barrel addresses take the following form:

NATIONAL ARMS CO, BROOKLYN N.Y.

Values

Not particularly successful, due to the appearance of a number of metal cartridge revolvers after the expiration of White's patent in 1867, so few were made and antique examples are rare.[13]

NRA Good: $4,000

Plant's Manufacturing Company revolvers

Plant's "Cup-Primed" revolvers

Manufactured by Plant's Manufacturing Company, New Haven, Connecticut, to use a unique "cup-primed" cartridge. Merwin and Bray acted as agents for Plant as well as providing financial backing, so revolvers also bear this company's stamp. The priming in these cartridges lies between the walls of the case, within a fold made at the base of the round to form the "cup." Cylinders had an opening bored in their rear wall to allow access for the hammer nose, which was arranged so as to strike the surface of the cup, thus firing the cartridge, which was loaded from the front of the cylinder. The design was essentially unreliable, although Plant's various companies and licensees sold nearly 30,000 weapons of this type before production ceased in 1870.

Plant Manufacturing Co. front-loading "Army" revolver

Serial numbers: 1–8000. Single-action, solid-frame revolver, with spur trigger and in .42 caliber. Frames either iron or brass, often silver-plated, with a 6-inch, octagonal, ribbed barrel. Cylinders with six chambers, plain and unfluted. These revolvers were usually supplied with an additional percussion cylinder. Butt plates in walnut or sometimes rosewood.

Cartridge ejectors were of two types. The earliest design used on the First Model, which features a hinged frame, was a simple, under-barrel rod. In this model, the cylinder had to be removed for loading, and the rod was used to simply knock out the case in a manner analogous to a .22 caliber Smith & Wesson revolver. A better design was introduced with Second Model, consisting of an ejector rod contained within a housing fixed to the right side of the frame behind the cylinder. The ejector rod moves through the hole pierced in the rear cylinder wall for the hammer nose to eject the cartridge.

FIRST MODEL

Found with brass or iron frame. Approximately 250 produced.
Barrel marked on top flat:

PLANT'S MFG. CO. NEW HAVEN, CT.

Barrel marked on side flat:

M & B

Iron framed examples marked on side of barrel:

M & B
NY

Cylinders are stamped:

PATENTED JULY 12, 1859

SECOND MODEL

Also found with iron or brass frame rounded at breech and fitted with later design of cartridge ejector. Approximately 400 weapons produced.
Barrel marked on top flat:

PLANT'S MFG. CO. NEW HAVEN, CT.

Frame is stamped in front of cylinder:

MERWIN & BRAY, NEW YORK

Cylinders are stamped:

PATENTED JULY 12, 1859 & JULY 21, 1863

THIRD MODEL

Frames only in brass with square breech. Two types, known to collectors as Standard (or Heavy) frame Model and Light Frame Model.

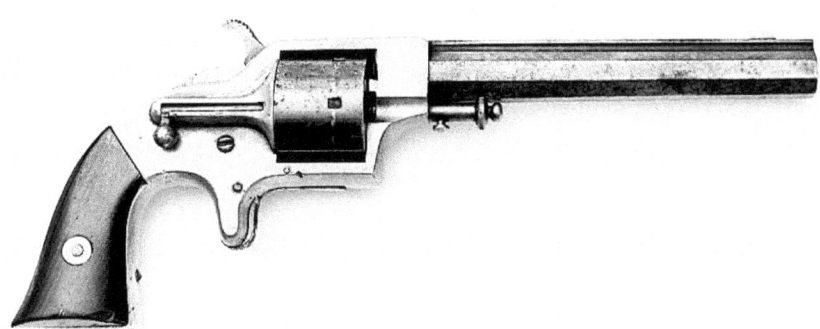

3rd Model Plant's "front-loading" revolver, showing the cartridge ejector on the right side (courtesy James D. Julia Auctioneers, Fairfield, Maine. www.jamesdjulia.com).

Serial numbers:

Heavy Frame Model: 700–6800
Light Frame Model: 6800–8000

Frame markings correspond to Second Model and other minor differences, such as the top-strap sight groove and cylinder, are described in Flayderman.

Plant Manufacturing Co. front-loading Pocket Model revolver

Similar in conformation to Plant's Third model Army, with its square-fronted breech. Despite being known to collectors as Plant's Pocket Model, these small-caliber revolvers were, in fact, manufactured by the Eagle Manufacturing Company, New York, in the mid-1860s, although Plant's company did act as their sales office.

Total manufactured: approximately 20,000 weapons, between 1864 and 1866, although in view of the later cartridge ejector and frame conformation, the Pocket Model was probably made in parallel with the Third Model Army.

These are solid-frame, single-action revolvers, fitted with a spur trigger and chambered for a .30 caliber cup-primed cartridge. Frames are silver-plated brass, with a square front to the breech. Barrels are octagonal, ribbed on the top flat, and 3½ inches long. Cylinders are plain, not usually engraved. Weapons made by the Eagle Arms Co. are six-chambered, all other types having cylinders with five chambers. Butt plates are either rosewood or walnut.

Barrels bear a variety of stamps on the top flat, such as:

EAGLE ARMS CO., NEW YORK

or:

MERWIN & BRAY FIREARMS CO., N.Y.

or:

REYNOLDS, PLANT & HOTCHKISS, NEW HAVEN, CONN.

Cylinders are stamped:

PATENTED JULY 12, 1859 & JULY 21, 1863

Merwin & Bray advertised the Army Model in *Harper's Weekly* as "officially adopted by the U.S. Revenue Service." No official record exists of any U.S. Government contract purchase of Plant revolvers, and although the *Harper's* advert did appear, it may well have been part of the company's marketing strategy. It follows, then, that any Plant revolver that seems to have U.S. government and/or U.S. Revenue Service markings should be examined very carefully, especially if a premium is being asked for the weapon on the basis of its service history. However, Plant revolvers were also privately purchased and carried during the Civil War, so authentic weapons with that type of history may be encountered. In addition, some Plant revolvers were converted to take breech-loading rimfire cartridges.[14]

VALUES: ARMY MODEL REVOLVER

First and Second Models: NRA Good: $850; NRA Fine: $2,000
Third Model: NRA Good: $300; NRA Fine: $950
Pocket Model revolver: NRA Good: $200; NRA Fine: $500

L.W. Pond front-loading revolvers

Manufactured by Lucius Pond in Worcester, Massachusetts, to use a conventional rimfire cartridge in either .22 or .32 caliber, which was loaded into the front of the cylinder and retained in place by individual steel sleeves, which were pushed into the chamber after the cartridge had been loaded.

Pond front-loading .22 caliber rimfire model revolver

Total production: Estimated at approximately 2,000. Frame numbers absent.

Single-action, solid-frame revolver, with spur trigger and chambered for a conventional .22 caliber rimfire cartridge. Frame is silver plated brass with a 3½-inch octagonal barrel. The cylinder has seven chambers, with push-in steel inserts. Butt plates are walnut or rosewood.

Barrel is stamped in one line:

L.W. POND, WORCESTER, MASS. PAT'D SEPT. 8, 1863, PAT'D NOV. 8, 1864.

Pond front-loading .32 caliber rimfire model revolver

Total production: estimated at approximately 5,000 weapons.

Similar in conformation to the .22 caliber weapon, except cylinder has six chambers and barrels are longer, at 4, 5 or 6 inches. Barrel stamps are the same.[15]

Values

NRA Good: $400; NRA Fine: $900

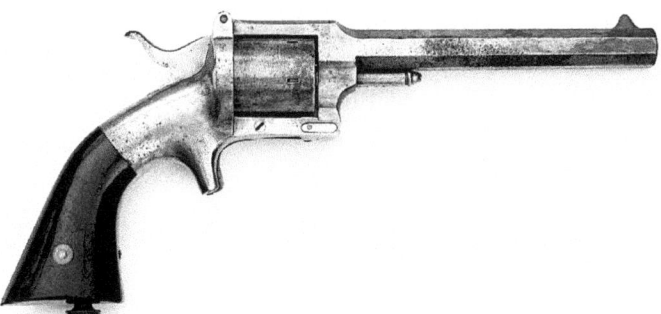

Pond .22 rimfire revolver (courtesy James D. Julia Auctioneers, Fairfield, Maine. www.jamesdjulia.com).

Silas Crispin's 1865 revolver

Not all the devices produced to circumvent White's patent were practical or even safe. One extraordinarily dangerous cartridge invented to circumvent White's patent was described by Silas Crispin in an American patent he registered in 1865.

Crispin's cartridge was of a type best described as "belted." The fulminate was enclosed in a ridge or raised band around the approximate middle of the cartridge case and the revolver was loaded by opening the top-break frame, which split the cylinder, inserting the cartridge and then closing the weapon, which resulted in the band being wedged between the two parts of the cylinder. The weapon was fired (in the unlikely event that one or all of the cylinders had not discharged prematurely when the weapon was closed) by a hammer that was designed to reach over the narrower, rear section of the cylinder and strike the primer band. Fortunately, Crispin's revolver never passed out of the experimental stage, although examples are occasionally encountered at auction.

Reported to have been manufactured by the Smith Arms Company of New York City

(barrels of some weapons are stamped with this name), although the actual numbers produced is not recorded in the relevant literature.

Solid-frame, single-action, top-break revolver, with spur trigger and chambered for the .32 caliber "Crispin" cartridge. Barrel is octagonal, five inches long. Cylinder has six chambers and is of a characteristic design, being constructed in two unequal parts that split when the revolver is opened to allow the unique cartridges to be loaded. Hammer also has a characteristic shape being elongated to allow it to pass over the rear section of the cylinder and strike the union between the two parts.

Frames may be stamped, in a single line:

SMITH ARMS CO., NEW YORK CITY. CRISPIN'S PAT. OCT. 3, 1865

although authentic examples are recorded which do not bear these stamps.

Values

Despite the highly dangerous nature of the weapon, they are sought after and their rarity means they can fetch considerable sums at auction.[16]
NRA Good: $8,000; NRA Fine: $20,000

Cartridge for Crispin revolver, showing the "belt" containing the fulminate that fired the charge (courtesy of: www.old ammo.com).

CHAPTER SEVEN

Pinfire and Centerfire Revolvers

The Pinfire Cartridge

The first cartridge for use in a breech-loading weapon was patented in 1812 by a Swiss gun maker, S.J. Pauly.

He intended that his cartridge should be used in a shotgun that had fixed barrels and was loaded by lifting the breech block. Several improvements on this design were made subsequently, although many who used the gun felt that a cartridge that was permanently ready to shoot was unsafe. They reverted to using unprimed paper cartridges, with ignition being achieved by a conventional percussion cap.

Improvements in the design of breech-loading weapons continued, however, and in 1832, Casimir Lefaucheux patented an improved breechloader. It was partially based on Pauley's design, but incorporated a pair of barrels that hinged downwards to reveal the breech ends, although these still used a percussion cap for ignition. He continued his experiments, and in 1835 was granted an addition to the original 1832 patent, covering a new type of cartridge. The priming compound in the new cartridge was ignited when struck by a pin that protruded radially from just above the base of the cartridge, the pins fitting into a small groove machined into the top of the breech of each barrel. Lefaucheux's original cartridge had a copper base with a paper body to hold the load, which meant they were not particularly gas-tight.

In 1846, Benjamin Houllier was awarded a French patent for an improved pinfire round made with brass walls and base. These new cartridges made the guns using them cleaner and quicker to load than the old muzzleloading weapons, and consequently pinfire shotguns began to gain in popularity with French shooters.

The British shooting public remained indifferent, however, and it was not until some pinfire shotguns were seen at the Great Exhibition of 1851 that their popularity with the English sporting set began to improve. This acceptance of the pinfire cartridge began when a young apprentice gunmaker, Charles Hodges, saw a Lefaucheux shotgun at Crystal Palace. Realizing its potential, Hodges made a copy of the weapon with a number of improvements, which he subsequently persuaded Joseph Lang to produce. Lang made the first pinfire shotguns for his aristocratic clients in 1853 and was soon imitated by other London gunmakers, such as Lancaster, Blanch, Reilly, Boss, Egg, Purdey, and the Army and Navy stores.[1] Pinfire cartridges became obsolete once reliable rimfire and centerfire ammunition began to be available. The later types were quicker to load and safer, having no protruding pin that could cause the ammunition to accidentally detonate during rough handling, particularly if cartridges were kept loose in a pocket or bag. Although favored by Continental gunmakers,

Pinfire revolver by an unknown Continental maker, showing the "swing-out" case ejector and the closed loading gate (courtesy James D. Julia Auctioneers, Fairfield, Maine. www.jamesdjulia.com).

few American or English revolvers of this type were produced. The French Lefaucheux revolver typifies the design, being an open-frame, gate-loading weapon, with a cylinder chambered for six cartridges.[2]

The Lefaucheux Revolver

DEVELOPMENT

Having seen the improvement which Houllier made to the pinfire cartridge in his 1846 French patent, Casimer Lefaucheux (1802–1852) and his son, Eugene, began work on a revolving pistol. By 1851, they had produced a design of pepperbox revolver, which was shown at the Great Exhibition. Colt's products proved more popular, but undeterred by this indifference, the Lefaucheux duo produced a conventional revolver that was eventually tested by the French Navy. It was accepted into service with that force in 1858, the first revolver using a metal cartridge to be adopted by a national government. Although the French Army still refused to adopt the revolver, some French cavalry units were equipped with it before beginning service in Mexico in 1862, and over 12,000 Lefaucheux revolvers were used by both sides during the U.S. Civil War. Pinfire revolvers became increasingly popular in Europe, and were produced in calibers from the 12mm military Lefaucheux down to a tiny 2mm pistol for use in tavern shooting galleries.

OPERATION AND SPECIFICATION

The Lefaucheux revolver is a single-action, open-frame design with a cylinder chambered for six 12mm pinfire cartridges. Cartridges were loaded via a top-hinged loading gate on the right side of the frame, and an under-barrel ejector rod was fitted. Barrels were round, approximately six inches long, and rifled with six deep, clockwise grooves, giving a slow rate of twist to the conical bullet. Butt plates were in two parts, usually of walnut and fixed with a single screw, held in place by a bolt inset into the right-hand plate, with lanyard rings often fitted from new to military weapons. A rudimentary pillar front sight was fitted, with a rear sight groove milled in the top of the hammer, allowing the sight picture to be made only when the weapon was cocked. These guns were produced by a number of French and Belgian gunmakers and manufacturers, with retail and patent marks usually be found on the standing breech. Belgian guns are distinguished from the French product by the presence of a Liege proof mark; French guns of this period were not required to undergo a proof check.[3]

Lefaucheux revolver showing detail of loading gate, with a cartridge inserted in the cylinder (courtesy Rama: License: CCASA-2.0).

Values

NRA Good: $800–$1,000; NRA Fine: $1,200–$1,500

Table Eleven: Specification of the Lefaucheux revolver

Period of production	1858 to 1870
Production	No records, but probably 100,000
Military service	French Navy from 1858 until 1870
	French Army: Maximillian in Mexico in 1862
	U.S. Civil war: Both sides, approximately 12,000 imported weapons
Weight	Approximately 2½ lbs (1.2 kgs)
Length/Barrel length	12 inches (25cms)/6 inches (12.5 cms)
Frame type	Open frame
Mechanism	Single action, with a cylinder turned and indexed by internal mechanism
Ammunition	12mm all-brass pinfire cartridge
	Six-chambered cylinder revolving clockwise
Sights	Post front sight
	Groove rear sight, milled into the top of the hammer
Maximum accurate range	25 meters
Rate of fire	A loaded Lefaucheux revolver may be discharged in between 5 and 10 seconds, depending upon the dexterity of the user. Reloading would take approximately 1 to 2 minutes, again depending upon the user's familiarity with the weapon.

The Centerfire Cartridge

Although they were a significant improvement over the earlier percussion arms, weapons that used the rimfire or pinfire cartridges still suffered from a number of disadvantages. The design of the rimfire case in particular, which necessitated a thin-walled base in order that ignition could occur, made it unsuitable for a heavy powder charge. Pinfire cartridges also tended to be low-powered because of limitations in their construction. Perhaps more importantly, both types cartridges were expensive and difficult to obtain, because they could only be manufactured with specialized machinery. These disadvantages ensured that neither type ever became popular enough to completely supersede the percussion revolver. The military were especially critical of weapons chambered for these cartridges, and they were still the major market for any sort of revolving pistol. Consequently, many users began to look for something better than these relatively low-powered cartridge designs, and weapons chambered for the new, powerful centerfire round began to predominate. Although rimfire weapons are still extensively manufactured, they tend to be used in the smaller hunting rifles and target pistols, while pinfire weapons are almost completely obsolete.[4]

Development

The centerfire cartridge is a type of self-contained ammunition in which both the powder load and ball are contained in a metal case and fired by a primer mounted in the center of the base or "head." Although centerfire cartridges are often designated "Boxer" or "Berdan" cartridges, this is really a misnomer, since what both Boxer and Berdan invented was not a type of centerfire cartridge, but rather two different primers for use in that round.

The Boxer primer

This pattern was developed by Colonel Edward Boxer while he was superintendent of the Royal Laboratory at the Royal Arsenal, Woolwich, England. He registered the British patent for his primer in October 1866. In a centerfire cartridge, the primer fits into a circular recess in the base or "head" of the cartridge and sits flush with its lower surface. Boxer primers have a small, concave cup or "anvil" integral with the primer, providing the necessary resistance to the impact of the firing pin, such that the fall of that component indents the primer body, crushing the pressure-sensitive ignition compound against the anvil and causing a flame to pass through the single flashhole in center of the cartridge base, firing the round.[5]

The Berdan primer

In contrast to the Boxer primer, Berdan's device requires that the anvil be incorporated into the case of the cartridge. Consequently, a Berdan primer is little more than a percussion cap inserted into the recess in the head of the cartridge, adjacent to its two flashholes and snug against the anvil. Berdan primers are easier to manufacture than the Boxer pattern, but the cases are much more complex to make, and although a Berdan case can be reloaded, it is significantly more difficult and time-consuming than the same process using Boxer-primed ammunition. Consequently, most of the cartridges currently manufactured use Boxer primers.[6]

The Centerfire Revolver

American developments

In America, after the expiration of White's patent, Colt, Remington and Smith & Wesson had the monopoly on centerfire revolver production during the latter part of the nineteenth century, although several smaller companies, such as Merwin & Hulbert, were also producing excellent weapons of this type. Colt's SAA (Single Action Army) revolver was adopted by the U.S. Army in 1872 after winning the U.S. government service revolver trials in that year.[7]

The English gunmakers

English centerfire revolver production centered around Philip Webley and William Tranter, who had been able to begin producing well-made, reliable centerfire revolvers in 1867, six years before the introduction of Colt's Model P, because White's patent was not in force in England. Tranter, in fact, had began producing a revolver of this type in 1862, when he recorded his first patent for such a weapon. He went on to produce a wide variety of models chambered for both centerfire and rimfire, many models offering the option of both types of cartridge according to the customer's preference.[8]

Webley's first metal cartridge revolver was the Royal Irish Constabulary Model, chambered for the company's own .442 centerfire cartridge. This first appeared in 1867, although the company had been making good copies of the Smith & Wesson .22 and .32 caliber rimfire revolvers since 1862 and of Tranter's "Boxer" revolver since 1866. The RIC proved a popular weapon, and it is said that George Custer was carrying a pair at the Battle of the Little Bighorn, although some authorities dispute this. Subsequent models included the short-barreled Bulldog, Express, and Webley-Pryse revolvers, as well as a range of small, hammerless six-shot pistols.

Large numbers of privately purchased Webley revolvers certainly saw service with officers in the British Army during the latter half of the nineteenth century. In 1892, a Webley revolver was officially adopted for British military use, although the weapon was first ordered by the British government in 1887. This was the Webley Mk I Government Model (accepted into the British Army as Pistol, Webley Mk I). Thus began a long association between the British Army and Webley's robust, reliable top-break revolvers, which replaced the unpopular, unreliable Enfield Mk I and Mk II. Webley's first contract called for 10,000 Mk I revolvers, at £3 1s 1d each (about £3.06). This revolver subsequently went through a series of minor changes and improvements, culminating in the Mk VI, introduced in 1915. An excellent weapon, it remained in service with the British Army until 1947. Another Webley, the Mk IV, this time chambered in .38/200, was still in service until 1963, when it was finally replaced by the Browning Hi-Power semi-automatic pistol.[9]

Operation

Centerfire revolvers are usually solid-frame and may be single- or double-action. Three designs of loading mechanism predominate: gate-loading, top-break, and types with a "swing-out" cylinder. Certain refinements were introduced by some manufacturers; for example, Merwin & Hulbert's "swing-open" ejection mechanism, in which the barrel and standing breech assembly can be swung sideways on the arbor to allow ejection of spent cartridges.

The gate-loading revolver

This type is the earliest design of cartridge revolver and weapons of this type may be found chambered for certain calibers of rimfire cartridges as well as the more common centerfire round. Cylinders are fixed in the breech and may not be removed without disassembling the weapon. Loading is accomplished by inserting cartridges into the rear of the cylinder via a loading slot. The slot is closed and the cartridge protected by a loading gate, which may be hinged at the top or bottom, spent cases usually being removed with the aid of an ejector. This type is well illustrated by Colt's famous "Peacemaker," designated by the Colt factory as the "Model P" revolver.

Colt's Single Action Army revolver or "Model P"

Production: approximately 400,000 of all models

MODELS

- Sheriff's, Banker's Special or Storekeeper's Model: 2½–4¾-inch barrel; cartridge ejector may be absent.
- Wells Fargo & Company: Bears a W.F & Co stamp on the butt; usually 5½-inch barrel.
- Civilian Model: 4¾ inch barrel in a variety of calibers. Cartridge ejector always present on right side of barrel.
- Artillery Model: 5½-inch barrel in a variety of calibers. Cartridge ejector always present on right side of barrel.
- Cavalry or Standard Model: 7½-inch barrel, in .45/28 or .45/40 caliber. Arms for the civilian market were produced in a variety of calibers including .45/40. Cartridge ejector always present on right side of barrel.
- Colt "Frontier" or "Frontier Six-Shooter": Barrel lengths variable, between 4¾ and 7½ inches, and with the usual cartridge ejector present on right side of barrel. This "Model P" was only sold chambered for the 44/40 WCF (Winchester Center-Fire) cartridge, which also fitted the Winchester Model 73 rifle, a deliberate marketing strategy aimed at allowing users to carry only one type of ammunition for both their rifle and revolver.

SPECIFICATION

Known by its factory designation of the Model "P," as well as a number of other nicknames, Colt's SAA revolver is a solid-frame, single-action weapon. It is fitted with a fluted cylinder chambered for six cartridges, and may be found in a variety of calibers, ranging from .45/40 to .44 and .22 caliber rimfire, the cylinder being accessed by a bottom-hinged loading gate on the right side of the weapon. Barrels are round, and vary in length from 2½ inches on the Sheriff's Model up to 7½ inches on the Standard revolver and "Bisley" target models. A cartridge ejector is fitted on the right side of the barrel, although short-barreled models tend to be without this device. Front sights are a conventional blade sight on all models, while rear sights usually consist of a groove milled in the top of the frame, although target weapons may have a more useful pattern of aperture sight fitted to the rear of the top strap. Serial numbers as well as patent and manufacturing marks are stamped or etched on frames and barrels and serve as a convenient means of identifying the model of a particular revolver. Butt plates are in one piece and found in a variety of material, although the most common is walnut.

Values

Difficult to estimate. An ordinary revolver with little provenance can be bought for between $2,000 and $5,000, depending upon condition, but any weapon with a special finish or unusual or desirable history will reach considerably more. Some Single Action Army revolvers and their differently chambered variants have sold at auction for well in excess of $200,000.[10]

Colt SAA revolver from the right, showing the loading gate and characteristic case ejector (courtesy James D. Julia Auctioneers, Fairfield, Maine. www.jamesdjulia.com).

Adams Model 1867 cartridge revolver, showing the top-hinged loading gate, plain cylinder and early case ejector. A later model of this revolver was adopted by the British army (courtesy James D. Julia Auctioneers, Fairfield, Maine. www.jamesdjulia.com).

The top-break revolver

This type of revolver typically features a robust hinge between the breech-piece and the lower frame and a catch between the lock assembly and the top strap of the barrel. To load the weapon, the frame catch between the lock and the top strap is opened, whereupon the barrel and cylinder assembly can be tilted forward, giving access to the breech end of the cylinder into which the cartridges are loaded. Usually a revolver of this type is also fitted with a self-ejecting mechanism that ejects the spent cases from the cylinder when the weapon is opened. Once loading is completed, the weapon is closed and is then ready to fire. Produced by Smith & Wesson and Webley, amongst others, a representative example of the type is the Webley Government model of 1887.

Webley Government Model

Webley Government Model, Mk I—Mk VI center-fire revolver (1887–1947)
Production: Serial number ranges and adoption dates:

- Mk I—Serial number range: 679–41000
  Accepted between May and July 1887, first order confirmed 18 July 1887 (sealed pattern approved: November 1887). Officially adopted 8 November 1892 as **"Pistol, Webley, Mk I, B.L Revolver,"** when it replaced all the older weapons. The original revolver was manufactured to use the Webley .442 centerfire cartridge and early production

also included revolvers chambered to use either the Enfield .455 or Enfield .476 cartridge. Later weapons (Mk IV, Mk V and Mk VI) were chambered only for the Webley .455 cartridge.

Initial order was for 10,000 revolvers, with a total of 40,000 weapons eventually supplied.

- Mk I*—Later Mk I revolver with modification to the recoil plate.
- Mk II—Serial number range (continuous from the Mk I): 44000–61000
  Adopted 21 May 1895.
- Mk III—Serial number range: 101–80000
  Adopted 5 October 1897.
- Mk IV—Serial number range (possibly as a continuation of the Mk II): 77000–130000.
  Adopted 21 July 1899, known to collectors as "Boer War" Model. Initial order unknown.
- Mk V—Serial number range: 129000–214000 (higher numbers in civilian arms are recorded).
  Adopted 9 December 1913 with an initial order of 20,000.
- Mk VI—135000–455000 (in a range shared initially with the Mk V revolver).
  Approved 24 May 1915 and produced until 1939.
  Government figures show over 300,000 made for World War I alone.
  From 1921, also manufactured by Royal Small Arms Factory, Enfield, as: "Pistol, Revolver, Webley, No. 1 Mk VI."

SPECIFICATION

The Webley Government Model revolvers are all top-break, hinge-frame, double-action, self-extracting revolvers, chambered for the various government-issue revolver cartridges, featuring a rebounding hammer and fitted with the characteristic lock, frame catch and self-extraction mechanisms based on patents of Webley and Carter (Br. Pt. 4070/1885) and Thomas and Henry Webley (Br. Pt. No 5143/1881). Barrels are octagonal, with a top-strap rib, rifled with seven clockwise grooves of the shallow Metford type, and may be 3, 4, 5, 6 or 7½ inches in length. The frame is hinged below the front of the cylinder and fitted with the characteristic stirrup-catch, operated by a single lever on the left side of the frame near the hammer. Cylinders are semi-fluted, with six chambers and fitted with an automatic ejector, actuated when the weapon is opened by operation of the thumb-operated frame catch lever. Cylinder bolt recesses are present on the rear surface of that component and there are also a second series of small rectangular slots near the middle of the cylinder also associated with the cylinder locking mechanism, which is similar to that fitted to the earlier Webley revolvers. A blade foresight and fixed rear sight are fitted, the front sight being an integral part of the barrel rib. Butts are two-piece, "Bird's-Head" conformation in Mks I - V, conventional in the Mk VI, and are usually of vulcanite (aka: "ebonite"), a rubber compound hardened by the inclusion of sulfur, although walnut plates were occasionally fitted to early weapons. Early weapons were designed to use black-powder cartridges, with a modification introduced during production of the Mk V to allow the use of a cordite round. A significant feature of these revolvers, which assured continued government interest, was that parts were largely interchangeable. Military or civilian proof marks are usually stamped on the barrel or frame and every chamber of cylinder, in a form characteristic for the date (a crowned "VR" or "GR," above crossed scepters, with a "P" beneath are most common for government-issue revolvers). Patent information, including the "Mk" of the revolver, is stamped on the left side of the barrel lug or frame and appears in a typical oval format. Government-issue revolvers produced after 1912 are found stamped on the top of the butt strap with the day and month of their year of issue (Ordnance marks) and corps marks ("R.S." for Royal Scots, "R.B." for the Rifle Brigade, etc.), and after 1914 (Mk V and Mk VI revolvers), they also bear a date below the patent stamp which will

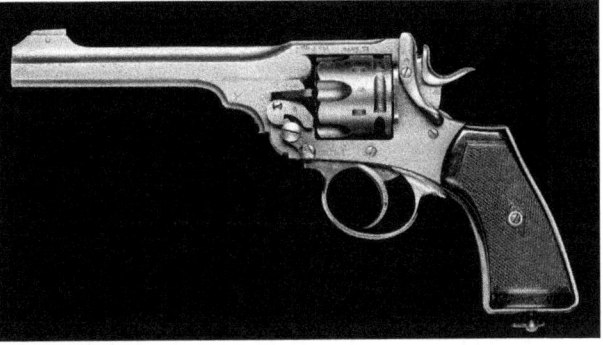

Webley MkVI revolver, showing frame stamps and conventional butt, with two ebonite butt plates (by kind permission of Bonhams).

correspond to the year of manufacture. Serial number stamps may be found on either the left or right side of the frame, usually below the cylinder, although their position is variable. Other stamps include: acceptance marks, the War Department's "Broad Arrow," and Webley's "Winged Bullet" trademark.[11]

VALUES

Webley Mk I—Mk V Government revolvers: NRA Good: $1,300–$1,500; NRA Fine: $1,800–$2,000

Webley Mk VI Government revolver: NRA Good: $900–$1,100; NRA Fine: $1,200–$1,250

The swing-out cylinder revolver

Most modern centerfire revolvers are of this type, although some shooters feel that the design is not as robust as Webley's old top-break model. Reasonable care certainly has to be exercised when opening and closing the cylinder to ensure that the pivot pin does not become bent, and the common practice seen in the cinema of snapping a cylinder shut under its own weight is certainly not to be recommended. Smith & Wesson's Military & Police Model is a commonly encountered example of this pattern of revolver. It should be noted that, because of their later development, swing-out revolvers are usually designed to use smokeless cartridges.

Smith & Wesson Military & Police

Production numbers: Over 6 million produced between 1899 and 2016, making it the most popular centerfire revolver of the 20th century.

- **1st Model 1899:** serial number range: 1–20975

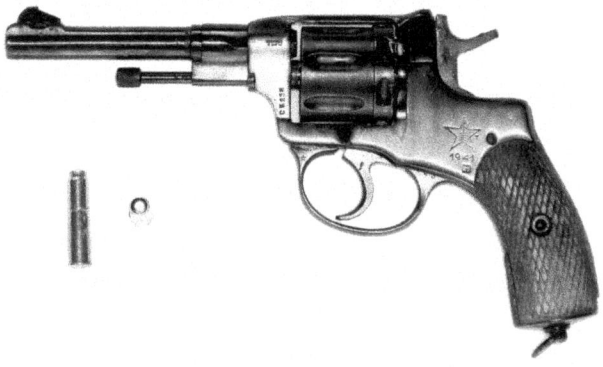

Nagant gate-loading revolver (courtesy Mascamon at lb.wikipedia).

- **2nd Model, 1902:** serial number range: 20976–33803
- **2nd Model, 1902, 1st Change:** serial number range: 33804–62449
- **Model 1905:** serial number range: 62450–73250
- **Model 1905, 1st Change and 2nd Change:** serial number range: 73251–146899
- **Model 1905, 3rd Change:** serial number range: 146900–241703
- **Model 1905, 4th Change:** serial number range: 241704–700000

SPECIFICATION

This revolver is a solid-frame, double-action weapon, fitted with a swing-out cylinder having six chambers, designed to accept either the .38 Long Colt, .38 Special or .38/200 (.38 S&W) cartridge. Cylinder release is by a thumb-actuated push button on the left side of the frame. Barrels may be 2, 3, 4, 5 or 6 inches in length. Sights are fitted, a blade front sight and the conventional milled groove in the top strap of the frame serving as the rear sight. Butts are in two pieces and usually walnut, although custom butt plates are available.[12]

VALUES

Depending upon model and designation (1st, 2nd, 3rd or 4th Change):
NRA Good: $125–$700; NRA Fine: $300–$2,000 (1st Model)

OTHER NINETEENTH-CENTURY MANUFACTURERS OF CENTERFIRE REVOLVERS

American manufacturers[13]

After the expiration of Roland White's patent, other U.S. manufacturers began to produce centerfire weapons. These companies included:

- Colt: Single- and double-action revolvers in calibers from .31 to .455, with four-, five- or six-chambered cylinders.
- Merwin Hulbert & Co.: Single- and double-action revolvers in calibers from .32 to .45, usually with six-chambered cylinders and an open frame, unusual in centerfire weapons.
- Remington: Single-action revolvers in .38, .44 and .45 caliber, with five- or six-chambered cylinders.
- Smith & Wesson: Double-action revolvers in calibers from .32 to .44, usually with six-chambered cylinders, although S&W also made weapons with five- and seven-chambered cylinders.

British manufacturers[14]

White's patent had not been registered in Britain nor in any Continental country, so revolver manufacturers in both these locations could produce conventional breech-loading revolvers, without resorting to the American makers' technological trickery. Such manufacturers included:

- John Adams: Produced Mk I and Mk II revolvers for the British army which were also sold as a civilian version.

- Tranter: Single- and double-action revolvers in calibers between .38 and .577, with five- and six-chambered cylinders.
- Webley: Single- and double-action revolvers in calibers between .38 and .455, usually with six chambers, although some early models, such as the Webley-Kaufman, featured variations chambered for five cartridges.

European manufacturers[15]

- Galand & Sommerville: Charles Francois Galand patented this open-frame, double-action revolver with a six-chambered cylinder in 1868. The weapon is usually referred to as the Galand or Galand & Sommerville Model 1870, since Mr. A. Sommerville of the Birmingham firm of Braendlin & Sommerville shared in the patent for the unique extractor system. Cartridge extraction was brought about by jerking down the trigger guard, which moved the barrel and cylinder forward, withdrawing all the cartridges simultaneously by means of a disc extractor connected to the rear of the cylinder). Galand revolvers were sold to the military chambered for a 9mm centerfire cartridge and as a civilian arm chambered in 12mm centerfire.
- Gasser: M1870 Gasser revolver was a single-action, open-frame, gate-loading revolver with a five-chambered cylinder designed for the 11.2 × 29.5mm centerfire cartridge. It was adopted by the Austro-Hungarian cavalry in 1870 and continued to be used by German forces until 1945.
- Nagant: The Nagant Model 1895 revolver was a solid-frame, gate-loading revolver, with an under-barrel ejector. It was produced in either a double- or single-action, and had a cylinder with seven chambers designed for the 7.63 × 38mmR cartridge. Over 2 million were produced, mainly for use by the Imperial Russian Army until 1917, and then by the Red Army and Soviet security forces until the end of World War II. It had a reputation for robustness, which led one former Imperial Russian officer to comment: "If anything went wrong with the M1895, you could fix it with a hammer."

Table Twelve: General specification of rimfire, pinfire and centerfire revolvers

Weapon	Rimfire revolver	Pinfire revolver	Centerfire revolver
Makers	USA: Remington, Smith & Wesson UK: Webley, Tranter, and smaller Birmingham makers	France: Lefaucheux Belgium, Liege: Auguste Francotte	USA: Colt, Remington, Merwin & Hulbert UK: Webley, Tranter Europe: Nagant
Period of production	1857–present day	1860–1880	1867–present day
Production	Reliable figures not available. Probably several hundred thousand, significantly less than either percussion or centerfire weapons	Approximately 250,000 in Europe. 12,000 12mm Lefaucheux imported for use by both sides in the U.S. Civil War	Reliable figures not available, probably at least 100 million. 6 million of S&W Military & Police produced alone
Military service	Only as private purchases. Do not appear to be any issue revolvers	Frequent amongst European armies: French Army and Navy—Lefaucheaux;	Extensive; all armies have issued this type at some period.

Weapon	Rimfire revolver	Pinfire revolver	Centerfire revolver
		U.S. Civil War—Variety of calibers between 12mm and 4mm	
Weight	Between 2 lbs and 4 lbs	Between 2 lbs and 4 lbs	Between 1lb and 3½ lbs (Pocket and Target Models)
Length/Barrel length	7 and 12 inches/ 3¼ and 7½ inches	7 and 12 inches/ 3¼ and 7½ inches	6–18 inches/2½–12 inches (Pocket and Target Models)
Frame type	Open or solid frame	Invariably open-frame, due to the requirements of the ammunition	Usually solid-frame, unless converted from an earlier percussion weapon
Mechanism	Single, self-cocking or double action. Cylinder turned and indexed by an internal mechanism.	Single-action, double-action or self-cocking. Cylinder turned and indexed by internal mechanism.	Single, self-cocking or double-action. Cylinder turned and indexed by an internal mechanism.
Ammunition	Variety of calibers: .22 short, .22 long, .230, .32, .38, .41, .44. Cylinders may have four, five or six chambers, usually accessed via a loading gate.	Pinfire cartridge: 4mm, 6mm, 7mm, 9mm, 11mm. Cylinders may have four, five or six chambers, usually accessed via a loading gate.	Variety of calibers: .22, .230, .32, .38, .44, .45. Cylinders may have four, five or six or seven chambers, accessed by either a loading gate, a top-break mechanism or swinging the cylinder out to the left.
Sights	Usually blade front sight, fixed rear sight on top of the frame	Blade or post front sight. Rear sight either fixed on frame or as groove milled into the hammer	Front: Usually blade sight, although post sights are also fitted. Rear sight: Variable. Most frequently a groove milled in the top strap, but target weapons often have an aperture sight on the lock frame or rear of the top strap
Maximum range	75 ft (25 m)	Between 20 and 30 meters	10–25 meters, depending upon conformation
Rate of fire	Generally discharged in 5–10 seconds. Reloading in approximately 2–4 minutes.	Generally discharged in 5–10 seconds. Reloading: 2 to 3 minutes, comparable to a rimfire revolver.	Generally discharged in 5–10 seconds. Reloading may take less than 10 seconds if a mechanical device, such as a speed-loader, is used.

CHAPTER EIGHT

Repeating Rifles and Shotguns

The development of early repeating rifles paralleled that of the repeating pistol, and both "Roman candle" guns and magazine weapons were produced by a number of gunmakers.[1] Of particular note are the "Roman candle" guns manufactured under a U.S. patent by Joseph Chambers, who sold 850 muskets, rifles and pistols of this design to the Commonwealth of Pennsylvania and the U.S. Navy, and which were actually used in action during the War of 1812. Of the magazine weapons, arms manufactured by the Florentine gunsmith Michele Lorenzoni around 1680 are most common, although it seems at least doubtful if Lorenzoni actually invented the gun which bears his name. They feature a double magazine system and were unique at the time for also incorporating a mechanism that cocked and primed the weapon in a single operation. The Lorenzoni rifle is also referred to as the Cookson rifle by American collectors, because the first rifle of this type recorded in America bore the name of a London gunsmith, John Cookson. One such weapon was recorded with the date 1666 (possibly 1686) stamped on the metalwork. It should also be noted that an American gunsmith, also named John Cookson, was making guns to this pattern in Boston 100 years later, in 1756, so care must be exercised in differentiating products of their respective workshops. An earlier weapon, produced by Peter Kalthoff sometime before 1650, also features two magazines, although its mechanism, being more complex and less robust than the later weapon, ensured that it never became as widespread or popular as the significantly more reliable Lorenzoni guns.[2]

Magazine Rifles

THE LORENZONI/COOKSON SYSTEM

A Lorenzoni/Cookson rifle or pistol was constructed with both the ball and powder magazines in the butt of the weapon, with a smaller magazine for priming powder in the lock. The two larger magazines were accessed by a revolving, cylindrical breech block in which there were two cavities.

To operate the weapon, one first held it with the muzzle pointing upwards and the operating lever of the breech block on the left side of the weapon pulled to the rear to its full extent, allowing the two cavities in the breech block to align with their respective butt magazines. The orientation of the gun was then reversed, with the muzzle pointing down, and this action allowed a ball to move into one cavity and a measured charge of powder to flow into the second. With the gun still held muzzle down, the operating lever is then

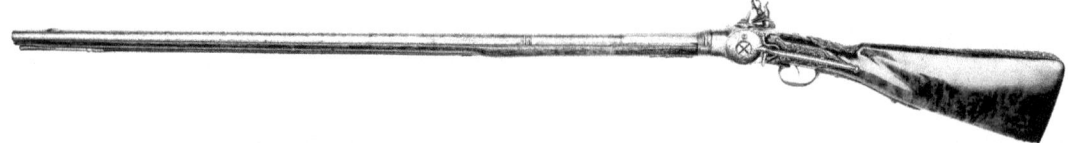

Lorenzeni breech-loading, repeating flintlock rifle from the left, showing the cycling lever (courtesy James D. Julia Auctioneers, Fairfield, Maine. www.jamesdjulia.com).

moved fully forward, delivering both the ball and powder to the chamber, whilst at the same time priming and cocking the weapon. All that is subsequently required to fire the weapon is to pull the trigger.[3] This was a remarkably innovative design, especially considering that the first examples of a gun based on this system began to appear in Italy about 1680, and that H.W. Mortimer Sr. was still making guns of this type in 1800, representing quite a remarkable span for the production of a flintlock repeater.

Harmonica Guns

These weapons were another attempt to produce a repeating firearm designed for magazine operation, which was also reliable and cheap enough for battlefield use. The guns were ostensibly breechloaders, although they were charged by having the load inserted into the front of each of the separate chambers, which were then capped separately in much the same way as a muzzleloading revolver. A harmonica or "slide" rifle consisted of a conventional barrel and butt, with a breech section in which a wide slot has been accurately machined, the breech end of the barrel communicating with this slot. The rectangular magazine that inserts into this slot, and whose appearance incidentally gives the weapon its name, has chambers at regular intervals, each chamber being provided with a percussion cone screwed into the top of the magazine, and communicating with its respective chamber via a conventional flashhole. To operate the weapon, the magazine is first loaded with powder and ball, the percussion cones capped, and the magazine is then inserted into the breech slot and either moved by hand or cammed forward by an internal mechanism. When the magazine is correctly lined up or "indexed" with the barrel, the hammer may then be cocked and the trigger pulled to fire the weapon. The magazine is then moved to its next position, the hammer cocked, and the whole procedure can begin again. The operation of a rifle of this design is essentially the same as a Jarre harmonica pistol. A number of gunmakers produced pistols and rifles of this type during the early nineteenth century. Most notable for the excellence of their design and production quality are the weapons made by Jonathan Browning, father of John Moses Browning.[4]

THE BROWNING SLIDE REPEATING RIFLE

Browning invented what he called his "sliding-breech" rifle sometime between 1834 and 1842, while he was living in Quincy, Illinois, and probably before he became involved with the Church of the Latter-Day Saints. His gun seems to have been a commercial success, even though each weapon took about two weeks to make and cost twenty-four dollars.

Despite this apparent popularity, examples are rarely seen at auction. The gun is similar in design and function to the more usual harmonica guns, having the appearance of a conventional rifle, with a slot manufactured in the breech to accept the five-chambered magazine or "slide."

Production numbers: Not accurately known, but possibly several hundred.

These weapons had a conventional percussion mechanism with a single trigger and an octagonal barrel of between 30 and 36 inches. Trigger guards and butt plates were in brass, and the stock and woodwork of recorded examples appear to have been patterned on the contemporary "Kentucky" rifle, with its characteristic shape to the butt and a forestock extending to the muzzle (i.e., fully stocked). Firing followed the usual procedure: the releasing lever on the right of the weapon was first lifted so that the magazine could be inserted and moved across the loading slot until the first chamber was correctly lined up with the barrel. The releasing lever was then depressed, which moved the magazine forward and sealed the protruding breech end of the magazine chamber against the recess machined in the end of the barrel that was designed to accept it, a system intended to minimize losses from escaping gas. The hammer was then cocked and the weapon fired, whereupon the magazine could be moved across manually and the whole cycle began again.

Military service

Although the weapon was never accepted formally by the military, it has been suggested that it was used during the 1850s by Mormons defending their homes from Native Americans.[5]

Values

Although rare at auction, examples do occasionally appear.
NRA Good: $30,000; NRA Fine: $150,000

MODERN HARMONICA GUNS

Harmonica guns are still manufactured today. Perhaps the best known examples are the Steyr range of semiautomatic air pistols and rifles.

Early Repeating Air Rifles

Air rifles offered several advantages over conventional muzzleloading arms. They were quieter than a flintlock, produced no smoke to reveal a rifleman's position, and the ammunition and rifle mechanism were both completely waterproof. Unfortunately, the technology necessary to reliably deliver air at high pressure was in its early developmental stages in the late seventeenth century, and only one air rifle, produced by an Austro-Italian inventor, ever saw military service.

GIRANDONI'S AIR RIFLE

This was the only magazine rifle to be used by a European army during the eighteenth century and as well as being a repeating weapon, it was also something of a departure from

A Girandoni air rifle from the right side, this example a well-made civilian arm (by kind permission of Bonhams).

the traditional muskets of the period, since it used compressed air instead of black powder as its propellant. The gun was developed by an Austrian inventor, Bartholomäus Girandoni (or Girardoni), who also produced a number of pistols to the same design. It was only the primitive technology associated with both the design of the containers used to hold the propellant and the means to pump them full, that fatally impeded the development of what was a very superior weapon indeed.

Production numbers: Not known, but 1,500 were issued to troops in the Austrian army and several hundred were produced by Continental gunmakers to Girandoni's original design.

Girandoni's rifle was 40 inches long and weighed about 10 lbs, which made it comparable to a contemporary flintlock musket. It fired a ball of between .46 and .51 caliber, which was supplied to the breech of the gun from a tubular, spring-loaded magazine holding approximately 20 rounds and mounted beside the barrel, its opening being adjacent to the breech. A transverse metal bar containing the chamber ran through this combined breech and magazine section, such that in the firing position the chamber communicated directly with the barrel and the chamber bar effectively closed the entrance to the magazine. The air supply was contained in the removable, cylindrical metal butt. Some weapons also appear to have been made in which the ball was fed to the chamber under gravity, although the construction of the chamber bar and the weapon's operating system were the same as in rifles with a spring-loaded magazine.

Having filled both the air reservoir and the magazine, the chamber was loaded by first pulling the transverse chamber bar out of the breech until it reached a position that would allow a ball from the magazine to position itself correctly in the chamber itself. The chamber bar was then allowed to return to its original position under the influence of a spring, the barrel and chamber, which now contained the ball, thus being in alignment. Pulling the trigger released a fixed quantity of air through the breech, sufficient to drive the ball down the barrel. The quantity of air held in the butt reservoir was sufficient to fire approximately 30 shots to a distance of around 125 meters, although how accurate the weapon was at such an extreme range is not recorded. When this reservoir was empty, it had to be laboriously refilled using a hand pump that needed around 1,500 strokes to completely charge the reservoir. Standard equipment for a rifleman using a Girandoni, according to regulations issued by the Austrian army in 1788, were:

three compressed air reservoirs (two spare and one attached to the rifle)
a cleaning rod
a hand pump

- a lead ladle
- 100 lead balls, 1 in the chamber, 19 in the magazine built into the rifle, and the remaining 80 in four tin tubes.

As well as keeping the gun scrupulously clean, a soldier also found it necessary to keep the leather gaskets of the reservoir moist in order to maintain a good seal and prevent leakage. As well as the hand pumps issued to individual troops, rifle companies were issued with a larger pump, mounted on a wheeled chassis, although these only appear to have been intended for emergency use.

Military service

Girandoni's air rifle was approved for service in the Austrian army and was in use with that body from 1780 until 1815. It had all the advantages of an air weapon over contemporary flintlock arms, having a high rate of fire, no muzzle flash or smoke, and no loud report, being almost completely silent. More importantly, contemporary muzzleloading muskets and rifles required the operator to stand up in order to reload, but another advantage of Girandoni's weapon was that it allowed the operator to reload a ball from the magazine by holding the rifle vertically while lying on his back and operating the ball delivery mechanism, without exposing himself to the enemy.

Unfortunately, despite its many advantages, the weapon proved fragile under battlefield conditions, particularly the brazed and riveted sheet iron air reservoirs, which needed to develop only the most minute of leaks to be rendered inoperative. The Austrians finally removed it from service after Waterloo. Lewis and Clark are claimed to have taken one of these weapons with them on their expedition and used it to impress the Native Americans they encountered, although some researchers have suggested that their weapon may not have been a Girandoni rifle, but rather a similar gun made by one of the Lukens family of Philadelphia.[6]

A Girandoni air rifle, this example a military weapon, showing signs of heavy wear (by kind permission of Bonhams).

Values

Although rare at auction, examples do occasionally appear.
NRA Good: $4,000; NRA Fine: $8,000

English gunmakers

Although Girandoni's weapon was the only repeating air rifle accepted for military service, his design was copied by a number of other gunmakers for use in hunting or recreational target shooting. These gunmakers included:

- **Staudenmayer, Samuel Henry:** Despite the European flavor of his name, Staudenmayer was a London gunmaker and former apprentice of John Manton. He was appointed gunmaker to the Prince of Wales and Duke of York, being well known for the production of fine rifles as well as repeating airguns.

  He had a number of premises during his career. His weapons are often found in cases that bear labels giving the address of the shop from which the gun originated, thus serving as a reliable means of dating the weapon:

  Premises:

  35, Jermyn St. London (1799 until 1802)

  35, Cockspur St. London (1802 until 1814)

  32, Cockspur St. London (1814 until his death in 1825)

  The business appears to have been carried on under his name by his executors from the premises at 32, Cockspur St. until 1834.

- **Reilly, Edward Michael:** A London gunmaker famous for his conventional airguns and air canes, although he is not generally associated with repeaters. He published one of the early books on air weapons, titled *A Treatise on Air Guns* in 1850.

  Premises:

  316, High Holborn, London (1835 until 1847, with his father)

  502, Oxford St. London (1848 until 1860)

  Became E.M. Reilly & Co. in 1861 at:

  277, Oxford St. London (These were the same premises as the original shop at 502 but became 277 after renumbering by the London Corporation.)

CONTINENTAL GUNMAKERS

As well as these English gunmakers, a number of smaller Continental gunmakers also produced weapons of this type, particularly in Germany and Liege, Belgium.

LATER DESIGNS OF REPEATING AIR RIFLE

Although air guns never had a significant military application, they were (and are) produced for game and recreational shooting by a very considerable number of companies.

Revolving Cylinder Rifles

Revolving cylinder rifles were an obvious development from the earlier Colt revolver, and several models were produced by Colt's Hartford factory between 1856 and 1864. They were never very popular, suffering a number of design faults, including "chain" fires and having a distressing tendency to spray the user's left hand with splinters from the ball after firing. Colt's Model 1855 is a good example of a percussion weapon of this type, although a number of revolving flintlock rifles and muskets are also recorded.[7]

Colt's Model 1855 Revolving Rifle

Production numbers: approximately 15,000 weapons of several types

Colt's 1855 rifle was a single-action, solid-frame weapon made in a variety of barrel lengths; 21, 24, 27, 31 and 37 inches were the most common. The barrels fitted to these guns are round with an octagonal breech and produced most commonly in .36, .44 and .56 caliber, although there were rare weapons made in .40, .50 and .64 caliber. Cylinders are fluted and have a variable number of chambers; rifles in .36 and .44 caliber usually have six chambers, while the .56 caliber weapons have only five. Butts and forestocks are of varnished or oil-stained walnut, and the finish is generally blue, with a case-hardened hammer and loading lever. Military weapons have sling swivels and are usually found with U.S. military markings.

Factory stamps are variable but are always stamped on the top strap, usually in this form:

**COLT'S PT. ADDRESS COL COLT
1856 HARTFORD CT. U.S.A.**

Variations

- Model 1855 "First Model" Sporting rifle: Made in .36 caliber, carbine 15- and 18-inch barrel, rifle 21, 24, 27 and 30-inch barrels.
- Model 1855 Half Stock Sporting rifle: Made in .36, .44 and .56 calibers, with 24, 27, and 30-inch barrels.
- Model 1855 Full Stock Sporting rifle: Made in .36, .40, .44, .50 and .56 calibers, with 21, 24, 27, 30 and 31⅜-inch barrels.
- Model 1855 Military rifle and rifled musket: Made in .44, .56 and a rare .64 calibers, with 21, 24, 27, 30, 31 and 37½-inch barrels (barrel sizes are approximate).
- Model 1855 Revolving carbine: Made in .36, .44 and .56 calibers with 15, 18, 21 and 24-inch barrels.[8]

Colt revolving rifle Model 1855, from the right, showing the side-hammer and fluted cylinder (courtesy James D. Julia Auctioneers, Fairfield, Maine. www.jamesdjulia.com).

Values

NRA Good: $3,000; NRA Fine: $20,000

Other Revolving Rifles[9]

- Remington revolving percussion rifle Model 1866: Made in .36 and .44 caliber with 24- and 28-inch barrels. May be found as a factory conversion to use either a .38 or

.44 caliber rimfire cartridge. A rare conversion designed to use a .46 caliber rimfire cartridge is also recorded.
- Le Mat revolving grapeshot rifle: Cylinder with nine chambers in .42 caliber firing through the top, rifled barrel, with a .63 caliber, smoothbore shotgun barrel under the conventional revolver barrel, similar in conformation to the more familiar Le Mat revolver.
- The Treeby "chain" gun: This was a .54 caliber (approximately 30 bore) single-action weapon with a conformation similar to a percussion carbine, although the loads are delivered to the chamber from a continuous chain containing 14 chambers. Not perhaps strictly a revolving rifle, Treeby's weapon incorporated a series of steel chambers linked into a circle that passed behind the breach of the weapon. Each chamber was loaded separately with powder and shot and fired by means of a conventional percussion lock striking a fulminate cap, the chambers being moved into position manually. Only two were made, and these prototypes performed so badly during Ordnance Board trials that the project was abandoned.

Metal Cartridge Magazine Repeaters

Although both Browning's slide repeater and Girandoni's air gun were magazine repeaters in the strictest sense, it was not until the appearance of a reliable metal cartridge that the breech-loading repeating rifle became a serious proposition for civilian and military personnel who wanted a little more firepower. Unfortunately, development of a reliable repeating rifle was beset with problems and, curiously enough, as with so many firearms produced in the period before Boxer's primer, it was ammunition that had failed to keep pace with the new refinements to the gunmakers' art. The Volcanic company's rather poorly performing original guns are a good example of this failure in ammunition technology, although the Volcanic lever action rifle was the original concept from which was developed first the Henry and then the ubiquitous Winchester range of lever-action repeaters.[10]

THE VOLCANIC PISTOLS AND RIFLES

The forerunners of the lever-action Volcanic rifles were the Hunt repeating rifle or "Volition repeater," the Jennings rifle, and the Smith-Jennings rifle. The last named owes part of its design work to Horace Smith, who later became a partner in Smith & Wesson. All three patterns used the original "Rocket-Ball" ammunition designed by Walter Hunt, who invented the first of these repeaters, which also incorporated an early lever-action mechanism. A Rocket-Ball cartridge consisted of a conventional bullet with a hollowed-out base that was filled with a powder charge and sealed with a cap. The cap had a small hole to allow access to the powder for the flash from the priming system, in the early weapons an automatic "pill" or pellet lock mechanism.[11] This early design of percussion lock was replaced in the Volcanic pistols and rifles, both now manufactured by the new Volcanic Repeating Arms Co., which had changed its name from the original designation of the Smith & Wesson Company. These new "Volcanic" weapons had a more recognizable lever-action mechanism, as a result of a modification to the ammunition: the original

Rocket-Ball cartridge now had an integral percussion cap, which made the ammunition self-contained and so more useful for magazine loading. However, even the self-contained Rocket-Ball cartridge suffered from a number of disadvantages; in particular, the hollow base of the bullet could not contain enough black powder to generate a powerful propulsive force. Consequently, the original Volcanic guns lacked both range and accuracy.[12]

Volcanic was forced into insolvency by one of its shareholders, Oliver Winchester, late in 1856. Winchester subsequently assumed control of the company and moved the plant to New Haven, Connecticut, where it was once again renamed, as the New Haven Arms Company, in April 1857. Winchester hired a former Volcanic employee, B. Tyler Henry, as plant superintendent. After some initial development work, Henry patented a new gun as the Henry .44 rimfire caliber repeating rifle, which used the rimfire ammunition Henry had devised for his weapon.

Henry and Winchester fell out over the royalty payments Winchester made to his colleague for the new repeater. After some legal squabbling the New Haven Arms Company was renamed once again, this time as the Winchester Repeating Arms Company. Under Winchester's enthusiastic direction now began producing the first rifle and carbine to bear that name, the Model 1866, a .44 caliber, rimfire arm using the same ammunition as Henry's repeater. Winchester went on to produce the huge range of lever-action rifles which bear his name, many of which are still in use today.

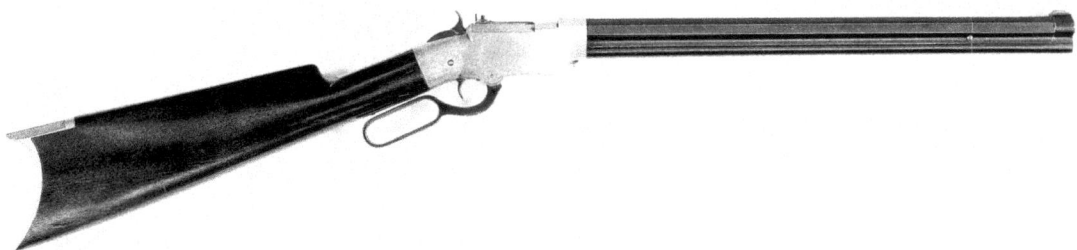

Volcanic Repeating Arms Co. lever-action repeating rifle, this one with a carbine barrel (courtesy James D. Julia Auctioneers, Fairfield, Maine. www.jamesdjulia.com).

The Henry rifle

Serial number range: 1–14,000 (1860 to 1866, in a serial number range overlapping the Winchester Model 1866).

The Henry .44 caliber rimfire repeating rifle is a lever-action weapon with cartridges supplied to the mechanism from a tubular, under-barrel magazine. Barrels are 24 inches long (no carbine model is recorded) and lack a foregrip, which is a characteristic feature of this weapon and serves to differentiate it from the later Winchester Model 1866. Later models were fitted with a latch that secured the cycling lever in place to prevent accidental misfires. Front sights are a fixed blade, with rear sights in the form of an adjustable leaf sight graduated to 500 yards. Finish is blue except for the brass frame, and the butt and forestock are in oil-stained walnut.

To load and operate a Henry repeating rifle, the end of the tubular magazine is first unscrewed and removed, together with the magazine spring. Fifteen rimfire cartridges are then placed base-down in the magazine, the spring and magazine plug are reinserted, and the end plug is secured. Forcing the cycling lever down allows the magazine spring to push a cartridge into the mechanism; subsequently raising the lever then moves the round into the chamber and closes the breech. After firing, the cycling lever is depressed and raised again, ejecting the spent case and moving a fresh cartridge into the chamber. A Winchester Model 1866 functions in an exactly similar way, the only difference being the later Model 1866 is loaded via a loading gate let into the brass frame on the right side.

Military service

Henry rifles were privately purchased by many who fought with federal forces in the U.S. Civil War, including units from Kentucky, Illinois, Indiana and Missouri. Confederate forces found that they had less use for these rifles, because ammunition for even conventional muzzleloading rifles was difficult for the Southern forces to acquire, and Henry rimfire cartridges could only be obtained from Union soldiers who had privately purchased such a weapon.[13]

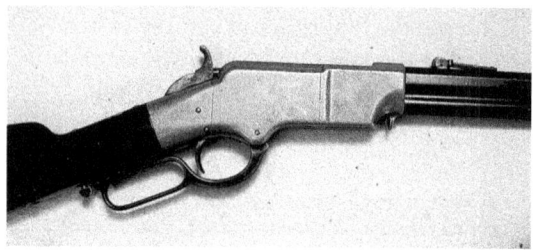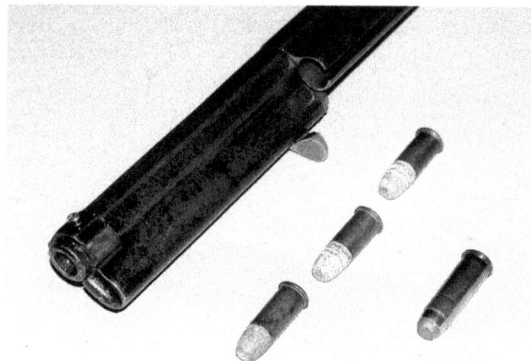

Left: Breech and loading lever of a Henry repeating rifle from the right, showing the loading lever and the safety button, which could be turned to prevent the lever from being accidentally depressed. *Right*: Muzzle of Henry rifle, showing magazine open and early .44 caliber rimfire cartridges (both photographs courtesy Hmaag).

Winchester lever-action rifles and carbines[14]

- Model 1866: Production: approx. 170,000 guns. Chambered in .44 caliber rimfire supplied from a tubular, under-barrel magazine loaded via the characteristic loading slot in the right side of the frame. Rifles have 24-inch octagonal barrels (round after

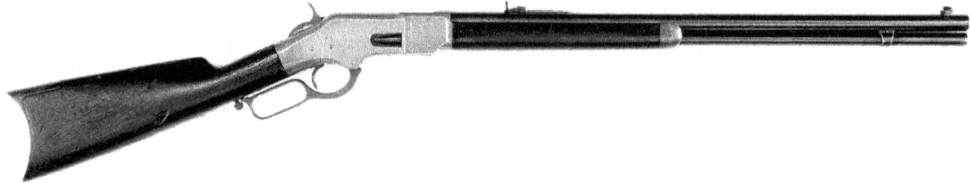

Winchester Model 1866 rifle from the right, showing the loading slot (courtesy James D. Julia Auctioneers, Fairfield, Maine. www.jamesdjulia.com).

serial no. 100,000), carbines 20-inch round barrels, fitted with two barrel bands, and muskets are fitted with a 27-inch barrel and 24-inch magazine. Cycling lever latch present on all types. Stocks and foregrip in oiled walnut.
- Model 1873: Production: approx. 720,000 guns. Chambered for .44–40 centerfire, .38–40 centerfire and .32–20 centerfire cartridges. Rifle and carbine same dimensions and characteristics as Model 1866, except musket has 30-inch round barrel and 27-inch magazine, and rifle may have round or octagonal barrel. "**MODEL 1873**" is stamped on the upper tang of the butt.

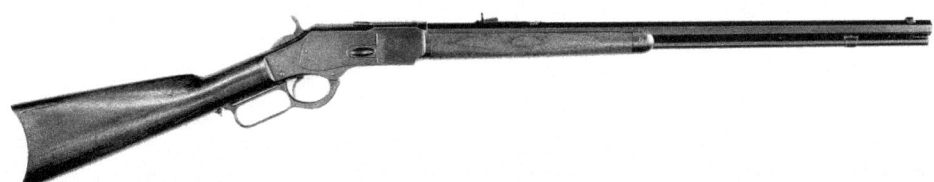

Winchester Model 1873 rifle, showing the conventional Winchester loading lever, loading slot and iron sights (courtesy James D. Julia Auctioneers, Fairfield, Maine. www.jamesdjulia.com).

Winchester Model 1873 rifle, with a barrel of musket length and its regulation bayonet (courtesy James D. Julia Auctioneers, Fairfield, Maine. www.jamesdjulia.com).

- Model 1876: Production: approx. 64,000 guns. Chambered for .50–95, .45–75, .45–60, .40–60 centerfire cartridges, rifle with 26- or 28-inch round or octagonal barrel, carbine with 22-inch round barrel and muskets with 32-inch round barrel. Other characteristics similar to Model 1873, with "**MODEL 1876**" stamped on the upper tang of the butt. The succeeding models are all similar to the Model 1876 and include Model 1886, Model 71, Model 1892, Model 53 and Model 65.[15]
- Model 1894: Production in excess of 7 million guns, the first Winchester produced for a smokeless powder cartridge. Made by Winchester from 1894 until 2006, but have been manufactured since that date under license by the Miroku Corporation of Japan. Chambered for .25-35, .30-30, .32-40, .32 WS (Winchester Special) and .38-55 centerfire cartridges. Huge number of variations, but generally, rifles have 26-inch octagonal barrels, carbines 20-inch barrels with a saddle ring on the left of the frame, while there are also short-barreled "Trapper" and "Take-down" Models. Upper butt tang stamped "**MODEL 1894, Winchester**" in some form.[16]

Values

Henry repeating rifle

Rare iron-frame Model: NRA Good: $25,000; NRA Fine: $85,000
Brass frame Models: NRA Good: $10,000; NRA Fine: $50,000

Winchester repeating rifles and carbines

Depending upon model and provenance, these weapons, particularly the "One of a Hundred" and "One of a Thousand" Models, can fetch astronomical prices at auction), although new Winchester Model 1894 rifles chambered for the .30-30 and .38-55 cartridge are available for less than $1,400.[17]

THE SPENCER RIFLE

Production: 144,500 rifles and carbines, of which 107,372 were sold to the U.S. government.

Produced initially by the Spencer Repeating Rifle Company of Boston, Massachusetts. Subsequent demand meant that production was also subcontracted to the Burnside Rifle Company of Providence, Rhode Island, and weapons made by this company are marked appropriately. The Spencer is a lever-action weapon, carbines being fitted with a 20- or 22-inch barrel, while the barrel of the rifle is 30 inches. They are chambered for a .52 or .50 caliber rimfire cartridge, although the original copper round is generally referred to as a "56-56," a measurement which refers to the diameter of the top and bottom of the case, rather than the size of the bullet. The front sight is a simple blade, the rear sight a conventional, graduated flip-up leaf. Both carbines and rifles are fitted with a case-hardened receiver and iron furniture (barrel bands, trigger, cycling lever), with a blued barrel and walnut butt and foregrip.

Early rifles and carbines produced by the Spencer Repeating Rifle Company are stamped on the top of the receiver:

> **SPENCER REPEATING**
> **RIFLE CO. BOSTON. MA.**
> **PAT'D MARCH 6. 1860**

Later weapons made by the Burnside company are similarly stamped on the receiver, but with the addition of the subcontractor's name:

> **SPENCER REPEATING RIFLE**
> **PAT'D MARCH 6. 1860**
> **MANUF'D AT PROV. RI**
> **BY BURNSIDE RIFLE CO.**
> **MODEL 1865**

Operation

To load and operate the weapon, seven cartridges of the appropriate caliber are first fed into the tubular magazine fitted into the butt. This could be accomplished either by loading individual rounds by hand or from a preloaded tube contained in a Blakeslee Cartridge Box, which contained between six and thirteen preloaded tubes, each containing the required seven rounds. With the tubular butt magazine loaded, the magazine spring and magazine end plug are pushed into the magazine and the end plug secured in position. The cycling lever, which also served as the trigger guard is then jerked down to its full extent and quickly returned to its original position, placing a cartridge in the chamber. This abrupt cocking action is necessary, because many users find that any hesitancy in

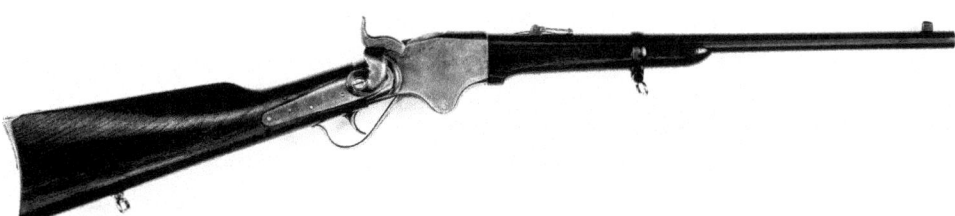

Spencer carbine from the right, showing the cycling lever, side-mounted hammer and the military pattern sling swivels (courtesy James D. Julia Auctioneers, Fairfield, Maine. www.jamesdjulia.com).

operating a Spencer can result in a jammed weapon. With the cartridge in the chamber, the hammer is then cocked and the weapon is ready to fire. Reloading is simply a repeat of the original procedure, operation of the cycling lever ejecting the spent round, after which the magazine spring pushes a fresh cartridge into the chamber, and the weapon only needs to be cocked to be ready to fire again.

Military service

Developed by Christopher Spencer, his final design for the rifle bearing his name was completed in 1860, although Spencer was unable to demonstrate the weapon to Abraham Lincoln until some time after the Battle of Gettysburg in 1863. Lincoln was extremely impressed with the effectiveness of the new repeater and ordered the Chief of Ordnance of the Army, Brigadier General J.W. Ripley, to adopt the weapon and begin production. However, Ripley, like so many of the elderly federal staff officers, considered that repeating firearms would encourage soldiers to waste ammunition. He was also sure that the federal army's logistics system could not stand the strain of supplying the extra ammunition that would be required by units equipped with the new guns. More importantly, the Army could buy several muzzleloading Springfield rifles for the cost of a single Spencer. Ripley decided to ignore the presidential order, and consequently, the Spencer was only purchased by the U.S. Navy and was not a weapon generally issued to the army until later in the war, after Ripley had been replaced. However, some units are thought to have been issued with the weapon even before the White House demonstration, in particular Custer's Michigan Brigade.[18]

Variations

Carbine

Characterized by the presence of a short foregrip (half-stocked), a single barrel band, and a conventional carbine "sling ring" on the left side with an accompanying sling swivel on the underside of the butt.

- Civil War Model: Production: 1863–1865 in a serial number range: 11000–61000 and manufactured by the Spencer Rifle Company. Barrels 22 inches, with six grooves and chambered in .52 caliber rimfire. Postwar alteration: Production: approximately 11,000 and manufactured by the Spencer Rifle Company. Alterations carried out at the Springfield Armory between 1867 and 1874, with barrels sleeved to accept .50 caliber rimfire cartridge and Stabler single-shot cut-off device fitted. Barrels with three groove rifling. Stock bears **ESA** inspector markings on left side of butt.

- Model 1865: Production serial numbers: 1 to 23,000. Manufactured by the Spencer Rifle Co between 1865 and 1866. Chambered for .50 caliber rimfire cartridge, with 20-inch barrel and six-groove rifling. Breech stamped: **M 1865**.
- Contract Model 1865: Production serial numbers: 1 to 34,000. Manufactured by Burnside Rifle Company during 1865 and consequently carries "BURNSIDE" receiver stamp. Chambered for .50 caliber rimfire cartridge, with 20-inch barrel and three-groove rifling.
- Model 1867: Production serial numbers: 91000 to 101000 in a serial number range with the Model 1867 rifles. Made by Spencer Rifle Co between 1865 and 1866. Chambered for .50 caliber rimfire cartridge, with 20-inch barrel and six-groove rifling. Breech stamped: **M 1867**.
- "New Model": Production serial numbers: 101000 to 108000 in a serial number range with the New Model rifles. Made by Spencer Rifle Co. during 1868. Chambered for .50 caliber rimfire cartridge, with 20-inch barrel and six-groove rifling. Breech stamped: **N.M.**

Military rifle or musket

Fitted with 30-inch barrel and a full stock or foregrip, ending in an iron tip at the muzzle. Barrel fastened with three bands and having a sling swivel at the butt and muzzle.

- Navy Model: Production serial numbers 1 to 750, manufactured by the Spencer Rifle Co between 1862 and 1864. Chambered in .52 caliber rimfire, with six-groove rifling and large lug on underside of muzzle for Naval Pattern saber bayonet.
- Army Model: Production serial numbers 700 to 11000 and small group in the 28000 range, both produced by the Spencer Rifle Co. between 1862 and 1864. Chambered in .52 caliber rimfire, with six-groove rifling. Front sight doubles as securing lug for a socket pattern bayonet, serving to differentiate this weapon from the Navy Model. Postwar alteration: Barrel sleeved to .50 caliber and Stabler single-shot cut-off device fitted.
- Contract Model 1865: Production: approximately 1,000 weapons, in Model 1865 carbine serial number range and manufactured by the Spencer Rifle Company. Chambered for .50 caliber rimfire cartridge, barrel with six-groove rifling. Breech stamped **M 1865**.
- Model 1867: Production: approximately 7,000 weapons, in Model 1867 carbine serial number range 91000 to 101000, and manufactured by the Spencer Rifle Company. Chambered for .50 caliber rimfire cartridge, barrel with six-groove rifling. Breech stamped **M 1867**.
- "New Model": Production: approximately 5,000 weapons, in New Model carbine serial number range 101000 to 108000, and manufactured by the Spencer Rifle Company. Chambered for .50 caliber rimfire cartridge, barrel with six groove rifling. Breech stamped **N.M.**

Values

NRA Good: $1,000; NRA Fine: $10,000

Table Thirteen: Comparison of the Spencer, Henry and Winchester repeating rifles

Weapon	Spencer Model of 1860	Henry Model 1860	Winchester: various Models 1866–1894
Makers	Spencer Company Burnside Rifle Company Winchester Repeating Arms Co.	New Haven Arms Co.	Winchester Repeating Arms Co.
Period of production	1860 until 1869	1860 until 1866	1866 until 1900s
Production	Approximately 150,000	Approximately 14,000	Approximately 9 million (7 million of the Model 1894)
Military service	United States Army United States Navy Confederate States Army	United States Army Confederate States Army Sioux Indians	American Indian Wars, Russo-Turkish War of 1877–78, North-West Rebellion, French intervention in Mexico, Spanish–American War, Mexican Revolution
Weight	Rifle: 8lbs 4oz Carbine: 7lbs 8oz	Rifle: 9lbs 4oz	Rifle: 9.5 lbs Carbine: 8 lbs
Length/Barrel length	Rifle: 47 inches/ 30 inches Carbine: 39 inches/ 22 or 20 inches	45 inches/24 inches	Rifle: 50 inches/30 inches Carbine: 42 inches/ 22 inches
Mechanism	Manually cocked, lever-action repeating mechanism	Automatically cocked, lever-action repeating mechanism	Automatically cocked, lever-action repeating mechanism
Cartridge	.56–56/.50 or .52 caliber Spencer rimfire cartridge. Seven cartridges loaded into the tubular magazine contained in the butt	.44 caliber Henry rimfire cartridge. 16 cartridges loaded into a tubular, under-barrel magazine from the muzzle	.22 rimfire .44 caliber Henry rimfire .44/40 Winchester CF .38/40 Winchester CF .32/20 Winchester CF 15 cartridges loaded into a tubular, under-barrel magazine via a loading slot in the side of the frame
Sights	Front sight: Flat blade Rear sight: Graduated leaf	Front sight: Flat blade Rear sight: Graduated leaf	Front sight: Fixed post Rear sight: Various designs
Maximum range	500 meters	100–200 meters	300–500 meters, depending upon equipment
Rate of fire	Between 14 and 20 rounds per minute, allowing for re-loading	16 rounds in 15 seconds, but then reloading could take several minutes	15 rounds in 15 seconds, but the weapon can be loaded after each round so is appreciably quicker than a Henry

Smaller American Manufacturers of Lever-Action Repeating Rifles and Carbines

Marlin

Model 1881 lever-action rifle with under-barrel tubular magazine: Chambered for .32–40, .38–55, .40–60, .45–70 and .45–85. Various barrel lengths. Also found as Model 1888, Model 1889, Model 1891, Model 1892, Model 1893, Model 1894, Model 1895 and Model 1897.[19]

Colt

Lever-action and pump-action rifles in a variety of calibers and barrel lengths, all using tubular, under-barrel magazines.[20]

Savage[21]

- Model 1895 lever action rifle : Production: approximately 5,000 between 1895 and 1899. Chambered for .303 caliber centerfire cartridge with a 26 inch round or octagonal barrel and a rotary magazine holding six rounds. Hammerless action with side ejection.
- Model 1899 lever action rifle: Production: several hundred thousand between 1899 and 2016. Chambered for a wide variety of centerfire cartridges, .303 and 30–30 being probably the most popular. Barrels are 20 inches and round on the carbine Model, 26 inches and round or partly round and octagonal on the Model 1899 Sporting Rifle. The Model 1899 has a hammerless action with side ejection and an internal rotary magazine which holds six cartridges. Many users consider it to be superior to the Winchester Model 1894 in a number of respects, although the weapons small magazine capacity can be a disadvantage.

Savage Model 1899 5-shot lever-action repeating rifle (courtesy James D. Julia Auctioneers, Fairfield, Maine. www.jamesdjulia.com).

Repeating Shotguns

Shotguns designed to fire a number of shots without reloading are of three basic types:

- **Multi-barrel weapons**: Usually two barrels, side-by-side or over-and-under being the most common configurations, these names referring to the placing of the barrels and being largely self-explanatory. They were commonly referred to as fowling pieces and first appeared as single-barreled, smoothbore arms in Europe during the 16th century. Antique weapons of this type may be found at auction as flintlock, percussion, rimfire, pinfire and centerfire guns.
- **Pump-action**: This pattern of shotgun has the foregrip replaced by a handgrip which can be pushed or "pumped" back and then forwards to eject a spent cartridge and sub-

sequently chamber a fresh round. Such a mechanism is faster than that used in either a bolt-action or lever-action weapon, because operation of the weapon does not require the rear hand to be removed from the trigger while reloading. In most weapons of this type, holding back the trigger and operating the handgrip will fire the weapon.
- **Semiautomatic/fully automatic:** This pattern of shotgun works in a manner similar to semiautomatic pistols and rifles, in that one the user has loaded the weapon and cocked the mechanism, all that is required to fire the gun is to pull the trigger. The mechanism then cycles automatically, chambering a fresh cartridge and cocking the action without any further action by the operator. Fully automatic shotguns are also available, but legislation in most countries confines their use to the police and military units, or limits the number of cartridges that can be used before reloading is necessary.

SHOTGUN MANUFACTURERS

American shotgun manufacturers

- **Browning:** Manufacturers of double-barreled, pump-action and semiautomatic weapons of this type. John Browning patented the Browning Auto-5, the first commercially successful semiautomatic shotgun, in 1900, with production begun by FN in 1902. The design was so successful that it remained in production until 1998.

  The Browning Auto-5 semiautomatic shotgun

  This was a self-loading shotgun, with a long-recoil mechanism and an under-barrel magazine designed to hold 5 cartridges, although a plug or cut-off is usually fitted in the magazine to allow only three cartridges to be loaded to comply with U.S. hunting regulations. The weapon is loaded via a port in the bottom of the receiver.
- **Colt:** Manufacturers of double-barreled, pump-action and semiautomatic weapons of this type.
- **Remington:** Manufacturers of double-barreled, pump-action and semiautomatic weapons of this type.
- **Smith & Wesson:** Began manufacture of pump-action shotguns in 1972, but quality issues caused them to cease production.

As well as these major manufacturers, there are a significant number of smaller American companies producing all three types of shotgun.[22]

British shotgun manufacturers

- **Holland & Holland:** Production includes both side-by-side and over-and-under shotguns as well as hand-made rifles.
- **James Purdey and Sons Ltd:** Perhaps the most famous maker of hand-made double-barreled shotguns in the world, Purdey also produce an excellent range of rifles.
- **Westley-Richards:** Production includes both side-by-side and over-and-under shotguns as well as hand-made rifles, in both side-lock and box-lock.

As well as these major manufacturers, there are a significant number of smaller British companies producing all three types of shotgun.

Italian shotgun manufacturers

- **Beretta:** Manufacturers of double-barreled, pump-action and semiautomatic weapons of this type.

In addition to the these larger manufacturers, there are a number of companies operating from Turkey, Italy and Spain, who manufacture good weapons of all three designs at a reasonable price.

Chapter Nine

Early Machine Guns and Repeating Cannon

The Eighteenth Century

Although flintlock ignition did not readily lend itself to operation in conjunction with weapons capable of repeating fire as opposed to multi-firing, this characteristic did not deter early eighteenth-century inventors. Lorenzoni and his contemporaries produced their reliable flintlock repeating rifle, Nock turned out his little 120 bore, seven-barreled pistol, Collier had his flintlock revolver, and most astounding of all, an English inventor, lawyer and essayist, James Puckle, invented a weapon which has since come to be referred to as the "first machine gun." However, despite this rather fanciful name, its operation bears little resemblance to a modern automatic recoil-operated weapon of that type, having in reality more in common with a percussion revolver.

The Puckle Gun

Invented and patented by James Puckle in 1718, this was the first weapon to be referred to as a machine gun. It was intended by its inventor to be used as an antipersonnel weapon against those attempting to board a ship equipped with the weapon. It was essentially a single-barreled, smoothbore flintlock revolver, mounted on a tripod, fitted with a cylinder that had to be revolved and indexed manually, and a barrel that was 3 ft long and 1.25 inches in caliber. The loads were delivered to the barrel directly from the cylinder, in a similar manner to a Colt's revolver. This cylinder had between six and eleven chambers, which were charged with powder and shot after the cylinder or "charger" had been removed from the weapon.

Operation was similar to a flintlock musket of the period, the weapon being fitted with a conventional trigger and flintlock ignition mechanism, incorporating the usual pan and frizzen. After firing the first shot in the cylinder, a large nut, which incorporated a handle, was loosened on the threaded shaft at the rear of the gun and the cylinder advanced by hand to the next chamber, whereupon the securing nut was re-tightened, locking the cylinder into the end of the barrel, which was shaped to receive it. The flintlock mechanism was then be primed and the weapon was ready to fire. Reloading the cylinder was accomplished by first unscrewing the securing nut completely from its threaded shaft. This procedure allowed the empty cylinder to be removed and replaced by one which was fully charged, the empty cylinder being reloaded by the crew with powder and ball in the conventional manner at their leisure. Puckle produced two designs for his gun, one firing round balls for use against Christian opponents, and a second chambered for square ammunition, specifically for action against the "Muslim Turks," the inventor considering that this would "convince the Turks of the benefits of Christian civilization." The gun seems also to have been capable of firing grapeshot; a cylinder was loaded with sixteen musket balls for this purpose.

Military service

Puckle's prototype was shown to the English Board of Ordnance in 1717, one year before the gun was patented. The board did not seem to have been overly impressed with the weapon. However, at a later public trial in 1722, Puckle demonstrated a gun capable of firing nine rounds per minute, which it achieved by discharging over 60 shots in a total of seven minutes. This was approximately three times the rate of fire which a trained soldier could achieve, a flintlock musket of the period being capable of firing only three or four shots per minute, in even the most experienced hands.

Despite this superior performance, Puckle's invention never entered mass production or saw service with Britain's armed forces. Its main disadvantage, as with many contemporary designs, was the clumsy and unreliable flintlock ignition. A leaflet of the period sardonically observed of the venture that *"they're only wounded who hold shares therein."* Production was very limited and may have been as few as two guns, one a crude prototype made of iron, the other a more finished weapon in brass, although two guns do appear to have been purchased by John Montagu, then Britain's Master of the Ordnance, for an expedition in 1722 to capture St. Lucia and St. Vincent. Shipping manifests from a vessel involved in supplying the expedition certainly state that "2 Machine Guns of Puckles" were among the cargo that departed from Portsmouth, although there is no evidence that the guns were ever used in battle.[1]

Surviving Puckle guns

- One original example is at Boughton House, former home of the Montagu family.
- A second original example is at Beaulieu Palace, another former home of the Montagu family.
- A replica is displayed at Buckler's Hard Maritime Museum in Hampshire.

The Nineteenth Century

The U.S. Civil War

Paralleling the search for a reliable repeating rifle, the period prior to the U.S. Civil War saw considerable energy expended on the search for a strategic multi-fire weapon, something of sufficiently large caliber that was capable of discharging sufficient ammunition in a reasonable period of time to destroy or at least decimate a company of troops armed with muskets. A considerable number of devices that claimed to meet these criteria were constructed and some were even patented, but only the weapons that actually saw military service will be described in this section, which may be conveniently considered to include all of the manually operated repeating guns.[2]

AGAR'S "COFFEE MILL" GUN

Agar's Coffee Mill gun was a gravity-fed, single-barreled weapon, manually operated by a firing handle and using a specially designed steel cylinder to house the weapon's load. To prepare the gun for firing, a number of these steel cylinders were loaded, either with loose powder and ball or a paper cartridge, and a percussion cap was placed on a cone that was screwed into the rear end of the steel container, so that in conformation they resembled a modern centerfire cartridge or a single cylinder of a percussion revolver. These loaded containers were then placed in a rectangular box, or hopper, mounted on top of the weapon so as to allow separate containers to move down into a recess formed in the rear of the gun barrel. With the first cartridge in this recess, a firing handle on the right side of the weapon was operated, which turned a system of cogged wheels and forced the charged cylinder forward against the end of the barrel, forming a gas-tight seal, while a wedge rose behind the cylinder and locked it in place. Further rotation of the firing handle kept the cylinder in place while simultaneously operating the hammer, which fell on the cap and fired the weapon. The wedge was then released and an ejector displaced the spent container, which was immediately replaced by a fresh cylinder. Agar's weapon was designed to operate at a firing rate of only 120 rounds per minute, because it used only one barrel, unlike the multi-barreled Gatling gun, and the heat generated by continued rapid firing could have serious consequences. To eliminate this problem, Agar incorporated a fan that was operated from the firing handle and served to cool both the barrel and its surrounding jacket. As another aid to prevent overheating, each gun came with two barrels, which could be quickly changed while the weapon was in action. The Coffee Mill gun also had a number of other features more usually seen in modern guns, such as a ball-and-socket joint mounting that allowed the gun to be quickly elevated or traversed, without moving the light, two-wheeled carriage. This carriage was another innovation, having two ammunition boxes conveniently mounted on either side of the gun and a metal shield to protect the gunner from small arms fire.

Despite these modern features, the gun was not a success. A report from a British officer, Major Fosbery, who was present at one of the trials where the gun was tested, highlights the problems. He was certain that the deployment of any gun consuming such quantities of ammunition would be prohibited because of the cost and problems with logistic supply. More importantly, he was skeptical that a single barrel would be able to stand the continual discharge of between 100 to 120 bullets a minute, without irreparable damage. He added: "The only thing forgotten seems to be that, when firing at the rate of 100 discharges a minute, the flame of 7,500 grains of exploded powder and nearly 7 pounds of lead would pass through a single barrel in that time. The effect during the trial proved that the barrel first grew red and nearly white hot, and large drops of fused metal poured from the muzzle, and the firing had to be discontinued from fear of worse consequences." The federal authorities seemed to have agreed with Fosbery, and the weapon was never purchased for active service. Its role was usually confined to guarding bridges and narrow passes, although on

Section III: The Black Powder Era

Above: Agar "Coffee Mill" gun showing the loading hopper and single octagonal barrel. *Below, left:* Magnified view of Agar "Coffee Mill" gun showing the firing handle and part of the mechanism. *Below, right:* Agar "Coffee Mill" gun from the left side, showing the loading hopper and ejection port. The shield fixed to the front of the gun seems more useful to protect the mechanism than the gun crew (all three photographs courtesy Amoskeag Auction Company, Inc.).

those rare occasions when it did see active service and was used within its safe operating parameters, it seems to have performed well.[3]

Values

Although rare at auction, examples do occasionally appear.
NRA Good: $40,000; NRA Fine: $150,000–$200,000

Table Fourteen: Specification of the Agar "Coffee Mill" gun

Manufacturer	Presumably Agar, using his original workshop
Period of production	1861–1863
Production	Sixty-four weapons are known to have been purchased by the federal government
Military service	Harpers Ferry skirmish (January 1862)
	Middleburg, VA skirmish (March 1862)
	McClellan's Peninsular campaign (1862)
	CSA captured 17 guns (1864)
Crew	Crew of four
	Gunner: aiming and firing
	Loaders: to keep the hopper filled and refill the cartridge tubes
Weight	1,000 lbs
Length/Barrel length	Total length: 6 ft/Barrel: 3 ft
Mechanism	Manually operated revolving cylinder supplying a single fixed barrel
Cartridge	Standard paper cartridges loaded into reusable steel tubes, which were then fitted with a percussion cap.
	These capped tubes were then placed in funnel-shaped hopper and turning the crank on the right of the breech delivered single cartridges to the mechanism.
Sights	None fitted
Maximum range	Between 800 and 1000 yds, similar to an Enfield P53 rifle
Rate of fire	120 rounds per minute

Mitrailleuse Guns

Mitrailleuse guns were the logical centerfire development of the earlier flintlock volley guns, having multiple barrels of rifle caliber capable of firing several rounds in very rapid succession (the earliest Montigny gun fired all its cartridges simultaneously; only in later guns was provision made for successive firing). Such weapons were constructed with a variable number of rifled barrels clustered together and mounted on a conventional artillery chassis or a tripod.

Loading was accomplished using ammunition that had been previously inserted into a specially constructed plate or removable breech block, this block being carefully positioned in the breech so as to ensure that the individual cartridges lined up with their respective barrels. The breech was then closed by means of a lever or horizontal screw, which caused all the barrels to be loaded simultaneously, each barrel being fitted with its own firing pin. With the weapon loaded, firing was achieved by turning a second, smaller crank or lever, mounted on the right side of the breech, which fired each barrel separately, the rate of firing being determined by the rapidity with which the gunner turned the firing handle. When the gun was empty, the loading plate or block was removed manually and another loaded plate inserted. Despite the necessity for so much manual operation,

Mitrailleuse gun mounted on a standard artillery carriage. This particular weapon is capable of discharging 20 shots (courtesy Chris O).

mitrailleuse guns could reliably operate at any rate of fire from single, aimed shots to approximately 400 rounds per minute in battlefield conditions. While this was slightly less than a Gatling's rate of fire, it was still respectable, although unfortunately, one significant problem with the weapon was that its volley of rifle balls did not spread significantly after leaving the muzzle. During the Franco-Prussian War, the only conflict in which mitrailleuse guns were deployed, in this case the 25-barreled Reffye mitrailleuse, a Prussian general was struck and killed by four bullets from a mitrailleuse, which was positioned 600 meters from its target. This characteristic made them much less effective than a Gatling gun. As a result, after the armistice with Prussia in May 1871, the remaining mitrailleuse were relegated to static defense duties on France's eastern border with Germany, where a number of weapons of this type were not replaced in these fortifications until 1908. It has also been suggested by some military historians that the weapon's ineffectiveness in the Franco-Prussian War resulted in longstanding opposition among European armies to adopting machine guns, particularly on the Continent.[4]

Hotchkiss 37mm Revolving Cannon

SPECIFICATION

The Hotchkiss revolving cannon was a manually operated, repeating-fire weapon, with revolving barrels, which was invented in 1872 by Benjamin Hotchkiss, the founder of the

Hotchkiss 37mm revolving cannon, this example mounted on a standard artillery carriage (courtesy James D. Julia Auctioneers, Fairfield, Maine. www.jamesdjulia.com). *Below:* Breech of Hotchkiss 37mm revolving cannon, showing the firing handle and elevating screw (courtesy James D. Julia Auctioneers, Fairfield, Maine. www.jamesdjulia.com).

French firearms company Hotchkiss et Cie. A Hotchkiss cannon chambered for the conventional shell had five barrels of 37mm caliber, and was capable of firing 68 rounds per minute, to an extreme range of about 2,000 yards (1,800 m). Ammunition was a self-contained cartridge, which consisted of a soldered tin cylinder, with one end closed to form a cup. This end was reinforced by two iron caps fixed inside and outside the case, and fastened with three rivets to a

wider, round iron plate, which formed the base of the cartridge and also served as the point of contact for the extractor mechanism. The cartridge was just over 6½ inches long and 2½ lbs in weight, and was loaded with a charge of 3½ ounces of black powder. The usual load was shrapnel, consisting of 24 lead balls, .71 inch in diameter, arranged in 8 tiers of 3 balls each, and having the interstices packed with sawdust, although an explosive shell was also available.

Operation

Although the Hotchkiss had multiple revolving barrels, the mechanism differed from the Gatling gun in having only one striker, bolt and extractor serving all the barrels and using a single, center cam wheel turned by the firing handle, which both rotated the barrels and held them in place during the separate parts of the firing cycle. This cam also turned a second gear on the left side of the breech block, which was pinned to 2 toothed shafts, the upper shaft being designed to remove a cartridge from the magazine and load it into the chamber of each barrel, while the lower shaft extracted the spent case from the barrels after firing and ejected it from the bottom of the breech. This mechanism was extremely strong and, in fact, it had been expressly designed by Hotchkiss to allow what he saw as the logical development of the rifle caliber machine gun into a weapon capable of firing larger caliber shrapnel rounds. In operation, a magazine containing ten of these specially designed explosive cartridges was fitted into the upper breech opening and a single rotation of the firing handle then loaded a cartridge, fired that round when the barrel was at the bottom of its cycle and extracted the spent case, although single rounds could also be loaded into the breech by hand, which allowed single ranging shots to be used to determine the distance to a new target.

Variations

Six models of the Hotchkiss 37mm revolving cannon were produced by Hotchkiss and Cie:

- The 37mm gun, supplied for shipboard use.
- A light 37mm for field use, usually supplied with a two-wheeled carriage.
- A high-velocity 37mm for use in flank defense and on fortifications.
- A 40mm for use in fixed mounts in fortifications.

HMS *Lightning*, an early torpedo boat built around 1877.

- A 47mm gun for naval use.
- A 57mm weapon, also for naval use.

MILITARY SERVICE

The Hotchkiss was bought and used by most European navies, including the Royal Navy, Imperial German Navy, Royal Netherlands Navy, Italian Royal Navy (Regia Marina), Royal Danish Navy, Austro-Hungarian Navy, Imperial Russian Navy, the navy of the Ottoman Empire, and the United States Navy. Most of these guns were purchased as a defense against the newly introduced torpedo boats, which were designed to cripple or sink the new ironclad warships then being built by many of these countries.[5]

VALUES

Although very rarely seen at auction, the Hotchkiss 37mm cannon does occasionally appear. One very good and complete example reached an auction price of $58,000.

Table Fifteen: Specification of the Hotchkiss 37mm revolving cannon

Manufacturer	Hotchkiss et Cie
Period of production	1874 to 1885
Production	Not clearly recorded but certainly many thousands
Military service	Most European navies including:
	Royal Navy; Imperial German Navy; Royal Netherlands Navy;
	Italian Royal Navy or *Regia Marina*; Royal Danish Navy;
	Austro-Hungarian Navy; Imperial Russian Navy; Ottoman Navy
	United States Navy
Crew	Crew of three
	Gunner: responsible for aiming and controlling the weapon
	Operator: responsible for turning the firing handle
	Loader: responsible for changing the magazine
Weight	1,200 lbs
Length/Barrel length	70 inches/40 inches
Mechanism	Operated by means of a firing handle, giving controlled, repeating fire
Cartridge	Shrapnel round, loaded with 24 balls in .71 caliber
	HE round
Sights	Front sight—none
	Rear sight—graduated ladder, set for 100 yds to 2,000 yds
Maximum range	2,000 yds
Rate of fire	Between 60 and 80 rounds per minute

Early Multi-fire and Repeating Strategic Weapons

AMERICAN MANUFACTURERS

Federal machine guns

- **The Billinghurst Requa Battery Gun:** This weapon is essentially a modern organ gun chambered in .50 caliber and having 25 barrels mounted in a single row on a lightweight, two-wheeled metal cart. The reusable cartridges were machined from a steel alloy with an oval base which was open in the center to allow access to the powder for ignition and held in specially designed 25-round "clips" that were designed to bring the cartridges into the correct position relative to the barrels. To operate the weapon, a 25-round clip was placed in position and the breech locked, resulting in each cartridge coming to rest with its opening aligned to a channel filled with priming powder and its front end correctly aligned with the adjacent barrel. The single hammer was then cocked and a percussion cap placed upon the single percussion cone. Pulling the lanyard attached to the trigger dropped the hammer, firing the percussion cap, which in turn ignited the powder train and fired all the barrels simultaneously.[6]

- **The Ripley volley gun**: Ripley took out a U.S. patent for this gun, but no example appears to have been constructed, although his weapon did demonstrate a number of features used by Gatling, amongst others, in their later weapons.[7]
- **The Gatling gun**: Only the early percussion version saw service in the U.S. Civil war.[8]

Confederate machine guns

- **The Gorgas machine gun**: a manually cranked machine gun, invented by CSA General Josiah Gorgas. It consisted of a single 1.25 caliber smoothbore barrel, which was fed from a horizontal revolving ring or cylinder, this cylinder containing 18 copper-lined, muzzleloaded chambers. The interior section of the chamber was lined with the corresponding 18 percussion cap cones and this ring-shaped cylinder was rotated by a complex mechanism terminating in a firing lever.[9]
- **The Pate repeating cannon**: Only one example produced, its mechanism based on that used in a percussion revolver, having a cylinder that held five rounds and a barrel with a two-inch bore. The weapon employed a screw mechanism that pushed the cylinder forward when it was in position, reducing the gap between the cylinder and the barrel and significantly reducing gas leakage during firing. Cylinder rotation was by means of a ratcheting mechanism, which incorporated a spring-loaded pawl, designed to lock into slots in the cylinder and ensure it was indexed correctly before firing. The single example was used in action once, at the siege of Petersburg, VA.[10]

BRITISH MANUFACTURERS

- **The Gardener machine gun**: Operation was by a firing handle, cartridges dropping into the breech from a hopper pattern magazine under gravity, whereupon turning the firing handle moved a cartridge into the breech, closed the bolt, fired the round and then extracted the spent case. The weapon was manufactured with a variable number of barrels, one, two or five, and was adopted for use by both the Royal Navy and British Army.[11]
- **The Nordenfeldt automatic machine gun**: Invented by a Swedish engineer, Heldge Palmcrantz, the gun became the Nordenfeldt after Palmcrantz was unable to finance his invention and turned to another Swede, Thorsten Nordenfeldt, for financial help. These guns were essentially modern volley guns, with a variable number of barrels and a hopper-fed mechanism that fired each barrel in very rapid succession. To operate a Nordenfeldt, the ammunition hopper, which had a separate column for each barrel, was first filled with the appropriate cartridges and the firing lever was then simply worked back and forth, chambering and firing the ammunition automatically until

the hopper was empty. Pulling the lever backwards extracted the spent cases and the subsequent forward motion first loaded fresh cartridges into all the barrels and then finally fired each barrel in very quick succession. Although the mechanism of the gun was out of date even before the first prototype was built, its design strength and quality of manufacture convinced the Admiralty to purchase a quantity, especially after one test in which a ten-barrel gun of rifle caliber fired at a rate of 1,000 rounds per minute for three minutes, without a stoppage.

Four-barreled Nordenfeldt machine gun showing the elevating screw, firing handle and magazine (courtesy Wikipedia, License: CC-BY-SA).

Five-barreled Nordenfeldt I action from the fighting top of a Royal Navy ship.

Variations

- Rifle caliber guns: Most commonly produced in .45 caliber, with five barrels, although weapons were produced with any number up to twelve.
- 1-inch caliber guns: Produced in one-, two- and four-barreled variants, the mechanism of these guns, which were designed for use against torpedo boats, was exactly similar

to the Nordenfeldts designed for rifle caliber ammunition. They were chambered for a solid steel bullet with a hardened tip, surrounded by a brass jacket, and although explosive shells would have been vastly more effective, no cartridge of that sort was used in the gun because the St. Petersburg Declaration of 1868 had banned exploding ammunition that weighed less than 400 grams.[12]

Four-barreled Nordenfeldt in 1-inch caliber (courtesy Wikipedia: GFDL CC-BY-SA).

FRENCH WEAPONS

- **The Montigny gun**: Produced in 1867 in the arsenal at Meu-

Woodcut of a four-barreled Nordenfeldt in operation.

Nine. Early Machine Guns and Repeating Cannon 127

dan, this modern volley gun or mitrailleuse consisted of 37 rifled barrels contained in a wrought iron tube, which were loaded from an iron plate bored with 37 matching holes corresponding in position and number to the barrels, each hole containing a specially designed Chassepot cartridge. The firing mechanism was operated by a firing handle, one clockwise turn serving to fire all 37 rounds simultaneously in the prototype weapons, although later guns were designed to fire each barrel separately at any speed required. The average rate of fire was recorded as 12 bursts, or 444 shots per minute. This weapon was subsequently developed into the 25-barreled Reffye mitrailleuse, which was deployed by the French army during the Franco-Prussian War (1870–1871).[13]

CHAPTER TEN

The Gatling Gun
Gatling's 150-Year-Old Masterpiece

In 1862, some months after the start of the American Civil War, a weapon was patented which its inventor claimed in a letter to a young friend was created to "reduce the size of armies and so reduce the numbers of deaths by combat and disease and thus show how futile war is." The name of this visionary arms manufacturer was Dr. R.J. Gatling. Unfortunately his brainchild, the Gatling gun, far from reducing deaths in action, was one of the devices responsible for setting the feet of the military establishment on the road that led to the mechanized carnage of World War I.

Development

Gatling was born in Hertford County, North Carolina, in 1818. His father was also an inventor, although of agricultural implements, and possibly as a result of his father's influence, Gatling's first patent was for a machine designed to plant rice. In 1849, he entered Ohio Medical College, and although awarded a degree, he never entered practice. By 1861, aged 43, he was deep in designs for the weapon that would revolutionize nineteenth-century warfare. Gatling appears to have studied earlier attempts to produce a weapon capable of continuous firing, since his gun incorporated some design features from two earlier weapons: the Ripley gun, a multi-fire weapon incorporating multiple barrels revolving around a common axis; and the Agar "Coffee Mill" gun, which used precharged percussion cylinders delivered to the firing chamber by a hopper.

Gatling's first prototype, the M1862 (Model 1862) had significant design flaws, although it appears to have functioned reliably. In particular, no effective seal was possible between the cylinder and the barrel, allowing significant gas leakage and loss of power, a feature the Gatling shared with all the percussion revolvers of the period. It was further handicapped by being chambered for paper cartridges, which were contained in steel cylinders and fired by percussion caps. Gatling contracted Miles Greenwood & Co. to produce six weapons to this design, but before he could take delivery, Greenwood's factory burnt down, taking Gatling's nearly completed weapons, design models and blueprints with it. Undeterred, Gatling found more financial backers, and this time had twelve M1862 guns made to his original percussion design by the Cincinnati firm of McWhinney, Rindge & Co. A few of these M1862 Gatling guns were bought privately for use during the Civil War, but even when they were completed, Gatling was still dissatisfied and immediately began to make changes, redesigning the guns to use a copper rimfire cartridge. These modifications resulted in the development of the Model 1865 Gatling, made by the Cooper Fire Arms Manufacturing Co., and incorporating a chamber and barrel in one piece to prevent gas leakage, a leaf-spring cartridge extractor, and an improved cam-loading design. This M1865 Gatling still used a rimfire cartridge, however, and under the influence of Col. S. V. Bénet, later Chief of Ordnance of the U.S. Army, Gatling converted the gun to use centerfire ammunition. He then entered into a contract with Colt's Patent Fire Arms Manufacturing Co. to build 100 of these M1866 guns for delivery to the U.S. Army in 1867. Fifty were to be in 1-inch centerfire caliber, while the rest were to be chambered for the Army's .50 caliber centerfire cartridge, then being adopted for the U.S. infantry's Springfield rifle. These arrangements proved so successful that in 1870, Gatling sold his patents for the gun to the Hartford Company, and all succeeding models of Gatling gun supplied to the U.S. Army and Navy were subsequently manufactured by Colt.

All the early models, the M1862, 1865 and 1866, were loaded through a simple hopper on top of the gun from tin boxes containing twenty cartridges each. However, after its adoption in 1866, the Gatling was the subject of a number of modifications to both improve loading performance and lighten the gun itself, resulting in a series of models that saw use with a number of European armies as well as the U.S. Army and Navy.

These modifications to the loading mechanism included:

- A curved box magazine introduced for the M1871. In early guns these magazines entered the hopper from the left and at a distinct angle, to avoid the sights. However, problems with the gravity-feed mechanism resulted in the aperture's being moved to the center of the gun, while the sights were shifted to the right side.
- The Broadwell "drum" magazine, patented in 1872 by its inventor, L.M. Broadwell. This device held 400 cartridges, in twenty separate stacks of 20. It was loaded from the underside by filling each stack with cartridges, the internal mechanism of the drum being turned to fill each subsequent stack through a slot in the bottom plate. The slot was then set between two stacks to prevent the loaded cartridges from falling out, and the magazine was secured to the gun with the slot over the loading port in the breech. The drum was then rotated to bring a stack of cartridges over the slot, the cartridges dropped into place, and the gun was ready to fire.
- The mechanically fed Accles "Drum" magazine, patented in 1883 and fitted to the M1883 Gatling. The Accles Drum was a good design in that it was the first Gatling magazine to force cartridges directly into the breech, rather than just dropping them in under gravity. This allowed the weapon to be angled away from the horizontal, which had not been possible with the gravity-fed magazines. Unfortunately, the magazine would only function properly when perfectly clean, and even a small dent in the thin brass wall would disable it completely. Consequently, those M1883 Gatlings originally purchased to use the Accles system were converted to use the later Bruce Feed system.
- The Bruce Feed, patented in 1886. Fitted to all subsequent models, this proved to be the most reliable and popular loading mechanism of all those designed for the gun. It consisted of a long, narrow steel box, open at the front and the top, its advantage being that cartridges could be loaded into the device from a standard, 20-round cardboard box, without interrupting its operation.

In parallel with these improvements in loading performance, in 1872, Gatling took out a U.S. patent for one of his most useful variants of the Gatling, the .45 caliber "Camel" gun. Weighing only 125 lbs, this 10-barreled weapon could be easily transported on horse-, mule- or camel-back. More importantly, it was mounted on a tripod, which allowed the weapon to be traversed, unlike the earlier models, which were mounted on the older, fixed artillery carriage.

By 1893, Maxim's invention of the first fully automatic machine gun had rendered the Gatling obsolete. Undeterred by his competitors, Gatling modified his brainchild once again, first fitting an electric motor to operate the mechanism in 1893, then, in 1895, designing a gas-operated system which, after being cocked by a single motion of the firing handle, would fire automatically without any further attention from the operator. Despite these innovations, all models of Gatling guns were declared obsolete by the U.S. Army in 1911.

Specification

The Gatling gun was a multiple-fire weapon rather than a machine gun, designed for manual operation instead of utilizing the residual cartridge gas and automatic mechanism of the Maxim and later fully automatic weapons. It consisted of a number of barrels (five, six or ten depending upon the model), chambered for a variety of cartridges, including the .45/70 caliber Springfield U.S. service rifle cartridge and the .30-06 Springfield U.S. service rifle cartridge. These barrels revolved around a central shaft, the mechanism delivering a cartridge to each barrel into its own separate lock when the user turned a handle mounted

M1895 Gatling gun from the right side. This weapon was mounted on a conventional artillery carriage, with a U-shaped bracket that allowed it to be traversed horizontally. The firing handle and the front sight on the right of the forward section of the main frame are also shown here (courtesy James D. Julia Auctioneers, Fairfield, Maine. www.jamesdjulia.com).

Ten. The Gatling Gun

Left: Magnified view of the breech of an M1895 Gatling, showing the firing handle, adjustable rear sight, and lever for opening the breech. The large round knob in the center was used to adjust the firing mechanism. *Right:* Breech of the M1895 Gatling gun, showing the cartridge carrier and the lock with its attached ejector (both photographs courtesy James D. Julia Auctioneers, Fairfield, Maine. www.jamesdjulia.com).

on the breech. To facilitate cooling, some of the early models had fibrous matting stuffed in between the barrels that could be soaked with water, although this device had its own problems and was discontinued in later production. Gatlings were usually mounted on a standard artillery carriage, although later variants included types that could be transported on horseback.[1]

Receiver Stamps

The rear of the receiver is engraved with a number of identifying marks in a circular configuration and having the following form:

> **GATLING GUN PATENTED**
> **Manufactured by**
> **Colt's Pt. F.A. Mfg. Co.**
> **HARTFORD, CONN. U.S.A.**
> **No XXXX**
> **Cal. .45**

Where "No XXXX" represents the serial number and "Cal. .45" is the caliber of the weapon.

An additional stamp is also found on the edge of the receiver mounting, indicating the model, and has the following form:

> **MODEL**
> **1895**

Operation

Patent information inscribed on the breech of an M1895 Gatling gun, showing the manufacturer's name, caliber (.30), serial number (No 1011) and the model number (Model 1895) (courtesy James D. Julia Auctioneers, Fairfield, Maine. www.jamesdjulia.com).

Operation was reasonably simple. In the early weapons, one member of the loading team dropped cartridges into the hopper; later weapons used a magazine that fed cartridges into the gun either under gravity or through the action of a spring. With the ammunition supply correctly in place, the user aimed the gun and turned the firing handle, the speed of revolution determining the rate of fire. As the barrels rotated in a clockwise direction as a result of the action of the firing handle, separate cartridges dropped into the grooves of the cylindrical carrier and the lock, of which there was a separate one for each barrel, and were moved forward by the action of a cam, pushing the adjacent cartridge into the chamber. The lock (which contained the bolt and firing spring) continued to move forward, compressing its internal firing spring, which, when fully compressed to its release point, drove the bolt and its firing pin forward, firing the cartridge, each barrel being discharged in turn as it reached the lower right-hand position. With continued rotation of the firing handle, the lock moved back, at which point the extractor on the side of the lock removed the empty case, carrying it down and ejecting it through an opening in the housing.

Gatling's mechanism was extremely reliable. At a series of trials supervised by senior U.S. Navy officers in 1873, at Fort Madison, near Annapolis, Maryland, the following results were observed[2]:

October 23, 10:33 a.m., commenced firing in the presence of Chief of Bureau of Ordnance and others. Ten drums, each holding 400 cartridges (making 4,000), were fired rapidly, occupying in actual time of firing ten minutes and forty-eight seconds. The firing was then discontinued to witness experimental firing of the 15-inch Navy rifle. The firing of the Gatling gun was resumed in the afternoon, when some 28,000 cartridges were fired. Commenced firing at 8:50 a.m., October 24, the gun having been cleaned.

One hundred and fifty-nine drums, of 400 cartridges each, making a total of 63,600 cartridges, were fired without stopping to wipe out or clean the barrels. At the close of the firing, which extended over a period of five hours and fifty-seven minutes, although the actual time of firing was less than four hours, the barrels were not foul to any extent; in proof of which a very good target was made at 300 yards range before cleaning the barrels. On the 25th day of October the remainder of the 100,000 cartridges were fired. The working of the gun, throughout this severe trial was eminently satisfactory, no derangements of any importance whatever occurring.

Variations

MODEL 1862

The first of Gatling's prototypes, designed to use percussion primed steel cylinders, rather than rimfire or centerfire cartridges.

MODEL 1865

Produced after significant design changes to the specification of the M1862 and chambered for a .58 caliber rimfire cartridge.

MODEL 1866

First Gatling accepted for use by the U.S. Army, 24 August 1866, and chambered for both 1-inch and .50 caliber centerfire cartridges. Some examples of this model produced with ten barrels.

M1871

First model designed to use a curved box magazine, containing between twenty and forty .50 caliber centerfire cartridges.

MODEL 1874

First model chambered for the U.S. Army's new .45/70 centerfire cartridge. Two common models: the short "Camel" gun with ten 18-inch barrels; and the long model, fitted with ten 32-inch barrels.

MODEL 1876

Almost unchanged from the previous weapon.

MODEL 1877

Five-barreled "Bulldog" Model, with barrels encased in a brass sleeve. Chambered for the .45/70 centerfire cartridge.

MODEL 1879

Little changed from the M1877 and still chambered for the U.S. Army's .45/70 centerfire cartridge.

MODEL 1883

Originally designed to use the innovative, spring-fed Accles magazine. In practice this proved too fragile for use on the battlefield, and most of these weapons were converted to use the new Bruce Feed system.

Model 1886

First model designed to use the Bruce Feed system for cartridge loading.

Model 1892

Fitted with Bruce Feed, and the last model chambered for the now outdated .45/70 black powder military cartridge. The Bruce Feed system was fitted to all subsequent models.

Model 1893

First model to be chambered for the .30 smokeless cartridge, then being adopted by the U.S. Army.

Model 1895

Little changed from the M1893, only 94 guns being produced for the U.S. Army by Colt. For the first time Gatlings were painted in the Army's olive drab (OD) green. This and all subsequent models could be mounted on an armored field carriage.

Model 1900

The Model 1900 was very similar to the model 1895, but with only a few components finished in OD Green, the rest being left with their original blueing.

Model 1903

In 1903, the Army converted all its M1900 guns in .30 Army to chamber the new .30-03 Krag-Jorgensen cartridge (standardized for the M1903 Springfield rifle) as the M1903.

Model 1903–'06

The later M1903–'06 was an M1903, rechambered for the new Springfield .30-06 spitzer ball cartridge, these conversions usually being carried out in the workshops of Army's Springfield Arsenal.

Military Service

American Civil War and the U.S. Army

R.J. Gatling's first approach to the U.S. army was during the Civil War, when he offered the weapon to Brig. Gen. J.W. Ripley, Chief of Ordnance. Ripley refused to even allow a trial of the gun. Undeterred, Gatling next approached General B. F. Butler in Baltimore.

Ten. The Gatling Gun 135

Oil painting of the U.S. Army's attack on San Juan Hill. Gatling guns were used in support and are shown in the background (courtesy James D. Julia Auctioneers, Fairfield, Maine. www.jamesdjulia.com).

Butler was impressed by the results of a demonstration Gatling organized and immediately purchased 12 guns, together with 12,000 rounds of ammunition, subsequently deploying the weapons during the siege of Petersburg, Virginia.

Despite its adoption in 1866, Gatling's brainchild saw little use with American forces until the Spanish-American War of 1898, when Captain J.H. "Gatling Gun" Parker organized a detachment equipped with four M1895 Gatling guns to serve in Cuba. The guns proved effective, particularly at the Battle of San Juan Hill, where Parker's detachment used three swivel-mounted Gatlings to decimate the Cuban defenders. Although the Gatling had proved successful at San Juan, its artillery-style carriage made it difficult to maneuver when accompanying infantry in the mountainous jungle terrain, so the decision was taken to replace the U.S. Army's Gatlings with M1895 Colt-Browning machine guns. These fully automatic machine guns had also been used in Cuba and found to be more effective than the Gatling because of their lighter weight and tripod mounting.[3]

British Army

The British Army was the most prolific user of Gatling guns during the nineteenth century, employing the weapon in a number of its "small wars" including, amongst others:

- The Second Afghan War (1878–1880)
- The Anglo-Zulu war (1879), where a Gatling gun was deployed by the Naval Brigade at the Battle of iNyezane and the final decisive engagement at Ulundi.
- The First and Second Matabele Wars.
- The Sudan Campaign (1881–1899).

British Army Gatling gun detachment, photographed during the Second Afghan War. These weapons are fitted with Broadwell drum magazines and appear to be mounted on a conventional fixed artillery carriage.

The British Army first bought the Gatling gun (chambered for the issue .577/450 Martini-Henry cartridge) in 1879. Considering their activity in what are usually referred to as the colonial "small wars" of the period, it seems probable that the Gatling would have been quickly replaced by the superior Maxim, which the British began using in 1893. Unfortunately, no reliable date for its declaration as obsolete by the British Army is readily available.[4]

Later Developments

Although the Gatling was superseded at the beginning of the 20th century by newer, fully automatic, recoil-operated machine guns, weapons using multiple rotating barrels began to be developed again after World War II, because of the superior rates of fire that could be achieved with such weapons. These trials resulted in the appearance of the M61 Vulcan 20mm autocannon and the ubiquitous M134 Minigun, a six-barrel rotary-fire weapon, chambered for the 7.62 × 51mm NATO cartridge and used extensively by U.S. forces in Vietnam.[5]

Table Sixteen: Specification of the Gatling gun

Manufacturers	Gatling Gun Company 1862–1870
	Colt's Patent Firearms Manufacturing Company 1870–1911
	Pagett & Co., Vienna (mostly ten-barrel guns)
	W.G. Armstrong & Co., Newcastle-upon-Tyne (mostly ten-barrel guns)
Period of production	1862–1911
Production	Probably several hundred thousand, including those copied under license or illicitly

Military service	U.S. Army and Navy, British Army, Royal Navy, various European forces, including the Russian Army
Crew	Operator and three subsidiaries
Weight	Between 70 and 270 kgs (150–600 lbs) depending upon the carriage
Overall length/Barrel length	0.75–1.08 ms (29–43 inches)/0.45–.82ms (18–32 inches), depending upon the model
Number of barrels	Five barrels–M1874, M1877 (Bulldog)
	Six barrels—all models from M1865 to M1903
	Ten barrels—M1865, 1895
Mechanism	Manually rotated multiple fire
Cartridge	.58 caliber percussion fired cylinders
	.58 caliber rimfire (M1865)
	.50 caliber centerfire (M1866)
	1.00 caliber centerfire (M1866)
	.45/70 caliber Springfield U.S. service rifle cartridge (M1874-M1890)
	.30-40 caliber Krag (M1893-M1900)
	.30-03 caliber Springfield (M1903)
	.30-06 caliber Springfield (1903-'06)
Cartridge loading system	Gravity-fed hopper (M1862-M1871)
	Gravity-fed box or Broadwell drum magazine (M1871 to M1883)
	Accles direct-feed drum magazine (M1883)
	Bruce Feed (M1883 to M1911)
Sights	Blade foresight
	Slotted rear sight, adjustable for elevation and windage
Maximum range	250 ms using rimfire ammunition
	500 ms when using centerfire ammunition
Rate of fire	1,200 rounds per minute, more usually 400 rpm in action

Section IV: The Smokeless Powder Era

CHAPTER ELEVEN

Maxim's Automatic Machine Gun
"The Devil's Paintbrush"

Sir Hiram Maxim

The inventor of the Maxim gun was an American, originally from Maine, who moved to England in 1881 at the age of 41. He became a naturalized British subject in 1900 and was knighted in 1901, nearly sixteen years before his death in 1916. Sir Hiram Maxim (February 1840–November 1916) patented a number of innovative designs, including an early "fire extinguishing" sprinkler system, although he was most famously responsible for the Maxim machine gun, which has been called by one historian "the weapon most associated with British Imperial conquest." More familiarly, Maxim's gun was also nicknamed "the Devil's Paintbrush" because anything that got into its field of fire was completely swept away. Maxim's gun was redesigned and improved by Vickers during the early part of the twentieth century, before being accepted by the British Army in 1912. It remained in service as its standard heavy machine gun until the end of 1968, when it was superseded by the L7 GPMG.[1]

Development

Maxim's inspiration for his lethal brainchild was claimed to be an accident he suffered as a child. While firing a heavy, centerfire rifle, the youthful Maxim was knocked over by the powerful recoil, and this is said to have suggested to him that the extra force generated by a weapon's "kick" might be used to operate it automatically. This story may be true, but a more likely reason for the development of the Maxim automatic machine gun is probably given in his own words, when he wrote: "In 1882 I was in Vienna, where I met an American whom I had known in the States. He said: 'Hang your chemistry and electricity! If you want to make a pile of money, invent something that will enable these Europeans to cut each other's throats with greater facility.'"

Maxim had previously made an all but permanent move to England in 1881, and upon his return from Vienna, he established a small factory and experimental workshop in London's Hatton Gardens. By June 1883, Maxin had made sufficient progress in his development work to register several patents covering various features of the design of his machine gun,

Eleven. Maxim's Automatic Machine Gun

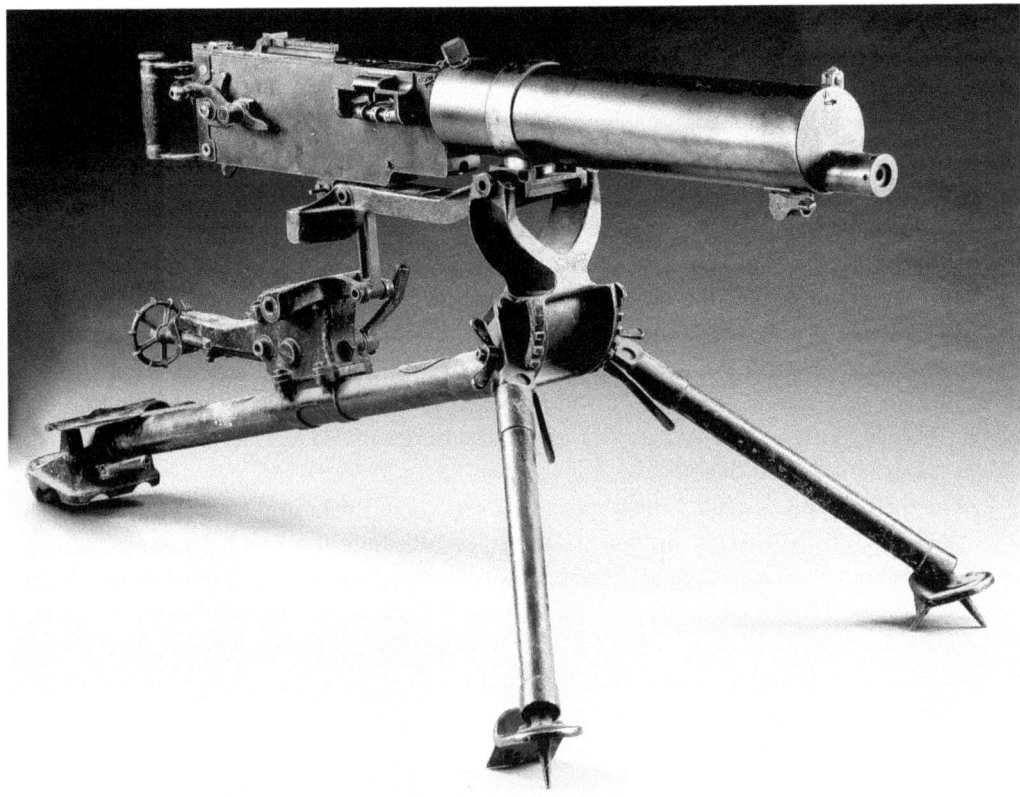

Maxim automatic machine gun from the right, showing the tripod leveling screws, water jacket and charging handle at the rear of the breech (courtesy James D. Julia Auctioneers, Fairfield, Maine. www.jamesdjulia.com).

and by 1884, the first prototype was ready to be shown to a select audience. This initial design attracted considerable interest, especially from the British Army in the person of General Lord Garnet Wolseley, who attended a demonstration that same year, accompanied by the Inspector General of Fortifications, Lt. Gen. Sir Andrew Clarke. Clarke must have recognized the possibilities inherent in Maxim's weapon because he advised the inventor to "simplify the gun as much as possible and do not be satisfied until it can be disassembled, examined and cleaned with no other instrument than the hands." Maxim seems to have thought that this was good advice and redesigned much of the mechanism so that any damaged component could be replaced and the gun made ready to fire again in a matter of a few seconds. Further changes followed to decrease the overall weight of the gun. Having now developed what he considered to be a salable prototype, Maxim gave a number of demonstrations to representatives of European powers, using black powder cartridges and achieving a rate of fire of around 600 rounds per minute.[2]

Smokeless cartridges

Maxim was able to chamber his new invention for any cartridge in service with the military during this period, but all of the ammunition he used had a major drawback. Black powder was the standard propellant of the day, and one of the main disadvantages of this material is the enormous quantity of residue that is left after firing. Maxim's gun does not seem to have been affected unduly by residue accumulation during its operation, although cleaning the weapon after use must have been a major problem. However, in 1885 a French chemist, Paul Vielle, developed a new smokeless propellant for use in firearms, and this proved to be a turning point both for Maxim and the designers of automatic machine guns in general. Smokeless powder produces little or no residue upon ignition and generates about three times the power of an equivalent weight of black powder, which meant that the development of guns using more finely machined, recoil-operated mechanisms became possible. Maxim quickly exploited this advantage and produced a version of his own machine gun that used the French 8mm Lebel cartridge and had a rate of fire of 1,100 to 1,200 rounds per minute. This impressed a French officer so much at one of the first tests using smokeless cartridges that he told Maxim that his gun fired too fast and that the mechanism should be slowed down![3]

The British Amy accepted the Maxim into service in 1888, on the recommendation of its new C-in-C, British Army, Sir Garnet Wolseley, although the first 120 guns he ordered were chambered for the necked .577/.450 black powder cartridge then used in the British Army's Martini-Henry rifle. After the adoption of his gun by the British, Maxim also received orders from a number of other countries. By the outbreak of World War I it was the German army that had shown most foresight, being equipped with a total of 50,000 rifle-caliber guns made to the Maxim pattern, principally by DWM.[4]

Production

Maxim moved from his tiny Hatton Garden premises to a site in Crayford, Kent, in 1884, using money provided by Albert Vickers, who became the company's first chairman. In 1888, the company expanded by taking over the Nordenfelt Guns and Ammunition Company. This conglomerate went on to produce the Maxim as the Maxim-Nordenfelt Guns and Ammunition Company until 1897, when the company was bought by Vickers. That

Maxim showing the fusee spring cover and the port through which the canvas belt leaves the weapon (courtesy James D. Julia Auctioneers, Fairfield, Maine. www.jamesdjulia.com).

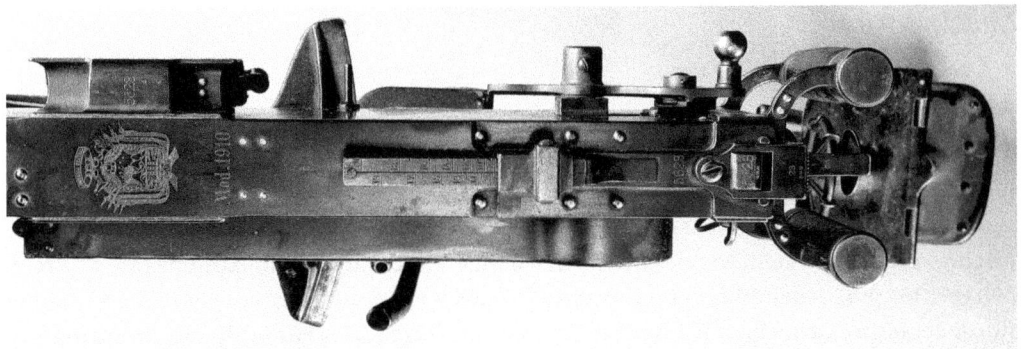

Maxim from above showing the sights, operating handles, and safety catch in the "SAFE" position. The model number "Mod 1910" is stamped below the company trademark (courtesy James D. Julia Auctioneers, Fairfield, Maine. www.jamesdjulia.com).

Left: Maxim from the right showing details of the charging or cocking handle. *Right:* Maxim from the rear showing the firing handles, safety catch (this gun has an Argentinian provenance; consequently the catch is stamped FUEGO) and firing button, with its position for both thumbs (both photographs courtesy James D. Julia Auctioneers, Fairfield, Maine. www.jamesdjulia.com).

company became Vickers, Sons & Maxim, which first produced the Maxim-Vickers, subsequently modified and lightened to become the British Army's long-lived and ultra-reliable Vickers medium machine gun, first introduced in 1912.

A number of international companies were also licensed to produce the Maxim. In particular, the German arms firms DWM and Waffenfabrik Bern produced copies designated MG 01, MG 08 and MG 11 (numbers indicating the year of production), and there were also Russian, Finnish and Chinese versions of the gun. In America, Colt was licensed to produce a version of Sir Hiram's gun, designated the Maxim Machine Gun, Caliber .30, Model of 1904. The first of these guns was made by Vickers and chambered for the inferior .30-30 cartridge, although by the time Colt had their manufacturing operation in place, which was unfortunately not until 1908, the specification had been changed to allow the new machine gun to use the recently introduced and far superior .30-06 cartridge.[5]

Specification

PRODUCTION

Precise records not available, estimated at over 3 million weapons by all manufacturers, including those using Maxim's design in a modified form.

The Maxim MG is a belt-fed, water-cooled, heavy machine gun, fitted with Maxim's original recoil-operated, toggle-locked mechanism and having a maximum rate of fire of 500 to 600 rpm, depending upon the model. Guns were chambered for the .577/.45 caliber Boxer centerfire cartridge, .303 British rimmed cartridge (7.7 × 56mmR), .30-06 Springfield cartridge, as well as a number of others. Rounds were delivered to the weapon from a canvas belt, a single belt holding 333 cartridges and entering the right side of the weapon. Operation was by means of "spade" firing handles with the firing button or "thumb piece" mounted between them. Maxims were usually fitted with conventional iron sights.

IDENTIFYING STAMPS

Identification stamps on Maxim guns are quite variable, but usually include the maker's name and the serial number. Stamps on guns made by DWM are quite typical and have the following form, usually being stamped or inscribed on a brass plate with the "DEUTSCHE WAFFEN—UND MUNITIONSFABRIKEN" surrounding the other stamps in a circular configuration:

DEUTSCHE WAFFEN—UND MUNITIONSFABRIKEN
No XXXX
MAXIM'S PATENT
1898
BERLIN

Where "No XXXX" is the serial number and "1898" is the date of production.

Operation

To operate an automatic machine gun with a mechanism based upon Maxim's original prototype, the loader first inserted a loaded ammunition belt into the right side of the breech. The gunner then pulled the tab of the belt as far to the left as it would go and held it in that position while the cocking handle, located on the right of the weapon, was operated twice, forwards and then backwards. He then raised the safety catch, thus allowing the "thumb piece" (effectively a button that serves to fire the weapon) to be pushed forward, actuating the trigger bar and sear and firing the weapon.

When the first cartridge in the belt had been fired, the barrel and lock immediately moved to the rear a short distance. At the end of this recoil movement the lock unbolted from the barrel and was drawn back from the chamber, simultaneously opening the breech, drawing a loaded cartridge from the belt and extracting the empty case from the chamber. As the lock reached the end of its recoil movement, both the empty case and live round were lowered until the spent case was in line with the ejection opening and the live cartridge was adjacent to the chamber, this rearward motion also serving to cock the firing pin. The recoil having also extended the fusee spring, that spring now returned to its former position, pressing the lock forward, which simultaneously pushed a fresh cartridge into the chamber and ejected the empty case. It also caused a cammed lever to move the belt forward one round and returned the lock and barrel to the firing position, with the bolt and barrel locked together. If the trigger was still depressed, the sear was struck as the lock reached its final position, releasing the firing pin and firing the weapon, whereupon the firing cycle began again. Automatic fire continued while the thumb piece was depressed, there being no provision to fire single shots from a gun with this type of mechanism, except by controlling the period of depression of the thumb piece trigger.[6]

Cartridges for these weapons were delivered to their mechanism in a canvas belt, each belt being seven yards long, holding 333 cartridges and fitted with a clip on each end for the attachment of a second loaded belt. In the earliest commercial Maxim, the rate of fire could be controlled by a selector lever that could be moved against a graduated quadrant scale marked on the side of the gun. Pulling the selector to the rear until the fire-selector reached "1" gave a firing rate of 1 round per minute; this rate increased as the selector lever was pulled further back, until at the end of the scale a rate of 600 rounds per minute was achieved. This mechanism had little military value and consequently was not fitted to later models.[7]

Table Sixteen: Specification of Maxim medium/heavy machine gun

Manufacturers	Maxim Gun Company
	Maxim Nordenfeldt Guns and Ammunition Company
	Vickers, Sons & Maxim
	Colt (M1904)
	Various overseas manufacturers
Period of production	1886–1914
Production	Estimated at 3 million weapons.
Users	Almost every country with a modern army has used the Maxim.
Military service	Boer War (1899–1902)
	Boxer Rebellion (1899–1901)
	Russo-Japanese War (1904–1905)
	World War I (1914–1918)
Crew	Eight:
	1 gunner
	1 or 2 loaders
	1 or 2 ammunition and water carriers
	4 additional men to move the weapon
Weight	27 kgs (60 lbs)
Length/Barrel length	108 cms (42 inches)/67 cms (26 inches)
Mechanism	Recoil-operated, toggle-locked mechanism, firing from a closed bolt.
Cartridge/Delivery system	.45/.577 caliber Boxer centerfire cartridge
	.303 British rimmed cartridge (7.7 × 56mmR)
	.30-06 Springfield cartridge
	Delivered from a canvas belt, a single belt holding 333 cartridges and entering the right side of the weapon.
Sights	Front sight: iron blade
	Rear sight: graduated leaf sight
Maximum range	1,500 meters
Rate of fire	500–600 rpm (rounds per minute)

Military Service

Although Maxim gave an early prototype of his gun to the Emin Pasha Relief Expedition in 1886, the weapon was first issued by the British army to the Singapore Volunteer Corps in 1889. The first use of the gun in action occurred during the First Matabele War (1893–1894) in Rhodesia, at the Battle of Shangani, as a result of Matabele forces conducting raids into British South Africa. As a consequence of the Matabele operations, a British column consisting of 700 paramilitary policemen of the British South Africa Police and a number of native auxiliaries were sent into Matabeleland on a reprisal raid. The column advanced towards Bulawayo, the capital city of the region, but were compelled to camp at the Shangani river, arranging themselves in a defensive circle or *laager*, where they were attacked during the night by approximately 5,000 Matabele warriors. The new Maxim guns with which the force was equipped proved so effective that before the Matabele withdrew, they had suffered over 1,500 fatalities. The Maxims, as one eyewitness put it, were "mowing them down literally like grass." The South Africans lost four men. A week later, the Matabele attacked the column again and were driven off for a second time, leaving behind over 2,500 dead. The Maxim was used extensively by the British during this period of predominantly colonial warfare. It proved particularly effective in engagements in which native forces could be persuaded to charge headlong at numerically inferior British detachments, a situation that occurred at the Battle of Omdurman in 1898. Maxim guns were also used by British forces against the Boers in the both the First and Second Boer Wars, as was another of Sir Hiram's inventions, the quick-firing 1-pounder gun usually known as the Pom-Pom. Unfortunately for the British, the Boers had got their hands on about fifty of these weapons first, and during the Second Boer War (1899–1902), the British found themselves being fired on by a weapon their own Ordnance Committee had rejected!

Russia also found the Maxim to be effective during the Russo-Japanese War of 1904–1906, and its use resulted in heavy Japanese losses, particularly at Nanshan in 1904. The Battle of Nanshan took place across the two-mile defensive perimeter that protected Port Arthur, a vital Russian possession because it was their only port which remained ice-free for the whole year. Japanese forces began their assault on the port by capturing the walled city of Chinchou, just north of the Russian defensive line. With their flank secured, the Japanese assaulted the Russians' main defensive position on Nanshan Hill on the 26 May 1904. The Russians, however, although numerically inferior, had their Maxims entrenched behind barbed-wire obstacles and further protected by mine fields. Using their Maxims to good effect, the Russian troops inflicted over 6,000 casualties on the attacking Japanese and by 6 p.m. had beaten off nine assaults. They were still firmly entrenched, if short of ammunition, when their commander Colonel Tretyakov was informed that his reinforcements were in full retreat back to Port Arthur and that his reserve ammunition had been blown up on the orders of his superior, General Fok. Tretyakov and his men were forced to retreat without support to their second defensive line outside Port Arthur, sustaining more casualties in the process than had died defending the hill. A series of land and naval engagements followed until the Russian Fleet was all but annihilated in the Battle of Tsushima Straits on 28 May 1905 and the Russians were forced to accept a humiliating peace.

America adopted its first Maxims in 1904, with the acceptance of 50 guns made by

Vickers, Sons & Maxim and chambered for the unreliable .30-03 Krag cartridge. The Colt's Manufacturing Company had been selected to produce the gun for the U.S. Army, but changes to schematics and specification delayed production. The first of the Colt-made guns did not reach the Army until 1908, and even then total production was only 287 weapons. Troops equipped with the M1904 were deployed in operations in the Philippines, Hawaii, Mexico, and Central and South America, but the weapon itself did not see much use in any of the actual fighting involved in these operations. Despite a paucity of modern automatic weapons, the U.S. Army's Maxims remained at home during World War I, the American generals preferring to place their faith in vastly inferior types such as the Chauchat light machine gun.

Machine guns that were direct copies of the Maxim were used in World War I, however, exemplified by weapons like the British Vickers medium/heavy machine gun, essentially a lightened and improved Maxim; the German Army's M 08; and the Russian Pulemyot Maxim. By this time, however, despite its reliability and rugged construction, the Maxim in its original form had been largely replaced in modern warfare by the new generation of lighter, more versatile medium machine guns such as the Hotchkiss M1909, the Browning M1917 and the Lewis gun.[8]

Maxim QF 1-Pounder "Pom-Pom"

Maxim's quick-firing gun, which had been designed to use a 37 × 94mmR, 1lb (454 grm) shell, supplied to the breech from a conventional canvas belt, was simply an enlarged

Maxim QF 1-pounder, designed for use in an antiaircraft role (courtesy Andrew Gray: License: CC:A-S-A 2.0G).

Maxim-Nordenfelt 37-mm 1-pounder autocannon, mounted aboard USS *Vixen*.

version of his original machine gun. Early production was sold by Maxim-Nordenfeldt, while weapons sold for British service from about 1900 were labeled "Vickers Sons and Maxim," although they were the same gun. The weapon saw some minor service in World War I, but began to be replaced from 1918 by the QF 2-pound gun.

Military service

American service

Adopted sometime before 1898 as the 1-pounder Mark 6, it saw service as a naval antiaircraft gun in World War I.

British service

Second Boer War

Rejected by the British government. Vickers sold about 50 of these guns, mounted on conventional field gun carriages, to the government of the South African Republic (Transvaal), in time for the Battle of Paardeburg in 1900.

World War I

Deployed in Britain as an early form of antiaircraft gun, they met with little success, because the small, 37mm shell fired from Maxim's Pom-Pom was not powerful enough to shoot down the German Zeppelins. Officials at the Ministry of Munitions were disparaging about the gun's performance, one of these men noting in 1922: "The pom-poms were of very little value. There was no shrapnel available for them, and the shell provided for them would not burst on aeroplane fabric but fell back to earth as solid projectiles.... [They] were of no use except at a much lower elevation than a Zeppelin attacking London was likely to keep." Maxim's little quick-firer was also considered too small for use in France with the Royal Artillery, who preferred the QF 13-pound gun and the 18 pound field gun, both firing shrapnel, as their main anti-personnel weapon.

German service

World War I

Introduced into service with the German military as the Maxim Flak M14 and used as an antiaircraft gun, it also saw service with the German army in South West Africa 1915.

Variations

- **QF 1½ pounder:** This was the first modification of the QF 1-pounder to be considered for naval service. Designated the QF 1.5-pdr Mark I, it was of 37mm caliber with a barrel 1.6 meters long. The weapon underwent trials in the *Arethusa*-class light cruisers HMS *Arethusa* and HMS *Undaunted*, but did not enter full service, being replaced instead by a larger weapon, the QF 2-pdr Mark II.
- **QF 2-pounder Mark II:** this was in all essentials an enlarged version of the Vickers QF 1-pounder Maxim gun, designed to use a 40mm shell. It incorporated the same water-cooled barrel and a Vickers-Maxim mechanism as the original Pom-Pom, but this resulted in problems with the early guns because the unmodified Maxim QF mechanism was rather light and prone to faults, such as rounds falling out of the belts. The weapon was originally designed to have cartridges delivered from hand-loaded fabric belts, but these were later replaced by belts with disposable steel links. Originally accepted by the Royal Navy in 1915 for service as an antiaircraft weapon in ships of cruiser size and below, the weapon was modified between 1923 and 1930 to produce the QF 2-pounder Mark VIII or "Multiple Pom-Pom."
- **QF 2-pdr Mark VIII:** This was essentially eight modified QF Mark IIs installed in an eight-barreled mounting and controlled by remote director. When the original eight-gun mounting had been introduced into Royal Navy ships in the 1930s, it was found to have a gratifyingly large volume of fire and considerable destructive force, but unfortunately, it was almost impossible to aim the weapon successfully because of the smoke and vibration created when it was firing. The solution was to operate the mounting from a remote location, using some form of "director," which, in the early versions, would allow the gun to be aimed at the target aircraft by causing a pair of pointers that determined altitude and direction to rotate on the gun mount, the gun crew then moving the mount to match the pointers rather than trying to aim at the target aircraft. The early Mark I, II and III directors were aimed by eye, using a simple ring sight, but the Mark IV saw the introduction of gyroscopes and radar control, which significantly improved the Royal Navy's shoot-down rate. Later versions also controlled the move-

ment of the pom-pom remotely, requiring the gun crew to simply act as loaders. The first Mark V and Mark VI eight-gun mountings weighed between 11 and 18 tons, which made them suitable only for larger ships such as cruisers and aircraft carriers, but by 1935 a smaller version using four guns and designated the Mark VII had been developed for light cruisers and destroyers, along with a power-operated, single-barreled version, the Mark XVI. These mountings also incorporated a large magazine, containing 140 shells for an eight-barreled mounting and 56 for the single-barreled type, which gave the larger gun a fire duration of 73 seconds without reloading. The guns designed to fit these mountings of necessity were of four distinct designs, left- and right-hand belt loading and inner and outer, so the ejection and loading slots were compatible. By the beginning of World War II, the Maxim was showing its age, but improvements to the director system and the introduction of a HV (high velocity) 1.8 lb shell ensured that the old gun continued in service with the Royal Navy until the later stages of World War II, when it began to be replaced by the 40mm Bofors gun. Incidentally, the forces generated by the new HV ammunition required that older mountings be modified, although the newly manufactured mounts were improved in the factory to fire the new shell. A mount modified or designed for HV ammunition was given a "star" designation; for example a Mk VI mount modified for HV ammunition would be designated Mk VI*.[9]

Table Seventeen: Comparison of the specifications of the QF 1-pounder and QF 2-pounder guns

Weapon	Maxim QF 1-pound gun	Vickers QF 2-pounder Mark II	Vickers QF 2-pounder Mark VIII
Manufacturers	Maxim-Nordenfelt Vickers, Sons & Maxim DWM	Vickers, Sons & Maxim	Vickers Armstrong
Period of production	1890 until 1918	1915 until 1944	1923 until 1945
Production	3–5 thousand guns	7,000 guns	20,000 guns
Military service	Spanish–American War (U.S.) Second Boer War (South Africa) World War I (Britain and Germany)	World War I World War II	World War I World War II
Crew	Gunner and loader, with ancillaries for movement and ammunition carriage.	Gunner and loader, with ancillaries for movement and ammunition carriage.	Gunner and loader, with ancillaries for movement and ammunition carriage.
Weight	410 lbs (185 kgs)	530 lbs (240 kgs)	850 lbs (390 kgs)
Length/Barrel length	Length: 6 ft (1.8 meters) Barrel: 3.5 ft (1.1 meters	Length: 8ft (2.5 meters) Barrel: 5ft (1.5 meters)	Length: 8.5 ft (2.6 meters) Barrel: 5ft (1.5 meters)
Mechanism	Single-barreled autocannon, using automatic recoil operation	Single-barreled autocannon, using automatic recoil operation	Single-barreled autocannon, using automatic recoil operation and mounted in a bank of 4 or 8 guns
Shell/Delivery system	37 × 94R, 1 lb (0.45 kg) shell, filled with black powder and with a fuse in the nose.	40 × 158mmR Initially designed to use the conventional canvas belt of the	40 × 158mmR Steel-linked belt, holding 14 shells.

Weapon	Maxim QF 1-pound gun	Vickers QF 2-pounder Mark II	Vickers QF 2-pounder Mark VIII
	Shells were delivered to the breech in a canvas belt, holding 25 shells.	QF 1-pounder, this was later replaced by a steel-linked belt, holding 14 shells and giving superior performance.	The mountings for these guns often incorporated a magazine, holding 56 rounds for a single gun. Magazines for the 8-barreled guns held 140 rounds, giving a firing time between loadings of 73 seconds.
Sights	Fore sight: steel acorn point Rear sight: Crosshead with traversing screw	Fore sight: steel acorn point Rear sight: Crosshead with traversing screw	Fore sight: steel acorn point Rear sight: Crosshead with traversing screw
Maximum range	Between 4,000 and 4,500 meters	1,200 meters	6,200 meters As AA gun: 4,000 meter ceiling
Rate of fire	300 rpm (rounds per minute)	200 rpm	115 rpm

Maxim's Competitors

AMERICA

- Colt-Browning 1895.
- Browning Model 1901.

AUSTRIA

- Skoda Model 1893 machine gun: A water-cooled, single-barreled machine gun with delayed blowback operation and usually chambered for the 8 × 50mmR cartridge supplied from a unique design of overhead magazine. It was capable of between 180 and 250 rounds per minute depending upon the rate selected by the user. Austrian tests showed it to be reliable: "The weapon fired a considerable number of bursts of 3 minutes' duration, and on one occasion operated continuously for 9 minutes before a stoppage occurred to put it out of action. It also passed the dust and mud test and was fired successfully in temperatures ranging from 32° Fahrenheit to 20° below zero." Despite the success of these trials, the weapon use was limited and it was considered to be suitable only for defending fixed positions within fortifications.[10]

FRANCE

- Hotchkiss machine guns: These include the early Model 1897, which was later developed into the Hotchkiss M1909, also known as the Hotchkiss Mark I in the British army and M1909 Benét–Mercié in the U.S. army.[11]

SWEDEN

- Nordenfeldt Model 1897 automatic machine gun: Only produced as a prototype.[12]

Chapter Twelve

Smokeless Powder and Repeating Rifles

Until the end of the nineteenth century, black powder was the propellant used in the overwhelming majority of firearms since their introduction into European warfare during the fourteenth century. Despite its widespread acceptance, it had a number of inherent disadvantages. Smoke generated after firing several black powder volleys was sufficient to obscure the action in front of a line of troops, making it difficult to see the enemy. Also, the residue left after firing tended to clog any complex mechanism and render it inoperative after very few rounds had been fired, which complicated the manufacture and use of a repeating black powder firearm.

A possible answer to the problems associated with black powder made its first appearance in 1847 when an Italian chemist, Ascanio Sobrero, first synthesized nitroglycerine. Unfortunately, it was found to be unsuitable as a propellant in firearms designed for black powder, because when nitroglycerine detonates it releases its energy as a shock wave, which in practical terms means it would shatter any gun that it was used in, before sufficient force was exerted on a projectile to drive it up the barrel. Gunpowder, by contrast, does not detonate in the breech of a gun, but rather burns almost instantaneously to produce a huge volume of gas in a process termed deflagration, which was the main reason it was found to be suitable for use as a propellant in early firearms, with their fragile iron barrels. Nitroglycerine is also highly unstable, making it dangerous when carried onto a battlefield in a cartridge pouch. Another explosive, nitrocellulose or gun cotton, also appeared in 1847, produced by treating cotton with a mixture of nitric and sulfuric acid and then very thoroughly washing the resulting material in order to remove the excess acid. After drying at moderate temperatures, the resulting product could be flaked and was then ready for use. Initial manufacturing processes for nitrocellulose were not scrupulous enough in its final washing, however, resulting in an explosion in the first factory designed for its manufacture, and it was not until Sir Frederick Abel improved the process that manufacturing could safely be resumed. Gun cotton was subsequently used in all British military warheads, although it was still not stable enough to be used as a small-arms propellant.

Both nitroglycerine and gun cotton were potentially too useful to be abandoned as propellants, however, and in 1884, a French chemist, Paul Vielle, invented a smokeless powder that came to be referred to as Poudre B (poudre blanche or white powder, referred to currently as pyrocellulose). It consisted of a combination of insoluble and soluble nitrocellulose, which had been transformed into a colloidal or gelatinous composition by treatment with an alcohol/ether mixture. This gelatinous product was stabilized with amyl alcohol before being rolled into thin sheets, dried and then cut into small flakes, which were greenish-gray in color, rather than white. This variation had the useful property of deflagrating rather than exploding when ignited, which made it suitable as a propellant. It was first used in the cartridge of the Lebel Model 1886 rifle, but proved so successful that it became the standard load for all French ordnance, including naval guns and artillery pieces. Found to be three times more powerful than gunpowder and producing almost no smoke and little residue, it was also rapidly adopted by many European armies. There were a number of improvements to the original composition, which resulted in the final formula, termed Poudre BPF 1, which remained in service with the French army until 1960.[1]

The British government was also interested in smokeless powder and formed an Explosives Committee specifically to examine the characteristics of Poudre B and an explosive invented by Alfred Nobel, which he had called Ballistite. After testing, both substances were considered to be unsatisfactory. In 1889, three members of the committee, Sir Frederick Abel, Sir James Dewar and Dr. W. Kellner, patented a new propellant, consisting of nitroglycerine, nitrocellulose and petroleum jelly, which was similar to the composition of Nobel's Ballistite. After being dispersed in acetone, the new composition could be extruded as thin, brittle rods, which were initially referred to as "cord powder" or "the Committee's modification of Ballistite," although this was quickly shortened to "Cordite." The new propellant was adopted for British service use as "Cordite Mk 1" in 1899, although when increased wear was found in the barrels of guns using it, a new composition designated "Cordite MD" was introduced in 1901.[2]

In America, a significant variety of smokeless powders were produced between 1890 and 1897, all based on nitrocellulose powder that had been dispersed or colloided in a variety of organic liquids, before being dried and converted to granules (corned). The end result of all these experiments was the appearance in 1897 of a powder colloided with a mixture of ether and alcohol, devised by Lieutenant John Bernadou, USN, and which proved to be superior to all other formulas. The U.S. government sold or licensed the patents for this new propellant to the DuPont chemical company, who modified and improved the formula, eventually marketing the product as Improved Military Rifle Powder, more usually abbreviated to "IMR," which was produced in a variety of grades for both military and civilian use. Both the U.S. Army and Navy adopted the new powder, although manufacture of the military propellants was carried out for the Navy at their Naval Powder Factory in Maryland and for the Army at the Picatinny Arsenal in New Jersey.[3]

Types of Propellants

Propellants containing only nitrocellulose as their active ingredient are termed single-base powders, while those containing both nitrocellulose and nitroglycerine are termed double-base. There is another type composed of nitrocellulose, nitroglycerine and nitroguanidine, termed a triple-base powder, which saw considerable use in British large-caliber guns, such as artillery and naval weapons, after World War II, although it was never used in small-arms ammunition.

Smokeless Powders

White Powder or *Poudre B*

The constituents of this propellant were 68 percent insoluble nitrocellulose and 30 percent soluble nitrocellulose. Used by the French army from 1886 until 1960. Poudre B was unstable after long-term storage, and was soon replaced for military applications. Poudre BN3F and BPF1 were later, more stable substitutes, the final formulation, BPF1, remaining in service until 1960.

Cordite

Produced in 1889 by combining 58 percent nitroglycerine, 37 percent nitrocellulose and 3 percent petroleum jelly. The resulting material was then dispersed in acetone and subsequently extruded as thin rods or "cords." Cordite was used as propellant in British service pistol cartridges until 1941 and in the .303 British cartridge, designated CARTRIDGE S.A. BALL .303 INCH MARK VII until 1916, when a nitrocellulose version was introduced, designated the MARK VIIZ, although cordite was the preferred loading throughout the service life of this type of ammunition. Nitrocellulose cartridges were made for British military use during this period because of a shortage of cordite and may be identified by the "Z" included in the head stamp. Double based cordite propellants were phased out of general use after World War II, with the appearance of more stable nitrocellulose products such as the various grades of IMR, which are now used in the British service round, the NATO 5.56 × 45mm cartridge.

Variations

- Cordite Mk I and Cordite MD (Modified): The first form of cordite, Cordite MkI, was replaced in 1901 by Cordite MD, with a composition of 65 percent nitrocellulose, 30 percent nitroglycerine and 5 percent petroleum jelly, because the early formulation caused excessive barrel wear.
- Cordite RDB (Research Department formula B): Acetone was difficult to obtain during World War I and a new explosive, Cordite RDB, was developed in 1916 with a composition of 52 percent collodion (guncotton dissolved in an ether/alcohol mixture), 42 percent nitroglycerine and 6 percent petroleum jelly. Unfortunately, it was found to be unstable if stored for long periods, and new techniques for synthesizing acetone allowed a return to Cordite MD.
- Cordite SC (Solventless Cordite): A more stable development of Cordite RDB, it was commonly used in World War II as a propellant in naval guns.
- Cordite N: This was a triple-base explosive, incorporating nitroguanidine, as well as nitrocellulose and nitroglycerine. It was more powerful than the earlier formulations, with a reduced muzzle flash and a lower operating temperature, which reduced erosion in the barrel of the gun designed to use it. It remained in use after World War II and is still used in a number of modern designs of artillery ammunition, such as the ammunition for the 105mm L118 light field gun, the British army's standard field gun.[4]

Nitrocellulose

This was a formulation produced for use as a propellant when nitrocellulose powder is dissolved to form a colloid or gel in a variety of organic solvents.[5]

Variations

- Ballistite: Produced in 1887 by Alfred Nobel and made by dissolving nitrocellulose in a solution of nitroglycerine, after which 10 percent camphor was added. A modification of ballistite called W.A. was produced in 1897 by the U.S. army and was the standard U.S. service loading from 1897 until 1908, when it was replaced by Improved Rifle Powder.
- Indurite: Produced in 1891 and manufactured by dissolving nitrocellulose in nitrobenzene to form a colloid, the resulting solution being treated to form a variety of grain sizes.
- Peyton powder: Produced in 1893 and made by combining a mixture of nitroglycerine and nitrocellulose with ammonium picrate, which gave it corrosive properties.
- Ruby powder: Produced in 1893 and made by combining a mixture of nitroglycerine and nitrocellulose. An improvement on Peyton powder, because the absence of any picrate salt made it less corrosive.
- Military Rifle powder and Improved Military Rifle powder: Patented in 1897, this propellant was manufactured by dispersing nitrocellulose in a mixture of ether and alcohol to form a colloidal solution, which was subsequently treated to produce grains in a variety of sizes, thus ensuring that the powder type was suitable for the gun in which they were used. DuPont began manufacturing their Military Rifle powder 1909 Military or Pyro DG using this process in 1909, with the U.S. Army producing their version at a separate establishment from 1908. MR or IMR powders were used in all U.S. Army and Naval cartridges after 1908, replacing "WR" powder which had been the previous loading for cartridges in both services.
- Modern IMR powders are coated with dinitrotoluene (DNT) to slow initial burning and graphite to minimize static electricity during blending and loading. They contain 0.6 percent diphenylamine as a stabilizer and 1 percent potassium sulfate to reduce muzzle flash. Military Rifle 20 (MR # 2) was a nitrocellulose powder of this type with a grain diameter of 0.03 inches and length of 0.084 inches which was used in the .30-06 Springfield rifle cartridge until 1926, when the M1 bullet was introduced for loading in that ammunition.[6]

Revolvers and Magazine Rifles Using Smokeless Ammunition for Civilian Purchase

AMERICAN MANUFACTURERS

Colt

Single Action Army revolver (SAA): Designed and guaranteed for smokeless powder in weapons produced after 1900, weapons having serial numbers above approximately 192000 being claimed to be safe for such loads. However, care must always be exercised when using modern smokeless cartridges in older guns, and it is recommended that an appropriate expert be consulted before pursuing such a course.[7]

Marlin

Winchester's most effective competitor, Marlin produced an early range of top-ejecting rifles, which although certainly comparable in construction never sold as well as their larger competitor. Marlin's

Model 1899 introduced a side-ejection mechanism, an innovation that gave it a considerable advantage over the similar Winchester guns, because the Marlin could now be fitted with a telescopic sight.[8]
Marlin rifles and carbines include:
- **Model 1881:** Top-ejecting gun, produced as both rifle and carbine variants.
- **Model 1888:** Top-ejecting weapon, produced as rifle and carbine variants.
- **Model 1889:** First side-ejecting Marlin rifle, produced as rifle and carbine variants.
- **Model 1894:** Top-ejecting weapon, produced as rifle and carbine variants, with various magazine capacities, barrel lengths and rifling.
- **Model 1895 Military Repeater:** Top-ejecting weapon, produced as rifle and carbine variants, all chambered for the .45/70 military black powder cartridge.
- **Model 1897:** Top-ejecting weapon, produced as rifle and carbine variants.

Marlin also produced a number of bolt-action rifles for civilian use as well as several bolt-action shotguns.

Remington

Model 8 semi-automatic rifle: This was a semi-automatic rifle designed by John Browning and introduced by Remington in 1906. It had a long-recoil mechanism and was sold with either a five- or fifteen-round fixed box magazine and in a wide variety of calibers.[9]

Savage

Model 1899 rifle.[10]

Smith & Wesson

- Military and Police 1st Model revolver and all its later variations: Chambered for .38 S&W Special cartridge, which was introduced in 1898 as an improvement over the .38 Long Colt cartridge. Originally loaded with black powder, its popularity caused Smith & Wesson to retail it with a smokeless powder loading in 1899.
- Hand Ejector First Model revolver, also known popularly as the "Triple Lock": Chambered for the .44 S&W Special cartridge, a smokeless cartridge introduced in 1907, specifically for use in this revolver.

All Smith & Wesson revolvers chambered for the .38 S&W Special and the .44 S&W Special cartridges are considered to be chambered for smokeless cartridges, although, as usual, care must always be exercised when using modern smokeless cartridges in older guns, consultation with an expert being recommended before shooting.[11]

Winchester

- Model 1894 rifle
- Model 1895 rifle: Production: 425,881, between 1896 and 1931. Produced in a variety of calibers including: .30-03, .30-06, .30-40 Krag, .303 British and for several 7.62 Russian cartridges. The Model 1895 was a lever-action rifle, which differed from all its predecessors in having a fixed box magazine beneath

Hand Ejector First Model revolver, also known as the "Triple Lock." Chambered for the .44 S&W Special cartridge, a smokeless cartridge introduced in 1907, specifically for use in this revolver (Adamsguns.com).

the breech, instead of the under-barrel, tubular magazine. It was produced in a variety of models, which included:
- Standard rifle: Production approximately 150,000. Chambered for .30-03, .30-06, .30-40 Krag, .303 British MkII–MkVII cartridges, barrel lengths being dependent upon chambering.
- Carbine: Production approximately 5,000. Chambered for .30-03, .30-06 and .303 British cartridges, with a 22-inch barrel.
- Russian Model musket: Production 293,816, manufactured to complete an order from the Imperial Russian government. Chambered for the 7.62 × 54mmR rimmed cartridge, with a 28-inch barrel.[12]

BRITISH MANUFACTURERS

Webley
- Webley Government Models V and VI revolvers, which were also sold to civilian purchasers. **Production:** over 3 million revolvers.
  The first cordite pistol cartridge introduced into the British Army was the CARTRIDGE, S.A., BALL, PISTOL, WEBLEY, CORDITE (MARK I), which had a solid drawn-brass case, containing a 265-grain bullet with three cannelures and a load of 6.5 grains of Mark I Cordite. A letter "C" was added to the head stamp to differentiate this cartridge from the earlier black powder round. The first revolver cartridge using nitrocellulose as an alternative to cordite was introduced in 1941 as a variant of the CARTRIDGE, S.A., BALL, REVOLVER, .455 inch MK.VI, with a propellant load of 5.2 grains. All rounds loaded in this manner were designated as MKVI.Z, with a "Z" also included in the head stamp.
- Webley-Government or Webley-Green revolvers.
- Webley-Wilkinson revolvers.[13]

Bolt-Action Service Rifles

The first bolt-action rifle designed for military use was the Dreyse needle gun, accepted into service by the Prussian army in 1841, although not issued to the troops until 1848. Dreyse's gun was a single-shot, breech-loading weapon, in which the cartridge consisted of a paper case, powder charge, percussion cap and bullet. The bullet, of .61 inches caliber and shaped like an acorn, had a primer attached to its base and was wrapped in a paper case, termed a sabot, which separated it from the powder charge. Both the powder charge and wrapped bullet were enclosed in a second, outer paper case, which was rolled up and tied in a way similar to a conventional, muzzleloading cartridge of the period. To operate the weapon, the bolt was pulled back and a paper cartridge inserted into the breech. The bolt was then pushed forwards and turned, locking the breech closed. Squeezing the trigger resulted in the needle-shaped firing pin being driven forwards, piercing the rear of the cartridge and continuing through the powder charge, before striking the primer fixed to the base of the sabot, the powder charge thus burning from the front to the rear of the cartridge. Although Dreyse's gun had some significant advantages, such as an improved rate of fire when compared to conventional muzzleloaders (10–12 rpm as compared to 3–4 for an Enfield P53 rifle), problems with powder residue and cartridge paper accumulation, the fragility of the firing pin and various other difficulties meant its success on the battlefield was limited. This became readily apparent when its performance was compared to the later French Fusil Modèle 1866 or Chassepot needle gun, which operated on a similar principle

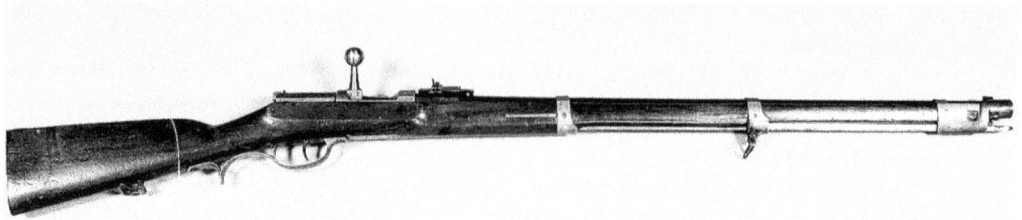

Dreyse needle gun from the right.

Breech and bolt of a Chassepot rifle (courtesy Rama: License: CC-A-S-A-2.0).

and had been adopted by the French in 1866, just in time for the Franco-Prussian War. The French army replaced their Chassepot rifles in 1874, with the single-shot, bolt-action Gras Modèle 1874 M80, which was chambered for a superior 11 × 56mmR black powder, centerfire cartridge, replacing those in turn with the Lebel Model 1886, the first military rifle to use a cartridge loaded with smokeless powder.[14]

A French Model 1866 Chassepot needle gun. These weapons were unpopular with the troops who were issued with them, as the needle-pointed firing pin had a tendency to break at the most inopportune moment (courtesy Rama: License: CC-A-S-A-2.0).

The Lebel 8mm Model 1886 Service Rifle

The Lebel Model 1886, known in the French army as the Fusil Modèle 1886, was a conventional bolt-action repeating rifle with a tubular, under-barrel magazine, capable of holding ten rounds, eight in the magazine, one in the transporter and the tenth in the chamber. It was chambered for the 8 × 50mmR Lebel cartridge, which was produced by reducing the neck diameter of an 11mm Gras black powder cartridge and loading this modified case with a flat-nosed, full-metal jacket bullet, which could withstand the heat generated by the new explosive without deforming in the barrel. The original bullet jacket, designated "Balle M" and made of cupro-nickel, was replaced in 1898 by a brass Spitzer bullet, designated the "Balle D." The new bullet necessitated a modification to the case, in

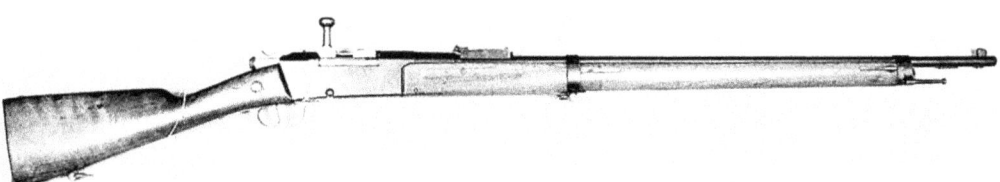

Model 1886 Lebel rifle from the right.

the form of a circular groove machined around the primer cup, to prevent the sharp tip of the bullet from accidentally igniting a primer within the magazine. As a further safeguard, all Balle M and Balle D French military cartridges have convex primer covers crimped over the primer itself.

When it first appeared, the Lebel proved to be a significant advance in military weapons technology, its new, smokeless ammunition giving it a longer range and better accuracy than contemporary black powder rifles.

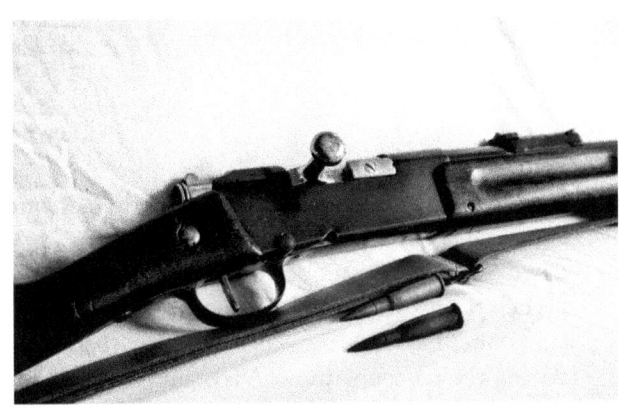

Breech of Lebel Model 1886 rifle.

Troops equipped with the Lebel were both out of range of an enemy carrying rifles chambered for black powder and virtually invisible at longer ranges, because the Lebel produced no visible smoke. Men equipped with the new rifle were also able to carry more ammunition, since the 8mm Lebel cartridge was significantly lighter than any conventional black powder round. However, other countries, in particular Germany, were not slow to appreciate the new technology and were soon producing bolt-action repeaters of their own chambered for smokeless ammunition. Both the rifles and cartridges they used were in many respects superior to the 8mm Lebel.

Breech stamps

Proof marks and acceptance and inspector's stamps are found on both the barrel and the breech. The manufacturer's stamp is usually on the left side of the breech and has the following form:

MANUFACTURE D'ARMES
St Etienne

The model designation (either Mle 1886 or Mle 1886/93) is also stamped on the left side of the receiver and has the following form:

M^{LE} 1886

or

M^{LE} 1886/93

Variations

- **Fusil Mle 1886 M (modifié) 93**: This was a slightly modified version of the original M1886 rifle, incorporating an improvement to the rear sight and a change to the bolt head, which now diverted any hot gases escaping from a ruptured cartridge case away from the shooter's face.
- **Mle 1886 M93-R35**: This was a carbine version with an 18-inch barrel, produced at the Tulle Arsenal (MAT or Manufacture d'Armes de Tulle), between 1935 and 1940. The shorter barrel of necessity caused an associated shortening of the magazine, which could consequently hold only three cartridges.

Military service

Despite its antiquated design, the Lebel Model 1886 remained in service with the French army for the whole of World War I. Economic pressures and the incompetence of Phillippe Pétain, then serving as War Minister, meant that replacement of the severely outdated Lebel with a modern, bolt-action rifle, the MAS-36, did not begin until 1937, and French troops were still awaiting supplies of the new gun when World War II broke out in September 1939. As late as 1949, Lebel M1886 rifles were still in service with civilian militia during the reoccupation of Vietnam (1945–1946) and the Algerian War (1954–1962).[15]

The Gewehr Model 1898 Service Rifle

Also known as the G98, Gew 98 or M98, and developed as an improvement on Mauser's original Model 1888, the Gewehr '98 or Model 98 rifle was a conventional bolt-action repeating rifle, with an internal magazine originally holding five 88/M cartridges, until 1905, when it was rechambered for the superior 7.92 × 57 Mauser cartridge. It featured Mauser's final definitive bolt action, considered by many users to be one of the best designs of this type ever invented. The Gewehr '98 was in use with the German army until 1935, when it was replaced by Mauser's Karabiner 98k, which was also a development of the Gewehr '98. Mauser's bolt action formed the basis for a significant number of other rifle designs between 1902 and 1903, including the Springfield M1903 service rifle.[16]

Breech stamps

Gewehr 98 rifles will usually be found with a stamp on the left side of the breech denoting the model and having the following form:

Gewehr Model 1898 German service rifle, showing the bolt mechanism and rear sight (courtesy James D. Julia Auctioneers, Fairfield, Maine. www.jamesdjulia.com).

G e w. 98.

The letters have the appearance of an older Germanic script.

VARIATIONS

- **Gewehr '98:** The first model and one most commonly encountered by collectors.
- **Sniper rifle:** Production approximately 18,000, during spring 1915.

Breech stamp on Mauser Model 1898 rifle: "G e w. 98" (courtesy James D. Julia Auctioneers, Fairfield, Maine. www.jamesdjulia.com).

These weapons were G98s converted to use a telescopic sight, which were mounted high above the receiver to accommodate the action of the bolt and safety catch. However, trials showed that to mount the 'scope successfully, the bolt handle had to be turned down from its original position, a slot being cut in the stock to accommodate the modified bolt.

- **Karabiner 98a:** Produced in 1908, this was a shorter version of the G98 with a 23-inch barrel and a turned-down bolt handle, which also required a corresponding recess in the stock. The bayonet receiver ring and stacking lug were also modified.
- **Karabiner 98b:** Produced in 1923, this was a G98 that was termed a carbine in order to comply with the terms of the Treaty of Versailles, which stipulated that Germany could only manufacture carbines. It featured slight modifications to the rear sight and sling swivels as well as having a turned-down bolt handle.

The Springfield M1903 Service Rifle

Designated in U.S. army service as the "United States Rifle, Caliber .30-06, Model 1903," the M1903 was a conventional bolt-action repeating rifle, with an internal magazine holding five cartridges and chambered for the .30-06 Springfield cartridge, although earlier weapons may be encountered that are chambered for the unsuccessful .30-03 Krag cartridge. Sharing a number of features with the successful Gewehr '98 rifle as well as the earlier Krag, it was fitted with an internal magazine, loaded by means of a five-round charger and a strong bolt mechanism with two retaining lugs. This arrangement makes it suitable for more powerful ammunition than the U.S. army's previous rifle, the unsuccessful Springfield

Springfield M1903 U.S. service rifle from the right, showing the Mauser pattern breech and mechanism (courtesy James D. Julia Auctioneers, Fairfield, Maine. www.jamesdjulia.com).

1892 Krag-Jørgenson. In reality, the Springfield is a Mauser in all but name, as the German company proved when it sued the U.S. government and received $250,000 in settlement of its claim. The Springfield M1903 remained in service with all branches of the U.S. military until its replacement by the M1 Garand in 1936.

Breech stamps

Springfield 1903 rifles accepted into service with the U.S. army are stamped on the breech behind the front sight with the Springfield Armory mark in the following form:

U.S.
SPRINGFIELD
ARMORY
MODEL 1903.
MARK I -
XXXXXX

The "XXXXXX" denoting the serial number.

Springfield M1903 showing the breech stamp: "US SPRINGFIELD ARMORY MODEL 1903. MARK I" and the serial number (courtesy James D. Julia Auctioneers, Fairfield, Maine. www.jamesdjulia.com).

Variations

Only the main variations are listed here.
- **M1903**: Introduced in 1903 and developed for the .30-03 (also known as the .30-45) cartridge.
- **M1903**: Introduced in 1905 and modified to use the knife pattern Model 1905 bayonet and featuring an improved Model 1905 sight.
- **M1903**: Introduced in 1906 and rechambered for the new M1906 .30-06 cartridge ("Ball Cartridge, caliber .30, Model of 1906").
- **M1903 Mark I**: Produced between 1918 and 1920 and designed to use the Pedersen device, a specialized insert that replaced the bolt and allowed the user to fire .30 caliber pistol cartridges semi-automatically from a detachable magazine.

- **M1903 NM:** Produced between 1921 and 1940 at Springfield Armory, specifically for National Match shooting competitions. These guns were fitted with standard production barrels that had been measured with star gauges, those meeting specified tolerances being stamped with an asterisk-shaped star on the muzzle crown. Sometimes referred to as "Star Gauge Springfields."
- **M1903A1:** Produced between 1929 and 1939, and fitted with a stock that had been changed from the straight pattern to a pistol grip pattern stock (designated the "Type C" stock).
- **M1903A3:** Produced between 1942 and 1944, with stamped metal parts and somewhat different grip and stock (late model Type S stock; no finger grooves) to make production easier and thus quicker.[17]

The Lee-Enfield .303 Service Rifle

The British Army's first bolt-action repeating rifle was the Lee-Metford, introduced in 1888. It combined a rear-locking, conventional bolt-action mechanism, which cocked the action when the bolt was closed, and a detachable, ten-round box magazine, both designed by J.P. Lee, with W.E. Metford's barrel, featuring an innovative, seven-groove polygonal rifling. It was originally designed for a .303 black powder cartridge, the "Cartridge, S.A., Ball, Magazine Rifle, Mark 1.C. Solid Case, .303inch," but the success of the Lebel Model 1886 prompted the British to begin experiments with a smokeless round in the same caliber. The result was the introduction of the British army's first smokeless cartridge in 1891, the "Cartridge S.A. Ball, Magazine Rifle Cordite Mark 1." Unfortunately, trials quickly showed that the shallow, polygonal rifling of the Lee-Metford became dangerously worn after only about 5,000 of the new rounds had been fired through it. In 1895 the Lee-Metford was replaced by a new rifle, the Magazine Lee-Enfield or MLE, in which the original Metford barrel was replaced by a barrel designed at RSAF, Enfield. The new barrel featured deeper, square profiled rifling better able to stand the increased heat and pressure generated by the new smokeless cartridge.

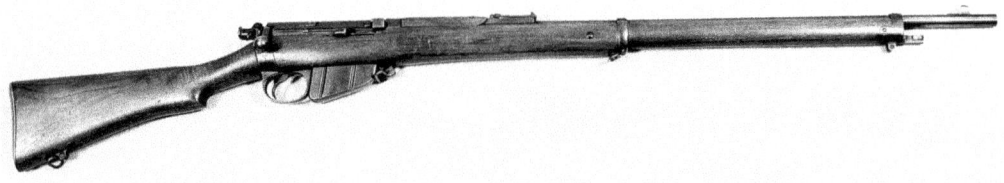

Lee-Metford .303 caliber British service rifle. Although this was a good weapon, the polygonal Metford rifling was insufficiently robust to accommodate the later smokeless .303 cartridge.

THE S.M.L.E.

The Short, Magazine Lee-Enfield rifle, which succeeded the earlier MLE, was a conventional bolt-action weapon, chambered for the .303 caliber Mk VII British cartridge and fitted with a ten-round detachable magazine, loaded from two five-round chargers. Its bolt-action mechanism was a significant improvement over most of the contemporary designs, featuring a bolt with rear-mounted lugs that placed the operating handle over the trigger and made it quicker to cycle than weapons like the Mauser G98, which required the rifleman to move his hand forward to operate the bolt. Moreover, the distance the bolt was required to travel was just the length of the cartridge, and it was only necessary to rotate it through 60 degrees rather than the full 90-degree turn required in the Mauser G98 and Lebel M1886. Lee's design also incorporated a detachable box magazine holding ten cartridges, while most of his rivals had opted for an integral magazine only holding five rounds. In addition, the mechanism incorporated a magazine cutoff, which allowed the user to load single cartridges, while retaining a full magazine against the time when reloading single rounds would be inconvenient.

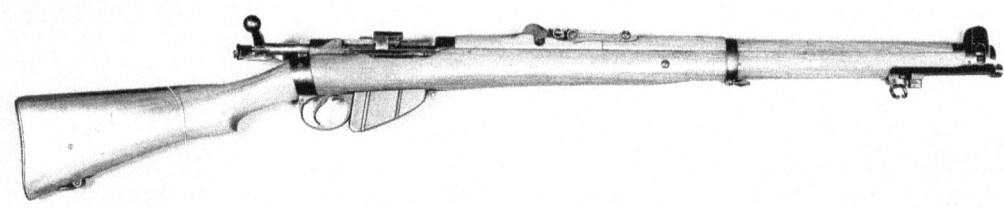

The Short Magazine Lee-Enfield MkI (SMLE) British Army service rifle, chambered for the .303 smokeless service cartridge.

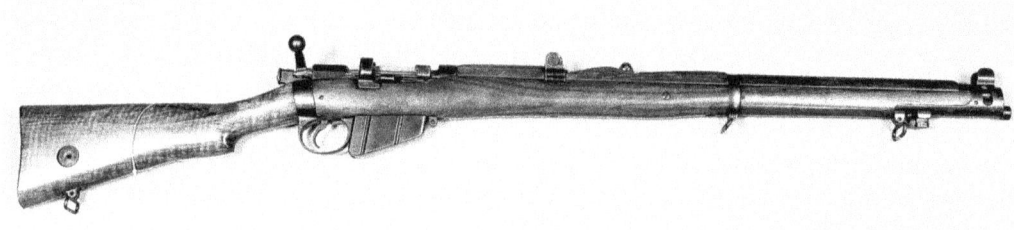

SMLE MkIII from the right-hand side, showing the characteristic muzzle cap.

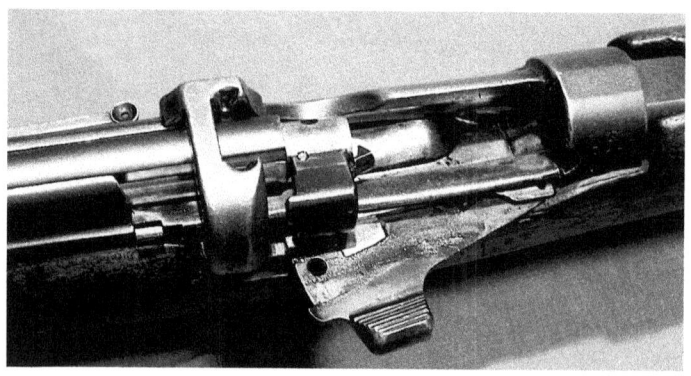

Breech of an SMLE Mk III, showing the breech cut-off device, intended to encourage soldiers to conserve ammunition (courtesy Commander Zulu).

These design features made the Lee-Enfield the fastest bolt-action military rifle available at that time, so that an experienced rifleman using one was able to fire between 20 and 30 aimed shots in a minute. This characteristic of the Lee-Enfield was embodied in a rapid-fire exercise known in the British army as the "Mad Minute," which entailed firing as many aimed shots as possible in one minute, and for which the record is somewhere between 36 and 38 shots on a 48-inch target at 300 yards. This sort of training meant that most British regular soldiers before the beginning of World War I could out-shoot their European opponents and allies. It is reliably recorded that many of the German infantry at Mons believed they were facing British battalions heavily equipped with machine guns rather than riflemen well trained in the use of the SMLE.

Breech stamps

Lee-Enfield rifles are found with a variety of stamps on both the breech and barrel, including proof marks, acceptance stamps, inspector's marks, manufacturer's stamps and serial numbers. Serial numbers, in particular, are found stamped on the breech, receiver and stem of the bolt handles. Model designation and other details are found stamped on the right of the receiver ring, also termed the butt socket, which surrounds the stock just to the rear of the bolt mechanism and is attached to the rear of the trigger guard. The following is an example from a SMLE MkIII* made at RSAF, Enfield in 1917.

GR
ENFIELD
1917
S^{HT}L.E.
III*

Where:
  "GR" is the acceptance mark and stands for "George Rex."
  "ENFIELD" is the manufacturer.
  "1917" is the date of manufacture.
  "SHTL.E." is the model, in this case Short, Magazine Lee Enfield.
  "III*" is the variant.

Models

- **Magazine Lee-Enfield**: Introduced in November 1895 as the ".303 caliber, Rifle, Magazine, Lee-Enfield" this rifle was designed to be loaded with single cartridges rather than the five-round chargers used in later models and was fitted with a 30-inch barrel. It is easily differentiated from the later SMLE by its longer barrel, although it is fitted with the short bayonet fitting or boss, which is all that protrudes beyond the nosecap of the barrel, and which was a feature of all Lee-Enfield rifles until the No. 4 appeared in 1941. The MLE was in production until 1906, although some examples were still in service in 1926. A short version was introduced in 1896 as the Lee-Enfield Cavalry Carbine Mk I, or LEC, with a 21.2-inch barrel. The Mk I* followed in 1899, which omitted the cleaning rod. Some were converted to load with chargers (aka: stripper clips) and designated the "Charger Loading Lee-Enfield" or CLLE.
- **Short, Magazine Lee-Enfield Mk I**: Officially designated the "Rifle, Short, Magazine, Lee-Enfield," or SMLE, introduced on 1 January 1904 and produced until 1926. Fitted with a 25-inch barrel and incorporating a charger loading system, with the charger clip loading guide mounted on the face of the bolt-head.

- **Short, Magazine Lee-Enfield Mk II**: In service from 1906 until 1927.
- **Short, Magazine Lee-Enfield Mk III**, changed in 1926 to Rifle No. 1 Mk III: Introduced on 26 January 1907, this is the most familiar of all the SMLEs, which featured improvements to the design of the magazine and handguards as well as incorporating a simplified rear sight. Most importantly, the charger guide was now fixed, rather than mounted on the bolt-head, and the weapon was rechambered to accept the new Mk VII ammunition, loaded with a spitzer bullet.
- **Short, Magazine Lee-Enfield Mk III*,** changed in 1926 to Rifle No. 1 Mk III*: Costing £3.75 to produce in 1914, the Mk III was found to be too expensive for use in World War I. A number of modifications were made to simplify production, which resulted in a cheaper weapon, designated the SMLE Mk III*. Changes included the omission of the magazine cutoff device, the long-range volley sights, and the windage adjustment of the rear sights. A change was also made to the cocking handle, which was modified from a round knob to a serrated slab.
- **Short, Magazine Lee-Enfield Mk V**: Produced between 1922 and 1924, but used only for trials, with a total production of 20,000.
- **Rifle, No. 1 Mk VI**: Produced between 1930 and 1933, but used only for trials, with a total production of just 1,025.
- **Rifle, No. 4 Mk I**: Officially adopted in 1941, the No. 4 features the Lee bolt-action mechanism of the earlier SMLE, including the magazine cutoff, although a number of modifications were made that produced a lighter, stronger rifle that was cheaper to produce, although it was slightly heavier than the original No. 1 Mk III. The No. 4 is easy to differentiate from the SMLE, because the muzzle protrudes from the end of the forestock. Other modifications included an aperture sight that was fitted to the rear of the receiver, with an additional ladder sight for long-range shooting; and a heavier, "floating" barrel, which was mounted independently of the forestock, so that when it expanded during prolonged firing it would not alter the "zeroing" or accuracy of the rifle. A barrel band was also added to reinforce the union between the barrel and forestock at the muzzle and facilitate the use of the 1907 bayonet, although a new spike bayonet was designed and issued for the No. 4.

Lee-Enfield No. 4 MkI, from the right side.

- **Rifle, No. 4 Mk I***: Produced in America from 1942 until 1944, differing from the original No 4 in having the bolt release catch replaced by a simpler notch on the bolt track of the rifle's receiver.
- **Rifle, No. 4 Mk 2**: Postwar improvement on the original No. 4, featuring a trigger

hung forward from the butt collar rather than the trigger guard, as well as beechwood stocks in which the original reinforcing strap and center piece of wood in the rear of the forestock were replaced by a simpler screw and nut. This rifle was also fitted with a brass butt plate, which replaced the original zinc component.

- **Rifle, No 5 Mk I "Jungle Carbine"**: Produced between 1944 and 1947, the No. 5 was a shorter, lighter development of the No. 4, featuring a cut-down stock, flash hider and a lightened receiver that had been machined to remove all unnecessary metal. Combined with the same aperture and long-range ladder rear sight, these changes resulted in a rifle that was shorter and 2 lbs lighter than a standard No. 4, but with a similar range and accuracy.

Lee-Enfield No. 4 Mk1, with the rear sight raised and a five-round stripper clip in place, prior to loading (Wikipedia: License: CC-A-S-A 3.0).

The Lee-Enfield No 4 rifle was converted during the period from 1960 to 1970 to chamber the 7.62 × 51mm NATO cartridge. These rifles belong to a separate series designated L8, which includes the L8A1, a converted No. 4 Mk2 rifle; the L8A4, a converted No. 4 Mk1 rifle; and the L8A5, a converted No. 4 Mk1* rifles, as well as a number of models originally upgraded to No. 4 Mk2 specification from the MkI and Mk1*.[18]

Table Eighteen: Comparison of the Lebel, Mauser, Springfield and Lee-Enfield rifles

Weapon	Lebel M1886	Gewehr '98	Springfield M1903	Lee-Enfield MK III 1907 (SMLE)
Makers	**Civilian production:** None **French Government production:** Manufactured in the French government arsenals at Châtellerault St-Etienne Tulle (MAT)	**Civilian production:** Mauser Deutsche Waffen und Munitionsfabriken Haenel Sauer & Sohn, Waffenwerke Oberspree V. Chr. Schilling Co. Simson **German Government production:** The Imperial German arsenals at Amberg Danzig Erfurt Leipzig Spandau	**Civilian production:** Remington Smith-Corona **U.S. Government production:** Springfield Armory Rock Island Armoury	**Civilian production:** Birmingham Small Arms (BSA) London Small Arms Co. Ltd. **UK and Commonwealth Government production:** RSAF, Enfield Lithgow Small Arms factory, Australia The Rifle Factory, Ishapore, West Bengal
Period of production	1887 until 1916	1898 until 1935	1907 until 1949	1907–2016

Weapon	Lebel M1886	Gewehr '98	Springfield M1903	Lee-Enfield MK III 1907 (SMLE)
Production	Production recorded as 3.45 million	Production recorded as over 5 million	Production recorded as over 1.3 million	Production recorded as over 17 million of all types
Military service	Boxer Rebellion Monegasque Revolution World War I Franco-Turkish War Polish–Soviet War Spanish Civil War World War II Algerian War In use for the period covering 1900 until 1962	Boxer Rebellion Mexican Revolution World War I 1918 German Revolution Finnish Civil War Russian Civil War Turkish War of Independence Spanish Civil War World War II Second Sino-Japanese War Chinese Civil War In use for the period covering 1900 until 1950 In use for the period covering 1899 until 1973	Philippine-American War Banana Wars Mexican Revolution World War I World War II Second Sino-Japanese War Chinese Civil War Korean War Cuban Revolution Vietnam War	Second Boer War World War I Irish War of Independence Irish Civil War World War II Indo-Pakistani Wars Greek Civil War Malayan Emergency French Indochina War Korean War Arab-Israeli War Suez Crisis Mau Mau Uprising Sino-Indian War Bangladesh Liberation War Soviet invasion of Afghanistan In use for the period covering 1899 until 2014
Weight	Loaded: 9.7 lbs Empty: 9.2 lbs	Loaded: 9.5 lbs Empty: 9.0 lbs	Loaded: 9.3 lbs Empty: 8.7 lbs	Loaded: 9.3 lbs Empty: 8.8
Length/Barrel length	Length: 51 inches Barrel: 31 inches, rifled with four clockwise grooves	Length: 49 inches Barrel: 29 inches rifled with 4 clockwise grooves	Length: 43 inches Barrel: 24 inches, originally rifled with 4 or 6 clockwise grooves, 2 groove rifling in Smith-Corona M1903-A3 guns	Length: 44 inches Barrel: 25 inches, rifled with 5 counterclockwise grooves
Mechanism	Bolt action, action cocked on opening	Bolt action, action cocked on opening	Bolt action, action cocked on opening	Bolt action, action cocked on closing
Cartridge	8 × 50mmR Lebel Cartridges delivered from an under-barrel magazine holding 8 cartridges	M/88 (8.07 × 57mm) until 1905 7.92 × 57mm Mauser from 1905 until 1935 Cartridges delivered from an integral box magazine holding 5 rounds, loaded with a 5-round stripper clip	.30-03 in a few early weapons from 1903 until 1906 .30-06 Springfield (7.62 × 63mm) From 1906 until 1973 Cartridges delivered from a detachable box magazine holding 5 rounds, loaded with a 5-round stripper clip	.303 MkVII SAA Ball Cartridges delivered from an integral box magazine holding 10 rounds, loaded with 5-round stripper clips
Sights	Rear sight: ladder adjustable from 850 to 2,400 meters	Rear sight: curved tangent pattern Front sight: blade	Rear sight: Flip-up sight graduated to 2,500 meters	Rear sight: sliding ramp Front sight: fixed post

Weapon	Lebel M1886	Gewehr '98	Springfield M1903	Lee-Enfield MK III 1907 (SMLE)
	Front sight: blade		Front sight: Barleycorn pattern	
Maximum range	Accurate range: 300 meters Max range: 1,800 meters	Accurate range: 500 meters Max range: 2,000 meters	Accurate range: 500 meters Max range: 5,000 meters	Accurate range: 550 meters Max range: 2,800 meters
Rate of fire	Approximately 10 rounds in one minute, but reloading took a relatively long time, because of the under-barrel magazine	10–15 rounds per minute, the use of stripper clips facilitating the process	10–15 rounds per minute, the use of stripper clips facilitating the process	20–30 rounds per minute, the use of stripper clips facilitating the process
Cost	Record unavailable	$28 (£6) in 1940	$15 (£3) in 1914	Record unavailable

Other Bolt-Action Service Rifles

AMERICAN MANUFACTURERS

Krag–Jørgensen rifle

Production: recorded as approximately 700,000 weapons, from 1892 until 1930, mostly for the U.S. army.

This weapon was a bolt-action repeating rifle, chambered for the .30-40 Krag cartridge. It had a characteristic side-loading, internal 5-round magazine with an opening on the right-hand side protected by a hinged cover. To load the weapon, single cartridges were inserted through the side opening, before being pushed up and into the action by a spring-loaded follower. Loading was slow compared to most other contemporary designs, and the Krag was only in service with the U.S. Army as the Springfield Model 1892, from 1892 until 1903, when it began to be replaced by the Springfield M1903 rifle.[19]

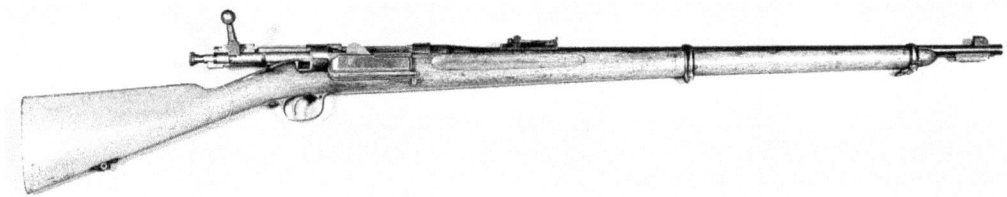

Krag–Jørgensen rifle, an early inferior bolt-action weapon adopted by the U.S. army in 1892 and replaced by the M1903 eleven years later. Shown with the bolt open.

BRITISH AND COMMONWEALTH MANUFACTURERS

Ross rifle

Production: recorded as approximately 420,000, between 1903 and 1918.

This rifle was produced for use by Canadian forces during World War I and manufactured in a factory erected by Sir Charles Ross, the inventor of the rifle. This was a straight-pull bolt-action repeating rifle, fitted with an internal magazine, holding five .303 caliber British cartridges, which were charger-loaded. It was extremely accurate in trained hands, but suffered a number of design defects that made it unsuitable for use in the conditions experienced in trench warfare. One officer described it as the "contemptible Ross rifle," before going on to say, "Those in the front line with that rifle will never forget ... what it is like to be charged by the flower of the German army ... and be unable to fire a shot in return."[20]

P14 rifle

Production: precise records not available, but estimated at over 1.2 million weapons.

More correctly designated "Rifle, .303 Pattern 1914," this rifle was a conventional bolt-action repeating rifle with a five-round integral magazine and chambered for the .303 British cartridge. Unlike the Mauser rifles upon which its mechanism was based, the action of the P14 cocked on closing like the SMLE. It was produced in America as the M1917 Enfield and chambered for the .30-06 Springfield cartridge, its formal designation in the U.S. army being "United States Rifle, cal .30, Model of 1917."[21]

Pattern 1914 Enfield rifle, showing left and right sides.

French manufacturers

Fusil modèle 1866 or Chassepot

Production: recorded as over 1 million weapons between 1867 and 1874.

This rifle was produced exclusively for the French army, which adopted the weapon in 1866. It was a single-shot, bolt-action needle-fire rifle chambered for a 11mm lead bullet in a paper cartridge loaded with black powder.[22]

Fusil Gras Modèle 1874 M80

Production: precise records not available, but estimated at 400,000 weapons.

All of these rifles were converted from the original Chassepot M1866, and accepted into service with the French army in 1874. This was a single-shot, conventional bolt-action centerfire rifle chambered for the 11 × 59mmR Gras black powder cartridge, although some were rechambered later for the 8mm Lebel cartridge.[23]

Berthier rifles

Models:
Carbines: Mle1890, Mle1892, Mle1892/M16
Rifles: Mle1902, Mle1907, Mle1907/15 and Mle1916
Production: recorded as approximately 2 million of all models.

The first carbine was accepted into service with the French army in 1890, and two rifles with longer barrels were accepted in 1902 and 1907. All these weapons were conventional bolt-action repeating rifles with an internal box magazine capable of charger loading and holding either three or five rounds, depending upon the model. Originally chambered for the 8 × 50R mm Lebel cartridge, although some weapons were manufactured to chamber the later 7.5 × 54mmFrench cartridge, introduced in 1924.

Fusil Automatique Modèle 1917

Production: recorded as approximately 87,000 weapons in 1918, total production being supplied to the French army.

This was a semiautomatic, gas-operated rifle with a five-round internal box magazine, which could be loaded from a charger, and which was chambered for the 8 × 50mmR Lebel cartridge. It has the distinction of being the first self-loading service rifle.[24]

German Manufacturers

Mauser

Mauser Model 1871

Production: precise records not available, but estimated at 500,000 weapons.

Adopted by the Army of the German Empire in 1871, this was a single-shot, bolt-action centerfire rifle, chambered for a 11 × 60mm black powder cartridge.[25]

Mauser M1888

Production figures not accurately known, but probably approximately one million, all supplied originally to the German army.

Forerunner to the famous Gewehr '98, the M98 shared many design features with this earlier rifle, being a conventional bolt-action repeating rifle, fitted with a five-round external magazine capable of charger loading and chambered originally for the round-nosed M/88 smokeless cartridge.[26]

Karabiner 98k

Production recorded as over 14½ million weapons.

This rifle was accepted by the German army in 1935 to replace the M98, although it was largely based upon Mauser's earlier design. This was a conventional bolt-action repeating rifle, fitted with an internal magazine holding five cartridges that were capable of charger loading, and chambered for the 7.92 × 57 Mauser cartridge. It was the main German service rifle during World War II and was available with a number of accessories, including a grenade launcher and a noise suppressor.[27]

Japanese Manufacturers

The Arisaka service rifle

Production: not accurately known, but probably in excess of 10 million weapons of all models.

All these weapons were originally supplied to the Japanese Army and Navy between 1897 and 1945. All models were conventional bolt-action, repeating rifles with an internal box magazine containing five rounds and chambered for a variety of Japanese service cartridges[28]:

Variations

Only the most common variants are described.

- **Type 30 rifle and carbine:**
  Production: recorded as 554,000 rifles and 45,000 carbines from 1897 until 1905.
  Both weapons were chambered for the 6.5 × 50mmSR Type 30 cartridge as well as the .303 British and 6.5 × 54mm Mannlicher–Schönauer cartridges.
- **Type 35 rifle:**
  Production: recorded as approximately 38,000 rifles from 1902 until 1905.
  This was a modification of the type 30, with improvements to the rear sights, receiver mechanism and safety catch. This weapon was only chambered for the 6.5 × 50mm Arisaka cartridge.
- **Type 38 rifle and carbine:**
  Production: recorded as 3½ million rifles and carbines, from 1905 until 1939.
  Chambered for the 6.5 × 50mmSR Type 38 cartridge, it was also claimed to be safe with the original 6.5 × 50mmSR Type 30 cartridge.
- **Type 99:**
  Production: recorded as 2½ million rifles, from 1939 until 1945.
  Produced in response to a perceived need by the Japanese military authorities for a service rifle using a larger, more powerful cartridge, this weapon was chambered for the rimless 7.7 × 58 mm Arisaka cartridge, although manufacturing difficulties and a lack of raw materials meant that the earlier 6.5 mm cartridge was never entirely phased out.

Manufacturers in the USSR

The Moisin-Nagant service rifle:

Production: 37 million weapons between 1882 and 1945.

This was a conventional bolt-action rifle, chambered for the 7.62 × 54mmR cartridge and fitted with a five-round integral magazine that was loaded from a five-round charger. Its simple, strong construction has ensured that it has remained in use to the present (2016). Like the Mauser M98, its mechanism has two front locking lugs, although these lugs lock in a horizontal position, instead of vertically like the Mauser. There are a number of other differences, such as the operation of the bolt head cycling mechanism. Like the Mauser, the bolt is moved through 90 degrees to operate the mechanism, making it slower to operate than a SMLE.[29]

Variations

- **Model 1891 Infantry Rifle**: Russian service rifle from 1891 until 1930. Substantially unchanged from its first adoption, minor modifications included improved sights, a reinforcing piece in the stock to accommodate the new 147-grain spitzer bullet, new stronger barrel bands, and slot pattern sling mounts to replace the earlier swivel type. Shorter, lighter versions were produced for cavalry as the Dragoon and Cossack rifles.
- **Model 1907 Carbine**: A lighter, shorter version of the M1891, designed for issue to cavalry, engineer, signals, and artillery regiments.
- **Model 1891/30 rifle**: The most common of the Moisin-Nagant rifles and issued between 1930 and 1945. This rifle has dimensions similar to the earlier M1891 Dragoon rifle, being nearly one lb lighter at 7½ lbs and 2½ inches shorter than the original M1891 rifle, at only 45½ inches.
- **Model 1938 Carbine**: A shortened version of the M1891/30 rifle produced between 1939 and 1945. Both stock and barrel were reduced in length to give a weapon only 40 inches long overall. A Model 1944 Carbine was also produced between 1944 and 1948, which differed from the M1938 Carbine in having a permanently fixed, cruciform pattern spike bayonet, which folded along the side of the weapon.
- **Model 1891/59 Carbine**: Thought to have been produced during 1959 in Bulgaria, these were originally M1891/30 rifles, with barrels shortened to 40 inches and with the

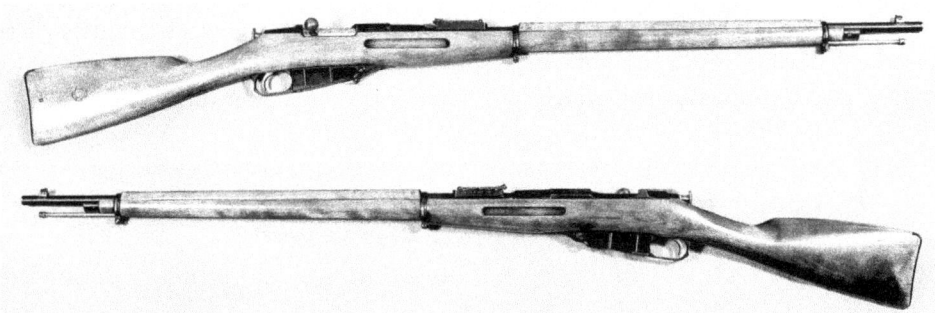

Moisin-Nagant M1891 Russian service rifle, showing right and left sides.

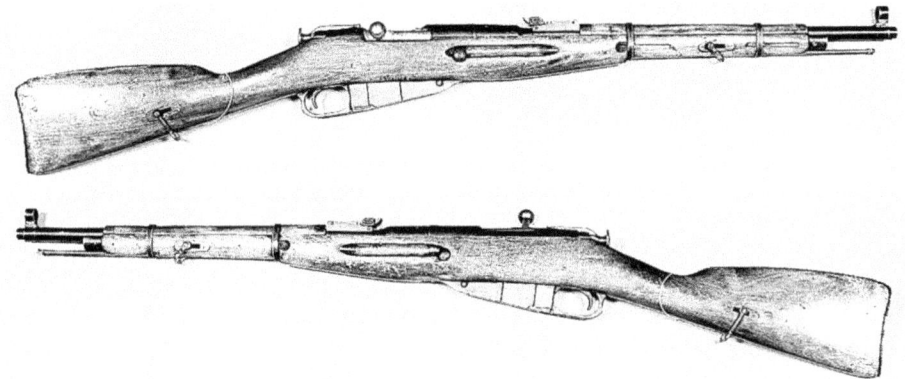

Moisin-Nagant M1938 Russian service rifle, showing right and left sides.

upper section of the rear sight numbers ground off to reflect the reduced range inherent in the shorter barrel. Receivers are usually stamped "**1891/59**," which serves to differentiate them from the earlier models.

The "Stopping Power" of Smokeless Ammunition

Until the introduction of the Lee-Metford rifle, augmenting the damage done by the ammunition supplied for the British army's small arms was not a problem given much attention by members of the military establishment.

Undeniably, there was a certain amount of justification for this attitude. Being shot either by the soft lead ball used in the Brown Bess musket or an officer's flintlock pistol, or by the shaped Minié bullet from an Enfield P53 or Springfield M1861 rifle, was not a pleasant experience, although the effects of the two types of projectile were significantly different. A Minié ball tended to cut a straight path through any tissue it encountered, regardless of obstructions, usually driving completely through any object it struck. In particular, bone would often be completely shattered by this type of projectile, almost invariably necessitating the amputation of any limb that received such a wound, and ushering in the usual nineteenth-century battlefield complications of shock and gangrene. By contrast, owing to their lower muzzle velocity and slightly lighter weight, the almost spherical balls used in a smoothbore musket or pistol tended to take a less direct path through the body, because any sort of obstruction, such as a bone, tendon or even a flexed muscle, could cause such a projectile to deviate from a straight passage through the tissue of the victim. Consequently, wounds caused by a musket ball were often much less severe than those from a rifle bullet.

Left: **The ball, powder and percussion cap used to load a conventional smoothbore musket.** *Right:* **A Minié ball, showing the flattened tip and three cannuleres or grooves characteristic of this projectile.**

This pattern of injury was also typical of wounds received from the Snider-Enfield and Martini-Henry rifles, which were the first weapons using metal cartridges to be accepted into service with the British Army. The Snider was a conversion of the P53 Enfield rifle and was designed to accept a .577 caliber centerfire black powder cartridge, while the Martini-Henry was originally chambered for the .577/.450 centerfire black powder cartridge, a modified .577 caliber Snider cartridge, which was "necked" or reduced in size to accept the .450 caliber bullet designed for the Martini-Henry rifle and carbine. Cartridges for both these rifles continued to use an unjacketed soft lead bullet, which caused much the same degree of damage as the earlier Minié bullet.

However, in 1889, a new black powder cartridge was accepted into service with the British Army, designed for use in its new .303 caliber Lee-Metford rifle. Originally, this cartridge had been designed to use cordite as its propellant, and it was also loaded with a much smaller bullet than had been used in any previous British Army long arm. In order to increase the accuracy of the new weapon, the original lead bullet was encased in a full metal jacket, which tended to deform less than a solid lead bullet when it was driven up the shallow Metford rifling. As well as the new rifles, a large number of Martinis were withdrawn from service and rechambered for this cartridge, although they were not in use for very long because, in 1891, the cartridge propellant was changed from black powder to cordite. This new smokeless cartridge was then designated "Cartridge SA (Small Arms) Ball .303 Inch Cordite Mark II" and, unfortunately, was directly responsible for ending the service life of the Lee-Metford.[30]

Left: Snider .577 cartridge. *Right*: Martini-Henry .577/.450 cartridge, this one in a later drawn brass case, showing the "necked" conformation.

THE LEE-METFORD IN SERVICE

This weapon was the first of the British Army's bolt-action, magazine service rifles, and although it was a considerable improvement over the single-shot Martini-Henry, it could not stand the strain of the new .303 caliber Mark II smokeless cartridge. In addition, and of considerably more practical importance, the bullet in the new cordite round was not very effective at killing the opposition. The provision of a steel jacket for the Metford bullet certainly produced a very accurate rifle while the rifling lasted, but when the British were forced to conduct a campaign in the mountainous region of Chitral, the troops found that their rifles were disconcertingly ineffective. Although the steel bullets seemed to penetrate the bodies of the tribesmen perfectly, they produced relatively little effect on anybody shot with one. This was particularly so when the Metford was used at close range. One tribesman, who was reported by the *British Medical Journal* as having been shot six times, still went on to recover, although admittedly only after extensive treatment in a British field hospital. Clearly, something was amiss, and investigation soon showed that the problem with the new steel-jacketed round was a lack of deformation on impact. Lead balls spread or "mushroomed" when they were fired into a human body, but the steel-jacketed Mark II bullet kept its shape after striking its victim and, consequently, traveled almost straight through a human body without causing significant tissue damage. Faced with these difficulties, the British military authorities decided on a redesign exercise, the Ordnance Board insisting that the new bullet should not just have more stopping power but must also retain all the accuracy of the original.[31]

THE DUM-DUM ARSENAL

Captain Neville Bertie-Clay was the officer responsible for solving the British Army's bullet problem. During 1896, Bertie-Clay was Superintendent of the Royal Artillery Arsenal at Domdoma in West Bengal, a name usually Anglicized from the original Bengali as "Dum-Dum." Using the facilities available to him in the arsenal at Domdoma, he produced a bullet in which the metal jacket was absent from just the tip, thus exposing the soft lead underneath. This design ensured that when the bullet struck human flesh it would "mushroom" uncontrollably and cause damage out of all proportion to its original size, while the retention of the steel jacket over the rest of the bullet ensured that it would retain its accurate shooting characteristics. Hollow-point "Express" bullets working on a similar principle had been used previously on heavy game such as elephants and buffalo, but this was the first military application of the idea. Trials in 1896 of the new "Dum-Dum" bullet confirmed its effectiveness, and this led to the adoption of the "Cartridge S.A. Ball .303 Cordite Mark III," which was simply a Mark II cartridge in which the lead tip of the bullet had been exposed. This was effectively a "soft-point" bullet. Intermittent problems with the jacket being stripped from the bullet upon firing, and consequently being left in the bore, led to the introduction of the hollow-point Mark IV bullet, although the problem of jacket-stripping had not been solved by the time the cartridge was withdrawn from use in 1899.

Commercial MkVII .303 British R cartridge, showing the covered tip of the bullet.

The British Army used the Mark III, Mark IV and Mark V on a number of occasions, most notably at the Battle of Omdurmen, where many of the British troops cut away the tops of their issue Mark II cartridges in order to convert them into the Mark III "Dum-Dum." However, in 1899, the Hague Convention prohibited the use of expanding ammunition against signatories of the treaty, declaring them "inhumane," and the remaining stocks, approximately 45 million rounds, were subsequently used only for target practice.[32]

BRITISH ARMY REVOLVER CARTRIDGES

The British army was not just concerned with the stopping power of its rifle cartridges. Revolver cartridges also came in for scrutiny, and development of the .455 caliber "Manstopper" bullet followed a process similar in many ways to the development of the .303 caliber Mark III.

The first revolver using a self-contained metal cartridge accepted into service by the British army was adopted in 1868, and was a conversion of the old percussion Beaumont-Adams revolvers already in use. No new weapons were ever purchased for this purpose, and conversion of the existing weapons consisted of the addition of a new cylinder, along with a loading gate and cartridge ejector. Since these revolvers were predominantly chambered in 54 bore, which was effectively .450 caliber, a new black powder cartridge was introduced. It was originally termed the .450 Boxer but was accepted into service as the .450 Adams, its official designation being "Cartridge, SA, Breech-Loading Boxer (Mark I)." This cartridge proved under-powered and largely ineffective, and was quickly replaced by the Mark II and Mark II, which were only slightly better, even when used in the new Adams Mark I and Mark II revolvers, which had been designed by John Adams, brother of Robert, and adopted by the Army in 1872.

In 1880, the British Army adopted another new revolver, the Enfield Mark I. This weapon and the later Mark II both used a new, slightly more powerful cartridge, the Enfield Mark I, in .476 caliber, later replaced by the Mark II, in .455 caliber, and the Mark III, which reverted to .476 caliber. Despite the apparent difference in size, the Enfield Mark I and Mark II revolvers would use all of these cartridges, because the case used by the Mark I, II and III was of .455 caliber and the changes only referred to a difference in the place where the bullet was measured. Unfortunately, the Enfield Mark I and Mark II revolvers proved unreliable when used in military service, and in 1887, yet another new revolver was accepted into service as "Pistol, Webley, MKI, B.L. Revolver." This was the Webley Mark I government-issue top-break revolver, the first of the long series of Webley service revolvers (Mark I to Mark VI) chambered for the familiar .455 Webley cartridge. The Mark I, Mark II and Mark III revolvers were stamped ".450/.476," and were thus also able to use the earlier Enfield .476 caliber black powder ammunition.[33]

Left: Webley Mark III, Mark IV and Mark V pistol cartridges, showing the conformation of the bullet. *Right*: Webley Mark III, Mark IV and Mark V pistol cartridges, from the side (both photographs, Wikipedia: License: CCA-S 3.0).

The Webley .455 Cartridge and Development of the "Manstopper" Bullet

The first Webley .455 cartridge, the Webley Mark I, was introduced into service in 1891 and designed to use black powder as the propellant, although some of the later Webley Mark I cartridges were loaded with cordite. These later cordite cartridges may be differentiated from the black powder round because they have a "C" included in the head stamp on the base of the cartridge. The first Webley cartridge specifically designed for cordite was the Webley Mark II, accepted into service in 1897 and now using a Berdan primer, rather than Boxer's device, and a shorter case than the earlier black powder round. The combination of the Webley Mark III and Mark IV revolvers together with this cartridge resulted in a weapon with a relatively mild, controllable recoil, but which still had good penetration characteristics, and hence excellent stopping power. Despite the excellent record of the Webley Mark II cartridge, however, the British Army's experience of the .303 Mark II convinced some senior figures that a more lethal round was required, and this led to the introduction in 1898 of what came to be known as the "Manstopper" bullet.[34]

Webley "Manstopper" Bullets: the Mark III, Mark IV and Mark V Cartridges

The Webley Mark III .455 cordite cartridge was approved for use by the British army on 5 February 1898, the same date as the Mark II cartridge, the later being declared obsolete later in the same year. Designated as "Cartridge, S A, Ball, Pistol, Webley, Cordite (Mark III)." it used the same .750 × .477-inch case as the Mark II but was loaded with a slightly smaller propellant charge, 7 grains of Mark I Cordite, as opposed to the 7.5 grains of the early Mark II cartridge. Its bullet also differed markedly from the earlier round, being of Webley's patented "Manstopping" pattern (British Patent 14754/1897), which featured a deep cavity in the nose and a similar depression in the base. It was also lighter, being 218.5 grains instead of the 265 grains of the conventionally shaped Mark II bullet. In combat the Mark III was shown to have considerable stopping power. Trials conducted by Thompson and Le Garde, to determine the caliber of pistol round which should be adopted by the U.S. military, obtained the same result. Unfortunately, the nature of the wounds produced by the bullet meant that, like the Mark III .303 cartridge, it contravened the 1899 Hague Convention. The British government was forced to order its withdrawal from service on 14 July 1900, finally declaring it obsolete on 18 November 1902. This led to the reintroduction of the Mark II cartridge with a lighter propellant charge of 6.25 grains of cordite, which was retained as the British army's pistol cartridge until the introduction of the Mark IV cartridge.

The Webley Mark IV .455 cartridge was introduced into British Army service on 23 November 1909, but not officially approved until 20 May 1912 as "Cartridge, S A, Ball, Pistol, Webley, Cordite (Mark IV)." This cartridge was also loaded with a pattern of "Manstopper" bullet which, although retaining the hollow base of the original bullet, was now flat-nosed and similar in conformation to a modern "wad-cutter" target bullet. This meant it had a less extreme effect when used against an opponent, although despite this modification it was declared obsolete after only two years service, again because of concerns about the

1899 Convention. The Mark II was reintroduced once more to replace it and remained in service until the jacketed Mark VI cartridge replaced it in 1939.

Although the Mark II was to remain the issue pistol cartridge after 1914, the British were still experimenting, and on 9 April 1914 another pistol cartridge with a "Manstopper" bullet was introduced. This was the Mark V, designated as "Cartridge, S A, Ball, Pistol, Webley, Cordite (Mark V)," and loaded with the same pattern of "Manstopping" bullet as the Mark IV. However, instead of being cast in the original 1:12 tin/lead alloy, as was the case for all the previous Webley bullets, this was made from a harder alloy of 99:1 lead/antimony. It proved remarkably unsuccessful and was declared obsolete on 9 November 1914, the remaining rounds being used for target practice.

The main problem with the .303 caliber Mark III and IV cartridges and Webley's "Manstopper" rounds was that they proved to be too effective. After the use of the Mark III at Omdurman and other battles, Germany lodged a protest against their use, claiming the wounds produced by such bullets to be "excessive and inhumane." Despite opposition from all the delegates at the Hague Convention of 1899, with the marked exception of the Americans, the British representative, Sir John Ardagh, attempted a vigorous defense of the round, explaining: "[M]en penetrated through and through several times by our latest pattern of small caliber projectiles, which make small clean holes, were nevertheless able to rush on and come to close quarters and some means had to be found to stop them." He went on: "The civilized soldier when shot recognizes that he is wounded and knows that the sooner he is attended to the sooner he will recover. He lies down on his stretcher and is taken off the field to his ambulance, where he is dressed or bandaged. Your fanatical barbarian, similarly wounded, continues to rush on, spear or sword in hand; and before you have the time to represent to him that his conduct is in flagrant violation of the understanding relative to the proper course for the wounded man to follow—he may have cut off your head." Despite these cogent arguments, the Convention voted to ban the future use of the Dum-Dum bullet in war by a majority of 22–2, a decision which also relegated the Webley "Manstopper" to obsolescence.

It was not just the British Army who were concerned about the stopping power of available small arms ammunition, however. In 1892, the U.S. Army had adopted a new pistol cartridge, the .38 caliber LC (Long Colt), for use in its new Colt New Army M1992 revolver, the weapon issued to officers at the beginning of the Philippines Campaign in 1899. Doubts soon arose over the effectiveness of this round, and the results of the Thompson-La Garde Tests in 1904, as well as conservative attitudes amongst senior U.S. army officers, led first to the reintroduction of the .45 caliber Colt Model P revolver and the adoption later of the famous Colt 1911 and 1911A self-loading pistols.

However, the U.S. Army learned from the British experience. The cartridge issued for the new 1911 self-loading pistol was loaded with a conventional, round-tipped bullet, which would not offend the delegates of the 1899 Convention, and relied upon its 230-grain bullet and 850 ft/sec muzzle velocity to disable its victim.[35]

CHAPTER THIRTEEN

Self-Loading or Semiautomatic Pistols

A semiautomatic or self-loading pistol is a handgun that requires only a single squeeze of the trigger to fire the weapon after loading and chambering a cartridge. It may then be fired continually until the magazine is empty by simply squeezing the trigger, since cycling the cartridge and cocking the hammer are carried out by the mechanism of the pistol. Such a weapon differs from a double-action pistol because the hammer of a semiautomatic pistol is cocked by residual cartridge gas operating the mechanism and not by the pressure of the user's finger pulling back the trigger, which in turn operates the hammer.[1]

John Browning

The man most associated with the development of the semiautomatic pistol was born in Ogden, Utah, on 23 January 1855. John Browning began working in his father's gun shop in 1862, at the age of seven, and in 1883, he sold the patent for a single-shot rifle he had developed to the Winchester Repeating Arms Company, and so began his distinguished career in firearms design. In 1898, after an altercation with Winchester over royalty fees, Browning moved to FN (Fabrique Nationale de Herstal), a new Belgian firearms manufacturer that was desperate for well-designed weapons. Browning found FN suited his innovative approach and spent the rest of his working life with the Belgian firm. He died of heart failure in 1926, while at a bench in his son's workshop, characteristically developing refinements for what would later become the Browning Hi-Power pistol.[2]

EARLY BROWNING "BLOWBACK" PISTOLS

Browning's first semiautomatic pistol design was the FN Browning M1900. It was a single-action, semiautomatic pistol with a simple blowback mechanism, chambered for Browning's .32 caliber ACP cartridge, and was the first design to use a slide surrounding the barrel and holding the bolt. He followed this with a procession of successful pistols for both FN and Colt, culminating in his M1911 self-loading pistol, adopted by the U.S. army in 1911 as the "Automatic Pistol, Caliber .45, Model of 1911" and retained as the U.S. military's service pistol until replaced by the 9mm Beretta M9 pistol in 1986.

Simple Blowback Operation

In a weapon with a blowback mechanism, the bolt rests against the rear of the barrel, but is not locked in place. When a cartridge is fired, the expanding gases from the charge push the bullet forward through the barrel while simultaneously pushing the case backwards against the bolt, driving it to the rear. The speed of the bolt's motion is determined by the mass of the bolt, internal friction, and the force required to compress the recoil spring, the design of the weapon ensuring that this delay is long enough for the bullet to exit the barrel before the cartridge case is ejected from the chamber. The empty case having been ejected as the slide, which also contains the bolt, travels to the rear, a recoil spring then drives the slide forward, stripping a cartridge from the magazine and forcing it into the chamber as the bolt returns to its original position, readying the pistol for firing. Blowback mechanisms are only practical for pistols using relatively low-power cartridges with lightweight bullets. Higher-power cartridges require heavier bolts to keep the breech from opening prematurely, and with the larger, more powerful cartridges, a point is reached where the bolt becomes too heavy to be practical, at least in a pistol designed to be operated with one hand. However, there are a number of reliable submachine guns produced in pistol calibers, such as 9mm Parabellum and .45 ACP, which do use a simple blowback mechanism, usually firing from an open bolt. These types include the British STEN, the Sterling, the Israeli UZI and later versions of the Thompson.

In light of the drawbacks of simple blowback operation, a number of designers tried to use the system as the basis for a mechanism that delayed the rearward passage of the bolt and consequently allowed the use of a more powerful cartridge. Not surprisingly, such systems are referred to as "delayed" blowback, and include roller-delayed, lever-delayed, gas-delayed, and a number of other types.[3]

Colt's M1911 Self-Loading Pistol

Development

The Colt M1911 pistol was designed to compete in a series of trials instigated by the U.S. military in 1906 to find a new pistol chambered for a .45 caliber pistol round.

During the Philippine-American Insurrection (1899–1902), the Americans had encountered problems with the stopping power of their service revolver, the Colt M1892 chambered for the .38 caliber Long Colt black powder cartridge. In light of this salutary experience, a series of tests, known as the Thompson-LaGarde tests after the men who conducted them, were carried out to determine the effectiveness of a variety of pistol cartridges. The ammunition tested included:

- 7.65 × 22mm Parabellum (.30 Luger)
- 9 × 19mm Parabellum
- .38 caliber Long Colt
- .38 caliber ACP
- .45 ACP in both blunt and hollow-point conformations

- .476 caliber Eley
- .455 caliber Webley Mk III "Manstopper"

Although the Webley Mk III "Manstopper" proved superior to all the other cartridges, the U.S. Army adopted the .45 caliber ACP cartridge as their standard pistol round. However, clearly the cartridge was of little use without a reliable pistol to fire it. In 1906, the U.S. Army conducted a further series of trials on semiautomatic pistols chambered for this cartridge submitted by Colt, Bergmann, DWM, Savage, Knoble, Webley (the Webley-Fosbery revolver) and White-Merril.

Browning's small pistols based on his "blowback" mechanism could not be modified to fire the .45 caliber ACP cartridge. Although the mechanism was simple and robust, it was unsuitable for this more powerful cartridge, because the bolt would need to be made prohibitively heavy for the mechanism to operate safely, such that the bullet left the barrel before the cartridge case was extracted from the chamber. Aware of the disadvantages of his blowback system, Browning designed a pistol for the 1906 competition with a much stronger short-recoil, toggle-locked mechanism, which Colt submitted as their entry.

The final choice was between the Savage Arms Company's Model 1907, which had a fragile, delayed blowback mechanism, and the Colt pistol. In a final test, six thousand rounds were fired from a single pistol over the course of two days, the weapons being cooled by immersion in water when they became hot. Browning's pistol was reported as having no stoppages during this test, while the Savage M1907 had a total of 37. Consequently, the Colt pistol was accepted into service with the U.S. Army on 29 March 1911 as the "Automatic Pistol, Caliber .45, Model of 1911." In 1917, this was changed to "Automatic Pistol, Caliber .45, Model 1911," later changed to "Automatic Pistol, Caliber .45, M1911" in the mid–1920s. In 1924, a new modified pistol was introduced and designated the Model 1911A1, incorporating changes to the original design which consisted of:

- a shorter trigger
- cutouts in the frame behind the trigger
- an arched mainspring housing
- a longer grip safety spur, specifically designed to alleviate the tendency in the early model to trap the web of the shooter's thumb between the hammer and the frame when the weapon cycled
- a wider front sight
- a shortened hammer spur
- simplified grip checkering, which eliminated the complex "Double Diamond" pattern.

Examination of the grip for these diamonds at the top and bottom of the butt plates is the quickest way to differentiate between a M1911 and a M1911A1.

Colt New Army Model 1892, chambered for .38 caliber Long Colt black powder cartridge, which proved so unreliable during the Philippines campaign (Wikipedia: License: CC-A-S-A 3.0).

Both models remained in service with the U.S. armed forces until 1986, when the Beretta M9, chambered for that old favorite, the 9 × 19mm Parabellum cartridge, was adopted as the "Pistol, Semiautomatic, 9mm, M9." The M1911 pistol has been copied by manufacturers in a number of countries including Argentina, Brazil, Mexico and Spain.[4]

Specification

Production:
Serial number ranges: Military pistols:
Colt factory and other contractors: 1-22693613
Remington-UMC: 1-21676
Springfield Arsenal: X72751–X133186
Serial number range: Civilian pistols:
Serial number range: C1-C336169, all M1911 pistols manufactured for the civilian market are "C" prefixed.[5]

The M1911 pistol is a semiautomatic weapon, with a short recoil, toggle-link mechanism, fitted with a magazine holding seven rounds and chambered for .45 caliber ACP cartridge. It is a single-action weapon, which means that even with a round in the chamber, the weapon must be cocked by the user to begin the first cycle of operation, although subsequent cartridges are fired by simply squeezing the trigger. Later designs of automatic pistol, such as the Beretta M9, have a double-action mechanism, such that they can be safely carried with a round chambered and the hammer not cocked, since it is only necessary to draw the weapon and squeeze the trigger to fire the chambered cartridge. Early military M1911 pistols usually have a blue finish, while later guns are "Parkerized"; weapons sold commercially are much more variable. Iron sights are fitted and butt plates are in two pieces, military weapons featuring either walnut or hard rubber, commercial weapons once more showing a much wider variation.

Frame Markings

Military pistols

Right side stamped, below the slide:

UNITED STATES PROPERTY M1911A1 U.S. ARMY

An unprefixed serial number is stamped below "UNITED STATES PROPERTY" and the "U.S. ARMY" stamp may be substituted for "U.S. NAVY" or "U.S.M.C," depending upon the provenance of the weapon. Weapons made in the Springfield Arsenal have a serial number with an "X" prefix.

Left side stamped, on slide:

PATENTED APR.20.1897. SEPT.9.1902 COLT.S PT.F.A. MFG.CO.
DEC.19.1905. FEB.14.1911. AUG.1913 HARTFORD.CT.USA

The "Dancing Colt" trademark is stamped between the patent dates and the manufacturer's details.

Civilian pistols

Right side stamped, on the slide:

COLT AUTOMATIC

and underneath "AUTOMATIC" is stamped:

CALIBRE .45

followed by the "Dancing Colt" trademark.

Below the slide is stamped:

GOVERNMENT MODEL
C XXXXX

"C XXXX" represents the "C" prefixed serial number.

Left side stamped, on slide:

PATENTED APR.20.1897. SEPT.9.1902 COLT.S PT.F.A. MFG.CO.
DEC.19.1905. FEB.14.1911. AUG.1913 HARTFORD.CT.USA

The "Dancing Colt" trademark is stamped between the patent dates and the manufacturer's details. The stamp may also appears as:

COLT'S PT. FA. MFG CO. HARTFORD. CT. U.S.A
PAT'D APR.APR.20.1897. SEPT.9.1902. DEC.19.1905. FEB.14.1911. AUG.1913.

The lower letters are sized so that the lines are of corresponding lengths. Patent dates were not included in this stamp after 1938.[6]

Colt M1911, the first semiautomatic pistol accepted into service with the U.S. military and chambered for the .45 caliber ACP cartridge (Wikipedia: License: CC-A-S-A 3.0).

Thirteen. Self-Loading or Semiautomatic Pistols

Colt 1911A1 self-loading pistol, introduced 1924, after some minor improvements had been incorporated into the design (Wikipedia: License: CC-A-S-A 3.0).

M1911 field stripped to show the component parts.

Operation

To fire the weapon, a loaded magazine is first pushed firmly into the butt cavity until the magazine catch is heard to click, indicating the magazine is properly seated. The slide is then pulled back to its full extent and released, which removes a cartridge from the magazine and pushes it into the chamber. The manual safety may now be operated, rendering the weapon safe to carry with the hammer either up or down. To fire the weapon with the hammer cocked, the manual safety catch is depressed, the butt is gripped firmly to operate the butt safety mechanism, and the trigger is squeezed. Subsequent shots are fired by simply squeezing the trigger, although care must be taken to grip the butt firmly, otherwise the butt safety mechanism is insufficiently depressed and the gun will not operate.

The short-recoil mechanism

The short-recoil, toggle-locked mechanism of the M1911 pistol consists of a barrel and slide which initially recoil together for a short distance until the barrel is unlocked and moved vertically downward away from the slide by a toggle link mechanism, a system which was copied in a number of later pistols.

When a cartridge is fired, the barrel and slide recoil together until the toggle mechanism causes the chamber and the barrel to be drawn downward and stopped. This downward movement of the barrel disengages it from the locking recesses in the slide, which continues rearward, the spent case being removed from the chamber and ejected from the weapon by the operation of the extractor, while the slide reaches the end of its travel and recocks the hammer. Having also reached the limit of its travel, the recoil spring pushes the slide forward again, removing (stripping) a new round from the magazine and pushing it into the chamber, while simultaneously pushing the chamber and barrel forward. As the barrel and chamber move forward, the toggle mechanism in turn moves them upward and the lugs on the barrel re-engage those in the slide, locking the slide and barrel together prior to firing. The weapon is now cocked and ready to fire.[7]

Variations

Military issued weapons are either the M1911 or M1911A1, with the standard finish and butt plates. Civilian weapons, as might be expected, show considerably more variation, with modified weapons being produced by a number of U.S. companies.

Values

NRA Good: $1,000; NRA Fine: $2,000

Weapons made by the North American Arms Company and Singer Manufacturing Company are rare and may reach in excess of $10,000 at auction.[8]

Luger Self-Loading Pistol

Development

Designated the Pistole Parabellum 1908, this design was a development of the C-93 pistol patented by Hogo Borchardt in 1893. Borchardt's original pistol was accurate and reliable, with a good rate of fire using his own 7.65 × 25mm cartridge, but was awkward to shoot because of its weight distribution and powerful recoil. Despite these shortcomings, over 3,000 weapons were manufactured by Loewe and Company of Berlin and DWM, who took over the later production of the pistol. The management of DWM appointed Borchardt's assistant, one Georg Luger, to go to America and sell the pistol to the U.S. military. It was tested by both the U.S. Navy, in 1904, and later by the Army, but was rejected because of its awkward shooting characteristics. Borchardt refused to make any design changes, and DWM requested that Luger modify the gun, which he did initially by adopting DWM's new 7.65 × 21mm Parabellum cartridge for the weapon, a cartridge designed as a result of a collaborative effort between Luger and Borchardt. This allowed him to shorten the stroke of the toggle mechanism and incorporate a narrower, more angular grip, resulting in a weapon that finally became the Luger Parabellum pistol. The name "Parabellum" incidentally is derived from the Latin motto of DWM: "Si vis pacem, para bellum" ("If you seek peace, prepare for war").

Above: Borchardt self-loading pistol, one of the first weapons of this type designed to use a high-power cartridge. *Below:* Borchardt self-loading pistol with the breech open, showing the similarities in construction with the later Luger pistol (courtesy James D. Julia Auctioneers, Fairfield, Maine. www.jamesdjulia.com).

The early OPOO pistol was adopted by the Swiss army in 1900, still chambered for the 7.65 × 21mm Parabellum cartridge. By 1902 Luger had developed his famous 9 × 19mm Parabellum round, which was adopted by German Navy in 1904 and the German Army in 1908. All Luger pistols supplied to those two arms of the German military were subsequently chambered for the new 9mm cartridge.[9]

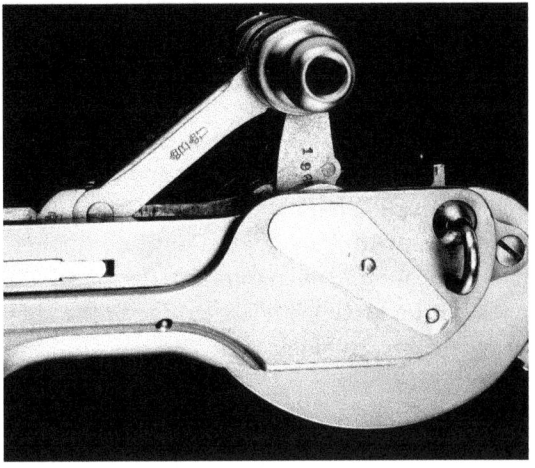

Specification

Production: precise records not available, but estimated at approximately 3 million weapons.

Serial numbers: Lugers usually bear a four- or five-digit serial number, stamped on the frame. This numbering was repeated monthly by the various manufacturers, some weapons also bearing a letter prefix or suffix that identifies the maker. Serial numbers were often stamped on both the receiver and barrel, and thus numbers on any of these components that do not match indicate a pistol assembled from parts taken from several other weapons and may significantly decrease its value.

Although based upon the Borchadt self-loading pistol, Luger's weapon shares a number of characteristics with the M1911 pistol, being a semiautomatic weapon with a short-recoil, toggle-link mechanism, although it differs from the Colt in being fitted with a slightly larger magazine holding eight rounds. Barrels are between 100mm and 200mm depending upon the model, and a safety catch is fitted to the rear of the breech, which consists of a short lever pivoted at the lower end. With the lever pushed down, the safety catch is operative and the word "GESICHERT" (trans: made safe) is revealed on the frame. Pushing the lever up covers the word and renders the weapon ready to fire. Finish is usually standard blue, but commercially produced guns may have a variety of more expensive treatments. Iron sights are fitted and butt plates are separate and of walnut, beech or plastic, depending upon date of manufacture; the bottom of the magazine is usually a wooden plug matching the butt plates. Lugers were chambered for a variety of cartridges, including 7.62 × 21mm Parabellum, and a few rare arms chambered for the .45 caliber ACP cartridge. However, most of these pistols were designed for the ubiquitous 9 × 19mm Parabellum cartridge, also designated the 9 × 19mm Luger, which is probably the world's most popular and widely used military handgun cartridge.[10]

Frame markings

Manufacturers' names or their trademarks are usually stamped on the top of the toggle mechanism, with a date of manufacture on the front of the breech. Proof marks are also present, stamped on the forward portion of the receiver.

Operation

To operate the weapon, a loaded magazine is pushed into the butt cavity until the magazine catch is heard to click, indicating the magazine is properly seated. With the pistol held in the right hand, the knurled knobs on either side of the toggle joint are pulled firmly to the rear with the left hand until no further movement is possible. Releasing the knobs allows the joint to snap forward, chambering a cartridge. The safety may now be operated or the pistol fired. With a cartridge in the chamber, the front end of the extractor projects above the breech block, exposing the word "GELADEN" (trans: loaded) on the left side of the extractor.

The Luger uses a jointed arm to lock the mechanism when firing, as opposed to the slide actions of almost every other semiautomatic pistol. After a cartridge has been fired,

Above: **Luger Parabellum 9mm self-loading pistol, a development of the earlier Borchardt (courtesy James D. Julia Auctioneers, Fairfield, Maine. www.jamesdjulia.com).** *Below:* **Toggle link system of a Luger pistol, shown with the breech open (courtesy Rama, Wikimedia Commons, CC-BY-SA-2.0-Fr).**

the locked barrel and toggle assembly are driven backwards until the toggle strikes a cam built into the frame, causing the jointed arm to operate, unlocking the barrel and toggle assembly, which holds the bolt and firing pin. Simultaneously, the barrel impacts the frame and stops, while the jointed toggle assembly continues moving, extracting the spent case from the chamber and ejecting it. The toggle and breech assembly are subsequently driven forward by the recoil spring, stripping the next round from the magazine

and loading it into the chamber. The Luger mechanism works reliably when used with ammunition containing relatively large powder loads, but the use of low-powered cartridges can result in stoppages, because they do not generate enough recoil to work the action properly, resulting in the breech block's either not clearing the top cartridge of the magazine, or jamming open on the cartridge's base.[11]

Variations

- **Ordonnanzpistole 00 or OP00:** Adopted by the Swiss army in 1900, this model was fitted with a 120mm barrel.
- **Pistole 04:** Accepted by the Imperial German Navy in 1904, this model, known as the

"Navy" Model, had a 150mm barrel and a two-position rear sight, with settings for 100 and 200 meters.
- **Pistole 08 or P.08:** Accepted by the German army in 1908, this model was fitted with a 100mm barrel and chambered for the 9 × 19mm Parabellum cartridge. The P.08 was the usual side arm for German Army officers and specialized NCOs in both World Wars, though it was replaced by the Walther P38 from 1938. DWM (Deutsche Waffen und Munitionsfabriken) were the original manufacturers of the P.08, until Mauser began manufacture in 1930, continuing in this role until 1943.
- **Lange Pistole 08 or LP.08, the Artillery Model:** This was a slightly later model designed for use by German artillerymen as a useful compromise between the short-range P.08 and a G.98 rifle, which had longer range but was more awkward for an artilleryman to carry and handle. This version of the P.08 had a 200mm barrel, an 8-position tangent rear sight calibrated to 800 meters, and a shoulder stock which doubled as a holster, in a manner similar to Mauser's C96. It used the standard Luger 8-round box magazine, but could also be fitted with a 32-round drum-pattern magazine, designated the Trommelmagazin 08. Early LP.08s had micrometer front and rear sights which required a 2-pin tool for adjustment, and the pistol was also available commercially with longer barrels.[12]

Values

Difficult to assess, but expect to pay between $1,500 and $2,000 for a standard P.08 with a 4 inch barrel, with prototypes and carbines considerably more expensive, possibly as much as $20,000.

NRA Good: $1,500–$2,000; NRA Fine: $4,000–$5,000

Mauser C96 Self-Loading Pistol

Development

Mauser's C96 series of semiautomatic pistols was the product of the combined talents of the three Federle brothers, who were working for Mauser in 1894. Patented by Mauser in 1895, the gun was originally chambered for the 7.65 × 25mm Borchardt cartridge, but design problems forced the company to introduce a new, more powerful cartridge for the pistol, the 7.63 × 25mm Mauser. These early guns were produced with magazines holding 6, 10 or 20 cartridges, although this was soon standardized to the 10-round version. The new, more powerful cartridge solved the cycling problems inherent in the mechanism of the C96 when using the earlier Borchardt cartridge, giving the pistol an accurate range of approximately 150 meters when used with the shoulder stock. The C96 was produced from 1895 until 1937, exclusively by Mauser. Since it is a popular gun with a strong, reliable action made for a cartridge that can be obtained without trouble, there are many still in use by civilian owners.[13]

Specification

Production: precise records not available, but estimated at over 1 million weapons.

Serial numbers: 1–1000000, in an indeterminate number of series, some of which are associated with the most important contracts entered into by Mauser for these pistols. Serial numbers are found stamped on the sight, back of sight cursor, bolt stop, firing pin retainer, hammer, and frame, as well as a number of internal components. Guns with matching serial numbers on all components are highly valued, and this is reflected in their auction price.

The Mauser C96 was a short-recoil, cam-operated semiautomatic pistol, with an internal box magazine holding ten cartridges and chambered most commonly for either the 7.63 × 25mm Mauser cartridge or the 9 × 19mm Parabellum cartridge. Barrels varied in length from 99mm up to 140mm, frames usually being blued and the butt having two separate, characteristically shaped plates.

Mauser C-96 self-loading pistol, this example the Commercial Model 1895 with 140mm barrel and ten-round magazine (courtesy James D. Julia Auctioneers, Fairfield, Maine. www.jamesdjulia.com).

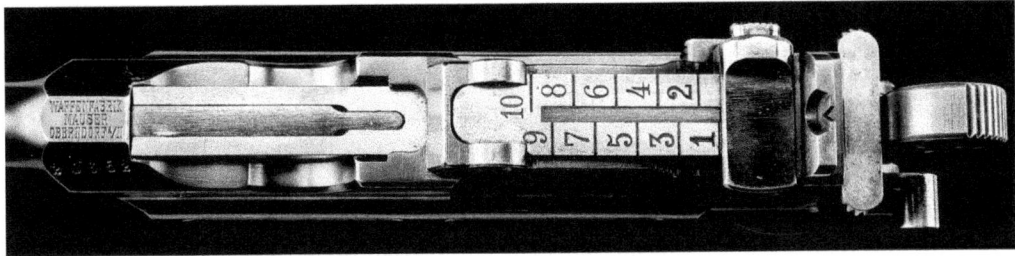

Standard adjustable sights fitted to a Mauser C-96 pistol (courtesy James D. Julia Auctioneers, Fairfield, Maine. www.jamesdjulia.com).

Frame Markings

The top of the chamber is stamped:

WAFFENFABRICK
MAUSER
OBERNDOR^A/N

Military weapons will be found stamped with the relevant proof marks, usually on the left side of the receiver, while acceptance marks are stamped on the right for any weapon with a German Imperial Army provenance, although this position may be variable with weapons made for other contracts.

Operation

To operate a Mauser C96, the slide is first pulled back to its full extent and locked. This opens the breech and reveals the charger clip guide. A charger containing ten cartridges in the appropriate caliber is inserted into the guide and the cartridges are pushed into the internal magazine. The slide release is then operated and a cartridge is chambered. With the hammer being already cocked, the pistol can now be fired, although there is a safety catch on the left side which allows the gun to be carried safely with a round chambered and the hammer cocked.

Upon firing, the barrel and bolt, which are locked together, are moved backwards by the cartridge gases against a substantial spring, the weight of the bolt and force in the spring being designed to allow the bullet to travel down the barrel and exit the gun before the spent case leaves the breech. Rearward movement of the barrel and bolt assembly operates a cam, which separates the barrel and bolt, allowing the bolt to move completely to the end of its travel, compressing the bolt recoil spring and extracting and ejecting the spent case, while simultaneously cocking the hammer. The recoil spring then pushes the bolt forward, removing a fresh cartridge from the magazine, chambering it and leaving the gun ready to fire again.

Variations

- **Commercial Model 1895**: Production approximately 1 million guns between 1895 and 1937, and the most common of the Mauser C96 variants. Chambered for the 7.63 × 25mm Mauser cartridge with a 140mm barrel and an internal magazine holding ten cartridges.
- **M1896 Kavallerie Karabiner**: Experimental design intended for cavalry use and featuring a permanently fixed wooden stock and 300mm or 370mm barrel. There were also a number of C96 carbines produced fitted with a permanently attached stock and wooden foregrip.
- **1896 Compact Mauser**: Produced until 1899, this version of the M1895 was fitted with a full-sized grip, 6-shot internal magazine, and a 120mm barrel. This variant was also produced as the **M1896 Officer's Mauser**, which was fitted with wooden or hard rubber butt plates and a curved grip similar to a revolver.

- **M1898 Pistol Carbine:** First M1895 Mauser C96 to have the butt modified to accept the combination wooden stock/holster.
- **M1912 Mauser Export Model:** Conventional M1895 C96 Mauser pistol, rechambered for the Mauser 9 × 25mm Mauser cartridge.
- **M1920 Mauser Rework:** C96 modified from previously issued guns, to comply with the Treaty of Versailles, which imposed a barrel length of less than 100mms and stipulated that pistols must be smaller than 9mm in caliber if sold in Germany or issued to German forces. Consequently, these pistols have barrels which have been reduced in length to 99 mm, along with a fixed sight, and are rechambered for the early 7.63 × 25mm Mauser cartridge.
- **M1921 "Bolo" Mauser:** Production from 1921 until 1930, being designed to comply with the Versailles Treaty requirements. This version was produced by Mauser as a new pistol, fitted with a 99mm barrel and chambered for the 7.63 × 25mm Mauser cartridge. It became commonly associated with the Bolshevik movement and was hence designated the "Bolo" Model.
- **M1930 Mauser:** Production from 1930 until 1937. This was a modification of the M1921, with a longer 132mm barrel, the conventional butt of the original M1895 and the omission of several expensive machining operations during production, which had been found to be unnecessary. Later weapons were fitted with a 140mm barrel.
- **M1932/M712 Schnellfeuer:** Production from 1932 until 1936, with nearly 100,000 guns being manufactured. This was a select fire (automatic and semiautomatic) weapon, with a detachable magazine replacing the internal component of the older guns, although it was still chambered for the original 7.63 × 25mm Mauser cartridge and fitted with a 132mm barrel.

In addition to these variations, there were a number of pistols made under specific contracts.

- **1897 Turkish Army Mauser:** Production: 1,000 guns with their own serial number range, for the Ottoman government, 1897. Six-pointed star on both sides of chamber, with crossed Turkish flags and "1314" on the left rear frame panel.
- **1899 Italian Navy Mauser:** Production: 5,000 guns in their own serial number range during 1899.
- **1910 Persian Contract Mauser:** Production: 1,000 guns in a serial number range from 154000 to 154999 during 1910 for the Persian government. Stamped with Persian "Lion and Sun" insignia.
- **M1916 Austrian Contract Mauser:** Production: 50,000 guns, chambered for the 7.63 × 25mm Mauser cartridge. A small number were rechambered for the 8mm Gasser cartridge, probably because supplies of the Mauser round were hard to obtain in the later stages of World War I.
- **M1916 Prussian "Red 9" Contract Mauser:** Production: 137,000 guns, so the most important of the contract guns, more especially because the guns were ordered in 9 × 19mm Parabellum to compensate for the slow production of the Luger P08. These guns are easily recognizable, having a large figure "9" burnt into the butt plates, this figure being subsequently lined out in red paint, which resulted in this variant receiving the designation "Red 9." The guns were marked in this way to ensure that only 9 ×

19mm Parabellum ammunition was used in the guns and not the more usual 7.63 × 25mm Mauser cartridge.
- **1920 French Police Contract:** Production: 1,000 weapons with 99mm barrels and ebonite butt plates for the French Gendarmerie Nationale.
- **World War II Luftwaffe Contract:** Production: 7,800 of the later Model 30 pistols, stamped with Wehrmacht proof marks.[14]

"Red" Mauser C-96, chambered for the ubiquitous 9x19mm Parabellum cartridge, with stripper clip in position for loading. The red "9" scored into the handle serves to differentiate this model from those chambered for the 7.63x25mm Mauser cartridge (Wikipedia: License: CC-A-S-A 2.5).

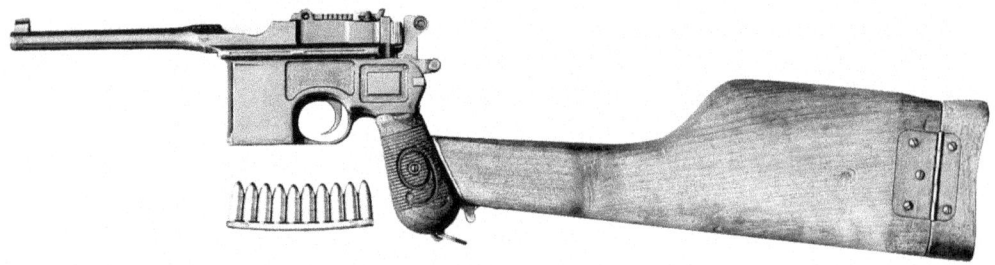

"Red" Mauser C-96, with a shoulder stock fitted (Wikipedia: License: CC-A-S-A 2.5).

VALUES

Difficult to assess, but expect to pay between $2,000 and $4,000 for the most common commercial Model in 7.63 × 25mm Mauser and correspondingly more for rare models and any weapon with 9 × 19mm Parabellum chambering. Models with a six shot magazine may reach in excess of $30,000.

NRA Good: $2,000–$3,000; NRA Fine: $4,000–$5,000

Table Nineteen: Comparison of the specification of the C96, Luger p.08 and Colt 1911 pistols

Weapon	Mauser C96	Luger	Colt 1911
Makers	Mauser, Hanyang Arsenal, China	DWM, Mauser (from 1930), Vickers, Simson (BSW), Kreighoff, Imperial arsenals at: Efurt and Spandau	Colt's Manufacturing Company, Springfield arsenal, Remington UMC, Remington Rand, Itahaca Gun Co., Konsberg Vaapenfabrikk
Period of production	1896–1961	1898–1942	1911 until present day
Production	Approximately one million made by Mauser; Chinese-made guns not recorded	Not recorded, but certainly several million	Recorded as over 2.7 million weapons
Military service	Spanish-American War, Second Boer War, Boxer Rebellion, Xinhai Revolution, World War I, Anglo-Irish War, Finnish Civil War, Mexican Revolution, Philippine Revolution, Philippine-American War, Russian Civil War, Spanish Civil War, Second Sino-Japanese War, World War II, Chinese Civil War, Korean War, Vietnam War, Soviet war in Afghanistan	**German service pistol:** World War I German Revolution Spanish Civil War World War II **Other users:** Second Sino-Japanese War Chinese Civil War Rhodesian Bush War	**U.S. service pistol:** World War I World War II Korean War Vietnam War **Other users:** Persian Gulf War War in Afghanistan Iraq War Syrian Civil War
Weight	Approximately 2½ lbs	Approximately 2 lbs	2.4 lbs empty 3 lbs with full magazine
Length/Barrel length	12.5 inches/ Barrel 4–5.5 inches	8.75 inches/ Barrel 3.75–8 inches	8.25 inches/ Barrel 5 inches
Mechanism	Semiautomatic, short recoil, toggle-locked mechanism	Semiautomatic, short recoil, toggle-locked mechanism	Semiautomatic, short recoil, toggle-locked mechanism
Cartridge	7.63 × 25mm Mauser 9 × 19mm Parabellum	7.65 × 21mm Parabellum	.45 caliber ACP 7 round box magazine

Weapon	Mauser C96	Luger	Colt 1911
	.45 ACP (China) 8mm Gasser 10-round internal magazine fed by charger. Removable magazine in the M1932	.45 ACP (very rare) 9 × 19mm Parabellum 8-round box magazine 32-round detachable drum magazine	located in the butt
Sights	Front sight: inverted V Rear sight: V-notch tangent sight adjustable up to 1000 meters	Front sight: Inverted "V" blade Rear sight: Non-adjustable open "V" notch	Front sight: Blade Rear sight: Simple notch pattern, with no adjustment
Maximum range	150–200 meters with shoulder stock	50 meters with 4-inch barrel	25 meters
Rate of fire	20 rpm, depending upon experience of user	20 rpm, depending upon experience of user	20 rpm, depending upon user's experience
Cost in 1940	Record not readily available	$13 (£5.50)	$20 (£4)

Other Self-Loading Pistols

Self-loading pistols were produced in a number of countries. Firearms manufacturers and companies offering such arms for sale before World War II included a number of well-known and long-established manufacturers.

AMERICAN MANUFACTURERS

Colt

Most of Browning's early semiautomatic pistols were manufactured by FN, with variants and some new models also offered by Colt[15]:

- **Colt M1900**

  Production: over 4,000 weapons, in their own serial number range. Single-action, short-recoil operated, semiautomatic pistol chambered for the .38 caliber ACP cartridge. Barrel was 6 inches with a magazine holding seven cartridges. Colt's first semiautomatic pistol; approximately 250 were purchased for U.S. military service.

- **Colt M1902**

  Production: approximately 25,000 of both the Sporting Model (1902–1907) and the Military Model (1902–1928).

Colt 1900 from the right side, showing the ejection port (courtesy James D. Julia Auctioneers, Fairfield, Maine. www.jamesdjulia.com).

Thirteen. Self-Loading or Semiautomatic Pistols 195

Essentially an improvement on the M1900 with the same short-recoil operation and six-inch barrel, only the Military Model differed from its predecessor in having an 8-round magazine.

- **Colt Model 1903 Pocket Hammer**

  Production: 26,000 weapons between 1902 and 1929.

  Essentially a short-barreled M1902, with a magazine holding seven .38 caliber ACP cartridges and with a 4½-inch barrel. The internal mechanism differed from later Colts in having two toggle links and a retaining wedge in the slide near the muzzle. It was not uncommon for less experienced shooters to reassemble the pistol after cleaning without inserting the wedge, resulting in the slide leaving the frame to the rear past the hammer, resulting in injury to the operator.

- **Colt Model 1903 Pocket Hammerless**

  Production: over 570,000 pistols between 1903 and 1946.

  Fitted with a hammer covered by the rear of the slide and a magazine designed to hold eight .32 ACP cartridges, with either a 4-inch or 3¾-inch barrel, this was a semi-automatic, single-action pistol, with a simple blowback

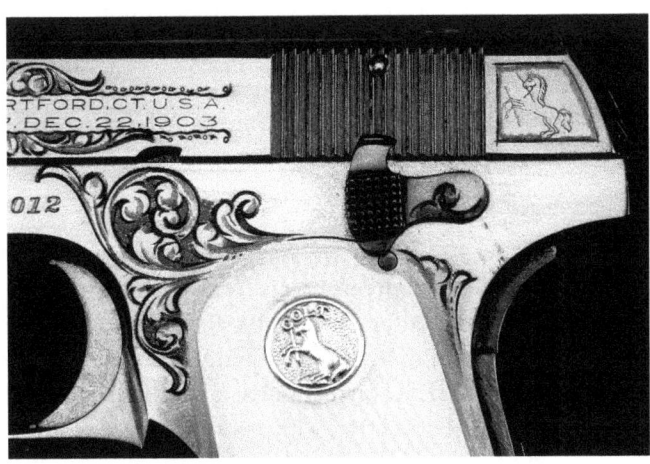

Top: Colt 1903 Pocket Hammerless semiautomatic pistol from the right side, showing the ejection port and caliber information. *Middle:* Colt 1908 Pocket Hammerless semi-automatic pistol from the right side, showing the ejection port and caliber information. *Bottom:* Colt 1908 Pocket Hammerless semiautomatic pistol from the left side, showing detail of the safety catch (all three photographs courtesy James D. Julia Auctioneers, Fairfield, Maine. www.jamesdjulia.com).

mechanism. A similar weapon was produced in 1908, chambered for .380 caliber ACP and designated the "Model 1908 Hammerless" or Model "M."

- **Colt Model 1908 Vest Pocket**
  Production: over 400,000 pistols between 1908 and 1941.

  This was a hammerless semiautomatic single-action pistol with a striker mechanism, chambered for the .25 ACP cartridge, with a box magazine holding six cartridges and a 2-inch barrel. Weighing only 13 ounces and with a total length of only 4½ inches, it was a favorite weapon for "concealed carry," as its name implied.

Colt 1908 Vest Pocket pistol from the right, showing the ejection port and caliber information (courtesy James D. Julia Auctioneers, Fairfield, Maine. www.jamesdjulia.com).

- **Colt Model 1909**
  Production: 10 guns.

  Prototype pistol developed for testing by the U.S. army. Similar in conformation and operation to the M1911.

- **Colt Model 1910**
  Production: 23 guns.

  A second prototype, modified after the faults in the M1909 had developed during the 1906 test, this was the successful version which was accepted as the "Colt Model of 1911."

- **US M1911 and M1911A:** The U.S. military's service pistol between 1911 and 1986.

Remington

- **1911 R1:** This was a licensed copy of the Colt M1911, produced for use in World War I between 1910 and 1919.[16]

Savage

- **Model 1907**
  Production: precise records not available, but estimated at 100,000 weapons.

  A competitor in the 1906 U.S. army trials, this is a development of the pistol used in that event. It was a semiautomatic, delayed blowback pistol, chambered in .32 ACP or .38 ACP, featuring a box magazine holding ten cartridges (nine in weapons using .38 ACP) and fitted with a 3.75-inch barrel. It was unique in using no bolts or screws in its assembly. Later automatic pistols from Savage included the hammerless .32 caliber Model 1915 and the Model 1917 in .38 ACP. The Model 1917 is almost identical to the Model 1907, except for a larger butt.

Smith & Wesson

Only two produced before World War II, the .35 caliber Model 1913 automatic pistol and the .32 caliber Model 32 automatic pistol.[17]

- **.35 caliber automatic pistol**
  Production: 8,350 weapons, between 1913 and 1921.
  Chambered for the unfamiliar .35 S&W Auto centerfire cartridge, with a magazine holding seven cartridges, a short 3.5 inch barrel and a semi automatic, blowback operated mechanism. Unpopular because it used a cartridge which was not very readily available, eight "Types" are recognized by collectors, based on entirely superficial changes to the original pistol.
- **.32 caliber automatic pistol**
  Production: under 1,000 weapons, between 1924 and 1936.
  An improved version of the Model 1913, generally designated the S&W 32 Automatic pistol, with a magazine holding seven .32 caliber ACP cartridges, although most other features are similar to the earlier .35 caliber Model 1913.

Belgium Manufacturers

FN (Fabrique Nationale d' Herstal)

Established in 1889 to manufacture Mauser Model 89 rifles for the Belgian government, FN began its ascendancy in the world of firearms manufacturing when it established a long-term relationship with John Browning in 1897.[18]

- **FN M1899/M1900**
  Production: 700,000 guns between 1899 and 1911.
  This was a single-action semiautomatic pistol with a 4-inch barrel, a box magazine holding seven .32 ACP cartridges, and incorporating a simple blowback mechanism. It was the first commercially successful pistol to use a slide surrounding the barrel.
- **FN Model 1903**
  Production: over 150,000 weapons between 1902 and 1927.
  This was a single-action semiautomatic pistol, fitted with a box magazine holding seven 9 × 20mm SR Browning Long cartridges and having a 5-inch barrel. Its mechanical design was the same as the Colt Model 1903 Pocket Hammerless, with a number of components enlarged and strengthened to allow the pistol to use the 9 × 20mm cartridge. With a total weight of 2 lbs and an overall length of only 8 inches, the pistol was the issue weapon of a number of police forces and military formations.
- **FN M1905**
  Production: precise records not available, but estimated at between 300,000 and 500,000 weapons.
  Essentially a copy of the Colt Model 1908 Vest Pocket, a design Browning sold to FN and Colt, this is the only pistol produced by both companies without any changes. It served as the basis for the later FN Baby Browning, produced by FN from 1931 until 2016.

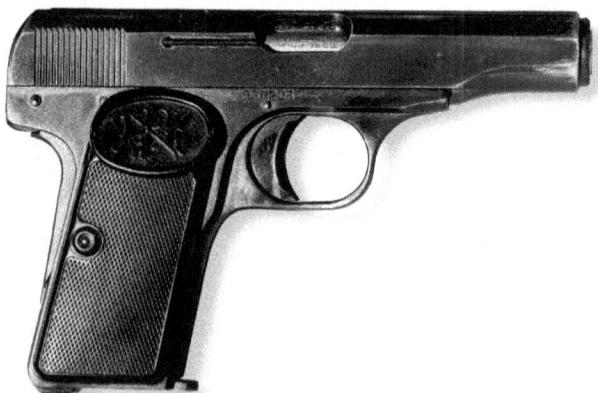

FN Model 1910, single-action semiautomatic pistol chambered for either .32 caliber ACP or .38 caliber (courtesy Rama: License: CCA-S-A-2.0).

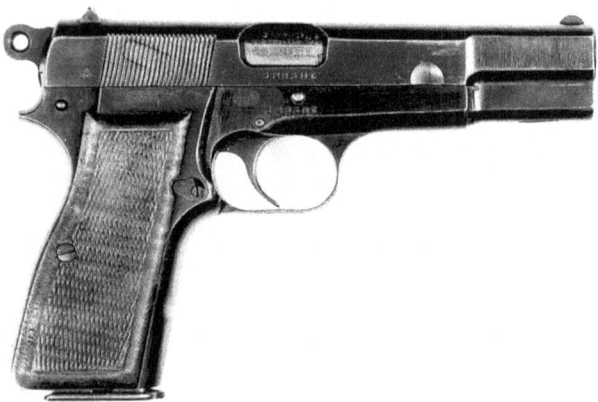

Browning Hi-Power, made by FN and usually chambered in 9 × 19mm Parabellum (courtesy James D. Julia Auctioneers, Fairfield, Maine. www.jamesdjulia.com).

- **FN Model 1910**

  Production: precise records not available, but estimated at several million between 1910 and 1983, as Model 1910, Model 1910/22, Model 1955 (U.S.) and Model 1971.

  All were essentially hammerless, single-action semi-automatic pistols with blowback operation and a striker mechanism. They were fitted with a box magazine holding either seven .32 ACP cartridges or six .38 ACP cartridges in the original FN Model 1910. This was expanded to nine .32 ACP or eight .38 ACP cartridges in the M1910/22 and its successors.

- **FN Browning Hi-Power**

  Production: well over 1 million weapons, between 1935 and 2016.

  This is a single-action semiautomatic pistol with short-recoil, cam-locked mechanism and a magazine holding thirteen cartridges. It was chambered in either 9 × 19mm Parabellum (most common), 7.62 × 21mm Parabellum or .40 caliber S&W.

  In operation the Hi-Power differs from the Colt M1911, with which it shares a number of features, in using a hardened bar or cam to unlock the barrel from the slide, instead of the slightly weaker, toggle-link system. When a cartridge is fired in the Hi-Power, the barrel and slide move backwards, until a slot under the chamber contacts a hardened bar that forces the barrel and breech down, disengaging the slide, which then continues its backward progress, extracting the spent case and cocking the hammer as it reaches the full extent of its rearwards travel. The recoil spring then pushes the slide forward, removing a cartridge from the magazine, chambering it and simultaneously pushing the chamber and barrel forwards. The action of the cam then pushes the barrel and chamber assembly upwards, re-engaging the locking lugs in the barrel and slide and leaving the weapon cocked, with a cartridge chambered and ready to fire.

British Manufacturers

Webley & Scott

Manufacturers of the world's only semiautomatic revolver, the Webley-Fosbery, and a group of small semiautomatic magazine pistols produced from 1905, all using a simple blowback action and chambered for .25 caliber ACP, .32 caliber ACP and 9 × 20mm Browning Long. Another group of pistols was produced after 1910, using a short-recoil mechanism and chambered for the more powerful .38 caliber ACP and .455 MK II Webley cartridge, although poor performance with the rimmed case meant that later weapons were chambered for a case of semi-rimmed pattern, specifically designed for that pistol.[19]

- **Webley & Scott Model 1905, 1907, 1908**
  Production: precise records not available, but estimated at 10,000 weapons.
  Chambered for the .32 ACP cartridge, all of these pistols have simple blowback operation, with a short, exposed 89mm barrel, a single-action trigger and an external hammer. The manual safety was located on the left side of the frame, above the butt plates, where it could be operated by the user's thumb. The detachable, single-column 8-round magazine was inserted into the bottom of the butt, with its release on the bottom of the magazine itself. Front and rear sights are fixed.

- **Webley & Scott Model 1906**
  Production: precise records not available, but estimated at 3,000 weapons.
  Chambered in .25 ACP, this model has a simple blowback mechanism with a 54mm exposed barrel, a single-action trigger and an external hammer. The manual safety catch was located on the left side of the frame, above the butt plates, where the safety catch could be operated by the user's thumb. A single-column, detachable box magazine holding six cartridges was contained in the butt, with its release button on the bottom of the magazine itself. Front and rear sights were fixed.

- **Webley & Scott Model 1909, 9mm Model**
  Production: precise records not available, but estimated at 10,000 weapons.
  Chambered for the 9 × 20mm Browning Long cartridge, this pistol had a simple blowback mechanism, an exposed 140mm barrel, a single-action trigger and an external hammer. An automatic safety mechanism is fitted at the rear of the butt, actuated when the user gripped the weapon. The detachable, single-column magazine contained 8 cartridges, and was fitted into the bottom of the butt, with the release button on the bottom of the magazine itself. Rear sights were adjustable and a lanyard ring was fitted to the base of the butt.

- **Webley & Scott Model 1909, .25 ACP Model**
  Production: precise records not available, but estimated at 10,000 weapons.
  Chambered for the .25 ACP cartridge, this pistol had a short, 140mm exposed barrel and a single-action trigger, operated by a simple blowback mechanism. The internal hammer was concealed inside the frame and the weapon was fitted with a manual safety catch on the left side of the frame above the butt, which could be operated by the user's thumb. The detachable, single-column magazine contained 8 cartridges, and was fitted into the bottom of the butt, with the release button on the bottom of the magazine itself. Sights were fixed.

- **Webley & Scott Model 1910**
  Production: precise records not available, but estimated at 3,000 weapons.

  Chambered for the .38 ACP cartridge, this was the first of the Webley self-loading pistols fitted with the stronger, short-recoil toggle locked mechanism. This model also featured a single-action trigger, a concealed hammer and a butt safety mechanism, although later guns made after 1913 reverted to a manual safety mechanism. The detachable, single-column magazine contained 8 cartridges, and was fitted into the bottom of the butt, with the release button on the bottom of the magazine itself. Rear sights were adjustable and a lanyard ring was fitted to the base of the butt.

- **Webley & Scott Model 1912, 1913, Mark 1 Navy (Mk.I N)**
  Production: precise records not available, but estimated at 10,000 weapons, since it was accepted as a service pistol.

  Chambered for the .455 Mk II pistol cartridge and fitted with the short-recoil toggle-locked mechanism. This model featured an exposed 127mm barrel, a single-action trigger, an external hammer and a butt safety mechanism. The detachable, single-column magazine contained 7 cartridges, and was fitted into the bottom of the butt,

Top, left: Webley Model 1905 semiautomatic pistol, chambered in .32 ACP. *Top, right:* Webley Model 1909 semiautomatic pistol from the right side, showing the ejection port. *Bottom, left:* Webley Model 1909 semiautomatic pistol, chambered in 6.35 × 16mmSR, from the left side, showing the robust safety catch. *Bottom, right:* Webley Model 1910 semiautomatic pistol, chambered in .38 ACP, from the left side, showing the butt safety catch.

with the release button on the bottom of the magazine itself. Rear sights were fixed on the Mk 1 but adjustable on the Mk.I Mod. 2.
- **Webley & Scott Model 1922:**
  Production: precise records not available, but estimated at 3,000 weapons.

  Chambered for the 9mm Browning Long cartridge, these pistols had a simple blowback mechanism, a single-action trigger, an external hammer and a manual safety catch, located on the left side of the slide. Magazines were detachable, single-column, holding eight cartridges and with the magazine release next to the trigger guard. Rear sights were adjustable and a lanyard ring was fitted to the base of the butt.

Austrian and German manufacturers

Germany's technical and engineering expertise had always been in the forefront of advancement in the field of firearms manufacture during the late nineteenth and early twentieth centuries, resulting in the production of a number of superior self-loading pistols.[20]

Bergmann

- **Bergman Bayer Model 1903 or Bergman-Mars pistol:**
  Production: precise records not available, but estimated at 1,000 weapons.

  Produced in 1903 from a design by Louis Schmeisser. This was a semi-automatic, recoil-operated single-action pistol chambered for the 9 × 23 Bergmann or Largo cartridge, with an external hammer and manual safety catch mounted on the left side of the weapon, near the hammer. Cartridges are delivered from a staggered double-column detachable box magazine holding six or ten cartridges located in front of the trigger guard, although the weapon could also be loaded from a charger, via the ejection port. Later weapons included the Model 1908 and Model 1910/21, although their complexity and consequent expense prevented them from achieving any sort of popularity.

Bergmann Bayer Model 1908 semiautomatic pistol. *Bottom:* **Bergmann Bayer Model 1910/21 semiautomatic pistol.**

DWM (Deutsche Waffen—und Munitionsfabriken Aktien-Gesellschaft)

- **P.08 Luger:** Service pistol for the German military from 1908 until about 1935, when it began to be replaced by Walther's P38.

Mannlicher-Steyr

- **Roth Steyr Model 1907**
  Production: 90,000 pistols.
  Single action pistol with a short-recoil, rotary locking mechanism and an integral magazine holding ten cartridges, loaded from a charger. Chambered for the 8mm Roth cartridge.
- **Steyr Hahn M1911 and M1912:**
  Production: precise records not available, but estimated at 30,000 weapons.
  Essentially a development of the earlier Roth Steyr pistol, this weapon was also a single-action pistol with a short-recoil, rotary-locking mechanism and an integral magazine holding ten cartridges, loaded from a charger.
  Originally chambered for the 9 × 23mm Steyr cartridge, many were converted to 9 × 19mm Luger.

Mauser

- **C96 Mauser pistol:** One of the first semiautomatic pistols, much prized for its accuracy.
- **Model 1910**
  Production: precise records not available, but estimated at 10,000 weapons.

  Chambered for .25 ACP, this was a single-action semiautomatic pistol, with a simple blowback mechanism and a striker firing mechanism. A manual safety catch is fitted on the left just behind the trigger and the detachable magazine holds nine cartridges, the magazine release button being located at the base of the pistol's butt. Front and rear sights are fixed. Butt plates on early guns were of walnut, with plastic being used on some later guns.

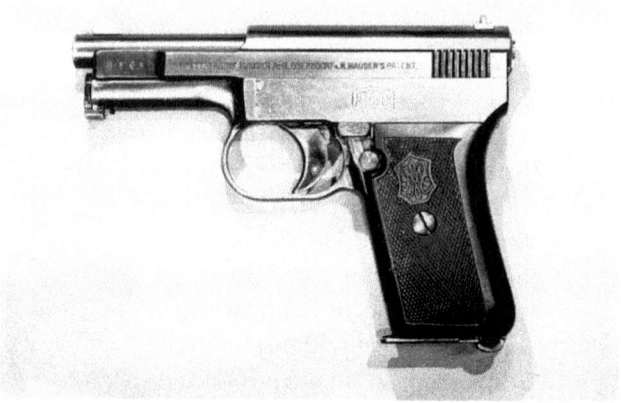

Mauser Model 1910 semiautomatic pistol (courtesy Rama: License: CCA-S-A-2.0).

- **Model 1914 and Model 1934**
  Production: precise records not available, but estimated at 31,000 weapons.
  Chambered for the .32 ACP cartridge, this was essentially a model of 1910, chambered for the more powerful cartridge and fitted with a magazine holding eight cartridges.

- **HSc**

  Production: precise records not available, but estimated at 1,000 weapons.

  Known by the factory designation Hahn-Selbstlspanner pistole ausfurung C, or self-cocking hammer pistol, model C, this was a double-action pistol with a blowback mechanism, 86mm barrel and a concealed hammer. It was chambered for either the .32 ACP or the .380 ACP cartridge, and had a detachable, single-column magazine, which fitted into the butt and held eight cartridges, with the release button on the bottom of the butt.

Sauer

- **38H**

  Production: precise records not available, but estimated at 1,000 weapons.

  Produced in 1938. This was a double-action pistol with a simple blowback mechanism, fitted with a stationary 83mm barrel and concealed hammer. Chambered in .32 ACP, with a detachable, single-column magazine containing eight cartridges. Sights were fixed and the butt plates were in black plastic with the "Double S" Sauer trademark impressed into the lower section.

Walther

- **Model 9**

  Production: precise records not available, but estimated at 200,000 weapons, between 1921 and 1945

  Chambered for the .25 ACP cartridge, this was a double-action, hammerless pistol with a striker mechanism, simple blowback operation and fixed sights. Overall length was only 100mm, with a barrel of 50mm, so this was a good weapon for clandestine operations. The detachable box magazine held six cartridges in a single column, with a magazine release button on the left side, which also operates the magazine safety mechanism.

- **PP and PPK pistols**

  Production: precise records not available, but estimated at several million weapons between 1929 and 1945.

  The PPK is a smaller version of the PP, with a 84mm barrel instead of the 99mm component of the larger gun and a slightly different design of butt backstrap. These were double-action weapons with an external hammer and a simple blowback mechanism chambered for a variety of cartridges, including .25ACP, 7.65 × 17mm Auto and .38ACP, although pistols cham-

Walther PPK semiautomatic pistol (courtesy Adams guns.com).

bered for the 7.63mm Auto cartridge are significantly more common than other types. Magazines are of the single-column, detachable box pattern and hold between six and ten cartridges, depending upon the chambering, with a release button on the left side of the frame just below the slide and in front of the butt plate. Sights were fixed and the butt plates were in brown plastic. Both the PP and PPK were fitted with a loaded chamber indicator and a lanyard loop.

- **P38**

    Production: over 1 million weapons—between 1938 and 1945 by Walther, then from 1945 until 2000 at the French Manurhin factory.

    Walther P38 semiautomatic pistol (courtesy Adamsguns.com).

    This was a steel-framed, double-action weapon with an external hammer and a single-column, detachable magazine holding eight 9 × 19mm Parabellum cartridges. Sights were fixed and butt plates were in wood or plastic. Later weapons were constructed with aluminum frames.

Italian Manufacturers

Beretta

- **Model 418**

    Production: precise records not available, but estimated at 800, 000 weapons based upon serial numbers, made between 1919 and possibly as late as 1945.

    This was a double-action hammerless "pocket" pistol, with a blowback mechanism, chambered for the .25 ACP cartridge and fitted with a butt-safety mechanism. The single-column detachable box magazine held seven cartridges in the early models, increased to eight in later weapons. Sights were fixed but largely superfluous, and butt plates were produced in a number of materials, including walnut and ivory. Has the distinction of being the gun used by James Bond in the first five books of the series.[21]

- **Model 1934**

    Production: precise records not available, but estimated at over 1 million weapons between 1934 and 1991.

    Chambered in .380 ACP or 9mm Corto (its Italian equivalent), this was a single-action pistol, with a stationary 88mm barrel, external hammer, and a simple blowback mechanism. The single-column detachable box magazine held seven cartridges, sights were fixed and the butt plates were usually of black plastic. The M1935 variant was an M1934 pistol modified to chamber the smaller .32 ACP cartridge.

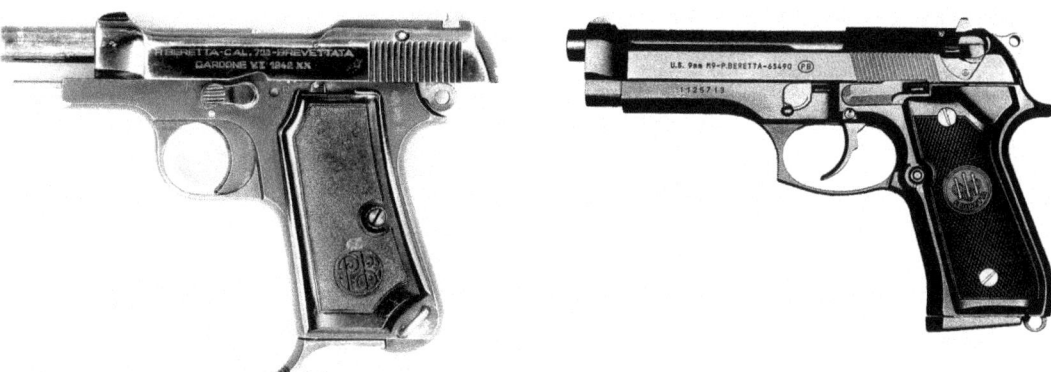

Left: Beretta M1935 semiautomatic pistol from the left side, with the slide open (Wikipedia: License CC-A-S-A 2.5). *Right:* Beretta M9 semiautomatic pistol, the weapon adopted by the U.S. military to replace the M1911. Chambered in 9x19mm Parabellum, but many in the U.S. army preferred to retain their old .45 caliber M1911A automatics rather than adopt the new pistol, which was thought to lack stopping power.

Japanese Manufacturers

Nambu pistols

A pistol series invented by Lt. General Kijiro Nambu, and first entering production in 1902. It was claimed to have originated during the "30 year Automatic Pistol Plan" of 1897 in Japan. Production of all types was approximately 400,000 weapons, between 1906 and 1945. These pistols were all locked-breech, recoil-operated semiautomatic weapons, usually chambered for the 8 × 22mm Nambu cartridge, which was difficult to obtain outside Japan. The single-column detachable box magazine was housed in the butt and contained either 7 or 8 cartridges, depending upon the model. Sights were fixed and butt plates were usually in walnut, and a butt safety mechanism was fitted to all but the Type 14. The weapon was cocked by inserting a loaded magazine and then pulling the cocking knob mounted at the rear of the breech as far to the rear as it would move, before releasing it, in a manner analogous to the toggle mechanism of the Luger P.08.[22]

- **Type A**
  Production: several thousand, from 1903 until 1906.
  Known as "Granpa Nambus" by collectors and featuring a magazine with a wooden base and a welded lanyard loop.
- **Type A Modified**
  Production: approximately 4,500 pistols, between 1906 and 1923, initially at the Tokyo Artillery Arsenal.
  Known as "Papa Nambus" by collectors, these pistols featured a magazine with an aluminum base and a lanyard ring.
- **Type B**
  Production: approximately 6,000 weapons between 1909 and 1929, initially at the Tokyo Artillery Arsenal, production later being moved to the Koishikawa Arsenal.
  Known to collectors as the "Baby Nambu" and chambered for the less powerful 7 × 20mm Nambu cartridge, with a detachable box magazine holding seven cartridges, this was essentially a scaled-down version of the earlier Type A.

- **Type 14**

  Production: approximately 400,000 weapons between 1927 and 1945 and officially adopted by Japanese military in 1927.

  Nambu pistol, chambered for the 8x22mm Nambu cartridge (courtesy Olegvolk at en. Wikipedia).

  This was a further modification of the Type A Modified pistol designed to be produced by a simplified manufacturing process and so reduce cost. Changes included an enlarged trigger guard to make the weapon easier to use while wearing gloves, a knurled cocking knob instead of the slotted component, and the removal of the butt safety mechanism.

Spanish Manufacturers

Astra

- **Model 400 and Model 600 pistols**

  Production: over 100,000 weapons between 1921 and 1950.

  Chambered for the 9 × 23mm Bergman or Largo cartridge, this was a single-action weapon with a concealed hammer and simple blowback operation, despite being chambered for a cartridge with a loading usually considered unsuitable for a pistol using a blowback mechanism. The weapon is fitted with a single-column, detachable box magazine holding eight cartridges, fixed sights and separate plastic butt plates. The Astra Model 600 was a variation chambered for 9 × 19mm Parabellum, while a smaller Astra 300 was also produced, chambered for .32 ACP and .380 ACP.[23]

Top: Astra 300 semiautomatic pistol. *Bottom:* Astra 400 semiautomatic pistol (both photographs courtesy James D. Julia Auctioneers, Fairfield, Maine. www.jamesdjulia.com).

Manufacturers in the USSR

Tokarev

- **TT-30**

    Production: approximately 1.7 million weapons between 1930 and 1952, at state arsenals in the USSR.

    This was a single-action, short-recoil, locked-breech pistol chambered for the 7.62 × 25mm Tokarev cartridge, with a 116mm barrel, fixed sights and plastic butt plates usually stamped with five-pointed star. It is fitted with a detachable box magazine, contained in the butt of the pistol and holding 8 cartridges.[24]

Left: A Soviet-produced TT-33 pistol made by the Tula Arsenal in 1937 (Wikipedia: License CC-A-S-A 4.0). *Right:* A crude "knockoff" copy of the TT-33 pistol made in Pakistan (Wikipedia: License CC-A-S-A 3.0).

The Webley-Fosbery Semiautomatic Revolver

Originally designed by Lt. Colonel George Fosbery and patented in 1895, Webley & Scott began production of this unique revolver in the early years of the twentieth century. Fosbery produced the original weapon because his experience while serving in India with the British Army convinced him of the need for a pistol combining the rapid fire and simple operation of Browning's automatic pistols with the powerful .455 caliber British service revolver cartridge. The simple blowback mechanism of most early automatic pistols meant that they could only be chambered for low-power cartridges such as the .32 ACP or .38 ACP, and Fosbery was convinced that a larger round was necessary for military

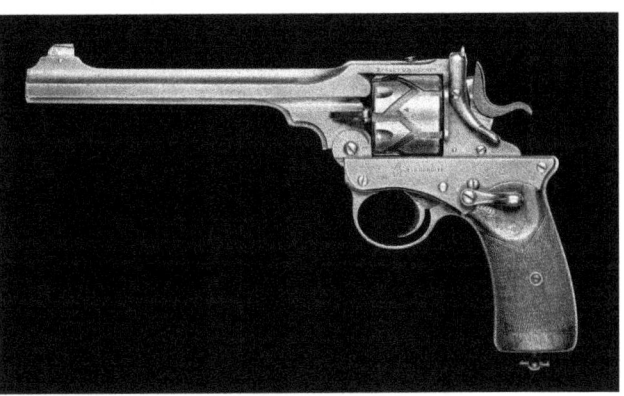

Webley-Fosbery semiautomatic revolver (courtesy James D. Julia Auctioneers, Fairfield, Maine. www.jamesdjulia.com).

service. Rather than trying to design an automatic pistol with a stronger mechanism incorporating the bolt and firing pin in a slide surrounding the barrel, as Browning did with the Colt 1911, Fosbery produced a design based on a Colt SAA (Single Action Army) revolver, which cocked the hammer and rotated the cylinder by using the residual energy generated from explosion of the weapon's cartridge. Unfortunately, the Colt company rejected his prototype as too complicated for economic manufacture. Fosbery took the idea to the English firm of P. Webley & Sons (Webley & Scott from 1899) and they began producing a gun incorporating Fosbery's system and based on their top-break, double-action revolvers, which was subsequently exhibited at Bisley in 1900.[25]

Operation

Fosbery's automatic revolver differed from the more conventional designs of semiautomatic pistol in using a conventional revolver cylinder to deliver cartridges to the firing mechanism, which necessitated some fairly unique design features. Being operated by the residual energy generated by the recoil of the cartridge, unlike a conventional revolver, the Webley-Fosbery was divided into two distinct sections: the upper barrel, cylinder and hammer mechanism, and the lower trigger and butt assembly. The barrel, cylinder and hammer were fixed together during operation and slid on rails machined in the top surface of the lower frame, which housed the trigger mechanism.

The weapon was loaded by operating the frame locking lever on the left side of the lock, allowing the barrel and cylinder assembly to tilt forward, a star-shaped ejector simultaneously expelling the spent cartridges, using a mechanism similar to the Webley service revolvers. Fresh cartridges were then either pushed into the chambers individually or inserted using an auto-loader and the barrel and cylinder assembly was returned to its original position and locked. The upper barrel assembly could now be pulled back to its fullest extent, cocking the hammer and indexing the cylinder, whereupon this assembly was pushed forward by an internal recoil spring, thus making the weapon ready to fire. A Fosbery revolver may also be manually cocked in a manner exactly similar to a conventional single-action revolver, although this would not operate the indexing mechanism of the cylinder, which only cycled when the barrel and lock assembly were pulled to the rear. Consequently, simply cocking the hammer would only allow the weapon to be fired if the cylinder had an unused cartridge already in the firing position. (Unlike the very similar Webley Government revolvers, the Fosbery is fitted with a safety catch on the left side of the butt, which only operates when the revolver is cocked. This mechanism allows it to be safely carried with the hammer at full cock, so that all that is required to fire the weapon is for the safety catch to be moved up from the "SAFE" position and the trigger pulled.)

When a cartridge was fired, the residual force from the explosion moved the barrel, cylinder and hammer assembly backwards, while a pivoting lever connected to the frame cocked the hammer and a diamond-shaped stud mounted on the frame below the cylinder simultaneously pushed on one of the diagonal grooves milled on the outer surface of the cylinder, partially revolving the cylinder. The recoil spring then returned the whole assembly to its original position, such that the stud encountered a second groove, which indexed the cylinder to its final, firing position. This mechanism was simple and reliable as long as it was kept scrupulously clean, but it would only fully cycle the mechanism if the gun was firmly gripped when firing. If the gun was allowed to lift under the force of recoil in the normal manner, so as to lessen the "kick" delivered to the shooter's arm, the gun's mechanism would often fail to operate and the revolver would need to be manually cycled before it could be fired again.

Specification

Serial number range: 1–5000. Manufactured from 1900, possibly until 1924. The Webley-Fosbery revolver was still included in Webley's catalogue of 1939.

Solid-frame, top-break, self-extracting semiautomatic revolver in .445 or .38 caliber, with barrel length varying from 4 to 7½ inches. Cylinder is semi-fluted, with six chambers, machined on the external surface with a series of zigzag grooves, making this arm easy to recognize. A later version was designed for the .38 ACP cartridge and had a shorter cylinder with 8 chambers. There is a thumb-operated frame locking lever on the left side, exactly similar to Webley Government revolvers but with a safety catch, also thumb-operated, on the lower left side of the frame. This safety catch can only be operated when the hammer of the weapon is at full cock.

Frames are stamped on left side of the top-strap:

"WEBLEY-FOSBERY AUTOMATIC"

which became, on arms made in 1902 and later:

"WEBLEY-FOSBERY"

On left side of frame below the cylinder is stamped:

.455 CORDITE ONLY

which became on weapons made in 1902 and later:

.455 CORDITE

or, on the revolvers chambered for .38 ACP:

".38 AUTOMATIC"

indicating the chambering of the weapon. Proof marks, usually of the Birmingham Proof House, are stamped on both barrel and cylinders. The lower frame of the revolver was fixed, while the hexagonal barrel, cylinder and upper frame assembly moved on machined rails under the force of the weapon's recoil, cocking the hammer and rotating the cylinder, so the action was analogous to a modern semiautomatic pistol. Incidentally, the weapon seems to have only functioned correctly with the higher power smokeless or cordite rounds, hence the stamp on the frames of the early weapons.

Variations

- **Webley-Fosbery .445 caliber Model**
  Cylinder with six chambers for the government issue Webley .455 cartridge, barrel lengths between 4 and 7½ inches. These weapons worked best when using the Mk 1 pistol cartridge, with a load of 6.5 grains of Cordite and a 265-grain bullet. However, they would still shoot adequately when using the earlier black-powder rounds, although with some detriment to automatic function.

Serial range: 1–600.
Left side of top strap stamped:

"WEBLEY-FOSBERY AUTOMATIC"

Left side of frame stamped:

.455 CORDITE ONLY

- **Webley-Fosbery .445 caliber Model**
  Serial range: 600–5000.
  Top-strap stamp:

"WEBLEY-FOSBERY"

On left side frame stamp:

.455 CORDITE

A number of further variations were produced of the 1902 Model, involving changes in barrel length and designated Mk I to Mk VI.

This revolver was also produced as a 'Short-Frame' Model, with a cylinder having similar dimensions to the .38 ACP Model but with only six chambers, for the .455 service cartridge.

- **Webley-Fosbery .38 caliber Model**
  Manufactured for .38 ACP cartridge, cylinder with eight chambers, various barrel lengths.

MILITARY SERVICE

Although Fosbery's revolver was very accurate and fast to shoot, the precise machining necessary to produce the revolver made it both expensive and susceptible to stoppages in muddy conditions, so that it proved to be unsuitable for service use. It was also heavy and unwieldy, at 11 inches in length and 2½ lbs in weight, and that made it unpopular with many British officers, who were responsible for the purchase of their own side arms during the period before World War I. Some officers did purchase it for use during both the Second Boer War and World War I, but reports appear to have quickly circulated about the weapon's unreliability in dirty or wet conditions, the fine tolerances of the sliding mechanism proving particularly susceptible to the ingress of dirt or sand.

However, it quickly became popular with target shooters, who preferred it to the Colt and Browning semiautomatic pistols because of the Fosbery's much reduced recoil. Good results were obtained by experienced shooters, with records showing that it was possible to discharge twelve shots through a four inch target in as little as 20 seconds.

VALUES

NRA Good: $2,800–$3,350; NRA Fine: $3,300–$3,700; Cased: $4,500–$4,900

Section V: The Machine-Gun Era

CHAPTER FOURTEEN

The Development of Repeating and Multi-fire Weapons in the Early 20th Century

The Road to Mechanized Carnage

The opening phase of World War I began on 28 July 1914 as a classic war of movement, and, as such, was quite familiar to all the senior military figures responsible for its conduct. In the first weeks, German forces made rapid advances through Belgium and into France, but were checked on the outskirts of Paris by a combined French and BEF (British Expeditionary Force) counterattack along the river Marne. This resulted in both sides moving north in an attempt to outflank each other in a series of battles and advances known to military historians by the misleading designation "the Race to the Sea." Rather than a "race," these maneuverings were, in fact, attempts to complete mutual enveloping movements which led to the two armies eventually facing each other in northern France, with neither having gained a decisive advantage. After a succession of battles along this line, which culminated in the First Battle of Ypres in late November 1914, both forces began the construction of a meandering line of fortified trenches that stretched from the North Sea to the Franco-Swiss border. It was this miscellaneous collection of trenches, mud holes, machine gun posts, ammunition dumps and shell-torn buildings which was to become known to history as the Western Front. By the beginning of 1915, the German and Allied armies had both become bogged down there in an indecisive stalemate, the original war of movement having changed into a battle of attrition for which the senior military staffs on both sides were largely unprepared, both physically and mentally.[1]

Much of this mental stagnation revolved around the new weapons technology that had become available at the beginning of the 20th century, and this was particularly reflected in the Imperial General Staff's perception of the role of machine guns. The British army was not, as is generally believed, unfamiliar with multi-fire weapons when World War I broke out. They had been using Gatling guns since 1879; those weapons were originally chambered for the British army's .577/.450 Martini-Henry black powder service cartridge. As early as 1888 they had begun replacing those Gatling guns with the Maxin, the first batch also chambered for the British Army's black-powder Martini cartridge, although subsequent purchases were designed to use the new smokeless .303 caliber British service rifle cartridge. These guns had proved particularly effective when used against uncivilized opponents whose main tactic was to charge British positions in large, tightly packed groups. Consequently, there should have been sufficient senior officers in the British army capable of recognizing the threat to their men from machine gun posts and barbed wire, and more importantly, who should have been able to think of ways to counteract such a lethal combination. Despite the presence of considerable expertise of this sort in the old Regular army, it was not until the Battle of Vimy Ridge in 1917 that new tactics began to be introduced to circumvent the threat of machine guns and barbed wire. As Churchill suggested in his *World Crisis*, greater use of tanks, as at Cambrai, could have been an alternative to blocking enemy machine-gun fire with "the breasts of brave men."[2] Enthusiasm for the machine gun was not noticeable during this period amongst many British senior officers either. Such weapons apparently were considered "unsporting," as well as encouraging defensive fighting rather than an aggressive war of movement, which was what was considered necessary to win in Flanders. Douglas Haig typified this attitude, and is often claimed to have said in 1915: "The machine gun is a much overrated weapon; two per battalion is more than sufficient." Although this quote may not have originated with the British commander, it certainly typifies the stance of the majority of the British Imperial General Staff. Certainly, if this was his attitude in 1915, it changed abruptly after events on the Somme.[3] The German army, in contrast, had taken readily to the machine gun in the period before World War I. By 1904, they had sixteen units equipped with "Maschinengewehr," with machine gun crews taken from elite infantry units and attached to Jaeger (light infantry) battalions.[4]

When war was declared in 1914, British infantry regiments were armed with two machine guns for each battalion, while comparable units in the Imperial German Army had six and the Russians eight. The U.S. Army had lagged even further behind, and as late as 1917, many American infantry units were still equipped with only one machine gun, usually the vastly inferior Chauchat, which was only a light machine gun. Offensives such as the First Battle of Ypres, Loos, the Somme and Passchendaele soon showed the monstrous errors in this kind of thinking. At the Somme, in particular, it was noted that the horrendous casualties suffered by British troops on the first day, with over 57,000 killed or wounded, were mostly "lost under withering machine gun fire," although the British army had begun to substantially increase the number of machine guns available to their troops well before July 1916.[5]

Vimy Ridge saw the beginnings of a more rational approach to machine gun posts and barbed wire. It was the Canadians who had learnt the most from the mistakes made previously by the British and French, pioneering area denial and indirect fire with Vickers machine guns (soon adopted by all Allied armies) under the guidance of former French Army Reserve officer Major General Raymond Brutinel. Minutes before the attack on Vimy Ridge, for example, the Canadians increased the artillery barrage by aiming machine guns indirectly to deliver plunging fire on to the German positions. They had also significantly increased the number of machine guns per battalion, and to meet this demand, production of the Vickers machine gun was contracted to the Colt PFA Manufacturing Co. in the United States.

Fourteen. The Development of Repeating and Multi-fire Weapons

Tactical Use of the Heavy/Medium Machine Gun

Although the British army began World War I with its infantry battalions and cavalry regiments equipped with a single machine gun section containing just two guns each, by November 1914 these forces were being supplemented by the formation of the MMGS (Motor Machine Gun Service). This service was a branch of the Royal Artillery and consisted of motorcycle-mounted machine gun batteries, with personnel trained at a specialist machine gun school located in France. Each battery consisted of 18 motorcycle and sidecar combinations as well as eight motorcycles without sidecars, and several cars or trucks. Six of the motorcycle combinations in a battery had a single Vickers machine gun mounted in the sidecar, while the rest transported ammunition and spare parts. However, a year of warfare on the Western Front showed that to be fully effective, machine guns should be

Matchless motorcycle combination from the right, showing the hand gear change, the spare wheel and bulb horn. This bike also has bicycle pattern brakes, which bear on the rim of the wheel and must have been less than effective, considering the total weight of the machine! (by kind permission of Bonhams).

Matchless motorcycle combination from the left (by kind permission of Bonhams).

14th Battery Motor Machine Gun service, showing the types of vehicle in use by these units.

deployed in larger units, crewed by specially trained men who were not only thoroughly conversant with their weapons but also understood how to site them in order to achieve maximum effect. To achieve this, the Machine Gun Corps was formed in October 1915 with Infantry, Cavalry, and Motor branches, followed in 1916 by the addition of the Heavy Branch. A depot and training center was established at Belton Park in Grantham, Lincolnshire, and a base depot at Camiers in France.[6]

The Machine Gun Corps

Of the three groups, the Infantry Branch was significantly larger than the other two, being formed by the transfer of all battalion machine gun sections to the MGC, these sections, of two guns each, then being grouped into brigade machine gun companies. Three machine gun companies were allotted to each division, a division consisting of two brigades, or between six and twelve battalions, consequently giving each division between twenty-four and forty-eight machine guns each. By 1917, however, it had been found to be expedient to add a fourth company to each division, and during March 1918, the four companies in each division were formed into a Machine Gun Battalion. The cavalry branch was less well equipped, having only a single machine gun squadron serving with each cavalry brigade.

The Motor branch was formed originally from the motorcycles and mounted Vickers guns of the MMGS, together with the armored car squadrons of the RNAS. These variegated units were then reformed into new motorcycle batteries, light armored motor batteries and light car patrols, the last two using vehicles as diverse as the Model T Ford and Rolls Royce Silver Ghost. In March 1916, a Heavy section was also formed, and men from this unit were responsible for crewing the first tanks in action during the Battle of Flees in September

1916. Shortly after Flees, in November 1916, the Heavy section became the Heavy branch, and less than a year later, in July 1917, this unit was removed from the MGC and became the Tank Corps, which became in turn the Royal Tank Corps in October 1923 and the Royal Tank Regiment in April 1939. The MGC itself saw out the war but was disbanded in 1922.

Although the usefulness of machine guns had been clearly demonstrated, many senior officers still insisted upon confining them to a role delivering direct fire in support of massed infantry movements and ignored the weapon's potential for delivering indirect fire. By firing over the heads of advancing infantry as short-range artillery, a Vickers could be effective at ranges of about three miles (approximately 4,500 yards). Until Vimy Ridge saw a radical change in military thinking, machine guns and the members of the MGC who manned them were often placed in flimsy emplacements constructed of a few sandbags, where the effect of their firing could be seen by the men advancing towards the enemy, despite the obvious danger to the highly trained and therefore extremely valuable machine gunners. This was reflected in the casualty rates incurred by the MGC—out of a total of 170,500 men of all ranks, 62,049 became casualties, including 12,498 killed or died of wounds. With the characteristically macabre humor of the British army, the Corps became known as "the Suicide Club."

It was not until nearly the end of the war, in 1918, that British and particularly Commonwealth troops were able to use their "plunging fire" techniques effectively as a matter of routine. Favorite targets included road junctions, trench systems, forming-up points, and other locations that could be spotted by a forward observer, "zeroed in" prior to a later attack during the hours of darkness, or estimated by experienced men with detailed trench maps. A favorite technique of Commonwealth troops was to set up a white disc on a pole near the machine gun with a mark on it for the gunner to aim at, which corresponded to the desired target. Later versions of the Vickers machine gun were fitted with an inclinometer back-sight incorporating a tall extension for this purpose.

The French army does not seem to have organized their heavy machine guns in a similar pattern to the British army, instead relying upon their distribution at battalion level, and not making much use of indirect fire, although the German army was aware of the advantages of this technique. Later versions of their MG '08 machine guns were fitted with a chronometer and range calculator similar to that supplied for the British Vickers gun, although circumstances, in particular the entry into the war of the U.S. army, ensured that the German generals were not able to make much use of this potentially lethal addition to their soldier's tactical equipment.[7]

The Heavy Machine Gun

Considered to be very much a specialist weapon, heavy machine guns (HMGs) were usually deployed in the static warfare of the trenches as part of a regular, carefully controlled system, except when part of a British mobile machine gun battery. They were positioned with clearly defined fields of fire, so that accurate bursts could be directed at any part of the enemy's trench system, such as a poorly constructed parapet or an accidental break in the wire stretched across No Man's Land. Unfortunately a team of approximately eight men was required to move and operate this type of a weapon, making HMGs impractical for offensive forward action, which also served to prolong the stalemate on the Western Front.

Heavy machine guns in use during World War I

American forces

The main U.S. HMG was the M1917 Browning, chambered for the Springfield .30–06 cartridge, although the introduction of this weapon was delayed until late in the war. U.S. army units on the Western front were often equipped with the elderly Maxim M1904, or if they were fortunate, the Colt-made M1915 Vickers gun.

British and Commonwealth forces

The main British HMG was the Vickers, chambered for the .303 service rifle cartridge and based on the earlier Maxim. Commonwealth forces were similarly equipped, although later in the war, Canadian units in particular were using a Vickers gun produced under license by Colt.

French forces

The main French HMG was the Hotchkiss M1914, chambered for the 8 × 50Rmm Lebel, the French service rifle cartridge. Prior to the adoption of the M1914 in 1917, the French army used the vastly inferior St. Étienne M1907 heavy machine gun.

German and Austro-Hungarian forces

The main German and Austro-Hungarian HMG after 1915 was the Maschinengewehr '08 (M08), a copy of the original Maxim. Other German and Austro-Hungarian HMGs included the Maschinengewehr (Schwarzlose) M. 7, the Skoda M1909 and M1913, and the Parabellum MG 14, a specialist modification of the MG '08 for use in aircraft.

Tactical Use of the Light Machine Gun (LMG)

The British army

Removal of the battalion heavy machine gun complement left a significant shortfall in the firepower of the British infantry. Consequently, the significantly more portable Lewis gun was issued to replace the original Maxim and Vickers guns. Beginning in July 1915, four Lewis guns were issued to each British infantry battalion or cavalry regiment, although by July 1918, this had increased to 36 for each infantry battalion, approximately three for each infantry company. With new weapons came new tactics, although it was not until after the disaster of the Somme offensive, in January 1917, that Haig established a BEF Training Directorate, which began issuing the revised training manuals SS143 and SS144. These publications marked the beginnings of a system that avoided attacks made by vulnerable lines of infantry. The new tactics encouraged individuals to learn the jobs of those around and above them and included an emphasis on every soldier's being fully aware of the nature of the battlefield, thus considerably reducing the disastrous "command and control" problems which had plagued operations at the Battle of Loos in September 1915 and on the Somme in the summer of 1916.

At platoon level in particular, changes were radical during 1917. Platoons were divided into a small headquarters unit and four other sections: the first with two grenade-throwers and several assistants carrying extra grenades; the second consisting of a single Lewis gunner and nine loaders with 30 drums of ammunition; a third rifle section made up of a sniper, a scout and nine riflemen; while in the fourth section were nine men with four rifle-grenade launchers. The platoon advanced in a diamond formation: the rifle section in front, rifle grenade and grenade or bombing sections to the sides, and the Lewis gun section behind, until resistance was met. The Lewis gunner and rifle grenade section then advanced, using all available cover, and engaged the enemy, while the riflemen and hand-grenade sections moved sideways around the flanks of the resistance and attacked the enemy from the side and rear.[8]

Despite these greatly improved "fire and movement" tactics, Passchendaele proved to be another costly, bloody shambles, although the lack of success in this offensive seems to have been due mainly to the unseasonably poor weather conditions and badly coordinated support for the advancing infantry, particularly at Messines Ridge. Later operations, in particular those at Vimy Ridge and during the Hundred Days offensive, used the new tactics, including more effective inter-arms coordination, and were significantly more successful, although it has been argued that this was due to innovations introduced by officers like the Canadian Julian Byng, rather than a sudden *volte-face* by Haig. However, Haig was in overall command, and he could have quite easily prevented the changes urged upon him by younger, more scientific soldiers like Byng. It must be to his credit that he approved their plans and encouraged them in their new approach, although his earlier, more spectacular failures have blackened his name in the eyes of the general public.[9]

THE FRENCH ARMY

The French army was also plentifully supplied with light machine guns, although initially these were the inferior Chauchat machine rifle, which proved unreliable in the conditions encountered in the trenches. They also adopted a new tactic that emphasized the role of their LMGs and which the French military referred to as *"du feu de marche"* or "marching fire," a simpler variant of the "fire and movement" technique the British were using in conjunction with their Lewis machine guns and grenade and rifle platoons. Later in the war, after the German offensive in March 1918, the French army reorganized its infantry tactics once again, using methods similar to the those of the British army. They introduced small combat groups known as *"Demi-Sections de Combat,"* which contained eighteen men, four operating an improved version of the unreliable Chauchat machine gun, four carrying Lebel 1886 rifles equipped to fire rifle grenades from a VB (Viven-Besseieres) grenade launcher, and ten conventional riflemen, who also carried grenades. Tactics employed by these groups were similar to those used by the British Lewis gun/rifle grenade squads and appear to have met with the same level of success.[10]

THE GERMAN ARMY

German use of the light machine gun does not appear to have been quite so sophisticated as the British approach, although a single Madsen light machine gun was issued to each infantry company, and this gun was used later to equip mountain troops and storm troopers. In addition to this issue of LMGs to conventional front-line troops, in August 1915, a number of infantry units were converted to specialized Musketoon battalions, trained to operate these Madsen light machine guns. These battalions were composed of approximately 500 men organized into three companies, each company being equipped with thirty machine guns. A single machine gun was operated by a team of four men, composed of a gunner, a loader and two ammunition carriers. Their role in any operation was to act as a mobile defensive reserve, ready to close any breaches in the front lines by engaging the advancing Allied forces and stopping them by the volume of fire laid down by the Madsen LMGs. However, this sort of tactical deployment proved unsuccessful as the air-cooled Danish gun, although lightweight and easy to move forward, could not match the sustained rate of fire of the water-cooled Vickers machine guns used by the Allied forces. LMGs in general were unsuited for this kind of defensive role and the British deployments, with their Lewis gun squads, quickly showed that there was a better way. Unfortunately, the German High Command persisted in their defensive use of the Madsen, and this misjudgment inevitably resulted in heavy casualties amongst the Musketoon battalions, with many of their Madsen LMGs also being destroyed, forcing the German army to re-equip those units with captured Lewis guns. By 1916 and the beginning of the Somme Offensive, only two of the original three battalions remained operational. These units were eventually broken up in early 1918, and their personnel sent to various machine gun sharpshooter detachments. Despite this lack of success, the Madsen LMG continued to be used by the German army, most notably by mountain troops in the Vosges, the Carpathians and the Balkans. German trench warfare operations on the Western Front did, however, begin to show a marked degree of success after the introduction of their "Stormtrooper" tactics, which shared some of the characteristics of the British tactical changes. They were used with particular success during Operation Michael in March 1918 and almost resulted in a German breakthrough, although a bad choice of the site for the initial assault, exhaustion of the leading troops, a slow advance, heavy casualties and the capture of a large quantity of alcohol left by the British allowed the Allies to close the gap that had been made initially in their lines.[11]

THE U.S. ARMY

American appreciation of the possibilities of both types of machine gun unfortunately came a little too late. Writing some time after World War I, Major General Julian Hatcher was moved to comment[12]:

> Now, if at that time we had known the least thing about the tactical role of machine guns, we would have realized that we ought to have two kinds in the Army at the same time: the heavy type for one kind of action and the light type, for a totally different use. We didn't, however, realize this or anything else much about these matters, so we adopted this light gun as THE machine gun of the Army. In those days, every regiment had a machine gun platoon, made up by detailing men from regular companies for temporary duty in the machine gun platoon. This platoon had four guns. It was not a regular authorized company, but just a scraped together aggregation of men who could best be spared from their places. Many times the temptation to get rid of unwanted problem children was solved by company commanders by sending them to the machine gun platoon. A pretty sorry outfit it was, as a rule.

This is no reflection on American perspicacity or tactical thinking, however. Haig himself is always claimed to have stated categorically in 1915 that the machine gun was an overrated weapon and two per battalion was quite sufficient. It was only the mistakes made by the British generals between 1914 and 1917, and the horrendous casualty rates resulting from those errors, that made them appreciate the need for a coherent approach to automatic weapons, not a superiority in training, strategic appreciation or intelligence over their U.S., French or even German counterparts.

The U.S. army did learn from its experiences, however. After an abortive invasion of the U.S. by Pancho Villa during which the performance of their Hotchkiss M1909 machine guns and the men trained to use them was less than useful, the U.S. military re-evaluated their former methods of training and established a machine gun school at Harlingen, Texas, in the Rio Grande Valley in August 1916. This machine gun instruction school taught the proper operation of the Colt Automatic Gun Model of 1895/1914, the Maxim Model of 1904, the Automatic Machine Rifle Model of 1909 and the Lewis Gun Model of 1916, so that the men trained there would form one of the most important components of the AEF when it reached the trenches of the Western Front. In addition to improved training, the company machine gun platoons were disbanded and a machine gun company was formed in each regiment, composed of men interested in assuming such a role rather than the misfits allotted to machine gun duties, as had previously been the case.

Despite these preparations, American troops arrived in France singularly ill-equipped to fight what had become a machine-gun war. The total inventory of machine guns in the U.S. when war was declared in 1917 was:

670 Model of 1909s for the Army
282 Maxim Model of 1904s
143 Colt Automatic Guns Model of 1985/1914s
353 Lewis guns, but they were chambered for the British .303 cartridge.

It was only after their arrival in France that U.S. units began to be issued the inferior Chauchat automatic machine rifle, which most of them thoroughly despised.[13]

Light machine guns in use during World War I

Although not introduced until July 1915, light machine guns soon became an essential feature of the tactical situation on the Western Front. Easy to move and set up, such weapons complimented the infantry role in trench warfare, being used in both defensive and offensive situations as well as during the almost constant trench raids that typified much of the period between January 1916 and the end of 1917.

American forces

The principal U.S. light machine gun was the Chauchat machine rifle, chambered for the Springfield .30–06 caliber cartridge, the Browning Automatic Rifle not being issued until too late in the war to be effective. Some Hotchkiss M1909 light machine guns also appear to have been in use with U.S. troops, retained after service in the battles against Pancho Villa. Some of these M1909s were also fitted to Indian motorcycles, but no record has so far been found of where or when they saw service.

British and Commonwealth forces

The main British light machine gun was the American-made Lewis gun, chambered for the British Army .303 caliber service rifle cartridge. Cavalry and the Tank Corps were issued with the superior Hotchkiss M1909, also chambered in .303 caliber British, a French machine gun produced by Hotchkiss et Cie. Commonwealth forces were similarly equipped.

French forces

The main French light machine gun was the Chauchat automatic machine rifle chambered for the 8 × 50mmR Lebel cartridge, although the Hotchkiss M1909 was also in service with the French army and chambered for the same cartridge. French aircraft were usually equipped with the Hotchkiss Model 1909.

German and Austro-Hungarian forces

The main Austro-Hungarian light machine gun was the Hotchkiss M1909. German forces used a number of light machine guns including the Madsen machine gun, Bergmenn MG 15nA, and the Knögen automatic rifle.

Machine Guns and the Air War

THE BEGINNING OF AIR COMBAT

In the early stages of the war, air combat was rare, because neither side had been able to produce an aircraft capable of effectively utilizing a machine gun, and pilots during this early period had to content themselves with waving or shaking their fists at each other. Clearly, a more aggressive attitude was necessary, and a surprising variety of weapons soon began to make an appearance in aircraft cockpits, including rifles, pistols, grappling hooks, grenades and even large stones! Perhaps a little surprisingly, the first aircraft destroyed during World War I was brought down on 8 September 1914, not by one of these conventional weapons, but when a Russian pilot, Pyotr Nesterov, *rammed* an Austrian reconnaissance aircraft in midair, resulting in the deaths of both the crews.[14]

This somewhat haphazard approach to war in the air changed forever in October 1914, when a French pilot, Louis Quenault, became the first flier to shoot down an enemy aircraft with a machine gun. Although some little way behind the French, the RFC began receiving their first purpose-built fighter aircraft, the Vickers FB5 or "Gunbus," in December 1914. It dominated the skies over the Western Front, alongside the French Morane-Saulnier monoplane, which was fitted with the first machine gun capable of forward firing through the arc of the propeller. Although the FB5 had the advantage of a Lewis gun mounted in the observer's cockpit at the front of the machine, its engine conformation was of the "pusher" type, making the plane comparatively slow, with a poor rate of climb. Despite giving the RFC a strategic advantage over the Western Front early in 1915, by the middle of the year it was being outperformed by the newer aircraft, particularly Anthony Fokker's Eindecker monoplane, the Fokker E.I, with its synchronized machine gun firing through the propeller arc, like the Morane "L" type.[15]

The "Fokker Scourge"

The British and French air corps had initially possessed all the advantages over the Western Front early in 1915, because they were operating the only aircraft equipped with machine guns capable of forward firing. The Morane-Saulnier L was particularly innovative in this respect, being fitted with a machine gun capable of firing through the arc of the propeller, which was fitted with armored deflector wedges, thus preventing the bullets from its Hotchkiss M1909 machine gun from destroying the propeller. Unfortunately, while flying a type "L" over German lines, the designer of the aircraft, Roland Garros, was forced down and his machine captured, despite the pilot's attempts to burn it. The German aviation authorities quickly circulated details of the forward-firing mechanism to a number of aircraft manufacturers, including Anthony Fokker, asking them for a similar design.

Fokker's answer was a significant improvement upon Garros's idea, the Dutch designer devising a system that allowed the bullets from a Parabellum MG 14 machine gun to be interrupted when the propeller was in line with the muzzle of the weapon. This allowed almost uninterrupted fire from the machine gun, without endangering the propeller, giving the pilot equipped with this system a considerable advantage over his more conventionally armed opponents. Later the Parabellum was substituted for the IMG '08, Imperial Germany's Maxim copy.

Fokker's interrupter or synchronization gear was fitted to a monoplane of his own design, the Fokker E.I. This aircraft, and the succeeding derivative machines, did not have very good performance when compared to their German and Allied contemporaries, being tricky to fly and not particularly maneuverable, but its rotary engine and overall conformation made it a perfect platform for the installation of Fokker's new system. The forerunner of the Eindecker monoplanes, the prototype E.5/15, began operations in July 1915, and the first recorded destruction of an Allied aircraft by this type was on 15 July 1915, when a Morane "L" type was shot down by Lt. Kurt Wintgens of FFA 48. Despite this initial success, the RFC did not report the appearance of large numbers of the new Fokkers until almost the end of the Battle of Loos in October 1915.

In the six months between August 1915 and February 1916, pilots now flying the improved Fokker E.I. claimed a total of 61 aircraft shot down, mostly from the French air force. But when compared with "Bloody April" in 1917, when 275 RFC aircraft of all types were shot down in a single month, the number of aircraft lost during the "Fokker scourge" was almost trivial. It was not, however, the material losses but rather the effect on the morale of Allied pilots that made the period of the "Fokker

The Oberursel U.0 seven-cylinder rotary engine of the Fokker E.I, with the *Stangensteuerung* synchronizer drive unit behind the engine crankcase, shown here with the engine cowling removed.

Scourge" so important. The E.I. was perceived by many French and British pilots as impossible to destroy or evade, and this caused the RFC to both restrict its operations and increase the number of escorts accompanying single reconnaissance or artillery observation aircraft, which had a corresponding effect on the efficiency of Allied air operations.

During this period, the RFC's best aircraft, the Vickers FB5 "Gunbus" carrying a single forward-firing Lewis gun, had a top speed of only 70 mph at 5,000 ft, compared to the 81 mph of the E.I. The Fokker also had a significantly better rate of climb, and the Germans had developed the technique of attacking British artillery spotter aircraft and their escorts from above and "out of the sun," which added significantly to their success. However, new, improved designs of aircraft were on their way to both the British and French air forces, and the arrival, in the early months of 1916, of the Nieuport 11 and Airco DH2 with their top speeds of around 90 mph and greater maneuverability, signaled the end of the Fokker's dominance of the skies. By April 1916, two months after the beginning of the Battle of Verdun, the Allies were in control of the skies over the Western Front once again, just in time to participate in the aerial reconnaissance and artillery spotting that was intended to be a vital part of the Somme offensive. The RFC continued to dominate the skies over the Somme during the most significant period of the offensive and were able to supply Haig and his staff with detailed maps of the German trench system, although this information does not appear to have been well used by the British generals. By November 1916, the Somme offensive had ground to a halt and had resulted in an advance of six miles into German-occupied territory for the loss of nearly 800,000 Allied troops and over 500,000 Germans.[16]

Sir Hugh Trenchard and "Bloody April"

Operations began again in January 1917 at Ancre, which was to serve as a diversion from Allied preparations to mount a major offensive at Arras, which began on 9 April 1917 and lasted until 16 May 1917. During this period the RFC supported British operations by flying close air support and aerial reconnaissance sorties as well as conducting strategic bombing missions of selected German military targets. Unfortunately, this aggressive strategy, which was carried out almost wholly over enemy lines at the insistence of the commanding officer of the RFC, Sir Hugh Trenchard, resulted in the loss of 275 British aircraft and the death or wounding of 400 aircrew. Most of these casualties were amongst inexperienced pilots, leading one British pilot to remark: "The worst carnage was amongst the new pilots—many of whom lasted just a day or two."

Methods of pilot training in the RFC left much to be desired. This lack of foresight in equipping the newly recruited British pilots with the skills necessary to carry out their duties in reasonable safety is claimed to have largely accounted for their excessively high attrition rate. In May 1915, there were 11 training stations in Britain, with a total of 234 pilots undergoing instruction. By March 1916, six months after Trenchard's appointment, there were 15 training stations, but the number of pilots undergoing instruction had risen to a massive 963.[17]

In March 1916, Trenchard also revised the level of qualifications required to qualify as a pilot officer (see box). As a consequence of his ruthless demands for pilots to carry the

Fourteen. The Development of Repeating and Multi-fire Weapons 223

> **Qualification Tests in Flying required as of March 23, 1916**
> 1. The pilot must have spent at least fifteen hours in the air solo.
> 2. He must have flown a service aeroplane satisfactorily.
> 3. He must have carried out a cross-country flight of at least 60 miles successfully. During this flight he must land at two outside landing places under the supervision of an officer of the Royal Flying Corps.
> 4. He will climb to 6,000 feet and remain at that height for at least fifteen minutes, after which he will land with his engine stopped, the aeroplane first touching the ground within a circular mark of fifty yards diameter.
> 5. He will make two landings in the dark assisted by flares. [The CFS and Administrative Wing commanders had the authority to dispense with this test if the weather conditions caused an unwarranted delay.]
> 6. He will attain a standard of eight words a minutes signalling on the buzzer [Morse code].[18]

fight to the Germans, however inadequately trained they might be, a new pilot usually found himself at the Western front after having done only 15 hours solo, although he was expected to be able to send Morse at 8 words per minute, because the army could then rely upon him for artillery spotting! Many in the RFC were critical of this haphazard approach, which also came to mean that pilots were being sent to France without having the most basic skills, such as formation flying, and often having never flown the type of aircraft they were expected to pilot over enemy lines. Sir Sefton Brancker, during his short-lived tenure as Director of Air Operations, acknowledged the deficiency in pilot training in a memorandum to Lt. Col. C.J. Burke, then head of the Central Flying School, on 21 March 1916. Burke was unhappy about the requirement of only 15 solo hours required to qualify as a pilot officer in the RFC, regarding 50 hours as much more realistic. Brancker argued that this was not feasible: "I am absolutely with you in principle, but I fear that at the moment we cannot make graduation more difficult than laid down in the draft which I sent you. Already the output [of pilots] is not equal to the demand, and thanks to too rapid expansion during the past six months we are very nearly bankrupt at the moment. The standard has been allowed to drop too low, hence my memorandum, but the time has not come yet to raise it to a really satisfactory basis."

Another factor that contributed significantly to the loss of British pilots was the disparity in aircraft. The German air force was equipped with the superior Albatross D.II and D.III fighters, with their twin forward-firing IMG '08 machine guns, superior rates of climb and higher top speeds when compared to the best available British aircraft, the Airco DH2 and the F.E.2. It was not until late in 1917 that the new Sopwith Camel and SE5a, both equipped with forward-firing Vickers guns, began to appear in sufficient numbers to move the balance of air superiority back to the RFC.

However, despite these frightful losses, the German air force did not succeed in preventing the RFC from carrying out its initial objectives. The British air corps continued to support the army throughout the Arras offensive with effective contact patrolling during British offensives, up-to-date aerial photographs, reconnaissance information, and bombing raids against the German trenches and other military targets.[19]

Chapter Fifteen

Light Machine Guns in World War I

Light Machine Guns in Use by British Forces in World War I

The British army used two light machine gun during World War I, the American-designed Lewis gun and the French Hotchkiss Mk 1, a version of the Hotchkiss M1909, chambered for the .303 British Mark VII service rifle cartridge.

The Lewis Gun, Model 1914

The Lewis gun was the invention of a U.S. Army officer, Colonel Isaac Lewis, who patented the gun in 1911, although some of its features were copied from the design of another inventor, Samuel McClean. McClean had produced a weapon for the Automatic Arms company, incorporating many of the design features used later in the Lewis gun, which he called the McClean-Lissak automatic rifle. Unfortunately, he had introduced so many modifications into the weapon's original design that it became too heavy to use in the role of a light machine gun. However, McClean had by this time signed over all his patents for the weapon to Automatic Arms, and the company's directors then approached Lewis with the suggestion that he produce a lightweight automatic machine gun based on patents already held by the company or, as an alternative, from an original idea of his own. By 1911 he had a satisfactory prototype based on the McClean-Lissak, which he took to Washington, D.C., where he showed it to Maj. Gen Leonard Wood, who was the Army's Chief of Staff. Lewis subsequently conducted a series of informal test firings in the presence of senior officials of the U.S. government, using four guns produced to his own design and chambered for the Army's Springfield .30–06 service rifle cartridge. He also used one of his guns in the very first firing of an automatic machine gun from an aircraft at the U.S. Army's College Park Airport in June 1912.[1]

Despite the success of the demonstrations, no orders were forthcoming from the U.S. government. Despairing of his own military establishment, in 1913, Lewis took his guns to Europe, where he first established a small company to manufacture the guns in Liege, Belgium, which he called *Armes Automatique Lewis*. With the German invasion of Belgium imminent, he moved his operation to England, and in 1914, BSA (British Small Arms Company) purchased a license from Lewis to manufacture the weapon at their factory in Birmingham. After some development work by BSA, it was approved for service with the British army on 15 October 1915 under the designation: "Gun, Lewis, .303-cal."

During World War I, the Lewis was produced in Britain by BSA and in the United States by the Savage Arms Company. The two versions were largely similar, but the weapons produced by BSA were chambered for .303 British service rifle cartridge and the Savage guns used the .30–06 Springfield round. As a result, there were differences in the magazine, cartridge delivery mechanism, bolt, barrel, extractors and gas operation system. This meant parts were not interchangeable, although this was rectified when Lewis guns were being produced by both companies during World War II. However, Savage did make a number of Lewis guns in .303 British caliber; the Model 1916 and Model 1917 in particular were exported to Canada and the United Kingdom, and a few were also supplied to the U.S. military, particularly the Navy, while Savage's Model 1917 was produced in .30–06 caliber. A number of these weapons were also supplied to the UK under the terms of lend-lease during World War II.[2]

Specification

Production: precise records unavailable, but estimated at 350,000 weapons.

The Lewis gun is a fully automatic light machine gun, with a single barrel and a gas-operated recoil mechanism, cartridges being delivered from a drum-pattern magazine mounted on the upper surface of the receiver, which contains either 47 (land service) or 96 (air service) cartridges. There is no provision for adjusting the rate of fire or switching to semiautomatic operation; adjustment of the rate of fire is possible only by careful manipulation of the trigger. The barrel was fitted with a finned aluminum heat sink at the breech and a shroud, both devices being incorporated into the design of the gun to encourage cooling during firing. There is an adjustment knob on the return spring casing in front of the trigger to allow the tension of the unusual spiral return spring to be adjusted to compensate for temperature and wear and a gas regulator tap on the front of the barrel shroud to allow more gas into the piston cylinder when the mechanism becomes fouled by cartridge residue. Originally manufactured to fire either the .303 MkVII British service rifle cartridge

Lewis gun from the right side, showing the magazine and carrying handle, with the characteristic barrel shroud fitted (courtesy James D. Julia Auctioneers, Fairfield, Maine. www.jamesdjulia.com).

or the .30–06 Springfield U.S. service rifle cartridge, some Lewis guns were exported by Britain during World War I, first to Russia, chambered for the 7.62 × 54mmR Russian service rifle cartridge, and subsequently to Japan, chambered for the 7.7 × 58mm Arisaka Japanese army service rifle cartridge. A number of these weapons were also captured during World War II by German forces and subsequently rechambered for the 7.92 × 50mm Mauser German service rifle cartridge.[3]

Frame Markings

Guns from the BSA factory

Serial number range: 1–160000 (numbers are approximate). The serial number itself number may also have an "E" prefix.

A manufacturer's stamp is usually found applied to the top of the receiver at the rear, having the following form:

> **Manufactured by**
> **The Birmingham Small Arms Co Ltd**
> **ENGLAND**
> **for**
> **Armes Automatic Lewis**
> **BELGIUM**

The receiver is also stamped just in front of the rear sight:

> **LEWIS AUTO GUN**
> **MOD. 1914—PAT**

A serial number is usually found beneath this stamp, and a serial number may also be found on the upper rear surface of the barrel shroud, adjacent to the magazine. The "Broad

Lewis gun from above, showing the adjustable sights, manufacturer's stamp (Birmingham Small Arms Co) and the model (Model 1914) (courtesy James D. Julia Auctioneers, Fairfield, Maine. www.jamesdjulia.com).

Arrow" acceptance mark of the War Office will also be stamped on any gun that has been in service with the British army, most frequently on the pistol grip and breech. Magazines will also be stamped with a Broad Arrow.

Guns from the Savage factory

Serial number range: 1–30000 (numbers are approximate).

The receiver is stamped with the manufacturer's details just in front of the rear sight, having the following form:

LEWIS MACHINE GUN
MFG. BY SAVAGE ARMS CORP. UTICA. NY.U.S.A.
.30 U.S. GOV'T.

This stamp is repeated on the right side of the receiver, just in front of its union with the butt, a serial number being stamped beneath and the caliber designation omitted:

LEWIS MACHINE GUN
MFG. BY SAVAGE ARMS CORP. UTICA. NY.U.S.A.
00000

Patent information is found stamped on the right side of the receiver, below the ejection port, in a complex collection, which is also found stamped on the butt plate.

OPERATION

Firing a Lewis gun is a relatively simple process. The magazine is first placed on the magazine spigot located on the upper surface of the breech and locked in place, this action ensuring that the magazine is correctly orientated so that a cartridge is placed over the breech slot, ready for delivery. The cocking handle is then drawn back, which also moves the gas piston and bolt assembly backwards, allowing it to be retained by the sear, and also operating a cog that compresses the spiral return spring contained in a semicircular housing in front of the trigger. Pulling the trigger causes the bolt and gas piston assembly to move forward under the action of this return spring, the bolt lip removing a cartridge from the magazine and driving it into the breech. The bolt is then stopped and locked to the barrel with a rotating motion that engages its locking lugs with the locking slots in the receiver, the firing pin continuing its forward motion until it strikes the primer and fires the cartridge.

The bullet now moves up the rifling until it passes a vent in the barrel, which allows some of the gas generated by the charge in the cartridge to pass into the under-barrel cylinder. This increase in pressure causes the piston contained in the cylinder to be forced backwards, pushing the firing pin back into its original position and rotating and unlocking the bolt from the barrel. Movement of the piston also operates an extractor that removes the spent case from the breech, before it is struck by a pivoting ejector that knocks the case out of the ejection port on the right side of the weapon. The piston then continues its movement to the rear, driving the bolt and piston assembly back on to the sear mechanism, while simultaneously tightening the spiral recoil spring and operating the feed arm, which turns the magazine to position the next cartridge. If the trigger is still depressed, the sear

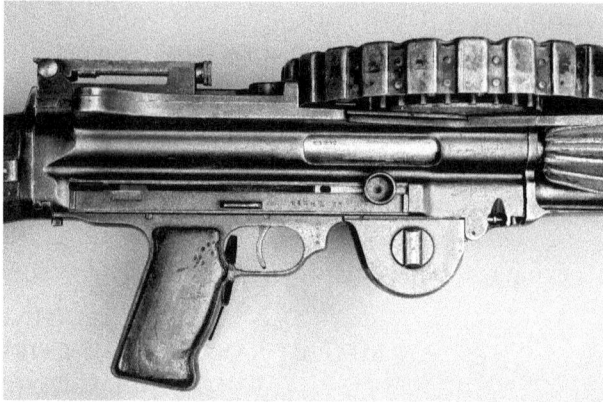

Left: Empty Lewis gun magazine. *Right:* Receiver of Lewis gun, showing the charging or cocking handle, ejection port and the return spring housing, with its adjustment key (both photographs courtesy James D. Julia Auctioneers, Fairfield, Maine. www.jamesdjulia.com).

does not operate, and the bolt and piston are driven forward by the recoil spring to begin the operating cycle again.[4]

VEEDER CARTRIDGE COUNTER

One design flaw in the Lewis gun's otherwise excellent mechanism was the absence of some means of determining when a drum was nearly empty. This flaw quickly became apparent to pilots who used the weapon, and they clamored for a modification that would indicate the number of rounds left in the drum magazine, because unlike a gun that was belt-fed, no estimate of the remaining cartridges was possible by eye. Many devices were tried, the most successful being a system designed and built by the Veeder Manufacturing Co., Hartford, Conn. The Veeder counter was mounted on top of the magazine plate of a Lewis drum and operated by a small gear, which engaged in the notches of a latch lock located in the spacer ring. Upon loading, this indicator was set to zero and as the Lewis was fired, the magazine revolved, operating the indicator, which showed a luminous figure "1" when 19 rounds were left, changing to a red marker when only 9 cartridges remained to be fired.[5]

Loaded drum magazine, ready to be fitted to a Lewis gun (Wikipedia: License: CC-A-S-A 3.0).

Major variations

Lewis guns used by the British armed forces

- **Mark I, Model 1914**: The Lewis Mk I, Model chambered for the .303 caliber British service cartridge was the model used by British and Commonwealth forces from 1915 until 1942, although improvements were introduced with the production runs of later weapons.
- **Mark II**: The first purpose-built aircraft version of the Lewis, earlier versions having been modified Mk Is. Cooling fins were omitted to save weight, but the lightweight protective shroud around the barrel was retained, while the wooden butt was replaced with a T-shaped "spade" butt, with the pistol grip retained. A 97-round drum magazine was introduced, requiring a larger magazine spigot on the body of the gun.
- **Mark II***: An improved Mk II with an increased rate of fire introduced in 1918, for aircraft use.
- **Mark III**: A further upgrade of the Mk II with an even faster rate of fire and the barrel shroud removed, introduced later in 1918.
- **Mark III***: The British designation for the US .30–06 caliber M1918 aircraft gun, which was modified for use in land service (i.e., the army or Home Guard), by exchanging the spade grip for a metal skeleton stock and adding a simple wooden fore-grip. The barrel shroud, originally fitted to cool the barrel, was not replaced and the weapon's performance seems to have been unaffected. The British government imported over 80,000 of these guns to replace weapons left behind at Dunkirk and 46,000 of these weapons were issued to the Home Guard in 1940.
- **Mark III****: The designation for the .303 caliber Mark III modified for land service by replacing the spade grip with a rudimentary skeleton stock and addition of a simple wooden fore-stock, using the same type of modification as the Mark III* Lewis gun.
- **Mark III DEMS**: Intended for Defensively Equipped Merchant Ships (DEMS), it was similar to the Mark III** but with the addition of a pistol grip on the fore-stock, so that the weapon could be fired free-standing from the shoulder, from any part of the deck of a ship.
- **Mark IV**: Constructed from surplus parts and incomplete guns, these weapons closely followed the design of the Mk III** Lewis gun, intended for use by land forces. There was a particular shortage of the fragile spiral recoil springs for the Lewis, so a simpler spring was manufactured and housed in a straight tube which extended into the skeleton stock. Many of these guns were fitted with a simple, light tripod which had been specially produced for this Model.

Lewis guns used by Canadian forces

- **Model 1915**: This was the designation given to .303 Lewis Mk I weapons manufactured for Canada in the USA by the Savage Arms Company. Large numbers of these guns were also produced by Savage for the British Army and for France and Italy, although these were guns designed for air service.

Lewis guns used by U.S. forces

- **M1917 Lewis:** Savage produced a version of the Lewis Mk I for U.S. forces, rechambered for the .30–06 Springfield U.S. service rifle cartridge, with a modified gas operation due to the greater power of the U.S. cartridge. Most of these weapons were modified for aircraft use.
- **Lewis Mark IV:** U.S. Navy designation for the M1917 Lewis gun.
- **M1918 Lewis:** A version of the M1917, designed for use in aircraft with the barrel shroud omitted and a modified butt.[6]

MILITARY SERVICE

World War I

Initially used in Belgium during the first two months of the war, Lewis guns were fitted to a number of vehicles that were in action against the forces of the Central Powers. However, the Lewis was not adopted for both land and air service by the British army until October 1915, with a general issue not beginning until spring 1916. At this point the weapon was supplied to infantry battalions as a replacement for their Vickers medium/heavy machine guns, which were then being assigned to the Machine Gun Corps. Lewis guns also replaced the original Hotchkiss M1909 and Vickers on the MkIV male and female tanks introduced in 1917.

Royal Navy ships began to be fitted with Lewis guns during 1916. HMS *Cockchafer* was one vessel equipped with such armament, and was described in 1916 as having eight Lewis guns for antiaircraft defense. By 1918 all the ships of the Grand Fleet had Lewis guns for dealing with attacks from low-flying aircraft. They were installed in the following configurations:

- Capital ships: 10 Lewis guns, some fitted into twin mountings.
- Cruisers and light cruisers: 8 Lewis guns, some fitted into twin mountings.
- Destroyers: 4 Lewis guns, all using single mounts.

Lewis guns were also fitted to submarines, mine sweepers and patrol boats operating in the southern sector of the North Sea, and to defensively equipped merchant ships (DEMS), operating on the east coast as a defense against aircraft, which were attacking these craft at low level and short range. All of these classes of ship were usually fitted with single weapons.[7] Both the U.S. Navy and the Marine Corps also used the gun at different periods, as did the German army, who included instructions on operation and care of the Lewis gun in their training regime for machine-gun crews during World War I and World War II.

Lewis guns fitted to aircraft

Used extensively in aircraft during World War I as either an observer's weapon or as an addition to the air service Vickers guns, the Lewis gun was popular with the RFC due to its light weight, air-cooled configuration, and self-contained drum magazine, which were easily changed while in flight, unlike the much more cumbersome Vickers belt.

Unfortunately, the open-bolt design of the Lewis meant it could not be modified to use the synchronization equipment then being introduced to allow a machine gun to fire through the arc of a propeller. Consequently, aircraft equipped with a Lewis gun either had it installed on a forward-firing Foster mount or on a Scarff ring mounted in the observer's cockpit of a two-seater observation or reconnaissance aircraft, the Foster mount soon proving to have significant advantage over other forward-firing systems. Foster's system utilized an arc-shaped beam which allowed the gun to be pulled down and unloaded in flight. Pilots soon found that a Lewis gun on this type of mounting could also be locked and fired in this position, with the barrel at approximately 45° from the horizontal. This was a useful feature for attacking aircraft and especially airships from directly underneath where neither pilot or observer could see an enemy coming, in the aircraft's "blind spot," because the orientation of the gun resulted in a flat

Right: **Foster mount for a Lewis gun fitted to an Avro 504.** *Below:* **Lewis gun fitted into the front cockpit of a Royal Aircraft Factory FE2d.**

trajectory and made aiming at a target much simpler. This was to prove an essential factor for the RFC in the battle against what became known as the "Zeppelin menace."[8]

Zeppelin raids and the "Buckingham" cartridge

The potential threat posed by the airships designed by Ferdinand von Zeppelin had begun to concern the British as early as 1909, and the RNAS had made their first attack on a Zeppelin base soon after war was declared, during October 1914. Despite these bombing raids, Zeppelins were still being produced in significant numbers, and on 7 January 1915, Kaiser Wilhelm signed the order approving attacks by airships upon Britain, although he specified that London should not be a target. Although attacks were only intended to be directed against military targets, navigation was problematic. The first raid, which took place on 19 January 1915, saw bombs dropped on Great Yarmouth, instead of Humberside, resulting in the deaths of four civilians and serious injury to another sixteen residents. Raids on the London docks were subsequently authorized in February 1915, but the Zeppelins were so inaccurate that civilian casualties were still the usual result of an attack by airships. During this period the Zeppelins were able to carry out their missions with relatively little danger: RFC fighters had inadequate performance when faced with these giant airships, which operated at heights far above the service ceilings of existing British aircraft.

During 1915, the Zeppelins had seemed unassailable, but in the following year ground defenses were improved, searchlights were introduced, and the RFC began to use new aircraft with improved performance. They also had two new incendiary cartridges for their Lewis guns, the Buckingham Mark I (RFC designation: Cartridge S.A. Incendiary Buckingham .303 inch Mark I) and the Buckingham Mark VIIB (RFC designation: Cartridge S.A. Incendiary Buckingham .303 inch Mark (VII.B)), named after their inventor. Both bullets contained yellow phosphorus, which began to burn on firing and produced a clear smoke trail or "trace" visible up to 1,000 meters. Unfortunately, the round nose of the Mark I cartridge made it unsuitable for use in Lewis guns, and the Mark VIIB had to be introduced to overcome this problem. These bullets and the improved designs that followed were able to ignite the hydrogen gas contained in the envelope of the Zeppelins, something conventional Mark VII ball ammunition had been unable to do.

Despite the civilian deaths caused by the night raids carried out by these airships, the British government was obliged to modify the use the RFC and RNAS were allowed to make of the new Buckingham ammunition. Orders were issued to RFC and RNAS squadrons, banning the use of incendiary ammunition during air-to-air combat with another aircraft, as their use against personnel was considered initially to be a violation of the St. Petersburg Declaration. Pilots were permitted to use the new incendiary cartridge only against Zeppelins and balloons, and they were additionally restricted to shooting at the gas envelope rather than the crew. Furthermore, they were required to carry written orders on their person when engaging these targets and were liable to be sentenced to death by military tribunal if they were found using this type of ammunition without proper authorization.

Despite these restrictions, the RFC and RNAS began to be increasingly successful against the Zeppelins. In an attempt to prevent the losses to their airships, in 1917 the German airship service introduced a new type capable of operating at 5,000 meters. They proved relatively unsuccessful, with altitude sickness and extreme cold causing the crews more problems than the British fighters. In May 1917 the Kaiser, alarmed by the Zeppelin

Zeppelin flying over London.

losses, ordered that airship raids should only be attempted in favorable circumstances. The last major Zeppelin raid of World War I was made on the night of 19 October 1917 by 13 craft that were intended to bomb Liverpool, Sheffield and Manchester. Only one, the L45, reached Britain, dropping its bombs on North London before crashing in France on its return journey. Three more of the formation were lost from engine failures or ground fire, while another, the L55, was damaged on landing. Four minor raids followed in 1918, but they were insignificant when compared to the operations conducted in previous years. The Armistice saw the end of German dirigible technology, with the Allies demanding the abolition of all German air forces and the surrender of Zeppelin's remaining airships as part of the war reparations.[9]

World War II

Prior to Britain's entry into World War II, most of the Lewis guns previously in use for land service had been replaced by the new Bren gun, and in aircraft by the

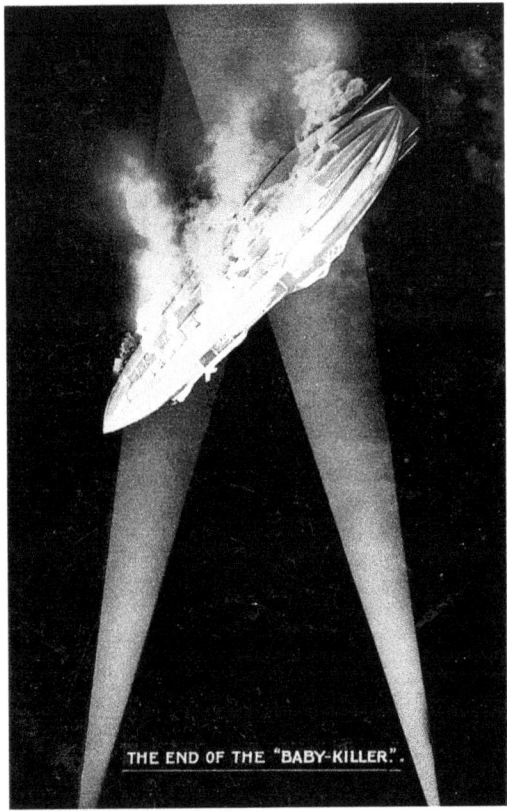

World War I propaganda postcard called "The End Of the Baby-Killer," depicting a Zeppelin shot down in flames.

Vickers K or G.O. However, due to the massive loss of equipment suffered at Dunkirk, Lewis guns were removed from storage and refurbished before being issued to Home Guard and antiaircraft units. The Lewis was also retained in service with some Commonwealth forces, especially in the Pacific Theater.

The Royal Navy retained the Lewis gun as their standard close-range air defense weapon for much of the war, until it was replaced by the Oerlikon 20mm cannon. It was fitted to major warships, armed trawlers and defensively equipped merchant ships, often using twin mountings, and a quadruple mount was also developed for motor torpedo boats (MTBs). British submarines generally carried two guns on single mounts, and the weapon was also installed aboard the Royal Air Force's air-sea rescue launches. Although Lewis guns were gradually being replaced by the more modern Oerlikon, new corvettes were still being fitted with Lewis guns in twin mounts as late as 1942. U.S. naval forces also used the Lewis gun during World War II to arm merchant cruisers, small auxiliary ships, landing craft and submarines, as well as U.S. Coast Guard vessels. A total of 145,000 new Lewis guns were produced by BSA during World War II, with approximately 3,500 manufactured by Savage in both calibers.[10]

The Lewis was officially withdrawn from British service in 1946, but continued to be used by forces operating against the United Nations in the Korean War. It was also used against French and U.S. forces in the First Indochina War and the subsequent Vietnam War.

Values

Under the 1986 American legislation, a fully functional Lewis gun may be owned and fired. Consequently, at auction, a gun capable of firing will command a significantly higher price than a deactivated weapon. Local regulations as they apply to these weapons should be consulted before purchase.

Prices quoted here are for a working gun.

BSA Lewis guns

- **Land service**
  NRA Good: $10,000–$12,000; NRA Fine: $30,000–$45,000
- **Air service**
  NRA Good: $10,000–$12,000 NRA; Fine: $20,000–$25,000

Savage Lewis guns

NRA Good: $10,000–$12,000; NRA Fine: $20,000–$30,000

Light Machine Guns in Use by French Forces in World War I

Hotchkiss M1909/Hotchkiss Mk 1

Also known in U.S. service as the M1909 Benét-Mercié machine gun, this weapon was effectively the culmination of a series of machine guns produced by Hotchkiss et Cie.

The original idea for all the later automatic machine guns made by the company came from a gun designed by a Captain Odkolek von Ujezda and presented to the company sometime in the early 1890s. This was not a very good weapon, but Laurence Benét and Henri Mercié, two of the Hotchkiss company's designers, liked the basis of the captain's gun, which had a mechanism worked by a piston housed beneath the barrel and operated by residual gas from the cartridge. Hotchkiss bought the patent for the weapon for a lump sum and Benét and Mercié began to adapt the mechanism for use in an improved automatic machine gun, chambered in 8mm Lebel, which they showed to the U.S. Navy in 1896. The gun had a number of problems which the USN suggested be referred to a Mr. Edward Parkhurst, who had been involved with the development of the Gardner manually operated quick-firing gun. He made some suggestions that Hotchkiss et Cie. gratefully accepted, resulting in the first Hotchkiss automatic machine gun, the Model 1897, which also began the Hotchkiss company's predilection for metal strip magazines and air-cooling. This was followed by a succession of weapons based on the M1897: the Model 1900, Model 1903, Model 1907 St. Etienne, finally resulting in the Model 1909, which was accepted into service by the French Army in 1909, accounting for the model designation. It was also adopted by the U.S. army, although these weapons were made in America under license to the Springfield Armory and the Colt Patent Firearms Manufacturing Co.[11]

Specification

Production: precise records unavailable, but estimated at 100,000 weapons.

The Hotchkiss M1909 is a gas-operated, air-cooled light machine gun, firing from a closed bolt and chambered for a variety of cartridges, including 8mm Lebel, .303 British, .30–06 Springfield, 7.92 × 57mm Mauser and 7 × 57mm Spanish Mauser. Ammunition is delivered to the breech of the gun from a metal strip magazine containing 30 rounds, although later weapons were modified to use belt loading, employing a single metal belt containing 251cartridges (3 strips, each containing 84 rounds) and constructed of disposable wire links. The barrel was designed to be changed quickly when it overheated, and was fitted with numerous wide, circular metal rings that served to cool both that component

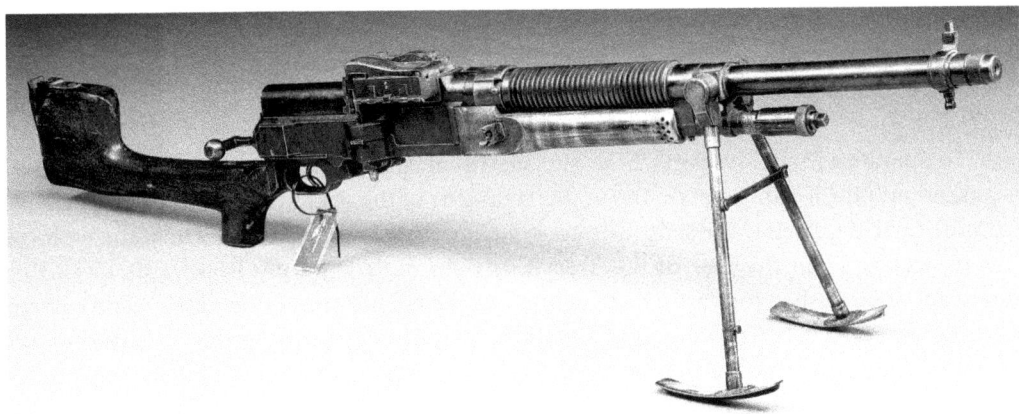

Hotchkiss Model 1909 LMG, showing the finned barrel, gas cylinder, skid-footed bipod and characteristically shaped butt (courtesy James D. Julia Auctioneers, Fairfield, Maine. www.jamesdjulia.com).

Model and caliber stamps on the receiver of a Hotchkiss Model 1909 LMG (courtesy James D. Julia Auctioneers, Fairfield, Maine. www.jamesdjulia.com).

and the breech, prolonging the service life of the rifling and also giving the gun its characteristic appearance. A shoulder stock of black walnut was fitted, with an integral pistol grip, so that any soldier familiar with a conventional rifle could operate a Hotchkiss with a minimum of practice. The piston and bolt assembly are also fitted with a safety block, allowing the mechanism to be made safe with the breech either open or closed, and a gas regulator with manual operation was fitted between the barrel and piston cylinder. Guns made for land service by the Springfield Armory, Colt, and both British and European manufacturers had a bipod at the muzzle, while M1909s intended for use by the British cavalry were supplied with a tripod. This tripod was mounted under the barrel of the gun and could be folded back and moved with the weapon, much like the later supports fitted to the Bren gun and BAR. Weapons intended for use in tanks were fitted to those vehicles by means of a substantial, three-sided bracket, the guns being hinged so as to be capable of vertical movement and using the spigot mounting intended for the tripod mounting of the cavalry gun.[12]

Operation

To operate a Model 1909 machine gun, a strip of cartridges, or a belt in later weapons, is pushed into the loading slot on the upper right side of the breech, the strip being inserted with the cartridges below the strip. The cocking handle, which is on the right of the weapon and projecting from the rear of the breech, is then pulled sharply backwards to its full extent and then pushed forwards, cocking the weapon against the action of the recoil spring. Turning the cocking lever to the right and lining it up with either the letter "A" (Automatic) or "R" (Repeater or semiautomatic fire) determines the firing mode, and the weapon is then ready to fire.

Pulling the trigger releases the bolt and piston assembly, which starts forward under compression of the recoil spring. The face of the bolt strikes the base of the first cartridge in the magazine strip, forcing it into the chamber, while the claw of the extractor moves into the groove or cannelure in the base of the cartridge. As soon as the bolt engages the breech locking nut, also referred to as the fermature nut, the firing pin and its large lug contact a ramp or machined projection in the receiver, causing the firing pin to rotate partially and disengage the firing pin lug from its transverse slot in the bolt. Immediately after this operation, the bolt is locked rigidly behind the chambered cartridge and the firing pin moves forward, striking the primer and discharging the weapon.

After the bullet has passed the gas port in the barrel, residual cartridge gas is vented into the gas cylinder, forcing the piston contained in that component to the rear, unlocking the bolt and causing the firing pin to turn and move backwards, where it is held stationary. The extractor then removes the empty case from the chamber and operation of the ejector knocks it out of the ejection slot on the left side of the receiver. When the gas piston has moved halfway through its travel, it operates the spurred wheel in the breech, which advances the magazine strip sufficiently to move the next round into position for subsequent loading into the firing chamber. With the piston fully retracted and the recoil spring compressed, the firing cycle can begin once again, continuing for as long as there is ammunition and the trigger is depressed.[13]

The cartridge delivery system

Instead of delivering its cartridge from a fabric belt or box magazine, all Hotchkiss machine guns originally used metal strips made of spring-tempered sheet steel. Thirty cartridges were loaded into each of these 15-inch strips, which were then packed into cardboard boxes. The strips were so arranged that they could be fed directly into the gun from the box or into a wooden box, which held 10 loaded magazine strips in 5 partitions, arranged on edge. The delivery mechanism within the breech of the gun consisted of a spurred wheel, which engaged with the openings milled in the magazine strip and the two cams on the piston, and this had the additional advantage of ensuring that magazine strips could be loaded with the breech either open or closed. The strips were constructed so that they could be locked together in a single continuous length so that a whole series of strips could be fired without the necessity of cocking the gun between strips, although using this device with more than two or three strips at one time must have been extremely awkward.[14]

Major variations[15]

Hotchkiss M1909 light-machine gun

Serial number range: No record currently available.

- **Mle1909:** This version was accepted by the French army in 1909, chambered for the 8mm Lebel cartridge.

Receiver markings:
Left side of breech stamped:

MITRAILLEUSE LEGERE HOTCHKISS
BREVETEE S.G.D.G CALIBRE 8m/m
No XXXX

Where "XXXX" denotes the serial number and "BREVETTE S.G.D.G" indicates a French technical patent: "Breveté Sans Garantie Du Gouvernement," i.e.: "Patented Without Guarantee of the Government," effectively a weapon made under contract and not by the patentee. Many weapons are also found stamped "CALIBRE 7m/m," indicating that they were chambered for the 7mm Spanish Mauser cartridge and consequently designed for use by either the Austro-Hungarian army or are of later provenance and intended for South America, typically Argentina.

Hotchkiss Mk 1

Serial number range: No record currently available.

- **Hotchkiss Portable Machine Gun Mk 1:** This version of the French Model 1909 was manufactured by RSAF, Enfield and chambered for the .303 British service rifle cartridge. It had a conventional wooden stock, a bipod at the muzzle and was designed to use magazine strips. Usually issued to land forces.
  Receiver markings:
  Left side of breech stamped:

  HOTCHKISS PORTABLE MACHINE GUN Mk I*
  PATENTED CALIBER .303
  NoE XXXXX

Where "XXXXX" denotes the serial number. A serial number is also found stamped on the barrel band and British military proof marks will be found stamped on the barrel itself, usually just forward of the barrel band.

- **Hotchkiss Portable Machine Gun, Cavalry, No2 Mk 1:** Another version of this gun was also made by RSAF, Enfield, chambered for the .303 British cartridge, but fitted with a removable, straight metal stock and separate, brass pistol grip which could use either a strip magazine or the articulated metal belt, composed of disposable wire links and holding 249 cartridges. Usually issued to cavalry units, although some later weapons were installed in tanks.
  Receiver markings:
  Left side of breech stamped:

  HOTCHKISS PORTABLE MACHINE GUN Mk I*
  PATENTED CALIBER .303
  NoE XXXXX

Where "XXXXX" denotes the serial number. A serial number is also found stamped on the barrel band and British military proof marks will be found stamped on the barrel itself, usually just forward of the barrel band.[16]

Benét-Mercié machine rifle, Model 1909

Serial number range: 1–670.

Adopted by the U.S. army as the "Automatic Machine Rifle, Model of 1909" in 1909, with an initial order to Hotchkiss et Cie. for 29 guns chambered in .30–06 Springfield. Colt and the Springfield Armory were both eventually contracted to produce the guns. Colt guns have smooth barrels in front of the cooling fins, while M109s made by Springfield have sharply pointed checkering in that area, a modification intended to provide a better grip when changing barrels. Records show 670 guns produced for U.S. service, but this may only include guns sold to the Army, with additional weapons purchased by the USN.

Frame markings:
- **Guns from the Springfield Armory**
Left side of breech stamped:

> AUTOMATIC MACHINE RIFLE
> CAL..30, MODEL OF 1909
> No XXX
> SPRINGFIELD ARMORY

Where "XXX" denotes the serial number.
- **Guns from the Colt factory**
Left side of breech stamped:

> AUTOMATIC MACHINE RIFLE
> CAL..30, MODEL OF 1909
> No XXX
> COLT PT. FRMS. MFTG. CO.

Military service

In use by the French army throughout World War I as their principal light machine gun, the M1909 was also issued to British tank and cavalry formations. Some Commonwealth forces also received the Hotchkiss, in particular the Australian Light Horse brigades, the New Zealand Mounted Rifles Brigade, and the Imperial Camel Corps Brigade, who all saw action in Sinai and Palestine between 1915 and 1917.

U.S. forces also used the gun during the Villa Expedition into Mexico between 1916 and 1917. Initially, the gun was found to be unreliable, but after some retraining its performance during combat was found to have improved significantly. Unfortunately, by the time the U.S. had entered World War I, production had been terminated. The U.S. Army was forced to accept the Chauchat as the only replacement available, although the USN continued to use the M1909 during this period.[17]

Values

The U.S. government ruling of 1986 means that a gun capable of firing will fetch considerably more than a deactivated weapon. French and British guns appear so far to be comparable in value, unless an early weapon appears with some special provenance. Local regulations as they apply to these weapons should be consulted before purchase.

Prices quoted here are for a working gun.
NRA Good: $7,000–$9,000; NRA Fine: $11,000–$12,500

Chauchat Automatic Machine Rifle

Often referred to as "the worst machine gun ever invented," Chauchat's machine rifle Model 1915 CSRG was first issued to French troops in June 1916, with the specific intention of increasing the firepower of the individual rifle platoons then fighting in the trenches on the Western Front. Senior French infantry officers also felt that the weapon would be particularly useful when implementing their new tactic of "marching fire," which involved troops advancing in line, firing their weapons from the hip, confusing the enemy and preventing any return fire until the attackers were close enough to charge and overrun the opposing trenches. Success in this maneuver particularly depended upon the ability of the attacking forces to deliver a high rate of fire, and the generals considered that the Chauchat would be ideal for this purpose.

The initial prototype was, for its time, a reasonably reliable weapon, incorporating a number of innovative features that were to feature in later, better-designed weapons, such as a pistol grip, in-line rifle-pattern butt, detachable 20-round magazine, and a selective fire capability, giving both fully automatic and semiautomatic fire. Unfortunately, the French army's desperate need for a machine gun meant it was rushed into production, with inevitable and unfortunate effects upon its efficiency. Changes made to the design to both lower the cost and increase the speed of manufacturing resulted in a weapon that particularly in its .30–06 chambered variant, has been described by many experts as "the worst machine-gun ever fielded in the history of warfare."

U.S. Marine Corps Maj. Gen. Lemuel Shepherd served as a lieutenant with the AEF (American Expeditionary Force) during World War I and was wounded several times. He was clear about what *he* thought of the Chauchat: "I spent the last few weeks [of World War I] back in the hospital, but I'll tell you one thing the boys later told me: The day *after* the Armistice they got the word to turn in their Chauchats and draw Browning Automatic Rifles. That BAR was so much better than that damned Chauchat. If we'd only had the BAR six months before, it would have saved so many lives."

Development

Design work on the Chauchat machine rifle began in 1903 at a French Army weapons research establishment near Paris, by a design team led by Colonel Louis Chauchat, after whom the weapon was initially named. Its mechanism was based on Browning's long-recoil design for the Remington Model 8 self-loading rifle, since the project was intended to produce a light automatic rifle, chambered for the French issue 8 × 51mmR Lebel cartridge, which could be fired and deployed by an individual soldier. Between 1903 and 1909 Chauchat and his assistant, Charles Sutter, developed eight different prototypes. After a final design was approved in 1912, one hundred of the new CS (Chauchat-Sutter) machine rifles were produced by the French government's Manufacture d'Armes at Saint-Étienne (MAS), intended for issue to the crews of military observation aircraft.

Like so many European armies in 1914, when war broke out the French Army did not have a light machine gun in general use, although it quickly became apparent that they were certainly going to need one. Under stimulus from General Joffre, the decision was taken to adopt the Chauchat because small numbers were already in use, so its reliability was considered proven. Also, it was chambered for the French Army's 8mm Lebel rifle cartridge, which meant ammunition supply should not provide major logistic headaches, of which the French Army already had more than enough already. More importantly, its mechanism was considered to be simple enough to allow the gun to be produced cheaply and quickly at a factory converted from peacetime industrial use, rather than needing a purpose-built military plant. There was a factory of just the right sort near Paris, at Pre-Saint-Gervais and owned by the Gladiator Company, which had been used to manufacture cars, motorcycles and bicycles before 1914. Converted to arms manufacture in 1915, it became the main supplier of Chauchat machine rifles during World War I, although a second facility in the Loire valley, a subsidiary of FAMH called SIDARME, also produced significant numbers during 1918. The Chauchat was also known as the C.S.R.G, a designation made up of the initials of Chauchat, Sutter, Ribeyrolles and Gladiator; Charles Ribeyrolles was the general manager of Gladiator during the period the gun was constructed at that factory.

Many of the faults encountered by troops issued with the Chauchat were the result of inconsistent manufacturing controls, particularly at the Gladiator factory. Some parts were of high quality, such as the steel recoiling-barrel sleeve and the bolt, which was composed of a number of complex, intricate moving parts. These components were precision machined and also subject to scrupulous quality control to ensure that they were fully interchangeable. Barrels were of a similar quality, being a standard component from the Lebel rifle that had been shortened from the muzzle end, and the barrel radiators were also produced from high-quality, ribbed, cast aluminum. Unfortunately, other parts were not so carefully made. Outer breech housings were a simple tube, and the parts like the receiver assembly were constructed of plates stamped out of poor-quality steel. Side plate assemblies in particular were put together with screws that become loose and dropped out after prolonged firing. In addition, sights were never properly adjusted on guns made at the Gladiator factory, and correction had to be made by the gunner when firing.

Specification

Production: precise records not available, but estimated at 265,000 weapons from all sources.

Chauchat automatic machine rifle (AMR) from the right side, showing the magazine slot, cocking lever and cartridge ejection port (courtesy James D. Julia Auctioneers, Fairfield, Maine. www.james-djulia.com).

Position of serial number on Chauchat AMR chambered for 8mm Lebel. The selective fire switch is on the right. Curiously, the first position after "S" (safe) is for fully automatic fire (courtesy James D. Julia Auctioneers, Fairfield, Maine. www.jamesdjulia.com).

Chauchat AMR, the type issued to the AEF. This weapon has the rectangular box magazine and is chambered for the .30–06 Springfield cartridge (courtesy James D. Julia Auctioneers, Fairfield, Maine. www.jamesdjulia.com).

The Chauchat automatic machine rifle was an air-cooled, selective-fire light machine gun firing from an open bolt. It was chambered for either 8mm Lebel or .30–06 Springfield, which were contained in a 20-round, open-sided box magazine. It was unique amongst light machine guns in use during World War I, which were almost exclusively operated by residual cartridge gas, in being the only fully automatic light machine gun having a spring-operated, long-recoil mechanism. Its unique, open-sided magazine was famous for collecting much of the accumulated refuse of trench warfare, including, if one U.S. soldier is to be believed, a dead mouse! A fragile bipod was fitted, and both stock and foregrip were of walnut.

Operation

To operate the weapon, a loaded magazine is inserted between the side plate and bottom of the barrel, its rear end being pushed up until the catch snaps home, thus holding the magazine in position. For semiautomatic fire, the fire regulator lever is then moved from "S" (for "sur," or safe) to "C" (for "controle" or controlled fire), and if automatic fire is required, the regulator is moved to "M" (for "mitrailleuse" or machine gun). With the magazine properly in place, the short cocking lever on the right is pulled to the rear until the sear engages and holds the action in the cocked-bolt position, which leaves the chamber open. Pulling the trigger causes that portion of the bolt body that carries the firing pin to be driven forward, stripping a cartridge from the magazine and directing it into the chamber, whereupon the firing pin strikes the primer and fires the cartridge. The mechanism then causes the barrel and bolt to recoil, while remaining locked together, compressing the recoil spring. Following this rearward movement, the bolt is locked to the rear by the trigger sear, while the barrel is forced forward by the recoil spring. The bolt is held in position until the barrel completes its forward movement, during which operation the spent cartridge is extracted and ejected by the spring-loaded ejector. If fully automatic fire is selected, the sear of the trigger is then tripped automatically, the next cartridge is stripped from the magazine and enters the chamber, and the whole cycle proceeds as before. In semiautomatic operation, the sear retains the bolt assembly until the trigger is squeezed again.

Firing a Chauchat is definitely an acquired skill, principally because of the long recoil action. Getting a cheek too close to the stock would result in the recoiling bolt/barrel assembly striking the gunner in the face, a phenomenon the French infantry called "*la gifle*" or "the slap," and even if the operator avoided the slap, operation of the recoil mechanism was so abrupt that careful aiming was almost impossible. In addition to its idiosyncratic mechanism, firing between 100 and 150 rounds (5–8 magazines) without a break would overheat the barrel sufficiently to jam the recoiling barrel/bolt mechanism, although this is a common fault with air-cooled light machine guns, even modern-day arms. Moreover, it is easily avoided by firing the Chauchat in short 4- or 5-round bursts, which is the firing procedure recommended by the official French government instruction manual. The bipod was also too high for safety and often badly fitting, but what really condemned it in the eyes of the "vulgar soldiery" who were equipped with it was that magazine. Made from ultra-thin, poor-quality pressed steel, it could easily be dented if handled roughly, which resulted in a jammed follower spring and left the cartridges stuck in the magazine. More importantly, the open sides allowed the ingress of mud and anything else lying around the trenches, which fouled even the loosely made mechanism of the Chauchat. A poll of French soldiers early in World War I found, perhaps not surprisingly, that over 75 percent of all stoppages were caused by problems with the magazine.

The weapons manufactured to use the U.S. .30-06 cartridge were even worse, despite being supplied with a better, fully enclosed, straight box magazine, although this only held

16 rounds. Despite the improved overall design of the U.S. magazine, unfortunately, in most of the magazines made by Gladiator, the lips of that component were too short to allow the cartridges to cycle properly. Even worse, the firing chambers of the weapon itself had been incorrectly machined, causing extraction failures after only a few rounds were fired. This usually resulted in a hot case becoming so tightly stuck in the chamber that the extractor would remove just the head of the spent cartridge, leaving the rest of the brass immovably fixed in the weapon.

Major variations

Production: Approximately 263,000 Chauchat automatic rifles were manufactured between 1916 and 1918 for two types of cartridge, the rimmed 8 × 50mmR Lebel cartridge and the rimless .30–06 Springfield.

French 8 × 50mmR Lebel Chauchat

Gladiator serial number range: 1–2257000 (including 19,000 guns chambered in .30–06).

SIDARME serial number range: 1–18600.

Produced between 1916 and November 1918, by Gladiator and SIDARME.

Gladiator produced 225,7000 in 8 × 50mmR Lebel cartridge between April 1916 and November 1918. SIDARME produced 18,600 chambered exclusively for 8 × 51mmR Lebel between October 1917, and November 1918, the SIDARME guns being reputed to be better quality than those made by the Gladiator factory. Weapons produced in the two factories *appear* to have separate serial number series.

Receiver stamps:

Receiver above trigger and barrel stamped:

C.S.R.G No XXXXXX

Where "XXXXXX" indicates the serial number, which in French weapons may be six digits.

French-made Chauchats used by the AEF were designated "Automatic Rifle, Model 1915 (Chauchat)," the Gladiator factory delivering approximately 16,000 Chauchats in 8mm Lebel to the AEF between August 1917 and November 1918.

American .30-06 Springfield Chauchat, .30 Model 1918

Produced by Gladiator between April 1916 and November 1918, these were not guns converted from weapons originally chambered for the Lebel cartridge, but newly manufactured guns with original .30-06 chambering. Official U.S. Army designation was the "Caliber .30 Model 1918," although U.S. troops always referred to the gun as the "Sho-Sho." U.S. records show that American inspectors at the Gladiator factory rejected about 40% of the .30–06 Chauchat production, while the remaining 60% proved problematic whenever they reached the front lines.

Receiver stamps:

Receiver above trigger and barrel stamped:

C.S.R.G A^{No} XXXXX

Where "XXXXX" indicates the serial number, which in U.S. weapons will be only five digits. The "A" after the CSRG indicates a weapon chambered for the Springfield cartridge.

Gladiator delivered approximately 19,000 Chauchats in .30–06 to the AEF before the end of World War I.

MILITARY SERVICE

Almost immediately after its introduction, the French troops who received it began to complain about the Chauchat's poor performance. Their complaints were mostly about the possibilities of fouling inherent in the open-sided design of the magazine and the gun's propensity to overheat and jam open after a few hundred rounds. Added to this was a tendency for a magazine loaded with a full twenty rounds to exhibit a failure to feed the first round, so that most of the French gunners using Chauchats only loaded 18 or 19 rounds to a magazine as a matter of routine. Experienced gunners also oiled the magazines internally before use, and although this helped to alleviate the problems of cartridge feeding, the oil also made the mechanism more prone to attract dirt and other fouling material. Many soldiers found it awkward to handle and almost impossible to shoot with any degree of accuracy, because of the short butt, poorly designed pistol grip and excessively tall bipod, while the long recoil system must have added to the difficulties encountered in keeping the weapon on target. As the final insult, the sights fitted in the Gladiator factory always caused the gun to shoot low and right, which, needless to say, added considerably to the difficulties for inexperienced gunners. Later in the war, reorganization of French infantry tactics introduced the deployment of four-man Chauchat squads, which, along with movement out of

U.S. infantryman firing Chauchat AMR. The two men on the gunner's left are using Springfield .30-06 rifles.

the muddy environment of the trenches, resulted in a significant improvement in the gun's contribution to the French army's strategic successes.

Captured Chauchats were also used by German flame-thrower units, and nearly 7,000 were issued to the Belgian army, some also being converted to chamber their 7.65mm Mauser cartridge. Several European countries acquired Chauchats after World War I, and these included Bulgaria, Finland, Greece, Italy, Romania, the USSR, Serbia and Poland.

Modern opinion

Although many experts have criticized the Chauchat, recent tests have shown that its poor performance is associated more with mishandling by inexperienced gunners and poor manufacturing of certain components than inherent design faults, although the magazine is certainly a significant flaw. Weapons chambered for the 8 × 50mmR Lebel cartridge, with a carefully maintained magazine and fired according to the official French government manual, in short bursts of only 4 or 5 rounds' duration, will certainly operate reliably. Even so, the rate of fire is slow compared even to contemporary weapons, such as the BAR (Browning Automatic Rifle), which had a rate of fire of between 500 and 600 rounds per minute.

Reasonable performance has been described by a number of recreational shooters, and an account from one such shooter in the Midwest is particularly instructive in this context. This individual was using a Chauchat chambered for 8mm Lebel and describes the weapon's jamming after firing approximately 5 or 6 magazines continually (approximately 100–120 rounds), whereupon the weapon was made safe and left to cool. Some minutes after the suspension of firing, a loud click was heard, and upon examination, the Chauchat was found to have cooled sufficiently to release the bolt back into the chamber. After a further five minutes, the gun was found to be operating perfectly once again.

Values

The U.S. government ruling of 1986 means that a gun capable of firing will fetch considerably more than a deactivated weapon. Otherwise, Chauchats from all the important manufacturers seem comparable in value so far, unless an early weapon appears with some special provenance. Local regulations as they apply to these weapons should be consulted before purchase.

Prices quoted here are for a working gun.

- **Chauchat chambered for 8mm Lebel**
NRA Good: $5,500; NRA Fine: $9,000

Guns may be found stamped with acquisition stamps from a number of European countries other than France.

- **Chauchat chambered for .30-06 Springfield**
NRA Good (deactivated): $5,500; NRA Fine (safe to shoot): $7,500

The Chauchat chambered for the U.S. cartridge is by far the more rare of the two weapons, although it does not seem to be seen as more desirable by auction buyers.[18]

Table Twenty: Comparison of the Lewis gun, Hotchkiss M1909 and Chauchat automatic machine rifle

Weapon	Lewis gun	Hotchkiss M1909	Chauchat AMR
Maker	The Birmingham Small Arms Company Limited; Savage Arms Co.	Hotchkiss et Cie.; RSAF, Enfield; Springfield Armory; Colts Patent Firearms Manufacturing Co.	Gladiator Company, Pre-Saint-Gervais, Paris (225,000 weapons); SIDARME Company, Saint-Chamond, Loire (19,000 weapons)
Period of production	1913 until 1942	1909 until 1918	1915 until 1922
Production	Approximately 200,000 weapons during World War I and World War II	British and French guns: Not recorded. U.S. guns: Records suggest a total of 670 guns but this may be only the U.S. Army purchase.	Approximately 265,000 weapons
Operators	America, Australia, Britain, Belgium, Canada, Finland, France, German Empire (World War I), Nazi Germany (World War II), New Zealand, Poland and the USSR	America, Austria-Hungary, Australia, Belgium, Brazil, Britain, France, India, Ireland, New Zealand, China and Spain	America, Belgium, Britain, Finland, France, Greece, Italy, Poland, Russian Empire, USSR
Military service	World War I; Irish War of Independence; Irish Civil War; World War II; Korean War; Malayan Emergency; 1948 Arab-Israeli War	World War I; U.S. border war against Pancho Villa (1916); World War II	World War I; Greco-Turkish war (1920–1922); World War II
Crew	A single soldier could carry and use the gun, but more usually each gun had a crew of two, gunner and loader	Originally a crew of two: Gunner and loader. Additional men were probably required to carry the ammunition boxes	Original crew of two: Gunner and loader. Crew of four from 1917: squad leader, gunner, assistant gunner, magazine carrier
Weight	13 kg (28 lbs)	12 kg (26.5 lbs)	9 kg (20lbs) with the bipod
Length	1,280mm (50 inches)	1,230 mm (48 inches)	1,143 mm (45 inches)
Barrel length	670mm (26.5 inches)	640 mm (25 inches)	470mm (19 inches)
Mechanism	Gas-operated recoil mechanism. No selector switch, fire control by trigger manipulation	Gas-operated recoil mechanism. Selector switch giving fully automatic or semiautomatic settings	Gas-assisted long-recoil mechanism. Selector switch giving fully automatic or semiautomatic settings
Cartridge/ Delivery system	.303 BritishR; .30-06 Springfield. Delivered from: 47-round pan magazine; 97-round pan magazine (aircraft guns); 30 round Bren magazine	8mm Lebel; .303 BritishR; .30-06 Springfield; 7.92 × 57mm Mauser; 7 × 57mm Spanish Mauser. Delivered from: A single metal strip containing 30 cartridges; A linked metal belt, holding 251 cartridges	8 × 50mmR Lebel (245,000 weapons); .30-06 Springfield (19,000 weapons); 7.92 × 57mm Mauser; 7.65 × 53mm Argentine. Delivered from: An open-sided, crescent-shaped magazine containing 20 rounds.

Weapon	Lewis gun	Hotchkiss M1909	Chauchat AMR
			A straight box magazine containing 16 rounds, in guns manufactured for the .30-06 cartridge.
Sights	Fronts sight: Blade Rear sight: Tangent leaf	Front sight: Blade Rear sight: Adjustable leaf sighted to 2,800 yds	Front sight: Blade Rear sight: Sliding leaf
Effective range	800 meters	150 meters	200 meters
Maximum range	3,200 meters	3,800 meters	2,000 meters
Rate of fire	500–600 rpm (rounds per minute)	Claimed 400 to 600 rpm, but usually no more than 150 rpm	240 rpm
Cost for a single gun in 1914	£165	£100–120, depending upon manufacturer	£60–80, depending upon manufacturer

Light Machine Guns Used in World War I by the Allies and Central Powers

AMERICAN FORCES

Lewis gun

Production: 200,000 weapons.

Almost identical to the model used by the British army but chambered for the .30-06 Springfield cartridge and only in service with the U.S. Navy.

Chauchat automatic machine rifle

Production: 40,000 weapons.

Similar in conformation to the model used by the French army but chambered for the .30-06 Springfield cartridge.

American guns adapted or designed for aircraft: Lewis gun

Production: figures not readily available, possibly 10,000 weapons.

Cooling sleeves were removed from barrel for use in U.S. aircraft and the weapon was chambered for the .30-06 Springfield cartridge.

BRITAIN

Lewis gun

Production: 200,000 weapons.

Produced as a number of variants for land and air service.

Hotchkiss Mk 1

Production: figures not readily available, possibly 100,000 weapons.

This weapon was a Hotchkiss M1909 rechambered for the .303 Mark VII British rifle cartridge and manufactured by RSAF, Enfield.

British guns adapted or designed for aircraft: Lewis gun

Production: figures not readily available, possibly 10,000 weapons.

Cooling sleeves were removed from barrel for use in RFC and RNAS aircraft but otherwise the weapon was similar to the model issued for land service, except a 96-round drum magazine replaced the 47-round magazine issued to land forces.

FRANCE

Chauchat automatic machine rifle

Production: 265,000 weapons.

Made by two separate manufacturers and chambered for the 8 × 50mmR Lebel cartridge.

Hotchkiss M1909 light machine gun

Production: figures not readily available, possibly 100,000 weapons.

Adopted by the French army in 1909 and chambered for the 8 × 50mmR Lebel cartridge.

French guns adapted for use in aircraft: Hotchkiss M1909 light machine gun

Production: figures not readily available, possibly 10,000 weapons.

This weapon was used without any modification in the aircraft flown by members of the French air force. Although it had the advantage of being air cooled and was without the cumbersome barrel sleeve that was fitted to the Lewis gun, its strip-loading system was clumsy and did not contain enough cartridges for a prolonged air combat.

GERMANY AND AUSTRO-HUNGARY

Germany never seems to have opted for a light machine gun in the same way as the Allies embraced the Lewis and the Hotchkiss, relying more on their perceived ability to deploy their M'08 medium/heavy machine guns effectively and using their light machine guns in a similar defensive role until late in the war. However, they did use some weapons of this type with selected units.

Bergmann MG 15nA automatic machine gun

Production: figures not readily available, possibly 10,000 weapons.

The MG15 is an air-cooled, fully automatic LMG, with a short-recoil mechanism, firing from a closed bolt, although the original design used an open-bolt mechanism which performed poorly in military trials. It was chambered for the 7.92 × 57mm German service rifle cartridge, ammunition being delivered from either a cloth belt (which was also used by the MG '08) or a similar metal belt, and the weapon could also be fitted to the bipod used with the MG08/15. This weapon was introduced after the Somme offensive when it became clear to the German generals that some weapon was needed, besides the MG'08, to support their rifle companies. The Bergmann was designed to fire from a metal-link belt holding 100, 200 or 250 cartridges, which gave a firing rate of 500 rpm, and also meant the weapon was acceptable for both land and air service. The German army ordered 6,000 MG15nA machine guns in November 1916. The weapon saw most service with Germany's Asia Korps in Palestine and the Near East, rather than on the Western Front where, arguably, it would have been of more use.[19]

Madsen Model 1903 automatic machine gun

Production: figures not readily available, possibly a total for all users of 100,000 weapons.

The Madsen or Schoube light machine gun was a recoil-operated, magazine-fed, air-cooled weapon that fired from a closed bolt. The magazine curves towards the muzzle of the gun, giving a characteristic appearance somewhat reminiscent of a Bren gun, although mechanically the guns bear no other relation to each other. Adopted in 1902 by the Danish army, the Madsen was the first commercially successful light machine gun and was subsequently adopted for use by another 34 countries, including Imperial Germany, Russia, Finland, France, Norway and Italy. Consequently it may be found chambered for twelve different cartridges types, from 6.5mm up to 8mm in caliber and including 7 × 57 Mauser, 7.92 × 57 Mauser, 7.62 × 54mmR, .303 British and even the modern 7.62 × 51mm NATO cartridge used in the British L1A1 service rifle and the US M60 GPMG (General-Purpose Machine Gun), amongst others. The mechanism is a combination of short and long recoil operation which was both robust and reliable in service conditions as long as good quality

Madsen LMG from the right, showing the curved box magazine, reminiscent of the later Bren gun, and the cocking handle (courtesy James D. Julia Auctioneers, Fairfield, Maine. www.jamesdjulia.com).

ammunition was used, although its construction was complex, with a number of intricate machining operations that made the weapon expensive to manufacture. Despite the cost and the age of the design, it was still being advertised for sale by the Madsen Company in 1950, and there is also a record of Brazilian police using the old gun in an action against members of a drug cartel in 2009.[20]

CHAPTER SIXTEEN

Medium and Heavy Machine Guns in World War I

The protagonists began World War I with the heavy machine gun as the only automatic weapon available for use in the conditions encountered on the wholly new battlefields of the Western Front. They were invariably sited in fixed positions commanding good fields of fire and did considerable damage in the early years of the conflict, particularly during the first day of the Somme offensive in 1916, when the deployment of Maxim M '08 machine guns by the Central Powers resulted in nearly 60,000 casualties in the British sectors alone. Changes in tactics after the Somme and Passchendaele saw less reliance being placed on heavy machine guns in fixed positions and began to emphasize a more modern war based on movement and the deployment of light machine gun and rifle grenade squads. However, heavy machine guns continued to be used in defensive positions where there was no necessity for rapid relocation, and as secondary weapons on some tanks and armored cars.

Heavy Machine Guns in Service with American Forces in World War I

The American army was poorly equipped with machine guns when war began in 1914, although a number of Vickers machine guns were produced by Colt for the AEF (American Expeditionary Force), as the Model 1915 automatic machine gun. Apart from these modern Vickers, however, the U.S. army's machine gun provision consisted of some M1895 Browning "Potato Digger" machine guns, a number of M1904 Maxims, and even a few Gatling guns left over from the Mexican War and the Philippines Insurrection. Adoption of a modern, reliable heavy machine gun would be delayed until the appearance of another John Browning brain child, designated the Model 1917 by the U.S. army, although the design was adopted far too late to be of any use to the men of the AEF mired in the trenches of the Western Front.

The Browning M1895: The "Potato Digger"

Very loosely based on the mechanism that John Browning had perfected for the Winchester Model 1894 lever-action rifle, the first prototype of the M1895 was finished in 1889 and weighed only 12 lbs, which made it suitable for deployment in the role of a light machine

Sixteen. Medium and Heavy Machine Guns in World War I

gun. It was chambered for a black powder cartridge and claimed to have a firing rate of nearly 1,000 rpm. The weapon proved unsatisfactory in a number of ways, and it was not until 1892 that Browning felt he had a design worth offering to Colt. Unfortunately this version now weighed 35 lbs, with the standard tripod and seat for the gunner adding a further 56 lbs and giving a total weight of over 90 lbs. This made the Colt far from portable and placed it in the medium/heavy machine gun class.

This weapon was accepted into service with the U.S. Navy and Marine Corps in 1896 as the "Colt-Browning Model 1895 machine gun," and saw some service with all branches of the U.S. armed forces. Although the U.S. army never officially adopted the weapon, training in the operation of the Colt M1985 was included in the course of instruction at the U.S. machine gun school when it was opened in Harlingen, Texas, in August 1916. It was produced in a variety of calibers as the Colt M1895, including 7 × 57mm Mauser and even .30-06 Springfield, although guns chambered for the U.S. service rifle cartridge did not make an appearance until 1914.

The Marlin Firearms Company bought the machinery for producing the Model 1895 from Colt around this time and, as well as producing the original weapon, began making an improved version of the M1895 which was designated the Model 1895/14 in 1916. Care must be taken when examining such a weapon because they were also designated simply the "Marlin gun" or "Model 1917." This version was fitted with an easily detachable barrel, a more generous side plate cutout, and a sliding door on the opening in the enlarged right side plate to improve access to the mechanism. Despite these improvements, the Marlin was still limited to 500 rounds of continuous fire due to its tendency to overheat. Although adopted in 1917 by the U.S. army, it never saw military service and was relegated to the role of a training weapon.

Another, much more radical version of the old "Potato digger" was produced in 1917, incorporating a linear gas piston mechanism and aluminum cooling fins, specifically intended for service in tanks and aircraft, although the advent of the Browning M1919 air-cooled machine gun meant that the Colt quickly became obsolete for this and all other military purposes.[1]

SPECIFICATION

Production: 100,000 weapons, by all manufacturers.

The M1985 is an air-cooled, belt-fed, fully automatic, gas-operated machine gun that fires from a closed, rear-locking, tilting bolt, giving a cyclic firing rate of 450 rounds per minute. Originally developed to fire a .44 caliber black powder cartridge, the final prototype was chambered for the 6mm Lee Navy cartridge. It was also produced to use the .30–40 Krag service rifle cartridge, when that inferior cartridge was adopted for U.S. service use in 1895. Subsequently, versions made after 1914 were chambered for the new .30–06 Springfield cartridge.

OPERATION

To operate the weapon, the gunner pushes the brass tip of the loaded belt through the opening in the left side of the breech, simultaneously swinging the loading lever down to the rear until it strikes the bottom plate of the gun, in a manner reminiscent of the technique used to cock a lever-action rifle or carbine. This lever, which is spring loaded, is released when it has reached the limit of its travel, whereupon it will return to its original position, chambering the first cartridge, cocking the weapon, and finally, locking the breech. The safety catch may then be pushed to the "FIRE" position and the gunner pulls the trigger, disconnecting the sear and dropping the hammer, which fires the cartridge. The bullet now moves up the barrel, passing an orifice that connects the barrel and the cylinder containing the piston, the increase in pressure from this residual gas driving the piston backwards and, in turn, forcing the cocking lever down and to the rear. The action of the lever then opens the breech, extracts the empty case, ejects it, and feeds the incoming round into position in the carrier, as before, in a manner analogous to the action of a Winchester repeating rifle. The lever is then returned to its original position by its associated spring, in the process chambering a fresh cartridge from the belt and closing and locking the breech, before releasing the sear of the firing mechanism. The cycle continues as long as the trigger is held back and ammunition is supplied.

Unfortunately, one of the disadvantages of the M1895 was that the breech remained closed at the end of the firing cycle with a cartridge in the chamber. If the weapon had been fired for a sufficient length of time for the barrel and breech to become overheated, this would result in the cartridge "cooking off" and firing the gun spontaneously without the gunner pulling the trigger. This unfortunate design flaw meant that a Colt M1895 had to be unloaded immediately after an extended burst of firing; otherwise the weapon had a tendency to discharge five or six cartridges before the gun cooled sufficiently to be safe. The operation of the loading lever also brought disadvantages, because when the later M1895/14 variant was mounted on a lower tripod, the loading lever would dig into the ground when the gun was fired, which apparently led to its original nickname of the "Potato Digger."

Colt-Browning Model 1895 machine gun with spare barrel (courtesy James D. Julia Auctioneers, Fairfield, Maine. www.jamesdjulia.com).

Manufacturer's stamp on Colt-Browning Model 1895 HMG (Marlin Arms CO.) (courtesy James D. Julia Auctioneers, Fairfield, Maine. www.jamesdjulia.com).

Major variations

Colt-Browning Model 1895 machine guns made by Colt

Serial number range: 1–5000 (estimated)

- **Colt-Browning Model 1895**

Incorporating Browning's original lever action design, this weapon only saw service with the U.S. navy and Marine Corps, although a small number were purchased by the U.S. army for experimental and training purposes.

Barrels are stamped in front of the rear sight:

COLT AUTOMATIC GUN
BROWNING PATENTS

This is followed by a second stamp:

MANUFACTURED BY
COLT'S' P.T. F.A. MFC. CO
HARTFORD. C0NN U.S.A

Which was then followed by a third stamp:

PATENTED IN THE UNITED STATES
JULY 30. AUGUST 20.1895.

Caliber and serial numbers are also found stamped on the barrel, usually between the three manufacturer's stamps and at right angles to them, taking the following form:

CAL 30
U. S. A
NO. XXXXX

Where "XXXXX" represents the serial number.

- **Colt-Browning Model 1895/14**

This version differed from the earlier variant in being chambered for the U.S. army's .30–06 service rifle cartridge and fitted with a lower tripod, although in all other respects it was the same as the original M1895. Some of the Colt M1895/14 machine guns were also chambered for the .303 caliber MKVII British service rifle cartridge, as were some of the guns of this type manufactured by Marlin.

Barrels are stamped in front of the rear sight:

MODEL 1914
COLT AUTOMATIC GUN
MANUFACTURED BY
COLT'S' P.T. F.A. MFC. CO
HARTFORD. CN U.S.A

This is followed by a second stamp:

BROWNING PATENTS.
PATENTED IN THE UNITED STATES
JULY 30. AUGUST 20.1895.

Caliber and serial numbers are also found stamped on the barrel, usually between the three manufacturer's stamps and at right angles to them, taking the following form:

CAL 30
U. S. A
NO. XXXXX

Where "XXXXX" represents the serial number.

Colt-Browning Model 1895/14 machine guns made by Marlin-Rockwell

Serial number range: 1–10000 (estimated)

- **Colt-Browning Model 1895/14**

Produced by Marlin, this version also differed from the earlier variant M1895 machine gun in being chambered for the U.S. army's .30–06 service rifle cartridge and fitted with the smaller, lower tripod, although in all other respects the gun was the same as that produced by Colt as the Model 1895/14. These weapons are sometimes referred to as the "Marlin Gun" or "Model 1917," although the last designation strictly refers to the later Model 1917, fitted with the linear gas piston.

Barrels are stamped in front of the rear sight:

MARLIN ARMS CORPORATION
NEW HAVEN, CONNECTICUT

and include a caliber stamp, having the following form:

CAL 30
U. S. A
NO. XXXXX

Where "XXXXX" represents the serial number.

- **Colt-Browning Model 1917/Model 1918**

Produced by Marlin with extensive modifications to the original design, this weapon was specifically intended for service in tanks and aircraft. It was also produced in .30-06 Springfield but bore little external resemblance to the original gun, its modifications including a linear gas piston mechanism with the cylinder installed under the barrel and aluminum cooling fins.

Barrels are stamped in front of the rear sight:

MARLIN ARMS CORPORATION
NEW HAVEN, CONNECTICUT

and include a caliber stamp, having the following form:

CAL 30
U. S. A
NO XXXXX

Where "XXXXX" represents the serial number.

Military service

The Colt M1895 first saw service with the Marine Corps during the Spanish-American War in Cuba, as well as the Philippines Insurrection and the Boxer Rebellion. It was also used extensively on the United States mainland by various militia and National Guard units. In particular, in what came to be known as the "Ludlow massacre," a Colt M1895 that had come into the possession of one of the private "militias" organized by the mining companies to break the strike, was used to murder women and children at the Ludlow miners' camp. In a similar type of operation, the Baldwin-Felts Detective Agency had an M1895 fitted to a specially built armored car which they used during this and other labor disputes to terrorize workers striking over legitimate grievances.

World War I

By the time America entered the war, the M1895 was obsolete, having been succeeded by superior air-cooled weapons, although the Model 1917/1918 was fitted to a significant number of SPAD XIII fighter planes and some of the U.S. army's M1917 tanks.[2]

Values

The U.S. government ruling of 1986 means that a gun capable of firing will fetch considerably more than a deactivated weapon. Otherwise, Colt and Marlin guns are comparable in value, unless an early weapon appears with some special provenance. Local regulations as they apply to these weapons should be consulted before purchase.

Prices quoted here are for a working gun.
NRA Good: $20,000–$25,000 NRA; Fine: $30,000–$45,000

The Browning M1917 .30-06 Caliber Medium Machine Gun

Development

John Browning registered his first patent for a recoil-operated automatic machine gun that was the basis for the Model 1917 as early as 1900. Unfortunately, a lack of government funding caused him to abandon work on the new weapon in order to take up other, more lucrative projects. He did no more development work on the weapon until 1910, when he built a water-cooled prototype of the earlier design. This version had a few flaws and Browning subsequently modified the design, incorporating an ejection port which opened out of the bottom of the breech and a two-piece firing pin instead of the original hammer, as well as making a number of other minor improvements.

Browning took this gun to Washington, D.C., in 1917, along with his prototype for the BAR (Browning Automatic Rifle), both weapons being chambered for the Springfield .30-06 U.S. service rifle cartridge. He arranged a live-firing demonstration at Congress Heights in southern Washington on 27 February 1917, in front of a crowd of military and government officials from various countries. The test proved so successful that the BAR was adopted for U.S. service on the spot. Additional tests were conducted on what was to become the Model 1917 in May 1917 at the Springfield Armory, where a Model1917 fired a total of 40,000 rounds without a single stoppage. Not surprisingly, the new water-cooled machine gun was immediately recommended for adoption by the U.S. military.[3]

Specification

Production: 128,000 weapons, by all manufacturers.

The Browning Model 1917 was a water-cooled, fully automatic heavy machine gun with a short-recoil mechanism, firing from a closed bolt and having a cyclic rate of between 450 and 600 rpm. Its total length was only 30 inches, and so it was shorter and handier than the older Vickers, although surprisingly, it weighed approximately 10 lbs more, with a tripod and water in the cooling jacket. It was the only automatic machine gun produced during World War I that did not work on Maxim's well-tried toggle-locked recoil principle. This mechanism was also used in the later, very successful air-cooled Model 1919 and .50 caliber M2.

Operation

The M1917 is loaded by inserting the tab of an ammunition belt into the left side of the gun until the pawl at the receiver opening or feedway engaged the belt.

With a belt loaded, the cocking handle is pulled to the rear and then released, positioning a cartridge for loading. Operating the cocking handle a second time moves the first cartridge into the chamber and the second round into the position previously occupied by the first round, making it ready for chambering after

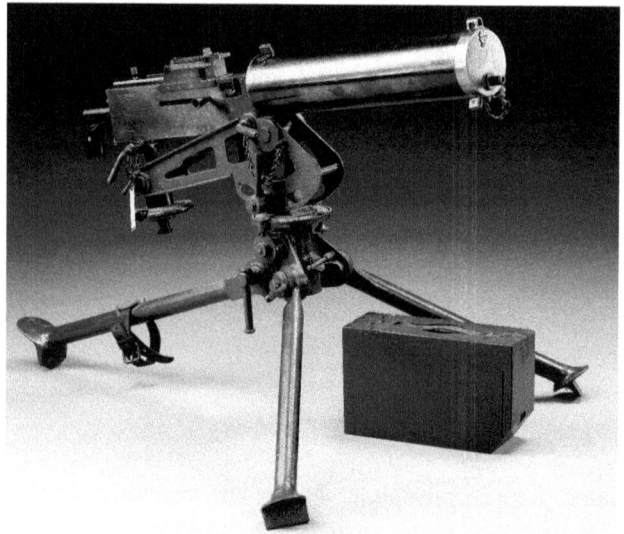

Browning Model 1917 HMG, showing the cocking handle, water jacket, tripod and an ammunition box (courtesy James D. Julia Auctioneers, Fairfield, Maine. www.jamesdjulia.com).

Receiver stamp on Browning M1917 HMG, showing this weapon to have been made by Westinghouse (courtesy James D. Julia Auctioneers, Fairfield, Maine. www.jamesdjulia.com).

the first cartridge has been fired. The M1919 is now ready to fire with a round in the chamber, the bolt and barrel group locked together, and the locking block at the rear of the bolt. Operating the trigger lever fires the cartridge and the mechanism recoils, cocking the striker and ejecting the spent case from the chamber and positioning a new cartridge in the extractor, before the bolt recoil spring pushes the bolt forward, chambering the fresh round. With a cartridge in the chamber, the bolt and barrel are locked together by the locking block, and if the trigger is still depressed, the striker moves forward, firing the cartridge. As with all weapons of this type, firing continues as long as the trigger is depressed and there is ammunition in the belt.[4]

Major variations

Military variants

U.S. military weapons

M1917

This was the original gun offered to the U.S. military authorities in 1917, although many of these guns were modified with either a U-shaped metal bracket or right-angled steel straps riveted to the bottom of the receiver to strengthen that structure, in order to prevent the bottom plates of the receiver from becoming displaced during prolonged firing.

Production of these guns began in 1917, with three manufacturers receiving substantial contracts: Colt, Remington and Westinghouse. Problems with assembly lines and tooling meant that by June 1918, the total output of all three companies was only 4,000 weapons, although by November 1918, this had risen to over 42,000 guns.

Model 1917 machine guns made by Colt. Production by November 1918: 600 guns.
Side-plate stamp:

COLT
CAL .30
1917 Model 1917
Nº XXX
COLT AUTOMATIC MACHINE GUN
COLT'S PAT. FIREARMS MFG. CO.
HARTFORD, CONN. U.S.A

Where "No XXX" is the serial number. The Colt badge for the period appears between the "CAL" and ".30" and the year of manufacture and Model designation were varied as was appropriate, for example a Model 38 is stamped "1928 MODEL 38," with the Colt company badge between.

Model 1917 machine guns made by Remington. Production by November 1918: 12,000 guns.

Side-plate stamp:

NO. XXXXX U.S. INSP.
BROWNING MACHINE GUN
U.S. CAL .30 MODEL OF 1917
MAN'F'D. BY REMINGTON ARMS CO.
PATENTS APPLIED FOR

Where "NO. XXXXXX" is the serial number and "U.S. INSP." is a U.S. inspector's stamp signifying that the gun has been inspected and subsequently accepted for service. Model designations will also vary depending upon the nature and date of production of the weapon.

Model 1917 machine guns made by Westinghouse. Production by November 1918: 30,150 guns.

Side-plate stamp:

NO. XX N.A.C. U.S. INSP.
BROWNING MACHINE GUN
U.S. CAL.30 MODEL OF 1917
MANFD. BY N.E. WESTINGHOUSE CO.
PATENTS APPLIED FOR

Where "NO. XX" is the serial number and "N.A.C. U.S. INSP." is a U.S. inspector's stamp signifying that the gun has been inspected and subsequently accepted for service. Model designations will also vary depending upon the nature and date of production of the weapon.

M1917A1

Introduced after 1930, this version of the M1917 featured a new receiver bottom plate, with side flanges riveted to the side plates, and thus ensuring that the bottom plates remained in their correct position while the gun was being operated. In addition it had a rear sight modified for the U.S. army's new M2 cartridge, which was the usual ammunition for the M1917 during World War II. An all-steel water jacket, developed by RIA (Rock Island Arsenal), was also introduced to replace the earlier, brass-capped component.

These guns were manufactured by a variety of companies, but the side-plate stamps are broadly similar. Guns made at Rock Island Arsenal, for example, are stamped in the following form:

> NO. XXXXX U.S.INSP.
> BROWNING MACHINE GUN
> U.S. CAL. .30 M1917A1
> MAN'F'D BY ROCK ISLAND ARSENAL
> PATENT 1,621,478

Weapons from the Rock Island Arsenal are probably the most common variation, but stamps from other makers will have a similar configuration, the only change being the name of the gun maker. As with the M1917 machine guns, the stamp "NO. XXXXX" is the serial number, while "U.S. INSP." is an inspector's stamp indicating that the gun has been inspected and subsequently accepted for service. Model designations will also vary depending upon the nature and date of production of the weapon.

M1918

This was an air-cooled version of the M1917 designed for air service.

Chinese military weapons

Type 30

An M1917 was produced in China, designated "Type 30" and chambered for the 7.92 × 57mm Mauser, the German service rifle cartridge.

Swedish military weapons

Ksp m/14–29

This weapon was a licensed copy of the M1917A1, with the riveted bottom plate on the receiver and chambered for the 6.5 × 55mm Swedish service rifle cartridge. It was designated "Kulspruta m/14–29" by the Swedish military authorities and manufactured by Carl Gustafs Gevärsfaktori in Eskilstuna. Modifications from the original U.S. version of the M1917A1 included "spade" firing handles instead of a pistol grip, and a cooling jacket and tripod originally designed for the M14 Schwarlose machine gun.

Ksp m/36

Similar to the original Ksp m/14–29, except for modifications associated with rechambering for the more powerful 8 × 63mm patron m/32 cartridge. This version was also used successfully as an AA (antiaircraft) gun, usually operated from a double mounting.

Polish military weapons

Ckm wz.30

Production: Precise records unavailable, estimated at 8,000 weapons produced by the state rifle factory, FK (*Państwowa Fabryka Karabinów*).

This weapon was an unlicensed copy of the M1917, chambered for the 7.92 × 57mm Mauser service rifle cartridge. Modifications from the original M1917 included a lengthened pistol grip and barrel; modified iron sights, featuring a V-notch rather than a loophole; a simplified rifle lock for easier exchange of over-heated barrels; and better handles and mountings adapted for use in both an antipersonnel and antiaircraft role.

Norwegian military weapons

M/29

Production: 1,800 weapons, imported from the Colt company and in use by 1940, when the Nazis invaded Norway.

This weapon was the Colt version of the M1917, designated the M/29 by the Norwegian military authorities and chambered for the 7.92 × 57mm Mauser service rifle cartridge. It was in service with the Norwegian army from 1929 until 1942, replacing their original Hotchkiss 1914 heavy machine guns.

Civilian production

- **Colt Model 1917:** Colt also produced the M1917 for sale to civilian and smaller military purchasers.
- **Colt Model 1928:** Produced for sale to Argentina, with modifications that included a safety catch operated by the gunner's thumb, a Type A flash hider, and an improved rear sight.
- **Colt MG38 and MG38B:** Intended for general commercial sale, both these weapons were improvements on the Model 28, although the only modifications appear to have been to the water jacket, which was threaded inside the trunnion, and the addition of "spade" firing handles.
- **Colt MG38BT:** This version of the Model 28 was fitted with a short, very heavy, air-cooled barrel and spade firing handles. Similar in conformation to the Model 1919, it was specifically designed to be fitted on the new generation of armored vehicles.[5]

AMMUNITION

The .30–06 Springfield U.S. service rifle cartridge is available in a number of types, including:

M2 ball: this is a conventional rifle cartridge.
Armor-Piercing, M2: An armor-piercing round for use against lightly armored vehicles.
Incendiary, M1: For use against flammable targets without armor.
Tracer, M2: Tracer for observing fire, signaling, target designation, and incendiary purposes.

All of these cartridge types could be fired from an M1917, and the weapon is known to have used four-to-one tracer for targeting purposes and the armor-piercing cartridge during World War II.[6]

MILITARY SERVICE

The Browning Model 1917 was accepted into service with the U.S. army too late to be of significant use on the Western Front, although it saw sufficient service to demonstrate that the U.S. service cartridge, despite its reliability, was inferior in range and stopping power to the ammunition in use by the British and French armies.

The Model 1917 was still in service with the U.S. army at the outbreak of war in 1941, although now it was as the superior Model 1917A1, chambered for the new M2 ball, tracer and armor-piercing ammunition introduced between 1937 and 1943. Despite the significant modifications to the old Model 1917, it was still a heavy machine gun, with all that implied about its lack of tactical resilience, and its deployment was limited to supplying continuous fire from a static position—not conditions typical of the highly mobile warfare that characterized most of the fighting during World War II.

The elderly Browning also saw some service during the Korean War (1950–1953), but by 1960 it was being replaced by the lighter M60 GPMG, chambered for the 7.62 × 51mm NATO cartridge.[7]

Values

The U.S. government ruling of 1986 means that a gun capable of firing will fetch considerably more than a deactivated weapon, with older weapons having the most provenance generally achieving the best price at auction. Local regulations as they apply to these weapons should be consulted before purchase.

Prices quoted here are for a working gun.

NRA Good: $20,000–$30,000; NRA Fine: $35,000–$60,000

Prices, as is usual, are largely dependent on provenance, and to a lesser extent, condition.

Table Twenty-one: Comparison of the specification of the Browning M1895 and M1917 machine guns

Weapon	Browning M1895	Browning M1917
Principal Manufacturers	Colt Patent Firearms Manufacturing Co. Marlin Firearms Co.	Colt Patent Firearms Manufacturing Co. Remington Arms Company The New England Westinghouse Company
Period of production	1895–1914 Last use in action: U.S. National Guard 1921	1917 until 1968
Production	In excess of 100,000	128,369 as: M1917 M1917A1 M1918
Operators	Australia, Canada, Spain, France, Italy, Mexico, Russian Empire (pre-1917), UK, USA	Australia, Belgium, Brazil, Britain China, South Korea, North Vietnam, Norway, Poland, Sweden, USA
Military service	U.S. civil disturbances, World War I, World War II	World War I, World War II, Korean War, Vietnam War
Crew	Two men: operator and loader, as well as others for carrying gun and tripod	Two men: operator and loader, as well as others for carrying gun and tripod
Weight	Gun: 16 kgs (35 lbs) Tripod: 25 kgs (56 lbs)	103 lbs, including gun, tripod, water and ammunition
Length/ Barrel length	41 inches overall	35 inches (98 cm)/24 inches (60 cm)

Weapon	Browning M1895	Browning M1917
Mechanism	Gas operated, lever actuated	Short recoil, automatic mechanism
Cartridge	6mm Lee Navy	.30–06 Springfield cartridge
	7 × 57mm Mauser	Cartridges supplied to mechanism by a 250-round fabric cartridge belt, entering the gun on the left side of the breech.
	.30–40 Krag	
	.30–06 Springfield	
	.303 British	
	7.62 × 54mmR	Later weapons used the M1 disposable metal link
	6.5 × 52mm Mannlicher-Carcano	
	Cartridges supplied to mechanism as a belt	
Sights	Front sight: simple blade	Front sight: simple blade
	Rear sight: elevating leaf graduated to 1,000 yards	Rear sight: elevating leaf graduated to 1,000 yards
Rate of fire	400–450 rounds per minute (rpm)	M1917: 450 rpm
		M1917A1 and M1918: 600 rpm
Effective range	1,000 meters	3,500–5,500 meters

OPERATION

The M1917, M1919 and .50 caliber M2

All three weapons are based on an original design by Browning, patented in 1901, this original prototype being referred to as the Browning Model 1901 and the firing mechanism of all the later Models, the M1917, M1919 and the .50 caliber M1921, which became the air-cooled M2, are exactly similar to this early prototype, with some small refinements.

Loading is carried out by inserting the tab of an ammunition belt into the left side of the gun until the pawl at the breech opening or feedway engaged the belt. In the early M1917, M1919 and M2, this was a conventional canvas belt, although all these weapons could also use the disintegrating belt of steel links that was introduced in 1950, designated the M1 link for the M1917 and M1919.

After loading the belt, the cocking handle is pulled backwards and released, which causes the belt to move through the receiver and the extractor mounted on the bolt to engage the groove in the base of the first cartridge in the belt. The cocking handle is then pulled and released a second time, which extracts the first cartridge from the belt, lowers it into a T-shaped slot in the bolt face, and then moves the bolt forward, pushing the cartridge into the chamber. A second round takes up the position previously occupied by the first cartridge, with the extractor claw engaged in the groove of this round, the belt having been pulled to the right by the required distance to allow the next round to be extracted from the belt.

The weapon is now ready for firing with a round in the chamber, the bolt and barrel locked together, the locking block at the rear of the bolt and the claw of the extractor engaged in the groove of the next cartridge in the belt. Lifting the trigger lever disengages the sear, and the spring-loaded striker moves forward and fires the cartridge. The bullet moves up the barrel, the residual force from the cartridge simultaneously driving the bolt and barrel to the rear, compressing the bolt and barrel springs, extracting the spent case from the chamber and cocking the striker mechanism. As the bolt and barrel assembly recoils, the locking block is drawn out of engagement by a cam in the bottom of the gun's receiver, which allows the bolt to unlock from the barrel and begin to travel backwards, while the barrel is stopped by the accelerator assembly before being moved partway forwards towards its original position by the barrel recoil spring, the barrel's initial momentum imparting additional force to the bolt's rearward passage via this accelerator assembly. The bolt continues to move backwards, further compressing the bolt recoil spring, and causing the combined extractor-ejector mechanism, the claw of which is already engaged in the base of the next cartridge in the belt, to move backwards as well, removing the engaged cartridge from the belt. At this point the extractor moves vertically down, lowering the fresh cartridge into the T-shaped slot in the bolt face. The fresh cartridge pushes the expended case down and out of the bolt slot, whereupon it leaves the receiver via the ejection port cut in the bottom of that component, the new cartridge now being in line with the chamber.

The lever controlling the movement of the belt is connected to a pawl at the front end, with a pin at the rear end running through a track in the top of the bolt and a second pin in the receiver cover acting as a pivot between the two ends. Rearward movement of the bolt causes the rear end of this lever to be pulled to the right, so that the pawl at the other end moves to the left over the belt. This pawl then engages the belt and pulls it further to the right as the bolt comes forward again, positioning a fresh cartridge for extraction from the belt and pushing the belt out of the right side of the gun. When a gun was loaded with a disintegrating belt, this mechanism caused the loose M1 link of the previous round to be taken out of the belt and projected from the receiver via the ejection port on the right side, which originally accommodated the empty canvas belt.

Having reached the limit of its rearward travel, the bolt then moves forward, pushing the fresh cartridge into the chamber, while the extractor moves up and over the base of the next cartridge, before dropping down and engaging its claw in the grooved base of this round. The bolt and barrel are then locked together by the locking block, the barrel is released from the accelerator by the action of another cam, and the entire locked bolt/barrel assembly moves forward into its firing position. If the trigger is still depressed, the striker in turn moves forward, firing the cartridge, and the cycle is repeated until the trigger is released or the ammunition supply runs out. A recoil buffer tube extending from the back of the receiver was fitted to the three production models to make the cycling of the bolt smoother than in the original M1901 prototype, as well as absorbing some of the recoil from the bolt and forming a place for the pistol grip to be fitted.

Absence of the heavy, complex lock mechanism of the Maxim and the guns based upon that principle meant that the M1917 was significantly lighter than both the MG '08 and the Russian version of the Maxim and was soon proven to be just as reliable.[8]

Heavy Machine Guns in Service with British Forces in World War I

Britain's heavy machine gun during the whole of World War I and World War II was the ubiquitous and much-loved Vickers. Its reliability and firepower became the stuff of legends on the Western Front, and it remained in service with the British Army until 1968, when it was replaced by the L7-A1 version of Fabrique Nationale's MAG (Mitrailleuse d'Appui Général or General Purpose Machine Gun).

The Vickers Heavy/Medium Machine Gun

Development

Hiram Maxim began building the famous machine gun that bears his name at his Crayford factory in 1884. Having absorbed the Nordenfelt Guns and Ammunition Company four years later, he looked ready to begin a considered expansion. Circumstances worked against him, however, and in 1896, Maxim sold his operation to Albert Vickers, the original chairman of Maxim's first company, and this conglomerate now became Vickers, Sons and Maxim. The original Maxim was starting to show its age, so Vickers implemented a series of changes, improving and simplifying the weapon. These included inverting the toggle mechanism of the lock, consequently allowing the breech casing to be reduced in depth and producing a smaller, lighter weapon. Some components were also manufactured from lighter, stronger alloys, and a muzzle booster was added to increase the force of the recoil that cycled the action, subsequently resulting in a weapon originally designated the Model 1908 Light Pattern.

Vickers became Vickers Ltd. in 1911 and began manufacturing the new Light Pattern machine gun as the Model 1908 Light Pattern Vickers. It proved an instant success and was adopted by the British Army as the Vickers Mk1 in 1912, final issue of the weapon to infantry units being completed shortly before the assassination in Sarjevo sparked the outbreak of World War I. Vickers continued to manufacture what was now the British Army's medium machine gun until 1927, when the company merged with Armstrong Whitworth to become Vickers-Armstrong. The last Vickers machine gun sold to the British army was apparently manufactured at that company's Crayford works in 1945.[9]

Specification

Production: 500,000 weapons, by all manufacturers.

The Vickers is a belt-fed, water-cooled, fully automatic, medium/heavy machine gun, fitted with a modification of Maxim's recoil-operated, toggle-locked mechanism and firing from a closed bolt. Cartridges were loaded into a fabric belt containing 333 rounds, and the gun had "spade" firing handles with the firing button mounted between them. It weighed between 80 and 100 lbs with its tripod attached and a full water jacket. It was originally chambered for the .303 British Mk VII or

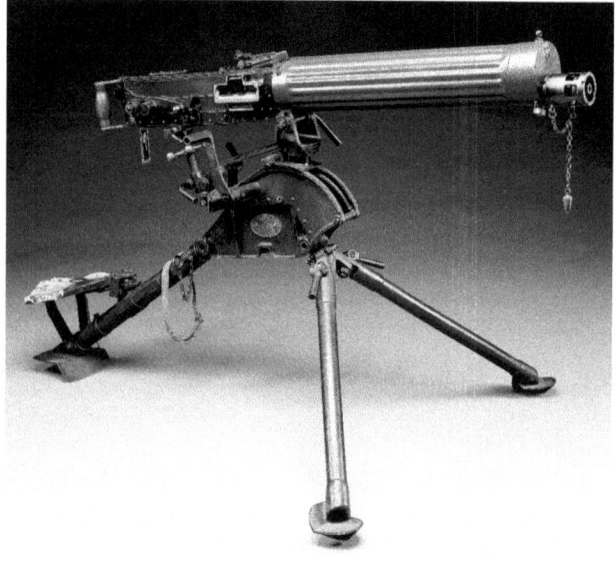

Vickers HMG and tripod showing elevation screw water jacket and cocking handle at rear of breech (courtesy James D. Julia Auctioneers, Fairfield, Maine. www.jamesdjulia.com).

Mk VIIz ball cartridge, which was also used in the British Army's Lee-Enfield rifle, although later weapons were manufactured for a very wide variety of cartridges.

Serial numbers

Most Vickers machine guns will bear a serial number, usually on the water jacket, although the position of this stamp is variable. Serial numbers take the form of a number with a single letter prefix, e.g., L677; the letter prefix identifies the site where the gun was manufactured. Five factories made the Vickers:

- Vickers Ltd., factories at Crayford and Erith, in Kent 1911–1927. Serial numbers from this factory were prefixed: A, B, C, D, E, ET, F, G, IK, S, V, W.
- Vickers Armstrong, one factory at Crayford, Kent 1927–1945. Serial numbers from this factory were prefixed: A, B, H, K, L, though some commercial guns were made here without any prefix.
- Colt Patent Firearm Manufacturing Company. Serial numbers from this factory were prefixed: A, N; some M1915 guns were made here without any prefix.
- Small arms Factory, Lithgow, Australia. Serial numbers from this factory were prefixed: A, B, T; some MkI Vickers were made here without any prefix.
- Fabrico de Braco de Prata, Portugal. Serial numbers from this factory were prefixed: A, N.[10]

Table Twenty-two: Site of manufacture and serial number prefixes

Manufacturer	Period of production	Letter prefixes and weapon types
Vickers Ltd./Vickers Armstrong Crayford factory	1918–1944	A: MkI 1916–1918 B: Commercial 1933–1934 C: MkI 1916–1918, Commercial 1935–1936 D: Mk I 1918, Commercial 1936–1937 E: Commercial 1937–1938 ET: MkI 1942 F: MkI 1918, Commercial 1939 G: MkI 1918, .5 inch MkI, MkII, Mk IV, Mk V IK: MkI 1942 S: .5 inch Mk III 1932–1935 V: MkI 1939–1944 W: MkI 1939–1944
Vickers Ltd, Erith factory	1916–1931	A: Mk II 1918–1919 B: Mk I 1917–1918 H: MkI 1918–1919 K: MkI 1918–1919 L: MkI 1911–1916 Early guns NO PREFIX: Commercial 1920–1931
Colt's Patent Firearm Manufacturing Company	1915–1936	A: M1918 N: Nepalese Special 1936 NO PREFIX: M1915 1915–1918
Small arms Factory, Lithgow, Australia	1933–1945	A: MkV 1935–1941 B: MkI 1944–1945 T: Mk XXI 1941–1944 NO PREFIX: MkI 1933–1945
Fabrico de Braco de Prata, Portugal	1930–1939	A: M/930 1939 N: M/930 1930

Other Stamps and Marks

Receiver plate markings

Vickers machine guns are often found with a brass plate riveted on to the top of the receiver, which describes the gun and the patents associated with it, typically appearing in the following format on the Mk1 infantry weapon:

VICKERS
AUTOMATICR.C.GUN
CLASS C
BRITISH PATENT N^{os}
12700 —— 1901
29423 —— 1904
7161 —— 1906
5637 —— 1907
18520 —— 1908
5815 —— 1910
24255 —— 1910

Patent plate mounted on receiver of Vickers HMG (courtesy James D. Julia Auctioneers, Fairfield, Maine. www.jamesdjulia.com).

Inspector's marks

Various stamps on separate components, usually composed of the initial of the inspector, a number with a letter prefix being the usual format, e.g., V520. RSAF Enfield, however, used a Crowned stamp which included a single number with a single letter prefix, having an "E" beneath. This mark may also be found stamped on the water jacket of guns refurbished by the Enfield factory.

Acceptance marks

Guns accepted into British service, whether land, sea or air, were stamped with the usual "Broad Arrow" of the War Office.

DP

These guns were assembled from unserviceable parts, the "DP" stamp, usually on the trunnion block, signifying that the weapon was for "Drill purposes only." Some weapons with this stamp will also have white bands painted on the water jacket.

EY

Suitable for firing ball ammunition in an emergency. Usually found stamped on the water jacket.[11]

Operation

Operation was fairly simple, the tripod first being set up on a level site and the legs either dug in or weighted with sandbags. The gun itself was then attached to the tripod and the water-jacket filled, total capacity about eight pints of water, although if water was not available other fluids were used, some of them not very genteel! With the gun set up and correctly positioned, the loader placed himself to the right of the gun and fed one of the hand-loaded canvas belts containing the cartridges into the gun's loading slot. With the first round in place, the gunner worked the cocking handle and thus charged the weapon, before moving the safety catch from the "SAFE" to the "FIRE" position and pressing the firing button located, like the Maxim, between the handles of the weapon. The mechanism of the Vickers was exactly similar to the earlier Maxim, pressing the firing button causing the recoil-operated, toggle-lock mechanism to draw in the belt, extract, chamber and fire a round, before expelling the empty brass case through a slot in the bottom of the breech, the mechanism continuing to operate as long as the firing button was depressed. As the firing cycle proceeded, the empty canvas belt was moved out of a second slot on the left side of the weapon, where it was available for reloading when emptied of cartridges. Like the Maxim, cartridges were delivered to the mechanism in a canvas belt seven yards long, holding 333 cartridges and fitted with a clip on each end for the attachment of a second loaded belt. Continuous firing rates of around 10,000 rounds per hour were possible, although to ensure that the gun worked reliably, the training manual recommended that the barrel be changed every hour, a job that took about two minutes for an experienced team. The Vickers' reliability was also helped by the cooling system: the water in the jacket reached the boiling point after the passage of about 600 rounds through the barrel and the steam produced was led out of the jacket via an external port, this evaporative loss thus serving to cool the barrel. Total capacity of the jacket was approximately eight pints, with about 1½ pints of this fluid lost for every 1,000 cartridges fired, although the external port through which the steam traveled was usually connected to a metal water container that collected the evaporated liquid so that it could be re-used. This recycling device also ensured that the clouds of steam that would otherwise have been produced did not give away the gunners' position, which was an important consideration during trench warfare on the Western Front.

The crew for a single Vickers consisted of eight men: a gunner and loader, with six riflemen to protect the crew as well as carrying the gun, tripod and ammunition boxes, no light task as a full box weighed 22 lbs. World War II saw a slight change to this pattern, Vickers guns and crews now being organized at platoon level and machine gun units usually consisting of a lieutenant in command of two sections, with two guns to each section. Each gun had a two-man crew, as before, together with the usual team of riflemen to protect the gun and keep it operational.[12]

The Vickers had a reputation for reliability that was unsurpassed by any of its contemporary rivals. In a test conducted on 15 March 1913, the U.S. Army's Board of Ordnance and Fortifications concluded: "[T]he Vickers rifle caliber gun, light model, stood the most satisfactory test. As to the merits of the Vickers gun there is no question—it stood in a class by itself. Not a single part was broken nor replaced. Nor was there a jam worthy of the name during the entire series of tests. A better performance could not be desired."[13] The gun was equally reliable in action, and it seems fairly certain that the men of 100th company of the Machine Gun Corps would have agreed with the U.S. experts when they found themselves in action on the Somme in August 1916. They sustained a German attack that went on continually for twelve hours, during which time the British fired their ten Vickers guns continuously, using 100 barrels and firing upwards of a million rounds without a single stoppage from any cause. It has been rightly said that "it was this sort of absolutely foolproof reliability which endeared the Vickers to every British soldier who ever fired one."[14]

The Vickers was widely sold commercially, seeing service with the armed forces of a number of countries who bought weapons chambered for the ammunition generally issued to their troops. Consequently, it was manufactured to use a number of foreign cartridges, which included .30–06 Springfield, 7 × 57mm Mauser, 8mm Lebel, 7.62 × 54mmR, 6.5 × 52mm Mannlicher–Carcano, 6.5 × 50mmSR Arisaka, 6.5 × 53.5mm R Dutch, 7.5 × 55mm Swiss, 7.62 × 51mm NATO and 7.65 × 53mm Argentine.

The armed forces of India, Pakistan and Nepal currently (2017) retain the Vickers as a reserve weapon, where it is to be deployed for emergency use in a major conflict.[15]

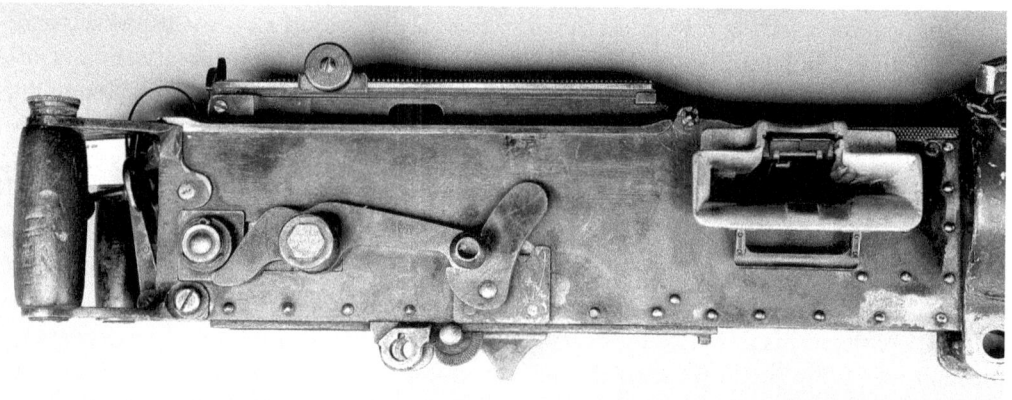

Cocking handle and receiver of Vickers HMG (courtesy James D. Julia Auctioneers, Fairfield, Maine. www.jamesdjulia.com).

Major variations

The infantry weapon

The Vickers Mk. I was accepted into service by the British army on 26 November 1912 and it remained largely unchanged during its service life, the only modifications to the basic design being attempts to decrease the weight of certain components by machining away the excess metal.

Gun, Machine, Vickers .303-inch, Mk.I

Originally designated the Model 1908 Light Pattern by Vickers in 1908, this Model was the standard machine gun issued to land forces between 1912 and 1968 and was produced in far greater numbers than any of the other succeeding models. It remained largely unchanged in that period, a tribute to the strength of the original design, although late in 1917, in an attempt to speed up production, a number of Vickers Mk.I machine guns were manufactured with smooth water jackets, instead of the usual fluted design.

Air Ministry Pattern Vickers guns

Gun, Machine, Vickers .303-inch, Mk.I*

Introduced in 1918, this weapon was designed for air service, and fitted to later RFC and RAF aircraft. Similar to the Mk.I but with vents cut in the rear of the water jacket to increase cooling.

Gun, Machine, Vickers .303-inch, Mk.II

Introduced in 1918, this weapon was also designed for air service, and fitted to later RFC and RAF aircraft. Internally similar to the Mk.I but the water jacket was replaced by a sleeve drilled with a number of holes to facilitate cooling when the gun was in the air. This method had been found to be more effective than the conventional water cooling system when a Vickers was fitted to an aircraft.

Gun, Machine, Vickers .303-inch, Mk.II*

Introduced in 1927, this weapon was another designed for air service, and fitted to RAF aircraft. Similar to the Mk.II but having a much larger cocking lever with a longer travel than the earlier gun, and a flash-hider.

Gun, Machine, Vickers .303-inch, Mk.III, Mk.V RH and Mk.V LH

These three patterns were all introduced in 1936 and are similar in almost every respect to the 1927 Mk.II*, the Mk.V RH and MkV LH being designed for mounting side-by-side, usually in front of an aircraft cockpit.

Vickers G.O.

Vickers also introduced another machine gun in 1935, the Vickers G.O. (Gas Operated), also termed the Vickers K machine gun for use in aircraft. However, it was not a modification of the original Vickers .303 and so is not discussed here.

Tank-mounted Vickers guns

All these guns were modifications of the Vickers Mk.I, their chief point of difference being the fitting of a pistol grip to the lower surface of the breech, replacing the original "spade" grips of the Mk.I. All of these weapons were declared obsolete in 1944 with the adoption of the Besa and Browning Model 1919 machine guns.

Gun, Machine, Vickers .303-inch, Mk.IV A

Introduced in 1930, this weapon was converted from a number of original Mk.I guns and issued with breech blocks loading from either the left or right. Originally the only machine gun fitted to the vehicles of the Royal Tank Corps, in addition to their 3-pounder gun.

Gun, Machine, Vickers .303-inch, Mk.IV B

Also introduced in 1930, it differed from the Mk.IV A in having the pistol grip mounted further forward, a padded shoulder rest at the rear of the breech, and minor changes to the cooling system. These guns were made as new weapons as well as being converted from original Mk.I guns and were produced with breech blocks loading from either the left or right, as required by their point of installation.

Gun, Machine, Vickers .303-inch, Mk.VI and Mk VI*

Introduced in 1936 and similar to the original Mk.IV B, both these guns were produced as new weapons as well as being converted from original Mk.I guns and were also manufactured with breech blocks loading from either the left or right, as required by their point of installation.

Gun, Machine, Vickers .303-inch, Mk.VII

Introduced in 1936 and similar to the original Mk.IV B, this guns differed from the previous weapons by having a better shoulder rest and a bipod. Only produced as new weapons, they were also manufactured with breech blocks loading from either the left or right, as required by their point of installation.

Vickers guns in .50 caliber

Chambered for the .50 caliber V/565 Vickers-Armstrong cartridge, these guns appeared successively as:

- the Mk.I, which was an experimental model.
- the Mk.II, introduced in 1933 and fitted with a dovetail mounting point to facilitate its use in armored vehicles and with a breech block loading from the right or left.
- the Mk.III, introduced in 1932 and used by the Royal Navy in banks of two or four as an antiaircraft gun.
- the Mk.IV, introduced in 1933 but quickly replaced by the Mk V.
- the Mk.V, the most successful of all the Vickers .50 caliber machine guns. It was introduced in 1933 and remained in service until 1944 when the lighter, potentially more rapidly firing Breda and Browning machine guns began to replace it.

Vickers tank gun from right, showing shoulder rest and pistol grip (courtesy James D. Julia Auctioneers, Fairfield, Maine. www.jamesdjulia.com).

Commercial Models

A number of guns were offered to nonmilitary organizations, and these were known as "Commercial" Vickers guns. Information about these weapons is not very detailed, but they were designated, in roughly chronological order: Class "A," Class "A/T," Class "C," Class "C/T" and then were placed in Classes "D" to "K" inclusive.[16]

Manufacturer's stamp on Vickers tank gun (courtesy James D. Julia Auctioneers, Fairfield, Maine. www.jamesdjulia.com).

MILITARY SERVICE

The British Army formally adopted the Vickers gun as its standard machine gun on 26 November 1912, using it alongside their Maxims, although there was still a considerable shortage of machine guns when the British Expeditionary Force went to France in 1914. So difficult did the situation become that Vickers was threatened with prosecution for war profiteering, because of the price the company was demanding for its weapons, and the cost of the weapon was finally reduced to a more reasonable level.

Vickers mounted as secondary weapon on an armored car.

As the war progressed, and numbers increased, it became the British Army's primary machine gun, and served on all fronts during the conflict. When the Lewis gun was adopted as a light machine gun and issued to infantry units, the Vickers guns were redefined as heavy machine guns, withdrawn from infantry units, and grouped in the hands of the new Machine Gun Corps. This unit was disbanded in 1918, but the Vickers remained in service with the British Army until 30 March 1968, its last operational use being in Radfan during the Aden Emergency.[17]

The Vickers with the RFC

The Vickers was the first automatic machine gun to be tried in service with the RFC, when, in 1913, a Vickers machine gun was installed in an experimental version of the Vickers F.B.5, although when this aircraft entered service its armament had been changed to a Lewis gun. Despite this early setback, the Vickers went on to become the standard machine gun fitted to British and French military aircraft during World War I, principally because its closed-bolt firing mechanism made it easier than the Lewis to synchronize for firing through aircraft propellers, and the belt feed was less liable to wind damage as it was enclosed right up to the breech. Wind speed also meant that the cooling water used in land service guns was largely redundant, and although the water jacket had to be retained, cooling was facilitated by cutting a series of slots in the empty water jacket, allowing improved air flow over the heated barrel. Later in the war, steel disintegrating-link ammunition belts replaced the canvas device, and this improved reliability even further, especially when fighters like the Sopwith Camel and the SPAD XIII types were introduced with their twin synchronized Vickers. During the interwar years, aircraft machine guns were moved from the cockpit to the wings, and the Vickers came to be replaced by the lighter, air-cooled Browning Model 1919 for use in RAF aircraft.[18]

VALUES

The U.S. government ruling of 1986 means that a gun capable of firing will fetch considerably more than a deactivated weapon. Prices range from $20,000 for a weapon in reasonable condition with a tripod, to around $80,000 for a gun with a significant or unusual provenance. Local regulations as they apply to these weapons should be consulted before purchase.

Prices quoted here are for a working gun.
NRA Good: $20,000–$25,000; NRA Fine: $35,000–$80,000

Heavy Machine Guns in Service with French Forces in World War I

The French army began World War I with possibly the two worst machine guns ever devised for military use: the Chauchat Automatic Machine Rifle as their light machine gun, and the St. Étienne Mle 1907 as their heavy weapon. The St. Étienne was a controversial design, because it used a unique, blow-forward gas piston, rather than the conventional blowback system of contemporary LMGs. It soon proved to be too fragile for the hard use it received on the Western Front. It was replaced in 1916 by another gun from Hotchkiss et Cie., the Model 1914, which was found to be so reliable that it was retained as the French army's heavy machine gun until 1942.

Hotchkiss Model 1914 Heavy Machine Gun

Like the Model 1909 light machine gun, the Model 1914 was one of the final contributions to a design series originally begun in 1896 with the first gas-operated air-cooled machine gun, the Hotchkiss Model 1897 automatic machine gun. The operating principles of this weapon were based largely upon the patents of Captain Baron Adolf Odkolek von Ujezda of Vienna, and featured an air-cooled barrel as well as the inventor's original reciprocating, gas-recoil piston.[19]

SPECIFICATION

Production: Estimated to be approximately 100,000 weapons in all calibers, all produced exclusively by Hotchkiss et Cie.

The Hotchkiss Model 1914 automatic machine gun was an air-cooled, gas-operated fully automatic weapon, with a cyclic rate of 450 rpm. Model 1914s were without provision for semiautomatic operation, and fired from an open bolt, thus preventing "cook off," the infantryman's perennial nightmare when using early machine guns that operated from a closed bolt. It was fitted with a single "spade pattern" firing handle and a combined brass pistol grip and trigger guard, the trigger being contained within this trigger guard and mounted on the bottom plate of the receiver. The weapon was usually mounted on a tripod for land service, one of three types being commonly found with antique weapons. Another advantage of the Hotchkiss from the senior military viewpoint was its simplicity of construction. Excluding the tripod, a Hotchkiss M1914 was composed of only 32 parts, which included just four coil springs and no screws or pins whatsoever.[20] All parts of the gun were constructed in such a manner that it was impossible to assemble them incorrectly, a distinct advantage for a weapon that was to be issued to troops who needed to learn how to clean and maintain their equipment as quickly as was humanly possible.

Initially accepted by the French army in 1916, it was consequently chambered for the 8×50mmR Lebel cartridge, although subsequently Model 1914s were produced to use the 7×57mm Spanish Mauser, 6.5×50mmSR Arisaka, 11mm Gras, and 6.5×55mm Swedish Mauser cartridges, as well as the 7.92×57mm Mauser German service rifle cartridge in weapons made by the Chinese government. As with all Hotchkiss machine guns, cartridges were supplied to the mechanism from a metal strip containing 30 rounds, which was loaded into the left side of the breech. Later weapons were designed to use a belt composed of disposable metal links, which held 251 cartridges, 3 strips joined into a single belt, with each strip holding 84 rounds, and unlike the Hotchkiss Model 1909, cartridges entered the breech of the Model 1914 on the top surface of the belt. Although the M1914 was capable of a sustained rate of fire of approximately 450 rpm, this firing rate soon overheated the air-cooled barrel and destroyed the rifling. Consequently, firing rates were reduced in practical operation to between 100 rpm and 120 rpm, which allowed the gun to be operated continually,

Hotchkiss Model 1914 HMG from the right (courtesy James D. Julia Auctioneers, Fairfield, Maine. www.jamesdjulia.com).

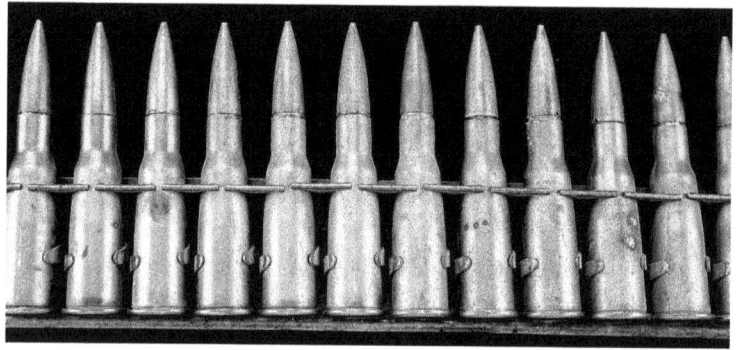

Loaded ammunition belt for the M1914 (courtesy James D. Julia Auctioneers, Fairfield, Maine. www.jamesdjulia.com).

apart from barrel changes after 1,000 rounds had been fired. Although the barrel tended to glow a dark red from the heat generated by firing at this rate, giving an operating temperature of approximately 400°C, heat dissipation was equal to the rate of generation, and so the barrel continued to perform well without significant damage to the lands and grooves of the rifling. Heat dissipation was also helped by the addition of five thick circular metal rings at the base of the barrel, which gives Hotchkiss machine guns their characteristic appearance. The weapon is also fitted with a gas regulator between the barrel and the piston cylinder, a switch to lock back the trigger during automatic firing, and a manual safety catch on the left side of the receiver.

Receiver Stamps

The receiver is stamped on the left side:

MITRAILLEUSE AUTOMATIQUE HOTCHKISS
BREVETEE S.G.D.G
CALIBRE 8 m/m

With a serial number and production date on the right side of the receiver above the trigger guard, in the following form:

N° XXXXX
1918

Where "XXXXX" represents the serial number and "1918" is the production date.

Operation

A magazine strip is first placed in the left side of the breech and the lever of the cocking handle is pulled back to its full extent. The gunner then pushes the cocking handle forwards, these actions serving to cock the weapon and making the Model 1914 ready to fire.

Pulling the trigger releases the sear on the underside of the piston, and the recoil spring then drives the piston forward, which causes the front face of the breech block to force the forward end of the ejector out of the path of the operating mechanism. The lower part of the breech block face then strikes the base of the cartridge, removing it from the metal magazine strip and driving it forward into the chamber. As the breech block chambers the round, the extractor moves over the rim of the cartridge, the breechblock in turn tilting up and locking into its firing position, while the wheel actuating the mechanism that moves the magazine strip also advances through the first half of its travel, carrying the magazine strip with it. The piston continues to move forward, carrying the firing pin, which then detonates the primer in the cartridge. As the bullet travels up the barrel, it passes a port connecting the barrel with the piston cylinder and some residual gas passes into this cylinder, driving the piston to the rear and compressing the recoil spring. The rearward movement of the piston withdraws the firing pin from the primer and tilts the breechblock down, unlocking it and carrying it to the rear. The extractor withdraws the empty case from the chamber, while the rear end of the ejector moves out of its groove in the breechblock, striking the base of the spent case and projecting the empty case out of the ejection slot in the receiver to the right of the weapon. A small cam on the piston now completes the rotation of the wheel that moves the magazine strip and places the next cartridge into position ready to be moved into the chamber on the next cycle. If the trigger is still held back manually or the automatic trigger catch is set, the mechanism begins its firing cycle again; otherwise the sear on the piston is engaged and the gun is held with the bolt locked open. When the magazine strip has been fed entirely through, the upper lug of the arrester catch engages a corresponding lug on the piston, locking back the piston and allowing the next strip to be loaded.[21]

Major variations

Hotchkiss Model 1914 machine gun

Production: approximately 55,000 guns.

Adopted by the French army in 1916 as the Mle 1914 Hotchkiss, this was the standard French heavy machine gun from 1916 until 1942, with 47,000 guns being delivered to the French army between 1916 and the end of 1918, for use by the infantry as well as being mounted in all French tanks and armored cars during World War I. Land service and tank-mounted weapons were chambered for the 8mm Lebel cartridge, although several hundred guns were also made for anti-balloon duties in 11mm Gras, which was the smallest incendiary bullet available in 1916. The U.S. army also used the larger Hotchkiss between 1917 and 1918, purchasing approximately 7,000 weapons in the period during which the AEF served in France.

Japanese Model 1914 machine guns

Japan began to produce a variation of the Model 1914 in 1914, called the Type 3 Heavy Machine Gun, under license from Hotchkiss, chambered for the 6.5 × 50mm Arisaka cartridge. Later, they produced another weapon based on the Hotchkiss, the Type 92 Heavy Machine Gun, chambered in 7.7 × 58mm Arisaka.

Chinese Hotchkiss Model 1914 machine guns

Between 1930 and 1935 the Chinese government bought 1,192 Hotchkiss M1914 machine guns in 8mm Lebel from Hotchkiss et Cie. and during the same period, they also copied the gun, modifying it to accept the 7.92 × 57mm Mauser German service rifle cartridge.

Polish Hotchkiss Model 1914 machine guns

Poland began to buy the Model 1914 from Hotchkiss et Cie. in 1919, chambered in 8mm Lebel and by 1936 the Polish army was equipped with 2620 weapons of this type. Between 1920 and 1925, they also ordered 1250 weapons chambered in 7.92 × 57 Mauser, although poor training resulted in bad performance by these weapons, which were consequently relegated to rear echelon units.[22]

MILITARY SERVICE

Hotchkiss Model 1914 machine guns chambered for the 7 × 57mm Spanish Mauser cartridge were used by both governmental and rebel forces during the Mexican Revolution (1910–1920). Later, between 1930 and 1936, Hotchkiss M1914 machine guns chambered in 7mm Spanish Mauser and built under license in Spain were the standard medium machine gun used by the conflicting parties involved in the Spanish Civil War. This goes some way to explain the preponderance of weapons stamped "7m/m" at American auctions.[23]

VALUES

The U.S. government ruling of 1986 means that, as is usual, a gun capable of firing will fetch considerably more than a deactivated weapon. Local regulations as they apply to these weapons should be consulted before purchase.

Prices quoted here are for a working gun.
NRA Good: $8,000–$10,000; NRA Fine: $10,000–$12,000

Heavy Machine Guns in Service with German and Austro-Hungarian Forces in World War I

In common with the British army, the armies of the Central Powers relied upon a single design of heavy machine gun, which was also based on Maxim's recoil-operated, automatic mechanism. Designated the Maschinengewehr 08 or MG 08, it was produced by a number of German state arsenals and the German munitions company DWM (Deutsche Waffen und Munitionsfabriken, trans: German Weapons and Munitions).

Maschinengewehr 08 or MG 08

Also known as the Spandau MG 08 after the factory where many of the weapons were produced, the original MG 08 was a design based on the Maxim gun of 1884, although, like the British army's Vickers, it had undergone a number of modifications and improvements. It was the German army's standard machine gun during World War I and also saw extensive service during World War II, although by the end of the war it was being largely superseded by the superior MG 34 and MG 42.

SPECIFICATION

The MG 08 was a belt-fed, water-cooled, medium/heavy machine gun, fitted with a modification of Maxim's recoil-operated, toggle-locked, fully automatic mechanism and having "spade" firing handles with the firing button mounted between them. Cartridges were loaded into a fabric belt that held 250 rounds, and the gun was chambered for the 7.92 × 57mm Mauser German service rifle cartridge, the 7.65 × 53mm Argentinian/Belgian Mauser cartridge, and the 13.2 × 92SR antitank cartridge. The weapon's lack of maneuverability was heightened because, instead of a tripod like the Vickers, the MG 08 was usually mounted on a sled (trans: Schlittenlafette) that was ferried between locations either on carts or else carried above men's shoulders in a manner similar to that used for a stretcher. Operation and protocols for water cooling were similar to those used for the Vickers auto-

German MG 08 HMG with ammunition boxes. A more faithful copy of Maxim's original gun, this was heavier than the British Vickers, requiring four men to move it on its usual sled mounting (courtesy James D. Julia Auctioneers, Fairfield, Maine. www.jamesdjulia.com).

matic machine gun, although the use of the sled mount sometimes made siting the weapon significantly more difficult than would have been the case with the British weapon.[24]

Receiver Stamps

The top of the receiver is usually stamped:

XXXXX
d
M.G.08.
Gwf.
SPANDAU.
1917.

The "XXXXX" representing the serial number, "SPANDAU" being the place of manufacture, and the "1917" representing the date of manufacture, which could vary from 1908 to 1918. There may be some weapons produced after this date, which will consequently bear the appropriate date stamp. The "*d*" may be an inspector's stamp or early manufacturer's code number.

When the war began in August 1914, approximately 12,000 MG 08 machine guns were available to German army units, although wartime production quickly increased. By 1914, around 200 MG 08s were being produced on a monthly basis. Further improvements in production followed, and by 1916, production had risen to 3,000 weapons each month, finally reaching a peak in 1917 of approximately 14,400 guns every month, an increase of over seventy times when compared to the first year of the war.[25]

Breech of German MG 08, showing serial number (4189), place of manufacture (SPANDAU Arsenal), and the date of manufacture (1917) (courtesy James D. Julia Auctioneers, Fairfield, Maine. www.jamesdjulia.com).

The MG 08/15

Production: precise records not available, but estimated at 150,000 weapons.

In 1915 a lightened and considerably more portable version of the MG 08 was produced by modifying and cutting down the upper rear and lower forward corners of the original MG 08's receiver and breech assembly, and reducing the cooling jacket's diameter from 105mm to 92.5mm. Designated the MG 08/15, the weapon was designed to be operated by four trained infantrymen working from a prone position. To facilitate this change, the new gun was fitted with a short-legged bipod, together with a wooden butt and pistol grip. Weighing

Sixteen. Medium and Heavy Machine Guns in World War I 281

MG 08/15, with characteristic bipod and magazine (courtesy James D. Julia Auctioneers, Fairfield, Maine. www.jamesdjulia.com).

only 18 kg, the MG 08/15 was lighter than the standard MG 08, although it still possessed all the attributes of a heavy machine gun and so was cumbersome, as well as still being awkward to both site and operate with any degree of safety. More importantly, its redesign had incorporated features, in particular the bipod, which made it difficult to achieve even a reasonable standard of accuracy with the weapon.

Receiver stamps

The top of the receiver is usually stamped:

XXXXX

a

M.G.08/15

Gwf.

ERFURT

1917.

The "XXXXX" representing the serial number, "ERFURT" being the place of manufacture, and the "1917" representing the date of manufacture, which could vary from 1908 to 1918. There may have been some weapons produced after this date, and they will consequently bear the appropriate date stamp. The "*a*" may be an inspector's stamp or early manufacturer's code number.

Military service

Despite its inherent disadvantages the MG 08/15, quickly superseded the older MG 08 in service with German units on the Western Front. It began to be issued in in increasingly large numbers to all front-line infantry regiments in the spring of 1917 and subsequently during the German offensives of the spring and summer of 1918. The MG 08/15 became the most common German machine gun deployed in World War I, reaching an allocation of six guns per company or 72 guns per regiment in 1918, such that there were four times more MG 08/15 light machine guns than the earlier MG 08 heavy machine guns in each infantry regiment. In order to achieve this figure, approximately 130,000 MG 08/15 were manufactured during World War I, most of them at the government arsenals of Spandau and Erfurt. This is the weapon usually referred to as the "Spandau MG 08," rather than the earlier weapon with the rectangular receiver.[26]

The MG 08 in aircraft

The lMG 08 and lMG 08/15 (*luftgeküht maschinengewehr 08*: trans; *air-cooled MG 08*)
Production:
lMG 08: Precise records not available.
lMG 08/15: Precise records not available but estimated at 23,000 weapons.

A lightened, air-cooled version of the original MG 08 was put into production by the Spandau arsenal in 1915 for use in the Fokker Eindecker monoplane, which was the first aircraft fitted with its designer's synchronization system. The gun was modified by having the original firing handles and mounting system removed, while sections of the water jacket were also cut away to allow it to operate as an air-cooled weapon. In the initial conversions, too much of the jacket was removed, which reduced the metal required to support the barrel to a disastrous extent, but later modifications rectified this problem, and such weapons worked well in the later Albatross aircraft. After the final development of the MG 08/15 was complete, this weapon was also modified for air service, and both the MG 08 and MG 08/15 were also used in dual mounts.[27]

lMG 08/15, a development of the original MG 08/15 for use in air service (courtesy James D. Julia Auctioneers, Fairfield, Maine. www.jamesdjulia.com).

MAJOR VARIATIONS

MG 08/18

This weapon was an air-cooled version of the original MG 08 for use by infantry units. A small number were tested between July and November 1918, but the barrel of the weapon was excessively heavy and could not be changed quickly, so no further development took place after the few prototypes had proven unsuccessful.

MG 08 antitank rifle

A variant of the MG 08 chambered for the same 13.2 × 92mmSR cartridge as the Mauser Anti Tank Rifle was introduced in 1918. Designated MG 18 TuF (Tank und Flieger: trans; tank and aircraft), it was issued in limited numbers late World War I.

The Chinese MG 08

Germany supplied China with the original MG 08 during WW1 and by 1935, the Chinese were making their own variant, the Type 24 Heavy machine gun, chambered for the 7.92 × 57mm Mauser German service rifle cartridge. It was exactly similar to the original German MG 08.

MILITARY SERVICE

Both the MG 08 and MG 08/15 were in use with the armies of the Central Powers in World War I, becoming the standard German heavy machine guns during this period. The Wehrmacht began World War II with the MG 08/15 as the standard machine gun with many infantry units, but the demands of the "Blitzkrieg" meant that most of these weapons were soon replaced by the excellent MG 34 and later MG 42 machine guns. Both types were also exported, particularly to the Far East and Eastern Europe, where they remained in service long after heavy machine guns had become obsolete in the armies of better equipped European forces.[28]

VALUES

The U.S. government ruling of 1986 means that, as is usual, a gun capable of firing will fetch considerably more than a deactivated weapon. Local regulations as they apply to these weapons should be consulted before purchase.

Prices quoted here are for a working gun.

MG 08: NRA Good: $10,000–$15,000; NRA Fine: $20,000–$25,000
MG 08/15 (Land service): NRA Good: $7,000–$8,500; NRA Fine: $10,000–$12,000
MG 08/15 (Air service): NRA Good: $7,000–$8,500; NRA Fine: $10,000–$12,000

Table Twenty-three: Comparison of the specification of the Vickers, MG 08 and Hotchkiss M1914 heavy machine guns

Weapon	Vickers HMG	MG 08 and MG 08/15	Hotchkiss M1914
Makers	Vickers, Son and Maxim. Colt's Manufacturing Company. Small Arms Factory, Lithgow, Australia. Fabrico de Braco de Prata, Portugal.	Deutsche Waffen und Munitionsfabriken (DWM). Spandau and Erfurt arsenals. Hanyang Arsenal, China.	Hotchkiss et Cie.
Period of production	1912–1945	Germany: 1908–1945 China: 1911–1960	1914–1920
Production	Difficult to accurately estimate but probably in excess of 500,000 weapons, including all chambering variants	In excess of 175,000 weapons	In excess of 100,000 weapons
Operators	Australia, Belgium, Britain, Canada, China, Czechoslovakia, France, India, Ireland, Italy, Malaya, Mexico,	Germany (1914–1918 and 1933–1945), Austria-Hungary, China, Korea, Turkey, Norway, Poland,	Belgium, Chile, China, France and Vichy France, Greece, Italy, Japan, Mexico,

Weapon	Vickers HMG	MG 08 and MG 08/15	Hotchkiss M1914
Military service	New Zealand, Pakistan, South Africa, USA **British Army 1912–1968:** World War I (1914–1918) World War II (1939–1945) Malaya (1948–1966) Aden (1963–1967) Korean War (1950–1953) **U.S. Army 1913–1919:** World War I (1917–1918)	North Vietnam (1963–1975) Xinhai Revolution (1911) World War I (1914–1918) Finnish Civil War (1918) Polish-Soviet War (1919–1921) Chinese Civil War (1927–1950) World War II (1939–1945) Second Sino-Japanese War (1937–1945) Korean War (1950–1953) First Indochina War (1946–1954) Vietnam War (1955–1975)	Norway, USSR, Sweden, Turkey, USA Mexican Revolution (1910–1920) World War I (1914–1918) Polish-Soviet War (1919–1921) World War II (1939–1945) Constitutionalist Revolution (1932) Second Italo-Ethiopian War (1935–1936) Spanish Civil War (1936–1939) Second Sino-Japanese War (1937–1945) First Indochina War (1946–1954) Algerian War (1954–1962)
Crew	Eight men: Gunner, loader and four to six others to carry the gun, tripod and ammunition boxes	Four men: Gunner, loader, two ammunition carriers	Three men: Gunner and two loaders
Weight	Gun: 30 lbs empty, 40 lbs with full water jacket Tripod: 40–50 lbs Total weight: 70–90 lbs	Gun: 58 lbs empty, 67 lbs with full water jacket Tripod: 85 lbs Total weight: 160 lbs	Gun: 54 lbs Tripod: 56 lbs Total weight: 110 lbs
Length/Barrel length	Total length: 43½ inches Barrel: 28½ inches	Total length: 46 inches Barrel length: 28 inches	Total length: 55 inches Barrel length: 31 inches
Mechanism	Water-cooled, automatic blowback operated, short recoil	Water-cooled, automatic blowback operated, short recoil	Air-cooled, gas operation using residual cartridge gas
Cartridge	Originally .303 British Mk VII ball cartridge, but also chambered for a large number of foreign cartridges. Cartridge delivery by means of a fabric belt, holding 333 cartridges, entering the right side of the breech	7.92 × 57mm Mauser cartridge 7.65 × 53mm Argentine cartridge 13.2 × 92mm, Tank and aircraft (TuF) cartridge Cartridge delivery by means of a fabric belt, holding 250 cartridges, entering the right side of the breech	8 × 50mmR Lebel 7 × 57mm Mauser 6.5 × 50mmSR Arisaka 11 mm Gras 6.5 × 55mm Cartridge delivery by means of: Metal strip holding 30 rounds Articulated steel belt, belt, composed of metal strips and holding 251

Weapon	Vickers HMG	MG 08 and MG 08/15	Hotchkiss M1914
			cartridges, both systems entering the left side of the breech
Sights	Front: Blade sight Rear: Adjustable, aperture sight	Front: simple blade Rear: Leaf, graduated up to 4,000 meters	Front: simple blade Rear: Leaf, graduated up to 4,000 meters
Maximum range	Approximately 2,000 yards for aimed shots, with a maximum lethal range of about 4,500 yds or 3 miles	Approximately 2,000 yards for aimed shots, with a maximum lethal range of about 4,500 yds or 3 miles	Approximately 2,000 yards for aimed shots, with a maximum lethal range of about 4,500 yds or 3 miles
Rate of fire	Approximately 450–550 rounds per minute (rpm)	500–600 rpm	450 rpm
Cost of manufacture in 1914	Approximately £100	Approximately £150	Approximately £250

Heavy Machine Guns in Service with the Allies and the Central Powers in World War I

AMERICAN HEAVY MACHINE GUNS

The 1903–'06 Gatling gun

Production: precise figures not available, estimated at 1,000 weapons.

Some of the Model 1903-'06 Gatling guns previously used in the Philippines were used for training at the U.S. machine gun school in Texas, although they never saw service in France with the AEF.

The Maxim M1904

Production: precise figures not available, estimated at 1,000 weapons.

This weapon was a U.S.–made version of the Model 1884 Maxim, which was used for training at the U.S. Machine Gun School.

The Colt-Browning Model 1895 machine gun

Production: precise figures not available, estimated at 100,000 weapons.
Used only for training.

The Browning Model 1917 machine gun

Production: precise figures not available, estimated at 130,000 weapons.

Accepted for U.S. land service in 1917, although not extensively used by AEF in World War I. Some Model 1917 guns were deployed during World War II, but they were being largely replaced by the Model 1919 and .50 caliber M2 during this period.

British heavy machine guns

The Vickers heavy/medium machine gun

Production: precise figures not available, estimated at 500,000 weapons.

Used in a variety of configurations, the Mk1 was the usual weapon issued for land service, with modified weapons used by the RFC and RAF.

French heavy machine guns

The St. Étienne Mle 1907

Production: 39,700 weapons.

This was a gas-operated air-cooled machine gun, chambered for the 8 × 51mmR Lebel cartridge, which was the standard French machine gun between 1907 and 1917, when it was replaced by the far superior Hotchkiss M1914 machine gun.[29]

The Hotchkiss Model 1914

Production: in excess of 65,000 weapons.

Used in a variety of configurations by the French and U.S. armies.

German and Austro-Hungarian heavy machine guns

The MG 08 and MG 08/15

Production: precise figures not available, estimated at 200,000 weapons.

The principal heavy machine gun in use by the Central Powers and manufactured in a variety of configurations for both land and air service.

The Maschinengewehr (Schwarzlose) M. 7

Production: precise figures not available, estimated at 50,000 weapons.

Also known as the Schwarzlose MG, the M.7 was a fully automatic, belt-fed, water-cooled medium machine gun with a tripod mounting. It was one of the principal machine guns used by the Austro-Hungarian Army throughout World War I, as well being in service with the armies of Greece, the Netherlands and Sweden. Chambered for a variety of cartridges, including the 7.92 × 57mm Mauser and the .303 British, it differed from contemporary weapons such as the MG 08 and Vickers in having a simpler, delayed blowback mechanism, which gave it a firing rate of between 400 and 600 rpm.[30]

Guns in air service: The Gast gun

Production: precise figures not available, estimated at 10,000 weapons.

This weapon was a twin-barreled machine gun which had its two barrels combined into a single mechanism so that the recoil from firing the first barrel loaded and fired the second. Ammunition was supplied to the breech from two vertically mounted cylindrical drums, one on each side of the weapon, which held 180 rounds of German 7.92 mm rifle ammunition. A Gast could be set to fire single shots if one side of the mechanism developed a fault, although a firing rate 1,600 rpm was possible with a properly adjusted weapon. A modification of the Gast mechanism was also adapted for use in the Soviet 25mm Gryazev-Shipunov Gsh-23L automatic cannon.[31]

The Parabellum MG14

Production: precise figures not available, estimated at 10,000 weapons.

The Parabellum MG14 was a 7.9 mm caliber World War I machine gun built by Deutsche Waffen und Munitionsfabriken. It was a complete redesign of the MG 08 and intended for use on aircraft and Zeppelins. It incorporated a new toggle-action mechanism that broke upwards rather than downwards as in the original 08, making for a much more compact receiver. An internal spring replaced the original fusee spring and the breech block was also redesigned, so that spent cases dropped out the bottom of the receiver. Ammunition was supplied from a drum and the water jacket was modified to allow the barrel to benefit from air cooling. The rate of fire was an improvement on the conventional MG 08 at 700 rounds per minute.[32]

RUSSIAN HEAVY MACHINE GUNS

The PM M1910

Production: precise figures not available, estimated at 500,000 weapons.

Adopted in 1910 by the Imperial Russian army, this weapon was a copy of the Maxim gun, chambered for the Russian 7.62 × 54mmR service rifle cartridge. Instead of the more portable tripod used with the MG 08 and Vickers, the M1910 was usually mounted on a wheeled carriage with a gun shield, reminiscent of an artillery field piece. In addition to this infantry weapon, there were also versions designed for air and naval service, some weapons in land service being fitted with a tractor radiator cap sealing the water jacket to allow handfuls of snow to be packed in, where it would melt during firing.[33]

CHAPTER SEVENTEEN

Submachine Guns, Semiautomatic Rifles and Postwar Changes

American Submachine Guns and Garand's Semiautomatic Rifle

UNHELPFUL ATTITUDES

The men in control of the nineteenth century's armies were, at best, a conservative bunch. Military thinking during that period always found innovation of any sort difficult, and nowhere was this predilection so marked as in the area of repeating rifles.

The British Army did not introduce a magazine rifle until 1888, when the Lee-Metford, with a magazine holding 10 rounds, began its service life. Unfortunately, the Metford's barrel was not suitable for the new smokeless ammunition then being introduced, and the rifle began to be replaced in 1895 by the Lee-Enfield, a weapon that will be familiar to many both in and out of Britain's armed forces. Even after the issue of this new rifle, the generals still were concerned about soldiers issued with a magazine rifle wasting ammunition, so the Lee-Enfield was fitted with a magazine cutoff to allow the rifle to be loaded with a single cartridge between shots, thus conserving the contents of the magazine.

The U.S. army also suffered from a tendency amongst its senior officers to be unreceptive to new ideas, and it was not until 1892 that their single-shot Springfield was wholly replaced with the Krag-Jørgenson rifle, which featured a five-round magazine amongst its other improvements. By the time America was involved in World War I, its troops had been equipped with a replacement for the Krag, the significantly better Springfield Model of 1903. Unfortunately, although both the M1903 Springfield and Lee-Enfield were excellent weapons, their long barrels proved a cumbersome liability at close quarters in the trenches. Something different was needed, and fortunately for its soldiers, the American Army had in General John Thompson, its chief of small arms for the Army Ordnance Department, a man who was clear about the shortcomings of conventional rifles ... and not afraid to say so.[1]

The Thompson Submachine Gun: "A One-Man, Hand-Held Machine Gun"

What was needed for trench warfare, according to the General Thompson, was "a small machine gun, a gun that will fire 50 to 100 rounds, so light that he can drag it with him ... and wipe out a whole company single-handed. A one-man hand-held machine gun."[2] Thompson had left the Army in 1914, upon the outbreak of World War I in Europe. In 1916, he and his son began a firearms manufacturing company they called the Auto-Ordnance Corporation. He was recalled to the Army in 1917, with the rank of brigadier general, and appointed to serve as director of arsenals.

By now thoroughly dissatisfied with the performance of the standard military rifle as a weapon for trench warfare, he gave orders to his staff at Auto-Ordnance to begin development of a new, hand-held *automatic* rifle, using the .30–06 U.S. Army service rifle cartridge. Unfortunately, problems with this powerful military round meant that the new weapon, now chambered for the .45 Automatic Colt Pistol (ACP) cartridge, did not begin production until March 1921. It was named the Thompson and designated a "submachine" gun, because it used a pistol cartridge, which was shorter and less powerful than the standard rifle cartridge, although it was of a larger caliber and later proved to have at least as much stopping power. These first weapons were produced by the Colt Patent Firearms Co. at their Hartford factory and are known to collectors as the "Model of 1921A" or M1921 A. They feature a unique delayed blowback mechanism patented by a former USN officer, John Blish, which was fitted to all Thompsons until production began of the much simplified M1 and M1A1 models.[3]

Like most innovative designs, the M1921 A had its problems, one of the most significant being its tendency to rear upwards when fired on fully automatic. This unfortunate shortcoming was alleviated, if not fully cured, by the development of a "compensator" by Col. Richard Cutts, which could be simply screwed onto the muzzle of a standard Thompson, without any modification. The Cutts compensator had four vent slots in its top surface through which the muzzle gases were expelled, causing a significant downdraft and counteracting the new machine gun's tendency towards "muzzle-lift" when firing.[4]

A new version of the "Tommy gun," the M1928, was introduced in 1928, with a lower, more controllable rate of fire, 600 rounds per minute (rpm), as opposed to the 800 rpm of the M1921. It was that model that was accepted into U.S. Navy service with the Marine Corps in 1932 and sold subsequently in small numbers to the military and civilian users.

The outbreak of World War II in 1939, and in particular British matériel losses at Dunkirk, meant an increased demand for small arms. As Colt had by this time ceased production of the Thompson, the new owner of what was now called the Thompson Automatic Arms Corporation, one Russell Macguire, approached the Savage Arms Corporation with a plan to offer them a license to manufacture the weapon. After some very careful negotiation, Macguire's slightly unsavory reputation having apparently preceded him, Savage agreed to produce the Thompson, with Remington also responsible for a number of parts, in particular the barrels and wooden stocks. Production began in May 1940 with a Thompson designated the M1928A1. This weapon underwent a number of changes in the period between 1940 to 1942, mostly associated with simplifying production and reducing costs, before being accepted by the U.S. Army Ordnance Board as "Gun, Submachine, Caliber

.45, Thompson, M1." A later, simplified variant was designated the Thompson M1A1. Levels of production required to supply the U.S. Army with the new gun were so high that a new Auto-Ordnance factory was opened in Bridgeport, Connecticut, in January 1941. Most of the later Thompsons were assembled here, although Remington still made the barrels, stocks and many internal components. The M1A1 was the last model to be manufactured, production ending in 1944, after nearly 1.4 million guns had been produced.[5]

SPECIFICATION

The Thompson submachine gun is an air-cooled hand-held weapon, capable of fully automatic or semiautomatic fire, with a unique delayed blowback mechanism firing from an open bolt, except the wartime M1 and M1A1 models, which had a simple blowback mechanism, also firing from an open bolt. Except for an experimental model, the M1923, produced in small numbers by Remington in 1923, Thompsons are chambered for the .45 caliber ACP U.S. service pistol cartridge. Early models can use a 20- or 30-round box magazine or a drum magazine holding either 50 or 100 cartridges, although the M1 and M1A1 models will not accept either of these drum magazines. Butts and foregrips are of walnut in the M21 and M28 Thompsons and a rear pistol grip is fitted, while the wooden fittings on the M1 and M1A1 Thompsons were of a cheaper hardwood. Early models have a carved pistol grip fitted to the barrel, while in the later weapons this was replaced by a simpler, cheaper wooden foregrip.[6]

Thompson, model of 1928A1, showing the frame stamps from the left side and the early form of the fire control lever and safety catch (courtesy James D. Julia Auctioneers, Fairfield, Maine. www.jamesdjulia.com).

Table Twenty-four: Specification of the Thompson pistol caliber machine gun

Manufacturers	Auto Ordnance Company, Colt's Patent Firearms Mnfg Company, Savage Arms Company, BSA
Period of production	1921 until 1945
Production	Approximately 2 million weapons
Operators	Australia, Belgium, Brazil, Britain, India, Canada, China, France, Ireland, Italy, Japan, Korea, Netherlands, New Zealand, North Vietnam, Poland, South Vietnam, USSR, U.S., West Germany.
Military service	Irish Civil War, World War II, Chinese Civil War, First Indochina War, Greek Civil War, Korean War, Vietnam War, Northern Ireland conflict

Weight (empty)	M1928 A1: 10.8 lbs (4.9 kgs) M1A1: 10.6 lbs (4.8 kgs)
Length/Barrel length	M1928 A1: Length: 33.5 inches (850 mm) Barrel: 10.5 inches (270 mm) (12 inches with compensator) M1A1: Length: 32 inches (810 mm) Barrel: 10.5 inches
Mechanism	M1928 A1: Blish delayed blowback M1A1: Simple blowback
Cartridge	.45 caliber ACP Delivered from: Box magazine containing 20 cartridges Box magazine containing 30 cartridges Drum magazine containing 50 cartridges (not M1 or M1A1) Drum magazine containing 100 cartridges (not M1 or M1A1)
Sights	Fore sight: simple blade Rear sight: Various designs
Maximum effective range	100 to 150 meters
Rate of fire	M1921: 1,000 rpm M1928: 700 rpm M1: 700 rpm
Cost	£50–£60 ($200–$240) in 1939 £11 ($44) in 1944

Operation

To operate a Thompson, a magazine is first placed into the magazine housing under the receiver and pushed firmly home. The cocking handle is then pulled back, where it is retained by the sear, the fire selector switch is pushed to either the "SINGLE" or "AUTO" position, and the safety catch is moved from "SAFE" to "FIRE."

Pulling the trigger releases the sear, driving the bolt forward and chambering a cartridge. The bolt and breech are then locked together by a unique wedge arrangement and the firing pin strikes the primer, firing the cartridge. Decreasing pressure in the breech causes the two wedges to move slightly apart, allowing the bolt to move backward against the action of the return spring, separating from the breech, while the spent case leaves the breech and drops out of the ejection port in front of the magazine. The bolt then continues to move backwards until it encounters the sear. If the weapon is set for semiautomatic fire, the sear engages and the bolt is held back, while with a weapon set to the "AUTO" position, the bolt moves forward and the operating cycles begins again. The later M1 and M1A1 models operate in a similar way, except the bolt and breech are not impeded from unlocking. The design characteristics of the bolt and return spring serve to keep the breech closed until the bullet has left the muzzle, as is usual in weapons with a simple blowback operation.[7]

Major variations

Total production: approximately 2 million weapons.

Model 1921 A

Production: approximately 15,000 weapons.

This was the first production model of the Thompson, using the complex Blish lock, and manufactured exclusively by the Colt Patent Firearms Company of Hartford, Connecticut. All models of the Thompson are capable of semiautomatic and fully automatic fire.

Characteristic features include a barrel with deep cooling fins, a blade foresight and Lyman "ladder-pattern" rear sight, a central, cocking lever with a milled center slot on top of the receiver, and front and rear pistol grips. A fire-selector switch and safety lever were fitted on the left side, and the receiver was machined to accept a drum magazine. Serial numbers were stamped on the left side of the magazine receiver, on the frame under the detachable butt, and on the barrel under the foregrip. Rate of fire was 800 rpm.

The right side of the frame bears patent information and the stamp:

AUTO-ORDNANCE CORPORATION
NEW YORK. U.S.A.

The left side of the frame is stamped:

THOMPSON SUBMACHINE GUN
CALIBRE .45 AUTOMATIC COLT CARTRIDGE
MANUFACTURED BY
COLT'S PATENT FIREARMS MFG. CO
HARTFORD. CONN., USA

Above the magazine receiver, also on the left side, is stamped:

MODEL OF 1921
NO. XXXXXX

The "XXXXXX" denoting the serial number.

Some of these early weapons were converted to operate only in semiautomatic mode. Finish on all these weapons is a deep blue with polished walnut fittings.

Model 1921 AC

Thompsons made from 1927 were all fitted with a Cutts compensator to make them easier to control when used in automatic fire mode. They were designated M1921 AC and are similar to the original M1921 in all other respects.

Model 1928

This group of guns includes the 1,500 first accepted into U.S. Navy service (for the Marine Corps) on 14 March 1932, designated "Gun, Submachine, Caliber .45, US Navy Model of 1928."

Similar in outward conformation to the M1921A and M1921 AC, but with a riveted steel block on the actuator and smaller recoil and buffer springs, designed to slow the rate of fire to a more manageable 600 rpm.

"Postal Service" Thompsons

Prior to acceptance by the Navy, 200 M1921A Thompsons were sold to the U.S. Marine Corps, who were assigned to protect the trains of the U.S. Postal service after a series of violent robberies in 1926. The guns were later converted to use the M1928 mechanism and the original "Model of 1921" mark on these guns is over-stamped "1928."

Model 1928A1

Production: 562,511 weapons

This group of Thompsons marks the beginning of the Savage Company's involvement with Thompson manufacture, and they characteristically have a "S" prefix to their serial numbers, most components also being stamped with a "S." In all other respects they are exactly similar to the Model 1928 Thompsons produced by Colt, although some have a gray "Parkerized" finish rather than being blued.

The right side of the receiver bears patent information and the stamp:

**AUTO-ORDNANCE CORPORATION
NEW YORK, N.Y. U.S.A.**

The receiver is stamped on the left side:

**U.S. MODEL OF 1928 A1
NO. S-XXXXXX**

"S-XXXXXX" denoting the serial number.

Above the rear pistol grip, also on the left side, is stamped:

**THOMPSON SUBMACHINE GUN
CALIBRE .45 AUTOMATIC CARTRIDGE**

Thompsons made by Savage between 1940 and 1942

Although the M1928A1 and M1A1 are seen by collectors as distinct weapons, the final, definitive version of the M1A1 was not really in production until late in 1942. In the intervening period, Savage introduced a number of modifications and improvements, and guns were produced with new components fitted as and when they became available, rather than as part of a coherent process of improvement. This means that perfectly authentic, "hybrid" guns may sometimes be encountered fitted with components not usually thought to be characteristic of a particular model.

Production of the Thompson was begun in a new Auto-Ordnance factory in Bridgeport, Connecticut, in January 1941, and weapons made in this new facility bear the appropriate factory stamp.

Model M1

This was the Thompson most commonly carried by Allied troops in World War II.

Externally, it differs from the M1928A1 in having a simple horizontal foregrip, with a groove on both sides, a non-adjustable rear sight and a barrel without cooling fins. The position of the cocking handle was also changed from the top of the receiver to the right-hand, side and the fire-selector and safety levers were changed to rotating studs.

The right side of the receiver bears patent information and the stamp:

**AUTO-ORDNANCE CORPORATION
NEW YORK, N.Y. U.S.A.**

Later weapons may be stamped:

AUTO-ORDNANCE CORPORATION
BRIDGEPORT, CONNECTICUT, U.S.A.

The receiver is stamped on the left side:

U.S. MODEL OF 1928 A1
NO. XXXXXX

"XXXXXX" denoting the serial number.

Above the rear pistol grip, also on the left side, is stamped:

THOMPSON SUBMACHINE GUN
CALIBRE .45 AUTOMATIC CARTRIDGE

Later weapons may bear a simpler stamp on the left side, which includes the serial number:

THOMPSON SUBMACHINE GUN
CALIBRE .45 M1
NO. XXXXXX

Internally, the mechanism was greatly simplified. The complex and hence expensive Blish lock mechanism was eliminated and the breech block and recoil spring were redesigned, so these weapons now had a relatively simple, open-bolt "blowback" mechanism, similar to the British Sten. Model M1 Thompsons all have a gray "Parkerized" finish, with a stock and foregrip of a cheap hardwood rather than polished walnut. These changes brought the unit price of an M1 Thompson down from $225 (£56) to $44 (£11).

Model M1/A1

Externally similar to the M1, in this model the breech-block and firing pin are in one piece, replacing the "floating" firing pin of the earlier M1.[8]

Member of the USMC at Okinawa, using a later Thompson M1A1 SMG.

BRITAIN AND THE THOMPSON

Agents of the British Purchasing Commission placed their first order for a number of M1928 Thompsons in February 1940, with total British orders eventually rising to 514,000. Guns intended for transport to Britain bear the stamps of British Ordnance inspectors, although many guns bearing these marks were never sent overseas. By April 1942, only around 100,000 of the guns that had been ordered had arrived in the UK. By now, however, the need for small arms had become so desperate that the Royal Small Arms Factory, Enfield had produced a lighter, cheaper machine gun of their own design, the Sten, and it was this weapon that was issued to the majority of British and Commonwealth units. Thompsons were still issued to commando units and, rather surprisingly, the Home Guard, as they became available. BSA was also licensed to make a variant chambered for 9mm Parabellum, although only small numbers were produced.[9]

The M1 Garand

DEVELOPMENT

The M1 Garand was the first semiautomatic rifle to be generally issued, replacing the U.S. army's bolt-action .30–06 caliber Springfield rifle. The "Semi-Automatic Rifle, caliber 30, M1" debuted in May 1934, although problems with the design meant that the first production model was not successfully proofed and tested for both function and accuracy until July 1937.

Production of this weapon began at the Springfield Armory in September 1937, but the original design incorporated a "gas trap" that resulted in a significant number of stoppages, mostly of the "failure to eject" variety. This problem necessitated a change to the mechanism used to direct the gas into the piston chamber, incorporating a much simpler "gas port" system that proved significantly more reliable. Earlier rifles were usually modified to this new specification, so any M1 Garand with the older "gas trap" system is rare and thus very collectible. By the end of 1941, the U.S. army had been completely re-equipped with M1 Garand rifles built at the Springfield Armory, although following the outbreak of World War II in Europe, the Winchester Repeating Arms Company was awarded an "educational" production contract for 65,000 rifles, with deliveries beginning in 1943.

Production was stopped after the end of World War II, but began again in 1952, when there was a shortage of weapons for the Korean War (1950–1953). The Springfield Armory increased production, and contracts were also awarded to two U.S. firearms manufacturers, International Harvester and Harrington & Richardson. Production was terminated again in 1957 when the M14 was adopted as the U.S. army's new service rifle.[10]

SPECIFICATION

The M1 Garand is a gas-operated semiautomatic rifle originally chambered for the .30–06 caliber Springfield U.S. service rifle cartridge and fitted with a rotating bolt mechanism. Its fixed box magazine held eight cartridges, delivered to the magazine by a stripper

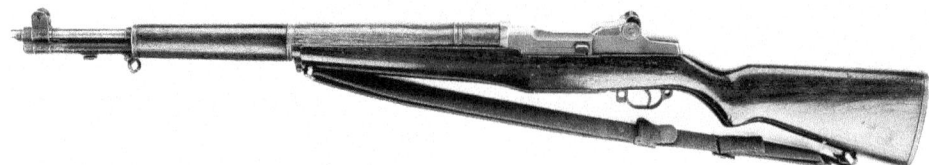

M1 Garand rifle, showing the rear sight and carrying sling (courtesy James D. Julia Auctioneers, Fairfield, Maine. www.jamesdjulia.com).

clip, which remained in the weapon until the last round was fired, when it was ejected. A safety catch was fitted on the front of the trigger guard, which was pushed forward to make the weapon ready to fire. The front sight was a simple blade with dual protecting "wings," dovetailed into the gas block at the muzzle, and rear sights were of an adjustable aperture pattern, built into the rear part of the receiver and adjustable from 100 yards to 1,200 yards, in 100-yard increments. Both the butt and foregrip were of walnut, and a steel butt-plate was fitted as well. Provision was made for attaching a bayonet. M1 Garands usually have a "Parkerized" finish.[11]

Receiver stamps

The rear of the receiver behind the rear sight bears a stamp in the following form:

U.S. RIFLE
CAL. .30 M1
SPRINGFIELD ARMORY
XXXXXX

where "SPRINGFIELD ARMORY" is the place of manufacture and "XXXXX" represents the serial number.

Operation

To fire an M1 Garand, the safety catch is first moved back, rendering the weapon safe. The cocking lever is then pulled back until it locks, and the stripper clip, containing eight cartridges, is inserted into the breech. The cocking lever is then released, causing the bolt to move forwards, chambering a cartridge and then rotating to lock the bolt and breech together. The safety catch is pushed forward and pulling the trig-

Upper receiver of M1 Garand rifle, showing the model designation, place of manufacture (Springfield Armory), and serial number (courtesy James D. Julia Auctioneers, Fairfield, Maine. www.jamesdjulia.com).

ger releases the firing pin, which strikes the primer of the chambered cartridge, the bullet then moving up the barrel, releasing a quantity of gas into the piston chamber via the gas port as it leaves the muzzle. This gas drives the piston backwards, unlocking the bolt, operating the extractor, which ejects the spent case, and cocking the firing pin mechanism. Reaching the end of its travel, the bolt moves forward again, removing a cartridge from the clip and chambering it, before rotating so that breech and barrel are locked together ready for firing. Pulling the trigger completes the cycle, which can be continued until the last cartridge is expended, whereupon the breech remains open and the empty stripper clip is ejected. Ejection of this clip results in a distinctive "pinging" sound, which was thought to be used by enemy soldiers to determine when an opposing U.S. soldier had an empty rifle, although a number of former members of the Wehrmacht claimed that this sound was inaudible during an engagement. Nor was it particularly useful, since, even if one man's Garand was empty, other platoon members would have been ready to fire.

In the hands of an experienced operator, a M1 Garand could fire between 40 and 50 aimed shots per minute, with a good expectation of a hit at 300 meters, a rate of fire far superior to any of the bolt-action service rifles in use during World War II. (NB: the best result for an SMLE, the fastest firing rifle up to the introduction of the M1, was 34 aimed shots in one minute.)[12]

Major variants

Total production of all types: approximately 5.5 million.

M1

This is the usual variant encountered by collectors, with the gas system modified to the more reliable gas port. Unmodified weapons fitted with the "gas trap" system are very rare and collectible.

M1E2

Standard M1 designed to accept a telescopic sight.

M1E3 and M1E4

M1 Garands with internal modifications to the bolt and gas recoil system.

M1E5

Standard M1 fitted with 18-inch barrel and folding stock, designed for use by airborne forces and tank crew.

Later variants mostly involved weapons modified to accept a variety of improved telescopic sights or with changes to the gas system and operating mechanism, although there were at least two later variants, the M1E14 and the T35, re-chambered to use the 7.61 × 51mm NATO cartridge.[13]

Table Twenty-five: Specification of the M1 Garand self-loading service rifle

Manufacturers	**Civilian production:** Winchester, Harrington & Richardson, International Harvester, Beretta, Breda, F.M.A.P. **U.S. government production:** Springfield Armory
Period of production	1936–1959 as standard U.S. service rifle
Production	Over 6.25 million
Operators	Argentina, Brazil, Cambodia, Canada, China, Cuba, Denmark, France, West Germany, Israel, Italy, South Korea, USA
Military service	World War II, Indonesian National Revolution, Korean War, Arab-Israeli War (1948), Hukbalahap Rebellion, First Indochina War, Suez Crisis, Lebanon crisis (1958), Cuban Revolution, Vietnam War, Cambodian Civil War, Angolan Civil War, Iran–Iraq War, Gulf War, Northern Ireland conflict, Syrian Civil War
Weight	Loaded : 10 lbs–12 lbs, depending upon model Empty: 9.5 lbs–11.5 lbs, depending upon model
Length/Barrel length	Total length: 43.5 inches Barrel: 24 inches
Mechanism	Semiautomatic, gas-operated rotating bolt
Cartridge	.30–06 Springfield (7.62 × 63mm) cartridge Delivered from an 8-round en-bloc clip contained in an integral magazine.
Sights	Front: wing-protected post Rear: adjustable aperture
Maximum range	500 meters
Rate of fire	40–50 rounds per minute
Price in 1942	$83 (£17)

British Submachine Guns: The Sten Gun

Produced in the aftermath of Dunkirk to replace the huge numbers of weapons lost during the evacuation, the Sten submachine gun was the brainchild of Major R.V. Shepherd OBE and Mr. Harold Turpin, its name being an acronym composed of the initial letters of the inventors' surnames and "EN" from Enfield. It was accepted into service with British forces in 1941 as the "9mm STEN Machine Carbine, Mark I." Cheapness and speed of manufacture had to be the inventors' main concerns, with Britain in such desperate need of weapons, and it is perhaps surprising that they managed to incorporate these characteristics into a submachine gun which, on the whole, performed remarkably well. Its assembly only required minor welding of simple parts stamped from sheet metal, with only minimal machining being required for parts such as the bolt and main and trigger springs. Later developments centered around simplifying the manufacturing process and reducing costs even further, rather than improving performance, and these measures were so effective that one of the later variants, the Mk III, could be produced in five man-hours for just over £2.[14]

SPECIFICATION

In common with its competitors, the Thompson M1 variants and the German MP40, the Sten was a simple blowback design, firing from an open bolt and with a fixed firing pin

Seventeen. Submachine Guns, Semiautomatic Rifles and Postwar Changes 299

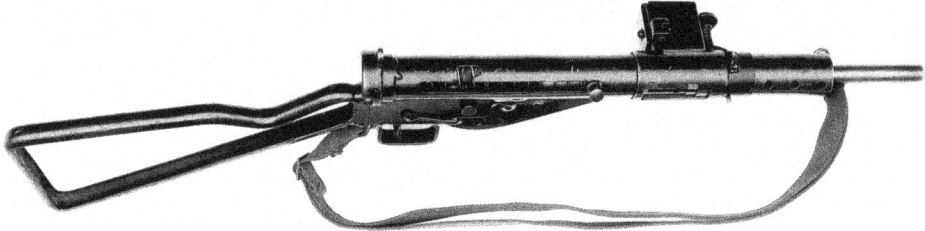

Mk II Sten from above (courtesy James D. Julia Auctioneers, Fairfield, Maine. www.jamesdjulia.com).

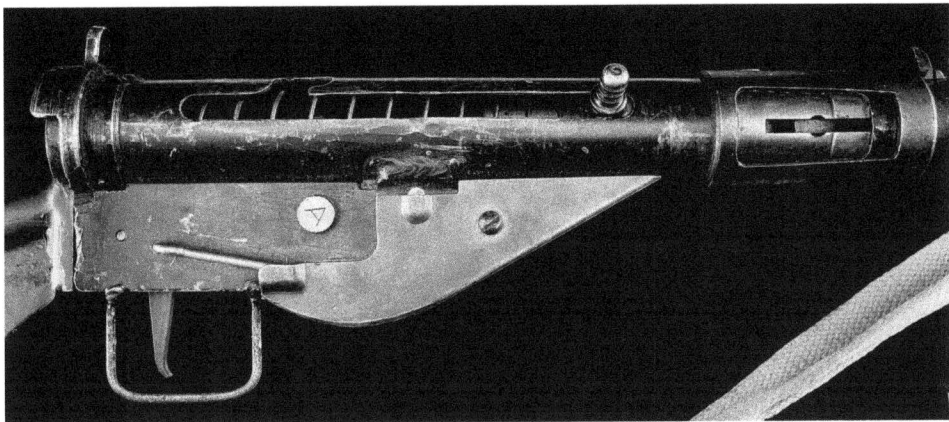

Mk II Sten from the right side, showing the ejection port, the cocking lever in its slot with the associated safety cut-out, and the fire change button. The poor quality of finish, particularly the rough welds, is apparent on this weapon (courtesy James D. Julia Auctioneers, Fairfield, Maine. www.jamesdjulia.com).

on the face of the bolt. It was air-cooled, with a detachable 30-round box magazine, and could be switched between semiautomatic or fully automatic fire by means of a button on the right of the weapon above the trigger. Machining operations were reduced to a minimum, the only precision components being the bolt, barrel and recoil spring, the tubular receiver and the barrel shroud being made from rolled steel with welded joints. Early weapons had a wooden butt and foregrip, but these were replaced in later weapons with a steel skeleton butt, the foregrip being abandoned altogether and replaced in some cases with a leather sleeve guard. Between 3.6 and 4.7 million Stens had been man-

Upper surface of magazine housing, showing the model designation (STEN MKV) (courtesy James D. Julia Auctioneers, Fairfield, Maine. www.jamesdjulia.com).

ufactured by RSAF Enfield and other sources by the time the British Army began replacing them with the Sterling submachine gun in 1953.[15]

IDENTIFICATION STAMPS

The upper surface of the magazine housing is often found stamped with the model number, in the following form, although the stamp may be indistinct:

STEN M*k*5
M/78

Where the "M*k*5" indicates the model designation and the M/78 is probably an inspector's stamp. These guns also usually bear a War Office "Broad Arrow" acceptance stamp. In addition, the lower surface of the magazine housing is usually stamped with a maker's name and the serial number, in the usual form.

Table Twenty-six: Specification of the STEN pistol caliber machine gun

Manufacturers	**British manufacturers:**
	RSAF Enfield, BSA, ROF Fazakerley, ROF Maltby, ROF Theale, Lines Brothers Ltd.
	Canadian manufacturers:
	Long Branch Canada
Period of production	1940 until 1950, depending upon model
Production	Between 3 and 5 million weapons
Operators	Argentina, Australia, Britain, Canada, Cuba, Cyprus, China, Denmark, Finland, France, Greece, Israel, Italy, Nazi Germany, New Zealand, Norway, Poland, South Africa, North and South Vietnam, Viet Cong, USA
Military service	World War II, Second Sino-Japanese War, Chinese Civil War, Malayan Emergency, Korean War, Mau Mau Uprising, Suez Crisis, 1948 Arab-Israeli War, First Indochina War, Vietnam War, Northern Ireland
Weight	Mk I: approximately 10 lbs (4.5 kg)
	Mk II: approximately 7 lbs (3.2 kg)
	Mk V: approximately 8.5 lbs (3.86 kg)
Length/Barrel length	Overall length: 30 inches (760mm)
	Barrel length: 7.7 inches (196mm)
Mechanism	Simple blowback mechanism, firing from an open bolt
Cartridge	9 × 19mm Parabellum service pistol cartridge
	Delivered to the breech from a detachable box magazine holding 32 cartridges (usual loading: 27–28 rounds)
Sights	Front sight: simple post
	Rear sight: fixed aperture
Maximum accurate range	Approximately 100 meters
Rate of fire	Mks I–III—approximately 500 rpm
	Mk V—approximately 600 rpm
Cost	£2–£4 ($8–$16) in 1942

OPERATION

Firing the weapon involves fitting a loaded magazine into the magazine slot on the left, then simply drawing the bolt to the rear of the cocking lever slot, against the action of the mainspring, where it is retained by the trigger sear. Squeezing the trigger releases the bolt, which is driven forward by the main spring, stripping a cartridge from the magazine, chambering and then firing it in the same operation, whereupon the recoil of the spent case pushes the bolt backwards and the spent case is ejected. If the Sten is set to automatic fire, the bolt will move forward again, chambering and firing a cartridge until either the trigger is released or the magazine is empty. If set to semiautomatic operation, the trigger sear will hold back the bolt and the trigger will need to be pulled to fire a second round. Rate of fire was between 550 and 600 rpm, depending upon the model, a 30-round magazine being emptied in approximately 3 seconds.

The Sten's design embodied a number of advantages: the firing chamber remains empty until the trigger is pulled, which means there is no possibility of a round being discharged through overheating or "cook-off"; the open ejection port allowed increased air flow to cool the mechanism; and manufacture was cheap and relatively simple. Unfortunately, this simplicity, together with the 9mm pistol ammunition it was chambered for, brought its own disadvantages, most notably a severely restricted accuracy, the effective range of the weapon being 100m.[16]

VARIATIONS

Mark I

Production: approximately 100,000 weapons.

This first model Sten was characterized by the use of wood for the construction of the foregrip, forward handle and part of the stock. The design also incorporated a clumsy flash hider and the barrel sleeve (or shroud), which had three small holes in the top, extended all the way to the end of the barrel, unlike the succeeding weapons in the series.

Mark I*

A simplified version of the Mark I, with the foregrip, wooden furniture and flash hider replaced with cheaper, steel components.

Mark II

Production: approximately 2 million weapons.

The most common variation, this type differed from the Mark I in having a removable barrel that projected beyond the barrel sleeve. This sleeve was shorter than in the Mark I and had three sets of holes equally spaced around the circumference to improve cooling. A Canadian variant of the Mark II, fitted with a "skeleton" type butt, and a suppressed (silenced) version, the Mark IIS, were also produced.

Mark III

Production: approximately 1 million weapons.

The most simplified of the wartime designs, and the gun with the biggest production numbers after the Mark II. Characterized by a magazine receiver, ejection port and barrel sleeve constructed in one piece, the barrel projecting only slightly past the muzzle end of its sleeve. The cheapest to produce of all the Stens, a MkIII could be produced in five man-hours for just over £2.

Mark IV

A smaller, lighter variant intended for use by airborne troops, which never progressed beyond its initial prototype.

Mark V

Produced in 1944, when the threat from Nazi Germany was less immediate, these were a better quality version of the Mark II, with a wooden pistol grip, foregrip and stock. A No. 4 Lee-Enfield foresight and a bayonet mount were also fitted.

Mark VI

A suppressed (silenced) version of the Mark V, the clumsy suppressor increasing its weight from seven to nearly 10 lbs.

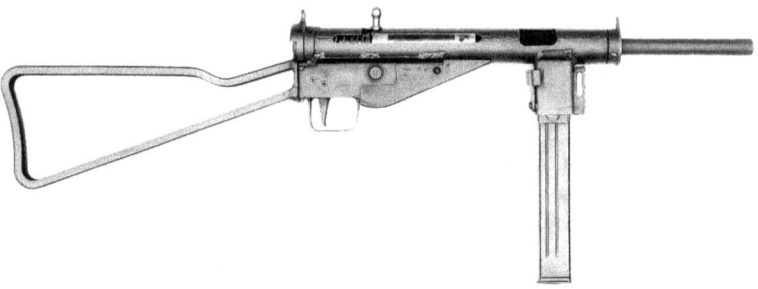

MP 3008 SMG, a German copy of the Sten (courtesy James D. Julia Auctioneers, Fairfield, Maine. www.jamesdjulia.com).

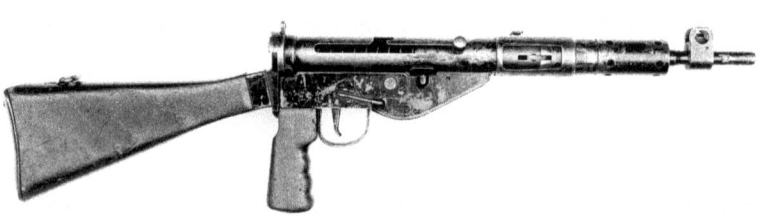

Mk V Sten from the right, showing the wooden butt and pistol grip (courtesy James D. Julia Auctioneers, Fairfield, Maine. www.jamesdjulia.com).

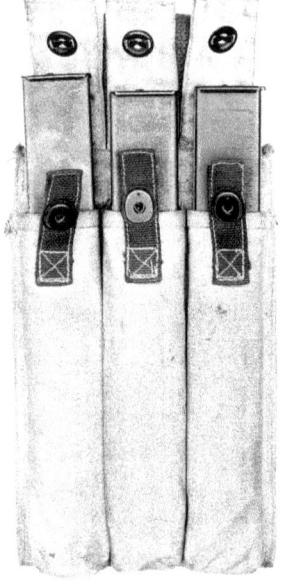

Carrying pouch for Sten magazines (courtesy James D. Julia Auctioneers, Fairfield, Maine. www.jamesdjulia.com).

Sten gun magazines showing the inferior quality of construction. The lips in particular were of thin gauge steel and prone to bending, which caused the weapon to malfunction (courtesy James D. Julia Auctioneers, Fairfield, Maine. www.jamesdjulia.com).

Foreign Copies

Argentina

Production: precise records unavailable.

Sten MkIIs were made under license in Argentina by Pistola Hispano Argentino. Known as the Modelo C.4, they may be recognized with a wooden handguard in front of the trigger guard.

Australia

Production: approximately 20,000 weapons.

The Austen MkI was a copy of the Mk III Sten gun developed during the Second World War by the Lithgow Small Arms Factory. Externally resembling the Sten and chambered for the 9 × 19mm Parabellum cartridge, it differed from the original in being fitted with twin pistol grips and folding stock more closely resembling those of the German MP40. A Mk II version was also produced which had a different appearance and made more use of die-cast components.

Belgium

Production: precise records unavailable.

Copies of the MkII Sten were produced in Belgium by the State Military Arsenal (l'Arsenale Militaire Belga). They are stamped on the top surface of the receiver housing with the name of the manufacturer, the Belgium royal cipher mark and the serial number, in the usual form.

Denmark

Production: precise records unavailable.

Resistance fighters in Denmark manufactured the Sten for their own use from raw material obtained locally.

France

Production: precise records unavailable.

The motorcycle and airplane engine manufacturer Gnome et Rhône (SNECMA) produced a copy of the Sten MkIII that was fitted with a forward pistol grip, distinctive wooden stock and a sliding bolt safety, added to secure the bolt in its forward position.

Germany

Gerät Potsdam Sten submachine guns:

Production: approximately 28,000 weapons.

These weapons were copies of the MkII Sten produced by the Mauser works, apparently for deception and sabotage purposes and intended to duplicate the British original as closely as possible, even including authentic stamps on the barrel and magazine housing.

MP 3008 Sten submachine guns

Production: approximately 10,000 weapons.

This weapon was based on the MkII Sten submachine gun, but was redesigned at the

Mauser factory, with a magazine fitted vertically into the bottom of the receiver and a stronger skeleton butt.

Norway

Production: precise records unavailable.

The resistance movement in German-occupied Norway made a significant number of Sten submachine guns, from the basic raw materials, mainly to equip the Norwegian underground army, the Milorg.

Palestine

Production: precise records unavailable.

Sten Mk II and Sten Mk V submachine guns were manufactured clandestinely in both Tel Aviv and on various kibbutzim between 1945 and 1948 for use with Jewish paramilitary groups. British paratroopers who served in Palestine during that period claimed that the Sten copies were better than their own issued weapons.

Poland

Production: precise records unavailable.

Polish resistance workers produced copies of the MkII Sten at approximately 23 underground factories, although all these weapons were marked with English stamps to disguise their origin.[17]

MILITARY SERVICE

It has become widely accepted as fact that all the men who used Shepherd and Turpin's "Woolworths gun" loathed it, so it is something of a surprise to find that, in truth, many preferred it to the much heavier Thompson. In a section of 10 men in the Parachute regiment, for example, the sergeant and corporal always carried a Sten gun, as did most of the officers. At least one member of the Parachute Regiment found the Sten to be a good weapon at close quarters, claiming: "When you went into a village or went into a house, whatever it was, it was a reliable weapon. It wasn't a reliable instrument for anything over 100 yards, but for anything close-quarters it was very reliable."

True, the Sten had faults. It had to be kept clean or stoppages would occur due to dirt on the face of the breech, in the bolt raceway or in the chamber itself. Magazines could be temperamental and had to be loaded and treated carefully after fitting. The poorly tempered springs in the magazines of early weapons were cited as a particular problem. (Experienced users tended to load magazines with only 25–27 cartridges, rather than standard 32 rounds.) In addition, holding the weapon by the magazine when firing tended to bend the lips of that component, often resulting in a stoppage, and hands had to be kept well clear of the cocking lever slot, or the result might be a severed finger or thumb. Even more worrying, in earlier Mks, the simple, open-bolt blowback mechanism was prone to firing spontaneously if dropped or handled carelessly, since the bolt could move back far enough to chamber and fire a cartridge without the need to fully cock the weapon if it was dropped on the butt.[18]

The Sten was not alone in having problems, however. Thompsons were also prone to stoppages, especially if poorly maintained or the subject of heavy use, and the complex mechanism would quickly jam if dirt or mud was introduced into it. They were heavy, 10½ lbs compared to the 7 lb Sten, and Resistance fighters also found them hard to conceal. In particular, they were at an especial disadvantage in desert environments, like the North African theater. Here, their carefully lubricated mechanism attracted dust and sand, a combination that formed a perfect grinding paste and wore out the guns' precisely machined components in an incredibly short space of time. The Sten, which had no fine tolerances inherent in its mechanism and was fired without lubrication, proved much more useful and reliable in the desert. Allied armorers certainly learned from their units' experience with the Thompson, however, subsequently modifying them to prevent the ingress of sand and issuing them free of lubricant. Guns subjected to this treatment then worked reliably, without any of the previous refinements.

Stens also possessed another significant advantage, in that they were chambered for Luger's 9 × 19mm Parabellum cartridge, the same ammunition as the German Army's Luger pistol and all of its issue submachine guns, such as the MP34, MP 35 and MP40. This made it very convenient for Resistance groups, who could replenish their supply of cartridges from the enemy's own ammunition pouches.

Perhaps most importantly for the British was the question of cost. RSAF Enfield and its subsidiaries were finally able to make a Sten for as little as £2, whereas, in November 1940, the cost of manufacture was such that the Americans were selling the Thompson to Britain for £27.50 ($110) each. This was, in fact, half what they had been asking for smaller quantities in January 1940, although by August 1942, the new Auto-Ordnance factory was able to offer the new M1 and M1A1 to the British for a unit price of just £11 ($44).

The Sten saw considerable service in World War II, and although it was withdrawn from service with the British army and replaced by the Sterling in 1953, it remained in use with the armed forces of a number of countries as well as paramilitary organizations such as the IRA.[19]

German Submachine Guns

Although Colonel Thompson had clearly enunciated the problems associated with the use of conventional, long-barreled rifles in trench warfare and by 1917 was even beginning to develop his pistol caliber machine gun to alleviate the problem, he was not alone in his conclusions. German designers were also aware of the need for a weapon developed for use during fire and movement operations, specifically for the task of clearing trenches where combatants were usually within a few feet of each other. In 1915, the German Rifle Testing Commission at Spandau began to develop a new weapon for trench warfare, using two semiautomatic pistols, the Luger and C96 Mauser as a starting point, although their efforts soon proved a resounding failure. This was principally because these relatively light weight pistols were extremely inaccurate when modified for fully automatic fire. Consequently, the Commission determined that a completely new approach to the problem of a new weapon capable of rapid fire was needed.

Hugo Schmeisser, together with Theodor Bergmann and a few other technicians, designed such a weapon, the world's first submachine gun, which was subsequently designated the Maschinenpistole 18/I or MP 18. Although it fulfilled the Commission's requirements and performed successfully during its initial trials, demands made on German industry by the war meant that full-scale production of this first submachine gun designed for military service did not begin until early 1918. Consequently, the weapon had little effect on the outcome of the war for the German army.

Despite failing to play a decisive role on the Western front, the M18 was a well-made, effective weapon that was adopted by the German police and a number of paramilitary forces after World War I, such as the German *Friekorps*. Its success in the trenches during World War I and its subsequent role in urban warfare ensured that the MP18 was soon followed by improved versions such as the MP 28, MP 34 and MP 38, culminating in its final metamorphosis as the excellent MP 40.[20]

The MP 40 Machine Pistol

The MP 40, more correctly referred to as the Maschinenpistole 40 (trans: Machine pistol 40), was not an original design, but was a modification of an earlier weapon, the excellent MP 38. Although the MP 38 was reliable and well made, its machined components increased production costs, so it was redesigned as the MP 40, with many components replaced with parts made from welded sheet steel. As the war progressed and Germany became increasingly desperate for weapons, a number of production changes were introduced to decrease the unit cost of the weapon. Although production ceased at the end of World War II, many MP 40s were retained in service or distributed to paramilitary or irregular forces in developing countries, until the appearance of the AK-47 soon made it the weapon of choice amongst these groups.[21]

SPECIFICATION

Production: approximately 1 million weapons made by the three factories, based upon the highest serial numbers recorded on weapons from the respective factories.

Erma: approximately 300,000 weapons.
Haenal: approximately 150,000.
Steyr: approximately 550,000 weapons.

However, further analysis of the serial numbers also suggests that complete blocks of serial numbers were sometimes omitted, for reasons known only to the manufacturers, and when this is taken into account, the most accurate estimate for total production of the MP 40 is approximately 800,000 weapons.

The MP 40 was an air-cooled, hand held submachine gun, chambered for the 9 × 19mm Parabellum service pistol cartridge which was delivered from a 32-round, detachable box magazine. It had a simple blowback mechanism, firing from an open bolt, which was only capable of fully automatic fire at a rate of 500 rounds per minute, although the low rate of fire made it possible to fire single shots by careful manipulation of the trigger. This mechanism could be made safe by pushing the cocking handle into one of two separate notches above the main opening, either locking the bolt to the rear in the fully cocked position or forward, leaving the mechanism uncocked. A pistol grip was fitted adjacent to the trigger guard, which projected at an angle from the rear of the gun, and a bakelite handgrip was mounted between the magazine housing and this pistol grip. In addition, a skeleton butt will be found on most weapons, which could be folded forward against the body of the gun when not in use, although this was found to be fragile under service conditions. Sling swivels were fitted and a significant percentage of weapons offered for sale will be found with a leather sling, which was designed to facilitate the weapon's fully automatic operation. As well as these more usual items of furniture, a supporting bar made of metal or bakelite was also fitted under the barrel and was used to steady the weapon when firing over the side of a vehicle, such as a halftrack.[22]

Table Twenty-seven: Specification of the MP 40 machine pistol

Manufacturers	Erma Werk, Haenel, Steyr
Period of production	1940 until 1945
Production	Over 1.1 million weapons
Operators	Austria, China, Czechoslovakia, France, Greece, Israel, South Korea, Nazi Germany, Norway, Poland, USSR, Spain, Vietnam, West Germany
Military service	World War II, Korean War, Vietnam War
Weight	8.75 lbs (4 kg)
Length/Barrel length	Total length with extended stock: 33 inches (833mm)
	Total length with stock folded: 25 inches (630mm)
	Barrel length: 10 inches (250mm)
Mechanism	Fully automatic, simple blowback, firing from an open bolt
Cartridge	9 × 19mm Parabellum service pistol cartridge
	Delivered to the breech from a detachable box magazine holding 32 cartridges
Sights	Front sight: hooded blade
	Rear sight: iron sight mounted on receiver
	Maximum accurate range 100m
Rate of fire	500 rpm
Cost	£6 ($20) in 1942

Operation

To fire an MP 40, a magazine was first inserted into the housing, and the bolt drawn back until secured by the sear. Pulling the trigger allowed the bolt to move forward, removing a cartridge from the magazine and chambering and firing it in one operation. Force from the cartridge's recoil drove the spent case out of the chamber, pushing the bolt backward against the recoil spring. The case was then thrown clear via the ejection port, and the bolt having reached the end of its rearwards travel, it moved forwards again, repeating the firing cycle until either the trigger was released or the magazine was empty.

Although the MP 40 was generally reliable, like its major competitor the Sten, one of its major weaknesses was the magazine. The MP 40 used a double-column magazine with a single-feed insert, which resulted in increased friction against the remaining cartridges moving upwards towards the magazine lips. This occasionally resulted in a stoppage, a problem that was exacerbated by the presence of dirt or other debris. Like the Sten, holding the magazine to steady the weapon while firing could also cause a stoppage, hand pressure on the magazine body causing the magazine lips to move out of line, because the magazine housing did not keep the magazine firmly locked. Consequently, German soldiers were

German MP 40 from the left showing the magazine, its housing, and the folded skeleton butt (courtesy James D. Julia Auctioneers, Fairfield, Maine. www.jamesdjulia.com).

MP 40 from the right with the butt extended (courtesy James D. Julia Auctioneers, Fairfield, Maine. www.jamesdjulia.com).

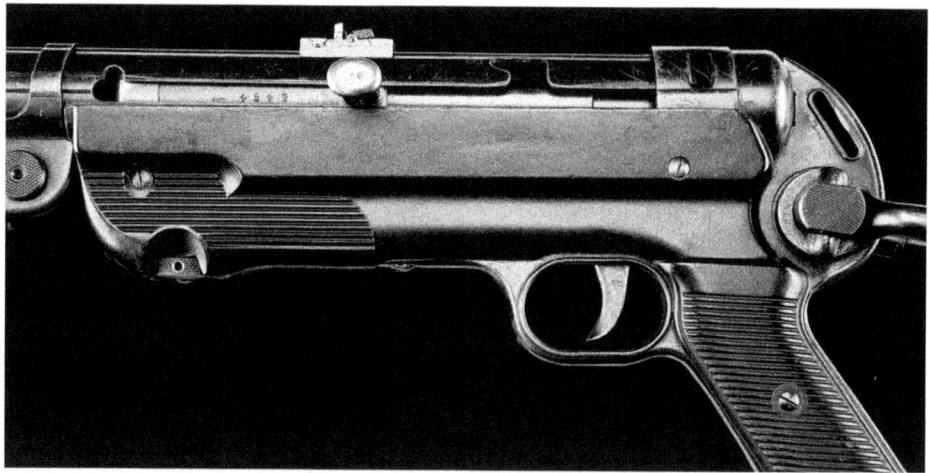

MP 40 showing the cocking lever within its slot, the two safety cut-outs, and the rear sight (courtesy James D. Julia Auctioneers, Fairfield, Maine. www.jamesdjulia.com).

trained to grasp either the handgrip or the magazine housing with the supporting hand to avoid this sort of malfunction.[23]

VARIATIONS

MP 40

This was the standard model produced by Erma Werk, Styer and Haenal.
The rear of the receiver is stamped in the following form:

M.P. 40
bnz. 42
XXXXX

Where the "M.P. 40" is the Model designation (MP 38s are stamped "M.P.38," MP 18s are stamped "M.P. 18" and so on), "bnz" is the later code for the Steyr factory, "42" is the date of production and "XXXXX" is the serial number. In addition, there may also be a Waffenamt code number stamped on the weapon to show it has been inspected and accepted into service with the Third Reich, and barrels and other parts may bear stamps from a manufacturer that do not match those on the receiver. This is not uncommon and is the result of refurbishment or replacement of worn-out components.

Weapons will be found with minor differences between the pistol grip and lower receiver, the bolt and mainspring, and the barrel. However, these were changes made to simplify production, not as improvements to the weapon, and so guns which have components made to these changed specifications are not really different types in a real sense.

MP40/l

This is a standard MP 40 that has been modified to hold two magazines, which gave a magazine capacity of 64 rounds. It was produced to compete with the Soviet PPSh-41 submachine gun, which was giving the Wehrmacht significant problems in Stalingrad. The magazines sit side-by-side in the normal position with a greatly enlarged magazine housing. To operate the weapon, both magazines were inserted in the housing, and the weapon was fired normally until the first magazine was empty. A button on front of the housing was then depressed, allowing the full magazine to be slid across, replacing the empty component. Operation could then recommence.

Production of these weapons seems to have been confined to Erma Werk and Steyr, no MP40/l having been located so far with a Haenel stamp on the receiver.[24]

Table Twenty-eight: Factory codes found on MP40 submachine guns

Factory	Early code number	Later code letters
ERMA Werk: Erfurter Maschinenfabrik B. Geipel GmbH	27	ayf
Steyr: Steyr Daimler Puch, A.G. Werk, Steyr, Austria	660	bnz
Haenel: C.G. Haenel, Waffen-u. Fahrradfabrik, Suhl	122	Fxo

These code letters are found stamped on the rear of the receiver in the format already described.[25]

MILITARY SERVICE

The MP 40 submachine carbine was introduced in 1940 as a weapon intended to be issued to specialized forces such as paratroops as well as senior infantry NCOs and platoon leaders, leaving the majority of conventional German troops armed with the Mauser 98k bolt-action rifle. However, the success of Russian troops armed with submachine guns at Stalingrad when fighting against the German forces operating there between 1942 and 1943 convinced the German High Command of the need to issue the MP 40 on a much wider basis. By September 1943, however, both weapons were being replaced by the StG 44 assault rifle, although production difficulties with the new weapon meant that the MP 40 remained in service with many units. Artillery units and tank crews retained their MP 40s, because the shorter length of the submachine carbine made it more convenient than the new assault rifle.

As well as being the standard weapon of the German army, many MP 40s that had been captured or surrendered to the Allied armies were redistributed to the paramilitary and irregular forces of some occupied countries. Estimates vary, but the consensus seems to be that over 200,000 MP 40s were captured or surrendered, and many of these weapons remained in service after World War II. In addition, significant numbers of Allied troops used a captured MP 40 in preference to their issued Thompson or Sten, an easy exchange since the Sten and MP 40 used the same ammunition.

These weapons were often referred to as "Schmeissers," and although Hugo Schmeisser appears not to have been actively involved in the design process, many of the most important features of the MP 40 were based upon his patents, including the delayed blowback mechanism, the design of the magazine and the folding stock. This confusion was compounded because guns made by Haenel were often stamped "PATENT SCHMEISSER" on the receiver.[26]

Table Twenty-nine: Comparison of the Thompson, Sten and MP40 pistol caliber machine guns

Weapon	Thompson M1921/M1928	Thompson M1A1	STEN	MP40
Rate of Fire (rpm)	600–800	500–600	500	500
Magazine capacity	20–30 round box 50–100 round drum	20- or 30-round box	32-round box (usually loaded with 25–27 rounds)	32 round box
Effective range (meters)	100	100	100	100
Weight (with full magazine)	11 lbs	11 lbs	7 lbs	8.75 lbs
Cost	£50–£60 ($200–$240) in 1939	£11 ($44) in 1945	£2–£4 ($8–$16) in 1942	£6 ($20) in 1942
Number produced	100,000–200,000	Over 1.2 million	Over 4 million	Over 1.1 million
Time to complete	35 hours	25 hours	5 hours	15 hours

Submachine Guns Developed Between World War I and World War II

America

The M3 or "Grease Gun"

Production: approximately 700,000.
Unit cost: $15 in 1945

Produced from 1942 as a U.S. alternative to the successful Sten and MP 40 machine carbines the M3 was an air-cooled submachine gun with a simple blowback mechanism, firing from an open bolt. It was fitted with a detachable box magazine holding 30 cartridges and was chambered for either the Colt .45 caliber ACP cartridge or 9 × 19mm Parabellum round. In common with the Sten and MP40, many of its components were of stamped and welded steel plate, and this meant that a finished gun only cost £5 ($20) in 1943. Unfortunately, the design was not a good one, and a significant number of complaints about its function and quality began to surface as soon as the gun was issued, so that it never fulfilled its intended role of replacing the Thompson in U.S. service.[27]

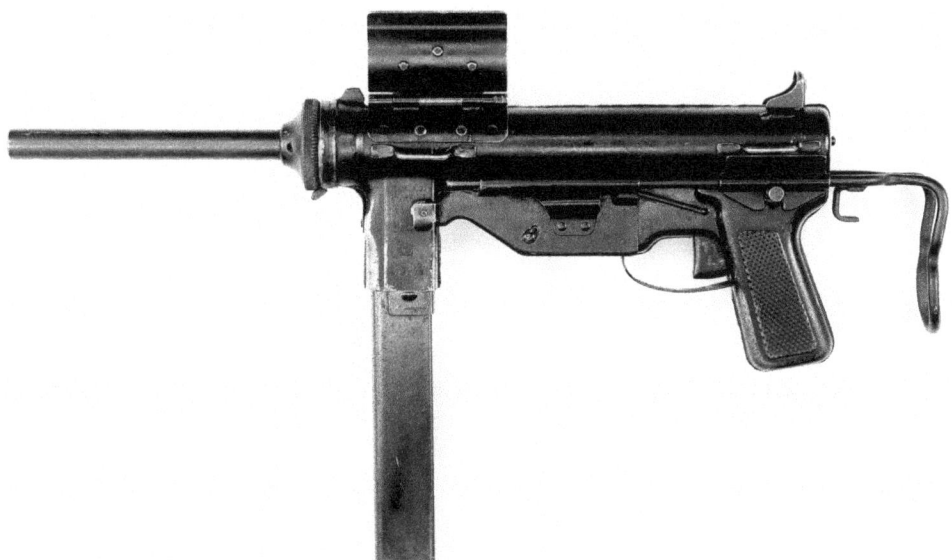

American M3 "Grease Gun," with the ejection port cover open, and the skeleton butt retracted, showing the stamped-steel welded construction (courtesy James D. Julia Auctioneers, Fairfield, Maine. www.jamesdjulia.com).

The Thompson submachine gun

Production; approximately 1.5 million.
Adopted by the U.S. army in 1921 and produced in a variety of models.

312   Section V: The Machine-Gun Era

Australia

Owen machine carbine

Production: approximately 45,000.

Built at the Lysaght Works in Port Kemba, this was an air-cooled submachine gun with a simple blowback mechanism firing from an open bolt, with a firing rate of 500 rpm. Chambered for the 9 × 19mm Parabellum service pistol cartridge, it was fitted with a detachable box magazine holding 33 cartridges, entering the top of the receiver to allow gravity to supplement the action of the magazine spring. A fixed wire skeleton stock and pistol grips were also fitted as part of the standard specification. Another unusual feature of this weapon was the separate compartment inside the receiver, which isolated the bolt from its retracting handle by means of a small bulkhead and prevented dirt and mud from jamming the mechanism. This unique design feature made the Owen a highly reliable weapon because dirt, sand or other foreign material entering the gun would collect at the back of the receiver, where it could either drain out or be expelled through a small opening. Independent tests showed that the Owen gun was able to continue firing despite being dipped in mud and sand, while a Sten and Thompson that were similarly tested stopped functioning at once. In jungle warfare, where both mud and sand were frequent problems, the Owen gun was popular and highly regarded by the Australian troops who used it.[28]

Owen SMG from the right showing two magazines and the unique conformation of this weapon (courtesy James D. Julia Auctioneers, Fairfield, Maine. www.jamesdjulia.com).

Britain

Lanchester Mk. 1 submachine gun

Production: approximately 95,000.

A copy of the German MP 28, the Lanchester was mainly used by the Royal Navy, having been accepted into service with them in 1941. It had a simple blowback mechanism firing from an open bolt and giving a firing rate of 600 rpm. Chambered for the 9 × 19mm Parabellum cartridge, were loaded into a detachable box magazine holding 50 cartridges, although the weapon could also use the 32-round magazine supplied for use with the Sten. A wooden stock, in the same pattern as the Lee-Enfield rifle, was fitted, and there was also a bayonet lug, centered below the muzzle and designed to accepted the Pattern 1907 sword bayonet used on the Lee-Enfield No.1 Mk. III*. The earlier Mk1 version had a selector fire switch, allowing a choice of fully or semiautomatic operation, but this was not fitted to the later MkI*, which could only be used as a fully automatic weapon.[29]

STEN submachine carbine

Production: over 4 million.

Produced Britain in 1940, as a direct result of the losses in France and manufactured in a number of types, including a silenced version for the Royal Marine Commandos.

FINLAND

Suomi KP/-31

Production: approximately 80,000 weapons.

Accepted into service with the Finnish army in 1931, the Suomi is considered by many experts to be one of the most successful submachine guns of World War II. It had a simple blowback mechanism chambered in 9 × 19mm Parabellum, giving a firing rate of between 750 and 900 rpm, and could be fitted with a 20-, 36- or 50-round detachable box magazine as well as either a 40- or 71-round drum magazine.[30]

Finnish Suomi SMG.

GERMANY

MP 18 submachine gun

Production: precise records unavailable, estimated at over 50,000 weapons.

Accepted in service with the German army in 1918, the MP 18 had a simple blowback mechanism, firing from an open bolt and only capable of fully automatic operation, with a firing rate of 500 rpm. Chambered for either the 9 × 19mm Parabellum cartridge or the 7.63 × 25mm Mauser cartridge, these were originally loaded into a 32-round detachable drum magazine of the same pattern as that designed for the Luger P08 semiautomatic pistol. Weapons made after World War I dispensed with this clumsy, "snail" drum magazine and used a detachable box magazine holding either 30 or 50 cartridges.

The MP 18 represented a significant milestone both in terms of armament technology and the new tactics being used in warfare, opening the way for a whole new class of weapons and triggering research into the deployment of lighter automatic weapons by mobile troops.[31]

MP 18 from the right, showing the ejection port and cocking handle within its slot (courtesy James D. Julia Auctioneers, Fairfield, Maine. www.jamesdjulia.com).

MP 34 submachine gun

Production: precise records unavailable, estimated at over 300,000 weapons.

Accepted in service with the Austrian army in 1934, the MP 34 has a simple blowback mechanism, firing from an open bolt, with a firing rate of 600 rpm. It was chambered for a variety of cartridges, including 9 × 19mm Parabellum, which were loaded into either a 20- or 30-round detachable box magazine. Unlike the later MP 40 machine pistol, this gun was manufactured with a one-piece, polished wooden stock and a correspondingly high standard of finish on the rest of its components. This earned it the nickname the "Rolls Royce of submachine guns," but meant that its production costs were excessively high.[32]

MP 35

Production: approximately 40,000, mostly supplied to Waffen SS troops.

A simplified and therefore less expensive version of the MP 34, the MP 35 SMG was adopted by the Wehrmacht in 1939. It had a selective-fire blowback mechanism, which fired from an open bolt and, unusually, the 24- or 30-round detachable box magazine was fitted into a slot in the right of the receiver. As with the MP 34, the butt and foregrip were manufactured from a single piece of timber.[33]

MP 38

Production: precise records unavailable, estimated at over 300,000 weapons.

Forerunner of the MP 40 and very similar in design and operation, except many of the expensive machined components in the MP 38 were replaced with welded, sheet steel parts in the MP 40.[34]

Seventeen. Submachine Guns, Semiautomatic Rifles and Postwar Changes 315

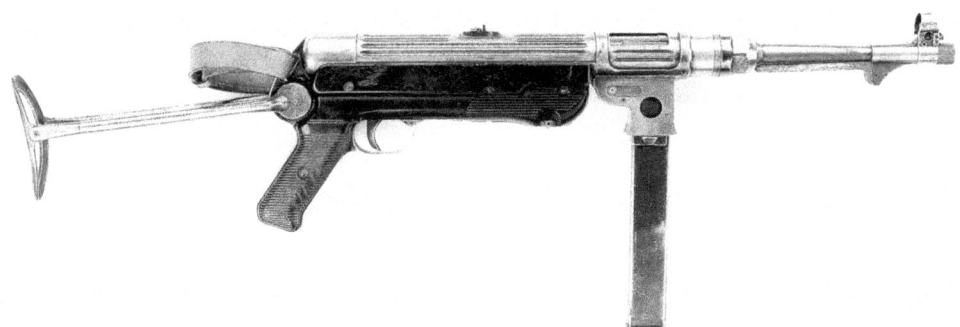

MP 38, showing the superior quality of construction of this SMG, when compared to the later MP 40 (courtesy James D. Julia Auctioneers, Fairfield, Maine. www.jamesdjulia.com).

MP 40

Production: Over 1.1 million weapons.

Wehrmacht's standard submachine gun during World War II and often referred to as the "Schmeisser" by Allied troops.

ITALY

Beretta OVP

Production: precise records unavailable, estimated at 100,000 weapons.

This weapon entered service with the Italian army in 1918, having been developed from the Villar Perosa air service machine gun, and was still in production in 1941. It had a delayed blowback, selective-fire mechanism capable of discharging 900 rounds per minute, using a detachable box magazine holding 25 rounds. Chambered for the 9 × 19mm Glisenti cartridge, a less powerful version of the 9 × 19mm Parabellum round, it weighed 8 lbs, slightly more than a Sten but less than the MP 40.[35]

Beretta M1918

Production: precise records unavailable, estimated at 20,000 weapons.

Similar to the OVP, except fitted with a wooden stock, the M1918 had a simple blowback mechanism which only delivered automatic fire. Also chambered for the 9 × 19 Glisenti cartridge, it had a gravity-fed, detachable box magazine holding 25 cartridges that was inserted into the top of the receiver.[36]

JAPAN

Type 100 submachine gun

Production: approximately 36,000 weapons of both types.

Based on the Bergmann MP 18 but with a simplified mechanism, the Type 100 was introduced into service with the Japanese army late in 1942. This was a fully automatic, air-cooled weapon with a blowback mechanism firing from an open bolt, which gave a rate of fire between 450 rpm (early Type 100/40) and 900 rpm (later Type100/44). It was chambered for the relatively ineffective 8 × 22mm Nambu Japanese service pistol cartridge, which were loaded into a detachable, half-moon box magazine holding 30 cartridges and entering the receiver on the left side. Unusually for a submachine gun, but typical of Japanese weapons of the era, a bayonet lug was fixed under the barrel, in this case with a heavy bar and lug. Some of the Type 100/40s also had a bipod as well as a complicated muzzle brake. The Type 100 was typical of a class of simple, inexpensive, wartime submachine guns produced by all military powers—designed for maximum ease of production, with less concern given to reliability or usefulness.[37]

USSR

PPSh-41

Production: approximately 6 million weapons.

Accepted into service with the Red Army of the USSR in 1941, this weapon had a selective-fire, simple blowback mechanism firing from an open bolt, with a maximum firing rate of 900 rpm. It was chambered for the 7.62 × 25mm Tokarov Soviet service pistol cartridge, which was loaded into either a detachable box magazine holding 35 cartridges or a 71-round detachable drum magazine. Like its contemporaries, the Sten and MP 40, as well as the later AK-47, many of its components were stamped from sheet steel and welded, although it did have a wooden butt, which extended over the receiver. It was replaced in service with the Soviet army by the Kalashnicov AK-47 in 1948.[38]

SVT 38/40

Production: 1.6 million weapons of all types.

This was a gas-operated semiautomatic rifle with a tilting bolt mechanism, chambered for the 7.62 × 54mmR Soviet rifle cartridge, cartridges being contained in a 10-round, detachable magazine. It was this rifle and its effectiveness during the German invasion of Russia that precipitated the development of the MG 44, although the weapon had a number of faults associated with poor quality control during production, despite the soundness of the original design.[39]

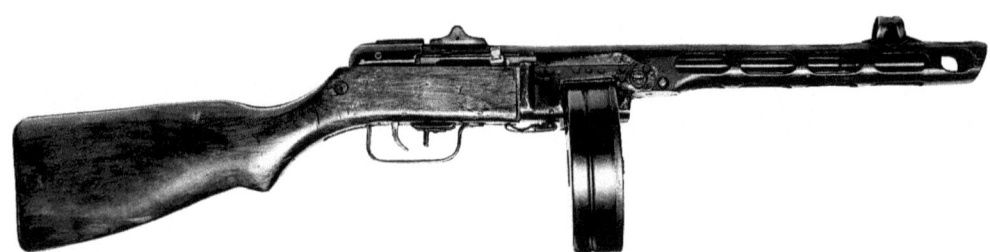

Russian PPSh-41 SMG, showing the poor quality of construction. Although quite roughly made, these were very reliable weapons and allowed the Red army to inflict significant casualties on the Germans at Stalingrad and during other operations (Wikipedia: License: CC-ASA-3.0).

CHAPTER EIGHTEEN

Light Machine Gun Development After World War I

Infantry Tactics and the Light Machine Gun

The infantry tactics developed by both the Axis and Allied armies before World War II and used during that conflict were based around the light machine gun team, supported by a squad of riflemen with grenades.

Costly advances by huge bodies of men against well-protected emplacements, which had been such a feature of World War I, were no longer considered desirable or feasible. The basic tactical theory evolved after World War I was much simpler: neutralize small groups of the enemy with superior firepower (known in modern military parlance as "suppressive fire"), and then send riflemen forward to finish off the opposition. This was to be accomplished without sustaining unnecessary casualties amongst the attacking troops. It was envisaged that such relatively small "fire and movement" offensives could be repeated indefinitely until total control was established over the enemy from suppressive fire delivered by the well-protected, highly mobile light machine gun teams. In this context the German army had a considerable advantage over most Allied forces in possessing the MG 34, a belt-fed light machine gun with a high rate of fire, and it soon became clear that German infantry tactics were as superior as their weapons.[1]

INFANTRY TACTICS

German infantry units at the beginning of World War II were divided into squads of 10 men, although by 1943, this had been reduced to squads of 9 men with a single light machine gun. These groups consisted of a squad leader and a 3-man MG (machine gun) team together with 5 riflemen, and in combat this unit tended to function as a 9-man MG unit. The tactical process usually began with the squad leader advancing with his unit until the enemy was encountered. With contact established, the machine gun crew engaged the enemy while the rest of the unit waited until the MG team had delivered sufficient suppressive fire to confuse and disorientate the opposition. In order to generate this sort of fire superiority, each man carried several spare belts of ammunition for the machine gun, which meant that there was at least 1,800 rounds ready for use, as well as 6 spare barrels carried by the MG team. With the enemy disorganized by the effects of the MG 34, the remaining members of the squad would then move forward in short rushes using available cover until they were sufficiently close to any surviving enemy troops to be able to finish the engagement with rifles, MP 40s and grenades. These tactics had the advantage of leaving the leader of the squad in a good position to control his men since he took no part in the attack. Even if he was killed or badly wounded, German infantry training emphasized individual initiative to such an extent that the squad could still function effectively even if severely depleted in strength. In addition, the "Blitzkrieg" system also relied upon effective cooperation between different service arms, so that the infantry was more closely integrated with other branches, such as the artillery, tanks and even the Luftwaffe, than was often the case with equivalent Allied forces. They were also more experienced, significant numbers of German troops and Luftwaffe personnel having been deployed since 1936 fighting for the Nationalists with the Condor Legion in the Spanish Civil War.[2]

British tactics were similar to those adopted by their German counterparts, being based around the Bren light machine gun team, although the function of the light machine gun was slightly different. It was used to protect the squad when it attacked, rather than as the principal offensive instrument, which was its function in the German system. A Bren gun squad consisted of the two-man Bren gun team and the squad's second-in-command, while the squad commander had control of the rest of the unit, composed of riflemen armed with bolt-action rifles and hand grenades. Upon encountering the enemy, the rifle squad would fall to the ground and then advance to an effective firing position, from where they would fire independently, while moving carefully forwards until they were close enough to successfully attack the occupied position with negligible casualties. Meanwhile, the Bren gun team would advance using cover to a position at 90 degrees to the line of assault which was to be taken by the main group, whereupon they would open fire on the enemy, thus providing covering fire for the advancing riflemen, who could also cover their colleagues who were using the Bren gun, if that became necessary. Having decimated and demoralized the enemy with fire from rifles and the light machine gun, the rifle squad would finish the attack by advancing on the position with fixed bayonets and firing their Lee-Enfields from the hip.[3]

American infantry tactics were similar in conception to the British plan, squads also being divided into teams: a scout team of two men, a second team consisting of the BAR operator and three riflemen, and a third team made up of five riflemen and the squad leader. Having located the enemy, the scout team would call up the BAR squad, who would lay down covering fire for the rifle squad, who were responsible for the final assault. Unlike the German troops, the inexperienced American soldiers could not be relied upon initially to continue an attack if their squad leader was killed or badly wounded; this was not an uncommon occurrence because, unlike the German MG unit commander, he was part of the final assault team.[4] Perhaps more significantly, the BAR and M1 Garands with which they were equipped also gave an insufficient volume of fire to ensure the all-important "fire superiority" that a belt-fed MG 34 or MG 42 was able to achieve. British troops must have faced similar problems, although in the battle for France in 1940, it was the degree of integration between different German military arms and the speed at which they were able to move, particularly the German Panzer units, that led to the British defeat rather than any deficiency in the tactics employed at platoon or company level.

Only the Royal Italian army differed slightly from the majority of European forces in its organization at platoon level, although tactics still centered around the squad light machine gun, in this case the very inferior Breda 30. Italian soldiers were issued with a single Breda 30 light machine gun for each squad, making a total of between 24 and 27 to a battalion, although this was later changed to two weapons per squad. By 1943, an Italian infantry platoon was divided into two large sections, each of twenty men, which were then further divided into rifle and light machine gun squads. Each section was commanded by a sergeant, who also controlled the light machine gun squad, which was composed of two Breda 30s, each weapon manned by a gunner—ranked as corporal and usually the squad's most reliable man—an assistant gunner, and two ammunition bearers, the remaining eleven men in the section or half-platoon constituting the rifle squad. The two squads were originally intended to operate as separate entities, with the two LMGs supporting the rifle squad in gaining its objective, in a manner similar to the tactics adopted by the British army. The Italian system was unnecessarily complex and inefficient, however, and most of the other European armies of that period found that deploying a single LMG with a much smaller group of about ten men gave better results. Experience had certainly shown the German Wehrmacht that this allowed the squad to operate more effectively.[5]

Tactical effectiveness

Undoubtedly of all the armies deploying LMGs during World War II, it was the German army who made the most effective use of the weapon, principally because the purpose of a German LMG squad was to protect the gun while it was being used to attack defensive positions, rather than simply providing covering fire for troops while they did the attacking. By contrast, Allied tactical doctrine insisted that the purpose of a British or U.S. LMG squad was to protect the men while they attacked a defensive position. Consequently, when Allied forces were deployed in this way, the LMG and its crew were often both unprotected and underused, and it was this tactical misconception that often resulted in just the sort of casualties an LMG deployed by German infantry units avoided.

American Light Machine Gun Development After World War I

The U.S. army retained the BAR as its squad light machine gun without modification, and its tactics at platoon level were based around this weapon. Although the BAR was a sound design and had given good service to both the U.S. army and the officers of various U.S. law enforcement agencies, by 1939 it was beginning to show its age. In particular the 20-round magazine and the lack of a quick-change barrel made it inferior to both the Bren and particularly the belt-fed MG 34 and MG 42 used by Axis forces.

The Browning Automatic Rifle

World War I has been referred to as the "Machine Gun War," and not without good reason. Unlike the foreign conflicts of the previous century, which were mainly wars of movement against relatively unsophisticated antagonists, World War I was a technological conflict conducted from trenches protected by barbed wire, with well fortified, fixed positions dominated by the fully automatic machine gun. Unfortunately, when the U.S. entered the war in April 1917, they had only about 1,000 serviceable machine guns, most of them antiquated designs like the M1904 Maxim, M1895 Colt and even a few M1912 Gatling guns. These were heavy machine guns in every sense, mounted on unwieldy tripods or conventional gun-carriages. Although they were reliable weapons, they were useless in the vicious hand-to-hand fighting that characterized trench warfare, so the search began for a more portable automatic weapon. Several designs for a fully automatic machine gun light enough to be carried into a trench fight were offered to the U.S. government, amongst them John Browning's Automatic Rifle, which he demonstrated to a group of Congressmen and government officials on 27 February 1917, along with what became the M1917 heavy machine gun. The group were so impressed by the performance of the BAR that it was immediately adopted and designated "Rifle, caliber .30, Automatic, Browning, M1918." Colt owned Browning's patent for the weapon and had secured an exclusive contract to manufacture it, but production difficulties meant that the contract was transferred to Winchester Repeating Arms Company, although Colt and Marlin-Rockwell also began to produce these weapons some time in June 1918. By 11 November 1918, 52,000 BARs had been delivered to U.S. forces, and by 1919, a total of over 152,000 of the M1918 variant had been produced by all three companies.

World War II saw the BAR still in service. In order to increase the stock of available weapons, a production contract was awarded to the New England Small Arms Corporation and the International Business Machines Corporation, who together produced over 168,000 new weapons. In 1943, in order to increase production, receivers were cast in a new process using a malleable pig iron called "ARMASTEEL," and components made by this process will be found with the appropriate stamps. The weapon was still in service in 1950 at the start of the Korean War, and BARs made for Korea were produced the Royal McBee Typewriter Co. and are marked accordingly.[6]

Specification

Production: approximately 100,000 in a number of serial number series.

The BAR is an air-cooled, selective fire, gas-operated light machine gun firing from an open bolt and weighing approximately 18 lbs with a full magazine and bipod. It was fitted with a three-position selective fire switch on the left side of the receiver: an "S" position for "safe," which blocked the trigger; "F" for semi-automatic fire; "A" for automatic fire. Early weapons were chambered for the .30–06 caliber Springfield cartridge, although later variants used the .303 caliber British rimmed cartridge. There was also a BAR chambered for the 7.92 × 57mm Mauser cartridge, probably intended for the Chinese army. Originally, the BAR was fitted with a conventional post front sight, although later weapons had a tunneled foresight, and a leaf rear sight that was adjustable from 100 to 1,500 yards in 100-yard increments. A wooden butt and handgrip were fitted as well as a bipod and flash suppressor.[7]

Receiver Stamp

The top of the receiver in front of the rear sight is stamped:

Eighteen. Light Machine Gun Development After World War I

BROWNING AUTOMATIC RIFLE
U.S. CAL..30. MODEL 1918
MAN'F'D. BY WINCHESTER
XXXXXX
PATENT APPLIED FOR

Where "U.S. CAL..30. MODEL 1918" is the model designation, the third line specifies the manufacturer, and "XXXXXX" denotes the serial number.

Trigger frame stamp

The forward frame of the trigger guard in those weapons produced from Armasteel are also found stamped **"ARMASTEEL,"** together with the weapon's serial number.

M1918A2 Browning automatic rifle from the right, showing the carrying handle, cartridge ejection port, and skid-footed bipod. This example has a "Parkerized" finish (courtesy James D. Julia Auctioneers, Fairfield, Maine. www.jamesdjulia.com).

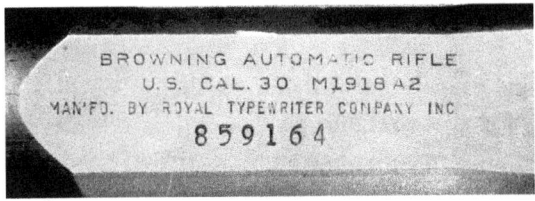 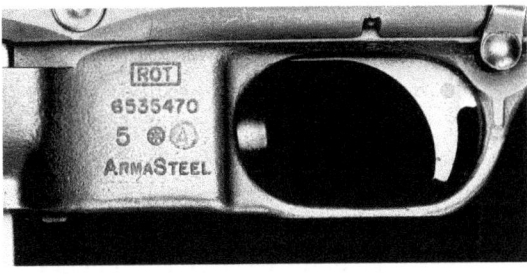

Left: Frame stamp for a BAR manufactured by the Royal Typewriter Company. *Right*: "ARMASTEEL" stamp on the receiver of a BAR, showing this gun is fitted with the later, malleable cast-iron receiver (both photographs courtesy James D. Julia Auctioneers, Fairfield, Maine. www.jamesdjulia.com).

Table Thirty: Specification of the Browning Automatic Rifle

Manufacturers	Colt Patent Firearms Manufacturing Company (16,000 guns)
	Winchester Repeating Arms Company (47,000 guns)
	New England Small Arms Corp.
	International Business Machines Corp (World War II: 168,000 guns)
	Royal McBee Typewriter Co (Korea: 61,000 guns)
	Marlin-Rockwell Corporation (39,000 guns)
	Carl Gustafs Stads Gevärsfaktori
Period of production	1917–1955
Production	Over 360,000 of all variants
Operators	Argentina, Austria, Belgium, Brazil, Britain, Cambodia, Canada, China, Finland, France, Nazi Germany, West Germany, Italy, Israel, South Korea, North Vietnam, USSR, USA
Military service	World War I, World War II, Chinese Civil War, Palestine, Korea, Vietnam, Cambodia
Crew	Two- or three-man crew: gunner and one or two loaders.
Weight	M1918: 16 lbs
	M1918A1/M1918A2: 19 lbs
	Crew usually carried 20 or more magazines, each weighing 1.5 lbs, so the total weight of gun and ammunition totaled 45–50 lbs.
Length/Barrel length	Overall length: 47 inches
	Barrel length: 24 inches
Mechanism	M1918: Gas-operated, air-cooled, open bolt design, with a selective fire switch giving either fully automatic or semiautomatic fire.
	M1918A2: Two position switch, giving two rates of fully automatic fire.
Cartridge	.30–06 Springfield (7.62 × 63mm)
	.303 British (7.62 × 56mmR)
	7.92 × 57mm Mauser
	20-round box magazine, with cartridges in a double column.
Sights	Front: Rectangular post sight, tunnel sight on later weapons.
	Rear: Leaf sight
Rate of fire	500–600 rpm (rounds per minute).
Effective range/Maximum range	100–1,500 yards/5,000 yards

OPERATION

To load and fire a BAR, the user first turned the selector switch to "S," before pushing the magazine into its slot below the breech, so that the retaining catch engaged. Pulling back the cocking handle on the left side cocked the weapon and the selective fire switch on the receiver could then be moved from "S" to "F" or "A," depending upon the user's requirements. Ammunition was fed to the breech from a 20-round box magazine entering the bottom of the receiver, ejection of the spent case being via the slot in the right side of that component. In common with many of Browning's automatic and semiautomatic weapons that also had an open-bolt mechanism, the bolt of the BAR was held open to the rear when the weapon was cocked, so that pulling the trigger caused the bolt to move forward, stripping a cartridge from the magazine and feeding it into the chamber before firing. Residual gas from explosion of the cartridge was then vented from the barrel on to the piston head, which was driven back, the associated mechanism simultaneously cocking the weapon and ejecting the spent case. Powder residue quickly fouled this gas vent after extended use, however, often resulting in a failure to eject the used case, so BARs were fitted with a three-port gas regulator to overcome this problem. If the gun failed to recycle after it had been in use for a considerable period, the case was ejected manually by working the cocking lever and the gas regulator was then moved to the next position, whereupon firing could be resumed. Care had to be exercised with this regulator, however, because if it was not repositioned to the lowest setting after cleaning, the increased recoil produced as a result of the excess gas made the weapon difficult to control when firing in fully automatic mode.[8]

Variations

Several attempts were made to improve the BAR after its service in World War I. These weapons will all be found with the appropriate model stamp on the top of the receiver.

M1922

This design differed from the original M1918 in having a heavier ribbed barrel, adjustable spiked bipod, a monopod mounted on the butt, a side-mounted sling swivel, and a redesigned butt plate. It was adopted by the U.S. Cavalry in 1922.

Colt "Monitor" R80

Originally intended for prison guards and the FBI, this design differed from the original in being lighter (16 lbs) and fitted with a pistol grip as well as a shortened barrel featuring a Cutts compensator. This compensator was a device that directed residual gas upwards from the barrel and was intended to control the weapon's tendency to lift when used in automatic fire mode. Only 125 were produced, with ninety going to the FBI and the rest sold to prisons, banks and police departments.

1919A1

An early attempt at improving the original M1918 by fitting a lightweight spiked bipod with adjustable legs, attached to the gas cylinder rather than the muzzle, and a hinged steel butt plate. Few of the original M1918 BARs were refurbished to this design.

1918A2

This weapon differs most significantly from the original M1918 in having a fire-selector system allowing only fully automatic fire, now housed in the butt, which was lengthened by one inch. This new selector switch had two settings: "Slow," giving a firing rate of 300–450 rounds per minute (rpm); and "Fast," giving a rate of 500–650 rpm. The bipod was skid-footed, instead of spiked, the foregrip was shortened, and a heat shield was added to help cool the barrel. Other minor changes included the addition of magazine guides to the receiver, a new flash suppressor, and a short monopod that was included for attachment to the butt. Sights were modified to accommodate the U.S. Army's new, more powerful M2 Ball ammunition introduced in 1938. Later weapons also featured a barrel-mounted carrying handle and those guns made after March 1942 were fitted with black plastic butts, instead of the more conventional walnut.[9]

Ammunition

Ammunition for the 1918A2 was also improved, at least four different types of cartridge being available for the new weapon:

- M2 50/150 Ball cartridge, a conventional ball cartridge with a 50-grain powder charge and 150-grain bullet.
- M25M1 Tracer: Intended for illuminating targets and signaling.
- M25 Armor Piercing: Intended for use against lightly armored vehicles and recognized by its black tip.
- M2 Armor Piercing Incendiary: Intended for use against lightly armored inflammable targets.[10]

Export Models

All produced by Colt Patent Firearms Company:

Automatic Machine Rifle Model 1919 (Model U)

Differs from 1918 in having return mechanism in the butt, rather than the gas tube under the barrel.

Model 1924

Similar to M1919. Chambered for .30–06 Springfield (7.62 × 63mm) U.S. service rifle cartridge, 7.65 × 53mm Belgian Mauser, 7 × 57mm Mauser, 6.5 × 55mm, 7.92 × 57mm Mauser and .303 British (7.7 × 56mmR) British service rifle cartridge.

Model 1925

Based on the M1924, but having a heavier barrel with cooling fins, and dust covers on the ejection port and in the magazine well. Chambered for .30–06 Springfield (7.62 × 63mm), 7.65 × 53mm Belgian Mauser, 7 × 57mm Mauser, 7.92 × 57mm Mauser, and .303 British (7.7 × 56mmR)

In addition, variants were manufactured under license by FN Herstal (Belgium) as the FN Mle 1930, which was a copy of the Colt M1925. Poland's State Rifle Factory and Carl Gustav (Sweden), also produced a version of the BAR, although these last two appear to have been making the FN Mle 1930 under license. The Polish government also bought a number of these weapons from FN.[11]

Bayonets

Since it was designed as an automatic rifle or light machine gun and intended to operate in an infantry support role, the M1918 was not fitted with a mount for a bayonet, nor was any pattern of bayonet ever issued for use with this weapon. However, one experimental bayonet fitting seems to have been made by Winchester, using an unmodified M1917 bayonet with a special muzzle ring, which was attached to a standard M1918 by an experimental flash hider assembly. This prototype assembly was found in the Winchester factory museum in New Haven, Connecticut, with a label printed on one side with the following description: "Winchester Repeating Arms Co./New Haven Conn." On the other side was a handwritten note: "Combined Flash Hider, Front Sight and Bayonet Mount for Browning Automatic Rifle Model 1918 with Bayonet and Scabbard–September 7, 1918." There is no evidence whatsoever of military adoption of this, nor any military documentation describing its development.[12]

Military service

World War I

The BAR saw its first use in combat in September 1918. Although it made a significant impression on America's allies, the French alone ordering 15,000 to replace their abominable Chauchat light machine guns, it arrived too late to see extensive use. After the war, it became popular with America's criminal underworld, and was said to have been a favorite with, amongst others, Clyde Barrow of "Bonnie and Clyde" fame.

World War II

The M1918A2 BAR was adopted by the U.S. army as its squad light machine gun in 1938, one BAR being issued to each 12-man squad, a single BAR team being composed of the gunner and one or two men assigned to carry magazines. Subsequent experience showed this arrangement to be ineffective, and by the end of the war, U.S. Army tactics were based around a thirteen-man squad equipped with three BARs. Compared to other weapons then in use, such as the Bren or belt-fed MG 34, the antiquated BAR had a number of faults, mainly involving its thin-walled, fixed barrel, which tended to overheat when the weapon was used for extended periods, and the small capacity magazine. Its mechanism was also complex to field-strip and clean, and the gas cylinder was especially prone to rust damage, because the M2 service ammunition used in BAR was fitted with a primer that produced an excessively corrosive residue after firing. Despite these disadvantages, the M1918A2 proved reliable enough if used by a man experienced in its operation and conscientious about regular cleaning, and it went on to continued service with the U.S. Army in Korea.

On the morning of D–Day (6 June 1944), a detachment of 200 U.S. Army Rangers were given the unenviable task of scaling the perpendicular cliff above the beach at Pointe du Hoc and silencing a battery of 155mm guns reported to be located there. Armed only with mortars and BARs, the Rangers climbed the sheer face of the cliff using ropes and ladders while under heavy fire, but upon reaching the top, they found the guns had been removed and replaced with telegraph poles, just as an earlier report had indicated.

Having sustained heavy casualties but still undeterred, the remaining Rangers moved towards their second objective, the Grandcamp-Maisy-Vierville-sur-Mer road. Walking in front of his unit, Sergeant William "L-Rod" Petty suddenly found himself faced with two German soldiers who had just leapt out of a deep shelter hole. Although the two Germans were right on top of him, Petty threw himself to the ground and fired a burst from his BAR. The .30-06 rounds passed harmlessly between the two men but the weapon's racket must have unnerved them, because they immediately dropped their weapons and surrendered. A friend of Petty's, who had been walking behind him, commented drily, "Hell, L-Rod, that's a good way to save ammunition—just scare 'em to death."[13]

The BAR was a popular weapon with the men who used it, and it remained in service with the U.S. Army from its introduction in 1918 until the end of the Korean War in 1953. Such was the popularity of the weapon that many were still in use by Special Forces personnel, while they were acting as advisers in Vietnam in 1963. The M1918A2 was still in use in the early stages of the Vietnam War, and the U.S. government also delivered a quantity of BARs as "obsolete," second-line small arms to the South Vietnamese Army and associated allies, including the Montagnard hill people of South Vietnam. U.S. Special Forces advisers frequently chose the BAR over more modern infantry weapons, as one Special Forces sergeant explained: "Many times since my three tours of duty in Vietnam I have thanked God for ... having a BAR that actually worked, as opposed to the jamming M16.... We had a lot of Viet Cong infiltrators in all our camps, who would steal weapons every chance they got. Needless to say, the most popular weapon to steal was the venerable old BAR."[14]

Values

U.S.-made machine guns manufactured before 1986 may still be transferred between owners in the United States. Consequently original, working BARs are sometimes offered for sale. Local regulations as they apply to these weapons should be consulted before purchase.

M1918: NRA Good: $20,000–$23,000 NRA Fine: $30,000–$35,000
M1918A2: NRA Good: $15,000–$18,000 NRA Fine: $24,000–$28,000
The M1918A1 is such a rare weapon that it is almost never offered for sale.

Prices may vary considerably, depending upon condition of the weapon and accessories, such as magazines or webbing, which are included in the sale.

British Light Machine Gun Development After World War I

At the close of World War I, the British Army was equipped with two machine guns, which were both beginning to show their age. Their medium/heavy machine gun was the ultra-reliable Vickers, chambered for the standard British .303 cartridge but weighing a fairly hefty 80 lbs. This meant it was only suitable in a defensive role, firing from a previously prepared position and could not be used to support troops as they were moving forward. The second weapon, the Lewis LMG, was lighter and could be moved up to support troops who were deploying, but it was becoming outdated. It was prone to unexplained stoppages, usually associated with the fragile, spiral-wound recoil spring and with significant overheating problems, which would often render the weapon completely inoperative. After two series of trials involving a number of weapons, in 1930 the Small Arms Committee of the British Army decided upon the Czechoslovakian ZB vz 26 as their new LMG. The British subsequently obtained a license to manufacture the gun from its original designers, the Holek brothers, and after a number of modifications, the weapon reached its final form, the ZB vz 33. This became the Bren, named for the first two letters of the two towns where it was originally manufactured, Brno and Enfield. By 1938, British Army units were receiving regular deliveries of its new LMG and training in its use, which included the improved "fire and movement" tactics introduced after World War I.[15]

The Bren Gun

SPECIFICATION

Production:
RSAF Enfield: approximately 220,000, over 50,000 in 1943.
Daimler (for B.S.A): records not readily available.
Lithgow Small Arms, Australia: 17,428 weapons.
John Inglis & Co., Canada: approximately 170,000 weapons.
Monotype: records not readily available.
Ichapore Rifle Factory, India: records not readily available.

The Bren light machine gun Mark 1 was an air-cooled, selective-fire, gas-operated light machine gun, which fired from a closed bolt with a cyclic rate of 500rpm. It was fitted with a fire-selector switch on the right side of the receiver, allowing either semiautomatic operation or fully automatic fire, as well as a gas regulator with four positions near the muzzle. Weapons in use during World War II were usually chambered for the British .303 caliber Mk VII service rifle cartridge, although RSAF Enfield also produced a version for the Chinese that was chambered for the 7.93 × 57mm Mauser Chinese service rifle cartridge. Ammunition was fed into the weapon from a characteristic curved, detachable box magazine which entered the top of the receiver, spent cartridges being ejected from a slot in the bottom of that component. These magazines were originally designed to hold 30 rounds, but were loaded usually with only 27 or 28, to prevent damage to the internal spring. One slight problem with the Bren was that these rimmed cartridges had to be positioned correctly, the rim of the new cartridge being forward of the rim of the previous round, otherwise a stoppage would inevitably result. The quality of manufacture ensured that problems were very infrequent, however, and many users claimed that any stoppage experienced with a Bren could be cleared by simply hitting the gun, turning up the gas regulator, or by doing both. Originally, sights were offset to bypass the magazine and consisted of a tunneled blade front sight and a calibrated drum rear sight, which was designed to emit a click for every 100 yards change in range. This was a useful feature for night fighting, although this as changed in the Mk.II to a simple graduated leaf in order to decrease production costs. Butts were in walnut and a rear monopod was fitted to the Mk1 and Mk1m.[16]

RECEIVER AND COMPONENT STAMPS

In early weapons, the left side of the receiver in front of the rear sight is stamped with the model designation and date of manufacture, in the following form:

M^K I
INGLIS
1943

Where "M$\underline{K}$ I" is the model designation, "INGLIS" is the manufacturer—in this case, John Inglis of Canada—and "1943" is the date of manufacture.

Later weapons may bear a stamp with a slightly different configuration, stamped on the left side of the receiver in front of the rear sight and having the following form:

Đ
1944 BREN Mᴷ III

Where "Đ" is the trademark of RSAF, Enfield (a joined "E" and "D"), "1944" is the date of production, and "BREN MK III" is the model designation.

A serial number is also found stamped on the left side of the receiver above the pistol grip, with a letter prefix denoting the place of manufacture. Serial numbers are also found on the barrel, magazine and a number of other components, serial number prefixes indicating the place of manufacture.[17]

Table Thirty-one: Factory codes found on Bren light machine guns

Manufacturer	Manufacturers' code stamp	Serial number prefix
Royal Small Arms factory, Enfield Lock	**ED** (This takes the form of a conjoined "E" and "D," appearing as "Đ")	A AA C F K L LB P U W X Z
Lithgow Small Arms, Lithgow, Australia	**LITHGOW**	A B
John Inglis & Co. Canada	**INGLIS**	N OT T (with a number in front; e.g., 4TXXXX)
Ichapore Rifle Factory, India	**SAF** (Indian Small Arms Factory)	
The Daimler company Ltd, as a subsidiary of BSA	**D**	R S T U W RA RB
Monotype Group, Canada	**M67**	

Operation

To load the weapon, the gunner or No. 1 first assumed a prone position, resting the butt on the ground and then sliding forward the cover of the magazine slot. Picking up a full magazine with his right hand, he checked the cartridges were placed correctly, before engaging the lip on the front of the magazine in the magazine slot and then tilting the magazine back until it engaged in the rear of the slot. The cocking handle was pulled back to its full extent, then released to its forward position and the selector switch moved from its "S" (safe) position to either "R" (rifle fire or semi-automatic) or "A" (fully automatic). Since the sights were offset in order to allow sighting past the magazine, this meant a Mk.I Bren could only be fired from the right shoulder. In firing, both elbows rested on the ground, and in this position elevation or depression of the gun was achieved by raising or lowering the forearms as required.

With a round chambered and the selector set, pulling the trigger disconnected the sear, allowing the firing pin to move forwards and fire the cartridge. When the bullet had progressed about two thirds of the way up the barrel, a proportion of the propulsive gas was expelled through a vent on to the piston head, which was then driven back sufficiently to operate the breech block and cock the striker. The breech block and bolt then moved forwards, driven by the return spring and chambering the next round, after which the bolt and barrel were locked together. When set to fire single shots, position "R," a sear was positioned to prevent the firing pin from moving forward until the trigger was squeezed, while in fully automatic mode the weapon fired every time a cartridge was chambered for as long as the trigger was depressed. Although a cyclic rate of around 500 rpm was possible, in battlefield conditions the necessity for changing magazines and barrels reduced this slightly.[18]

Variations

A number of changes were made to the Bren LMG during its service life, mainly to ease production problems, but only the main models are described here.

Mk 1

Manufacturer's stamps and serial number prefixes indicate that most of these guns were manufactured by RSAF, Enfield from 1938 and at Lithgow from 1940, although small numbers may have been produced by other makers.

Features

- Drum pattern rear aperture sight
- Folding cocking handle
- Bipod with adjustable, telescoping legs
- Canvas supporting strap for use over the shoulder when firing

Top: Mk1 Bren from the left-hand side, showing the carrying handle, flash excluder, spare magazine and rear sight adjustment dial. *Bottom:* Mk1 Bren from the right-hand, side showing the skid-footed bipod and the cocking handle (both photographs courtesy James D. Julia Auctioneers, Fairfield, Maine. www.jamesdjulia.com).

- Folding, rear securing point for the strap
- Rear supporting handle under butt
- Buffered butt plate

Mk 1m

Similar to the original Mk1, with slight changes to facilitate production, including a fixed securing point for the carrying sling rather than the folding component fitted to the Mk1. Serial numbers and manufacturer's stamps indicate that main production was at RSAF Enfield, although some weapons may have been produced by other manufacturers.

Mk II

Introduced in 1941 as a more easily manufactured version of the Mk1 and produced mainly in Canada by John Inglis & Co and the Monotype Group, although significant numbers may have been produced by other manufacturers. Also known as the "Garage hands" model.

Features

- Higher rate of fire than Mk1
- Folding leaf rear sight instead of the more complex drum design
- Fixed cocking handle
- Fixed height bipod with folding legs, rather than telescoping legs
- Supporting strap not fitted
- Rear handle under butt not fitted
- Simplified receiver with fewer machining operations compared to Mk1
- Simplified butt compared to Mk1
- Unbuffered steel buttplate

Mk III

Shorter, lighter weapon manufactured as a short-barreled conversion of the Mark 1 in 1944. Designed specifically for paratroop and glider forces, it was also used in Southeast Asia. Serial numbers and manufacturer's stamps indicate that main production was at RSAF, Enfield, although the weapon may have been manufactured elsewhere.

Mk VI

Another shorter, lighter weapon manufactured as a short-barreled conversion of the Mark II in 1944. Designed specifically for paratroop and glider forces, it was also used in Southeast Asia and is rarely seen at auction. Serial numbers and manufacturer's stamps indicate that main production was at RSAF, Enfield, although the weapon may have been manufactured elsewhere.

L4

The L4 was a version of the Bren that resulted from the conversion in 1958 of remaining Mark 1–4 Brens to use the 7.62 × 51mm NATO cartridge, which involved designing and fitting a completely new barrel, bolt and magazine. L4 Brens can be fitted with the magazine used with the L1A1 self-loading rifle, and later conversions had a chrome-lined barrel to increase service life. Serial numbers and manufacturer's stamps indicate that main center for conversion was RSAF, Enfield.[19]

Military Service

A Bren gun crew consisted of two men: the Number 1, who fired the weapon, and the Number 2, who carried the extra magazines, usually ten, together with a spare barrel and a tool kit. As well as the magazines carried by the No. 2, from 1937 British troops were also equipped with webbing that could hold two magazines for their section's Bren. One of the weapon's real strengths was its ease of operation. Every British soldier was trained both to fire a Bren and to act as loader, should such a need arise.

With a weapon set to fully automatic, the usual procedure was to fire short bursts of four or five rounds, which expended a full magazine in about one minute, and more importantly gave an opportunity to change magazines without unduly affecting the rate of fire nor overheating the barrel. Using a Bren in this way did require practice, however, the usual recommendation being for the gunner to depress the trigger for as long as it took to count "one hundred and one" fairly slowly. Fully automatic fire would empty 4 magazines in a minute and also necessitated a change of barrel after only 2½ minutes due to overheating, so it was rarely used. The Bren's idiosyncrasies with a hot barrel were well understood by those most experienced with it, as witnessed by the warning in the official instruction manual: "[D]o not fire for too long on automatic, as the gun may get so hot it starts playing tricks."

In order to change an overheated barrel, the No. 2 simply lifted the barrel-nut catch, grasped the handle and slid the barrel forward out of position, whereupon a cold barrel could be quickly reinserted. An overheated barrel could be cooled in a bucket of water without risk of damage, but as one member of No. 4 Commando recalled, sometimes more primitive methods were employed: "[T]he Bren was a good weapon, but if you fired it too long and too quick, the barrel heated up and the accuracy decreased. When that happened most of the boys just p...d on the barrel to cool it down."[20]

It was also easy to field-strip and clean. In order to disassemble a Bren, first the body-locking pin was drawn out sufficiently to remove the butt to the rear, the slot holding the pin being designed to retain that component after removal of the butt, which ensured the pin could not be put down and lost. With the butt removed, the breech block and piston could then be taken out, giving access to the rest of the mechanism. Barrel removal was also simple, requiring only that the barrel nut catch be raised, whereupon the barrel could be given a half-twist, before being lifted clear.

The Bren was certainly versatile. One of the places it proved its worth was in the defense of Dunkirk, at the Canal de Chats where Brigadier Beckworth Smith, commanding 1st Brigade Coldstream Guards, offered his men some instructions on shooting down enemy aircraft ... along with an incentive: "Stand up to 'em.... Shoot at them with a Bren gun from the shoulder.... Take them like a high pheasant and give them plenty of lead. Remember, £5 to anyone who brings one down." The Guardsmen must have taken him at his word, because the fighting around the canal was so intensive that a number of the Coldstreams' Bren guns became unserviceable when the firing pins *melted*.[21]

The Bren gun did have its detractors, however. During the British evacuation of

Dunkirk between 27 May and 4 June 1940, many civilians with boats volunteered to join the attempt to rescue the British Expeditionary Force from the beaches of the French seaside resort. Desperate for a way to protect his craft, one civilian visited an ordnance depot to ask a veteran Chief Petty Officer what he could recommend in the way of armaments. Probably tired of such requests at the end of a long day, the CPO demanded somewhat brusquely just what sort of gun his visitor wanted.

"What about a Bren?" the civilian demanded. "They're handy little tools, aren't they?"
"Ever fired one?" the CPO snapped.
"Well, no," the boat owner was forced to admit.
"Take my advice, chum," the Chief growled. "Fix yourself up with a Lewis. Brens are too bloody accurate. With a Lewis you get plenty of spray and that, plus the motion of your cockleshell, should get you out of trouble!"

Stories about the accuracy of the Bren are commonplace amongst the British and Commonwealth troops who came to rely upon it during the course of World War II. Some troops even claimed, "[I]f you fire a burst at oncoming troops, all the rounds will go through one man ... and leave only one hole." Although this is something of an exaggeration, it was certainly not unusual to find that a four- or five-round burst from an experienced operator resulted in a group similar to that achieved by firing five single shots. In fact, many users claimed to prefer an old gun with a worn barrel to a newer weapon, precisely because the older Bren spread its fire more widely and consequently was more effective against large bodies of troops.[22]

Later developments

The Bren gun was used very widely during World War II; as well as having an infantry support role, it was also employed as secondary armament by the Navy and as a short-range antiaircraft gun, firing from a fixed mounting. It continued as the British Army's main light machine gun until 1958, when changes in international relations made it necessary to both standardize cartridges to a NATO specification and supplement the British Army's Vickers medium machine guns and Brens with the FN MAG, designated in the British Army as the L7A2 GPMG (General Purpose Machine Gun). The Vickers was gradually phased out, finally leaving service in 1968, but the Bren was retained alongside the FN MAG, although modified to fire the new 7.62 × 51mm NATO cartridge, and subsequently redesignated the L4 LMG. As well as using the same cartridge as the new L1A1 Self Loading Rifle, the L4 could also accept its standard 20-round magazine, which added greatly to its versatility. It remained in service until 1990, when the adoption of the 5.56 × 45mm NATO cartridge and the new SA80 assault rifle resulted in the Bren's being withdrawn from service. Given the problems many serving British soldiers experienced initially with the unpopular SA80, there must have been not a few old sweats who mourned its passing.[23]

Values

Working Bren guns imported into the U.S. and registered before 1986 are transferable between owners. Consequently, these weapons are sometimes offered for sale, although only the Bren Mk 1 is seen with any frequency, and condition is quite variable. Local regulations as they apply to these weapons should be consulted before purchase.

Prices are for weapons capable of firing.

Mk1: NRA Good: $25,000; NRA Fine: $30,000

French Light Machine Gun Development After World War I

After the end of World War I, the French army decided to replace their problematic Chauchat LMGs with a better weapon, which could take advantage of the tactics used by the small LMG teams then being introduced into European armies during that period. Consideration was given to adopting the BAR, but eventually French military authorities decided that a locally developed weapon would be more expedient. MAC (Manufacture d'Armes de Châtellerault) won the contract with a weapon that used a modification of the mechanism of the BAR, designed by a Lieutenant Colonel Reibel and Chief Armorer Chosse and finally designated the FM Mle1924 (Fusil-mitrailleur Modèle 1924) when accepted into French service.[24]

The FM 24/M29 Light Machine Gun

The FM Modèle 1924 entered production in late July 1925 and first saw military service in Morocco in May 1926 during the later stages of the Rif War. It proved very popular and was favorably compared in performance with the heavier Hotchkiss M1909 light machine gun. However, the M1924 was chambered for a new cartridge, the 7.5 × 57mm MAS, which had replaced the 8mm Lebel, and unfortunately it was easy to mistake this round for a 8 × 57mm Mauser cartridge which was issued to French auxiliary troops for their Mauser rifles and MG 08/15 heavy machine guns. Loading and firing the Mauser cartridge in the FM1924 LMG tended to happen only once, with disastrous results, and after this had occurred on a number of occasions, the French quickly developed a new round for their FM1924s. This was the 7.5 × 54mm MAS cartridge, also known as the "7.5 French," introduced in 1929 and retained in use for all rifles and light machine guns in French service until 1990. A number of the older FM1924 LMGs were modified to use this new cartridge, with production of a new M1924/M29 (Fusil-mitrailleur modèle 1924 modifié 1929) gun chambered for the 7.5 × 54mm cartridge beginning in 1930.[25]

Specification

Production:
FM1924: 45,530 weapons converted to 7.5 × 54mm MAS cartridge.
FM1924/M29: 187,412 guns.

The FM1924/M29 was an air-cooled, selective-fire, gas-operated light machine gun firing from an open bolt, and having a unique fire selector mechanism consisting of two triggers. Operating the front trigger gives semiautomatic fire, while pulling the rear trigger delivers fully automatic fire at a cyclic rate of 450 rpm. A manual safety lever is fitted on the lower portion of the receiver and locks both triggers when engaged. Cartridges are delivered to the mechanism by a box magazine containing 25 rounds that fits into the top of the receiver, spent cases being ejected via an ejection port on the right side. Both apertures are protected by a single steel dust cover, which is hinged on the right side to cover the ejection port. The weapon is fitted with a wooden stock, pistol grip and foregrip under the receiver, as well as a folding bipod just behind the front sight.[26]

Receiver stamp

Model designation and serial number are stamped on the left side of the receiver, above the pistol grip, in the following form:

M^{LE} 1924/29
XXXXX

Where "M<u>LE</u> 1924/29" is the Model designation and "XXXXX" denotes the serial number.

Barrels are also stamped with the model designation and serial number, although in many weapons offered for sale, barrel numbers and even model designations may not match with other components.

Operation

Operation is similar to the Bren, a magazine being first placed in the magazine aperture and locked in place. The charging handle is then pulled back and locked to the rear by the trigger sear. Pulling the trigger releases the sear, removes a cartridge from the magazine, then chambers and fires the round. Part of the residual cartridge gas is used to operate the long-stroke gas piston, located in its tube beneath the barrel, which is driven backwards, causing the two swinging links connected to the rear operating rod of the piston to move the bolt down and back. The firing pin is also attached to the top of a projection on this operating rod, and as the bolt moves forward in fully automatic mode, it chambers a fresh round and is then moved up by the swinging links into a slot cut in the roof of the receiver, which serves to lock the bolt and the barrel together. With the bolt locked to the breech, the firing pin strikes the primer, firing the cartridge and beginning the cycle again, the firing rate on the automatic setting being adjusted to 450 rounds per minute, thus allowing more continuous firing without overheating. In semiautomatic mode, the bolt is locked back until the trigger is operated, in the usual manner. When the last cartridge in the magazine has been fired, the bolt is held open, thus giving both mechanism and barrel a chance to cool.

The FM1924/M29 proved to be both accurate and highly reliable, but since the barrel was not fitted with a quick-release mechanism like the Bren, it could not be exchanged once they were hot. This necessitated a slower rate of fire than could be achieved with the British weapon or the German MG 34. An instruction manual issued by the French Army for the FM1924/M29 in July 1925 recommended that the gunner should never exceed 400 rounds of uninterrupted firing because after such a period of extended operation, the gun

FM 24/M29 LMG from the right, showing the ejection port and wooden hand-grip (courtesy James D. Julia Auctioneers, Fairfield, Maine. www.jamesdjulia.com).

needs to be allowed to cool for a period of between ten to fifteen minutes. The manual goes on to recommend the following firing procedure for an FM1924/M29: "[F]ire between 4 and 5 magazines before taking a short pause, then repeat that firing pattern for the whole of the period of operation. This sort of firing pattern will permit steady, consistent performance, as well as allowing very extensive firing periods."[27]

Receiver stamps on FM 24 LMG (courtesy James D. Julia Auctioneers, Fairfield, Maine. www.jamesdjulia.com).

Variations

Model 1924/1929D light machine

Production: precise records unavailable.

This was a variant of the original FM1924/M29 adapted for firing from the interior firing ports in the bunkers of the Maginot Line. It was unique in being modified so that the cartridges were ejected from the bottom of the receiver, where they were led away via a flexible tube to the ditch surrounding the emplacement where the gun was mounted.

Model 1931

Production: precise records unavailable.

The MAC Model1931 (Mitrailleuse modèle 1931) was a gas-operated, air-cooled, fully automatic weapon, firing from an open bolt and based on the original FM1924. Chambered for the same 7.5 × 54mm MAS cartridge, it was fitted with two vertical pan magazines, each holding 150 cartridges and mounted vertically on the side of the gun. It was produced as a heavy machine gun for installation in tanks and fortified emplacements, particularly the Maginot line. Such a deployment required a number of modifications, and these included a different rifling to accommodate ammunition supplied with the heavier *Balle D* bullet; a heavier, thicker barrel to absorb the heat of sustained firing; an ejection port that directed the spent cases straight down, and a redesigned mounting to allow two guns to be mounted side-by-side. The original butt was removed and the pistol grip was made longer and given a sharper curve.[28]

VALUES

Working FM1924/M29 LMGs imported into the U.S. and registered before 1986 are transferable between owners. Consequently, these weapons are sometimes offered for sale, although only the FM1924/M29 is seen with any frequency, and condition is quite variable. Local regulations as they apply to these weapons should be consulted before purchase.

Prices are for weapons capable of firing.

Mk1: NRA Good: $10,000; NRA Fine: $15,000

German Light Machine Gun Development After World War I

Despite the restrictions imposed by the Versailles Treaty of 1919, firearms development continued in Germany after World War I, and one of the results of this necessarily clandestine research was a light machine gun designated the MG 30. This weapon and comparable guns such as the MG 13 and MG 15 were developed at the insistence of the Reichswehr or Imperial Defence organization, forerunner of the Wehrmacht (trans: Defense Force), in order to take advantage of the lessons learned in World War I regarding the use of the LMG as a central factor in small unit infantry tactics. These developments continued despite attempts by the European powers, particularly France, to both punish Germany and limit its development as modern military power. It has been claimed by modern historians that the extreme measures advocated after Versailles, particularly by the French, probably made the appearance of Adolf Hitler, or at least some figure with similar characteristics, almost inevitable.

Much of the research necessary to develop the MG 30 was carried out in Switzerland by Waffenfabrik Solothurn, a Swiss watchmaking company bought by the German company, Rheinmetall, specifically to serve as a R&D facility away from the scrutiny of the Allied Control Commission, which was responsible for enforcing German compliance with the terms of the 1919 Treaty. Germany industry also produced a modified version of the Dreyse Model of 1918 as the MG 13, which was introduced into service with the German army in

1930 and served until replaced by the much superior MG 34, although it was retained as the tailgunner's armament in Ju 87 Stukas and as a turret gun in the early Panzers.[29]

The MG 34

The MG 30 was a good weapon with a reliable mechanism, but the design was already antiquated, since it was designed only to fire from a 25-round box magazine, entering the receiver from the left side, and had a barrel that took a considerable time to change. It did have a number of outstanding features, however, and Henrich Volmmer of Mauser Industries was sufficiently impressed to begin work on modifying the design, which resulted in the first production version of the MG 34 in 1934. Unfortunately, the precise machining necessary to produce the parts for its construction meant it was prone to stoppages if used in a dusty or dirty environment, and also made it expensive to produce, the weapon being priced at £33 in 1942, and more importantly, requiring a total of 150 hours for completion.[30]

SPECIFICATION

Production: over 577,000 weapons.

Produced by a number of armaments companies, including Berlin-Suhler-Waffen, Carl Eickhorn, Maget, Mauser, Steyr and Waffenwerke Brünn, although individual production figures for these factories are not clearly established.

The MG 34 is a recoil-operated, selective-fire weapon, firing from an open bolt with a cyclic rate of 800 to 900 rpm and chambered for the 7.92 × 57mm Mauser German service rifle cartridge. Fire selection is simply achieved by operation of a two-part trigger, squeezing the top section giving semiautomatic operation, while operation of the lower section gives fully automatic fire. To facilitate this operation, the top section is stamped with the letter "E" (Einzelschussfeuer; trans: single-shot fire), while the bottom half is marked "D" (Dauerfeuer; trans: continuous fire). There is a safety catch on the left side just above the trigger; pushing the lever up moves it to "S" for safe and pushing down moves it to "F" for fire. Cartridges are supplied from a belt containing 250 rounds when the weapon is mounted on a tripod, and from a magazine containing either 50 or 75 rounds when deployed as a light machine gun fitted with a bipod, for service either with an infantry squad or as an AA weapon. A perforated cooling jacket surrounds the barrel, which is fitted with a muzzle booster to improve the recoil operation and designed to be changed quickly when overheating occurs. These weapons are also fitted with a pistol grip having bakelite or plastic plates and a substantial butt that was originally manufactured in wood, although in some later weapons this component may be in a heavy-duty plastic, and butt plates were never fitted, even to the wooden components. The standard front sight is a simple iron post, while the rear sight is a vertical leaf with an open V notch, graduated from 200 to 2,000 meters, in 100-meter increments. When it was deployed as a heavy machine gun on a fixed tripod, a telescopic sight was mounted on the tripod, giving the weapon accurate sighting up to 3,500 meters. In addition, the gun was often supplied with an antiaircraft (AA) ring sight, which fitted into a slot in the barrel jacket and was used with a folding aperture sight also incorporated into the rear sight.

The MG 34 features a unique system for quickly changing the barrel, and although slightly more complex and slower than the system designed for the Bren gun, barrel changing could be performed quickly and easily after a little practice. In order to change a barrel, the gun is first cocked and the safety lever set to the "SAFE" position. The gun is then inverted and the receiver catch, which is located on the left below the rear sight, is pushed in, the receiver is turned counterclockwise 180 degrees, and the gun is tilted until the barrel slides out of the barrel jacket. The hot barrel is removed using a heatproof pad or the asbestos glove supplied with the weapon, and is replaced with a cool barrel that is slid into the cooling jacket. The receiver is returned to its original position, and after ensuring that the receiver catch is locked, the gun is ready to fire.[31]

MG 34 from the right side, showing the ejection port, rear sight, spike bipod and a 50-round drum and 75-round saddle ammunition container (courtesy James D. Julia Auctioneers, Fairfield, Maine. www.jamesdjulia.com).

Left: Magnified view of an MG 34 from the left, showing the trigger and the opening in the receiver for the ammunition belt. The trigger markings indicate positions for fully and semiautomatic fire. *Right:* Ammunition containers for an MG 34 (both photographs courtesy James D. Julia Auctioneers, Fairfield, Maine. www.jamesdjulia.com).

Receiver and component stamps

Receivers are stamped on the top surface, adjacent to the rear sight with a proof mark in the form of a small German Imperial eagle, as well as the serial number and a code to designate the manufacturer, in the following form:

cra
1942
XXXX

Where "cra" is the manufacturer code, in this case MAGET, "1942" is the date of production, and "XXXX" denotes the serial number, which is also found on the barrel and various other components. In addition, the conventional eagle proof stamp of the Third Reich will be found on the receiver, barrel and other parts, and there may also be a Waffenamt code number stamped on the weapon to show it has been inspected and accepted into service with the Third Reich. Barrels and other components may bear stamps from a manufacturer that do not match those on the receiver. This is not uncommon and is the result of refurbishment or replacement of worn-out components.

Table Thirty-two. Factory codes found on MG 34 light machine guns

Factory	Code letters/numbers
Mauser: Mauser Werke AG	ar
	S/243
Steyr: Steyr Daimler Puch, A.G. Werk, Steyr, Austria	bnz
Waffenwerke Brünn: Waffenwerke Brünn, AG, Bystrica	dot
	dot VZ24
Berlin-Suhler-Waffen: BSW, Suhl, Germany	bsw
MAGET: Maschinenbau und Gerätebau GmbH, Berlin-Tegel	cra
Carl Eickhorn: Carl Eickhorn Waffenfabrik, Solingen, Germany	Cof

These code letters are found stamped on the rear of the receiver and adjacent to the rear sight, in the format and position already described. Although usually found in lower case, there are some instances of stamps with upper-case letters, and it should be noted that this may not be a complete list.[32]

OPERATION

An MG 34 could be fired using either a belt or double "saddle" pattern drum to hold the ammunition. In order to load a belt, the bolt is set in the forward position and the safety switch is set to "F." The top of the receiver is then opened by operating the receiver cover catch at the rear end of the receiver and lifting the receiver cover forwards. A belt of cartridges is loaded by laying the first three cartridge into the breech opening so that the first one rests against the cartridge stops, before the receiver cover is closed and locked. If the belt has a starter tab, this may be simply pushed through the breech opening until the first round is resting against the cartridge stops. With the belt or magazine loaded, the cocking handle is pulled to the rear to its full extent and then pushed forward, which results in the bolt being held back by the trigger pawl. Semiautomatic fire is achieved by pressing the top part of the double trigger, which is marked "E," fully automatic operation occurring when the lower section, marked "D," is operated.

Whichever firing mode is selected, pulling the trigger disengages the sear, allowing the bolt to move forward, driven by the recoil spring, and causing the bolt to remove a cartridge from the magazine or belt and push it into the chamber. As the bolt continues to move forward it rotates, engaging the bolt locking lugs with a corresponding set of slots in the chamber and locking the bolt and barrel together, whereupon the striker impacts upon the primer, firing the cartridge. Recoil from the cartridge causes the barrel and bolt to move backwards a short distance, rotating the bolt, disengaging the bolt locking lugs and thus unlocking the bolt from the barrel. The barrel returns to its forward position while the bolt recoils to the full extent of its rearward travel and the empty casing is ejected. If the weapon is operated in semiautomatic mode, the sear catches the bolt and retains it until the trigger is pressed again, while if a weapon is being fired in fully automatic mode, the recoil spring drives the bolt forward and the firing cycle is repeated. When the weapon is fired in fully automatic mode, the manual recommended that the legs of the bipod be held down, as the weapon had a marked tendency to jump![33]

MAGAZINES

Two types of magazine were issued for the MG 34: a magazine holding a belt containing 50 cartridges, and a double drum holding 75 cartridges, having a "saddle" configuration.

The 50-round drum

The 50-round drum is not a conventional magazine, but rather holds a belt of nondisposable links containing 50 cartridges. It is loaded by depressing the catch on the sliding lever of the drum, and then moving the cover protecting the opening of the drum to the open position, so that the tab end of the belt can be removed from the drum. The tab is inserted into the left side of the breech, with the open end of the links down, before engaging the hook on the front end of the drum with the lug on the front end of the receiver's lower assembly. The rear end of the drum is then turned towards the gun until the spring catch on the drum engages the lug on the rear end of the feedway. The cocking handle is then drawn back until the belt engages the cartridge pawls under the breech block and the weapon is ready to fire. These drums were usually used in weapons fitted to tanks or deployed as AA guns.

The 75-round drum

The 75-round drum is a conventional magazine, manufactured in the form of a double drum with a "saddle" configuration. Guns designed to use these drums are fitted with a special cover over the breech opening. To load, the drum is placed in position across the breech, which automatically opens the breech cover, and the cocking handle is moved back, then forwards. The gun is now ready to fire. These twin drums were usually fitted to weapons in land use with the Wehrmacht or to AA guns.[34]

VARIATIONS

MG 34/41 (MG34S)

This weapon was a conventional MG 34 that had been altered to give it a cyclical firing rate of 1,200 rpm, thus increasing its weight to 14kg, slightly more than the original weapon. Only a limited number were produced, production being discontinued after the development of the MG 42.

MG 34 Panzerlauf

This was a modification of the conventional MG 34 for use in tanks, the MG 42 having been found unsuitable for this role. Changes included a heavier barrel jacket, which had a much smaller number of cooling holes than the original component; removal of the front sight; and the absence of the wooden butt. A kit for quick conversion to land use was carried inside the tank, which contained a wooden butt and combined bipod and front sight assembly.

MG 81

This was a version of the MG 34 intended for use in aircraft and modified to allow cartridges to be fed into the mechanism from either side.

MG 81Z

This weapon consisted of two MG 81s bolted together and modified to operate from a single trigger. By 1943, the Luftwaffe had lost the battle for air superiority, and with that arm's decline in priority in the German war effort, both the MG 81 and MG 81Z LMGs were modified for ground land use with the German infantry. Such modifications as were produced do not seem to have been uniformly successful.[35]

MILITARY SERVICE

The MG 34 was specifically designed to be used as either a light machine gun fitted with a light bipod or mounted on a more massive tripod as a conventional heavy machine gun, in a defensive position. It also had a role as an antiaircraft gun, as well as being mounted on a number of modern tanks in service with the Wehrmacht. Consequently, it is considered to be the first of that modern group of automatic weapons categorized as the General Purpose Machine Gun or GPMG.

Adopted into service with the Wehrmacht in 1936, the MG 34 served in all major theaters where German troops were operating between 1936 and 1945. Although many of the older MG 34s were replaced by the new MG 42 when that became available, production of the MG 42 never succeeded in fulfilling demand, and the MG34 had to be retained in service by many units.[36]

VALUES

Working MG 34 light machine guns imported into the U.S. and registered before 1986 are transferable between owners. Consequently, these weapons are sometimes offered for sale, although condition is quite variable and price is dependent upon provenance. Local regulations as they apply to these weapons should be consulted before purchase.

Prices are for weapons capable of firing.

NRA Good: $25,000; NRA Fine: $30,000, depending upon provenance

Table Thirty-three. Comparison of the Bren, FM 24/29 and MG 34 light machine guns

Weapon	Bren	FM 24/M29	MG 34
Makers	RSAF, Enfield John Inglis & Co. Ichapore Rifle Factory Lithgow Small Arms	MAG (Manufacture d'Armes de Châtellerault)	Berlin-Suhler-Waffen, Carl Eickhorn Maget Mauser Steyr Waffenwerke Brünn
Period of production	1935–1958; chambered for .303 British 1958–2006; chambered for 7.62 × 51 NATO	1925 until 1957	1936 until 1945
Production	400,000 weapons **RSAF:** approximately 220,000 weapons. **Other manufacturers:** 190,000 weapons	190,400 weapons	577,120 weapons
Operators	Australia, Britain, Canada, China, Cyprus, Free French, Greece, India, Ireland, Israel, Italy (World War II), Germany (1939–1945), South Africa and others	France (Army and police), Greece, Poland, Spain, Germany (1939–1945), North Vietnam	Germany (1936–1945), China, North Korea, North Vietnam, Norway, Portugal, Spain
Military service	World War II, Chinese Civil War, Greek Civil War, Malayan Emergency, Korean War, Suez Crisis, Irish Troubles, Falklands War, Aden Conflict	Rif War, World War II, First Indochina War, Algerian War, Suez Crisis, Vietnam War, Cambodian Civil War	Spanish Civil War, World War II, Korean War, Arab-Israeli War (1948), Algerian War, Vietnam War
Crew	Two men: No. 1: gunner No. 2: loader and barrel changer. Spare magazines usually carried by platoon members	Two men: Gunner and loader, who also carried spare magazines	Capable of being operated by one man, although a crew of three, gunner and two loaders, was more usual. The rest of an MG squad also carried spare barrels and ammunition
Weight	Empty: 23 lbs With magazine: 25 lbs	Empty: 20 lbs With magazine: 22 lbs	Empty: 27 lbs (12 kg) With magazine: 29 lbs
Length/Barrel	Total length: 43 inches Barrel: 25 inches	Total length: 42 inches Barrel: 24 inches	Total length: 48 inches Barrel: 24.5 inches
Mechanism	Air-cooled, gas-operated, selective fire from a closed bolt	Air-cooled, gas-operated, selective fire from a closed bolt	Air-cooled, recoil-operated, selective fire from an open bolt
Construction	All parts machined, with small tolerances throughout, although the weapon remained reliable under extreme service conditions.	All parts machined, with small tolerances throughout, although the weapon remained reliable under extreme service conditions.	All parts machined, with small tolerances throughout, and this resulted in poor reliability under extreme conditions.

Cartridge	.303 British (7.7 × 56mmR)
	7.62 × 51 NATO
	Contained in
		7.5 × 57mm French (1924–1929)
		7.5 × 54mm French (1929–1950)
			7.92 × 57mm Mauser
			Contained in
			  Belt holding 250 rounds
			  Detachable drum magazine

Weapon	Bren	FM 24/M29	MG 34
	Detachable box magazine holding 30 cartridges Detachable pan magazine holding 100 cartridges. The later L4 could use also the standard 20-round SLR magazine	Contained in Detachable box magazine holding 25 cartridges	containing a belt holding 50 rounds Detachable tandem drum magazine holding 75 rounds
Sights	Mark 1: Front: iron blade Rear: adjustable drum Mark 2: Front: iron blade Rear: folding leaf	Front: simple post Rear: Flip-up adjustable leaf	Front: simple post Rear: Iron sight calibrated to 2,000 meters in 100 m increments. Additional components for operation in AA role
Maximum range	Approximately 2,000m	Approximately 2,000m	Approximately 2,000m
Rate of fire	500 rounds per minute (rpm)	450 rpm	Between 800 and 900 rpm
Price	£45 ($180) in 1941	£40 ($160)	£33 ($130) in 1942
Time to complete	55 man-hours	100 man-hours	150 man-hours

The MG 42 Light Machine Gun

Although the MG 34 was a very superior light machine gun with an especially good rate of fire, it was by no means perfect and had a number of features that sent the German military authorities looking for a better gun quite soon after its introduction.

It was time-consuming and considered relatively expensive to make, even though it was cheaper than its closest competitors, like the Bren. It was also unreliable under the sort of cold, filthy conditions the German army would encounter later, particularly in Russia, precisely because its precisely machined mechanism was easy to clog with dirt and other debris, unless the gunner took more than usual care of it.

Consequently, three companies were subsequently asked to submit new designs for a light machine gun, and the weapon produced by Werner Gruner of Johannes Grossfuss AG was accepted for further testing. Perhaps surprisingly, Gruner had no previous experience of firearms design; his company specialized in producing steel components made from stamped and pressed steel, rather than weapons. However, by combining what he learned on an army machine gunner's course and some information gained from ordinary soldiers who would use the weapon, by 1939 Gruner had a working prototype designated the MG 39, which was a significant improvement on the earlier weapon, being made from cheaply produced pressed steel components and without the need for the precise machining of the earlier weapon. Some further improvements were made to produce a second prototype, the MG 39/41, which was tested in combat trials and found to be exceptionally reliable, its looser mechanism being particularly resistant to stoppages caused by the ingress of mud and debris that had plagued the more temperamental MG 34. This was the weapon that was accepted in 1942 as the MG 42 and subsequently produced by a number of German armaments firms, with over 400,000 weapons produced before the end of World War II stopped production.[37]

Specification

Production: 423,600 weapons, although the numbers produced by each factory are not readily available.

The MG 42 is an air-cooled, recoil-operated, belt-fed, fully automatic light machine gun, firing from an open bolt with a cyclic rate of 900–1,500 rpm and chambered for the 7.62 × 57mm Mauser German service rifle cartridge. Cartridges are fed into the receiver from the left by a belt composed of non-disintegrating steel links, no magazine ever having been designed for the MG 42, although a 50-round belt container similar to that designed for the MG 34 was available for use when the weapon was deployed for land service. Firing rates were adjusted by the provision of bolts having different weights: a heavier bolt of 900 grm giving 900 rpm for ground use, and a lighter component weighing 650 grms for use in the AA weapon, which gave the MG 42 a firing rate of 1,500 rpm, although the bolts use different return springs and so are not readily transferable under service conditions. A recoil booster is fitted to the muzzle, which improved both the rate of fire and the weapon's reliability when cycling. A plunger-type safety catch is located on the receiver just above the pistol grip, which works from side to side and cannot be operated unless the gun is cocked. To put the gun on "safe," the gunner pushes the catch to the left until the letter "S" shows on its surface, while moving the catch to his right exposes the letter "F," showing that the gun is ready to fire.

Its high rate of fire made the weapon hard to control unless fired from a substantial mounting. It was fitted with a heavy, robust wooden butt, a pistol grip with plastic or bakelite plates and a substantial bipod which could be positioned either at the muzzle or under the receiver, all of which helped control its tendency to jump when firing was prolonged. A tripod fitted with a telescopic sight was also available when the weapon was deployed as either a heavy machine gun or AA weapon. Sights are simpler than the MG 34, the front sight consisting of an inverted "V" post that may be fixed, or folding and

MG 42 from the right, this weapon fitted with the AA sights (courtesy James D. Julia Auctioneers, Fairfield, Maine. www.jamesdjulia.com).

adjustable for height, while the rear sight is an open "V" notch on a sliding ramp, graduated from 200 to 2,000 meters, in 100-meter increments.[38]

Construction: another "Woolworth's" gun

The MG 42 was constructed of welded, pressed steel, the receiver and barrel jacket being made in one unit formed from a single piece of rolled steel, which was stamped out of a flat steel sheet and then pressed into shape, before being welded and pinned to give a component of generally rectangular cross-section. The front part of the housing serves as a barrel jacket and has a number of oval cooling slots on the top, bottom and left sides, the right side of the jacket having a single elongated slot which is used to remove the barrel. Barrels and bolts were produced by conventional machining techniques, while the butt was cut from a single piece of timber and often left unfinished.

This method of construction made the MG 42 about 30 percent cheaper to produce than the earlier MG 34, and it could be made in half the time: 75 hours instead of 150 hours.[39]

Receiver and component stamps

The left side of the receiver is stamped in the following form:

MG 42
XXXXX
cra

Where "MG 42" is the model designation, "XXXXX" denotes the serial number, and "cra" is the manufacturer's code, in this case MAGET. Serial numbers may also be found stamped on other components, including the cooling jacket, and the conventional eagle proof stamp of the Third Reich will also be found stamped on the receiver and barrel. There may also be a Waffenamt code number stamped on the weapon to show it has been inspected and accepted into service with the Third Reich. Barrels and other parts may bear stamps from a manufacturer that do not match those on the receiver. This is not uncommon and is the result of refurbishment or replacement of worn-out components.

Receiver stamps found on MG 42 (refer to text for precise designations) (courtesy James D. Julia Auctioneers, Fairfield, Maine. www.jamesdjulia.com).

Table Thirty-four. Factory codes found on MG 42 light machine guns

Factory	Manufacturers' code letters/numbers
Mauser: Mauser Werke AG	ar
	S/243
Steyr: Steyr Daimler Puch, A.G. Werk, Steyr, Austria	Bnz
	kls
	660
Berlin-Suhler-Waffen: BSW, Suhl, Germany renamed Wilhelm Gustloff Werke in 1939	337 (until 1939)
	bcd (1939–1945)
	936 (1940)
Johannes Grossfuss, AG: Döbeln, Sa	bpr
MAGET: Maschinenbau und Gerätebau GmbH, Berlin-Tegel	Cra

These code letters are found stamped on the left side rear of the receiver, in the format and position already described, although this may not be a complete list.[40]

Table Thirty-five. Specification of MG 42 light machine gun

Manufacturers	Mauser Werke AG
	Wilhelm-Gustloff-Stiftung
	Steyr-Daimler-Puch
	MAGET
	Johannes Grossfus AG
Period of production	1942 until 1945
Production	423,600
Operators	Germany (1942–1945)
Military service	World War II, Portuguese Colonial War, Yugoslav Wars, Syrian Civil War
Crew	Usually three men: Gunner, loader and spotter
Weight	25.5 lbs (11.57 kg)
Length/Barrel length	Total length: 48 inches (1.22m)
	Barrel: 21 inches (0.53m)
Mechanism	Air-cooled, recoil-operated, roller-locked fully automatic
Construction	Largely pressed steel and welded components, with only the bolt, barrel and some internal components requiring machining. This made the weapon much more reliable than the MG 34 under extreme conditions.
Caliber/Cartridge	7.92 × 57 Mauser German service rifle cartridge
Sights	Front: simple iron post
	Rears: Flip-up leaf
	Telescopic sight fitted when used as heavy machine gun
Accurate range	1,000 meters with telescopic sight
Maximum range	4.7 km (3 miles)
Rate of fire	Between 900 and 1,500 rpm depending upon bolt used
Price to manufacture in 1944	£25 ($100)
Time to complete	75 man hours

OPERATION

To operate a MG 42, the top of the receiver is first opened by operating the catch on the rear of the receiver cover. A belt of cartridges is then loaded in the same manner as the MG 34, before the receiver is closed and locked. The cocking handle on the right side is then drawn to the rear and pushed forwards until a click is heard, thus cocking the mechanism.

This weapon has a unique roller-locked bolt assembly consisting of a bolt head, two rollers, striker sleeve, bolt body, and a substantial return spring, which operates in the following manner: Pulling the trigger allows the bolt to move forward, removing a cartridge from the belt and chambering it, whereupon the rollers, which are positioned in grooves on the bolt head, are driven outwards into matching tracks in the barrel extension behind the breech by the striker sleeve, locking the bolt in place against the breech. The striker then moves forward, firing the cartridge. The recoil pushes the striker assembly back and the rollers move inwards, back to their previous position, unlocking the bolt head and allowing the bolt assembly to recoil, extracting the spent case and ejecting it. The return spring then pushes the bolt assembly forward again, pushing a new cartridge out of the belt into the breech, and the sequence is repeated for as long as the trigger is depressed, an MG 42 only being capable of fully automatic fire. Firing single shots by careful manipulation of the trigger is exceptionally difficult, even for experienced operators, due to the weapon's rate of fire, and gunners were usually trained so as to be able to fire a burst of no more than three rounds. Barrels, however, were designed to be changed quickly, being held in place by a simple hinged lock on the right side of the barrel jacket at the rear. To change a barrel, the gunner first cocks the weapon, before turning the barrel lock to the right and then pushing it forward, opening the barrel locking mechanism, which releases the breech, causing the barrel to move out of the jacket at an angle into the long slot on the right of the barrel jacket. The barrel is then removed, using some form of insulating material to protect the hands, and a cold barrel can then be inserted fully into the barrel jacket, after which the lock is snapped into its closed position and the gun is ready to fire.[41]

Military service

The MG 42 was accepted into service with the German armed forces in 1942 and it quickly proved to be a superior weapon. In particular, because its mechanism did not require the precise manufacturing tolerances of the MG 34, it was less susceptible to stoppages caused by the ingress of dirt and water and

Top: **Barrel release lever of MG 42.** *Bottom:* **Spare barrel for a MG 42, in its original cardboard box (both photographs courtesy James D. Julia Auctioneers, Fairfield, Maine. www.jamesdjulia.com).**

so proved far more reliable in combat conditions, particularly those encountered on the Eastern Front against Soviet troops. Its high rate of fire usually proved to be advantageous as well, not only because it was capable of providing a considerable degree of suppressive fire against the enemy, but the noise and general commotion caused when an MG 42 was fired also had a considerable psychological effect on the Allied troops who encountered it. Unfortunately, 1,200 rounds per minute used a lot of ammunition and caused excessive heating of the barrel, so firing rates often did not reflect the performance of which this truly innovative weapon was capable.[42]

Later developments

The MG 42 or derivatives of that weapon remained in service long after Germany's defeat and were copied by a number of manufacturers under license. Weapons based on the MG 42 include:

- MG 1 (MG42/51): This weapon was effectively a MG42 chambered for the 7.62 × 51mm NATO cartridge
- MG 1A3: A development of the MG1
- MG 3: A modified version of the MG1A3, manufactured in Germany by Rheinmetall and still in service with the German Bundeswehr
- Swiss MG 51

An MG3 in service with the German army.

- Zastava M53
- SIG MG 710–3
- Austrian MG 74
- Spanish Ameli light machine gun chambered for the 5.56 × 45mm NATO cartridge
- American M60
- Belgian FN MAG[43]

A pintle-mounted MG 3A1 on a Norwegian Leopard 1 armored recovery vehicle.

A Belgian FN MAG light machine gun, this weapon fitted with a C79 optical sight (courtesy Wikipedia: License: CC-A-3.0 U).

An American M60 GPMG (General Purpose Machine Gun).

Values

Working MG 42 light machine guns imported into the U.S. and registered before 1986 are transferable between owners. Consequently, these weapons are sometimes offered for sale, although condition is quite variable. Local regulations as they apply to these weapons should be consulted before purchase.

Prices are for weapons capable of firing.

NRA Good: $35,000; NRA Fine: $42,000 depending upon provenance

Light Machine Guns in Use By U.S. and European Armed Forces After World War I

Only the most commonly encountered weapons are included here and consequently this should not be regarded as a complete list.

American armed forces

Browning Automatic Rifle

Production: records not readily available, possibly 100,000 weapons.

Main US LMG in World War II and still in use in Vietnam some twenty years later.

British and Commonwealth armed forces

Bren gun

Production: 400,000 weapons.

Main British LMG and although a good weapon for the period, its lower rate of fire and magazine delivery system, convinced some operators that it was inferior to the German MG 42. In reality, the high rate of fire of the MG 42 was usually limited by both the ammunition supply and the tendency of the barrel to overheat after firing about 250 rounds. Under battlefield conditions, the Bren, with its five-round burst technique, could fire for longer periods and its barrel-changing mechanism was both quicker and more convenient than the system used in the German MG 34 and MG 42.

Lewis gun

British LMG of World War I vintage, mostly in use by the Home Guard and second-line forces during World War II.

Vickers-Berthier

Production: precise records unavailable, estimated at 10,000 weapons.

The Vickers-Berthier light machine gun was a gas-operated, selective-fired, air-cooled weapon, firing from an open bolt and having a firing rate of between 450 and 600 rpm. During firing, the bolt was tilted vertically and locked by a single lug on the top surface, the mechanism being powered by residual gas pressure acting upon a long-stroke piston contained in a cylinder fitted below the barrel. Cartridges were supplied to the breech from a box magazine mounted on top of the receiver, spent cases being ejected through an ejection slot in the bottom of that component. A wooden butt stock and a pistol grip were usually fitted, with a folding bipod attached to gas tube. The Mark 1 Vickers-Berthier also had short wooden foregrip under the front section of the receiver and a detachable monopod under the butt. The shape of the butt and foregrip was changed over time with introduction of successive versions of the gun.

Vickers-Berthier Mk.1

This was the first production model, introduced commercially in 1928 and fitted with a short foregrip under the receiver and a finned barrel.

Vickers-Berthier Mk.2

This weapon, which began production in 1931 at the request of the Indian government, has a lighter foregrip, no monopod under the butt, and a barrel without cooling fins.

Vickers-Berthier Mk.3

This was a modification of the Mk.2 Vickers-Berthier, introduced in 1933 and subsequently adopted by the Indian Army. Some parts were strengthened, the foregrip was omitted, and a carrying handle was added to the barrel, which had been redesigned to allow that component to be changed quickly. Vickers-Berthier Mk.3 light machine guns were produced by Nickers-Armstrong in Britain and the Ishapore Rifle factory in India.[44]

Vickers G.O. Machine gun

Production: precise records unavailable, estimated at 50,000 weapons.

Vickers G.O. No.1 air service machine gun

A modification of the original Vickers-Berthier light machine gun. The Vickers G.O. (Gas Operated) machine gun, also known as the Vickers "Class K" machine gun, was a gas-operated fully automatic weapon, firing from an open bolt, with the gas cylinder located below the barrel and containing a long-stroke gas piston operating the vertically tilting bolt mechanism and giving a firing rate of between 950 and 1,200 rpm. Cartridges are supplied to the breech from a flat pan magazine mounted on top of the weapon, which were designed to hold 100 cartridges, although it was customary to load only 96 or 97 rounds into each magazine to prevent stoppages. The Class K is fitted with a single spade grip at the rear of the receiver, which also incorporates the trigger. When air service weapons were used by the British army, they were normally mounted on single or twin pintle mounts and fitted to a variety of vehicles, vehicle allocation usually being determined by availability.

Vickers GO No.2 Mk.1 Land Service machine gun

This weapon differs from the earlier variant in having the spade grip replaced with short wooden stock and a pistol grip incorporating the trigger below the receiver. A short foregrip or a folding carrying handle was fitted below the piston cylinder, and a folding bipod was attached to the gas block. New iron sights are provided on folding bases.[45]

French armed forces

FM1924/M29

Production: precise records unavailable, estimated at 190,400 weapons.
The standard French light machine gun in use during World War II.

German armed forces

MG 13

Production: precise records unavailable, estimated at 20,000 weapons.
The MG 13 is an air-cooled, selective-fire light machine gun, with a short-recoil mech-

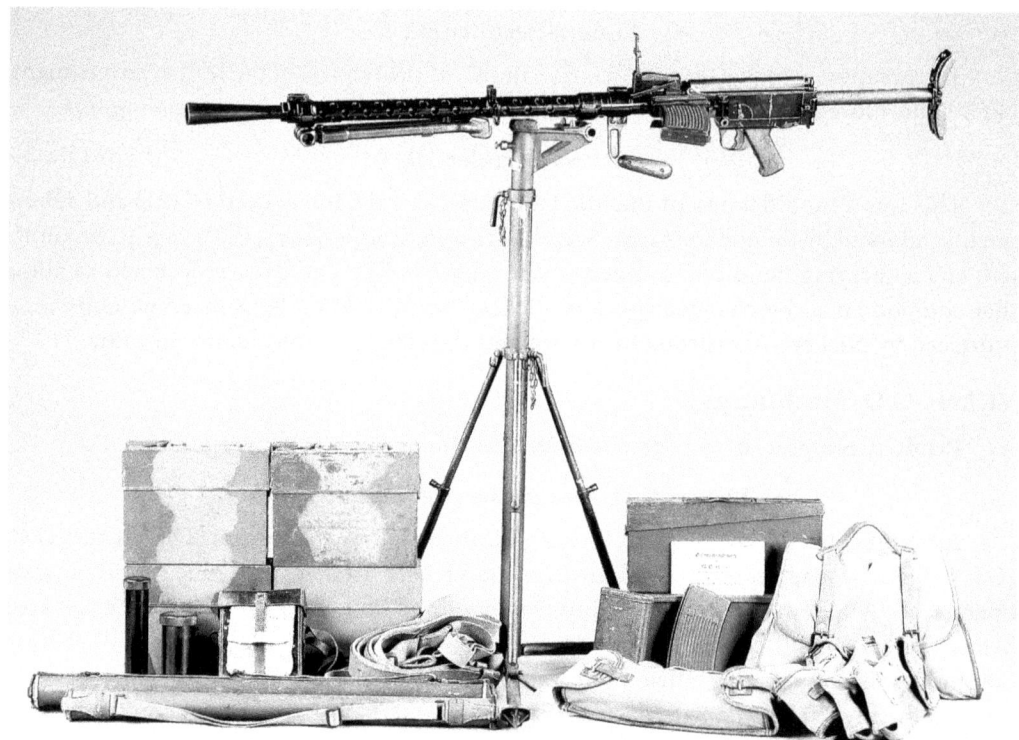

Mg 13 LMG mounted on a tripod and surrounded by ammunition boxes and other equipment (courtesy James D. Julia Auctioneers, Fairfield, Maine. www.jamesdjulia.com).

anism, firing from a closed bolt and with a firing rate of 500 rpm. It was chambered for the 7.92 × 57mm German service rifle cartridge, ammunition being delivered from either a detachable box magazine holding 25 cartridges or a 75-round "saddle" drum magazine, similar to that used with the MG 34. It has a "rocking trigger" similar to the MG 34 and a manual safety on the left side of the receiver, with a pistol grip and folding butt. Based upon the original water-cooled Dreyse 1918, the MG 13 was actually produced by simply rebuilding a number of these earlier weapons as air-cooled LMGs. The MG 13 designation was adopted in an attempt to represent this newly developed weapon as an older 1913 Model to the Allied Control Commission, which was enforcing the Versailles treaty.[46]

MG 15

Production: precise records unavailable, estimated at 50,000 weapons.

Although it shares the model designation with the Bergmann MG 15 used in World War I, this weapon has nothing else in common with the earlier weapon, having been devel-

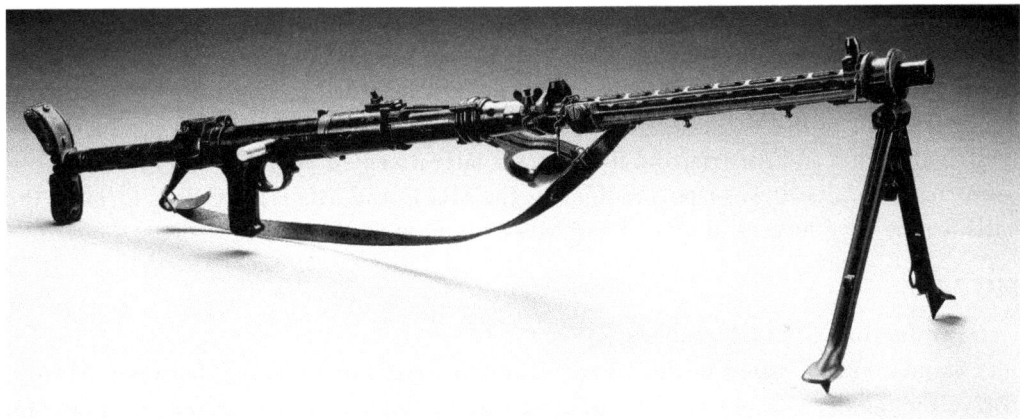

MG 15 from the left, showing the robust cocking handle and skeleton butt (courtesy James D. Julia Auctioneers, Fairfield, Maine. www.jamesdjulia.com).

oped from the earlier MG 30 designed by a R&D subsidiary of Rheinmetall. This later MG 15 is an air-cooled, fully automatic LMG, with a rotating bolt, locking ring mechanism firing from an open bolt, with a firing rate of between 1,000 and 1,050 rpm. It was chambered for the 7.92 × 57mm German service rifle cartridge, ammunition being delivered from a detachable 75-round "saddle" drum magazine, similar to that used with the MG 34. Since the weapon had a firing rate slightly in excess of 1,000 rpm, a drum magazine would be

Saddlebag ammunition drums for use with an MG 15 (courtesy James D. Julia Auctioneers, Fairfield, Maine. www.jamesdjulia.com).

emptied in just over 4 seconds. It was usual to provide at least 10 additional magazines for each MG 15 fitted to an aircraft, not including the magazine already on the weapon, which gave each gun about 45 seconds of sustained fire. The MG 15 was used in nearly all Luftwaffe aircraft with a flexible-mount defensive position, although by 1941 it was being replaced by more modern weapons based upon the MG 34. However, such was the shortage of equipment in the Werhmacht that many MG 15s originally used by the air force were modified for land use as better, heavier caliber weapons replaced them on German aircraft. A later variant, the MG 17, was designed to use both magazines and ammunition supplied in a 250-round belt and a rate of fire increased to 1,200 rpm.[47]

MG 30

Production: precise records unavailable, estimated at 50,000 weapons.

This is an air-cooled, recoil-operated, selective-fire weapon, chambered for the 7.92 × 57mm Mauser service rifle cartridge, which was supplied to the breech from a slightly curved magazine holding 30 cartridges inserted in the left side of the weapon and having a firing rate of between 600 to 800 rpm. Selection of either semiautomatic or fully automatic operation was controlled by manipulation of the two-position trigger, in a manner similar to the MG 34. Although the German government was forced to reject the design due to the restrictions of the Versailles Treaty, its designer, Rheinmetall, licensed production in both Switzerland and Austria, and the gun was later accepted by the armed forces of both countries. The MG 30 was later modified as the MG 15 and MG 17, as well as forming the basis for the very successful MG 34 and MG 42 light machine guns.[48]

MG 34

Production: 577,000 weapons.

Standard LMG issued at squad level to land forces of the Wehmacht between 1934 and 1942, although the MG 34 was still produced after the introduction of the superior MG 42.

MG 81

Production: precise records unavailable, estimated at 200,000 weapons.

Air-cooled, fully automatic, belt-fed variant of the MG 34, also chambered for the 7.92 × 57mm Mauser German service rifle cartridge and with a firing rate of between 1,400 and 1,600 rounds per minute. A version with a twin side-by-side mounting designated the MG 81Z was introduced in 1942, and fitted in the Dornier Do 217. It was also manufactured as an externally mounted pod holding three MG 81Zs and their ammunition, which was usually fitted to the Ju87 Stuka or Ju88 under the wing.[49]

MG 42

Production: 423,600 weapons.

The first really successful GPMG with a phenomenal firing rate of 1,200 rounds per minute, produced in Germany between 1942 and 1945.

MG 45 (MG 42V)

Production: Only 10 prototypes.

Using the same manufacturing processes as the MG 42, this was fitted with a different delayed blowback mechanism. This change, as well as the cheaper steel used in its construction, produced a weapon weighing only 9 kg and with an improved firing rate of 1,350 rpm in its standard configuration. Other factors operating against Germany's industrial capacity meant that only ten were produced, however, and it was never accepted into service.[50]

MG 3

Production: precise records unavailable, estimated at 100,000 weapons.

The MG 3 is a modern GPMG, developed from the MG 42, and manufactured by Rheinmetall from 1968. It is an air-cooled, fully automatic weapon with a roller-locked, recoil-operated bolt mechanism, firing from an open bolt with a rate of fire of between 700 and 1,200 rpm, depending upon the model. The weapon is chambered for the 7.62 × 51mm NATO cartridge and ammunition is supplied to the mechanism by a non-disintegrating 50-round belt or a 100-round belt with disintegrating links, both entering the receiver from the left. The barrel is chrome-lined to increase its service life and has a quick-change mechanism similar to that of the MG 42, but in the MG 3, the hot barrel can be dropped out of the gun by elevating the weapon, rather than needing to be grasped and then removed.

It is still in use with the armed forces of a number of countries as an infantry support weapon and vehicle-mounted machine gun (2017), but it has been replaced in service with the German military by the Heckler & Koch MG5 GPMG.

Earlier variants

- **MG1** (MG42/51): This weapon was effectively an MG 42 chambered for the 7.62 × 51mm NATO cartridge.
- **MG 1A1** (MG42/58): MG1 modified by fitting a chrome barrel and recalibrating the sights for the NATO cartridge.
- **MG 1A3:** MG1 with improvements to bolt, muzzle booster and bipod.
- **MG 2:** An MG 42 originally chambered for 7.92 × 57 mm Mauser and subsequently converted to use the 7.62 × 51 NATO cartridge.[51]

Italian Armed Forces

Breda M1930

Production: precise records unavailable, estimated at 30,000 weapons by 1940.

This was an air-cooled, fully automatic weapon with a simple blowback mechanism, firing from a closed bolt, with a rate of fire of 500 rpm. It was chambered for the relatively low-powered 6.5 × 52mm Carcano cartridge, which was delivered to the breech from a fixed, non-detachable magazine on the right side of the gun, hinged at the front and holding 20 rounds in two rows. There was no primary extraction mechanism, so each cartridge was lightly oiled before it entered the chamber to facilitate extraction. A wooden shoulder stock was fitted together with a pistol grip adjacent to the trigger and a folding bipod, attached to the barrel casing. To load a Breda M1930, the magazine is unlocked and swung forward until its opening is exposed to the operator. Fresh cartridges are then loaded into the magazine using special 20-round U-shaped "stripper" clips, which need to be pushed all the way into the magazine for loading, and then withdrawn manually, in a manner

Italian Breda LMG, one of the worst LMGs produced during World War II (courtesy Wikipedia: License: CC-A-S-A 3.0 U).

similar to a conventional bolt-action rifle. According to the men who used it, the Breda M1930 could have qualified for the worst machine gun ever invented, even worse in some ways than the deplorable old French Chauchat. The oiled cartridges had an almost supernatural attraction for sand and dust, and during service in North Africa the Breda proved to be almost useless, jamming after only a few rounds usually because debris of some sort had found its way into the mechanism. The closed-bolt blowback mechanism was prone to "cooking off" and recoiled violently when fired, making accuracy impossible, and both the rear and front sights were mounted on the body of the gun, which meant that the weapon had to be re-zeroed every time a barrel was changed.

The absence of any system for primary extraction, together with the weak cartridge, also frequently resulted in a cartridge jammed in the mechanism beyond the hope of a repair in the field.[52]

Japanese Armed Forces

Nambu automatic machine guns

Although these guns were manufactured in Japan between 1918 and 1940, they were based on the Hotchkiss designs, with a few modifications to deal with the specialized conditions under which the Japanese army found itself operating. Produced as:

Type11

Production: 29,000.

Based upon the Hotchkiss M1909, this was an air-cooled, gas-operated, selective-fire LMG, chambered originally for the 6.5 × 50mm Arisaka cartridge and having a firing rate of approximately 450 rpm. The loading mechanism differed from the standard Hotchkiss, the Type 11 having a hopper designed to hold six of the same five-round cartridge clips used on the Type 38 rifle, which were stacked so as to lie flat above the receiver before being secured by a spring arm. As the weapon was fired, a cartridge was removed from the lowest clip, the empty clip being ejected and the next clip automatically falling into place as the gun was fired.

Japanese light machine guns licensed for production from other manufacturers

Type 1

Production: precise records unavailable.
Based upon the German MG 15 and chambered for the 7.92 × 63mm Mauser cartridge, this weapon was designed for air service.

Type 92

Production: precise records unavailable.
Based upon the original Lewis gun, but chambered for a copy of the .303R British, the 7.7 × 56R Type 87 IJN cartridge, and designed for air service with the Japanese Navy. It performed poorly and was soon replaced by Type 1 and Type 2 weapons.[53]

SOVIET ARMED FORCES

DP28 machine gun (Degtyaryov infantry machine gun)

Production: 795,000 weapons of all variants (DP, DPM, DA, DT).
Designed by Vasily Degtyaryov, this is an air-cooled, gas-operated LMG that fires from an open bolt and is chambered for the 7.62 × 54mmR Russian service rifle cartridge, giving the weapon a firing rate of 550 rpm in its earliest variant. Cartridges are supplied to the mechanism from a pan magazine holding 47 rounds and the barrel was designed for quick changes when it overheated. This original version had several flaws, principally: the bipod tended to break, and the recoil spring tended to lose its temper and break, because it was located under the barrel in a position where it was prone to adverse changes in temperature.

Variants

DPM (DP, MODIFIED)

Production: precise records unavailable.
An improved version of the DP 28 adopted by the Red Army between 1943 and 1944. It was fitted with a stronger bipod fastened to the cooling jacket and the recoil spring was protected from heating by being housed in a tube projecting from the rear of the receiver, a change that necessitated a pistol grip for this model of the weapon.

Type 53: Production: precise records unavailable.
Copy of the DPM manufactured under license in China.

DA

Production: 1,200 weapons between 1928 and 1930.
A version of the DPM for use in air service and having a rate of fire of 600 rpm. It was also fitted in a in a tandem mount, when it was designated the DA-2, although both

types were quickly superseded by the ShKas heavy machine gun, which had a much higher rate of fire.

DT AND DTM

Production: precise records unavailable.
A version of the DPM designed to be mounted in an armored vehicle.

RP-46

This was a considerably modernized version of the DPM adopted in 1946. It was designed to use a metallic belt, with a heavier barrel allowing longer periods of sustained fire and an adjustable gas system, with three holes of increasing diameter designed to cope with varying environmental conditions and residue buildup. Approximately 500 rounds could be fired continuously before the barrel had to be swapped or allowed to cool. Although when empty the RP-46 was 2.5 kg heavier than a DPM, with a single ammunition box of 250 rounds, the RP-46 weighed 10 kg less than a DPM with the same amount of ammunition in five pan magazines. One useful feature of the gun was that, by removing its belt-feeding system, it could still fire from DP-pattern magazines. The RP-46 remained in Soviet service for 15 years before it was replaced by the PK machine gun.

Type 58: **Production:** precise records unavailable.
RP-46 made under license in China.
Type 64: **Production:** precise records unavailable.
RP-46 made under license in China.[54]

ShKAS aircraft machine gun:

Production:

The full name of this unusual weapon is the Shpitalny-Komaritski Aviatsionny Skorostrelny (trans: Shpitalny-Komaritski rapid fire for aircraft). It is a gas-operated, fully automatic LMG with a firing rate of 1,800 rpm, designed to be sited in the wing of an aircraft and chambered for the 7.62 × 54mmR Russian service rifle cartridge. The mechanism is unique in being based upon a revolving drum or cage holding ten rounds, which allowed the cartridges to be removed smoothly and precisely from their disintegrating-link belt. This mechanism, together with the light, recoiling portion of the gun, which weighs only 921 grams, was crucial in giving the gun its high rate of fire. The first prototype, designated "426," appeared in 1932, and the weapon proved to be remarkably successful, being fitted to most Soviet fighters of the period and with a number of later models entering production.

Variants

The prefix "KM" indicates that these were production models.

KM-33

Production: precise records unavailable.
This was the first production version, which was fitted into the Soviet version of a Scarff ring mounted in a turret and appeared in 1933.

KM-35

Production: precise records unavailable.

Also designed initially for use in a ring mounting, although the same weapon was modified to be used in a wing mounting in 1935.

KM-36

Production: precise records unavailable.

Another version designed initially for use in a ring mounting. The same weapon was also modified to operated as a propeller-synchronized weapon in 1937 and fitted with a longer barrel to facilitate this type of installation. It also had a higher cyclic rate of 2,000 rpm.

Ammunition supply: 750 rounds for the wing-mounted models and between 1,000 and 1,500 rounds for weapons mounted in a Scarff-pattern ring. Despite its excellent performance, the ShKAS was not without its problems, as one Soviet machine gun technician recalled: "The ShKAS machine gun had a high rate of fire but it also had 48 ways of jamming. Some of them could be fixed immediately, some could not. And 1,800 rounds a minute was an insanely high rate of fire. If you pulled the trigger too long, the ShKAS would fire all its ammo in one go and that would be it!!"[55]

Chapter Nineteen

Heavy Machine Gun and Automatic Cannon Development After World War I

Heavy machine guns did not show the same degree of innovation as their smaller, lighter counterparts except in America, where John Browning was continuing to show his usual design skill and flair for weapons development, with the production of the Model 1919 and .50 caliber M1921, which was the basis for the air-cooled M2.

The tactical use of the heavy machine gun had also changed during the interwar years, HMGs now being almost wholly confined to static roles, except in the U.S. army, where the M1919 was deployed in various configurations as an infantry support weapon, operated by a specialist machine gun platoon within an infantry company. Most of the other Allied armies and Axis forces had abandoned the HMG in this role and relied upon their excellent LMG designs, the MG 34 being the first modern GPMG which could be configured as both a light and heavy machine gun, as well as serving as a light AA gun.

American Heavy Machine Gun Development After World War I

Two heavy machine gun designs appeared in America between the wars, the Browning M1919 and the Browning M2. Both were usually deployed in static defensive positions or as aircraft gun, the weight of such weapons, particularly the M2, precluding a more mobile role.

The Browning M1919 .30 Caliber Machine Gun

The Browning M1919 was developed from Browning's original Model 1917 water-cooled heavy machine gun. The two weapons have an exactly similar mechanism, which was also used in the larger M2 machine gun, chambered for the .5 BMG cartridge (Browning Machine Gun, 12.7 × 99mm NATO).

Some time before World War II, the U.S. army had begun to develop the tank, with the intention that it should become a major factor in military operations, and they needed a reliable machine gun to supplement the vehicles' main armament. Unfortunately, the

Nineteen. Heavy Machine Gun and Automatic Cannon Development

original water-cooled M1917 proved unsuitable as a tank weapon because it was too heavy and the cumbersome water jacket got in the way. Consequently, Browning modified the M1917, using a shorter, heavier, air-cooled barrel to improve cooling under sustained fire, but retaining the basic operating mechanism. It was this modified weapon that was introduced into U.S. military service as the M1919.[1]

SPECIFICATION

Production: precise records not available, but estimated at more than 5 million weapons of all types.

The M1919 is an air-cooled, recoil-operated, fully automatic light machine gun with a cyclic rate of between 400 and 600 rpm, firing from a closed bolt. It has a perforated jacket with cooling holes surrounding the fixed barrel and the cocking handle on the right side of the receiver. It was originally chambered for the .30–06 Springfield U.S. service rifle cartridge when deployed with U.S. forces, but weapons made after 1938 were chambered for the .30 caliber M2 ball cartridge introduced in that year. Versions were also produced which used a number of other military cartridges. The top cover of the receiver is hinged

Water-cooled Model 1928 M1919, made by Colt, showing the adjustable tripod, cocking lever, pistol grip, rear sight and water tank plug (courtesy James D. Julia Auctioneers, Fairfield, Maine. www.jamesdjulia.com).

at the front so as to allow access to the mechanism in the event of a stoppage, cartridges being fed to the gun by a woven cloth belt, until the Korean War, when infantry units first began to use disintegrating belts of M1 links, although steel link disintegrating belts were used in M1919s designed for air service during World War II.[2] Butts were not fitted to the Model 1919 until the appearance of the M1919A6, the weapon being aimed and controlled by means of a pistol grip mounted on the rear of the receiver, with the triggering lever also being mounted on the back of the receiver below this component and fitted so that it could be conveniently operated by the gunner when he grasped the pistol grip. Some weapons may also be found converted to the older pattern of "spade" grips found on the M1917, especially guns sold or supplied in the postwar era to U.S. allies, such as Israel. Both firing systems require the Browning to be mounted on a substantial tripod when in use. A single pattern of tripod was issued with the M1919 for infantry use, designated the M2, which was adjustable for elevation by the use of a substantial screw fitting, although it could be freely traversed about its horizontal axis. Guns used in tanks or for air service were fitted with mountings designed for these applications. Iron sights were fitted, the front sight having the form of a small folding post at the front edge of the receiver, while the rear sight is an aperture sight mounted on a sliding leaf and calibrated from 200 to 1,800 meters in 200-meter increments, with a windage (left-right) adjustment dial on the right side. When folded down, the aperture in the rear sight formed a notch that could be used to fire the gun immediately without raising the leaf.[3]

Receiver stamps

Receiver stamps take a variety of forms, depending upon the company responsible for a weapon's manufacture. The side plate markings for the Saginaw Steering Gear division of General Motors are representative and have the following form, although all the markings will include the model, caliber and serial number, wherever they were manufactured:

NO. XXXXXXX U.S. INSP.
BROWNING MACHINE GUN
U.S.. CAL.30 M1919A
MAN'FD BY DLO MFG. STAMFORD, CT
SAGINAW STEERING GEAR DIV.
GENERAL MOTORS CORPORATION

Where "NO XXXXXX" is the serial number, "U.S. INSP." is the inspection mark, "US. CAL .30" is the cartridge for which the weapon is designed, and "M1919A" is the model designation.

Receiver stamp found on Model 1928 M1919 HMG (courtesy James D. Julia Auctioneers, Fairfield, Maine. www.jamesdjulia.com).

Nineteen. Heavy Machine Gun and Automatic Cannon Development

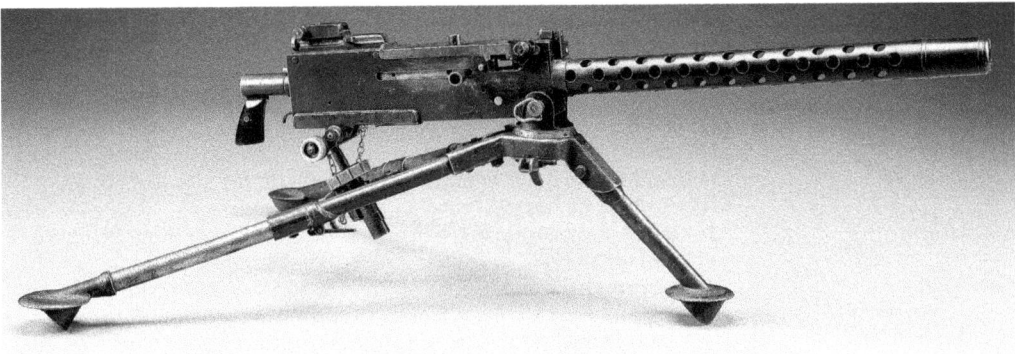

M1919 HMG mounted on the characteristic M2 tripod (courtesy James D. Julia Auctioneers, Fairfield, Maine. www.jamesdjulia.com).

Typical receiver stamp found on M1919 (courtesy James D. Julia Auctioneers, Fairfield, Maine. www.jamesdjulia.com).

Table Thirty-six. Specification of the Browning M1919 .30 caliber machine gun

Principal Manufacturers	**U.S. Government arsenals:** Rock Island Arsenal **Commercial manufacturers:** Saginaw Steering Gear division of the General Motors Corporation Buffalo Arms Corporation BSA (UK)
Period of production	1919–1945
Production	Estimated to be in excess of 5 million weapons of all types and calibers
Operators	Argentina, Australia, Brazil, Britain, Canada, Chile, France, Greece, Iran, Ireland, Israel, Italy, Rhodesia, South Africa, South Korea, USA, plus many others.
Military service	1919 until present (2017) Banana Wars, World War II, Korean War, First Indochina War,

	Congo Crisis, Vietnam War (1963–1975), Rhodesian Bush War, Six-Day War, Cambodian Civil War, Syrian Civil War
Crew	Usually two: gunner and loader, although extra personnel were required to carry the tripod and ammunition boxes
Weight	M1919A4: 31 lbs (14 kg)
	M1919A6: 32.5 lb (14.7 kg)
Length/Barrel length	M1919A4: 38 inches (964mm)/24 inches (610mm)
	M1919A6: 53 inches (964mm)/24 inches (610mm)
Mechanism	Air-cooled, fully automatic, belt-fed, short-recoil operation, firing from a closed bolt
Cartridge	.30–06 Springfield (U.S.), 7.62 × 51mm NATO, .303 British, 7.92 × 57mm Mauser, 6.5 × 55mm Swedish, 7.62 × 54mmR 8 × 63mm Patron m/32, 7.65 × 53mm Argentine, 7.5 × 54mm French Supplied to the gun by a 250-round belt, of either canvas or as a disintegrating belt composed of M1 links.
Sights	Front sight: simple post
	Rear sight: adjustable aperture leaf graduated from 200 to 1,800 meters in 200-meter increments
Rate of fire	400 to 600 rpm
Effective range	1,500 yards (1,400 meters)
Cost	$667 in 1919, decreasing to a final price of $141.44 in 1940

OPERATION

Operation is exactly similar to the earlier water-cooled M1917 and, like the M1917, the M1919 is loaded by inserting the tab of an ammunition belt into the left side of the gun until the pawl at the receiver opening or feedway engaged the belt.

With a belt loaded, the cocking handle is pulled to the rear and then released, positioning a cartridge for loading. Operating the cocking handle a second time moves the first cartridge into the chamber and the second round into the position previously occupied by the first round, making it ready for chambering after the first cartridge has been fired. The M1919 is now ready to fire, with a round in the chamber, the bolt and barrel group locked together, and the locking block at the rear of the bolt. Operating the trigger lever disengages the sear and allows the spring-loaded striker to move forward and strike the cartridge primer. The mechanism then recoils, cocking the striker and ejecting the spent case from the chamber and positioning a new cartridge in the extractor, before the bolt recoil spring pushes the bolt forward, chambering the fresh round. With a cartridge in the chamber, the bolt and barrel are locked together by the locking block and if the trigger is still depressed, the striker moves forward, firing the cartridge. As with all weapons of this type, firing continues as long as the trigger is depressed and there is ammunition in the belt.

Firing as it does from a closed bolt with an air-cooled barrel made the M1919 prone to "cook off." In order to prevent this, gunners were trained to fire an M1919 in controlled bursts of three to five rounds, with an interval between bursts to reduce barrel heating, which was necessary because the barrel could not be changed quickly. Gunners were also taught to cock the gun with the palm facing up, so that in the event of a cook-off, their thumb wouldn't be dislocated or broken by the reciprocating cocking handle.[4]

The M1 Link

The M1 link, was the U.S. military designation for a steel disintegrating link designed to hold the .30–06 Springfield cartridge fired by the M1917 Browning machine gun and M1919 Browning machine gun and introduced during World War II. Two links were held together by a single cartridge, more being added to make up a belt holding any number of cartridges, although a belt holding 250 rounds was most commonly used.

On the left side of each link was a circular loop that would hold the cartridge case, and an extension on the right was formed with two similar loops designed to form a link with the single loop of the next link. The rear loop on the right side of the link would be positioned on the cartridge case just above the base, with the left side loop of the next link above it. The front loop of the right side of the link was positioned on the neck of the cartridge, and was therefore slightly smaller in diameter.

In operation, the pawl designed to move the belt would pull the belt to the right as the gun was fired or cocked, sending the loose link out of the right side of the receiver, while the expended case was dropped vertically below the gun. This disintegrating system was a considerable improvement over the earlier canvas belts and contrasted with more modern designs like the system used in the excellent German MG 34 and MG 42 machine guns, which used metal links that did not detach from each other during the firing process.[5]

VARIATIONS

Seven variants of the basic M1919 machine gun have been produced since 1921 for land service, including the first M1919 Model.

M1919 Model

Production: precise records not available, estimated at fewer than 1,000 weapons.

The first standard model produced with a heavy 18-inch air-cooled barrel for fitting in tanks.

M1919A1

Production: precise records not available, estimated at fewer than 1,000 weapons.

A lighter version of the M1919, which was fitted with a lighter 18-inch barrel and a bipod.

M1919A2

Production: precise records not available, but estimated at fewer than 1,000 weapons.

Another lightweight version of the M1919, developed for cavalry units and fitted with the shorter 18-inch barrel and a special tripod, although it could also be fitted to the tripod used for the M1917, as well as the standard M2 tripod. It was in service for a short period after World War I, while the cavalry was converting to wheeled and tracked vehicles.

M1919A3

Production: precise records not available, estimated at fewer than 1,000 weapons.

An improved version of the M1919A2.

M1919A4

Production: precise records not available, estimated at over 4 million weapons.

The most common variant in the M1919 series, this weapon featured a number of improvements over the earlier weapons, which included:

- Increasing the length of the barrel to 24 inches.
- Repositioning the front sight on the front of the receiver and moving the rear sight to a mounting on the left side plate of the receiver.
- A fitting to allow the top cover to be held open.
- Improvements to the belt feed lever.
- Fitting a more convenient handle to the latch securing the top cover.
- The design of the rivets holding the rear of the top plate to the side plate was improved.

The M1919A4 was used in both fixed and flexible aircraft and vehicle mountings as well as by infantry units. It was also widely exported after World War II and continues to be used in small numbers around the world.[6]

M1919A5

A variant of the M1919A4 manufactured as a new weapon, and fitted with an extended charging handle for mounting in vehicles such as the Willys MB "Jeep."

M1919A4E1

An M1919A4 that was converted to the M1919A5 specification.

M1919A6

Production: precise records not available, estimated at 53,000 weapons.

This weapon was designed to provide U.S. forces with a more portable version of the M1919 and it incorporated a metal butt assembly fixed to the back plate of the gun, together with a lighter barrel fitted with a muzzle booster and a bipod similar to that used on the BAR. Despite these modifications the M1919A6 was an awkward weapon and heavier, at 15 kg (33 lb), than either the MG 34 or MG42, with which it was competing. It was eventually replaced in U.S. service by the vastly superior M60 machine gun in the 1960s.

T33

Production: precise records not available, estimated at 100,000 weapons.

Another version of the M1919 was produced for infantry use, designated the T33, which was an AM/M2 aircraft gun with a cyclic rate of 1,200 rpm, fitted with a butt from a M1919A6 and a set of sights from a BAR.

Adaptations of the M1919 for air service

The two most important adaptations of the M1919 for air service during World War II were the AN/M2 and the Browning .303 Mark II.

AN/M2

Production: precise records not available, estimated at 100,000 weapons.

This was a version of the Model 1919A4 specifically designed for aircraft and manufactured by Browning, with a cyclic rate of 1,150 rpm and thinner walls to both the barrel and receiver to keep down weight. It also incorporated a mechanism that allowed it to lift the loaded belt out of an ammunition box and feed it into the gun automatically. Perhaps as a result of this necessary complexity, amongst ordnance technicians the .30 caliber AN/M2 Browning was known for being the most difficult weapon to service and repair of all the U.S. military's small arms. It was used on U.S. combat aircraft early in World War II, but this lighter .30-caliber weapon was increasingly relegated to training duties as the war progressed, being replaced by an air service version of the M2. A derivative of this weapon was built by Colt for the civilian market and designated the MG40.

Browning .303 Mark II

Production: precise records not available, estimated at 500,000 weapons based upon the number of aircraft in service with the RAF.

The Browning Mark II was adopted by the Royal Air Force as a replacement for the .303 Vickers. Manufactured by Vickers Armstrong and BSA, it was chambered for the .303R British service rifle cartridge and had a cyclic rate of 1150 rounds per minute. Designated the Browning .303 Mk II in British service, it was essentially an AN/M2 modified to fire from an open bolt. Modifications were also introduced that allowed the Mark II to be fired both hydraulically as a wing mounted machine gun and as a manually operated weapon mounted in bombers and reconnaissance aircraft. The Browning .303 was fitted to:

- Early models of the Hawker Hurricane and Supermarine Spitfire, the RAF's "eight gun" fighters, as a wing-mounted machine gun.
- the Boulton Paul Defiant, Handley Page Halifax, Short Stirling, Avro Manchester, Avro Lancaster and the Short Sunderland flying boat as a turret gun, usually in a four-gun mounting.

POST–WORLD WAR II VERSIONS OF THE M1919

M37

Production: precise records not available, estimated at 50,000 weapons.

Between 1948 and 1952, the U.S. military were looking for an improved design of the M1919 that could be loaded from either side of the receiver for use on their M48 and M60 Patton medium tanks. The firm of Saco-Lowell developed a model that had the driving spring attached to the back plate (eliminating the need for a mainspring and driving rod on the back of the bolt), a bolt with dual tracks that could feed from either side, a feed cover that could also open from either side, together with a reversible belt feed pawl, ejector, and feed chute, as well as a solenoid trigger for remote firing. After the development of the T151 and T152 prototypes, the final T153 prototype was accepted into service as the M37, which was fitted with a pistol grip and back-up trigger like the M1919A4 and an extended charging handle similar to those on the M1919A5. The weapon was produced by SACO-Lowell and the Rock Island Arsenal between 1955 to 1957, being replaced by the M37E1, an M37 chambered for the 7.62 × 51 NATO cartridge, in the late 1960s. Subsequently, all the weapons based upon the M1919 were phased out and replaced by the M73A1 in the early 1970s.

M37C

Production: precise records not available, estimated at fewer than 2,000 weapons based upon the production of the OH-13 and OH-23 helicopters.

This weapon was a modification of the M37 without a sight bracket and designed for air service, typically with the XM1/E1 helicopter armament system, which was mounted on the skid landing gear of the OH-13 Sioux and OH-23 Raven helicopters.

Mk 21 Mod 0

Production: precise records not available, estimated at fewer than 100,000 weapons.

The Mk 21 Mod 0 was a conversion of the U.S. Navy's original .30 caliber M1919A4 Brownings, carried out during the period of the Vietnam War, so that those weapons could fire the new 7.62 × 51 NATO cartridge. The conversions were all performed at the Naval Ordnance Station, Louisville, Kentucky, and required the following changes:

- The barrel, bolt, and feed cover were replaced by new components of the appropriate size.
- A new chamber bushing, link-stripper and a second belt-holding pawl were fitted, to ensure that the NATO cartridge would both cycle and fire correctly.
- Spacer blocks were added to the front and back of the feedway to guide the shorter round and block the use of the longer .30–06 Springfield ammunition.
- A six-inch flash hider was also added to the barrel to reduce the muzzle flash from firing the shorter cartridge.

Modified M1919A4s had receivers stamped

Machine Gun, 7.62mm
Mk 21 Mod 0

Barrels were stamped

7.62mm NATO-G

The "G" indicating that the barrel had a grooved barrel bushing.

Versions of the M1919 produced outside the USA

In addition to the variations already described, there were an number of other weapons based upon the M1919 and manufactured by companies outside America, including:

- The Belgian FN30.
- The French FN-Browning Mle1938, chambered for the 7.5 × 54mm MAS cartridge.
- The Austrian MG A4.
- The South African MG4.
- The M/52–1, the designation of the M1919A4 in Danish service.
- The M/52–11, the designation for the M1919A5 in Danish service.
- The Ksp m/22, a M1919 built under license in Sweden, chambered for the 8 × 63mm patron m/22 cartridge and designed for air service.
- The Ksp m/39. A M1919A4 built under license in Sweden and available with the breech opening on either the right or left hand side of the receiver. The weapon was chambered

originally for either the 6.5 × 55mm Swedish Mauser cartridge or the 8 × 63mm patron m/32 Swedish heavy/medium machine gun cartridge, but from 1975 many of these weapons were rechambered for the 7.62 × 51mm NATO cartridge.
- The Ksp m/42. This was an M1919A6 built under license in Sweden. The weapon was chambered originally for either the 6.5 × 55mm Swedish Mauser cartridge or the 8 × 63mm patron m/32 Swedish heavy/medium machine gun cartridge, but from 1975 many of these weapons were rechambered for the 7.62 × 51mm NATO cartridge.
- The Ksp m/42B. This was a lighter version of the Ksp m/42, fitted with a bipod and conventional butt.
- The Ckm wz. 32. This was a Polish copy of the M1919, chambered for the 7.92 × 57mm Mauser German service rifle cartridge.[7]

Ammunition

The 30–06 Springfield U.S. service rifle cartridge is available in a number of types, including:

M2 ball: This is a conventional rifle cartridge.
Armor Piercing, M2: An armor-piercing round for use against lightly armored vehicles.
Incendiary, M1: For use against flammable targets without armor.
Tracer, M2: Tracer for observing fire, signaling, target designation, and incendiary purposes.

All of these cartridge types could be fired from an M1919, and it is probable that they were employed in a similar fashion to the rounds used in the M2HB heavy machine gun, in particular using four-to-one tracer for targeting purposes in both land and air service.[8]

Military service

When deployed as a company or battalion support weapon, the M1919 required at least a two-man machine gun team, although this was usually increased to four men: the gunner, responsible for operating the weapon and carrying the tripod and ammunition box; the assistant gunner, responsible for feeding the ammunition belt while in action as well as carrying the gun, spare parts and tools; and at least two other men, who carried extra ammunition.

The original M1919A1 had been introduced for land service in order to provide infantry units with a weapon that was easily transportable, and consequently, it was fitted with a light barrel and bipod. Unfortunately, it became clear very quickly that the weapon was too heavy to be easily moved and the barrel was too light to permit sustained fire. The gun was subsequently modified as the M1919A2, which included a heavier barrel and tripod, and could be continuously fired for longer periods. In 1940, a new version of the M1919, the M1919A4, was accepted into service with the U.S. military and this weapon saw action with infantry units and as secondary armament on jeeps, armored personnel carriers, tanks and amphibious vehicles as well as being modified for air service. The M1919A4 continued in service with U.S. forces after World War II and was rechambered for the 7.62 × 51 NATO cartridge for use as a tank gun and for U.S. naval service.[9]

Values

Working Browning M1919 fully automatic heavy machine guns registered in the USA before 1986 are transferable between owners. Consequently, these weapons are sometimes offered for sale, although only the M1919A4 is seen with any frequency and condition is quite variable. Local regulations as they apply to these weapons should be consulted before purchase.

Prices are for weapons capable of firing.

M1919A4: NRA Good: $25,000; NRA Fine: $30,000

There is also a considerable after-market trade in M1919s converted to semiautomatic operation, with kits available for DIY construction. The receivers of such weapons are modified so as to ensure that they cannot be converted to fully automatic operation.

The Browning M2 .50 Caliber Machine Gun

The development of a large-caliber heavy machine gun for U.S. forces began in 1918, at the direct request of General George Pershing, commander of the AEF, who wanted a gun capable of destroying military aircraft as well as the new, more heavily armored fighting vehicles then appearing on the Western Front. He specified that the weapon should be at least .50 inches in caliber, with a muzzle velocity of more than 2,700 fps (feet per second). Initial trials were conducted on some Colt machine guns, rechambered to use a French 11mm armor-piercing incendiary cartridge. This French round proved unsuitable because of its low muzzle velocity, and consequently the Winchester company began developing a cartridge to the necessary specification, which was to be fired from a modified M1917. It was this weapon that entered service with the U.S. military as the Model 1921 in 1929, chambered for the Winchester cartridge now designated the .50 caliber BMG (Browning Machine Gun) cartridge. Many in the U.S. military were doubtful of the weapon's effectiveness, and it was eventually relegated to the role of a static AA gun due to its excessive weight.

John Browning had died at his workbench in the FN factory in 1926. Development work on the M1921 was continued by

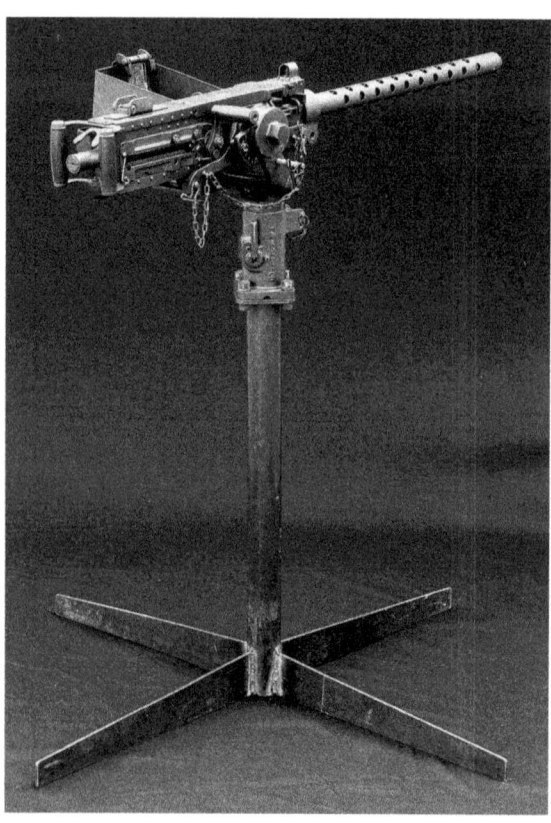

M2 on monopod mounting, showing the charging handle (courtesy James D. Julia Auctioneers, Fairfield, Maine. www.jamesdjulia.com).

Dr. S.H. Green, who produced a new version of the original M1921, designated the M2, with a receiver capable of accepting an ammunition belt from either the right or left side and which could be configured for a number of different roles. The most ubiquitous variant of this early weapon had a thick, air-cooled barrel and was designated the M2, Heavy Barrel or simply the "M2HB," and this was the type that proved most successful, being used as an infantry support weapon and in air and naval service with U.S. forces during World War II. After World War II, the .50-caliber M2HB was adopted by the armed forces of many countries and is still widely used as both an infantry support weapon and vehicle gun by many of the NATO allies, with production of new M2HB guns being continued in the USA by General Dynamics and in Belgium by FN Herstal.[10]

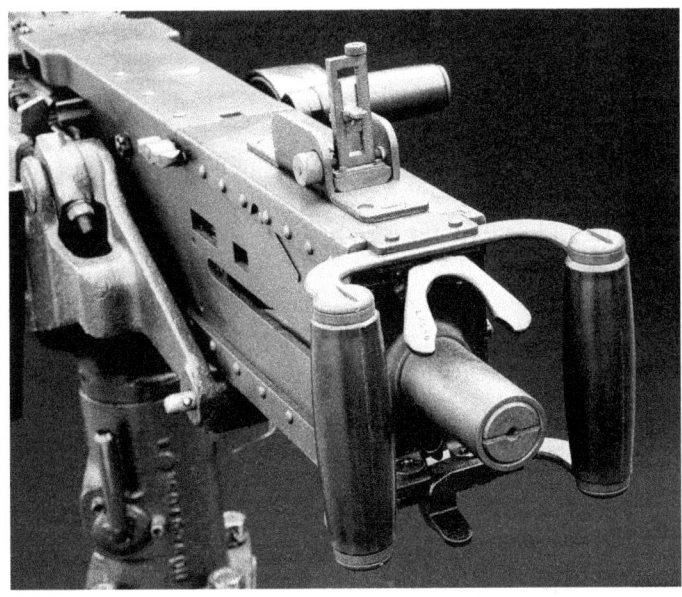

Operating handles of M2 HMG and the butterfly pattern firing lever (courtesy James D. Julia Auctioneers, Fairfield, Maine. www.jamesdjulia.com).

Specification

Production: precise records not available, but estimated at over 3 million weapons of all types.

The Browning M2 is a selective-fire, belt-fed, air-cooled heavy machine gun, firing from a closed bolt, with a short, perforated cooling shroud surrounding the barrel where it enters the receiver. It is chambered for the .50 caliber BMG cartridge, which was supplied to the mechanism by a canvas belt until 1950, when disintegrating belts composed of M2 links were introduced for land service, although like the M1919, disintegrating belts had been in use for air service since 1943. M2s have a short-recoil mechanism, which is exactly the same as the earlier water-cooled M1917 and air-cooled M1919 heavy machine guns, giving a cyclic rate on fully automatic of between 450 rpm for an AA gun and 1,200 rpm for an AN/M2 fitted with a feed booster. In addition to fully automatic operation, the M2HB has settings that allow it to fire single shots or operate as a fully automatic weapon firing at fewer than 40 rounds per minute. Firing is controlled by two "spade" handles, like the M1917, with a V-shaped, "butterfly" pattern trigger and a bolt release mounted below the trigger, between those handles. Depressing and locking down the bolt release causes the gun to function in fully automatic mode, while unlocking the release sets the weapon to single-shot operation. However, one disadvantage of the M2HB is that no trigger block is fitted, and gunners sometimes alleviate this problem by placing an expended cartridge case under the trigger to act as a safety block. On the infantry weapon, a folding blade front sight is mounted on the front edge of the receiver and protected by a semicircular sight cover. The rear sight is mounted on the rear of the receiver and takes the form of a substantial flip-up, leaf pattern sight, with a knurled elevating screw on top of the leaf frame and a windage adjustment knob mounted on the right of the sight frame. This rear sight is adjustable from 100 to 2,600 yards, in 100-yard increments. Various types of telescopic and night sights can also be installed, using appropriate the mountings.

An M2HB can be converted to load a cartridge belt from either the left or right, an experienced gunner being able to perform this conversion in a little under two minutes. It is also possible to change the charging handle from the right to the left side, and these two changes make it possible for the gun to be operated in a tandem mounting, a common configuration aboard USN vessels. Unfortunately, barrel changing on the original M2HB was a complex operation, so operating procedures and, consequently, firing rates were modified to minimize barrel heating and subsequent wear. However, in 2010, a new weapon was introduced, the M2A1, which incorporated a quick-change barrel with fixed head space and timing, thus improving the old design and bringing it more in line with its modern competitors.[11]

Receiver stamps

Browning M2HB heavy machine guns are stamped on the right side of the receiver, under the ejection port, in the following form:

U.S. NO. XXXXXXX GVT. INSP.
MACHINE GUN CAL .50-M3-AC-BASIC
SPRINGFIELD ARMORY
SPRINGFIELD MASS
PATENT NOS. REI9159 1803349
1803352 1919244 1936254 2110165

Where "U.S. NO. XXXXXXX" is the serial number, "GVT. INSP" is the inspection stamp, "MACHINE GUN CAL .50-M3-AC-BASIC" is the designation of the gun and "SPRINGFIELD ARMORY" is the place of manufacture.

In addition to the receiver stamp, serial numbers may be found on other components, such as the barrel.

Headspace and timing on the M2HB

The headspace is the distance between the face of the bolt and the base of the cartridge case, fully seated in the chamber,

Receiver stamps on an M2 HMG, this one by the Frigidaire division of General Motors (courtesy James D. Julia Auctioneers, Fairfield, Maine. www.jamesdjulia.com).

while timing refers to the adjustment required to ensure that firing takes place only when the recoiling parts are in the correct position. When Browning designed his original M1921 heavy machine gun, the available technology would not allow him to fix the head space or timing of the weapon, so that when the barrel was replaced both the headspace and the timing had to be reset manually with the aid of some simple "GO, NO GO" gauges supplied with the weapon. However, failure to carry out this procedure incurred significant danger for the gunner with the possibility of stoppages, or worse still, a cartridge exploding in the breech, which might result in death or injury to the crew and complete destruction of the weapon. Injuries from improperly adjusted weapons began to rise unacceptably towards the end of the 20th century. Consequently, in 1997, the U.S. military held a competition for a quick-change barrel conversion kit, incorporating a fixed headspace and timing, which resulted in the introduction of the new Browning M2A1 .50 caliber machine gun.[12]

Table Thirty-seven. Specification of the Browning M2 .50 caliber machine gun

Current Manufacturers	**U.S. makers:** General Dynamics, U.S. Ordnance **European and UK makers:** Fabrique Nationale (FN Herstal): from 1930 Manroy Engineering (UK)
Previous manufacturers	**Commercial manufacturers:** Buffalo Arms Corporation Colt's Patent Fire Arms Company High Standard Company Kelsey Hayes Wheel Company E.R. Maples Company (ERMCO) General Motors Corporation (Frigidaire, AC Spark Plug, Saginaw Steering, and Brown-Lipe-Chappin Divisions) Ramo Defence systems Inc. Sabre Defence Industries Savage Arms Corporation Wayne Pump Company **U.S. Arsenals:** Rock Island Arsenal Springfield Armory
Period of production	M1921: 1921 until 1930 M2HB: 1930 until present (2017)
Production	3 million weapons of all types
Operators	Argentina, Australia, Brazil, Britain, Canada, Chile, France, Greece, Iran, Ireland, Israel, Italy, Rhodesia, South Africa, South Korea, USA, plus many others.
Military service	1921 until present (2017) Banana Wars, World War II, Korean War, First Indochina War, Congo Crisis, Vietnam War (1963–1975), Rhodesian Bush War, Six-Day War, Cambodian Civil War, Falklands War, Syrian Civil War
Crew	Two-man crew: gunner and loader, although extra personnel would be required to carry ammunition and the tripod when a weapon was deployed in land service.
Weight	M1921: 78 kg (172 lbs), with tripod and full water jacket M2HB: 58 kg (128 lbs), with tripod
Length/Barrel length	M1921: 1,422mm (56 inches)/915mm (36 inches) M2HB: 1,650mm (65 inches)/1,145mm (45 inches) AN/M2: 1422mm (56 inches)/915mm (36 inches)

Mechanism	Air-cooled, selective-fire, belt-fed, short-recoil operation, firing from a closed bolt
Cartridge	.50 caliber BMG (12.7 × 99mm NATO)
	Cartridges delivered to mechanism by a disintegrating belt composed of M2 or M9 links
Sights	Variable, dependent upon application
Rate of fire	M2HB: 450 to 600 rpm
	AN/M2: 750 to 850 rpm
	AN/M3: 1,200 rpm
Effective range	1,800 meters
Maximum range	6,800 meters
Cost to the U.S. military in 2017	$14,002

Operation

Operation is similar to the M1919, the weapon being loaded by inserting an ammunition belt, either the early canvas component or the more modern version, made up of .50 caliber BMG cartridges and M2 links, into the left side of the gun. The cocking handle is then operated twice, chambering the first cartridge in the belt and positioning the second for loading, as well as locking the bolt and barrel together and correctly positioning the locking block. Pulling the trigger fires the cartridge in the chamber, causing the mechanism to recoil before chambering and firing a fresh cartridge in a manner exactly similar to both the M1917 and M1919 Browning machine guns, firing continuing until either the trigger is released or the ammunition is expended.

Until the development of the Browning M2A1 barrels on the M2HB could not be quickly changed and so gunners were trained to operate weapon in short bursts, which resulted in a firing rate of 50 rpm or less so as not to overheat the barrel or result in a "cook-off." Consequently, the gunner could fire five 10-round bursts, ten 5-round bursts, or a single long 50 round burst, although in the last case he would have to wait a full minute for the weapon to cool down before firing again.[13]

Variations

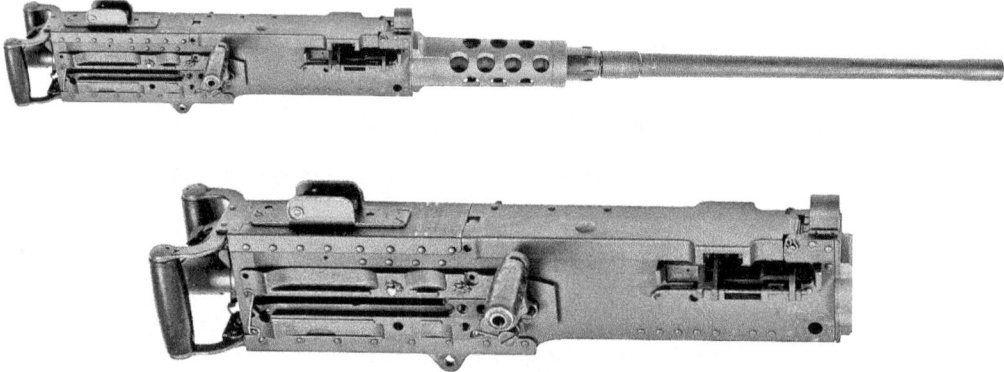

Top: M2HB HMG Showing rear sight, charging handle, ejection port and the short barrel shroud. *Bottom:* Magnified view of receiver of M2HB, showing the charging handle.

Nineteen. Heavy Machine Gun and Automatic Cannon Development

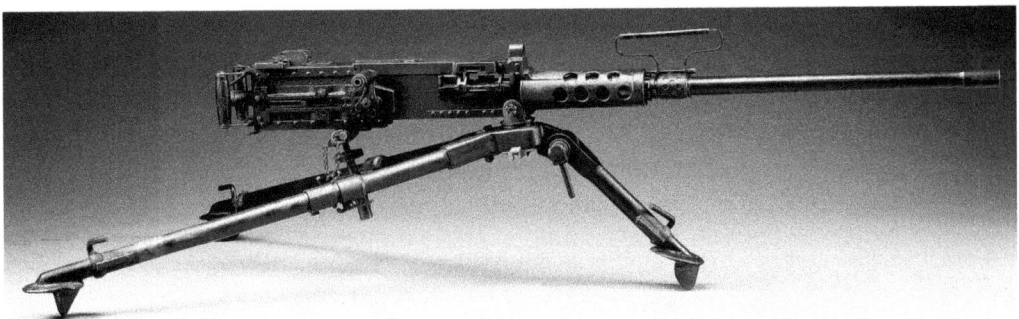

M2HB on a tripod mounting, possibly the M2 pattern (courtesy James D. Julia Auctioneers, Fairfield, Maine. www.jamesdjulia.com).

Browning M2s in military service

Browning Machine Gun, Cal. .50, M2, Water-Cooled, Flexible

Production: precise records not available.

This was the original water-cooled M2, first introduced in 1933, but quickly superseded by the M2HB.

Browning Machine Gun, Cal. .50, Flexible

Production: precise records not available, estimated at between 3 and 4 million weapons.

This was the basic model, chambered for the .50 caliber BMG cartridge with the feed slot on the left side and the charging handle on the right and deployed in land, air and naval service.

Browning M2A1 .50 caliber machine gun

Production: precise records not available, but estimated at possibly 100,000 weapons, since it is intended that all existing M2HB heavy machine guns should be converted to this specification, when it was introduced in 2010.

Formerly known as the M2E2 prototype, the M2A1 incorporates improvements to the design of the M2HB which include:

- A quick-change barrel, with removable carrying handle
- A slotted flash suppressor that reduces muzzle flash by 95 percent
- Fixed headspace and timing
- A modified bolt
- A manual trigger block safety device

Browning M2 in land service

Browning Machine Gun, Cal. .50, Flexible

Production: precise records not available, estimated at 2 million weapons.

This was the basic model, usually deployed by infantry in a fixed position and mounted on a tripod, the weight of even the M2HB making it difficult to use in a more mobile role.

Browning Machine Gun, Cal. .50, M2, HB, TT

Production: precise records not available.

The Browning M2HB was also modified as a "Turret type," for use in the turret of a tank and this weapon will be found designated "Browning Machine Gun, Cal. .50, M2, HB, TT" in documents originating from administration, manufacturing and supply sources, although it was apparently never an official military designation.

Receiver stamp on M2HB, this one showing the gun was built at the government's Springfield Arsenal (courtesy James D. Julia Auctioneers, Fairfield, Maine. www.jamesdjulia.com).

Browning Machine Gun, Cal. .50, M2HB, M48 Turret Type

Production: precise records not available, but estimated that at least 12,000 weapons were manufactured because this was the number of the M48 Patton main battle tanks that were produced.

This was a M2HB designed to use either a right- or left-hand feed system and fitted on the tank commander's station of the M48 Patton main battle tank.

Browning Machine Gun, Cal. .50, M2HB, M1 Turret Type

Production: precise records not available, but estimated that at least 10,000 weapons were manufactured because this was the number of the M1 Abrams main battle tanks that were produced.

This was an M2HB modified so that it could be mounted on the commander's position of the M1 Abrams main battle tank.

Browning Machine Gun, Cal. .50, Fixed

Production: precise records not available, estimated at less than 100 weapons.

This weapon is a "fixed" type designed to be fitted as a coaxial weapon mounted in the turret of the M6 heavy tank, an experimental model that was never put into production.

Browning M2 in naval service

Caliber .50 Machine Gun, Browning, M2, Heavy Barrel, Soft Mount (Navy)

Production: precise records not available.

This was an M2HB mounted on the U.S. Navy's MK 26 Mod 15, 16 and 17 gun mounts, which were originally designed for mounting the US Navy's 3"/50 and 3"/70 AA guns.

Caliber .50 Machine Gun, Browning, M2, Heavy Barrel, Fixed Type (Navy)

Production: precise records not available, but estimated at 10,000 weapons, because of its prevalence on USN and USMC craft.

This designation is applied to one of a pair of M2HBs, modified for right- or left-hand operation and deployed as one of a pair, mounted in tandem on the U.S. Navy's MK 56 Mod 0 and Mod 4 gun mounts. They are fired remotely by solenoid and consequently need to be installed with a 24–28 volt DC power source.

Browning M2s in air service

Browning AN/M2

Production: precise records not available, but estimated at 100,000 weapons, based upon the numbers of U.S. military aircraft to which it was fitted.

Officially designated the "Browning Machine Gun, Aircraft, Cal. .50, AN/M2 (Fixed) or (Flexible)," this was a weapon designed for air service in a fixed or flexible mounting with both the Army and the Navy (hence the "AN" designation). It had a cyclic rate of 750–850 rounds per minute and was designed to be fired by a remotely controlled solenoid trigger when installed as a fixed gun. It was also fitted with a lighter, shorter barrel because both the fixed and flexibly mounted guns were able to benefit from the cooling effect of an aircraft's slip-stream. This reduction in barrel size reduced the total weight of the gun to 28 kg (61 lbs) and was also the reason for the increased cyclic rate.

XM296/M269

Production: precise records not available, but estimated at 5,000 weapons, based upon the numbers of OH-58 helicopters manufactured for the U.S. military.

The XM296/M296 air service machine gun is a development of the AN/M2 designed to be fitted to the OH-58 Kiowa Warrior helicopter. Unlike most remotely fired machine guns, the M296 has adjustable firing rate between 500 and 850 rpm, although it can only be operated as a fully automatic weapon. Helicopters fly relatively slowly so air cooling is minimized. Consequently, an M296 mounted on a Kiowa is officially restricted to 50 rounds per minute sustained fire or 150 rounds per minute in a single burst while conducting peacetime training exercises. Firing rates are not restricted during active service, but a ten-minute cooling period after prolonged firing must be observed to avoid stoppages that will occur due to overheating.

XM213/M213

Production: precise records not available.

These weapons produced by modernizing and adapting a number of the original

AN/M2 air service weapons for service as a pintle-mounted door gun on helicopters equipped with the M59 armament subsystem. Subsequently, a number of improved versions were developed for service aboard helicopters, including:

GAU-15/A: Formerly designated the XM218, this was a lightweight version of the M2HB.
GAU-16/A: A development of the GAU-15 A, with improved grip and sight assemblies.
GAU-18/A: Another lightweight version of the M2, designed to be fitted to the USAF MH-53 Pave Low and HH-60 Pave Hawk helicopters. An EGMS (External Gun Mounting System) is used in the HH-60, and its recoil-absorbing cradle requires that the weapon to be fitted is adapted with the cocking handle on the right and the ammunition belt entering the receiver from either the right or left, depending upon which side of the aircraft the gun is mounted. An additional modification is the fitting of a feed chute adapter, attached to the left or right hand feed pawl bracket, allowing ammunition to be delivered to the weapon through this system from externally mounted ammunition containers holding 600 rounds each.

AN/M3

Production: precise records not available.

This is a machine gun based on the Browning M2 that was developed for air service during World War II with a mechanical or electrically enhanced cartridge feed mechanism that increased the cyclic rate to approximately 1,200 rpm. The AN/M3 was fitted to the F-86 Sabre, F-84 Thunderjet and F-80 Shooting Star, which saw service in Korea, and on the XM14/SUU-12/A gun pod, which was used in Vietnam. At present (2017), it is fitted to the Embraer EMB 314 Super Tucano. It has a number of modern variants, including:

M3P: This is a fixed, remotely fired version of the M3 also fitted to the OH-58D Kiowa Warrior helicopter.
M3M/GAU-21/A: A flexibly mounted version of the AN/M3 adopted by the U.S. Navy and U.S. Marine Corps for installation in a number if their helicopters under the GAU-21/A designation.[14]

Ammunition

The .50 caliber BMG cartridge is produced in a wide variety of types, all of which be used in the M2HB, and including[15]:

- **Tracer:** M1, M10, M17, M21 cartridges. Cartridges designed to allow the gunner to observe the trajectory of a projectile without using the sights or observing the impact on the target. Usually used in conjunction with other types of ammunition, often at a ratio of a single tracer cartridge for four other rounds in the belt and referred to as "four-to-one" tracer.
- **Incendiary:** M1, M23 cartridges: A bullet from this pattern of cartridge is designed to burn rapidly upon impact.
- **Ball:** M2, M33 cartridges.
- **Armor-Piercing (AP):** M2 cartridge. The bullet from this round was required to completely perforate 0.875 inches (22.2 mm) of hardened steel armor plate at a distance of 100 yards (91 m) and 0.75 inches (19 mm) at 547 yards (500 m)

- **Armor-Piercing Incendiary (API):** M8 cartridge. This round is designed to generate a flash and smoke on contact, which is useful for detecting an impact on an enemy aircraft, although it was primarily intended to penetrate the armor of thin-skinned and lightly armored vehicles and aircraft, as well as igniting their fuel tanks.
- **Armor-Piercing Incendiary Tracer (API-T):** M20 cartridge. This round is similar in design and application to the M8 API, except it has a tracer charge in the base of the bullet.
- **Saboted Light Armor Penetrator (SLAP):** M903 cartridge. The bullet from this round is fitted with a 7.6mm tungsten penetrator and can pierce 34mm of face-hardened steel plates at 500 meters. Should only be used in a tungsten-lined barrel.
- **Saboted Light Armor Penetrator Tracer (SLAP-T):** M962 cartridge. The bullet from this round is fitted with a 7.6mm tungsten penetrator with a tracer charge at its base. It can pierce 34mm of face-hardened steel plates at 500 meters. Should only be used in a tungsten-lined barrel.

Military service

The M2HB has been used in a variety of roles during its period of service, including infantry support weapon, ship-mounted AA gun, AA gun in land service, primary or secondary armament on an armored vehicles or naval patrol boats, spotting or coaxial mounted weapon on an armored vehicles, secondary armament on larger naval vessels, a fixed mounted primary aircraft weapon, and a flexibly mounted defensive aircraft weapon.[16]

Values

Working Browning M2 fully automatic heavy machine guns registered in the USA before 1986 are transferable between owners. Consequently, these weapons are sometimes offered for sale, although only the M2HB designed for land service is seen with any frequency and condition is quite variable. Local regulations as they apply to these weapons should be consulted before purchase.

Prices are for weapons capable of firing.

M2HB: NRA Good: $25,000; NRA Fine: $60,000

British Heavy Machine Gun Development After World War I

The only British-made heavy machine gun deployed by UK and Commonwealth land forces during World War II was the venerable old water-cooled Vickers, British requirements for air service being accommodated by the air-cooled Browning M1919 produced under license as the Browning .303 Mark II. From 1918, the .303 caliber Vickers was produced in variety of guises for both air service and as a tank gun, although the weight of the water jacket and lock work meant that the weapons were not as useful as the Browning M1919, which largely superseded the Vickers in these roles during the later stages of World War II.

Heavy Machine Guns in Military Service After World War I

Only the most commonly encountered weapons are included here, and consequently this should not be regarded as a complete list.

AMERICAN ARMED FORCES

Browning M1919

In use from 1919 until the present day, in a variety of roles and conformations.

Browning M2

In use from 1933 until the present day, in a variety of roles and conformations.

BRITISH AND COMMONWEALTH ARMED FORCES

Vickers .303 caliber heavy machine gun

In use from 1912 until 1964, in a variety of roles and conformations.

Browning M1919

In use from 1919 until the present day, in a variety of roles and conformations.

Browning M2

In use from 1933 until the present day, in a variety of roles and conformations.

Besa heavy machine gun, 7.92mm

Production: 39,332 weapons of all types.

This was a British version of the Czech ZB-53 machine gun. It is an air-cooled, gas operated, fully automatic weapon, chambered for the 7.92 × 57mm Mauser German service rifle cartridge, which was supplied to the weapon from a non-disintegrating belt holding 250 cartridges. Breda HMGs were fitted to British-made armored cars and tanks between 1940 and 1963.

The Breda Mark II entered service in 1940 and was fitted with a two-position fire selector, giving fully automatic fire at 750–850 rpm and 450–550 rpm. Later models were simplified to facilitate production, and included:

- **Mark II*:** Entering service in 1943, this weapon was similar in configuration to the Mark II, but with a simpler construction and parts interchangeable with the Mark II.
- **Mark III:** Entering service in 1943, this weapon was similar in conformation to the Mark II, but with no fire selector and consequently having a cyclic rate of between 750 and 850 rpm.
- **Mark III*:** Entering service in 1943, this weapon was similar in conformation to the Mark II, but with no fire selector and consequently having a cyclic rate of between 450 and 550 rpm. All weapons with Mark III specification were converted to Mark III* in 1951.

Mark III/2: This weapon was a Mark III*, fitted with a new mounting bracket and body cover and remaining in service as a vehicle gun until 1963.

Mark III/3: This weapon was a Mark III/2, which had been fitted with a new barrel and sleeve, together with larger vents in the gas cylinder, making it less problematic to use belts containing mixed ammunition.[17]

Besa heavy machine gun, 15mm

Production: 3,218 weapons of all types.

A heavier version of the original 7.92 mm Besa, this was an air-cooled, selective-fire weapon, chambered for a 15 × 104mm cartridge and capable of a cyclic rate of 450 rpm. Introduced into British service in 1940, it was fitted to the Light Tank Mk VIC and a number of armored cars before being declared obsolete in 1949.[18]

FRENCH ARMED FORCES

Hotchkiss M1914 HMG

Used by the French army as its main heavy machine gun in World War II.

Hotchkiss M1930 HMG

Production: precise records not available.

This was an air-cooled, fully automatic heavy machine gun with a cyclic rate of 450 rpm, chambered for a 13.2 × 96mm Hotchkiss cartridge, which were supplied to the weapon from a 30-round detachable box magazine. It saw service as a ground-based AA gun, a naval AA gun with vessels in the French and Japanese navies and as a vehicle gun on a number of tanks and armored cars deployed by both French and Japanese forces.[19]

GERMAN ARMED FORCES

MG 34

Its role as a GPMG meant it could be mounted on a tripod with a telescope sight for deployment as a heavy machine gun.

MG 42

Like the earlier MG 34, the design of the MG 42 meant that it could be mounted on a tripod with a telescope sight for deployment as a heavy machine gun.

MG 131

Production: 144,124 weapon produced for fitting to aircraft.

First produced by Rheinmetall in 1938, this was an air-cooled, belt-fed, fully automatic heavy machine gun with a short-recoil mechanism, firing from a closed bolt. It had a cyclic rate of 900 rpm and this was achieved in part by the adoption of electrically primed ammunition, when it was firing through the propeller hub of a single-engined fighter. It was the lightest of all the fully automatic heavy machine guns produced during World War II and was fitted in a number of German fighter and bomber aircraft, including later versions of the Messerschmidt Bf 109 and Folke-Wulf 190. When the need for automatic machine guns became critical, many of these guns were converted for land service by fitting a pistol grip and a bipod and reducing the cyclic rate.[20]

ITALIAN ARMED FORCES

Breda M37

Production: precise records not available.

The Breda M37 was an air-cooled, gas-operated, fully automatic heavy machine gun with a cyclic rate of 450 rpm, although in service it proved difficult to achieve a firing rate of more than 200 rpm. It was chambered for the 8 × 59mm RB Breda* cartridge, which were supplied to the mechanism by a clip containing 20 cartridges. Since it shared a number of features with the atrocious Breda M30, it was also slow to reload and prone to jamming in a dusty environment. Another version, the M38, produced for mounting on vehicles, used a magazine mounted on top of the weapon. As a consequence, it seems to have been more reliable.

The Breda M37 was the main Italian heavy machine gun throughout World War II and despite its shortcomings remained in service with Italian forces until the early 1950s, when it began to be replaced by better, modern weapons.[21]

JAPANESE ARMED FORCES

Type 89 Fixed HMG

Production: precise records not available.

This weapon is a licensed copy of the Vickers HMG, chambered for the 7.7 × 58mmSR Type 89 cartridge and used in air service fitted to the cowling of fighter aircraft or as a wing-mounted machine gun.[22]

Type 3 Heavy Machine Gun

Production: precise records not available.

Licensed copy of the Hotchkiss M1914, chambered for 6.5 × 50mm Arisaka cartridge. Usually deployed as an AA gun.[23]

SOVIET ARMED FORCES

PM 1910

Production: precise records not available, estimated at 500,000 weapons.

Heavy machine gun of WW 1 vintage, still in use by Soviet forces during World War II.

SG-43 Goryunov

Production: precise records not available, estimated at over 2 million weapons, based upon the size of the Red Army during this period.

In service between 1938 and 1968, this was an air-cooled, gas-operated, medium machine gun, with a cyclic rate between 500 and 700 rpm, and chambered for the 7.62 × 54mmR Russian service rifle cartridge, which was supplied to the gun from 200 or 250 round belts. Barrels could be changed quickly, and later improved versions included:

SGM-43 Goryunov: Introduced after 1945, this version was improved by fitting dust covers to the ejection port and receiver opening as well as an improved barrel catch and a splined barrel to improve cooling.

SGMT-43 Goryunov: This was a version of the SGM-43 designed to be fitted to a flexible mounting on tanks.[24]

DShK 1938

Production: precise records not available, estimated at over 1 million weapons, based upon the size of the Red Army during this period.

Serving as the standard heavy machine gun with Soviet forces during World War II, the DShK 1938 is an air-cooled, gas-operated heavy machine gun with a cyclic rate of 600 rpm and chambered for the 12.7 × 108mm Soviet heavy machine gun cartridge, which was supplied to the weapon from a belt holding 50 cartridges. It is comparable in both role and performance with the M2HB, but cost only $2,250 in 2012, compared to the $14,000 unit cost of the American weapon. It has been deployed as an AA gun, a vehicle gun, as secondary armament on tanks and self-propelled guns, and when mounted on a two-wheeled trolley, as an infantry support weapon. It is still in service with the armies of some smaller countries, although it was largely replaced in the Soviet army by the NSV and Kord GPMGs.[25]

The Development of Automatic Cannon Prior to World War II

In many ways, the automatic cannon was a direct and perhaps inevitable development from the heavy machine gun of the interwar years. Aircraft were becoming more difficult to shoot down because their increased speed and the use of armor to protect both the pilot and the aircraft's engine and control systems, so that a machine gun chambered for a service rifle cartridge was becoming largely ineffective in an AA role. Only the Browning M2HB was an exception to this general rule, since that weapon used a cartridge of considerably more power than the round used in a service rifle.

An automatic cannon is differentiated from an automatic machine gun by the size of its ammunition, any round of 20mm and above in diameter being designated a "shell" rather than a cartridge and thus fired from a cannon, rather than a machine gun. The designation is purely arbitrary and does not imply that any particular design feature is incorporated into either type of weapon. The designation applied to automatic cannon differs slightly from that used in small arms in that their barrel lengths are measured in calibers, so that the designation "Oerlikon 20mm/L60" describes an Oerlikon automatic cannon chambered for a 20mm cartridge with a barrel length equal to 60 calibers, i.e., 60 × 20 mm or 1,200mm.[26]

The Oerlikon 20mm Cannon

The Oerlikon 20mm cannon was based on a German 20mm automatic aircraft cannon, designed by Rheinhold Becker, which began to be fitted to German military aircraft during 1916. After the end of World War I, clauses in the Treaty of Versailles prevented the production of this type of weapon in Germany. Consequently the patents and tooling for the cannon were transferred from the parent company, Stahlwerke Becker, to the Swiss firm SEMAG, which was based in Zurich. SEMAG went on to produce an improved version of the cannon as the SEMAG L, but by 1924 the firm was bankrupt and another Zurich-based company, Oerlikon, acquired the rights to the weapon, along with SEMAG's manufacturing equipment and employees.

Oerlikon began production of an automatic cannon based upon the Becker design and designated the Oerlikon S in 1927. This led to the development in 1930 of aircraft guns with the designations AF and AL for use on flexible mounts in bombers and two-seater fighter aircraft. By 1935 Oerlikon had developed a series of wing-mounted guns—the FF, FFL and FFS—and they had also sold a number of manufacturing licenses to other armaments firms, including Hispano-Suiza in France and Ikaria in Germany.[27]

SPECIFICATION

Production: precise records not available, estimated at 200,000 weapons based upon the number of ships and aircraft fitted with Oerlikon 20mm cannon.

The Oerlikon cannon is an air-cooled, fully automatic cannon fitted with an API (Advanced Primer Ignition) blowback operating system, firing from an open bolt with a cyclic rate of 450 rpm, although later weapons were capable of firing at over 800 rpm. Under service conditions, however, this was reduced to a firing rate of approximately 250 rpm. It is chambered for a variety of 20mm cannon shells, depending upon type, which are delivered to the mechanism by a box magazine holding 15 shells in the early types, although this was replaced later by a selection of drum magazines holding between 15 and 100 rounds. There are two handles or grips used to steady the weapon as well as shoulder supports extending upwards from the back of the gun, plus a waist belt, the trigger being mounted on the right-hand grip. The intervals between barrel changes was reasonable, a new barrel having to be fitted only after a total of 9,000 rounds, and this could be done in about 30 seconds by an experienced crew.

Mounting types were variable and of three main types, although other configurations may have been used:

- **Single-gun mounting:** Exclusively a naval design, in this type the weapon was fitted to a single, fixed pedestal mounting allowing the gun to be elevated or traversed manually by the gunner, and with a flat, armored shield for crew protection. The cannon was aimed and fired by a gunner using a ring-and-bead sight, and he was attached to the weapon by a waist belt and shoulder supports.
- **Twin-gun mounting:** Used for both AA and naval applications, these mountings were traversed and elevated by a mechanical system. The Royal Navy also deployed a hydraulically operated twin mounting. Guns were configured for loading and charging from the left or right side as required.

- **Quadruple-gun mounting:** Used for both AA and naval applications, these mountings were traversed and elevated by a mechanical system. The USN deployed a quad-mounting originally designed for torpedo boats aboard some of their capital ships.[28]

Table Thirty-eight. Specification of the Oerlikon 20mm/L70 quick-firing cannon

Manufacturer	Oerlikon Contraves
	British government Oerlikon factory, Ruislip
	U.S. government manufacturing plants, various
Period of production	1940 until present (2017)
Production	Production records unavailable, estimated 200,000 weapons
Operators	Argentina, Australia, Brazil, Britain, Canada, Chile, France, Greece, Iran, Ireland, Israel, Italy, Rhodesia, South Africa, South Korea, USA, as well as a number of other users.
Military service	1927 until present (2017)
	World War II, Korean War, First Indochina War, Congo Crisis, Vietnam War (1963–1975), Rhodesian Bush War, Six-Day War, Cambodian Civil War, Falklands War, and the Syrian Civil War, as well as a number of other conflicts.
Crew	Five: Gunner and four loaders
Weight	With breech mechanism: 68 kg (150 lb)
	Without breech mechanism: 21 kg (46 lb)
Barrel length	Overall: 2210mm (87 inches)
	Rifled section: 1400mm (55 inches)
Barrel duration	Approximately 9,000 rounds
Mechanism	Air-cooled, magazine-fed, API blowback firing from an open bolt
Cartridge	20 × 70mmRB
	20 × 72mmRB
	20 × 110mmRB
	(RB: Rebated Rim)
	Delivered from:
	15-round box magazine
	15-, 30-, 60- or 100-round drum magazines
Sights	Variable, depending upon application
Rate of fire	Variable depending upon type:
	450–1,000 rpm
Effective range/	Effective range: 1,000–1,500 meters
Maximum range	Maximum range: 5,000 meters

Operation

To operate an Oerlikon 20mm cannon configured as an AA gun, the magazine is first attached to the receiver opening and locked by the operation of the magazine locking lever. The gunner then steps into the two shoulder supports and operates the cocking handle, locking the bolt in the firing position. Aiming is accomplished by moving the whole body, and the weapon is fired by the trigger, usually mounted on the right-hand grip, which operates the sear, allowing the bolt to move forward and remove a round from the magazine. However, in twin or quadruple mounting systems, the position of triggers, charging levers and magazine mounting may be changed as appropriate. The Oerlikon cannon has an advanced primer ignition blowback mechanism in which the striker hits the primer and fires the cartridge while the bolt is still moving forward and before the round is chambered. This means that the propellant gases have to overcome the forward momentum of the bolt before exerting sufficient force to start it on its rearward journey. This allows the designer of such a system to incorporate a much lighter bolt than would be necessary in a simple blowback weapon, and also results in a weapon with significantly reduced recoil. Although considerable care must be taken in the design of such a weapon, once it is constructed the mechanism is relatively simple, with no gas cylinders nor very much mechanical complexity. Oerlikons in particular are well known for their reliability in the most adverse conditions and the ease with which they could be maintained.[29]

Ammunition

One consequence of the use of the API design is that it requires a special cartridge with a rebated rim, in which the rear of the case is of a smaller diameter than the neck, and a chamber longer than necessary to contain the cartridge. This type of case is essential because the final period of forward motion and the first rearward motion of the case and bolt occur within the confines of the extended chamber, and although gas pressure in the barrel at this point is high, the walls of the case remain supported and the breach is sealed, even when the expended case is sliding backwards. However, when the case is moving backwards, the high internal gas pressure could cause a rupture of the case wall, and the usual solution to this problem is to grease the ammunition, thus reducing friction. The case needs to have a rebated rim because the front end of the bolt will enter the chamber, and the extractor claw hooked over the rim therefore has to also fit within the confines of the chamber. The case generally has very little neck, because this remains unsupported during the firing cycle and is generally deformed, whereas a case with a long neck would be likely to split. In service, cartridges are usually greased before they are loaded to facilitate extraction, ammunition used in the Royal Navy being lubricated with a specially produced antifreeze grease.

Cartridges of various types are available for the Oerlikon, and these include:

- High Explosive (HE)
- High Explosive Incendiary (HEI)
- Armor-Piercing (AP)
- Armor-Piercing Incendiary (API)[30]

Variations

The Oerlikon 20mm automatic cannon was too heavy to be used in land service and was used as either an AA gun or in air service as a wing mounted cannon or flexibly mounted for defensive purposes.

Weapons designed for naval service

Oerlikon S

Production: precise records not available, estimated at fewer than 1,000 weapons.

Produced in 1927, the first weapon produced by Oerlikon after purchase of SEMAG. Chambered for a 20 × 110RB cartridge and having a cyclic rate of 280 rpm.

Oerlikon 1S

Production: precise records not available, estimated at fewer than 1,000 guns.
Produced in 1930, this was an improved version of the Oerlikon S.

Oerlikon SS

Production: precise records not available, estimated at 180,000 weapons.

Introduced in 1938, this weapon was a modification of the Oerlikon FFS, with a total weight of 39lbs, and a cyclic rate of 470 rpm. Drum magazines with capacities of 45, 60, 75 and 100 rounds were available, with the 60-round drum proving the most popular. It was the most popular version of the Oerlikon and was in service with both the Royal Navy and the U.S. Navy.

ROYAL NAVY OERLIKON 20MM AA GUNS

20mm/70 Mark I: Production: precise records not available, estimated at fewer than 200 weapons.

Produced by Oerlikon before the fall of France, but not supplied in great numbers; fewer than 100 in service by November 1940.

20mm/70 Mark II: Production: precise records not available, estimated at 55,000 weapons.

Produced in Britain under license, with delivery begun in September 1941 and fitted to all Royal navy ships after this date.

U.S. NAVY OERLIKON 20MM AA GUNS

Production: precise records not available, estimated at 125,000 weapons of all types.

20mm/70 Mark 1: Prototype built in USA and based upon original Oerlikon design.

20mm/70 Mark 2: First fully automatic production version for the USN, fitted with cooling fins and two locking slots.

20mm/70 Mark 3: Improved version of the Mark 2, with fewer cooling fins and one locking slot.

20mm/70 Mark 4: Improved version of the Mark 3, with a single heavier buffer spring and fluted chamber to facilitate ejection of the spent case. This was the version produced in the highest numbers by the Americans until it began to be replaced by the 40mm Bofors in 1943.

Oerlikon 1SS

Production: precise records not available.

Improved version of the SS produced in 1942 with an increased cyclic rate, but not widely adopted.

Oerlikon 2SS

Production: precise records not available.

Improved version of the SS produced in 1945 with an increased cyclic rate of 650 rpm, although this weapon was not widely adopted either, the Oerlikon having proved inferior to the larger caliber 40mm Bofors.

Single 20mm Oerlikon, in naval service, showing the twin shoulder supports (courtesy Wikipedia: License: CC-A-S-A 3.0).

Weapons designed for air service

Oerlikon AF

Production: precise records not available.

Produced in 1930, this was a version of the original Oerlikon S, designed to be used on a flexible aircraft mount and fitted with a drum magazine holding 15 or 30 rounds.

Oerlikon AL

Production: precise records not available.

Another version of the original Oerlikon S produced at the same time as the AF, also designed to be used on a flexible aircraft mount and fitted with a drum magazine holding 15 or 30 rounds.

Oerlikon FF (FF: Flügelfest. trans: "wing-mounted")

Production: precise records not available.

Another version of the original Oerlikon S produced in 1935, but lightened to 24 kg. It was chambered for a 20 × 72RB cartridge, with a cyclic rate of 520 rpm and a muzzle velocity of 550 m/s (meters per second). These guns came to be known later by the designation FF F.

Oerlikon FFL

Production: precise records not available.

Second version of the original Oerlikon S produced in 1935, with a total weight of 30 kg and chambered for a 20 × 101RB cartridge. It had a cyclic rate of 500 rpm, but a slightly higher muzzle velocity than the FF at 750 m/s.

Oerlikon FFS

Production: precise records not available.

Final version of the original Oerlikon S produced in 1935. It had a total weight of 39kg and was chambered for a 20 × 110RB cartridge, with a cyclic rate of 470 rpm, but a significantly higher muzzle velocity than the FF at 830 m/s.

Changes to the design of these guns included modifications for wing-mounting and to allow remote firing. Larger capacity drum magazines were also introduced because wing-mounted guns could not be reloaded in flight, and magazines with 45, 60, 75 and 100 rounds capacity were available, most users opting for the 60-round capacity drum.

Licensed production

British and American production apart, licenses were also granted to the French firm of Hispano-Suiza, the German firm of Ikaria and to the Japanese navy.

Oerlikons produced by Hispano-Suiza

Hispano-Suiza was a manufacturer of aircraft engines, and marketed a moteur-canon combination of its 12X and 12Y engines with a H.S.7 or H.S.9 cannon installed between the cylinder banks for fitting in fighter aircraft. The weapon fired through the hollow propeller spinner and was elevated above the crankcase by the design of the gearing.

HS.7

Production: precise records not available.
This was a licensed copy of the Oerlikon FFS.

HS.9

Production: precise records not available.
This was another licensed copy of the Oerlikon FFS, produced later than the HS.7 and incorporating a number of improvements.

Oerlikons produced by Ikaria Werke Berlin

MG FF

Production: precise records not available, estimated at 70,000 weapons based upon the number of aircraft to which it was fitted.

This was a licensed copy of the Oerlikon FF that could be wing mounted for use in fighter aircraft or used as a defensive weapon in a flexible mounting. It was fitted to both the Messerschmidt Bf 109 and the Folke-Wulf Fw 190 fighters, although installation was not simple and ammunition storage had to be reduced initially, as only the 60-round drum would fit in the space available.

MG FF/M

Production: precise records not available, estimated at 50,000 weapons based upon the number of aircraft to which it was fitted.

A version of the MG FF chambered for the Minengesshoss shell.

Oerlikons produced by the Japanese Navy

TYPE 99-1

Production: precise records not available, estimated at 50,000 weapons based upon the number of aircraft to which it was fitted.

A licensed copy of the Oerlikon FF fitted to the Mitsubishi Zero.

TYPE 99-2

Production: precise records not available, estimated at 30,000 weapons based upon the number of aircraft to which it was fitted.

A licensed copy of the Oerlikon FFL.[31]

MILITARY SERVICE

One of the major advantages of this weapon from a maintenance point of view was that the forces used to operate the automatic mechanisms were quite high, which meant that such factors as friction, insufficient lubrication, cold weather, different elevations, rain and the like were small in proportion to the operating forces involved and therefore unlikely to cause stoppages. In addition, the barrel on the Oerlikon gun could be changed in 30 seconds or less.

Oerlikons of a number of types saw service with the Royal Navy, U.S. Navy, Royal Canadian Navy, and in small numbers with the Italian Navy and German Kriegsmarine. The RAF regiment used the weapon as an AA gun in the Middle East, Italy, Northwestern Europe and the Far East, with approximately 2,000 guns being sent to the USSR as part of the terms of lend-lease.[32]

VALUES

Not often seen for sale because the Oerlikon is both a destructive device and a restricted weapon under U.S. law, so possession can depend upon how the local police force feel about having a gun like this within their jurisdiction. That said, working examples are to be had after processing the appropriate paperwork for between $35,000 and $60,000. One consideration, however, may be the cost of ammunition, single 20 × 110mm shells starting at between $35 and $50 each. Local regulations as they apply to these weapons should very definitely be consulted before purchase.

The Bofors 40mm/L60 Cannon

Beginning production at AB Bofors during 1933, the Bofors 40mm gun was produced by a number of makers under license during World War II, including Britain and America. It largely replaced the Oerlikon in Allied naval service because the 40mm shell it used was more effective against the new generation of fast, heavily armored fighter aircraft being introduced.[33]

Specification

Production:

Bofors 40mm/L60

Precise records not available, estimated at 70,000 weapons, based upon the number of ships of all powers that were fitted with the Bofors 40mm/L60 and the number of AA guns deployed.

Bofors 40mm/L70

Precise records not available, estimated at 100,000 weapons, based upon the number of ships and vehicles from all countries that were fitted with the Bofors 40mm/L70.

The Bofors 40mm gun is a recoil-operated, selective-fire automatic cannon originally chambered for a 900 gm, high explosive 40 × 311mmR (rimmed) shell and having a cyclic rate of 120 rpm, which may be configured for air- or water-cooling depending upon the model. It utilized a unique gravity-fed mechanism designed to literally drop a shell into the breech at the beginning of each cycle, the empty case being subsequently ejected from the rear of the breech casing and guided via a semicircular chute out under the barrel of the gun. Shells were fed to the mechanism or "autoloader" manually, by dropping clips containing four rounds into the fixed magazine mounted on top of the breech. Sights were of a reflector pattern; the two men responsible for aiming the weapon and who operated the separate elevation and traverse controls were both provided with a set of sights so as to be able to orientate onto the target, while a third crew member standing behind them adjusted the gun to compensate for the speed of the aircraft using a simple mechanical computer, power for the sights being supplied from a 6V battery. AA guns were mounted on a towable carriage, which could be deployed immediately or stabilized for more precise control of the gun's targeting system, while weapons in naval service were fitted into a variety of mountings appropriate to their role.[34]

Table Thirty-nine. Specification of the Bofors 40mm quick-firing cannon

Manufacturer	**Early production:**
	Bofors Defence (1932–2000)
	U.S. production during World War II:
	Chrysler Corporation
	British production during World War II:
	Vickers-Armstrong Ltd.
Period of production	1932 until present (2017)
Production	Production records unavailable, estimated 60,000 weapons of all types during World War II
Operators	Argentina, Australia, Brazil, Britain, Canada, Chile, France, Greece, Iran, Ireland, Israel, Italy, Rhodesia, South Africa, South Korea, USA, as well as a number of other users.
Military service	1933 until present (2017)
	World War II, Korean War, First Indochina War, Congo Crisis, Vietnam War (1963–1975), Rhodesian Bush War, Six-Day War, Cambodian Civil War, Falklands War and the Syrian Civil War, as well as a number of other conflicts.
Crew	Dependent upon deployment.
	Land service: seven, two gun aimers, computer operator and four loaders
	Naval service: nine, two gun aimers, computer operator and six loaders

Weight	40mm/L60: 1,981 kg (4,367 lb)
Barrel length	40mm/L60: 2,400mm (95 inches)
	40mm/L70: 2,800mm (110 inches)
Barrel duration	Approximately 9,000 rounds
Mechanism	Air- or water-cooled, magazine-fed, recoil-operated, selective-fire cannon
Shell	40mm/L60: 40 × 311mmR shell
	40mm/L70: 40 × 364mmR shell
	Supplied to mechanism as a four-round clip inserted into the fixed magazine or autoloader
Sights	Variable, depending upon application
Rate of fire	40mm/L60: 120 rpm
	40mm/L70: 240 rpm
Effective range/ Maximum range	**40mm/L60:**
	Effective range: 3,800 meters
	Maximum range: 7160 meters
	40mm/L70:
	Effective range: 3,800 meters
	Maximum range: 12,500 meters

OPERATION

To operate a Bofors gun, a clip of four shells was fed into the autoloader of the weapon, located behind the breech block. A substantial lever on the side of the autoloader was then pulled back, cocking the rammer spring and opening the breechblock, at which point the clip was pushed down until the lowest round rested upon the loading tray. The gun was now ready to fire. The foot-operated firing pedal was then pressed, releasing the rammer, which projected the round into the breech, causing the breech block to close, releasing the striker and firing the shell. The recoil-operated mechanism then ejected the spent case, cocked the rammer, and turned a star-shaped wheel in the autoloader, allowing another round to descend on to the loading tray. If the gun was set on auto and the pedal still pressed, the gun would repeat its firing cycle until the pedal was released or the ammunition supply ran out. The mechanism in most Bofors 40mm guns was designed to stop firing when two rounds remained in the autoloader so as to allow firing to be quickly resumed when a fresh clip was dropped in, although the USN M1 guns had an interlock device that allowed this facility to be disabled.[35]

VARIATIONS

Bofors 40mm/L60

Standard production Bofors 40mm produced between 1933 and 1980.

Bofors 40mm/L70

First accepted into service with the Swedish armed forces in 1951, this was an improved version of the original Bofors 40mm, with a longer barrel, higher cyclic rate, and a larger shell, which gave the weapon a muzzle velocity of 1,021m/s, a great improvement on the 881m/s of the L60. The carriage was also modified so that it was now aimed by means of an electromechanical system, referred to as "power-laying." The earlier L60s had been successful against the piston-engined aircraft used during World War II, but improvements in the performance of the jet aircraft coming into service meant that the old gun did not get sufficient rounds into the air to disable a fighter before it had flown out of range. The new L70 solved most of these problems and served as NATO's standard AA gun from 1953 until the 1970s, and with the RAF regiment from 1957 until it was replaced by the Rapier air defense system in 1977.[36]

Military service

Designed as an AA gun, which could also be adapted for a multi-purpose role, the Bofors 40mm gun could be deployed for land service on a towable carriage that could be converted into a stable AA platform, using the tow bar and muzzle-locking bar, in less than one minute. Naval guns were deployed in a variety of fittings either as single or tandem mounted guns. The Bofors 40mm remains in service to the present day (2017), as the Bofors 40mm/L70.[37]

Values

Not often seen for sale because the Bofors 40mm is both a destructive device and a restricted weapon under U.S. law, so possession can depend upon how the local police force feel about having such a weapon within their jurisdiction. That said, working examples have been sold for between $35,000 and $60,000, while deactivated examples sell for between $5,000 and $10,000, depending upon condition. One consideration, however, may be the cost of ammunition. Single 40 × 311mmR shells start at between $50 and $75 each, so a day at the range could work out expensive. Local regulations as they apply to these weapons should very definitely be consulted before purchase.

Automatic Cannon in Military Service After World War I

Only the most commonly encountered weapons are included here, and consequently this should not be regarded as a complete list.

American Armed Forces

Oerlikon Mark 2, Mark 3 and Mark 4

Used in a variety of configurations as a naval AA gun and in a similar role by land forces.

Bofors 40mm/L60

Production: precise records not available, estimated at 60,000 weapons.

Produced under license by Chrysler, who adapted the design for mass production, and thereby reduced production time and costs by half.

Naval service

These were both water-cooled guns.

Bofors 40mm/56 Mark 1: Designed to be fitted on the left side of a twin mounting.
Bofors 40mm/56 Mark 2: Designed to be fitted on the right side of a twin mounting.

Land service

Bofors 40mm automatic gun M1: This was a single Bofors 40mm/L60 mounted on the standard carriage and firing high-explosive or armor-piercing shells.[38]

British and Commonwealth armed forces

Oerlikon Mk I and Mk II

Used in a variety of configurations as a naval AA gun and in a similar role by land forces.

Bofors 40mm/L60

Production: precise records not available, estimated at 4,500 weapons during World War II, with a significant number also produced after the war.

Similar in all respects to the weapon produced for service with the U.S. military, so that even the ammunition was interchangeable.

Originally designated the 40mm OQF (Ordnance, Quick-Firing) and produced in a variety of types for both land and naval service, British guns were made under license and also modified for mass production.

Naval service

The Royal Navy began using the air-cooled Bofors 40mm after their withdrawal from Norway, but quickly switched to the water-cooled version in 1940, after receiving a single example from Holland after Dunkirk. A number of different versions were fitted to Royal Navy ships, in a bewildering array of mountings.

Land service

QF 40mm Mark I: The original design from Bofors modified for mass production.
QF 40mm Mark III: Bofors 40mm fitted with the Kerrison Predictor, to improve targeting. This became the British army's standard light AA gun.
QF 40mm Mark IV: Improvement on the Mark III Bofors 40mm.
QF 40mm Mark VI: Bofors 40mm with a modified breech mechanism, mounted on a Crusader tank chassis and designated the Crusader III AA Mark I.
QF 40mm Mark XII: Bofors 40mm fitted with the "Stiffkey" sighting system and an improved elevating mechanism.[39]

Hispano Mk.1

Production: precise records not available, estimated at over 42,000 weapons.

British version of the HS .404i produced under license and fitted to a variety of aircraft in both fixed and flexible mountings.

Variants

Hispano Mk II: Belt-fed version of the Mk I.
Hispano Mk V: Manually cocked, belt-fed version of the HS .404, with a shorter barrel, lighter mechanism and a higher cyclic rate than earlier weapons.[40]

French Armed Forces

Hispano-Suiza HS .404i

Production: precise records not available, estimated at 80,000 weapons based upon the number of Allied aircraft to which it was fitted.

Produced by Hispano-Suiza from 1942, this weapon was an air-cooled, gas-operated, delayed-blowback, fully automatic cannon, chambered for a 20 × 110mm Hispano "A" cannon shell and having a cyclic rate between 600 and 700 rpm. Ammunition was originally contained in a magazine, but this was quickly found to be disadvantageous, and a belt-fed system was developed. Although its main deployment was as an aircraft gun, it was also used in an AA role by land forces. Ammunition types available included:

- Ball: This was designated the 20mm Ball Mk.I cartridge in U.S. service.
- Semi-Armor Piercing, Incendiary (SAPI): This was designated the 20mm Armor Piercing-Tracer M75 in U.S. service.
- High Explosive, Incendiary (HEI): This was designated the 20mm High Explosive-Incendiary Mk.I in U.S. service.[41]

German Armed Forces

MG FF

German version of the Oerlikon FF produced under license

3.7 cm Flak 18

First in a series of AA cannon produced by Rheinmetall from 1935, this was an air-cooled, fully automatic, gas-operated weapon with a cyclic rate of between 80 and 120 rpm, depending upon the model. It was chambered for a 37 × 263mm shell, which was supplied to the mechanism by a clip holding 8 shells. The Flak 18 was usually mounted on a cumbersome, twin-axle carriage, giving the weapon a total weight of 2,000 kg.

Variants

3.7mm Flak 36: Improved version of the Flak 18, with a lighter, single-axle carriage, weighing only 1,500 kg, and a higher cyclic rate of approximately 120 rpm.

3.7mm Flak 37: Improved version of the Flak 36, with a better sighting system.[42]

4cm Flak 28

Designation for Bofors 40mm guns captured and returned to service with the German Navy.

Japanese Armed Forces

Type 99–1 autocannon

Production: precise records not available.

Japanese version of the Oerlikon FF produced in Japan and used by the Japanese Navy.

Type 99-2 autocannon

Production: precise records not available.

Japanese version of the Oerlikon FFL produced in Japan and used by the Japanese Navy.

Type 5 autocannon

Designation for Bofors 40mm guns captured and returned to service with Japanese forces.

CHAPTER TWENTY

Assault Rifles and the Rise of the "Woolworth's" Gun

Consideration of multi-fire and repeating weapons produced after World War II do not come within the scope of this book, but the direction in which military firearms and, in particular, service rifles began to move after World War II really had its origin in the period before the start of that conflict, and so a short digression seems to be in order.

As with much of the innovation in weapons design that took place in the early years of the 20th century, it was German ingenuity, as well as the pressures placed on the Wehrmacht at the end of World War II, that produced the first in a group of weapons that later came to be referred to as assault rifles. Initially it had been submachine guns in pistol calibers such as the Thompson, German MP18, British STEN and U.S. M3 "Grease Gun" that had signaled a new attitude to equipment of this type by many in the military of both the West and Eastern Bloc countries. Although Britain in particular had originally been forced by wartime economies to produce the Sten, the success of what became known as the "Woolworth's" gun could not be ignored. This class of weapon now put a gun capable of firing 500 rounds per minute and weighing only 7 lbs into the hands of an individual soldier for a cost of £2, the sort of firepower that had only been possible previously using a four-man team and a Vickers weighing well in excess of 100 lbs and costing over £100. So it came as no surprise that forward-thinking military minds saw this type of weapon as potentially the service rifle of the future. Unfortunately, these pistol-caliber weapons had a number of disadvantages, mostly associated with the ranges over which accurate fire could be delivered and the relatively low power of the service pistol cartridge for which they were chambered.

Consequently in 1942, German firearms designers began to look for a way of producing a weapon that combined the firing rate of a submachine gun with a high-power service rifle cartridge. What they eventually came up with was designated the MP44 assault rifle. It was not quite the solution the military wanted, because although its stamped steel and welded construction made it cheap to make and it would operate as a fully automatic weapon, it could not be chambered for the 7.62 × 57mm Mauser German service rifle cartridge. Instead it had to use a shorter, weaker cartridge, the 7.92 × 33mm Kurz, a rimless, bottle-necked cartridge, which was developed specifically for the MP44 as a compromise between the 7.92 × 57mm service rifle cartridge and the 9 × 19mm Parabellum pistol cartridge. This type of intermediate cartridge came to be associated with the assault rifle. Selective-fire weapons chambered for a full-power service rifle cartridge are referred to as battle rifles, although this distinction is not always clearly adopted in some texts.

Kalashnicov's AK-47 was arguably the culmination of this process. It has been developed over a number of years and a huge variety of types, to produce the final refined production version of a gun that began its service life with significantly fewer flaws than some of its more sophisticated competitors.[1]

The StG 44 Assault Rifle

During World War I, many in the military establishments on both sides began to realize that the full-power rifle cartridges being used in service rifles and fully automatic machine guns were capable of firing a bullet far in excess of the distance at which an average soldier could consistently hit a man-sized target. The costs involved in producing such a cartridge were worrying as well. In the spring of 1918, a Germany army officer, Captain Piderit, submitted a memo to the General Staff, explaining that because a fire fight rarely took place with troops more than 800 meters apart, a weapon chambered for a smaller, less powerful cartridge would have significant advantages at these more typical combat ranges. These included a lighter cartridge, thus allowing more to be carried and saving both materials and money, along with the possibility of producing a selective-fire arm in this conformation. Piderit was ignored, but in 1923, the German army began looking for a replacement for its Mauser 98 rifle, specifying that it should be lighter, with a 20- or 30-round magazine, and having similar accuracy at 400 meters. Desultory interest in designing a new weapon was shown by some manufacturers, but by the start of World War II, the Wehrmacht was still equipped with a mixture of bolt-action Mausers, light machine guns and a few MP40 submachine pistols.[2]

However, in 1942, the German High Command became concerned about the high casualty rates amongst its airborne troops during the invasion of Crete. The paratroopers had been forced to land with their heavy weapons dropped in separate containers, often at some distance from the drop zone, and attempts to retrieve the canisters had resulted in a significant number of casualties. The High Command asked for a selective-fire weapon with a longer range than a submachine carbine, and light enough to be carried by the parachute troops during a descent. This request resulted in the development of the FG 42, a selective-fire weapon chambered for the 7.92 × 57mm German service rifle cartridge.

A few German units were issued with this weapon, but the heavy recoil of the cartridge made it difficult to use efficiently as a personal weapon. The answer to the problem of a long-range, selective-fire rifle seemed to lie with a redesigned cartridge, which could be used in a lighter, more maneuverable rifle that would be a good compromise between a submachine carbine and the bolt-action rifle, with acceptable accuracy up to the usual combat range of about 300 yards. Consequently, German firearms designers shortened the Mauser cartridge by 24mm while retaining the rest of the original dimensions of the case. With a cartridge now only 33 mm in length, the resulting Kurz round was found to have less recoil than the full-size cartridge while still being almost as effective at typical combat ranges. Such a cartridge could be fired effectively from a selective-fire weapon that weighed less than a machine gun, yet still had much greater range, velocity, and stopping power than a typical submachine gun. The Kurz was also significantly lighter than the standard rifle cartridge, which meant that more could be carried into combat without incapacitating the troops involved.

Unfortunately, the Russian invasion and the effective use the Red army made of its SVT 38/40 semiautomatic rifles and PPSh-1 submachine guns, which had been issued on a huge scale, made the introduction of such a weapon imperative. This led to the development of the MP 44, which used the 7.92 × 33mm Kurz cartridge, although the rifle was not produced without a certain amount of interference from the Fuhrer himself. However, once he had seen it demonstrated, he was impressed sufficiently to rename it the "Sturmgewehr" (trans: Storm, i.e., Assault Rifle), and it was renamed the StG 44, in order to take advantage of the potential for propaganda that seemed inherent in such a name.[3]

Specification

Production: 425,977 weapons of all types.

The MP44 or StG 44 assault rifle is a gas-operated selective-fire weapon, with a cyclic rate of 550 rpm when set to fully automatic, firing from a closed bolt with a hammer firing system and chambered for the 7.92 × 33mm Kurz intermediate rifle cartridge contained in a curved, detachable box magazine holding 30 cartridges. The cocking handle is on the left, with the ejection port on the right of the pressed steel receiver, with a fire selection switch positioned above the pistol grip on the left, which is used to set the weapon to deliver either semiautomatic or full automatic fire. The front sight is of the hooded post type, while the rear sight is an adjustable V-notch; later weapons were equipped with an infrared aiming device, designated "Vampir" (trans: Vampire). The original MP 44s had a wooden butt, although the plates on the pistol grip were of hard plastic, and guns from later production runs also appear to have had plastic butts. Sling swivels were included in the standard design and a significant percentage of weapons offered for sale will be found with a substantial leather sling, which was fitted to facilitate fully automatic operation.[4]

Operation

Operation was conventional for a gas-operated weapon firing from a closed bolt. A magazine is first inserted into its slot in the bottom of the receiver and a round is chambered by pulling back the cocking lever and then allowing it to return to its original position. Pulling the trigger fired the cartridge, and after the bullet had passed far enough up the barrel, residual gas moved through the gas port and entered the gas cylinder, which was mounted over the barrel, pushing the gas piston and its attached bolt backwards, unlocking the bolt from the barrel in the process, compressing the recoil spring and ejecting the spent case. Having reached the limit of its travel, the recoil spring pushed the bolt forward, causing it to chamber a cartridge, before the bolt and barrel were locked together once again. If the weapon is set to automatic fire and the trigger is still depressed, the hammer strikes the primer and fires the cartridge. With the weapon's setting at semiautomatic, the hammer is retained in its cocked position until the trigger is operated.[5]

Variants

Mkb 42 (H)

Production: precise records unavailable, estimated at 12,000 weapons.
This was the first prototype produced by Haenal in 1942.

MP 43

Production: precise records not available.
Almost exactly similar to the Mkb 42, but redesignated the MP 43 to convince Hitler that this was an upgrade of existing submachine guns.

MP 44

Production: precise records not available, estimated at 426,000 weapons.
This weapon was an MP 43, redesignated the MP 44 at Hitler's express orders. He later changed the name to Sturmgewehr 44 or StG 44 (trans: Storm or Assault rifle, Model 1944).

Krummlauf: a development of the StG 44 with a bent barrel, devised to shoot around corners. Versions were produced with 30-, 45-, 60- and 90-degree bends, although only the version with the 30-degree barrel was produced in significant numbers. The weapon had numerous disadvantages; barrels were useless after the passage of only 300 rounds, and bullets tended to disintegrate before leaving the muzzle.[6]

Military service

The StG 44 assault rifle proved a valuable weapon, especially on the Eastern Front, where it was first deployed, because a trained soldier with this gun had a wider tactical capacity. He was able to engage targets at longer ranges than with an MP 40 and to be much more useful than a soldier armed with a Kar 98k in close combat, as well as being able to provide suppressive fire in the manner of a light machine gun. It was also found to be exceptionally reliable in extreme cold and proved capable of countering the effective Soviet PPS and PPSh-41 submachine guns, which used the 7.62 × 25mm Tokarev service pistol round. These were more effective weapons than either the Kar 98 or MP 40 because of their 71-round drum magazine or 35-round box magazines. Although they lacked the long-range effectiveness of the Kar 98k rifle, they were more useful in close-quarter engagements, which were a predominant feature of the battle of Stalingrad and other engagements on the Eastern Front. However, the StG 44, while lacking the range of the Kar 98k, had a considerably longer range than the PPS/PPSh submachine guns, used a more powerful cartridge, had a comparable rate of fire, and was surprisingly accurate up to 300 meters. This was not sufficient to change the outcome of the Russian campaign, but it did serve to show all the major military powers that this type of weapon could provide an individual user with unparalleled firepower compared to earlier service weapons and heralded a move by other countries to investigate the concept of the assault rifle soon after the end of World War II.[7]

Values

Working StG 44s imported into the U.S. and registered before 1986 are transferable between owners. Consequently, these weapons are sometimes offered for sale, although only the products of the later period are seen with any frequency and condition is quite variable. Local regulations as they apply to these weapons should be consulted before purchase.

Prices are for weapons capable of firing.

NRA Good: $25,000; NRA Fine: $30,000

The Kalashnikov AK47 Assault Rifle: The Russian "Woolworth's" Gun

During World War II, the MP 44 assault rifle used by the Wehrmacht had made a deep impression on the Soviet forces opposing them. The German assault rifle was chambered for a new type of cartridge, intermediate in power between a service pistol round and a rifle cartridge, and combined the firing rate of a submachine gun with almost the range and accuracy of a service rifle. Soviet military officials were so enthusiastic about this new type of service weapon that they immediately ordered work to begin on developing an automatic rifle chambered for a cartridge of intermediate power to replace the PPSh-41 submachine guns and outdated Mosin-Nagant bolt-action rifles used by the Russian Army. A number of weapons resulted from this drive for improvement, such as the SKS semiautomatic carbine and RPD light machine gun, both chambered for a new 7.62 × 39mm M43 Soviet service rifle cartridge. But it was not until 1948 that the best weapon of what had, until then, been a rather mediocre collection made its appearance, Mikhail Kalashnikov's AK-47.[8]

Kalashnikov began his career as a weapon designer in 1941, while recuperating from a shoulder wound received during the Battle of Bryansk. He claimed: "I was in the hospital, and a soldier in the bed beside me asked: 'Why do our soldiers have only one rifle for two or three of our men, when the Germans have automatics? So I designed one. I was a soldier, and I created a machine gun for a soldier. It was called an Avtomat Kalashnikova, the automatic weapon of Kalashnikov—AK—and it carried the date of its first manufacture, 1947."

The AK-47 assault rifle was in reality a combination of a number of innovations previously developed for other service weapons, combining, as it did, the best features of the American M1 and the German StG 44, although Kalashnikov may have also used features from a number of other designs. By November 1947, the final prototype of the AK-47 was completed, featuring a long-stroke, large-diameter gas piston above the barrel and what had previously been the upper and lower receivers combined into a single unit. Selector and safety levers were also improved by combining them into a single control lever and dust cover on the right side of the rifle, and the bolt-handle was simply attached to the bolt-carrier, all these features being designed to simplify production and reduce the unit cost of the new rifle. The first series of trials by the Red Army began early in 1948, and the new rifle proved to have convenient handling characteristic as well as being reliable under a wide range of adverse service conditions, resulting in its adoption by the Soviet Army as the "7.62 mm Kalashnikov assault rifle (AK)."[9]

SPECIFICATION

Production: precise records not available, estimated at 100 million weapons of all types.

The Kalashnikov AK-47 is a selective-fire, gas-operated assault rifle with a rotating bolt mechanism firing from a closed bolt, with a cyclic rate on fully automatic of 600 rpm and the cocking handle on the right side of the receiver, with the ejection port on the left. It was originally chambered for the 7.62 × 39mm Soviet intermediate rifle cartridge, but weapons made after 1974 are chambered for the 5.43 × 39mm Soviet rifle cartridge. It is fitted with a characteristic curved magazine holding 30 cartridges, and there is a fire selector lever on the left hand side of the weapon that sets the weapon to deliver either semiautomatic or full automatic fire. The butt, foregrip and upper heat guard were originally in solid wood, usually walnut, but later weapons featured a laminated plywood stock, usually of birch, which was cheaper and proved more durable under service conditions. Front sights consist of a simple post, which can be adjusted for elevation without tools, while the rear sight is a conventional notched tangent fitting calibrated from 100 meters to 800 meters, in increments of 100 meters, although the "point blank" setting on a AK-47 is 300 meters. At that range, soldiers were simply instructed to aim at an enemy soldier's belt buckle, since any ballistic error would still result in a bullet striking the torso.[10]

OPERATION

To fire an AK-47, a loaded magazine is first inserted into the magazine housing and the charging handle is pulled back and released, chambering a cartridge. If the trigger is then operated, the sear is released and the firing pin moves forward, striking the primer and firing the cartridge. The bullet moves up the barrel and part of the propellant gas is diverted into the gas cylinder above the barrel through a series of radial ports, driving the long-stroke piston and bolt carrier backwards. A cam guide machined into the underside of the bolt carrier, along with an ejector spur on the bolt carrier rail guide, rotates the bolt approximately 35° and unlocks it from the barrel extension by means of a shaped pin on the bolt. This assembly has about 5.5 mm of free travel, which creates a delay between the initial recoiling of the piston and the bolt unlocking sequence, allowing gas pressures to drop to a safe level in the barrel before the chamber and bolt separate. The bolt continues to move backwards, compressing the recoil spring, at which point the empty case is removed from the chamber by the extractor and ejected. The bolt then reverses direction, removing a cartridge from the magazine and pushing it into the chamber, whereupon the bolt rotates, locking the bolt and barrel extension together. The firing pin then moves forward and the cartridge is fired. If the mechanism is set for automatic fire, this sequence continues until the trigger is released or the magazine is empty. When set to "semiautomatic," the firing pin is engaged by the sear at the end of its rearwards travel and the trigger must be operated to fire the next cartridge.

Kalashnikov's mechanism was not sophisticated, even by the standards of weapons designers in the 1950s, but it had one considerable advantage over its better-made competitors. Like those of the MkIII Sten, the manufacturing tolerances of the AK-47 are not very demanding, and because of the looseness of its mechanism, which only gets looser with age, dirt, sand and cartridge residue do not significantly affect its performance, unlike its main competitor, the M16. Experience showed that the American service weapon needed to be kept scrupulously clean to avoid the sort of stoppages that plagued it when it was first introduced and for much of its later service life.[11]

Variants

Early variants (1948–1955)

All these weapons are chambered for the 7.62 × 39mm Soviet cartridge.

Type 1: issued 1948–1949: This was the earliest model fitted with a stamped sheet metal receiver and is considered to be very rare by collectors.

Type 2: issued 1951: This weapon was the first fitted with a milled receiver, and the barrel and chamber were chrome plated to resist corrosion.

Type 3: issued 1954–1955: This model was fitted with a lightened, milled receiver, reducing the overall weight, with a loaded magazine, to 3.47 kg (7.7 lb).

AKS or AKS-47: May be found with a Type 1, 2, or 3 receiver, but was fitted with a downward-folding metal stock similar to that of the German MP40, for use in the restricted space in the BMP infantry combat vehicle, as well as by paratroops.

AKN or AKSN: An AKS fitted with a sight rail suitable for an infrared night sight.

Modern variants

All these weapons are chambered for the 7.62 × 39mm Soviet cartridge.

AKM: Considered to be the most ubiquitous variant of the AK-47, this was a simplified, lighter version of the original AK-47, weighing only 3.1 kg (6.8 lb). It was fitted with a redesigned Type 4 receiver manufactured from stamped and riveted sheet metal, which reduced its weight to 3.1 kg (6.8 lb) and a slanted muzzle device to counteract the weapon's tendency to rise up under the stress of automatic fire.

- **AKMS:** AKM fitted with an under-folding stock, intended for airborne troops.
- **AKMN:** AKM fitted with a telescope sight rail designed for a night sight.
- **AKMSN:** AKM fitted with an under-folding stock and a telescope sight rail designed for a night sight (night scope rail).
- **AKML:** AKM fitted with a slotted flash suppressor and a night scope rail.
- **AKMSL:** AKM fitted with a folding stock, a slotted flash suppressor and night scope rail.

RPK

Light machine gun version of the AKM, fitted with a longer barrel and bipod.

- **RPKS:** RPK fitted with a side-folding, wooden stock, intended for airborne troops.
- **RPKN:** RPK fitted with a telescope sight rail designed for a night sight.
- **RPKSN:** RPK fitted with a side-folding, wooden stock and a night scope rail.
- **RPKL:** RPK fitted with a slotted flash suppressor and a night scope rail.
- **RPKSL:** RPK fitted with a folding stock, a slotted flash suppressor and night scope rail.

Variants chambered in 5.45mm

All these weapons are chambered for the 5.45 × 39mm Soviet cartridge.

AK-74: Assault rifle

- **AKS-74:** An AK-74 fitted with a side-folding stock.
- **AK-74N:** An AK-74 fitted with a night scope rail.
- **AKS-74N:** An AK-74 fitted with a side-folding stock and a night scope rail.

AKS-74U: Compact carbine, fitted with a shorter barrel and stock

- **AKS-74UN:** AKS-74U fitted with a night scope rail.

RPK-74: Light machine gun, fitted with a longer barrel and a bipod

- **RPKS-74:** RPK-74 fitted with a side-folding stock.
- **RPK-74N:** RPK-74 fitted with a night scope rail.
- **RPKS-74N:** RPK-74 fitted with a side-folding stock and night scope rail.

The 100 Series: chambered for either 5.45 × 39mm, 5.56 × 45mm or 7.62 × 39mm cartridges

- **AK-74M/AK-101/AK-103:** Modernized AK-74s fitted with a rail designed to accept a telescopic sight and a side-folding stock.
- **AK-107/AK-108:** Redesigned AK-74 fitted with a balanced recoil mechanism.
- **AK-105/AK-102/AK-104:** Carbine version of the AK-107 and AK-108.
- **RPK-74M/RPK-201/RPKM and RPK-203:** Squad automatic weapon.[12]

MILITARY SERVICE

Military service has been extensive and would require a book to itself, but it is sufficient to say that the AK-47 and its later variants were the favored weapon of both terrorists and guerrillas during the late 20th century, and it was an AK-47 that was usually firing at U.S. troops during most of their operations in that period.

Table Forty. Comparison of the specification of the StG 44 and AK-47 assault rifles

Weapon	StG 44	AK-47
Manufacturer	**World War II:** C.G. Haenel Waffen und Fahrradfabrik Steyr-Daimler-Puch	Kalashnicov Concern Norinco Innumerable unlicensed gun makers
Period of production	1943 until 1945	USSR: 1949–1978 Worldwide: 1949–present (2017)
Production	425,977 weapons of all types	In excess of 100 million weapons of all types
Operators	Argentina, Czechoslovakia, Germany (1945–1945), East Germany, Hungary, USSR, Poland, Syrian National Coalition, Yugoslavia	USSR and almost every Third World country
Military service	World War II, Korean War, Algerian War, Vietnam War, Ogaden War, Iraq War, Syrian Civil War	Korean War, Algerian War, Vietnam War, Ogaden War, Iraq War, Syrian Civil War, together with many other conflicts and minor operations.

Twenty. Assault Rifles and the Rise of the "Woolworth's" Gun

RPK light machine gun, in service in Iraq. The soldier nearest to the camera is using a weapon that has the butt repaired with duct tape.

Weapon	StG 44	AK-47
Weight	Magazine empty: 4.6 kg (10 lb) Magazine full: 5.13 kg (11.3 lb)	Magazine empty: 3.9 kg (8.6 lb) Magazine full: 4.4 kg (9.9 lb)
Length/Barrel length	Total length: 940mm (37 inches) Barrel: 42cms (16.5 inches)	Fixed stock: 880mm (35 inches) Folding stock: 875mm Stock folded: 645mm (25.4 inches) Barrel: 415mm (16 inches)
Construction	Receiver made from pressed and welded steel, with machined components in the internal mechanism and a machined barrel	Receiver made from pressed and welded steel, with machined components in the internal mechanism and a machined barrel
Mechanism	Air-cooled, selective-fire, gas-operated, tilting-bolt mechanism, firing from a closed bolt.	Air-cooled, selective-fire, gas-operated, rotating-bolt mechanism, firing from a closed bolt.
Cartridge	7.92 × 33mm Kurz Delivered from a detachable box magazine holding 30 cartridges	7.62 × 39mm Soviet rifle cartridge Delivered from a detachable box magazine holding 30 cartridges 5-, 10-, 20- and 40-round box magazines are available, as well as a 100-round drum magazine.
Sights	Front: adjustable hooded post Rear: adjustable V-notch	Front: adjustable hooded post Rear: adjustable V-notch
Maximum range	Automatic fire: 300 meters Semi-automatic: 600 meters	Automatic fire: 100 meters Semi-automatic: 350 meters
Rate of fire	Between 550 and 600 rpm	600 rpm
Cost to manufacture	$30 (£6 or 66 Reich Marks)	Variable but between $20 and $50,

| Weapon | StG 44 | AK-47 |

although in Central Africa AK-47s can be exchanged for a bag of maize.

Values

Working AK-47s imported into the U.S. and registered before 1986 are transferable between owners. Consequently, these weapons are sometimes offered for sale, although only the products of the later period are seen with any frequency and condition is quite variable. Local regulations as they apply to these weapons should be consulted before purchase.

Prices are for weapons capable of firing.
NRA Good: $25,000; NRA Fine: $30,000

AK-47M assault rifle, this weapon with a full stock, the most commonly encountered Kalashnikov.

Later Developments: Assault and Battle Rifles

After the end of World War II, the success of the StG 44 meant that the assault rifle was being given serious consideration by forces deployed under the control of the newly formed NATO and its allies, both because of the relative cheapness of both the guns and ammunition they used, and because of their effective performance on the battlefield. British and American efforts in the field led to the development of the L1A1 self-loading rifle and M14 respectively, with European and Soviet bloc countries following design paths similar to the British and American small arms development programs. Details of these weapons are to be found in the books included in the bibliography, in particular the excellent works by the late Ian Hogg.

In many publications, the terms "assault" rifle and "battle" rifle are used indiscriminately, although originally the term battle rifle was used specifically to describe selective-fire infantry rifles that were chambered for a full-power rifle cartridge such as the FN FAL, M14 and H&K G3. An assault rifle used a less powerful cartridge, which was cheaper to manufacture and lighter, so more could be carried, but was powerful enough to be useful at the sort of ranges over which infantry generally found themselves fighting, usually between 100 and 300 meters. Battle rifles have declined in popularity since the end of World War II, principally because it has been found impossible to make a rifle chambered for such a powerful cartridge that was controllable when used to deliver fully automatic fire. American experience with the M14 was salutary in this respect, and the British seem to have duly taken note of this, their excellent L1A1 battle rifle being designed for semiautomatic operation only. Price is also still a significant factor in military logistic calculations, but the NATO powers seem incapable of learning that a little extra money and time spent on research and development is a saving in the long run. As evidence, consider the extensive modification programs undertaken by the Americans with their original M16 prototype, and by the British army experience during their disastrous adoption of the original SA80, although Heckler & Koch did manage to get them out of that one.

American Assault and Battle Rifles

M14

Production: precise records not available, estimated at 1.5 million weapons.

Accepted into service as the U.S. infantry service rifle in 1957, this is a selective-fire, gas-operated, magazine-fed battle rifle with a rotating bolt mechanism, firing from a closed bolt and with a cyclic rate of 700 rpm when set to fully automatic. It was chambered for the 7.62 × 51mm NATO service rifle cartridge, the ammunition being contained in a detachable box magazine holding 20 rounds. The fire selector switch was on the right side just above the trigger. Sights were fitted, the front sight being a conventional "barleycorn" pattern, while the rear sight was of the adjustable aperture pattern. Butt and foregrips were made of one piece of walnut. The M14 did not prove particularly effective, especially under adverse environmental conditions, such as Vietnam, where the heavy wooden stock tended to swell, affecting both accuracy and cycling. Its powerful service rifle cartridge made it hard to control when set to deliver fully automatic fire and it was replaced, by the lighter M16 in 1966.[13]

M14 from right, showing the bolt and muzzle suppressor.

M16

Production: precise records not readily available, but estimated at 8 million weapons of all types.

Based on Colt's original AR-15 Armalite design and accepted into service as the U.S. military standard service rifle in 1969, this is an air-cooled, selective-fire, magazine-fed, gas-operated assault rifle with a rotating bolt mechanism, firing from a closed bolt and with a cyclic rate of between 700 and 950 rpm when set to fully automatic. Charging handle and ejection port are both on the right side of the receiver. It is chambered for the 5.56 ×

51mm NATO cartridge, which was contained originally in a detachable, straight box magazine holding 20 rounds, although this was changed subsequently to a curved, detachable box magazine holding 30 rounds. There is a magazine release button mounted on the right side of the receiver above the magazine housing. Colt M16 magazines were designed to be disposable, lightweight items, and the design and manufacture of these components led to problems that exacerbated the M16's poor early performance. The sights are unique, the front sight being a simple post, while the rear sight is incorporated into the characteristic carrying handle mounted above the receiver. It is an elevating, aperture rear sight with windage adjustment, incorporating two settings in the original design, zero to 300 meters and 300 to 400 meters, although a variety of more sophisticated fittings have been developed for the weapon. One of the requirements of the early design was that the original M16 be as light as possible. Consequently the receiver is of aluminum alloy, with a steel barrel, bolt, and bolt carrier, while foregrip, pistol grip, and butt are in high-grade hard plastic, giving a total weight for a M16A1 of under 8 lb with a full 30-round magazine. A number of accessories are available, including a grenade launcher.

Variations

AR15

Production: precise records not available.

The forerunner of the M16, which was purchased in limited numbers by the U.S. government for its Special Forces teams.

M16

Production: precise records not available.

The original design adopted by the USAF, with characteristic triangular foregrip, three-pronged flash suppressor, fully automatic operation only, no forward assist to clear a fouled cartridge, and no storage compartment for a cleaning kit, since Colt insisted their original rifle required no cleaning. Army weapons were not chrome-lined, which was one of the causes of the excessive number of stoppages experienced by U.S. troops issued with this weapon in Vietnam.

XM16E1

Production: precise records not available.

The XM16E1 was essentially an M16 with forward assist.

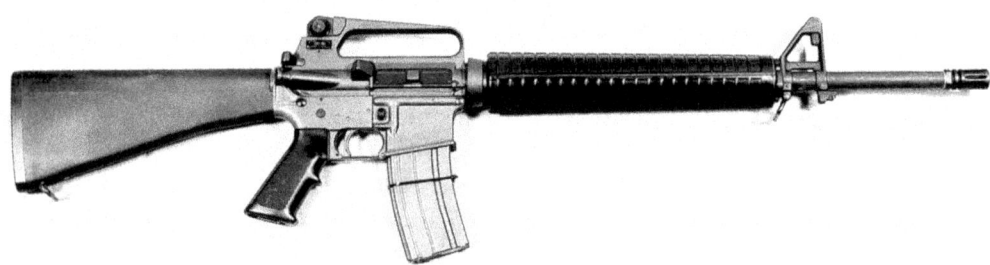

Early M16 from the right, showing pistol grip, magazine and characteristic front and rear sights.

M16A1

Production: precise records not available.

Improved version of the M16 with new improved flash suppressor, chrome-plated chambers (barrels also lined in weapons from later production), and a rib on the side of the receiver to prevent premature ejection of the magazine. Cleaning kits and lubricants were also developed and issued, the M16A1 being fitted with a compartment in the butt to hold these materials.

M16A2

Production: precise records not available.

Officially adopted by U.S. Department of Defense as "US Rifle, 5.56mm, M16A2" in 1982, this was a redesigned M16A1, with many of the weapon's original defects corrected. Improvements included a thicker barrel to allow longer periods of sustained fire; an improved rear sight with settings between 300 and 800 meters; a new flash suppressor; a smaller, round foregrip to accommodate personnel with small hands; an improved pistol grip; and a longer, much stronger butt. The mechanism was also modified, replacing fully automatic operation with a "3-round burst" setting.

M16A3

Production: precise records not available.

An M16A2 modified to deliver fully automatic fire instead of a 3-round burst.

M16A4

Production: precise records not available.

Latest variant of the M16, featuring amongst other improvements a removable carrying handle and full-length rail to mount optical sights; a new foregrip, allowing a variety of tactical accessories to be fitted; and a muzzle compensator to manage recoil, replacing the earlier flash suppressor.

M4

Production: precise records not available.

Adopted in October 2015 as the U.S. army's standard service rifle, this is essentially a M16A4 fitted with a shorter barrel and considered a carbine rather than a rifle.[14]

British assault and battle rifles

L1A1 SLR (Self-loading Rifle)

Production: precise records not available, estimated 500,000 weapons of all types.

Adopted by the British army in 1954, this weapon is a development of the FN FAL Light Automatic Rifle and is often referred to as the "Inch Pattern," because the design was adapted to use Imperial units in its manufacture. It is an air-cooled, magazine-fed, semi-automatic battle rifle with a gas-operated, tilting-breech block mechanism, chambered for the 7.62 × 51mm NATO cartridge, ammunition being contained in a detachable box magazine holding either 20 or 30 rounds. A magazine release catch is fitted on the right side above the magazine, and a fire selector switch with safe (marked "S") and fire (marked "R" for repetition) positions is located on the left side of the weapon. The cocking handle folds and a flash suppressor is fitted, with a carrying handle mounted over the receiver and designed to fold down next to the magazine housing. Front sights are of the iron post pattern in a "V" configuration, while rear sights are an adjustable aperture pattern, calibrated between zero and 800 yards, although a number of more sophisticated systems were also available. The butt, pistol grip, foregrip and carrying handle were originally made from walnut, which was treated with oil as a protection against moisture. Weapons produced later have synthetic furniture with an anti-slip finish, made from a nylon and fiberglass composite called Maranyl. These guns also feature an adjustable butt, available in four lengths. A number of accessories are available, including a grenade launcher.

The L1A1 was used by the armed forces of Australia, Britain, Canada, India, Jamaica, Malaysia and New Zealand, as well as a number of smaller countries.

Variations

L1A1

Production: precise records not available.

This is the standard weapon accepted into service with the British army in in 1954 and retained until 1998. Different models were produced for use by Commonwealth forces, those in use by the Canadian being designated the C1/A1.

L2A1/C2A1

L1A1 rifle adapted for use as a light machine gun and modified for fully automatic operation. Changes included a heavier barrel, square front sight, a foregrip that could be converted to a bipod, and a larger, 30-round magazine. Only in use with Australia and Canada, Canadian weapons being designated C2A1.[15]

SA 80 assault rifle

Production: precise records not available, estimated at 350,000 weapons.

In service with the British army from 1985 to the present (2017), this is a selective-fire, magazine-fed, gas-operated assault rifle with a rotating-bolt, hammer-fired mechanism. It is chambered for the 5.56 × 45mm NATO cartridge, contained in detachable box magazine holding 30 cartridges, and has a magazine release lever mounted on the left side of the receiver above the magazine housing. The weapon has a "Bullpup" configuration, with the action behind the trigger assembly and a fire selector switch giving either semiautomatic or fully automatic fire mounted on the left side of the receiver behind the magazine. Cocking handle and ejection port are both on the right of the receiver and a "cross-bolt" pattern safety catch is fitted just behind the trigger, the "safe" setting locking, rather than disconnecting, the trigger. The muzzle has a slotted flash suppressor that includes a mounting for launching rifle grenades or attaching a bayonet. Butt, pistol grip and foregrip are all synthetic, and the weapons construction is of welded, stamped sheet steel, only the barrel and parts of the mechanism being machined components. Optical sights are fitted to most weapons, the usual pattern being the SUSAT (Sight Unit Small Arms, Trilux), an optical sight with a 4× magnification, and an illuminated pointer. Iron sights are also fitted for some operational uses, and these consist of a blade foresight with a rear "flip-up" aperture sight.

Variations

L85 IW RIFLE

Production: precise records not available, estimated at 300,000 weapons.

The L85 IW (Individual Weapon) was originally accepted into service with the British army in 1985 as the L85A1 variant of the SA80, but this weapon proved so unreliable that a series of improvements were ordered. This resulted in the far superior L85A2, which is now the new L85 IW rifle, officially designated "Rifle, 5.56 mm, L85A2," and the standard rifle for British armed forces.

The upgrading exercise on the L85A1 was implemented by the BaE subsidiary Heckler & Koch and concentrated on improving both reliability and durability. Changes included a redesigned cocking handle, modified bolt and extractor, as well as a redesigned hammer assembly that produces a slight delay in the hammer's operation in continuous fire mode, which improved reliability. There were also improvements to the quality of the plastic furniture and magazines. These changes produced a weapon that has now been demonstrated to be more reliable than any of its contemporaries, including the M4 variant of the M16. It can be used with an LLM01 laser light module sighting device and the L123A1UGL 40mm under barrel grenade launcher.

L86 LIGHT SUPPORT WEAPON

Production: precise records not available, estimated at 50,000 weapons.

This weapon is a development of the infantry rifle fitted with a longer barrel and a bipod, shoulder strap and rear pistol grip, together with a shorter handguard. Apart from these changes the weapon is identical to the L85A1 on which it is based, and the same 30-round magazines and sighting systems are used. The extended barrel gives the weapon a greater effective range by increasing the muzzle velocity and improving the stability of the bullet's flight. The weapon also has a fire selector on the left side behind the magazine housing, enabling it to deliver either single shots or automatic fire. It was originally designed as a SAW (Squad Automatic Weapon), and after the period in which modifications were introduced to improve and upgrade the L85A1, the L86A1 was also improved to the L86A2 specification, incorporating the same improvements as those introduced for the infantry's individual weapon. Even in its improved form, however, the L86A suffered by comparison with similar arms, because it lacked both a quick-change barrel and a belt-feed system. It was subsequently replaced in service with the British Army by the FN mini machine gun.

L22A1 AND L22A2

Production: precise records not available, but estimated at 6,000 weapons.

A short-barreled version of the L85A2 (12.5 inches instead of 20.4 as in the original L85A2), designed to be used by tank, armored vehicle and air crews when in action out of their vehicles, and manufactured from surplus L86A2s. With the exception of the shorter barrel, it had the same configuration as the infantry weapon, except it was fitted with a vertical front grip instead of the conventional foregrip of the L85A2.

The was also a single shot Cadet rifle, designated the "L98A1 Cadet GP Rifle."[16]

Russian assault rifles

Kalashnikov AK-47

Produced in a variety of conformations, a total of 100 million weapons in use worldwide, making 1 in every 5 firearms on the planet an AK-47.

Chapter Twenty-one

Perspectives

Fully or semiautomatic repeating firearms have been developed to such an extent since World War II that they are now the preferred weapon within the armed forces of any country with an organized military establishment. The introduction and deployment of this type of weapon in military service shares a number of significant and interesting characteristics, even when considering those from the period before black powder, and although early weapons like the repeating crossbow and polybolos seem to have little in common with the MG 42 and Kalashnikov, there are distinct similarities in the ways in which their roles developed. In particular, throughout history, advances in repeating weaponry have often been associated with countries or organizations that wanted to accrue an advantage over a bigger, numerically superior opponent. This drive for technological supremacy was sometimes associated with a hasty restructuring of the forces for which the weapon was intended, dire necessity driving the development of a particular repeating arm, rather than considered progress. Consequently, the introduction of innovative repeating or automatic weapons into military service has occasionally been rushed and ill-considered, forced on politicians and senior military figures by wartime necessity, and frequently proving chaotic and ruinously expensive as a result.

The repeating crossbow probably came into existence as a result of financial upheaval and subsequent military operations between provinces within feudal China. It was certainly used both successfully and extensively in Asia from the 11th century, although it seems to have been a well-established weapon in China even before that period. Hwachas saved at least one outnumbered Korean army from ignominious defeat, although these early repeating arms were not uniformly successful, as evidenced by the defeat of the Yorkists at the second battle of St. Albans, despite their multi-barreled cannon. Nor was there much consensus about the technical nature of the weapons. Perkins tried steam as a propellant, Winan employed centripetal force, while Giradoni even used compressed air quite successfully. Gunpowder certainly had its place, but it was not until the development of a safe, hand-held weapon, using black powder and a self-contained ignition system in the form of a percussion cap, that repeating weapons began to achieve any sort of prominence.

Once that prominence was established, however, the repeater quickly became the *beau ideal* of the military establishment. Unfortunately, although senior officers quickly embraced innovations like the Gatling and Maxim guns, especially during wartime, financial expediency saw their ardor considerably dampened when it came to supplying these weapons to the rank and file in the front line of any battle being fought. Revolvers were certainly issued to cavalry units in Federal and Confederate forces during the U.S. Civil War and to British mounted regiments in the Crimea, but long arms seem to have been a subject for contention between those using the weapons and the politicians called upon to find the money for such equipment. During the American Civil War, when both Henry and Spencer repeating rifles were known to be reliable and available in significant numbers, only a small number of specialized units in the Federal army were issued with them. The majority of such arms used on the battlefield were private purchases or Confederate captures, despite the Spencer's having had the endorsement of Abraham Lincoln. The later engagements with the Plains tribes were also fought by cavalry armed with Colt revolvers and the single-shot, centerfire Springfield carbine, despite the development of an excellent American weapon, the Winchester Model 1876, which would probably have cost no more than the Springfield to supply to serving cavalry men and was chambered for the U.S. army service rifle cartridge. British experiences were little better, the British army retaining a single-shot, rising-block rifle in the shape of the Martini-Henry throughout the period of its colonial wars, until 1888 when the Lee-Metford was introduced. Subsequently, the ubiquitous Lee-Enfield appeared, although the Gatling gun was in use with the Royal Artillery from 1878, initially chambered for a black powder cartridge. Even then the Imperial General Staff were not without reservations over the adoption of a bolt-action rifle. The first of the Lee Model rifles, up until World War I forced the production of the MkIII*, was designed with a magazine cutoff to allow for the loading of single cartridges in order to prevent soldiers from wasting ammunition. It seems, perhaps inevitably, that technical innovations, even if they may save soldiers' lives, were always going to take second place to financial expediency.

The way in which semiautomatic weapons, especially light machine guns, were introduced to the fighting services, especially during World War I, was even more problematic. Haig is claimed to have said in 1915 that the machine gun was an "overrated weapon" and that the British army only needed two per battalion, until the disasters of 1915 and 1916 showed him the error in his thinking. Moreover, the stories behind the adoption of the BAR, which could have replaced the all-but-useless Chauchat as early as the end of 1917, and the Thompson, which did not have an acceptable working prototype until 1921, show clearly how outdated were some of the military and political minds overseeing the conflict, although undoubtedly the value of the light machine gun was beginning to be appreciated after Passchendaele by many younger minds in the military. However, even the present day provides examples of expediency overruling concern for the welfare of enlisted men. The introduction of the original M16 as the U.S. service rifle, and the extensive redevelopment program forced on the British government in order to render the original SA80 assault rifle fit for purpose, serve as perfect illustrations of rushed development programs paid for with the lives of the men using the early, inferior versions of these two weapons. The German Army in World War II is one of the few exceptions to this almost universal parsimony, although admittedly the National Socialists were caught in a trap of Hitler's own making. Unable to broker an acceptable peace with the Russians after Stalingrad and with the U.S. army on its way, they were forced to spend their dwindling financial resources equipping both the Wehrmacht and their elite SS troops with weapons capable of countering the numerically superior Allied forces. This led to the development and, more importantly, almost instantaneous introduction of the MG 42, and later the StG 44 assault rifle, both innovative weapons for the period and arms upon which much future development would be based.

Expense and the Rise of the "Woolworth's" Gun

Unquestionably, repeating arms are often more expensive than a comparable single-shot weapon, and certainly cost more to develop into a reliable weapon. In 1944, an M1 Garand could not be produced for less than $83, even with the cost saving made possible by production at the Government Arsenal at Springfield, while Germany could turn out a bolt-action Mauser rifle for only $28. Innovations and improvements also cost money, as evidenced by the price of a Lewis gun in 1914, at £165, when compared to the Vickers HMG, which cost only £100 to manufacture, despite a Lewis gun's being quicker to make. Even more important for the struggling European economies was the price of ammunition, although no politician seems to have been brave enough to suggest that economy should be made in that particular commodity, since it was easier to save money by supplying troops with substandard filth instead of decent rations.

Cost of the weapons and ammunition they were using was certainly a significant consideration amongst the high-ranking military after World War I, and the French debacle that necessitated the evacuation from Dunkirk also obliged the British to come up with some method of quickly and cheaply making up their resulting shortfall in weapons. The weapon that arose from this near disaster was the Sten, an adequate compromise between serviceability and cost mainly because of the cleverness of its designers, rather than any initiative by Churchill's government. Cheapness and ease of manufacture had to be the prime considerations, but despite the manifold financial concerns of government, a cheap, easily manufactured gun was only useful if it performed adequately. Fortunately, the Sten proved to be a reliable weapon in the hands of an experienced user who was wise to its faults, because the early Mks did suffer from a number of problems. These included poor quality magazines, a fault shared with the German MP 40, another cheaply made "Woolworth's" gun also produced as a result of the need for financial necessity, this time by Hitler's government. The AK-47 magazine, by contrast, is an extremely robust component and frequently has a service life longer than the average Kalashnikov. Russian troops even used them to open beer bottles without affecting their serviceability!

Whatever their disadvantages, the Sten and MP 40 were undoubtedly the way forward for the future of repeating military firearms. The original Thompson, for example, was a beautifully made, finely machined weapon, everything a nineteenth-century gun owner was looking for. Unfortunately, it was not private gun ownership that counted here but military contracts, and the military was perfectly happy with an inexpensive gun that wore out in a reasonable length of time, rather than something like the Thompson, which would last indefinitely. In reality, military purchasers both during and after World War II much preferred a cheap gun with a limited service life, because the rapid progress in firearms design and development meant that an infantry weapon was out of date and needed replacing after a much shorter time interval than had been the case in the twenties and thirties. Functional guns like the British Sten, the American M3 "Grease Gun," the German MP 40 and particularly the MG 42 light machine gun, with their cheap, welded pressed steel construction, would be the forerunners of the new generation of military weapons, while the rigorous construction techniques that had produced the Thompson, the Springfield M1903, Lee-Enfield and M14 would survive only in the world of the hand-built sporting gun, available to those who could afford the luxury of Purdey's or Westley-Richard's superb products.

These "Woolworth's" guns shared another characteristic that was becoming commonplace in weapons after World War II, in that they all employed similar operating principles. Simple blowback operation from an open bolt or one of its many developments is now the most common system used in automatic pistols, submachine guns, and some LMGs. This system has become so robust and reliable that further developments in the field have proven largely uncompetitive, although larger caliber weapons using a high-power cartridge are frequently designed with some form of locking bolt, often based upon one of John Browning's designs.

Weapons like the modern M16 and SA85 are certainly constructed to a more rigorous standard than a Sten or M3, but they are still "disposable" guns in a very real sense, while the most ubiquitous firearm on planet Earth, the AK-47, is the subject of unlicensed production in almost every Third World country, with Kalashnikov "knockoffs" being traded in some places for as little as a bag of maize. This low-cost manufacture has become an important factor in today's weapons market. No experienced professional soldier these days is satisfied with a personal weapon that is not capable of sustained, fully automatic fire using a reasonably powerful and hence expensive cartridge. The battlefield has certainly come a long way from the days when a soldier's only concern was whether the string of his repeating crossbow had incorporated enough duck feathers to last out the battle!

Chapter Notes

Chapter One

1. Jieming Liang, *Chinese Siege Warfare: Mechanical Artillery & Siege Weapons of Antiquity* (Da Pao Publishing, Leong Kit M; 1st edition, 2006), p. 205.
2. D. Campbell, *Greek and Roman Artillery 399 B.C.–A.D. 363* (Oxford: Osprey, 2003), p. 111.
3. J. Warry, *Warfare in the Classical World* (UK: Salamander, 1995), p. 178.
4. Wayne Reynolds, *Siege Weapons of the Far East: A.D. 612-1300* (Oxford: Osprey, 2001), p. 48.
5. Ibid., p. 50.
6. Syed Ramsey, *Tools of War: History of Weapons in Early Modern Times* (India: Vij Books, 2016), p. 105.

Chapter Two

1. Baker Perkins historical Society: www.bphs.net.
2. 2nd Maryland Infantry: www.2ndmdinfantryus.org/winans.html.
3. X542/40, *The Holman Projector for firing grenades* (Cornwall record office).
4. Ibid.

Chapter Three

1. D. Forrest, *Tiger of Mysore* (London: Chatto & Windus, 1970), p. 202.
2. Ibid., p. 200.
3. Frank Winter, *The First Golden Age of Rocketry: Congreve and Hale Rockets of the Nineteenth* Century (Washington and London: Smithsonian Institution Press, 1990), p. 108.
4. Ibid., p. 127.
5. Ibid., p. 105.

Chapter Four

1. H.B.C. Pollard, *Pollard's History of Firearms* (Middlesex, UK: Country Life Books, 1983), p. 33.
2. Ibid., p. 213.
3. Ibid., pp. 205, 213.
4. Ibid., p. 70.
5. Ibid., p. 73.
6. Ibid., p. 210.
7. Ibid., p. 166.
8. Ibid., p. 170.
9. Ibid., p. 171.
10. Ibid., p. 172.
11. N. Flayderman, *Flayderman's Guide to Antique American Firearms ... And Their Values* (Iola, WI: Krause Publications, several editions), pp. 312–313.
12. www.wikipedia, Grapeshot.
13. Pollard, pp. 154–155.
14. D.W. Bailey, *British Military Longarms 1715-1865* (London: Arms & Armour, 1986), p. 107.
15. F.O. Figes, *The Crimean War: A History* (USA: Picador, 2012).
16. John Keegan, *The American Civil War* (UK: Vintage, 2010).

Chapter Five

1. Pollard, p. 155.
2. Ibid., pp. 204, 210.
3. Ibid., p. 204.
4. A.W.F. Taylerson, R.A.N. Andrews, and J. Firth. *The Revolver 1816-1865* (London, UK: Herbert Jenkins, 1968), p. 22.
5. George Prescott, *The English Revolver: A Collector's Guide to the Guns, Their History and Values* (Atglen, PA: Schiffer, 2014), p. 21.
6. Taylerson, Andrews, and Firth, p. 39.
7. Prescott, p. 19.
8. Flayderman, p. 307.
9. See Chapter Six.
10. Pollard, p. 310.
11. Prescott, p. 11.
12. Ibid., p. 14.
13. William B. Edward, *The Story of Colt's Revolver: The Biography of Col. Samuel Colt* (Harrisburg, PA: Stackpole Company).
14. Flayderman, pp. 63–72.
15. Ibid., see relevant chapters on specific makers.
16. Prescott, see relevant chapters on specific makers.
17. Ibid., p. 39.
18. Ibid., p. 9.
19. Ibid., see relevant chapters on specific makers.

Chapter Six

1. Prescott, p. 239.
2. Ibid., p. 318.
3. Flayderman, p. 180.
4. Ibid., see relevant chapters on specific makers.
5. Prescott, see relevant chapters on specific makers.

6. Pollard, pp. 318–320.
7. Flayderman, see relevant chapters on specific makers.
8. Ibid., p. 82.
9. Ibid., p. 83.
10. Ibid., p. 83.
11. Ibid., p. 381.
12. www.oldammo.com.
13. Flayderman, p. 398.
14. Ibid., p. 402.
15. Ibid., p. 404.
16. Ibid., p. 414.

Chapter Seven

1. H.L. Blackmore, *A Dictionary of London Gunmakers* (London: Christie's, 1986), see relevant sections on specific makers.
2. Pollard, p. 240.
3. Ibid., p. 313.
4. Ibid., p. 315.
5. Ibid., p. 260.
6. Ibid., p. 262.
7. Flayderman, see relevant sections on specific makers.
8. Prescott, see relevant chapters on specific makers.
9. Ibid.,, p. 94.
10. Flayderman, p. 87.
11. Prescott, p. 127.
12. Flayderman, p. 193.
13. Ibid., see relevant sections on specific makers.
14. Prescott, see relevant chapters on specific makers.
15. Pollard, p. 335.

Chapter Eight

1. Pollard, p. 202.
2. Ibid., p. 207.
3. Ibid., p. 208.
4. Ibid., p. 206.
5. John Browning and Curt Gentry, *John M. Browning, American Gunmaker* (New York: Doubleday, 1964).
6. Pollard, p. 534.
7. Ibid., p. 210.
8. Flayderman, p. 79.
9. Flayderman, see relevant chapters on specific makers.
10. Pollard, p. 240.
11. Ibid., p. 166.
12. Flayderman, p. 265.
13. Ibid., p. 266.
14. Ibid., pp. 266–273.
15. Ibid., pp. 266–270.
16. Ibid., p. 272.
17. Ibid., pp. 266–273.
18. Ibid., p. 520.
19. Ibid., pp. 119–123.
20. Ibid., p. 104.
21. Ibid., 575.
22. Ibid., see relevant sections on specific makers.

Chapter Nine

1. G.M. Chinn, *The Machine Gun: History, Evolution, and Development of Manual, Automatic, and Airborne Repeating Weapons* (Washington, D.C.: Government Printing Office, 1951), The Puckle Gun, p. 18.
2. Chinn, p. 1.
3. Chinn, Agar "Coffee-Mill" Gun, p. 37.
4. Chinn, p. 64; J. Willbanks, *Machine Guns: An Illustrated History of Their Impact* (Santa Barbara, CA: ABC-CLIO, 2004), p. 56.
5. Chinn, p. 71.
6. Ibid., p. 35.
7. Ibid., p. 71.
8. See Chapter Ten.
9. Chinn, p. 46.
10. Ibid., pp. 44–45.
11. Ibid., p. 79.
12. Ibid., p. 110.
13. Ibid., p. 67.

Chapter Ten

1. Chinn, p. 48.
2. Ibid., p. 57.
3. Peter Smithurst, *The Gatling Gun* (Oxford: Osprey, 2015), p. 46.
4. Ibid., p. 21.
5. Ibid., p. 98.

Chapter Eleven

1. Chinn, p. 121.
2. Ibid., p. 123.
3. Ibid., p. 127.
4. Dolf Goldsmith, *The Devil's Paintbrush: Sir Hiram Maxim's Gun* (Ontario, Canada: Collector Grade, 2nd edition, 2002), p. 100.
5. Chinn, p. 123.
6. Ibid., p. 139.
7. Ibid., p. 141.
8. Ibid., p. p. 142.
9. I.V. Hogg and L.F. Thurston, *British Artillery Weapons & Ammunition 1914–1918* (London: Ian Allan, 1972), p. 115.
10. www.wikipedia.org: Salvator-Dormus M1893.
11. Chinn, p. 71.
12. Ibid., p. 204.

Chapter Twelve

1. Tenney L. Davis, *The Chemistry of Powder & Explosives* (London, UK: Angriff Press, 1992), p. 102.
2. Ibid., p. 105.
3. Ibid., p. 134.
4. Ibid., p. 176.
5. www.wikipedia.org: Smokeless powder.
6. Ibid.
7. Flayderman, p. 86; www.wikipedia.org: Colt Single Action Army.
8. Flayderman, p. 89.
9. David Miller, *The History of Browning Firearms* (London: Chartwell, 2014), p. 75.

10. Flayderman, p. 575.
11. Ibid., p. 197.
12. Flayderman, p. 272.
13. Prescott, pp. 110, 127.
14. Pollard, p. 251.
15. Ibid., pp. 267–269.
16. Ibid. pp. 272–276.
17. Ibid., p. 273.
18. Ibid., pp. 274–281.
19. Flayderman, p. 485.
20. Pollard, pp. 280–281.
21. John Walter, *Rifles of the World* (Iola, WI: Krause, 3rd edition), p. 110.
22. Pollard, p. 251.
23. Ibid., pp. 251–252.
24. Ibid., pp. 267–269.
25. Ibid., pp. 269–272.
26. Ibid., pp. 269–272.
27. Robert Ball, *Mauser Military Rifles of the World* (Iola, WI: Gun Digest Books. 5th edition, 2011), pp. 222, 227.
28. Fred L. Honeycutt Jr. and F. Patt Anthony, *Military Rifles of Japan* (Julin Books, 5th edition, 2006).
29. Terence Lapin, *The Mosin-Nagant Rifle* (Tustin, CA: North Cape, 3rd ed., 2003).
30. www.wikipedia.org: Dum-Dum Arsenal.
31. Ibid.
32. Ibid.
33. Prescott, p. 137.
34. Ibid., p. 138.
35. Ibid., p. 139.

Chapter Thirteen

1. Pollard, p. 340.
2. Ibid., pp. 269–272, 369.
3. Ibid., p. 370.
4. Ibid. p. 371.
5. Flayderman, p. 101.
6. Ibid. p. 101.
7. Pollard, p. 370.
8. Flayderman, p. 102.
9. *World Guns*: handguns—Luger pistol.
10. Richard Mann, *Cartridges of the World: A Complete and Illustrated Reference for Over 1500 Cartridges* (Iola, WI: Krause, 13th edition, 2012).
11. *World Guns*: handguns—Germany.
12. gundigest.com/thelugerpistol.
13. *World Guns*: handguns—Mauser C96.
14. Ask Mister Science: 1896 MauserC96.
15. Browning and Gentry.
16. *World Guns*: handguns—M1911 pistol.
17. Flayderman, p. 193.
18. *World Guns*: handguns—Belgium.
19. *World Guns*: handguns—Great Britain.
20. *World Guns*: handguns—Germany.
21. *World Guns*: handguns—Italy.
22. *World Guns*: handguns—Japan.
23. *World Guns*: handguns—Spain.
24. *World Guns*: handguns—Russia.
25. Prescott, p. 116.

Chapter Fourteen

1. A.J.P. Taylor, *English History 1914–1945* (London: Oxford University Press, 1965), pp. 1–118.
2. Winston Churchill, *The World Crisis 1911–1918* (London: Penguin Classics, 2007), p. 213.
3. Gary Sheffield, *The Chief: Douglas Haig and the British Army* (London, UK: Aurum Press, 2012). p. 33–40.
4. Taylor, pp. 1–118.
5. Ibid., pp. 73, 111.
6. www.1914–1918.net/mgc.htm.
7. www.1914–1918.net/mgc.htm.
8. Taylor, pp. 1–118.
9. Sheffield, pp. 33–40.
10. www.wikipedia.org: French Army in World War I.
11. Stephen Bull, *Trench: A History of Trench Warfare on the Western Front* (UK: Osprey, 2014), pp. 17, 151.
12. Julian Hatcher, *Hatcher's Notebook: A Standard Reference Book for Shooters, Gunsmiths, Ballisticians, Historians, Hunters, and Collectors* (Mansfield Centre, CT: Martino Fine Books, 2012).
13. John Eisenhower, *The Epic Story of the American Army in World War I* (New York: Free Press, 2002).
14. E.F. Cheeseman, ed., *Fighter Aircraft of the 1914–1918 War* (Letchworth, UK; Harleyford, 1960), p. 17.
15. Ibid., p. 27.
16. www.airwar1.org.uk.
17. www.wwiaviation.com/Bloody_April-1917.
18. www.airwar1.org.uk.
19. Ibid.

Chapter Fifteen

1. Chinn, p. 275.
2. Ibid., p. 280.
3. Ibid., p. 281.
4. Ibid.
5. Ibid., p. 291.
6. Ibid.
7. Norman Friedman, *Naval Anti-Aircraft Guns and Gunnery* (London: Seaforth, 2013).
8. Chinn, p. 295.
9. www.wikipedia.org: *Zeppelin*.
10. Chinn, p. 288.
11. Ibid., p. 195.
12. Ibid., p. 196.
13. Ibid., p. 198.
14. Ibid., p. 190.
15. Ibid., p. 195.
16. Pollard, p. 298.
17. Chinn, p. 197.
18. Ibid., p. 238.
19. *World Guns*: machine guns—Bergmann 1915 MG 15 n.a.
20. *World Guns*: machine guns—Madsen LMG.

Chapter Sixteen

1. Chinn, p. 160.
2. Ibid., p. 162.
3. Ibid., p. 173.
4. Ibid., p. 175.

5. Ibid., p. 176.
6. www.wikipedia.org: .30–06 Springfield.
7. Chinn, p. 178.
8. Ibid., 175.
9. www.vickersmachinegun.org.uk.
10. Ibid.
11. Ibid.
12. Ibid.
13. Chinn, p. 144.
14. Ian Hogg and John Batchelor, *Weapons and War Machines* (London: Phoebus, 1976), p. 62.
15. www.vickersmachinegun.org.uk.
16. Ibid.
17. Ibid.
18. Ibid.
19. Chinn, p. 200.
20. U.S. War Department Handbook of the Hotchkiss Machine Gun, Model of 1914.
21. Chinn, p. 201.
22. Ibid.
23. Chinn, p. 200.
24. *World Guns*: machine guns—MG 08, IMG 08/15 and IMG 08/15 Maxim machine gun.
25. Ibid.
26. Ibid.
27. Ibid.
28. Ibid.
29. Chinn, p.194.
30. Ibid., pp. 228–232.
31. Ibid., p. 379.
32. Ibid., p. 310.
33. *World Guns*: machine guns—Maxim M1910.

Chapter Seventeen

1. Martin Pegler, *The Thompson Submachine Gun: From Prohibition Chicago to World War II*. (Oxford: Osprey), p. 8.
2. Ibid., p. 9.
3. Ibid., p. 11.
4. Ibid., p. 15.
5. Ibid., pp. 22–25.
6. Pegler, p. 23.
7. ww.wikipedia.org, Thompson submachine gun.
8. Pegler, p. 30.
9. Pegler, p. 31: WO 185/12; *Thompson Submachine Guns*: WO 199/1906; *Ammunition and Weapons: Issue of Thompson submachine guns*.
10. *World Guns*: autoloading rifles—M1 Garand.
11. Ibid.
12. Ibid.
13. Julian Hatcher, *Book of the Garand* (U.S.: Gun Room Press, 1983), p. 120–150.
14. *World Guns*: submachine guns—the Sten.
15. CAB 122/227. Sten Gun programme.
16. *World Guns*: submachine guns—the Sten.
17. Ibid.
18. Ibid.
19. Ibid.
20. *World Guns*: submachine guns—Erma MP-38 and MP-40 submachine gun.
21. Die Maschinenpistole 40.
22. Ibid.
23. Ibid.
24. Ibid.
25. Ibid.
26. Ibid.
27. *World Guns*: submachine guns—M3 and M3A1 submachine gun.
28. *World Guns*: submachine guns—Owen machine carbine.
29. *World Guns*: submachine guns—Lanchester Mk.1 submachine gun.
30. *World Guns*: submachine guns—Suomi submachine gun.
31. *World Guns*: submachine guns—MP 18.
32. *World Guns*: submachine guns—MP 34.
33. *World Guns*: submachine guns—MP 34.
34. *World Guns*: submachine guns—MP 35.
35. Ian Hogg, *The Encyclopedia of Infantry Weapons of World War II* (Lincoln, NE: Bison, 1977), p. 66.
36. *World Guns*: submachine guns—Beretta M1918.
37. *World Guns*: submachine guns—Type 100 submachine gun.
38. *World Guns*: submachine guns—Shpagin PPSh-41 submachine gun.
39. *World Guns*: military rifles—Tokarev SVT-38 SVT-40.

Chapter Eighteen

1. Der Erste Zug: *Tactical Philosophies of the Squad*.
2. S. Bull and P. Dennis, *World War II Infantry Tactics: Company and Battalion* (Oxford: Osprey, 2005), p. 20.
3. Bull and Dennis, p. 38.
4. Der Erste Zug: *Tactical Philosophies of the Squad*.
5. Ibid.
6. J.L. Ballou, *Rock in a Hard Place: The Browning Automatic Rifle* (Ontario, Canada: Collector Grade, Canada, 2000).
7. *World Guns*: submachine guns—Browning Automatic Rifle BAR M1918.
8. Ibid.
9. Ibid.
10. www.wikipedia.org: .30–06 Springfield.
11. *World Guns*: submachine guns—Browning Automatic Rifle BAR M1918.
12. Ibid.
13. Stephen E. Ambrose, *D-Day: June 6, 1944: The Climactic Battle of World War II* (New York: Simon & Schuster, 2002), p. 142.
14. *World Guns*: submachine guns—Browning Automatic Rifle BAR M1918.
15. Bull and Dennis, p. 27.
16. Neil Grant, *The Bren Gun* (Oxford: Osprey, 2013), p. 28.
17. Bren serial numbers.
18. Grant, p. 28.
19. *World Guns*: light machine guns—the Bren.
20. Personal reminiscence.
21. Joshua Levine, *Forgotten Voices of Dunkirk* (London: Ebury Press, 2011).
22. Grant, p. 27.
23. Grant, p. 32.
24. *World Guns*: machine guns—MAC M. 1924/ 29 LMG.

25. Ibid.
26. Ibid.
27. Ibid.
28. Ibid.
29. www.lonesentry.com/manuals/german-infantry-weapons: MG34-machine-gun.
30. Ibid.
31. Ibid.
32. German Alphabetic Ordnance Codes: oldmilitarymarkings.com/codes_full_alpha_p-z.html.
33. Ibid.
34. Ibid.
35. Ibid.
36. Ibid.
37. www.lonesentry.com/manuals/german-infantry-weapons: MG42-machine-gun.
38. Ibid.
39. Ibid.
40. German Alphabetic Ordnance Codes: oldmilitarymarkings.com/codes_full_alpha_p-z.html.
41. www.lonesentry.com/manuals/german-infantry-weapons: MG42-machine-gun.
42. Ibid.
43. Ibid.
44. *World Guns*: machine guns—Vickers-Berthier LMG.
45. *World Guns*: machine guns—Vicker Class K/ VGO/ GO machine gun.
46. *World Guns*: machine guns—MG 13 "Dreyse" machine gun.
47. www.wikipedia.org: MG 15.
48. Terry Gander and Peter Chamberlain, *Weapons of the Third Reich: An Encyclopedic Survey of All Small Arms, Artillery and Special Weapons of the German Land Forces 1939–1945*. (New York: Doubleday, 1979), p. 37.
49. www.lonesentry.com/manuals/german-infantry-weapons: MG34-machine-gun.
50. www.lonesentry.com/manuals/german-infantry-weapons: MG42-machine-gun.
51. Gander and Chamberlain, p. 41.
52. *World Guns*: machine guns—Breda M1930 LMG.
53. *World Guns*: machine guns—Japan.
54. *World Guns*: machine guns—USSR gun.
55. www.wikipedia.org: ShKAS machine gun.

Chapter Nineteen

1. m1919tech.com/1501.
2. Ibid.
3. Ibid.
4. Ibid.
5. Ibid.
6. Ibid.
7. Ibid.
8. www.wikipedia.org: the 30–06 Springfield.
9. m1919tech.com/1501.
10. www.militaryfactory.com/smallarms.
11. Ibid.
12. *World Guns*: machine guns—Browning M1917 and M1919 machine gun.
13. Chinn, pp. 181–186.
14. Ibid., p. 531.
15. www.wikipedia.org: .50 BMG.
16. *World Guns*: machine guns—Browning M1917 and M1919 machine gun.
17. *World Guns*: machine guns—ZB 60.
18. Ibid.
19. *World Guns*: machine guns—Hotchkiss Model 1930 heavy machine gun.
20. www.wikipedia.org: MG 131 machine gun.
21. *World Guns*: machine guns—Breda M1937.
22. www.vickersmachinegun.org.uk.
23. Chinn, p. 200.
24. *World Guns*: machine guns—SG-43 Goryunov.
25. Leszek Erenfeicht, "Dushka: The Soviet Fifty Caliber" (*Small Arms Defense Journal* 4, No. 3 (August 2012).
26. Naval weapons: Oerlikon Mk 1, 2, 3.
27. Norman Friedman, *The Naval Institute Guide to World Naval Weapon Systems* (Annapolis, MD: Naval Institute Press, 2006), pp. 478–480.
28. Naval weapons: Oerlikon Mk 1, 2, 3.
29. Friedman, pp. 478–480.
30. Naval weapons: Oerlikon Mk 1, 2, 3.
31. Friedman, pp. 478–480.
32. Naval weapons: Oerlikon Mk 1, 2, 3.
33. Gander, *The 40mm Bofors Gun* (Wellingborough, UK: Patrick Stephens, 1990).
34. Naval weapons: Bofors 40mm.
35. Gander, *Bofors Gun*.
36. Naval weapons: Bofors 40mm.
37. Gander, *Bofors Gun*.
38. Naval weapons: Bofors 40mm.
39. Gander, *Bofors Gun*.
40. Chinn, p. 562.
41. Ibid., 567.
42. Gander and Chamberlain, p. 97.

Chapter Twenty

1. *World Guns*: assault rifles—Schmeisser MP 34/ MP44/ StG44.
2. Ibid.
3. Ibid.
4. Military factory/ small arms: StG 44.
5. Ibid.
6. Ibid.
7. *World Guns*: assault rifles—Schmeisser MP 34/ MP44/ StG44.
8. *World Guns*: assault rifles—AK-47, AKS, AKM and AKMS assault rifles.
9. Ibid.
10. Ibid.
11. Ibid.
12. Ibid.
13. *World Guns*: assault rifles—M14 rifle.
14. *World Guns*: assault rifles—Armalite / Colt AR-15 / M16 M16A1 M16A2 M16A3 M16A4 assault rifle.
15. *World Guns*: assault rifles—FN FAL automatic rifle.
16. *World Guns*: assault rifles—Enfield SA-80: L85A1 and L85A2 assault rifle, L22 carbine.

Bibliography

Bailey, D.W. *British Military Longarms, 1715–1865.* London: Arms & Armour, 1986. Includes information about early flintlock and percussion types as well as some British Army bayonets of the period. Exhaustive and informative.

Ball, Robert. *Mauser Military Rifles of the World.* 5th ed. Iola, WI: Gun Digest Books, 2011.

Ballou, James L. *Rock in a Hard Place: The Browning Automatic Rifle.* Cobourg, ONT: Collector Grade, 2000.

Berry, Henry. *Make the Kaiser Dance.* London: Arbor House, 1984.

Blackmore, Howard L. *A Dictionary of London Gunmakers.* London: Christie's, 1986. Just what it says: a complete list of every London gunmaker from the days of the Guilds, including a section on gunmakers' marks and a discussion of the development of the trade.

Bull, Stephen. *World War II Infantry Tactics: Company and Battalion.* Oxford: Osprey, 2005.

Campbell, Duncan B. *Greek and Roman Artillery 399 B.C.–A.D. 363.* Oxford: Osprey, 2003.

Cheeseman E.F., ed. *Fighter Aircraft of the 1914–1918 War.* Letchworth, UK; Harleyford, 1960.

Churchill, Winston. *The World Crisis 1911–1918.* London: Penguin Classics, 2007.

Davis, Tenney L. *The Chemistry of Powder and Explosives.* London: Angriff Press, 1992.

Demaison, G., and Y. Buffetaut. *The Chauchat Machine Rifle.* Cobourg, ONT: Collector Grade, 1995.

Figes, F.O. *The Crimean War: A History.* USA: Picador, 2012.

Flayderman, Norm. *Flayderman's Guide to Antique American Firearms ... And Their Values.* Iola, WI: Krause, 2008. An excellent book for the beginning collector. He discusses fakes, buying and selling, and much else that a newcomer to the arms collecting hobby needs to know. A good buy and a good read, even for those not mainly interested in American arms.

Forrest, D. *Tiger of Mysore.* London: Chatto & Windus, 1970.

Friedman, Norman. *Naval Anti-Aircraft Guns and Gunnery.* London: Seaforth, 2013.

_____. *The Naval Institute Guide to World Naval Weapon Systems.* Annapolis, MD: Naval Institute Press, 2006.

Gander, Terry, and Peter Chamberlain. *Weapons of the Third Reich: An Encyclopedic Survey of All Small Arms, Artillery and Special Weapons of the German Land Forces 1939–1945.* New York: Doubleday, 1979.

Goldsmith, Dolf. *The Devil's Paintbrush.* 2d ed. Cobourg, ONT: Collector Grade, 2002.

Hatcher, Julian. *Book of the Garand.* Highland Park, NJ: Gun Room, 1983.

_____. *Hatcher's Notebook: A Standard Reference Book for Shooters, Gunsmiths, Ballisticians, Historians, Hunters, and Collectors.* Mansfield Centre, CT: Martino Fine Books, 2012.

Hogg, Ian. *The Encyclopedia of Infantry Weapons of World War II.* Lincoln, NE: Bison, 1977.

_____. *Military Small Arms of the 20th Century.* Iola, WI: Krause, 2000.

_____, and John Batchelor. *Weapons and War Machines.* London: Phoebus, 1976.

Honeycutt, Fred L., Jr., and F. Patt Anthony. *Military Rifles of Japan.* 5th ed. Palm Beach Gardens, FL: Julin, 2006.

Keegan, John. *The American Civil War.* New York: Vintage, 2010.

Lapin, Terence. *The Mosin–Nagant Rifle.* 3d ed. Tustin, CA: North Cape, 2003.

Levine, Joshua. *Forgotten Voices of Dunkirk.* London: Ebury Press, 2011.

Liang, Jieming. *Chinese Siege Warfare: Mechanical Artillery & Siege Weapons of Antiquity.* Singapore: Leong Kit M, 2006.

Mann, Richard. *Cartridges of the World: A Complete and Illustrated Reference for Over 1500 Cartridges.* 13th ed. Iola, WI: Krause, 2012.

Pegler, Martin. *The Thompson Submachine Gun: From Prohibition Chicago to World War II.* Oxford: Osprey, 2011.

_____, and Peter Dennis. *The Vickers-Maxim Machine Gun.* Oxford: Osprey, 2013.

Pollard, H.B.C. *Pollard's History of Firearms.* Middlesex, UK: Country Life, 1983. Still one of the best and most thorough accounts of the history of firearms, especially early weapons.

Prescott, George. *The English Revolver: A Collector's Guide to the Guns, Their History and Values.* Atglen, PA: Schiffer, 2014.

Ramsey, Syed. *Tools of War: History of Weapons in*

Early Modern Times. New Delhi, India: Vij Books, 2016.

Reynolds, Wayne. *Siege Weapons of the Far East: A.D. 612–1300.* Oxford: Osprey, 2001.

Sheffield, Gary. *The Chief: Douglas Haig and the British Army.* London: Aurum Press, 2012.

Smithurst, Peter. *The Gatling Gun.* Oxford: Osprey, 2015.

Taylerson, A.W.F., R.A.N. Andrews, and J. Firth. *The Revolver 1816–1865.* London: Herbert Jenkins, 1968.

Taylor, A.J.P. *English History 1914–1945.* London: Oxford University Press, 1965.

Walter, John. *Rifles of the World.* 3d ed. Iola, WI: Krause, 1998.

Warry, John. *Warfare in the Classical World.* London: Salamander, 1995.

Willbanks, J.. *Machine Guns: An Illustrated History of Their Impact.* Santa Barbara, CA: ABC-CLIO, 2004.

Winter, Frank. *The First Golden Age of Rocketry: Congreve and Hale Rockets of the Nineteenth Century.* Washington and London: Smithsonian Institution Press, 1990.

Woodward, W Todd, ed. *Cartridges of the World.* Iola, WI: Gun Digest, 2014.

Websites

Ammunition: www.oldammo.com.
Ask Mister Science; detailed descriptions of antique firearms. http://askmisterscience.com.
Baker Perkins historical Society: www.bphs.net.
Bloody April: www.wwiaviation.com/Bloody_April_1917.
Bren serial numbers: weaponsonline.proboards.com/thread/242/bren-serial-number-database-marks.
Browning M1919: m1919tech.com/1501.html.
Chinn, G.M. *The Machine Gun: History, Evolution, and Development of Manual, Automatic, and Airborne Repeating Weapons:* www.ibiblio.org/hyperwar/USN/ref/MG/I/index.html#contents.
Cost of weapons in WW2: www.ww2f.com//topic/20451-cost-of-ww2-weapons.
Der Erste Zug: German WWII military research and enactment: www.dererstezug.com.
Die Maschinenpistole 40 (The MP 40 Machine pistol): www.mp40.nl.
German Alphabetic Ordnance Codes: oldmilitarymarkings.com/codes_full_alpha_p-z.html.
German infantry weapons: www.lonesentry.com/manuals/german-infantry-weapons.
Gun Digest: www.gundigest.com/gun-digest-classics-articles.
Infantry weapons–small arms: www.militaryfactory.com/smallarms.
The Machine Gun Corps: www.1914–1918.net/mgc.htm.
Naval weapons: www.navweaps.com/Weapons.
The RFC in France: www.apw.airwar1.org.uk/rfc.
The Royal Flying Corps: www.airwar1.org.uk.
2nd Maryland Infantry: www.2ndmdinfantryus.org/winans.html.
Small Arms Defense Journal, The Vickers machine gun: www.vickersmachinegun.org.uk.
World Guns: Handguns: world.guns.ru/handguns-e.html.
Machine guns: world.guns.ru/machineguns-e.html.
Military rifles: world.guns.ru/rifle-e.html.
Submachine guns: world.guns.ru/smg-e.html.

Public Record Offices in the UK

PRO, Kew

CAB 122/227. *Sten Gun programme.*
WO 185/12. *Thompson sub-machine guns.*
WO 199/1906. *Ammunition and Weapons: Issue of Thompson submachine guns.*

Cornish record office

X542/ 40. *The Holman Projector for firing grenades.*

Index

Agar's "Coffee Mill" gun 117
American Civil war 51
Archimede's steam gun (Architonnerre) 20
assault and battle rifles 407–412
automatic cannon 383; military service 393–396

Ballista, original 13
Berdan primer 88
Bofors 40mm/L60 cannon 390; variations 392
bolt-action service rifle manufacturers 167; Arisaka 170; Berthier 169; Krag-Jorgensen 167; Mauser 169; Moisin-Nagant 170; P14 168; Ross 167
Boxer primer 88
Bren gun 327; identifying stamps 327; major variations 329; military service 331–332
Brooklyn Firearms company 76
Browning, John 178
Browning automatic rifle 319; identification stamps 320; major variations 323; military service 325
Browning M1895, "Potato digger" 252; major variations 255; military service 257
Browning M1917 .30–06 caliber medium machine gun 257; military service 262; operation 258
Browning M1919 .30 caliber machine gun 360; military service 369; receiver stamps 362; variations 365–369
Browning M2 .50 caliber machine gun 370; receiver stamps 372; variations 374
Browning slide repeating rifle 98

canister and grapeshot 48
Caplock or Percussion system 43
centerfire cartridge 87
centerfire revolver 88; gate-loading 90; manufacturers 94; swing-out cylinder 93; top-break 91
Chauchat automatic machine rifle 239; major variations 244; military service 245

Chinese repeating crossbow 11
Cochran's Model 1837 percussion revolver 57
Collier's flintlock revolver 55
Colt's M1911 self-loading pistol 179; frame stamps 181
Colt's Model 1855 revolving rifle 103
Congreve's rocket 33
Crimean War 50
Crispin, Silas 83

Dragoon Colt revolvers 63
Dum-Dum arsenal 174; British Army revolver cartridges 174; British army rifle cartridges 172; "Manstopper" bullets 176

Flintlock or Snaplock system 42
FM 24/29 light machine gun 333; identifying marks 334

Gatling gun 128; centerfire 133; military service 135; percussion 133; receiver stamps 131; rimfire 133
Gewehr Model 1898 service rifle 158; breech stamps 158
Girandoni's air rifle 99

Hale, William 37
Hale's rocket 36
hand-turned revolving pistols 53
harmonica muskets and rifles 98
harmonica pistols 58
Hawacha or "Fire Cart" 15
heavy machine gun 215; American forces 216, 285; British and Commonwealth forces 216, 286; corps 214; development after WW1 380–383; French forces 216, 286; German & Austro-Hungarian forces 216, 286; Russian forces 287; tactics 213; use in WW1 216
Henry rifle 105
Holman Projector 26
Hotchkiss M1909/ Hotchkiss MK1 234; receiver markings 237
Hotchkiss model 1914 heavy machine gun 275; major variations 277; military service 278; receiver stamps 276
Hotchkiss 37mm revolving cannon 120

Kalashnikov AK47 assault rifle 401; military service 404; variants 403–404

Lebel Model 1886 service rifle 156; breech stamps 157; military service 158
Lee-Enfield .303 service rifle 161; breech stamps 163; models 163; S.M.L.E 161
Lefaucheux revolver 86–87
Lewis gun, Model 1914 224; aircraft 230; frame markings 226; military service 230
light machine gun 216; American forces 218; British forces 216–217; French forces 217; German forces 217–218; infantry tactics 317–319; manufacturers 350–359; tactical use in WW1 216, 317; types of weapon 219–220, 248–251
Lorenzoni/ Cookson system 97
Luger self-loading pistol 184; frame markings 186

M1 Garand 295; receiver stamps 296; major variations 297
machine guns: in air service 220; Bloody April 222; the Fokker scourge 221
magazine percussion pistols 57
magazine rifles 97
manufacturers: early multi-fire weapons 123; Gardener machine gun 124; Nordenfeldt machine gun 124; repeating rifles and shotguns 112–114
matchlock system 40
Mauser C96 self-loading pistol 188; frame markings 190
Maxim automatic machine gun 138; identifying stamps 142; military service 144; "Pom-Pom" 145; QF 1-pounder competitors 149; smokeless cartridges 139
Maynard's tape priming lock 45

metal cartridge magazine repeaters 104
MG 08 279; military service 281; receiver stamps 280
MG 34 general purpose machine gun 337; identifying marks 338; military service 341; variations 340
MG 42 general purpose machine gun 343; military service 347; post-war developments 348
Mitrailleuse guns 119
Moore's Patent Firearms company 78
MP40 machine pistol 306; military service 310; variations 309
Mysorean rocket technology 33

Napoleonic warfare 48
National Firearms Company 78
National Rifle Association antiques classification 2
Nock's flintlock pistol 54

Oerlikon 20mm cannon 384; military service 390; variations 386–390
organ guns 18

Paterson Colt revolvers 60
Percussion revolvers 59; manufacturers 65–66
Perkins, Jacob 22
Perkins' steam gun 21
pinfire cartridge 85
Plant Manufacturing Company 80
Polybolos (repeating ballista) 14

Pond, L.W revolvers 83
propellants 151; Cordite 152; Nitrocellulose 152; Poudre B 152
puckle gun 115

repeating air rifles 99; Continental makers 102; English makers 101
repeating and multi-barrel pistols 52
revolving cylinder rifles 102; makers 104
Richards Colt conversion 75
Richards-Mason Colt conversion 76
Rimfire revolver manufacturers 72
Rollin White 72
Rollin White's competitors 73

self-contained metal cartridge 69
self-loading pistol manufacturers 194; American 194–197; Austrian & German 201–204; Belgium 197–199; British 199–201; Italian 204; Japanese 205–206; Spanish 206; USSR 207
short-recoil mechanism 184
simple blowback operation 179
Smith & Wesson revolvers 70–71
Spencer rifle 108
Springfield M1903 service rifle 159; breech stamps 160
Sten gun 298; identification stamps 300; military service 304–305; variations 301–304
StG 44 assault rifle 398; military service 400; variants 400

sub-machine gun manufacturers 311; American 311–312; Australian 312; British 312–313; Finland 313; Germany 313–315; Italy 315; Japan 315; USSR 316
superimposed charge ("Roman Candle" guns) 53

tape primer 44
Thompson sub-machine gun 289; major variations and receiver stamps 291
Thuer Colt conversion 75
Tipu Sultan 32
transition percussion revolvers 59

Veeder cartridge counter 228
Vicker heavy/medium machine gun 266; major variations 270; military service 273–274; receiver plate markings 268; serial numbers 267
volcanic pistols and rifles 104
volley guns 49

Walker Colt revolvers 62
Webley-Fosbery semi-automatic revolver 207; military service 210
Wheelock system 41
Winan's centrifugal steam gun 24
Winchester rifles 106

Zeppelin raids 232; Buckingham cartridge 232

www.ingramcontent.com/pod-product-compliance
Ingram Content Group UK Ltd.
Pitfield, Milton Keynes, MK11 3LW, UK
UKHW051851210426
5322IPUK00025B/660